D1544226

Landmark Papers in Macroeconomics

The Foundations of 20ᵗʰ Century Economics

Prefaces by: Mark Blaug

      Professor Emeritus, University of London, UK
      Professor Emeritus, University of Buckingham, UK
      Visiting Professor, University of Amsterdam, The Netherlands
      Visiting Professor, Erasmus University of Rotterdam, The Netherlands

1. Landmark Papers in Economic Growth
   Selected by Robert M. Solow

2. Landmark Papers in Economic Fluctuations, Economic Policy and Related Subjects
   Selected by Lawrence R. Klein

3. Landmark Papers in General Equilibrium Theory, Social Choice and Welfare
   Selected by Kenneth J. Arrow and Gérard Debreu

4. Landmark Papers in Economics, Politics and Law
   Selected by James M. Buchanan

5. Landmark Papers in Macroeconomics
   Selected by James Tobin

Future titles will include:

Landmark Papers in Derivatives
Selected by Robert C. Merton

Landmark Papers in Human Capital Theory
Selected by Gary S. Becker

For a list of all Edward Elgar published titles visit our site on the World Wide Web at
http://www.e-elgar.co.uk

Landmark Papers in Macroeconomics

Selected by

James Tobin

Formerly Sterling Professor of Economics
Yale University, USA

THE FOUNDATIONS OF 20TH CENTURY ECONOMICS

An Elgar Reference Collection
Cheltenham, UK • Northampton, MA, USA

Published by
Edward Elgar Publishing Limited
Glensanda House
Montpellier Parade
Cheltenham
Glos GL50 1UA
UK

Edward Elgar Publishing, Inc.
136 West Street
Suite 202
Northampton
Massachusetts 01060
USA

A catalogue record for this book is available from the British Library.

Library of Congress Cataloging in Publication Data

Landmark papers in macroeconomics / selected by James Tobin.
    p. cm. — (The foundations of 20th century economics ; 5) (An Elgar reference collection)
Includes bibliographical references and index.
    1. Macroeconomics. I. Tobin, James, 1918– II. Series. III. Series: An Elgar reference collection
    HB172.5 .L357 2002
    339—dc21   2002028586

ISBN   1 84064 706 X

Printed and bound in Great Britain by MPG Books Ltd, Bodmin, Cornwall

Contents

Acknowledgements

The editor and publishers wish to thank the authors and the following publishers who have kindly given permission for the use of copyright material.

American Economic Association for articles: Don Patinkin (1948), 'Price Flexibility and Full Employment', *American Economic Review*, **38** (4), September, 543–64; Franco Modigliani and Merton H. Miller (1958), 'The Cost of Capital, Corporation Finance and the Theory of Investment', *American Economic Review*, **XLVIII** (3), June, 261–97; Edmund Phelps (1961), 'The Golden Rule of Accumulation: A Fable for Growthmen', *American Economic Review*, **LI** (4), September, 638–43; Robert M. Solow (1962), 'Technical Progress, Capital Formation, and Economic Growth', *American Economic Review*, **LII** (2), May, 76–86; William Brainard (1967), 'Uncertainty and the Effectiveness of Policy', *American Economic Review*, **LVII** (2), May, 411–25; Milton Friedman (1968), 'The Role of Monetary Policy', *American Economic Review*, **LVIII** (1), March, 1–17.

American Enterprise Institute for Public Policy Research for article: Arthur M. Okun (1980), 'Rational-Expectations-with-Misperceptions As a Theory of the Business Cycle', *Journal of Money, Credit, and Banking*, **12** (4, Part 2), November, 817–25.

Blackwell Publishers Ltd for articles and excerpt: J.R. Hicks (1935), 'A Suggestion for Simplifying the Theory of Money', *Economica*, **2** (5), New Series, February, 1–19; Nicholas Kaldor (1940), 'A Model of the Trade Cycle', *Economic Journal*, **50** (197), March, 78–92; A.C. Pigou (1947), 'Economic Progress in a Stable Environment', *Economica*, **XIV**, New Series, August, 180–188; A.W. Phillips (1958), 'The Relation Between Unemployment and the Rate of Change of Money Wage Rates in the United Kingdom, 1861–1957', *Economica*, **25** (100), New Series, November, 283–99; Richard G. Lipsey (1960), 'The Relation between Unemployment and the Rate of Change of Money Wage Rates in the United Kingdom, 1862–1957: A Further Analysis', *Economica*, **27** (105), New Series, February, 1–31; Franco Modigliani (1964), 'Long-run Implications of Alternative Fiscal Policies and the Burden of the National Debt', in James M. Ferguson (ed.), *Public Debt and Future Generations*, Chapter 5, Part A, 107–38, references.

Blackwell Publishers Ltd and the American Finance Association for article: Harry Markowitz (1952), 'Portfolio Selection', *Journal of Finance*, **VII**, March, 77–91.

Blackwell Publishers Ltd and the Canadian Economics Association for article: R.A. Mundell (1963), 'Capital Mobility and Stabilization Policy under Fixed and Flexible Exchange Rates', *Canadian Journal of Economics and Political Science*, **XXIX** (4), November, 475–85.

Eastern Economic Association for article: Dudley Dillard (1988), 'The Barter Illusion in Classical and Neoclassical Economics', *Eastern Economic Journal*, **XIV** (4), October–December, 299–318.

Econometric Society for article: J.R. Hicks (1937), 'Mr Keynes and the "Classics"; A Suggested Interpretation', *Econometrica*, **5** (2), April, 147–59.

Elsevier Science for excerpt: Robert E. Lucas, Jr (1976), 'Econometric Policy Evaluation: A Critique', in Karl Brunner and Allan H. Meltzer (eds), *The Phillips Curve and Labor Markets*, Carnegie-Rochester Conference Series on Public Policy, Volume 1, 19–46.

International Monetary Fund for article: Robert A. Mundell (1962), 'The Appropriate Use of Monetary and Fiscal Policy for Internal and External Stability', *IMF Staff Papers*, **IX** (1), March, 70–77.

MIT Press Journals for articles: William J. Baumol (1952), 'The Transactions Demand for Cash: An Inventory Theoretic Approach', *Quarterly Journal of Economics*, **66**, November, 545–56; John Lintner (1965), 'The Valuation of Risk Assets and the Selection of Risky Investments in Stock Portfolios and Capital Budgets', *Review of Economics and Statistics*, **XLVII** (1), February, 13–37; J. Hirshleifer (1966), 'Investment Decision Under Uncertainty: Applications of the State-Preference Approach', *Quarterly Journal of Economics*, **LXXX** (2), May, 252–77; Merton H. Miller and Daniel Orr (1966), 'A Model of the Demand for Money by Firms', *Quarterly Journal of Economics*, **LXXX** (3), August, 413–35; William Poole (1970), 'Optimal Choice of Monetary Policy Instruments in a Simple Stochastic Macro Model', *Quarterly Journal of Economics*, **84** (2), May, 197–216.

W.W. Norton & Company, Inc. for excerpt: Edmund S. Phelps (1972), 'Efficiency and Distributional Aspects of Anticipated Inflation', in *Inflation Policy and Unemployment Theory: The Cost-Benefit Approach to Monetary Planning*, Chapter 6, 170–228.

Pontificia Academia Scientiarum for article: Tjalling C. Koopmans (1965), 'On the Concept of Optimal Economic Growth', *Pontificiae Academiae Scientiarum Scripta Varia*, **28** (1), 225–300.

Review of Economic Studies Ltd for article: Kenneth J. Arrow (1962), 'The Economic Implications of Learning by Doing', *Review of Economic Studies*, **XXIX**, 155–73.

University of Chicago Press for articles: Lloyd A. Metzler (1951), 'Wealth, Saving, and the Rate of Interest', *Journal of Political Economy*, **LIX** (2), April, 93–116; Paul A. Samuelson (1958), 'An Exact Consumption-Loan Model of Interest With or Without the Social Contrivance of Money', *Journal of Political Economy*, **LXVI** (6), December, 467–82; David Cass and Menahem E. Yaari (1966), 'A Re-examination of the Pure Consumption Loans Model', *Journal of Political Economy*, **LXXIV**, August, 353–67; Robert J. Barro (1974), 'Are Government Bonds Net Wealth?', *Journal of Political Economy*, **82** (6), November–December, 1095–117; John B. Taylor (1980), 'Aggregate Dynamics and Staggered Contracts', *Journal of Political Economy*, **88** (1), February, 1–23.

Every effort has been made to trace all the copyright holders but if any have been inadvertently overlooked the publishers will be pleased to make the necessary arrangement at the first opportunity.

In addition the publishers wish to thank the Library of the London School of Economics and Political Science, the Marshall Library of Economics, Cambridge University and the Library of Indiana University at Bloomington, USA for their assistance in obtaining these articles.

Preface

Mark Blaug

James Tobin (1918–2002)

James Tobin was America's most distinguished Keynesian economist, meaning not only that he has refused to climb on the bandwagon of 'monetarism' but also that he has consistently held the view that the original Keynesian theory of income determination is capable of being extended and refined to deal with the macroeconomic problems of the 1980s and 1990s. His path-breaking theoretical work of the interest-elasticity of the demand for money, his empirical studies of consumption and saving, his analysis of the effects of financial variables on spending decisions, his efforts to incorporate money and business cycles in models of economic growth, his trenchant criticism of Milton Friedman's theoretical framework for monetarism, and his defence of demand management against the negative conclusions of the 'new classical macroeconomics' earned him the Nobel Prize in Economics in 1981. Many other honours have also come his way: the John Bates Clark Medal of the American Economic Association in 1955, President of the Econometric Society in 1958 and the American Economic Association in 1971, and honorary degrees from five American and European universities.

Tobin was born in Champaign, Illinois, and received his Bachelor's, Master's and Doctor's degrees from Harvard University in 1939, 1940 and 1947 respectively. As a graduate student, he was a teaching fellow at Harvard University in 1946–47. After a post-doctoral Junior Fellowship, he joined Yale University in 1950 where he remained as Sterling Professor of Economics except for 18 months in Washington as Member of President Kennedy's Council of Economic Advisers in 1961–62 and a year in Nairobi, Kenya, as Visiting Professor at the Nairobi Institute for Development Studies in 1972–73.

He published *National Economic Policy* (Yale University Press) in 1966. Apart from another more recent set of lectures, *Asset Accumulation and Economic Activity* (Basil Blackwell, 1980), his entire output has taken the form of articles in professional journals. They are collected together in his *Essays in Economics: Macroeconomics* (Markham, 1971; North-Holland, 1974), *The New Economics One Decade Older* (Princeton University Press, 1974), *Essays in Economics: Consumption and Econometrics* (North-Holland, 1975), *Essays in Economics: Theory and Policy* (MIT Press, 1982), and *Policies for Prosperity: Essays in a Keynesian Mode*, P.M. Jackson (ed.) (Wheatsheaf, 1987).

At the centre of Tobin's work has been the concept of asset-holding. Members of the public can hold money, bonds or capital in the form of stocks and shares. In most macroeconomic models these three assets are reduced to two – say, money and bonds as in Keynes' *General Theory*, on the assumption that bonds and stocks are perfect substitutes in the portfolio of investors and hence can be treated as equivalent. Denying this assumption,

Tobin was led to the conclusion that the effects of monetary policy on real output and income cannot be judged by looking only at the rate of interest, but that the ultimate gauge of monetary expansion or contraction is not the rate of interest but the rate of return that wealth-owners require in order to absorb the existing stock of bonds and shares into their portfolios. More generally, the ultimate measure of demand expansion or deflation is the relationship between the equities and debts of business enterprises as currently priced on the stock market, and the replacement cost of the real assets of these enterprises at current commodity prices: the ratio of these two global magnitudes he and his colleague William Brainard call 'q'. A change in q may occur because the financial sector changes the yield which investors require in order to hold equity capital but it may equally occur because of a change for any reason in investors' expectations. In 'A General Equilibrium Approach to Monetary Theory', *Journal of Money, Credit, and Banking*, February 1969, an article which synthesised his earlier work on financial flows, he concluded that the principal way in which events in the financial sector affect aggregate demand is by changing q. Monetary policy can lead to such a change but so can a change in asset preferences among money, bonds or equities. In this sense, the quantity of money is only one of the elements which alter the rates of inflation and unemployment, and it is not necessarily the most important element. This, in essence, is his reply to 'monetarism'.

In a classic paper, 'Liquidity Preference as Behavior Toward Risk', *Review of Economic Studies*, February 1958, Tobin suggested that investors trade off the mean against the variance of the returns on investment. Returns on financial assets depend on the interest rate and the capital gains or losses on the changing price of assets. These returns are, therefore, described in terms of mean returns, given by the interest rate, and the variance of these returns, given by the probability of capital gains and losses. Choice of an investment portfolio, made up of a mix of money, stocks and bonds, are hence made according to the preferences of investors for high mean/low variance versus low mean/high variance (money, generally, earns a zero mean and zero variance). Tobin's application of the concept of portfolio balance to the demand for money and assets in general in a whole series of papers since 1958 has figured heavily in the development of that branch of economics called the Theory of Finance.

Government debt and debt management, the economics of commercial banking, and active policies to stimulate economic growth have been Tobin's other areas of interest. Although an arch-opponent of Friedman's analysis of monetary problems, Tobin's studies of the poverty problem have led him to support Friedman's proposal for a guaranteed minimum annual income in the form of a negative income tax. He has also made a number of technical contributions to applied econometrics, originating a method known after him as TOBIT analysis for estimating statistical relationships involving explanations of dependent variables with large probabilities of being zero or some other limiting quantity.

James Tobin died in March 2002 in New Haven, Connecticut.

References

Primary Literature

Tobin, J. 'My Evolution as an Economist', in W. Breit and R.W. Spencer (eds), *Lives of the Laureates: Ten Nobel Economists* (MIT Press, 1990).

Secondary Literature

Purvis, D.D. 'James Tobin's Contributions to Economics', in H.W. Spiegel and W.J. Samuels (eds), *Contemporary Economists in Perspective*, vol. 1 (JAI Press, 1984).

Mark Blaug,
University of Amsterdam

[1]
The Economic Implications of Learning by Doing

It is by now incontrovertible that increases in per capita income cannot be explained simply by increases in the capital-labor ratio. Though doubtless no economist would ever have denied the role of technological change in economic growth, its overwhelming importance relative to capital formation has perhaps only been fully realized with the important empirical studies of Abramovitz [1] and Solow [11]. These results do not directly contradict the neo-classical view of the production function as an expression of technological knowledge. All that has to be added is the obvious fact that knowledge is growing in time. Nevertheless a view of economic growth that depends so heavily on an exogenous variable, let alone one so difficult to measure as the quantity of knowledge, is hardly intellectually satisfactory. From a quantitative, empirical point of view, we are left with time as an explanatory variable. Now trend projections, however necessary they may be in practice, are basically a confession of ignorance, and, what is worse from a practical viewpoint, are not policy variables.

Further, the concept of knowledge which underlies the production function at any moment needs analysis. Knowledge has to be acquired. We are not surprised, as educators, that even students subject to the same educational experiences have different bodies of knowledge, and we may therefore be prepared to grant, as has been shown empirically (see [2], Part III), that different countries, at the same moment of time, have different production functions even apart from differences in natural resource endowment.

I would like to suggest here an endogenous theory of the changes in knowledge which underlie intertemporal and international shifts in production functions. The acquisition of knowledge is what is usually termed " learning," and we might perhaps pick up some clues from the many psychologists who have studied this phenomenon (for a convenient survey, see Hilgard [5]). I do not think that the picture of technical change as a vast and prolonged process of learning about the environment in which we operate is in any way a far-fetched analogy; exactly the same phenomenon of improvement in performance over time is involved.

Of course, psychologists are no more in agreement than economists, and there are sharp differences of opinion about the processes of learning. But one empirical generalization is so clear that all schools of thought must accept it, although they interpret it in different fashions: Learning is the product of experience. Learning can only take place through the attempt to solve a problem and therefore only takes place during activity. Even the Gestalt and other field theorists, who stress the role of insight in the solution of problems (Köhler's famous apes), have to assign a significant role to previous experiences in modifying the individual's perception.

A second generalization that can be gleaned from many of the classic learning experiments is that learning associated with repetition of essentially the same problem is subject to sharply diminishing returns. There is an equilibrium response pattern for any given

155

stimulus, towards which the behavior of the learner tends with repetition. To have steadily increasing performance, then, implies that the stimulus situations must themselves be steadily evolving rather than merely repeating.

The role of experience in increasing productivity has not gone unobserved, though the relation has yet to be absorbed into the main corpus of economic theory. It was early observed by aeronautical engineers, particularly T. P. Wright [15], that the number of labor-hours expended in the production of an airframe (airplane body without engines) is a decreasing function of the total number of airframes of the same type previously produced. Indeed, the relation is remarkably precise; to produce the Nth airframe of a given type, counting from the inception of production, the amount of labor required is proportional to $N^{-1/3}$. This relation has become basic in the production and cost planning of the United States Air Force; for a full survey, see [3]. Hirsch (see [6] and other work cited there) has shown the existence of the same type of " learning curve " or " progress ratio," as it is variously termed, in the production of other machines, though the rate of learning is not the same as for airframes.

Verdoorn [14, pp. 433-4] has applied the principle of the learning curve to national outputs; however, under the assumption that output is increasing exponentially, current output is proportional to cumulative output, and it is the former variable that he uses to explain labor productivity. The empirical fitting was reported in [13]; the estimated progress ratio for different European countries is about ·5. (In [13], a neo-classical interpretation in terms of increasing capital-labor ratios was offered; see pp. 7-11.)

Lundberg [9, pp. 129-133] has given the name " Horndal effect " to a very similar phenomenon. The Horndal iron works in Sweden had no new investment (and therefore presumably no significant change in its methods of production) for a period of 15 years, yet productivity (output per manhour) rose on the average close to 2 % per annum. We find again steadily increasing performance which can only be imputed to learning from experience.

I advance the hypothesis here that technical change in general can be ascribed to experience, that it is the very activity of production which gives rise to problems for which favorable responses are selected over time. The evidence so far cited, whether from psychological or from economic literature is, of course, only suggestive. The aim of this paper is to formulate the hypothesis more precisely and draw from it a number of economic implications. These should enable the hypothesis and its consequences to be confronted more easily with empirical evidence.

The model set forth will be very simplified in some other respects to make clearer the essential role of the major hypothesis; in particular, the possibility of capital-labor substitution is ignored. The theorems about the economic world presented here differ from those in most standard economic theories; profits are the result of technical change; in a free-enterprise system, the rate of investment will be less than the optimum; net investment and the stock of capital become subordinate concepts, with gross investment taking a leading role.

In section 1, the basic assumptions of the model are set forth. In section 2, the implications for wage earners are deduced; in section 3 those for profits, the inducement to invest, and the rate of interest. In section 4, the behavior of the entire system under steady growth with mutually consistent expectations is taken up. In section 5, the diver-

THE ECONOMIC IMPLICATIONS OF LEARNING BY DOING   157

gence between social and private returns is studied in detail for a special case (where the subjective rate of discount of future consumption is a constant). Finally, in section 6, some limitations of the model and needs for further development are noted.

1. THE MODEL

The first question is that of choosing the economic variable which represents " experience ". The economic examples given above suggest the possibility of using cumulative output (the total of output from the beginning of time) as an index of experience, but this does not seem entirely satisfactory. If the rate of output is constant, then the stimulus to learning presented would appear to be constant, and the learning that does take place is a gradual approach to equilibrium behavior. I therefore take instead cumulative gross investment (cumulative production of capital goods) as an index of experience. Each new machine produced and put into use is capable of changing the environment in which production takes place, so that learning is taking place with continually new stimuli. This at least makes plausible the possibility of continued learning in the sense, here, of a steady rate of growth in productivity.

The second question is that of deciding where the learning enters the conditions of production. I follow here the model of Solow [12] and Johansen [7], in which technical change is completely embodied in new capital goods. At any moment of new time, the new capital goods incorporate all the knowledge then available, but once built their productive efficiency cannot be altered by subsequent learning.

To simplify the discussion we shall assume that the production process associated with any given new capital good is characterized by fixed coefficients, so that a fixed amount of labor is used and a fixed amount of output obtained. Further, it will be assumed that new capital goods are better than old ones in the strong sense that, if we compare a unit of capital goods produced at time t_1 with one produced at time $t_2 > t_1$, the first requires the co-operation of at least as much labor as the second, and produces no more product. Under this assumption, a new capital good will always be used in preference to an older one.

Let G be cumulative gross investment. A unit capital good produced when cumulative gross investment has reached G will be said to have *serial number G*. Let

$\lambda(G)$ = amount of labor used in production with a capital good of serial number G,
$\gamma(G)$ = output capacity of a capital good of serial number G,
x = total output,
L = total labor force employed.

It is assumed that $\lambda(G)$ is a non-increasing function, while $\gamma(G)$ is a non-decreasing function. Then, regardless of wages or rental value of capital goods, it always pays to use a capital good of higher serial number before one of lower serial number.

It will further be assumed that capital goods have a fixed lifetime, $\overline{T}$. Then capital goods disappear in the same order as their serial numbers. It follows that at any moment of time, the capital goods in use will be all those with serial numbers from some G' to G, the current cumulative gross investment. Then

$$(1) \qquad x = \int_{G'}^{G} \gamma(G)dG,$$

$$(2) \quad L = \int_{G'}^{G} \lambda(G)dG.$$

The magnitudes x, L, G, and G' are, of course, all functions of time, to be designated by t, and they will be written $x(t)$, $L(t)$, $G(t)$, and $G'(t)$ when necessary to point up the dependence. Then $G(t)$, in particular, is the cumulative gross investment up to time t. The assumption about the lifetime of capital goods implies that

$$(3) \quad G'(t) \geqq G(t - T).$$

Since $G(t)$ is given at time t, we can solve for G' from (1) or (2) or the equality in (3). In a growth context, the most natural assumption is that of full employment. The labor force is regarded as a given function of time and is assumed equal to the labor employed, so that $L(t)$ is a given function. Then $G'(t)$ is obtained by solving in (2). If the result is substituted into (1), x can be written as a function of L and G, analogous to the usual production function. To write this, define

$$\Lambda(G) = \int \lambda(G)dG,$$

$$(4)$$

$$\Gamma(g) = \int \gamma(G)dG.$$

These are to be regarded as indefinite integrals. Since $\lambda(G)$ and $\gamma(G)$ are both positive, $\Lambda(G)$ and $\Gamma(G)$ are strictly increasing and therefore have inverses, $\Lambda^{-1}(u)$ and $\Gamma^{-1}(v)$, respectively. Then (1) and (2) can be written, respectively,

$$(1') \quad x = \Gamma(G) - \Gamma(G'),$$

$$(2') \quad L = \Lambda(G) - \Lambda(G').$$

Solve for G' from (2').

$$(5) \quad G' = \Lambda^{-1}[\Lambda(G) - L].$$

Substitute (5) into (1').

$$(6) \quad x = \Gamma(G) - \Gamma\{\Lambda^{-1}[\Lambda(G) - L]\},$$

which is thus a production function in a somewhat novel sense. Equation (6) is always valid, but under the full employment assumption we can regard L as the labor force available.

A second assumption, more suitable to a depression situation, is that in which demand for the product is the limiting factor. Then x is taken as given; G' can be derived from (1) or (1'), and employment then found from (2) or (2'). If this is less than the available labor force, we have Keynesian unemployment.

A third possibility, which, like the first, may be appropriate to a growth analysis, is that the solution (5) with L as the labor force, does not satisfy (3). In this case, there is a shortage of capital due to depreciation. There is again unemployment but now due to structural discrepancies rather than to demand deficiency.

THE ECONOMIC IMPLICATIONS OF LEARNING BY DOING   159

In any case, except by accident, there is either unemployed labor or unemployed capital; there could be both in the demand deficiency case. Of course, a more neo-classical model, with substitution between capital and labor for each serial number of capital good, might permit full employment of both capital and labor, but this remains a subject for further study.

In what follows, the full-employment case will be chiefly studied. The capital shortage case, the third one, will be referred to parenthetically. In the full-employment case, the depreciation assumption no longer matters; obsolescence, which occurs for all capital goods with serial numbers below G', becomes the sole reason for the retirement of capital goods from use.

The analysis will be carried through for a special case. To a very rough approximation, the capital-output ratio has been constant, while the labor-output ratio has been declining. It is therefore assumed that

(7) $\qquad \gamma(G) = a,$

a constant, while $\lambda(G)$ is a decreasing function of G. To be specific, it will be assumed that $\lambda(G)$ has the form found in the study of learning curves for airframes.

(8) $\qquad \lambda(G) = bG^{-n},$

where $n > 0$. Then

$\qquad \Gamma(G) = aG, \Lambda(G) = cG^{1-n}$, where $c = b/(1-n)$ for $n \neq 1$.

Then (6) becomes

(9) $\qquad x = aG[1 - \left(1 - \dfrac{L}{cG^{1-n}}\right)^{1/(1-n)}]$ if $n \neq 1$.

Equation (9) is always well defined in the relevant ranges, since from (2'),

$\qquad L = \Lambda(G) - \Lambda(G') \leqq \Lambda(G) = cG^{1-n}.$

When $n = 1$, $\Lambda(G) = b \log G$ (where the natural logarithm is understood), and

(10) $\qquad x = aG(1 - e^{-L/b})$ if $n = 1$.

Although (9) and (10) are, in a sense, production functions, they show increasing returns to scale in the variables G and L. This is obvious in (10) where an increase in G, with L constant, increases x in the same proportion; a simultaneous increase in L will further increase x. In (9), first suppose that $n < 1$. Then a proportional increase in L and G increases L/G^{1-n} and therefore increases the expression in brackets which multiplies G. A similar argument holds if $n > 1$. It should be noted that x increases more than pro-portionately to scale changes in G and L in general, not merely for the special case defined by (7) and (8). This would be verified by careful examination of the behavior of (6), when it is recalled that $\lambda(G)$ is non-increasing and $\gamma(G)$ is non-decreasing, with the strict inequality holding in at least one. It is obvious intuitively, since the addition-al amounts of L and G are used more efficiently than the earlier ones.

The increasing returns do not, however, lead to any difficulty with distribution theory. As we shall see, both capital and labor are paid their marginal products, suitably defined. The explanation is, of course, that the private marginal productivity of capital (more strictly, of new investment) is less than the social marginal productivity since the learning effect is not compensated in the market.

The production assumptions of this section are designed to play the role assigned by Kaldor to his " technical progress function," which relates the rate of growth of output per worker to the rate of growth of capital per worker (see [8], section VIII). I prefer to think of relations between rates of growth as themselves derived from more fundamental relations between the magnitudes involved. Also, the present formulation puts more stress on gross rather than net investment as the basic agent of technical change.

Earlier, Haavelmo ([4], sections 7.1 and 7.2) had suggested a somewhat similar model. Output depended on both capital and the stock of knowledge; investment depended on output, the stock of capital, and the stock of knowledge. The stock of knowledge was either simply a function of time or, in a more sophisticated version, the consequence of investment, the educational effect of each act of investment decreasing exponentially in time.

Verdoorn [14, pp. 436-7] had also developed a similar simple model in which capital and labor needed are non-linear functions of output (since the rate of output is, approximately, a measure of cumulative output and therefore of learning) and investment a constant fraction of output. He notes that under these conditions, full employment of capital and labor simultaneously is in general impossible—a conclusion which also holds for for the present model as we have seen. However, Verdoorn draws the wrong conclusion: that the savings ratio must be fixed by some public mechanism at the uniquely determined level which would insure full employment of both factors; the correct conclusion is that one factor or the other will be unemployed. The social force of this conclusion is much less in the present model since the burden of unemployment may fall on obsolescent capital; Verdoorn assumes his capital to be homogeneous in nature.

2. WAGES

Under the full employment assumption the profitability of using the capital good with serial number G' must be zero; for if it were positive it would be profitable to use capital goods with higher serial number and if it were negative capital good G' would not be used contrary to the definition of G'. Let

$$w = \text{wage rate with output as numéraire.}$$

From (1') and (7)

(11) $\qquad G' = G - (x/a)$

so that

(12) $\qquad \lambda(G') = b\left(G - \frac{x}{a}\right)^{-n}.$

The output from capital good G' is $\gamma(G')$ while the cost of operation is $\lambda(G')w$. Hence

$$\gamma(G') = \lambda(G')w$$

or from (7) and (12)

(13) $\qquad w = a\left(G - \frac{x}{a}\right)^{n}/b.$

It is interesting to derive labor's share which is wL/x. From (2') with $\Lambda(g) = cG^{1-n}$ and G' given by (11)

THE ECONOMIC IMPLICATIONS OF LEARNING BY DOING   161

$$L = c \left[\ G^{1-n} - \left(G - \frac{x}{a} \right)^{1-n} \right],$$

for $n \neq 1$ and therefore

(14) $wL/x = a \left[\left(\frac{G}{x} - \frac{1}{a} \right)^n \left(\frac{G}{x} \right)^{1-n} - \left(\frac{G}{x} - \frac{1}{a} \right) \right]/(1-n)$ for $n \neq 1,$

where use has been made of the relation, $c = b/(1-n)$.   It is interesting to note that labor's share is determined by the ratio G/x.

Since, however, x is determined by G and L, which, at any moment of time, are data, it is also useful to express the wage ratio, w, and labor's share, wL/x, in terms of L and G.   First, G' can be found by solving for it from (2').

(15) $G' = \left(\ G^{1-n} - \frac{L}{c} \right)^{1/(1-n)}$ for $n \neq 1.$

We can then use the same reasoning as above, and derive

(16) $w = a \left(G^{1-n} - \frac{L}{c} \right)^{n/(1-n)}/b,$

(17) $\dfrac{wL}{x} = \dfrac{\left[\left(\dfrac{L}{G^{1-n}} \right)^{(1-n)/n} - \dfrac{1}{c} \left(\dfrac{L}{G^{1-n}} \right)^{1/n} \right]^{n/(1-n)}}{b \left[1 - \left(1 - \dfrac{L}{cG^{1-n}} \right)^{1/(1-n)} \right]} .$

Labor's share thus depends on the ratio L/G^{1-n}; it can be shown to decrease as the ratio increases.

For completeness, I note the corresponding formulas for the case $n = 1$.   In terms of G and x, we have

(18) $w = (aG - x)/b,$

(19) $wL/x = \left(\dfrac{aG}{x} - 1 \right) \log \dfrac{G/x}{(G/x) - (1/a)}.$

In terms of G and L, we have

(20) $G' = Ge^{-L/b},$

(21) $w = \dfrac{aG}{be^{L/b}},$

(22) $wL/x = \dfrac{L}{b(e^{L/b} - 1)}.$

In this case, labor's share depends only on L, which is indeed the appropriate special case ($n=1$) of the general dependence on L/G^{1-n}.

The preceding discussion has assumed full employment. In the capital shortage case, there cannot be a competitive equilibrium with positive wage since there is necessarily unemployment. A zero wage is, however, certainly unrealistic. To complete the model, it would be necessary to add some other assumption about the behavior of wages. This case will not be considered in general; for the special case of steady growth, see Section 5.

3. PROFITS AND INVESTMENT

The profit at time t from a unit investment made at time $v \leq t$ is

$$\gamma[G(v)] - w(t)\,\lambda[G(v)].$$

In contemplating an investment at time v, the stream of potential profits depends upon expectations of future wages. We will suppose that looking ahead at any given moment of time each entrepreneur assumes that wages will rise exponentially from the present level. Thus the wage rate expected at time v to prevail at time t is

$$w(v)\,e^{\theta(t-v)},$$

and the profit expected at time v to be received at time t is

$$\gamma[G(v)]\,[1-W(v)\,e^{\theta(t-v)}],$$

where

(23) $W(v) = w(v)\,\lambda[G(v)]/\gamma[G(v)],$

the labor cost per unit output at the time the investment is made. The dependence of W on v will be made explicit only when necessary. The profitability of the investment is expected to decrease with time (if $\theta > 0$) and to reach zero at time $T^* + v$, defined by the equation

(24) $We^{\theta T^*} = 1.$

Thus T^* is the expected economic lifetime of the investment, provided it does not exceed the physical lifetime, T. Let

(25) $T = \min(\bar{T}, T^*).$

Then the investor plans to derive profits only over an interval of length T, either because the investment wears out or because wages have risen to the point where it is unprofitable to operate. Since the expectation of wage rises which causes this abandonment derives from anticipated investment and the consequent technological progress, T^* represents the expected date of obsolescence. Let

$$\rho = \text{rate of interest}.$$

THE ECONOMIC IMPLICATIONS OF LEARNING BY DOING   163

If the rate of interest is expected to remain constant over the future, then the discounted stream of profits over the effective lifetime, T, of the investment is

$$(26) \quad S = \int_0^T e^{-\rho t} \gamma[G(v)] (1 - W e^{\theta t}) dt,$$

or

$$(27) \quad \frac{S}{\gamma[G(v)]} = \frac{1 - e^{-\rho T}}{\rho} + \frac{W(1 - e^{-(\rho - \theta)T})}{\theta - \rho}.$$

Let

$$(28) \quad V = e^{-\theta T} = \max (e^{-\theta \bar{T}}, W), \quad \alpha = \rho/\theta.$$

Then

$$(29) \quad \frac{\theta S}{\gamma[G(v)]} = \frac{1 - V^\alpha}{\alpha} + \frac{W(1 - V^{\alpha - 1})}{1 - \alpha} = R(\alpha).$$

The definitions of $R(\alpha)$ for $\alpha = 0$ and $\alpha = 1$ needed to make the function continuous are:

$$R(0) = -\log V + W(1 - V^{-1}), \quad R(1) = 1 - V + W \log V.$$

If all the parameters of (26), (27), or (29) are held constant, S is a function of ρ, and, equivalently, R of α. If (26) is differentiated with respect to ρ, we find

$$dS/d\rho = \int_0^T (-t) e^{-\rho t} \gamma[G(v)] (1 - W e^{\theta t}) dt < 0.$$

Also

$$S < \gamma[G(v)] \int_0^T e^{-\rho t} dt = \gamma[G(v)] (1 - e^{-\rho T})/\rho$$

$$< \gamma[G(v)]/\rho.$$

Since obviously $S > 0$, S approaches 0 as ρ approaches infinity. Since R and α differ from S and ρ, respectively, only by positive constant factors, we conclude

$$dR/d\alpha < 0, \quad \lim_{\alpha \to +\infty} R(\alpha) = 0.$$

To examine the behavior of $R(\alpha)$ as α approaches $-\infty$, write

$$R(\alpha) = - \frac{(1/V)^{1-\alpha}}{(1-\alpha)^2} [(1-\alpha)V + \alpha W] \left(\frac{1-\alpha}{\alpha} \right) + \frac{1}{\alpha} + \frac{W}{1-\alpha}.$$

The last two terms approach zero. As α approaches $-\infty$, $1 - \alpha$ approaches $+\infty$. Since $1/V > 1$, the factor

$$\frac{(1/V)^{1-\alpha}}{(1 - \alpha)^2}$$

approaches $+\infty$, since an exponential approaches infinity faster than any power. From (28), $V \geq W$. If $V = W$, then the factor,

$$(1 - \alpha)V - \alpha W = \alpha(W - V) + V,$$

is a positive constant; if $V > W$, then it approaches $+\infty$ as α approaches $-\infty$. Finally,

$$\frac{1 - \alpha}{\alpha}$$

necessarily approaches -1. Hence,

(30) $R(\alpha)$ is a strictly decreasing function, approaching $+\infty$ as α approaches $-\infty$ and 0 as α approaches $+\infty$.

The market, however, should adjust the rate of return so that the discounted stream of profits equals the cost of investment, i.e., $S = 1$, or, from (29),

(31) $R(\alpha) = \theta/\gamma[G(v)]$.

Since the right-hand side of (31) is positive, (30) guarantees the existence of an α which satisfies (31). For a given θ, the equilibrium rate of return, ρ, is equal to α 0; it may indeed be negative. The rate of return is thus determined by the expected rate of increase in wages, current labor costs per unit output, and the physical lifetime of the investment. Further, if the first two are sufficiently large, the physical lifetime becomes irrelevant, since then $T^* < \bar{T}$, and $T = T^*$.

The discussion of profits and returns has not made any special assumptions as to the form of the production relations.

4. RATIONAL EXPECTATIONS IN A MACROECONOMIC GROWTH MODEL

Assume a one-sector model so that the production relations of the entire economy are described by the model of section 1. In particular, this implies that gross investment at any moment of time is simply a diversion of goods that might otherwise be used for consumption. Output and gross investment can then be measured in the same units.

The question arises, can the expectations assumed to govern investment behavior in the preceding section actually be fulfilled? Specifically, can we have a constant relative increase of wages and a constant rate of interest which, if anticipated, will lead entrepreneurs to invest at a rate which, in conjunction with the exogenously given rate of interest to remain at the given level? Such a state of affairs is frequently referred to as "perfect foresight," but a better term is "rational expectations," a term introduced by J. Muth [10].

We study this question first for the full employment case. For this case to occur, the physical lifetime of investments must not be an effective constraint. If, in the notation of the last section, $T^* > \bar{T}$, and if wage expectations are correct, then investments will disappear through depreciation at a time when they are still yielding positive current profits. As seen in section 2, this is incompatible with competitive equilibrium and full employment. Assume therefore that

THE ECONOMIC IMPLICATIONS OF LEARNING BY DOING 165

(32) $\quad T^* \leqq \bar{T}$;

then from (28), $W = V$, and from (29) and (31), the equilibrium value of ρ is determined by the equation,

(33) $\quad \dfrac{1 - W^\alpha}{\alpha} + \dfrac{W - W^\alpha}{1 - \alpha} = \dfrac{\theta}{a}$,

where, on the right-hand side, use is made of (7).

From (16), it is seen that for the wage rate to rise at a constant rate θ, it is necessary that the quantity,

$$G^{1-n} - \frac{L}{c},$$

rise at a rate $\theta(1 - n)/n$. For θ constant, it follows from (33) that a constant ρ and therefore a constant α requires that W be constant. For the specific production relations (7) and (8), (23) shows that

$$W = a \frac{\left(G^{1-n} - \dfrac{L}{c}\right)^{n/(1-n)} bG^{-n}}{b} = \left(1 - \frac{L}{cG^{1-n}}\right)^{n/(1-n)},$$

and therefore the constancy of W is equivalent to that of L/G^{1-n}. In combination with the preceding remark, we see that

(34) $\quad L$ increases at rate $\theta(1 - n)/n$, G increases at rate θ/n.

Suppose that

σ = rate of increase of the labor force,

is a given constant. Then

(35) $\quad \theta = n\,\sigma/(1-n)$,

(36) $\quad$ the rate of increase of G is $\sigma/(1-n)$.

Substitution into the production function (9) yields

(37) $\quad$ the rate of increase of x is $\sigma/(1-n)$.

From (36) and (37), the ratio G/x is constant over time. However, the value at which it is constant is not determined by the considerations so far introduced; the savings function is needed to complete the system. Let the constant ratio be

(38) $\quad G(t)/x(t) = \mu$.

Define

$g(t)$ = rate of gross investment at time $t = dG/dt$.

From (36), $g/G = \sigma/(1 - n)$, a constant. Then

(39) $g/x = (g/G)(G/x) = \mu\,\sigma/(1 - n)$.

     A simple assumption is that the ratio of gross saving (equals gross investment) to income (equals output) is a function of the rate of return, ρ; a special case would be the common assumption of a constant savings-to-income ratio. Then μ is a function of ρ. On the other hand, we can write W as follows, using (23) and (13):

(40) $$W = a\,\frac{\left(G - \dfrac{x}{a}\right)^n}{b}\,\frac{bG^{-n}}{a} = \left(1 - \frac{x}{aG}\right)^n = \left(1 - \frac{1}{a\mu}\right)^n.$$

Since θ is given by (35), (33) is a relation between W and ρ, and, by (40) between μ and ρ. We thus have two relations between μ and ρ, so they are determinate.

     From (38), μ determines one relation between G and X. If the labor force, L, is given at one moment of time, the production function (9) constitutes a second such relation, and the system is completely determinate.

     As in many growth models, the rates of growth of the variables in the system do not depend on savings behavior; however, their levels do.

     It should be made clear that all that has been demonstrated is the existence of a solution in which all variables have constant rates of growth, correctly anticipated. The stability of the solution requires further study.

     The growth rate for wages implied by the solution has one paradoxical aspect; it increases with the rate of growth of the labor force (provided $n < 1$). The explanation seems to be that under full employment, the increasing labor force permits a more rapid introduction of the newer machinery. It should also be noted that, for a constant saving ratio, g/x, an increase in σ decreases μ, from (39), from which it can be seen that wages at the initial time period would be lower. In this connection it may be noted that since G cannot decrease, it follows from (36) that σ and $1-n$ must have the same sign for the steady growth path to be possible. The most natural case, of course, is $\sigma > 0$, $n < 1$.

     This solution is, however, admissible only if the condition (32), that the rate of depreciation not be too rapid, be satisfied. We can find an explicit formula for the economic lifetime, T^*, of new investment. From (24), it satisfies the condition

    $e^{-\theta T^*} = W$.

If we use (35) and (40) and solve for T^*, we find

(41) $$T^* = \frac{-(1-n)}{\sigma}\log\left[1 - \frac{1}{a\mu}\right]$$

and this is to be compared with $\bar{T}$; the full employment solution with rational expectations of exponentially increasing wages and constant interest is admissible if $T^* \leq \bar{T}$.

If $T^* > \bar{T}$, then the full employment solution is inadmissible. One might ask if a constant-growth solution is possible in this case. The answer depends on assumptions about the dynamics of wages under this condition.

We retain the two conditions, that wages rise at a constant rate θ, and that the rate of interest be constant. With constant θ, the rate of interest, ρ, is determined from (31); from (29), this requires that

(42) W is constant over time.

From the definition of W, (23), and the particular form of the production relations, (7) and (8), it follows that the wage rate, w, must rise at the same rate as G^n, or

(43) G rises at a constant rate θ/n.

In the presence of continued unemployment, the most natural wage dynamics in a free market would be a decreasing, or, at best, constant wage level. But since G can never decrease, it follows from (43) that θ can never be negative. Instead of making a specific assumption about wage changes, it will be assumed that any choice of θ can be imposed, perhaps by government or union or social pressure, and it is asked what restrictions on the possible values of θ are set by the other equilibrium conditions.

In the capital shortage case, the serial number of the oldest capital good in use is determined by the physical lifetime of the good, i.e.,

$G' = G(t - T)$. From (43),

$\qquad G(t - T) = e^{-\theta T/n}\, G.$

Then, from (1') and (7),

$\qquad x = aG(1 - e^{-\bar{\theta} T/n}),$

so that the ratio, G/x, or μ. is a constant,

(44) $\mu = 1/a(1 - e^{-\theta T/n}).$

From (43), $g/G = \theta/n$; hence, by the same argument as that leading to (39),

(45) $g/x = \theta/na(1 - e^{-\theta T/n}).$

There are three unknown constants of the growth process, θ, ρ, and W. If, as before, it is assumed that the gross savings ratio, g/x, is a function of the rate of return, ρ, then, for any given ρ, θ can be determined from (45); note that the right-hand side of (45) is a strictly increasing function of θ for $\theta \geq 0$, so that the determination is unique, and the rate of growth is an increasing function of the gross savings ratio, contrary to the situation in the full employment case. Then W can be solved for from (31) and (29).

Thus the rate of return is a freely disposable parameter whose choice determines the rate of growth and W, which in turn determines the initial wage rate. There are, of course, some inequalities which must be satisfied to insure that the solution corresponds to the capital shortage rather than the full employment case; in particular, $W \leq V$ and also the labor force must be sufficient to permit the expansion. From (2'), this means that the labor force must at all times be at least equal to

$$cG^{1-n} - c(G')^{1-n} = cG^{1-n}(1 - e^{-\theta(1-n)\bar{T}/n});$$

if σ is the growth rate of the labor force, we must then have (46)

(46) $\sigma \geq \theta(1 - n)/n,$

which sets an upper bound on θ (for $n < 1$). Other constraints on ρ are implied by the conditions $\theta \geq 0$ and $W \geq 0$ (if it is assumed that wage rates are non-negative). The first condition sets a lower limit on g/x; it can be shown, from (45) that

(47) $g/x \geq 1/a\bar{T};$

i.e., the gross savings ratio must be at least equal to the amount of capital goods needed to produce one unit of output over their lifetime. The constraint $W > 0$ implies an interval in which ρ must lie. The conditions under which these constraints are consistent (so that at least one solution exists for the capital shortage case) have not been investigated in detail.

5. DIVERGENCE OF PRIVATE AND SOCIAL PRODUCT

As has already been emphasized, the presence of learning means that an act of investment benefits future investors, but this benefit is not paid for by the market. Hence, it is to be expected that the aggregate amount of investment under the competitive model of the last section will fall short of the socially optimum level. This difference will be investigated in detail in the present section under a simple assumption as to the utility function of society. For brevity, I refer to the *competitive solution* of the last section, to be contrasted with the *optimal* solution. Full employment is assumed. It is shown that the socially optimal growth rate is the same as that under competitive conditions, but the socially optimal ratio of gross investment to output is higher than the competitive level.

Utility is taken to be a function of the stream of consumption derived from the productive mechanism. Let

$$c = \text{consumption} = \text{output} - \text{gross investment} = x - g.$$

It is in particular assumed that future consumption is discounted at a constant rate, β, so that utility is

(48) $$U = \int_0^{+\infty} e^{-\beta t}c(t)dt = \int_0^{+\infty} e^{-\beta t}x(t)dt.$$

$$-\int_0^{+\infty} e^{-\beta t}g(t)dt.$$

Integration by parts yields

$$\int_0^{+\infty} e^{-\beta t}g(t)dt = e^{-\beta t}G(t)\Big|_0^{+\infty} + \beta \int_0^{+\infty} e^{-\beta t}G(t)dt.$$

THE ECONOMIC IMPLICATIONS OF LEARNING BY DOING 169

From (48),

(49) $\qquad U = U_1 - \lim_{t \to +\infty} e^{-\beta t} G(t) + G(0),$

where

(50) $\qquad U_1 = \int_0^{+\infty} e^{-\beta t} [x(t) - \beta\, G(t)] dt.$

The policy problem is the choice of the function $G(t)$, with $G'(t) \geq 0$, to maximize (49), where $x(t)$ is determined by the production function (9), and

(51) $\qquad L(t) = L_0 e^{\sigma t}.$

The second term in (49) is necessarily non-negative. It will be shown that, for sufficiently high discount rate, β, the function $G(t)$ which maximizes U_1 also has the property that the second term in (49) is zero; hence, it also maximizes (49), since $G(0)$ is given.

Substitute (9) and (51) into (50).

$$U_1 = \int_0^{+\infty} e^{-\beta t} G(t) \left[a - \beta - a\left(1 - \frac{L_0 e^{\sigma t}}{c G^{1-n}} \right)^{1/(1-n)} \right] dt.$$

Let $\bar{G}(t) = G(t)\, e^{-\sigma t/(1-n)}.$

$$U_1 = \int_0^{+\infty} e^{-\left(\beta - \frac{\sigma}{1-n} \right) t}\, \bar{G}(t) \left[a - \beta - a\left(1 - \frac{L_0}{c \bar{G}^{1-n}} \right)^{1/(1-n)} \right] dt.$$

Assume that

(52) $\qquad \beta > \dfrac{\sigma}{1-n};$

otherwise an infinite utility is attainable. Then to maximize U_1 it suffices to choose $\bar{G}(t)$ so as to maximize, for each t,

(53) $\qquad \bar{G}\left[a - \beta - a\left(1 - \frac{L_0}{c \bar{G}^{1-n}} \right)^{1/(1-n)} \right].$

Before actually determining the maximum, it can be noted that the maximizing value of $\bar{G}$ is independent of t and is therefore a constant. Hence, the optimum policy is

(54) $\qquad G(t) = \bar{G}\, e^{\sigma t/(1-n)},$

so that, from (36), the growth rate is the same as the competitive. From (52), $e^{-\beta t} G(t) \longrightarrow 0$ as $t \longrightarrow +\infty$.

To determine the optimal $\bar{G}$, it will be convenient to make a change of variables. Define

$$v = \left(1 - \frac{L_0}{c \bar{G}^{1-n}} \right)^{n/(1-n)}.$$

so that

(55) $\hat{G} = \left[\dfrac{L_0}{(1 - v^{(1-n)/n})} \right]^{1/(1-n)}.$

The analysis will be carried through primarily for the case where the output per unit capital is sufficiently high, more specifically, where

(56) $a > \beta.$

Let

(57) $\gamma = 1 - \dfrac{\beta}{a} > 0.$

The maximizing $\hat{G}$, or v, is unchanged by multiplying (53), the function to be maximized, by the positive quantity, $(c/L_0)^{1/(1-n)}/a$ and then substituting from (55) and (57). Thus, v maximizes

$$(1 - v^{(1-n)/n})^{-1/(1-n)} (\gamma - v^{1/n}).$$

The variable v ranges from 0 to 1. However, the second factor vanishes when $v = \gamma^n < 1$ (since $\gamma < 1$) and becomes negative for larger values of v; since the first factor is always positive, it can be assumed that $v < \gamma^n$ in searching for a maximum, and both factors are positive. Then v also maximizes the logarithm of the above function, which is

$$f(v) = - \frac{\log (1 - v^{(1-n)/n})}{1 - n} + \log (\gamma - v^{1/n}),$$

so that

$$f'(v) = - \frac{v^{\frac{1}{n} - 2}}{n} \left[\frac{\gamma - v}{(1 - v^{(1-n)/n}) (\gamma - v^{1/n})} \right].$$

Clearly, with $n < 1$, $f'(v) > 0$ when $0 < v < \gamma$ and $f'(v) < 0$ when $\gamma < v < \gamma^n$, so that the maximum is obtained at

(58) $v = \gamma.$

The optimum $\hat{G}$ is determined by substituting γ for v in (55).

From (54), L/G^{1-n} is a constant over time. From the definition of v and (58), then,

$$\gamma = \left(1 - \frac{L}{cG^{1-n}} \right)^{n/(1-n)}$$

for all t along the optimal path, and, from the production function (9),

(59) $\gamma = \left(1 - \dfrac{x}{aG} \right)^n$ for all t along the optimal path.

This optimal solution will be compared with the competitive solution of steady growth studied in the last section. From (40), we know that

(60) $W = \left(1 - \dfrac{x}{aG} \right)^n$ for all t along the competitive path.

It will be demonstrated that $W < \gamma$; from this it follows that *the ratio G/x is less along the competitive path than along the optimal path.* Since along both paths,

THE ECONOMIC IMPLICATIONS OF LEARNING BY DOING   171

$$g/x = [\sigma/(1-n)] (G/x),$$

it also follows that *the gross savings ratio is smaller along the competitive path than along the optimal path.*

For the particular utility function (48), the supply of capital is infinitely elastic at $\rho = \beta$; i.e., the community will take any investment with a rate of return exceeding β and will take no investment at a rate of return less than β. For an equilibrium in which some, but not all, income is saved, we must have

(61) $\rho = \beta.$

From (35), $\theta = n\sigma/(1-n)$; hence, by definition (28),

(62) $\alpha = (1-n)\beta/n\sigma.$

Since $n < 1$, it follows from (62) and the assumption (52) that (63)

(63) $\alpha > 1.$

Equation (33) then becomes the one by which W is determined. The left-hand side will be denoted as $F(W)$.

$$F'(W) = \frac{1 - W^{\alpha-1}}{1 - \alpha}.$$

From (63), $F'(W) < 0$ for $0 \geq W < 1$, the relevant range since the investment will never be profitable if $W > 1$. To demonstrate that $W < \gamma$, it suffices to show that $F(W) > F(\gamma)$ for that value of W which satisfies (33), i.e., to show that

(64) $F(\gamma) < \theta/a.$

Finally, to demonstrate (64), note that $\gamma < 1$ and $\alpha > 1$, which imply that $\gamma^\alpha < \gamma$, and therefore

$$(1 - \alpha) - \gamma^\alpha + \alpha\gamma > (1 - \alpha)(1 - \gamma).$$

Since $\alpha > 1$, $\alpha(1 - \alpha) < 0$. Dividing both sides by this magnitude yields

$$\frac{1 - \gamma^\alpha}{\alpha} + \frac{\gamma - \gamma^\alpha}{1 - \alpha} < \frac{1 - \gamma}{\alpha} = \frac{\theta}{a}$$

where use is made of (57), (28), and (61); but from (33), the left-hand side is precisely $F(\gamma)$, so that (64) is demonstrated.

The case $a \leq \beta$, excluded by (56), can be handled similarly; in that case the optimum v is 0. The subsequent reasoning follows in the same way so that the corresponding competitive path would have $W < 0$, which is, however, impossible.

6. SOME COMMENTS ON THE MODEL

(1) Many writers, such as Theodore Schultz, have stressed the improvement in the quality of the labor force over time as a source of increased productivity. This interpretation can be incorporated in the present model by assuming that σ, the rate of growth of the labor force, incorporates qualitative as well as quantitative increase.

(2) In this model, there is only one efficient capital-labor ratio for new investment at any moment of time. Most other models, on the contrary, have assumed that alternative capital-labor ratios are possible both before the capital good is built and after. A still more plausible model is that of Johansen [7], according to which alternative capital-labor ratios are open to the entrepreneur's choice at the time of investment but are fixed once the investment is congealed into a capital good.

(3) In this model, as in those of Solow [12] and Johansen [7], the learning takes place in effect only in the capital goods industry; no learning takes place in the use of a capital good once built. Lundberg's Horndal effect suggests that this is not realistic. The model should be extended to include this possibility.

(4) It has been assumed here that learning takes place only as a by-product of ordinary production. In fact, society has created institutions, education and research, whose purpose it is to enable learning to take place more rapidly. A fuller model would take account of these as additional variables.

REFERENCES.

[1] Abramovitz, M., " Resource and Output Trends in the United States Since 1870," *American Economic Review, Papers and Proceedings of the American Economic Associations*, 46 (May, 1956): 5-23.

[2] Arrow, K. J., H. B. Chenery, B. S. Minhas, and R. M. Solow, " Capital-Labor Substitution and Economic Efficiency," *Review of Economics and Statistics*, 43 (1961): 225-250.

[3] Asher, H., *Cost-Quantity Relationships in the Airframe Industry*, R-291, Santa Monica, Calif.: The RAND Corporation, 1956.

[4] Haavelmo, T. *A Study in the Theory of Economic Evolution*, Amsterdam: North Holland, 1954.

[5] Hilgard, E. R., *Theories of Learning*, 2nd ed., New York: Appleton-Century-Crofts, 1956.

[6] Hirsch, W. Z., " Firm Progress Radios," *Econometrica*, 24 (1956): 136-143.

[7] Johansen, L., " Substitution vs. Fixed Production Coefficients in the Theory of Economic Growth: A Synthesis," *Econometrica*, 27 (1959): 157-176.

[8] Kaldor, N., " Capital Accumulation and Economic Growth," in F. A. Lutz and D. C. Hague (eds.), *The Theory of Capiatl*, New York: St. Martin's Press, 1961, 177-222.

THE ECONOMIC IMPLICATIONS OF LEARNING BY DOING   173

[9] Lundberg, E., *Produktivitet och räntabilitet*, Stockholm: P. A. Norstedt and Söner, 1961.

[10] Muth, J., " Rational Expectations and the Theory of Price Movements," *Econometrica* (in press).

[11] Solow, R. M., " Technical Change and the Aggregate Production Function," *Review of Economics and Statistics*, 39 (1957): 312-320.

[12] Solow, R. M., " Investment and Technical Progress," in K. J. Arrow, S. Karlin, and P. Suppes (eds.), *Mathematical Methods in the Social Sciences*, 1959, Stanford, Calif.: Stanford University Press, 1960, 89-104.

[13] Verdoorn, P. J., " Fattori che regolano lo sviluppo della produttività del lavoro," *L'Industria*, 1 (1949).

[14] Verdoorn, P. J., " Complementarity and Long-Range Projections," *Econometrica*, 24 (1956): 429-450.

[15] Wright, T. P., " Factors Affecting the Cost of Airplanes," *Journal of the Aeronautical Sciences*, 3 (1936): 122-128.

Stanford.   KENNETH J. ARROW.

[2]

Are Government Bonds Net Wealth?

Robert J. Barro

University of Chicago

The assumption that government bonds are perceived as net wealth by the private sector is crucial in demonstrating real effects of shifts in the stock of public debt. In particular, the standard effects of "expansionary" fiscal policy on aggregate demand hinge on this assumption. Government bonds will be perceived as net wealth only if their value exceeds the capitalized value of the implied stream of future tax liabilities. This paper considers the effects on bond values and tax capitalization of finite lives, imperfect private capital markets, a government monopoly in the production of bond "liquidity services," and uncertainty about future tax obligations. It is shown within the context of an overlapping-generations model that finite lives will not be relevant to the capitalization of future tax liabilities so long as current generations are connected to future generations by a chain of operative intergenerational transfers (either in the direction from old to young or in the direction from young to old). Applications of this result to social security and to other types of imposed intergenerational transfer schemes are also noted. In the presence of imperfect private capital markets, government debt issue will increase net wealth if the government is more efficient, at the margin, than the private market in carrying out the loan process. Similarly, if the government has monopoly power in the production of bond "liquidity services," then public debt issue will raise net wealth. Finally, the existence of uncertainty with respect to individual future tax liabilities implies that public debt issue may increase the overall risk contained in household balance sheets and thereby effectively reduce household wealth.

The assumption that government bonds are perceived as net wealth by the private sector plays an important role in theoretical analyses of monetary and fiscal effects. This assumption appears, explicitly or implicitly, in demonstrating real effects of a shift in the stock of public debt

I have benefited from comments on earlier drafts by Gary Becker, Benjamin Eden, Milton Friedman, Merton Miller, José Scheinkman, Jeremy Siegel, and Charles Upton. The National Science Foundation has supported this research.
[*Journal of Political Economy*, 1974, vol. 82, no. 6]

(see, e.g., Modigliani 1961, sec. IV; Mundell 1971; and Tobin 1971, chap. 5), and in establishing nonneutrality of changes in the stock of money (Metzler 1951, sec. VI). More generally, the assumption that government debt issue leads, at least in part, to an increase in the typical household's conception of its net wealth is crucial for demonstrating a positive effect on aggregate demand of "expansionary" fiscal policy, which is defined here as a substitution of debt for tax finance for a given level of government expenditure (see, e.g., Patinkin 1964, sec. XII.4; and Blinder and Solow 1973, pp. 324–25). The basic type of argument in a full-employment model is, following Modigliani (1961), that an increase in government debt implies an increase in perceived household wealth; hence, an increase in desired consumption (a component of aggregate demand) relative to saving; hence, an increase in interest rates; and, finally, a decline in the fraction of output which goes to capital accumulation. However, this line of reasoning hinges on the assumption that the increase in government debt leads to an increase in perceived household wealth. In a non-full employment context it remains true that the effect of public debt issue on aggregate demand (and, hence, on output and employment) hinges on the assumed increase in perceived household wealth.

It has been recognized for some time that the future taxes needed to finance government interest payments would imply an offset to the direct positive wealth effect. For example, in a paper originally published in 1952, Tobin (1971, p. 91) notes: "How is it possible that society merely by the device of incurring a debt to itself can deceive itself into believing that it is wealthier? Do not the additional taxes which are necessary to carry the interest charges reduce the value of other components of private wealth?" Bailey (1962, pp. 75–77) has gone somewhat further by arguing: "It is possible that households regard deficit financing as equivalent to taxation. The issue of a bond by the government to finance expenditures involves a liability for future interest payments and possible ultimate repayment of principal, and thus implies future taxes that would not be necessary if the expenditures were financed by current taxation. . . . If future tax liabilities implicit in deficit financing are accurately foreseen, the level at which total tax receipts are set is immaterial; the behavior of the community will be exactly the same as if the budget were continuously balanced."

There seem to be two major lines of argument that have been offered to defend the position that the offset of the future tax liabilities will be only partial.[1] One type of argument, based on finite lives, supposes that

---

[1] Of course, most analyses of government debt effects do not offer a specific defense for this position. For example, Blinder and Solow (1973, p. 325, n. 8) say: "This [analysis] includes government bonds as a net asset to the public. We are well aware of, but not persuaded by, the arguments which hold that such bonds are not seen as net worth by individuals because of the implied future tax liability."

the relevant horizon for the future taxes (which might correspond to the remaining average lifetimes of the current taxpayers) will be shorter than that for the interest payments.[2] Accordingly, a stream of equal values for interest payments and taxes will have a net positive present value. This argument has been used explicitly by Thompson (1967, p. 1200). The second type of argument, usually based on imperfect private capital markets, supposes that the relevant discount rate for tax liabilities will be higher than that for the interest payments. Hence, even with an infinite horizon for tax liabilities, a stream of equal values for interest payments and taxes will have a net positive present value. This argument has been used by Mundell (1971).[3]

The first part of this paper deals with the effect of government bond issue on the calculus of individual wealth in an overlapping-generations economy with physical capital where individuals have finite lives. No elements of "capital market imperfections" are introduced into this model. The key result here is that, so long as there is an operative intergenerational transfer (in the sense of an interior solution for the amount of bequest or gift across generations), there will be no net-wealth effect and, hence, no effect on aggregate demand or on interest rates of a marginal change in government debt. This result does not hinge on current generations' weighing the consumption or utility of future generations in any sense on an equal basis with own consumption, nor does it depend on current generations' placing any direct weight at all on the consumption or utility of any future generation other than the immediate descendant. Current generations act effectively as though they were infinite-lived when they are connected to future generations by a chain of operative inter-generational transfers.

The analysis then shows that social security payments are analogous to changes in government debt. Marginal changes in this type (or other types) of imposed intergenerational transfers have no real effects when current and future generations are already connected by a chain of operative discretionary transfers. The effects of inheritance taxes and of "transaction costs" for government bond issue and tax collections are also considered. It is shown that inheritance taxes do not affect the basic results, but that the presence of government transaction costs implies that the net-wealth effect of government bonds would actually be negative.

The second part of the paper deals with the existence of imperfect private capital markets. It is shown that, to the extent that public debt

---

[2] This type of argument applies to head taxes or to taxes based on wage income, but not to taxes which are based on the value of nonhuman assets. This distinction has been made by Mundell (1971, pp. 9, 10).

[3] A different line of argument that leads to a similar conclusion is that the government acts like a monopolist in the provision of the liquidity services yielded by its liabilities. I discuss this argument in part III, below.

issue entails a loan from low-discount-rate to high-discount-rate individuals, a positive net-wealth effect results if the government is more efficient than the private market in carrying out this sort of loan. If the government is more efficient only over a certain range, and if the public choice process determines the amount of government debt issue in accord with efficiency criteria, it is again true at the margin that the net-wealth effect of government bond issue is nil.

The third part of the paper discusses government debt as a bearer of nonpecuniary "liquidity services." It is shown that if the government acts like a competitive producer of these services, as would be dictated by a public choice process which reflects efficiency criteria, then the net-wealth effect of government bond issue would be zero on this count. More generally, the net-wealth effect would be positive if the government acts like a monopolist and would be negative if the government is an overproducer of liquidity services.

The last part of the paper deals with the risk characteristics of government debt and of the tax liabilities associated with the interest payments on this debt. It is argued that if relative tax liabilities are known, a change in government debt will not alter the overall risk contained in household balance sheets. When relative tax liabilities are uncertain, the effect of government debt issue on the overall risk may be positive or negative, depending on the nature of the tax system and on the transaction costs associated with private insurance arrangements.

I. The Effect of Finite Lives—a Model with Overlapping Generation

A. *Setup of the Model*

I use here a version of the Samuelson (1958)-Diamond (1965) overlapping-generations model with physical capital. Each individual lives two periods, which will be distinguished by the superscripts y (young) and o (old). Generations are numbered consecutively beginning with the generation which is currently old (subscript 1); followed by its descendant, which is currently young (subscript 2); followed by its descendant; and so on. I assume here that there are the same number of people, N, in each generation, and that all individuals are identical in terms of tastes and productivity. I also abstract from any technological change over time. The members of each generation work (a fixed amount of time set equal to one unit) only while young and receive an amount of wage income w. Expectations on w for future periods (i.e., for future generations) are assumed to be static at the current value. Asset holdings (A) take the form of equity capital (K). Subsequently, government bonds are introduced as an additional form in which assets can be held. The rate of return on assets is denoted by r and is assumed to be paid out once per period. Expectations on r for future periods are assumed to be static at the current value. A member of the ith generation holds the amount of assets A_i^y while young and the amount A_i^o while old. The asset holding while old constitutes the provision of a bequest, which is assumed to go to the immediate descendant, a member of generation $i + 1$. Since the focus of the analysis concerns shifts in tax liabilities and government debt for a given level of government expenditure, it is assumed for convenience that the government neither demands commodities nor provides public services. In this section, it is also assumed that the amounts of government debt and taxes are zero. Using the letter c to denote consumption, and assuming that consumption and receipt of interest income both occur at the start of the period, the budget equation for a member of generation 1, who is currently old, is

$$A_1^y + A_0^o = c_1^o + (1 - r)A_1^o. \tag{1}$$

The total resources available are the assets held while young, A_1^y, plus the bequest from the previous generation, A_0^o. The total expenditure is consumption while old, c_1^o, plus the bequest provision, A_1^o, which goes to a member of generation 2, less interest earnings at rate r on this asset holding.

The budget equation for members of generation 2 (and, more generally, for members of any generation $i \geq 2$) is, assuming that wage payments occur at the start of the young period,

$$w = c_2^y + (1 - r)A_2^y, \tag{2}$$

and, for the old period,

$$A_2^y + A_2^o = c_2^o + (1 - r)A_2^o. \tag{3}$$

A portion of the lifetime resources of a member of generation i goes to a bequest provision, A_1^o, which I assume is motivated by a concern for a member of generation $i + 1$. This concern could be modeled by introducing either the (anticipated) consumption levels or attainable utility of a member of generation $i + 1$ into the utility function for a member of the ith generation. For the purpose of the present analysis, the crucial condition is that this utility depend on the endowment of a member of generation $i + 1$ rather than, per se, on the gross bequest, A_1^o. (The distinction between the gross bequest and the net bequest, which determines the endowment of $i + 1$, will be discussed below.) So long as a member of generation i can transfer resources to a member of generation $i + 1$ only through the transfer of unrestricted purchasing power (which rules out the "merit good" case discussed in n. 8 below), the two types of models of interdependent preferences—concern with consumption levels and concern with attainable utility—will be equivalent in the sense of indirectly implying a concern for the endowment of a member of generation $i + 1$.

For present purposes, it is convenient to assume that the utility of a member of generation i depends solely on own two-period consumption, c_i^y and c_i^o, and on the attainable utility of his immediate descendant, U_{i+1}^*. The asterisk denotes the maximum value of utility, conditional on given values of endowment and prices. Hence, the utility function for a member of the ith generation has the form,[4]

$$U_i = U_i(c_i^y, c_i^o, U_{i+1}^*). \tag{4}$$

Subsequently, I consider the implications of entering the attainable utility of a member of the previous generation, U_{i-1}^*, as an additional argument of the U_i function.

Each member of generation 1 determines his allocation of resources to maximize U_1, subject to equations (1)–(4) and to the inequality conditions, $(c_i^y, c_i^o, A_i^o) \geq 0$ for all i. The key restriction here is that the bequest to the member of the next generation cannot be negative.[5] The choice of bequest, subject to this restriction, takes into account the effect of A_1^o on generation 2's resources, the impact of U_2^* on U_1, and the chain dependence of U_2 on U_3^*, of U_3 on U_4^*, etc. The solution to this problem will take the general form

$$c_1^o = c_1^o(A_1^y + A_0^o, w, r),$$

$$A_1^o = \frac{1}{1-r}(A_1^y + A_0^o - c_1^o) = A_1^o(A_1^y + A_0^o, w, r). \tag{5}$$

Similarly, for members of generation 2 (and, more generally, for members of any generation $i \geq 2$), the solution would take the form,

$$c_2^y = c_2^y(A_1^o, w, r),$$

$$A_2^y = \frac{1}{1-r}(w - c_2^y) = A_2^y(A_1^o, w, r),$$

$$c_2^o = c_2^o(A_2^y + A_1^o, w, r), \tag{6}$$

$$A_2^o = \frac{1}{1-r}(A_2^y + A_1^o - c_2^o) = A_2^o(A_2^y + A_1^o, w, r).$$

---

[4] A member of generation i is assumed to be concerned with own consumption and with the attainable indifference surface of his descendant. Further, it is supposed that a member of generation i can attach a metric to generation $i + 1$'s indifference surface which makes it comparable to c_i^y and c_i^o in terms of generating U_i in the form of eq. (4). The nature of this sort of utility function is discussed in the general context of interdependent preferences in Becker (1974, sec. 3.A).

[5] I have not imposed the condition, $A_i^y \geq 0$, so that young individuals are allowed to issue interest-bearing debt on themselves. If issued, these debts are assumed to be perfect substitutes for equity capital. These debts correspond to the consumption loans which have been discussed by Samuelson (1958).

Landmark Papers in Macroeconomics

The model can be closed, as in Diamond (1965, pp. 1130–35), by specifying a constant-returns-to-scale production function that depends on the amounts of capital and labor input, and by equating the marginal products of capital and labor to r and w, respectively. The value of r for the current period would then be determined in order to equate the supply of assets to the demand—that is,

$$K(r, w) = A_1^o + A_2^y, \tag{7}$$

where $K(r, w)$ is such as to equate the marginal product of capital to r. The current demand for assets, $A_1^o + A_2^y$, depends, from equations (5) and (6), on r, w, and the previous period's value of K, which is equal to $A_1^y + A_0^o$. Since the number of people in each generation is assumed to equal a fixed number N, it is not necessary to enter this number explicitly into the aggregate asset demand in equation (7). Similarly, N is omitted from the aggregate formulations below. Since N is constant and technical change is not considered, the current and previous periods' values of K would be equal in a steady state.

With the marginal product of labor equated to w and with constant returns to scale, output is given by

$$y = rK + w. \tag{8}$$

Equations (2), (3), (7), and (8) imply a commodity market clearing condition,

$$c_1^o + c_2^y + \Delta K = y, \tag{9}$$

where ΔK denotes the change in capital stock from the previous to the current period. The value of ΔK would be zero in a steady state, but the present analysis is not restricted to steady-state situations.

B. Government Debt

Suppose now that the government issues an amount of debt, B, which can be thought of as taking the form of one-period, real-valued bonds. These bonds pay the specified amount of real interest, rB, in the current period and the specified real principal, B, in the next period.[6] It is supposed that asset holders regard equity and government bonds as perfect substitutes. It can be assumed, for simplicity, that the government bond issue takes the form of a helicopter drop to currently old (generation 1) households. Equivalently, it could be assumed that the bonds were sold on a competitive capital market, with the proceeds from this sale used to effect a lump-sum transfer payment to generation 1 households.

---

[6] The amount of bond issue would be limited by the government's collateral, in the sense of its taxing capacity to finance the interest and principal payments (see n. 12 below).

Allowing some portion of the proceeds to go to generation 2 households would not alter any of the basic conclusions.

The future interest payments on the government debt must be financed in some manner. Further, the principal may eventually be paid off— that is, the government may not reissue the bonds when they come due in the next period. I assume, provisionally, that the current period's interest payments are financed by a lump-sum tax levy on generation 2 households (while young), and that the principal is paid off at the beginning of the next period by an additional lump-sum tax levy on generation 2 households (while old). In this setup there is no direct effect of the government debt issue and its financing on generation 3 and later generations. I examine, subsequently, the implications of imposing some part of the taxes on generations of the more distant future.

The generation 1 budget constraint is now

$$A_1^y + A_0^o + B = c_1^o + (1 - r)A_1^o, \qquad (10)$$

where B represents the lump-sum transfer payment, which is assumed to occur at the beginning of the period. For generation 2, the current budget constraint is now

$$w = c_2^y + (1 - r)A_2^y + rB, \qquad (11)$$

where rB represents the tax levy for the government interest payments. The next period's budget constraint for generation 2 is now

$$A_2^y + A_1^o = c_2^o + (1 - r)A_2^o + B,$$

where B represents the tax levy for repayment of principal. The two constraints on generation 2 can be combined into a single two-period budget equation,

$$w + (1 - r)A_1^o - B = c_2^y + (1 - r)c_2^o + (1 - r)^2 A_2^o. \qquad (12)$$

The form of equation (12) implies that the utility attainable by a member of generation 2 can be written in the indirect form,

$$U_2^* = f_2^*[(1 - r)A_1^o - B, w, r], \qquad (13)$$

that is, the "net bequest," $(1 - r)A_1^o - B$, determines the "endowment" for members of generation 2.

From equation (10), it is also clear that c_1^o varies inversely with $(1 - r)A_1^o - B$ for a given value of $A_1^y + A_0^o$. Hence, given the predetermined value of c_1^y, and using equations (4), (10), and (13), U_1 can be written in the form,

$$U_1 = U_1(c_1^y, c_1^o, U_2^*) = f_1[(1 - r)A_1^o - B; c_1^y, A_1^y + A_0^o, w, r].$$

For given values of c_1^y, $A_1^y + A_0^o$, w, and r, the choice problem for members of generation 1 amounts to the optimal selection of the net bequest,

$(1 - r)A_1^o - B$, subject to the constraint that the gross bequest, A_1^o, be nonnegative. In particular, if the solution to this problem is associated with a value of A_1^o in the interior—that is, if the constraint, $A_1^o \geq 0$, is not binding—any marginal change in B would be met solely by a change in A_1^o that maintains the value of the net bequest, $(1 - r)A_1^o - B$. This response in A_1^o will keep unchanged the values of c_1^o, c_2^y, c_2^o, and A_2^o. Hence, the utility levels attained by members of generations 1, 2, etc., will be unaffected by the shift in B.

In terms of the effect on r, the current asset market clearing condition of equation (7) would now be modified to

$$K(r, w) + B = A_1^o + A_2^y. \qquad (14)$$

The increase in B implies a one-to-one increase in the asset supply on the left-hand side of equation (14). However, A_1^o rises by $1/(1 - r)$ times the change in B in order to maintain the size of the net bequest, $(1 - r)A_1^o - B$. Further, with c_2^y fixed, the increase in rB (taxes) in equation (11) implies that A_2^y falls by $r/(1 - r)$ times the change in B. On net, total asset demand on the right-hand side of equation (14) rises one-to-one with B, so that no change in r is required to clear the asset market. Equivalently, the commodity market clearing condition, as expressed in equation (9), continues to hold at the initial value of r because the bond issue has no impact on aggregate demand.

Essentially, a positive value of B, financed by a tax levy on the next generation, enables a member of the old generation to "go out" insolvent by leaving a debt for his descendant. However, if, prior to the government bond issue, a member of the old generation had already selected a positive bequest, it is clear that this individual already had the option of shifting resources from his descendant to himself, but he had determined that such shifting, at the margin, was nonoptimal. Since the change in B does not alter the relevant opportunity set in this sense, it follows that—through the appropriate adjustment of the bequest—the values of current and future consumption and attained utility will be unaffected. On the other hand, if a member of generation 1 were initially at a corner where $A_1^o = 0$—in particular, if $A_1^o < 0$ would have been chosen had it been permissible—then an increase in B creates a relevant new opportunity. In this situation a generation 1 household would react by increasing c_1^o along with B, as long as the corner solution for A_1^o still applied. The upward shift in B would then correspond to an excess of earning-asset supply over demand (even after taking account of a shift in A_2^y), which would tend to raise the value of r. This increase in r would induce a drop in capital formation, which constitutes the real effect of government debt issue which has been described by Modigliani (1961). However, the main point is that the existence of this government debt effect hinges on a nonoperative bequest motive—that is, on households being at the corner where the amount of bequest is zero.[7]

It should be stressed that the crucial consideration for the above result is an operative intergenerational transfer, rather than an operative bequest motive per se. For example, the transfer could take the form of parental expenditure on children's education, etc., during the overlapping tenure of parent and child.[8] Further, the transfer could be occurring in the direction opposite to that specified above. In particular, U_1^* could be entered as an argument of the U_2 function, and the possibility of gifts from the young to the old generation could be introduced. In that case the same conclusions on the effect of a change in the government debt would be reached if a "gift motive" were operative.[9] The mechanism through which changes in B were offset would then be an alteration in the amount of gifts from young to old, rather than an alteration of the amount of bequests from old to young.

The results will now be extended to a situation where the taxes which finance the government debt affect some generations which are not currently alive. The extension will be made explicitly only to generation 3, since the extension to generations further advanced in the future is straightforward.

Suppose now that the current period's interest payments are financed by a lump-sum tax levy on (young) generation 2, the next period's interest payments (on the reissued bonds) are financed by a lump-sum tax levy on (young) generation 3, and the principal is paid off by a lump-sum tax levy on (old) generation 3.[10] The generalization of the earlier results to this situation can be demonstrated by working backward from generation 3. By analogy to equation (13), the attainable utility of generation 3 can

---

[7] When households are not identical, the aggregate effect of government debt issue will depend on the fraction of households at a corner. As long as some households are in this situation, a shift in B will have some upward effect on r in this model. However, this effect would be "small" if the fraction of households at a corner were small. The role of a bequest motive in eliminating the perceived net-wealth effect of government debt has also been discussed by Miller and Upton (1974, pp. 176–79).

[8] The previous results on the effect of B might not hold if parents were concerned with specific consumption components of their children ("merit goods"), rather than with their children's attainable utility. Formally, U_i in eq. (4) could depend on (components of) c_{i+1}^y or c_{i+1}^o, rather than on U_{i+1}^*. If generation i can tie its aid to generation $i + 1$ to a specific type of expenditure (as could be the case for education), the previous results would not hold if this tied aid were an effective constraint—in the sense of forcing the next generation to "purchase" more of the item than it otherwise would—and if the parents were not making any other transfers which were equivalent to the transfer of general purchasing power. Becker (1974, sec. 3.C) presents a detailed discussion of the merit goods case in an analogous context.

[9] A model which allows for a reciprocal dependence between U_i and U_{i+1} is formally similar to the model discussed by Becker (1974, sec. 3.A) in the context of transfer payments among members of a family.

[10] I do not deal here with the possibility of net government debt issue during the old-age tenure of generation 2. No new considerations would arise here (see however, n. 12 below).

be written in the indirect form,

$$U_3^* = f_3^*[(1 - r)A_2^o - B, w, r],$$

where $(1 - r)A_2^o - B$ now determines the endowment for members of generation 3. Since generation 2 no longer pays off the government debt principal, its budget equation is modified from the form of equation (12) to

$$w + (1 - r)A_1^o - B = c_2^y + (1 - r)c_2^o + (1 - r)[(1 - r)A_2^o - B].$$

For given values of w, r, and the net bequest from generation 1, $(1 - r)A_1^o - B$, generation 2 would select an optimal value of the net bequest to generation 3, $(1 - r)A_2^o - B$. This net bequest would be invariant with B as long as the solution for A_2^o were interior. Assuming that this solution is interior, the attainable utility of generation 2 can be written in the indirect form,

$$U_2^* = f_2^*[(1 - r)A_1^o - B, w, r],$$

which coincides in form with equation (13). The situation has therefore been reduced to the previous case in which marginal changes in B led solely to changes in A_1^o which kept $(1 - r)A_1^o - B$ constant without affecting any values of consumption or attained utility.

The three-generation results generalize to the case in which taxes are levied on m generations, with the mth generation paying off the principal. By starting with generation m and progressing backward, it can be shown for all $2 \le i \le m - 1$ that, if A_i^o is interior, U_i^* can be written in an indirect form as a function of $(1 - r)A_{i-1}^o - B$. As long as all inheritance choices are interior[11] (as anticipated by current generations), shifts in B imply fully compensating shifts in bequests, so as to leave unchanged all values of consumption and attained utility.[12]

[11] Intuitively, if this condition is violated for some generations, the impact of these violations on current behavior should be less important the further in the future the violating generations. I make no claim to having proved this conjecture.

[12] This line of proof does not apply as $m \to \infty$. The main issue seems to be whether the assumption that the principal is eventually paid off is crucial. If the amount of outstanding government debt were constant, the impact of the principal on current decisions would become negligible for large m as long as $r > 0$. However, a difficulty arises here when B is allowed to grow over time. Suppose that the growth of B were limited to the growth of the government's collateral in the sense of its taxing capacity, which depends in turn on the growth of real income. Suppose that the growth rate of real income is equal to n, which can be viewed as the combined effects of population growth and technical progress, which are now allowed to be positive. In that case the present value of the principal would have to become negligible as $m \to \infty$ if $n < r$. The situation in which $n > r$ applies is inefficient in that it is associated with a capital stock in excess of the golden rule level (see, e.g., Diamond 1965, p. 1129). It is possible in Diamond's model (p. 1135) that the competitive equilibrium can be in this inefficient region. However, this situation is not possible in growth models where individuals are infinite lived and utility is discounted (see, e.g., Koopmans 1965). As long as intergenerational transfers are operative, the overlapping-generations model would seem to be equivalent to the infinite-life model in this respect— that is, the possibility of inefficiency in Diamond's model seems to hinge on finite lives with inoperative intergenerational transfers. Hence, when these transfers are operative, $n < r$ would be guaranteed, and the possibility of perpetual government finance by new debt issue could then be ruled out.

The results in this section have demonstrated that changes in government debt would not induce any alteration in consumption plans even in a model where (1) the present generations have finite lives, (2) the present generations may, in some sense, give lesser weight to the consumption or utility of future generations than they give to own consumption, and (3) the present generation may give no direct weight at all to the consumption or utility of generations beyond their immediate descendants (who are also finite-lived).

A sufficient condition for changes in government debt to have no impact on consumption plans and, hence, no effect on aggregate demand and interest rates is that the solution for the current generations' inheritances be interior, and that the solutions for future generations' inheritances (as perceived by current generations) also be interior. More generally, the result will hold as long as current generations are connected to all future generations by a chain of operative intergenerational transfers, either in the direction from old to young or in the direction from young to old.

The derivation of conditions under which the solution for intergenerational transfer would be interior appears to be a difficult problem and would seem to require some specialization of the form of the utility functions in order to make any headway. However, it seems clear that bequests are more likely to be positive the smaller the growth rate of w (assuming that w is now viewed as variable across generations), the higher the interest rate, the higher the relative weight of U_{i+1}^* in the U_i function, and the larger the value of B.[13] The reverse conditions favor a gift from young to old.[14]

C. Social Security Payments and Other Imposed Intergenerational Transfers

The above results on government debt also apply to social security payments.[15] Suppose that a scheme is instituted which immediately begins payments to the current old generation (generation 1) of amount S, financed by a lump-sum tax levy of amount S on the current young

[13] In a more general context B should be viewed as outstanding public debt less the value of physical capital held by the government.

[14] There is an alternative argument, which Gary Becker refers to as the "enforcement theory of giving," which suggests that bequest motives would typically be operative. Suppose that, instead of receiving utility from the perceived utility of his child, a parent is concerned with own consumption and with the amount of attention, etc., shown by his child during their overlapping tenure. Suppose, further, that the child has some information on the size of his parents' estate and that—acting as a good optimal controller— he regulates the amount of attention as a function of the estate size. In this situation the estate would surely be positive if parents place a high value on getting at least a small amount of attention, and if the child provides no attention when the estate is zero. However, although a positive estate could be guaranteed in this fashion, it seems that the previous conclusions about the marginal effect of B on consumption plans would not hold in this model. The nature of the interactions between parents and children would have to be analyzed more fully for this case.

[15] The view of social security as analogous to government debt has also been taken by Miller and Upton (1974, pp. 182–84).

generation (generation 2). Generation 2 expects to receive a transfer of amount S while old, financed by a lump-sum tax levy on (young) generation 3, etc. It is assumed here that an individual's payment received while old is independent of his own contribution to the scheme while young, and that neither the old receipt nor the young payment depends on the amount of work, income, etc. Assuming interior bequests (which would be guaranteed by a sufficiently high value of S), a change in S would induce the current old generation (generation 1) to maintain its choice of c_1^o and, correspondingly, to raise A_1^o by $1/(1 - r)$ times the change in S. This increased inheritance would just offset the increased tax liability imposed on (young) generation 2. With its consumption unchanged, generation 2 would use its own higher social security receipt to raise its bequest to generation 3, A_2^o, by $1/(1 - r)$ times the change in S. As in the case of changes in government debt, if the solutions for bequest are interior, the impact of a marginal change in S would be solely on the size of bequests and not at all on the pattern of consumption.[16] The same results would follow in the case of operative intergenerational transfers from young to old, with a marginal increase in S implying a corresponding reduction in the size of gifts from young to old.

The results for social security payments would apply also to other programs which amount to imposed intergenerational transfer schemes. In particular, public support of education involves a forced transfer of resources from old to young. In the main, this sort of imposed transfer would be offset by adjustments in the opposite direction of discretionary transfers.[17]

D. Inheritance Taxes

Suppose now that inheritances (or gifts) are taxed at a proportionate rate τ. In particular, the bequest from a member of generation i, A_i^o, yields a

---

[16] As in the case of government debt issue, the formal proof depends on the assumption that the scheme is eventually liquidated (see n. 12 above). The consumption patterns would also not be affected by a social security scheme that involved the accumulation of a government "trust fund." Assuming that the fund were held in the form of earning assets, an increase in the fund would be equivalent to a negative government debt issue. Real effects of a social security system would arise if the payments were contingent on the work behavior of the old generation. In that case there would be allocative effects produced by the disincentive to work in later years.

[17] On a theoretical level, government education programs will involve real effects to the extent that (1) there is an efficiency difference between public and private production of education, (2) public expenditure on education is pressed sufficiently far so that a reduction of discretionary transfers cannot occur on a one-for-one basis, and (3) there are distributional effects involving relative educational expenditures and tax liabilities across families. As an empirical matter, Peltzman (1973) has shown that public subsidies for higher education are offset to an extent of about 75 percent by reductions in private expenditures for higher education. However, Peltzman's 75 percent figure does not coincide with the desired estimate of the effect on discretionary transfers, since other components of discretionary transfers may also be affected and (on the other side) since not all private expenditures for education constitute intergenerational transfers.

net receipt to his descendant, a member of generation $i + 1$, of size $(1 - \tau)A_i^o$. Of course, the tax receipts must also go somewhere. Suppose that these receipts are transferred to members of generation $i + 1$ (while old) in accordance with a rule that is independent of the size of each individual's inheritance.

Since an individual's contribution to general tax revenue will typically be valued by him at less than an equal amount of own income, it is clear that an increase in τ will tend to lower the amount of intergenerational transfers. In particular, the higher the value of τ, the less likely that a bequest or gift motive will be operative. Suppose, however, that the value of τ is sufficiently low that all intergenerational transfers are operative, even if at reduced levels. In this case the previous results on the effect of a change in government debt remain valid.

Consider the situation in which the principal on the government debt is paid off by generation 2. Equation (10) continues to apply in the presence of inheritance taxes, but equation (12) must be modified to

$$w + (1 - r)(1 - \tau)A_1^o + (1 - r)\tau\overline{A_1^o} - B$$
$$= c_2^y + (1 - r)c_2^o + (1 - r)^2 A_2^o,$$

where $\tau\overline{A_1^o}$ represents the transfer to a member of (old) generation 2 corresponding to his share of the receipts from the total taxes paid on the average generation 1 bequest, $\overline{A_1^o}$. In deciding on a plan for consumption and intergenerational transfers, an individual is assumed to treat $\tau\overline{A_1^o}$ as exogenous. Consider the conjecture that, when B rises, each member of generation 1 continues to respond by maintaining the value of c_1^o and, hence, by maintaining the value of the net pretax bequest, $(1 - r)A_1^o - B$. This response requires an increase in A_1^o by $1/(1 - r)$ times the increase in B. Each individual's net posttax bequest would fall in this case, but this fall would be offset, at least on average, by an increase in the transfers to generation 2 which are financed from the inheritance tax receipts, $\tau\overline{A_1^o}$. In this circumstance, the individual values of c_2^y, c_2^o, and A_2^o—and, hence, the attained value of U_2—would remain fixed. Hence, by maintaining the net pretax bequest, each member of generation 1 achieves the same combination of c_1^o and U_2^* as before the shift in B. On the other hand, if an individual member of generation 1 decided to increase his net pretax bequest, while all other members held their net pretax bequests fixed, it would turn out for this individual that U_2^* would increase, while c_1^o would decrease. The terms on which an individual can exchange c_1^o for U_2^* depend on τ and r, and these terms have not been altered by the change in B. Further, when the transfer to generation 2 of size $\tau\overline{A_1^o}$ is included, there is also no change in an individual's overall wealth position. Therefore, the pattern which maintains the net pretax bequest—and thereby involves no shift in c_1^o or U_2^*—must be the optimal pattern for an individual. It follows that constancy of the net pretax bequest for all members of generation 1 is the equilibrium solution.[18] In this case, a marginal shift in B again has no effect on consumption patterns.

The basic conclusion here is that the existence of taxes on intergenerational transfers makes less likely an interior solution for these transfers, but if these transfers are operative, even if at reduced levels, the marginal effect of B on consumption plans—and, hence, on r—remains nil.

E. Bond Issue and Tax-Collection Costs

Suppose now that the issue of government debt and the collection of taxes to finance this debt involve transaction costs. In particular, in the case where the principal is paid off by generation 2, suppose that a net issue of B to generation 1 is now associated with a tax levy of $(1 + \gamma)rB$ on (young) generation 2 and a levy of $(1 + \gamma)B$ on (old) generation 2. That is, γ amounts to a proportional transaction cost associated with government debt issue and tax collection.[19] For simplicity, suppose now that the inheritance tax rate is zero. Equation (10) again remains valid, but equation (12) is now modified to

$$w + (1 - r)A_1^o - (1 + \gamma)B = c_2^y + (1 - r)c_2^o + (1 - r)^2 A_2^o. \qquad (15)$$

Consider, again, the conjecture that, when B rises, c_1^o and, hence, $(1 - r)A_1^o - B$ remain fixed. From equation (15), $\gamma > 0$ implies a negative-wealth effect on generation 2, so that U_2^* would fall. Since this effect would be anticipated by generation 1, it can be supposed in the normal case that A_1^o would actually rise by somewhat more than $1/(1 - r)$ times B, so that c_1^o would fall. In general, $\gamma > 0$ implies that an increase in B amounts to an overall negative-wealth effect, which would

---

[18] The equilibrium satisfies two properties: (1) each individual chooses his bequest optimally, subject to a given choice of bequests by all other individuals; and (2) all individuals choose the same value for their bequests. It can also be shown that the solution that maintains the net pretax bequest for all individuals is the unique equilibrium. Finally, it can be noted that the solution involves the assumption that each individual perceives the shift in the transfer term, $\tau \overline{A}_1^o$, associated with the average response of bequests to the change in B. Alternatively, if individuals treated $\tau \overline{A}_1^o$ as fixed, they would view an increase in B as, effectively, a negative change in wealth. The typical response would be a reduction in c_1^o, which would be associated with an increase in A_1^o by more than $1/(1 - r)$ times the change in B. In the aggregate, there would be an increase in desired saving, $A_2^o + A_1^y$, which would lead to a reduction in r and to an increase in capital formation. In particular, if the shift in transfers associated with inheritance tax revenues, $\tau \overline{A}_1^o$, is not perceived, the effects would be opposite to the standard case in which perceived net wealth rises with B.

[19] If the initial debt issue is associated with a decrease in other taxes, rather than an increase in transfers, there could be an offsetting reduction in transaction costs. The parameter γ, which is assumed to be positive, must be interpreted in this net sense.

typically involve reductions in both c_1^o and U_2^*. This effect can be seen by combining equations (10) and (15) into the single two-generation budget equation,

$$A_1^y + A_0^o - \gamma B + w = c_1^o + c_2^y + (1 - r)c_2^o + (1 - r)^2 A_2^o. \quad (16)$$

The decline in total resources on the left-hand side of equation (16) produced by an increase in B would typically be reflected in declines in all terms on the right-hand side—c_1^o, c_2^y, c_2^o, and A_2^o.

In this circumstance the effect on r of a shift in B would be unclear. The commodity market clearing condition of equation (9) would now be modified to include the resources devoted to bond and tax transactions. The revised market clearing condition would be

$$c_1^o + c_2^y + \Delta K + \gamma r B = y.$$

The effect of B on current r will depend on whether, for a given value of r, the sum, $c_1^o + c_2^y$, falls by more or less than the increase in $\gamma r B$. This relationship seems to be ambiguous.[20]

II. Imperfect Capital Markets

This part of the paper analyzes the implications of divergences among individual discount rates. This source of a net-wealth effect for government bonds has been stressed by Mundell (1971), who argues that, because of high discount rates for some individuals, the taxes which finance the government debt will not be fully capitalized—hence, an issue of government bonds will involve a net-wealth effect. To analyze this effect, it is necessary to construct a somewhat different model. Suppose that there are now two types of individuals—those who have a low discount rate, r_l, and those who have a high discount rate, r_h. It can be supposed that the high-discount-rate individuals have relatively "bad collateral," so that loans to these individuals involve high transaction costs, which are reflected in high (net-of-default-risk) borrowing rates.[21] In particular, suppose that the two discount rates are related according to

$$r_h = (1 + \lambda)r_l,$$

where $\lambda > 0$ represents the proportional transaction costs involved in the loan process.[22] I suppose in this part of the paper that both types of

---

[20] From eq. (16), the negative wealth effect is γB, which is the present value of the flow, $\gamma r B$. The sum, $c_1^o + c_2^y$, will fall by as much as $\gamma r B$ if the total "propensity to consume" associated with the negative "income" flow, $\gamma r B$, is equal to one.

[21] In this respect see Barro (1974).

[22] I am assuming that the r_h individuals are actually borrowing, so that r_h represents both their borrowing rate and their marginal discount rate. Alternatively, r_h could be viewed as a marginal discount rate which could be somewhere between the borrowing and lending rates, as in Hirshleifer (1958).

individuals are infinite-lived, since the effect of finite lives has already been examined above.

It is convenient to suppose that government debt now takes the form of a perpetuity that carries a real interest payment of i per year. Suppose that the government issues an additional bond of this type. This bond would be purchased by a low-discount-rate individual and would be evaluated as $B = i/r_l$.[23] Suppose then that the government uses the lump-sum proceeds from this sale, B, to effect a lump-sum transfer (or lump-sum tax reduction) to individuals, and suppose that a fraction α of this transfer goes to r_l discount rate individuals and a fraction $(1 - \alpha)$ to r_h discount rate individuals. Finally, the taxes for financing the government interest payments are $(1 + \gamma)i$, where γ represents, as in section IE, the proportional transaction costs associated with government bond sale and tax collection. Suppose that these taxes are distributed across discount rates in the same manner as the lump-sum proceeds[24]—that is, a fraction α to r_l individuals and a fraction $(1 - \alpha)$ to r_h individuals.

Consider, in turn, the wealth effects for the r_l and r_h groups. The bond sale itself involves no wealth effect for the r_l group. The lump-sum transfer to r_l individuals is $\alpha B = \alpha i/r_l$, while the present value of the r_l share of tax liabilities, discounted at rate r_l, is $(1 + \gamma)\alpha i/r_l$. Clearly, if $\gamma > 0$, the net-wealth effect for r_l individuals is negative, as it was in the case discussed in section IE, where all discount rates were equal.

For the r_h group, the lump-sum proceeds are $(1 - \alpha)B = (1 - \alpha)i/r_l$, while the present value of the tax liability, discounted at rate r_h, is $(1 + \gamma)(1 - \alpha)i/r_h$. Using $r_h = (1 + \lambda)r_l$, the net-wealth effect here can be expressed as

$$\frac{(1 - \alpha)i}{r_l}\left(1 - \frac{1 + \gamma}{1 + \lambda}\right) = \frac{(1 - \alpha)i}{r_l(1 + \lambda)}(\lambda - \gamma),$$

which is positive if $\lambda > \gamma$. That is, the net-wealth effect for the r_h group is positive if γ, which measures the government transaction costs for bond issue and tax collection, is smaller than λ, which measures the private transaction costs implicit in the existing pattern of (net-of-default-risk) discount rates. To the extent, $1 - \alpha$, that the transfer payment and tax liability involve the r_h group, the government bond issue amounts to effecting a loan from the low-discount-rate to the high-discount-rate individuals. On the other hand, this sort of transfer could already have

---

[23] This analysis abstracts from any "liquidity yield" of bonds (see part III, below).

[24] If the fractions for transfer and tax liability vary, then the wealth effects on the two discount-rate groups are likely to be in opposite directions. The net effect on current consumption demand would depend, in part, on relative propensities to consume, which are not obvious. In any event, this case would amount to the effect of income distribution on consumption demand, rather than the effect of government bond issue per se on net wealth and consumption demand.

been accomplished privately, except that the transaction costs, as measured by λ, made this transfer marginally unprofitable. Hence, the government-induced transfer implied by its bond issue can raise net wealth only if the government is more efficient than the private capital market in carrying out this sort of lending and borrowing operation.

Some additional observations can be made concerning this result. First, if the government is really more efficient than the private market in the lending process (presumably because the benefits of economies of scale [in information?] and the ability to coerce outweigh the problems of government incentive and control), it may be able to exploit this efficiency better by a direct-loan program, rather than by the sort of bond issue described above. In my simple model, a fraction α of transfers and tax liabilities involved the r_l group, and this process entailed a dead-weight loss to the extent that $\gamma > 0$. A program which limited the loan recipients to high-discount-rate individuals would be more efficient in this respect. However, the information requirements for this sort of program may be much greater than those for a program which does not attempt to discriminate—in the transfer and tax liability aspects—among discount rates. The crucial point which can make the bond issue work as a loan program is that the purchasers of the bonds automatically discriminate among themselves as to their discount rates.

Second, the government may be more efficient than the private market only over a certain range of B. In particular, there may be a sufficiently large value of B such that, at the margin, the net-wealth effect of government debt is zero. If the public choice process leads to this value of B (as it should on efficiency grounds), then, at the margin, the net-wealth effect of government bonds would be zero, despite the continued existence of "imperfect private capital markets."[25]

III. A Government Monopoly in Liquidity Services

Suppose now that government debt provides a form of "liquidity service" to the holder, in addition to the direct interest payments. Suppose that, at the margin, these services are valued at the amount L per bond per year. Hence, in the context where all individuals have the same discount rate, r, an additional perpetual government bond would be evaluated as

$$B = (i + L)/r.$$

The taxes for financing the government debt can be thought of as the interest costs, i, plus any costs involved with the process of creating

[25] Of course, government debt issue would be "productive" in a total sense even in the case where the marginal net wealth effect was nil. However, it is this marginal effect which enters into analyses of (marginal) fiscal and monetary policies.

liquidity services (which could involve the γ-type costs discussed above).
Suppose that c denotes the marginal costs per bond per year associated
with the production of liquidity services. Hence, at the margin, the wealth
effect of a change in government debt will be

$$\frac{1}{r} (i + L) - \frac{1}{r} (i + c) = \frac{1}{r} (L - c).$$

If the public choice process is such as to motivate the government to act
like a competitive producer of liquidity services (as it should on efficiency
grounds), then $L = c$ and the marginal-wealth effect of government debt
would be nil. On the other hand, if the government operates mono-
polistically, so that $L > c$, then the marginal-wealth effect of government
debt would be positive.[26] However, it is also possible that the government
overextends its production of liquidity services, so that $L < c$ and the
marginal-wealth effect of government debt would be negative. This last
case corresponds implicitly to the one discussed above in section IE,
where $L = 0$ and $c > 0$ were assumed.

Of course, liquidity services can also be provided by private producers.
If the types of services rendered by private and public debt instruments
are close substitutes, and if the private market is competitive, then
governmental monopoly power can arise here only to the extent that, at
the margin, the government is more efficient than the private market as a
producer of liquidity services. Even if the government is a more efficient
producer over a certain range, a sufficient expansion of government
"output" would eliminate this efficiency differential at the margin if the
production of liquidity services is, at least eventually, subject to increasing
marginal costs. As in the case of an imperfect private capital market, as
discussed above, the net-wealth effect of government debt depends on the
relative efficiency at the margin of government versus private production.

IV. Risk and Asset Substitutability

The previous sections have dealt with the net-wealth effect of government
debt. I have not discussed explicitly in these sections the risk characteristics
of government bonds, tax liabilities, and the other types of available assets
and liabilities. Tobin (1971, p. 2) has argued: "The calculus of total
wealth is less important than the change in the composition of private
balance sheets that the government engineers by borrowing from the
public—forcing on taxpayers a long-term debt of some uncertainty while
providing bond-holders highly liquid and safe assets. Since no one else

---

[26] Of course, this observation would also apply to government money, which yields a
zero rate of explicit interest. The usual real balance effect for outside money assumes that
the marginal cost to the government of maintaining real balances is zero, and that the
government acts like a monopolist in determining its supply of real balances.

can perform the same intermediation, the government's debt issues probably do, within limits, augment private wealth. Another way to make the point is to observe that future tax liabilities are likely to be capitalized at a higher discount rate than claims against the government." I have already considered, above, arguments for effectively discounting tax liabilities at a higher rate because of finite lives, imperfect private capital markets, and a government monopoly in the production of liquidity services, and these arguments need not be repeated here. In this part of the paper, I will consider briefly some implications of the risk characteristics of government bonds and of the future tax liabilities associated with the finance of these bonds.

Suppose, first, that there were no uncertainty about the relative burden of the (lump-sum) tax liabilities that finance the government debt. In this situation the uncertainty in an individual's real tax burden associated with government interest payments would reflect solely the variability over time in the real-interest payments themselves. In terms of present values, the variability in the tax liabilities would reflect the variability in prices and interest rates—that is, the same factors which lead to variability in real bond values. In particular, holdings of government debt—amounting to a claim to a certain fraction of total government interest payments—would be the perfect hedge against variations in tax liabilities.[27] In this context a simultaneous increase in government interest payments (i.e., government bonds) and in the tax liabilities for financing these payments would not involve any net shift in the risk composition of private balance sheets.[28]

Suppose now that the tax liabilities are subject to an additional variability concerning the relative burden across individuals. Suppose, first, that the variation in relative taxes is purely random, in the sense of being unrelated to variations in relative income, etc. In that case, it is clear that an individual's tax liability associated with government interest payments would be subject to a source of variability above that of the total interest payments. In particular, the fractional holdings of government bonds which corresponds to the expected fraction of tax liabilities would no longer provide a perfect hedge against variations in the tax liabilities. Of course, it would be possible for individuals to utilize private insurance markets to reduce the risks associated with variations in relative tax liability. However, to the extent that insurance arrangements entail transaction costs, the risk associated with relative liability would not generally be fully eliminated. In this case an increase in government bonds would produce a net increase in the risk contained in household balance

---

[27] I am ignoring here effects which relate to the maturity structure of the government debt. In order to provide a perfect hedge, an individual's holding of debt by maturity would have to correspond to the overall maturity distribution.

[28] There could be an effect on individuals who do not hold any government bonds (or assets subject to similar risks).

sheets—that is, there would be a decline in effective household wealth. The typical household reaction would be twofold: first, an increase in desired total saving, and, second, a shift in portfolio composition away from more risky assets, such as equity capital, and toward less risky assets. The impact on the equity rate of return, and, hence, on capital formation would depend on which of these two responses was the dominant force.

The above discussion would be altered to the extent that variations in tax liability reflect variations in income. In this context the variation in relative tax liabilities can serve to reduce the net variability in disposable income—that is, the income tax works, in part, like a public program of income insurance. If the income-offsetting feature of taxes were the dominant element in relative tax variability, then a shift in government bonds could lead to a reduction in the overall risk contained in household balance sheets. In that case the effects on desired total saving and on portfolio composition would be opposite to those described above. However, it should also be noted that the public program of income insurance which is implied by an income tax system will also involve transaction costs. There are costs associated with administration and with individual reporting effort, as well as "moral hazard" costs associated with incentives for earning income. A full analysis of the wealth effect of government bonds under different tax systems would have to involve a comparison of these types of public transaction costs against the transaction costs associated with the pooling of income risks under private insurance arrangements.

One final observation can be made here. The argument in the early literature for a net-wealth effect of government bonds—for example, that given by Modigliani (1961)—involved a neglect of the tax liabilities associated with the financing of the debt. Similarly, Tobin's argument for effects based on the risk composition of household balance sheets seems to neglect the tax liabilities as an element of these balance sheets. It seems clear that, either in the sense of effects on perceived total wealth, or in the sense of the risk composition of household portfolios, the impact of changes in government debt cannot be satisfactorily analyzed without an explicit treatment of the associated tax liabilities. Once the variability in relative tax liability is considered, there seem to be no clear results concerning the effect of government debt issue on the overall risk contained in household balance sheets. The net effect hinges on the extent to which variations in relative tax liability reflect variations in relative income, and on the transaction costs for public programs of income insurance relative to those of private programs.

V. Summary and Conclusions

This paper has focused on the question of whether an increase in government debt constitutes an increase in perceived household wealth. The effect of finite lives was examined within the context of an overlapping-generations model of the economy. It was shown that households would act as though they were infinitely lived, and, hence, that there would be no marginal net-wealth effect of government bonds, so long as there existed an operative chain of intergenerational transfers which connected current to future generations. Net-wealth effects associated with imperfect private capital markets and with a government monopoly in the production of liquidity services were shown to depend on the assumption that the government was more efficient, at the margin, than the private market either in the loan process or in the production of liquidity services. Further, the introduction of government transaction costs for bond issue and tax collection implied that the net-wealth effect of government bonds could be negative. Finally, a consideration of the risk characteristics of government debt and of the tax liabilities associated with the financing of this debt suggested that an increase in government bonds could raise the overall risk contained in household balance sheets. However, this effect depends on the nature of the tax system and on the transaction costs associated with private insurance arrangements.

The basic conclusion is that there is no persuasive theoretical case for treating government debt, at the margin, as a net component of perceived household wealth. The argument for a negative wealth effect seems, a priori, to be as convincing as the argument for a positive effect. Hence, the common assertion (as in Patinkin 1962, chap. 12, p. 289) that the marginal net-wealth effect of government bonds is somewhere between zero and one and is most likely to lie at some positive intermediate value has no a priori foundation. If, in fact, the marginal net-wealth effect were negligible, the implications for monetary and fiscal analysis would be far-reaching. In particular, in the case where the marginal net-wealth effect of government bonds is close to zero, (1) the Metzler-type argument for nonneutrality of changes in the stock of outside money would not be valid, (2) a change in the stock of government debt would have no effect on capital formation, and, more generally, (3) fiscal effects involving changes in the relative amounts of tax and debt finance for a given amount of public expenditure would have no effect on aggregate demand, interest rates, and capital formation.[29]

References

Bailey, M. J. *National Income and the Price Level.* New York: McGraw-Hill, 1962.
Barro, R. J. "The Loan Market, Collateral, and Rates of Interest." Center for Math. Studies in Bus. and Econ., Univ. Chicago, Report 7401, January 1974.

[29] The usual fiscal analysis involves a shift in the flow of government debt rather than a one-time shift in the stock. The zero net-wealth effect applies also to the flow case if individuals perceive the implications of the current flow for the future time path of the stock of government debt.

GOVERNMENT BONDS   1117

Becker, G. S. "A Theory of Social Interactions." *J.P.E.* 82, no. 6 (November/December 1974): 1063–93.

Blinder, A. S., and Solow, R. M. "Does Fiscal Policy Matter?" *J. Public Econ.* 2 (November 1973): 319–37.

Diamond, P. A. "National Debt in a Neoclassical Growth Model." *A.E.R.* 60 (December 1965).: 1126–50.

Hirshleifer, J. "On the Theory of Optimal Investment Decisions." *J.P.E.* 66, no. 4 (August 1958): 329–52.

Koopmans, T. C. "On the Concept of Optimal Economic Growth." In *The Econometric Approach to Development Planning.* Amsterdam: North-Holland, 1965.

Metzler, L. "Wealth, Saving, and the Rate of Interest." *J.P.E.* 59, no. 2 (April 1951): 93–116.

Miller, M. H., and Upton, C. W. *Macroeconomics: A Neoclassical Introduction.* Homewood, Ill.: Irwin, 1974.

Modigliani, F. "Long-Run Implications of Alternative Fiscal Policies and the Burden of the National Debt." *Econ. J.* 71 (December 1961): 730–55.

Mundell, R. "Money, Debt, and the Rate of Interest." In *Monetary Theory,* edited by R. Mundell. Pacific Palisades, Calif.: Goodyear, 1971.

Patinkin, D. *Money, Interest, and Prices.* 2d ed. New York: Harper & Row, 1964.

Peltzman, S. "The Effect of Public Subsidies-in-Kind on Private Expenditures: The Case of Higher Education." *J.P.E.* 81, no. 1 (January/February 1973): 1–27.

Samuelson, P. A. "An Exact Consumption-Loan Model of Interest with or without the Social Contrivance of Money." *J.P.E.* 66, no. 6 (December 1958): 467–82.

Thompson, E. A. "Debt Instruments in Macroeconomic and Capital Theory." *A.E.R.* 67 (December 1967): 1196–1210.

Tobin, J. *Essays in Economics.* Vol. 1. *Macroeconomics.* Amsterdam: North-Holland, 1971.

[3]

THE TRANSACTIONS DEMAND FOR CASH: AN INVENTORY THEORETIC APPROACH

By WILLIAM J. BAUMOL

Introduction, 545. — I. A simple model, 545. — II. Some consequences of the analysis, 549. — III. The simple model and reality, 552.

A stock of cash is its holder's inventory of the medium of exchange, and like an inventory of a commodity, cash is held because it can be given up at the appropriate moment, serving then as its possessor's part of the bargain in an exchange. We might consequently expect that inventory theory and monetary theory can learn from one another. This note attempts to apply one well-known result in inventory control analysis to the theory of money.[1]

I. A SIMPLE MODEL

We are now interested in analyzing the transactions demand for cash dictated by rational behavior, which for our purposes means the holding of those cash balances that can do the job at minimum cost. To abstract from precautionary and speculative demands let us consider a state in which transactions are perfectly foreseen and occur *in a steady stream*.

Suppose that in the course of a given period an individual will pay out T dollars in a steady stream. He obtains cash either by borrowing it, or by withdrawing it from an investment, and in either case his interest cost (or interest opportunity cost) is i dollars per dollar per period. Suppose finally that he withdraws cash in lots of C dollars spaced evenly throughout the year, and that each time he makes such a withdrawal he must pay a fixed "broker's fee" of b

---

1. T. M. Whitin informs me that the result in question goes back to the middle of the 1920's when it seems to have been arrived at independently by some half dozen writers. See, e.g., George F. Mellen, "Practical Lot Quantity Formula," *Management and Administration*, Vol. 10, September 1925. Its significant implications for the economic theory of inventory, particularly for business cycle theory, seem to have gone unrecognized until recently when Dr. Whitin analyzed them in his forthcoming *Inventory Control and Economic Theory* (Princeton University Press) which, incidentally, first suggested the subject of this note to me. See also, Dr. Whitin's "Inventory Control in Theory and Practice" (elsewhere in this issue, *supra*, p. 502), and Kenneth J. Arrow, Theodore Harris, and Jacob Marschak, "Optimal Inventory Policy," *Econometrica*, Vol. 19, July 1951, especially pp. 252–255. In addition to Dr. Whitin, I am heavily indebted to Professors Chandler, Coale, Gurley, Lutz, Mr. Turvey, and Professor Viner, and to the members of the graduate seminar at Harvard University, where much of this paper was first presented.

dollars.[2] Here T, the value of transactions, is predetermined, and i and b are assumed to be constant.

In this situation any value of C less than or equal to T will enable him to meet his payments equally well provided he withdraws the money often enough. For example, if T is $100, he can meet his payments by withdrawing $50 every six months or $25 quarterly, etc.[3] Thus he will make $\dfrac{T}{C}$ withdrawals over the course of the year, at a total cost in "brokers' fees" given by $\dfrac{bT}{C}$.

In this case, since each time he withdraws C dollars he spends it in a steady stream and draws out a similar amount the moment it is gone, his average cash holding will be $\dfrac{C}{2}$ dollars. His annual interest cost of holding cash will then be $\dfrac{iC}{2}$.

The total amount the individual in question must pay for the use of the cash needed to meet his transaction when he borrows C dollars at intervals evenly spaced throughout the year will then be the sum of interest cost and "brokers' fees" and so will be given by

$$(1) \qquad\qquad \frac{bT}{C} + \frac{iC}{2}.$$

2. The term "broker's fee" is not meant to be taken literally. It covers all non-interest costs of borrowing or making a cash withdrawal. These include opportunity losses which result from having to dispose of assets just at the moment the cash is needed, losses involved in the poor resale price which results from an asset becoming "secondhand" when purchased by a nonprofessional dealer, administrative costs, and psychic costs (the trouble involved in making a withdrawal) as well as payment to a middleman. So conceived it seems likely that the "broker's fee" will, in fact, vary considerably with the magnitude of the funds involved, contrary to assumption. However, *some* parts of this cost will not vary with the amount involved — e.g., postage cost, bookkeeping expense, and, possibly, the withdrawer's effort. It seems plausible that the "broker's fee" will be better approximated by a function like $b + kC$ (where b and k are constants), which indicates that there is a part of the "broker's fee" increasing in proportion with the amount withdrawn. As shown in a subsequent footnote, however, our formal result is completely unaffected by this amendment.

We must also extend the meaning of the interest rate to include the value of protection against loss by fire, theft, etc., which we obtain when someone borrows our cash. On the other hand, a premium for the risk of default on repayment must be deducted. This protection obtained by lending seems to be mentioned less frequently by theorists than the risk, yet how can we explain the existence of interest free demand deposits without the former?

3. In particular, if cash were perfectly divisible and no elapse of time were required from withdrawal through payment he could make his withdrawals in a steady stream. In this case he would never require any cash balances to meet his payments and C would be zero. However, as may be surmised, this would be prohibitive with any b greater than zero.

Since the manner in which he meets his payments is indifferent to him, his purpose only being to pay for his transactions, rationality requires that he do so at minimum cost, i.e., that he choose the most economical value of C. Setting the derivative of (1) with respect to C equal to zero we obtain[4]

$$-\frac{bT}{C^2} + \frac{i}{2} = 0,$$

i.e.,

$$(2) \qquad C = \sqrt{\frac{2bT}{i}}.$$

Thus, in the simple situation here considered, the rational individual will, given the price level,[5] demand cash in proportion to the square root of the value of his transactions.

Before examining the implications of this crude model we may note that, as it stands, it applies to two sorts of cases: that of the individual (or firm) obtaining cash from his invested capital and that of the individual (or firm) spending out of borrowing in anticipation of future receipts. Since our problem depends on non-coincidence of cash receipts and disbursements, and we have assumed that cash disbursements occur in a steady stream, one other case seems possible, that where receipts precede expenditures. This differs from the first case just mentioned (living off one's capital) in that the individual now has the option of withholding some or all of his receipts from investment and simply keeping the cash until it is needed. Once this withheld cash is used up the third case merges into the first: the individual must obtain cash from his invested capital until his next cash receipt occurs.

We can deal with this third case as follows. First, note that any receipts exceeding anticipated disbursements will be invested, since, eventually, interest earnings must exceed ("brokerage") cost of investment. Hence we need only deal with that part of the cash influx which is to be used in making payments during the period

4. This result is unchanged if there is a part of the "broker's fee" which varies in proportion with the quantity of cash handled. For in this case the "broker's fee" for each loan is given by $b + kC$. Total cost in "broker's fees" will then be

$$\frac{T}{C}(b + kC) = \frac{T}{C}b + kT.$$

Thus (1) will have the constant term, kT, added to it, which drops out in differentiation.

5. A doubling of *all* prices (including the "broker's fee") is like a change in the monetary unit, and may be expected to double the demand for cash balances.

between receipts. Let this amount, as before, be T dollars. Of this let I dollars be invested, and the remainder, R dollars, be withheld, where either of these sums may be zero. Again let i be the interest rate, and let the "broker's fee" for withdrawing cash be given by the linear expression $b_w + k_w C$, where C is the amount withdrawn. Finally, let there be a "broker's fee" for investing (depositing) cash given by $b_d + k_d I$ where the b's and the k's are constants.

Since the disbursements are continuous, the $R = T - I$ dollars withheld from investment will serve to meet payments for a fraction of the period between consecutive receipts given by $\dfrac{T-I}{T}$. Moreover, since the average cash holding for that time will be $\dfrac{T-I}{2}$, the interest cost of withholding that money will be $\dfrac{T-I}{T} i \dfrac{T-I}{2}$. Thus the total cost of withholding the R dollars and investing the I dollars will be

$$\frac{T-I}{2} i \frac{T-I}{T} + b_d + k_d I.$$

Analogously, the total cost of obtaining cash for the remainder of the period will be

$$\frac{C}{2} i \frac{I}{T} + (b_w + k_w C) \frac{I}{C}.$$

Thus the total cost of cash operations for the period will be given by the sum of the last two expressions, which when differentiated partially with respect to C and set equal to zero once again yields our square root formula, (2), with $b = b_w$.

Thus, in this case, the optimum cash balance after the initial cash holding is used up will again vary with the square root of the volume of transactions, as is to be expected by analogy with the "living off one's capital" case.

There remains the task of investigating $R/2$, the (optimum) average cash balance before drawing on invested receipts begins. We again differentiate our total cost of holding cash, this time partially with respect to I, and set it equal to zero, obtaining

$$-\frac{T-I}{T} i + k_d + \frac{Ci}{2T} + \frac{b_w}{C} + k_w = 0,$$

i.e.,

$$R = T - I = \frac{C}{2} + \frac{b_w T}{Ci} + \frac{T(k_d + k_w)}{i},$$

or since from the preceding result, $C^2 = 2Tb_w/i$, so that the second term on the right hand side equals $C^2/2C$,

$$R = C + T\left(\frac{k_w + k_d}{i}\right).$$

The first term in this result is to be expected, since if *everything* were deposited at once, C dollars would have to be withdrawn at that same moment to meet current expenses. On this amount two sets of "broker's fees" would have to be paid and no interest would be earned — a most unprofitable operation.[5]

Since C varies as the square root of T and the other term varies in proportion with T, R will increase less than in proportion with T, though more nearly in proportion than does C. The general nature of our results is thus unaffected.[7]

Note finally that the entire analysis applies at once to the case of continuous receipts and discontinuous payments, taking the period to be that between two payments, where the relevant decision is the frequency of investment rather than the frequency of withdrawal. Similarly, it applies to continuous receipts and payments where the two are not equal.

II. Some Consequences of the Analysis

I shall not labor the obvious implications for financial budgeting by the firm. Rather I shall discuss several arguments which have been presented by monetary theorists, to which our result is relevant.

The first is the view put forth by several economists,[8] that in a

6. Here the assumption of constant "brokerage fees" with $k_d = k_w = 0$ gets us into trouble. The amount withheld from investment then is never greater than C dollars only because a strictly constant "broker's fee" with no provision for a discontinuity at zero implies the payment of the fee even if nothing is withdrawn or deposited. In this case it becomes an overhead and it pays to invest for any interest earning greater than zero.

For a firm, *part* of the "broker's fee" may, in fact, be an overhead in this way. For example, failure to make an anticipated deposit will sometimes involve little or no reduction in the bookkeeping costs incurred in keeping track of such operations.

7. If we replace the linear functions representing the "broker's fees" with more general functions $f_w(C)$ and $f_d(I)$ which are only required to be differentiable, the expression obtained for R is changed merely by replacement of k_w, and k_d by the corresponding derivatives $f_w'(C)$ and $f_d'(I)$.

8. See, e.g., Frank H. Knight, *Risk, Uncertainty and Profit* (Preface to the Re-issue), No. 16 in the series of Reprints of Scarce Tracts in Economic and Political Science (London: The London School of Economics and Political Science, 1933), p. xxii; F. Divisia, *Économique Rationelle* (Paris: G. Doin, 1927), chap. XIX and the Appendix; and Don Patinkin, "Relative Prices, Say's Law and the Demand for Money," *Econometrica*, Vol. 16, April 1948, pp. 140–145. See also, P. N. Rosenstein-Rodan, "The Coordination of the General Theories of Money and Price," *Economica*, N. S., Vol. III, August 1936, Part II.

stationary state there will be no demand for cash balances since it will then be profitable to invest all earnings in assets with a positive yield in such a way that the required amount will be realized at the moment any payment is to be made. According to this view no one will want any cash in such a stationary world, and the value of money must fall to zero so that there can really be no such thing as a truly static monetary economy. Clearly this argument neglects the transactions costs involved in making and collecting such loans (the "broker's fee").[9] Our model is clearly compatible with a static world and (2) shows that it will generally pay to keep some cash. The analysis of a stationary monetary economy in which there is a meaningful (finite) price level does make sense.

Another view which can be reëxamined in light of our analysis is that the transactions demand for cash will vary approximately in proportion with the money value of transactions.[1] This may perhaps even be considered the tenor of quantity theory though there is no necessary connection, as Fisher's position indicates. If such a demand for cash balances is considered to result from rational behavior, then (2) suggests that the conclusion cannot have general validity. On the contrary, the square root formula implies that

9. It also neglects the fact that the transfer of cash takes time so that in reality we would have to hold cash at least for the short period between receiving it and passing it on again.

It is conceivable, it is true, that with perfect foresight the difference between money and securities might disappear since a perfectly safe loan could become universally acceptable. There would, however, remain the distinction between "real assets" and the "money-securities." Moreover, there would be a finite price for, and non-zero yield on the former, the yield arising because they (as opposed to certificates of their ownership) are not generally acceptable, and hence not perfectly liquid, since there is trouble and expense involved in carrying them.

1. Marshall's rather vague statements may perhaps be interpreted to support this view. See, e.g., Book I, chap. IV in *Money, Credit and Commerce* (London, 1923). Keynes clearly accepts this position. See *The General Theory of Employment, Interest and Money* (New York, 1936), p. 201. It is also accepted by Pigou: "As real income becomes larger, there is, prima facie, reason for thinking that, just as, up to a point, people like to invest a larger proportion of their real income, so also they like to hold real balances in the form of money equivalent to a larger proportion of it. On the other hand, as Professor Robertson has pointed out to me, the richer people are, the cleverer they are likely to become in finding a way to *economize* in real balances. On the whole then we may, I think, safely disregard this consideration . . . for a close approximation. . . . ." *Employment and Equilibrium*, 1st ed. (London, 1941), pp. 59–60. Fisher, however, argues: "It seems to be a fact that, at a given price level, the greater a man's expenditures the more rapid his turnover; that is, the rich have a higher rate of turnover than the poor. They spend money faster, not only absolutely but relatively to the money they keep on hand. . . . We may therefore infer that, if a nation grows richer per capita, the velocity of circulation of money will increase. This proposition, of course, has no reference to *nominal* increase of expenditure." *The Purchasing Power of Money* (New York, 1922), p. 167.

THE TRANSACTIONS DEMAND FOR CASH 551

demand for cash rises less than in proportion with the volume of transactions, so that there are, in effect, economies of large scale in the use of cash.

The magnitude of this difference should not be exaggerated, however. The phrase "varying as the square" may suggest larger effects than are actually involved. Equation (2) requires that the average transactions velocity of circulation vary exactly in proportion with the quantity of cash, so that, for example, a doubling of the stock of cash will *ceteris paribus*, just double velocity.[2]

A third consequence of the square root formula is closely connected with the second. The effect on real income of an injection of cash into the system may have been underestimated. For suppose that (2) is a valid expression for the general demand for cash, that there is widespread unemployment, and that for this or other reasons prices do not rise with an injection of cash. Suppose, moreover, that the rate of interest is unaffected, i.e., that none of the new cash is used to buy securities. Then so long as transactions do not rise so as to maintain the same proportion with the square of the quantity of money, people will want to get rid of cash. They will use it to demand more goods and services, thereby forcing the volume of transactions to rise still further. For let ΔC be the quantity of cash injected. If a proportionality (constant velocity) assumption involves transactions rising by $k \Delta C$, it is easily shown that (2) involves transactions rising by more than twice as much, the magnitude of the excess increasing with the ratio of the injection to the initial stock of cash. More precisely, the rise in transactions would then be given by[3]

$$2 k \Delta C + \frac{k}{C} \Delta C^2.$$

Of course, the rate of interest would really tend to fall in such circumstances, and this would to some extent offset the effect of the influx of cash, as is readily seen when we rewrite (2) as

(3) $$T = C^2 i/2b.$$

Moreover, prices will rise to some extent,[4] and, of course, (3) at best

2. Since velocity equals $\dfrac{T}{C} = \dfrac{i}{2b} C$ by (2).

3. This is obtained by setting $k = C i/2b$ in (3), below, and computing ΔT by substituting $C + \Delta C$ for C.

4. Even if (2) holds, the demand for cash may rise only in proportion with the money value of transactions when all prices rise exactly in proportion, the rate of interest and transactions remaining unchanged. For then a doubling of all prices and cash balances leaves the situation unchanged, and the received argument holds. The point is that b is then one of the prices which has risen.

is only an approximation. Nevertheless, it remains true that the effect of an injection of cash on, say, the level of employment, may often have been underestimated.[5] For whatever may be working to counteract it, the force making for increased employment is greater than if transactions tend, *ceteris paribus*, toward their original proportion to the quantity of cash.

Finally the square root formula lends support to the argument that wage cuts can help increase employment, since it follows that the Pigou effect and the related effects are stronger than they would be with a constant transactions velocity. Briefly the phenomenon which has come to be called the Pigou effect[6] may be summarized thus: General unemployment will result in reduction in the price level which must increase the purchasing power of the stock of cash provided the latter does not itself fall more than in proportion with prices.[7] This increased purchasing power will augment demand for commodities[8] or investment goods (either directly, or because it is used to buy securities and so forces down the rate of interest). In any case, this works for a reduction in unemployment.

Now the increase in the purchasing power of the stock of cash which results from fallen prices is equivalent to an injection of cash with constant prices. There is therefore exactly the same reason for suspecting the magnitude of the effect of the former on the volume of transactions has been underestimated, as in the case of the latter. Perhaps this can be of some little help in explaining why there has not been more chronic unemployment or runaway inflation in our economy.

III. THE SIMPLE MODEL AND REALITY

It is appropriate to comment on the validity of the jump from equation (2) to conclusions about the operation of the economy. At

5. But see the discussions of Potter and Law as summarized by Jacob Viner, *Studies in the Theory of International Trade* (New York, 1937), pp. 37–39.

6. See A. C. Pigou, "The Classical Stationary State," *Economic Journal*, Vol. LIII, December 1943.

7. Presumably the "broker's fee" will be one of the prices which falls, driven down by the existence of unemployed brokers. There is no analogous reason for the rate of interest to fall, though it will tend to respond thus to the increase in the "real stock of cash."

8. The term "Pigou effect" is usually confined to the effects on consumption demand while the effect on investment demand, and (in particular) on the rate of interest is ordinarily ascribed to Keynes. However, the entire argument appears to antedate Pigou's discussion (which, after all, was meant to be a reformulation of the classical position) and is closely related to what Mr. Becker and I have called the Say's Equation form of the Say's Law argument. See our article "The Classical Monetary Theory; the Outcome of the Discussion," *Economica*, November 1952.

best, (2) is only a suggestive oversimplification, if for no other reason, because of the rationality assumption employed in its derivation. In addition the model is static. It takes the distribution of the firm's disbursements over time to be fixed, though it is to a large extent in the hands of the entrepreneur how he will time his expenditures. It assumes that there is one constant relevant rate of interest and that the "broker's fee" is constant or varies linearly with the magnitude of the sum involved. It posits a steady stream of payments and the absence of cash receipts during the relevant period. It deals only with the cash demand of a single economic unit and neglects interactions of the various demands for cash in the economy.[9] It neglects the precautionary and speculative demands for cash.

These are serious lacunae, and without a thorough investigation we have no assurance that our results amount to much more than an analytical curiosum. Nevertheless I offer only a few comments in lieu of analysis, and hope that others will find the subject worth further examination.

1. It is no doubt true that a majority of the public will find it impractical and perhaps pointless to effect every possible economy in the use of cash. Indeed the possibility may never occur to most people. Nevertheless, we may employ the standard argument that the largest cash users may more plausibly be expected to learn when it is profitable to reduce cash balances relative to transactions. The demand for cash by the community as a whole may then be affected similarly and by a significant amount. Moreover, it is possible that even small cash holders will sometimes institute some cash economies instinctively or by a process of trial and error not explicitly planned or analyzed.

2. With variable b and i the validity of our two basic results — the non-zero rational transactions demand for cash, and the less than proportionate rise in the rational demand for cash with the real volume of transactions, clearly depends on the nature of the responsiveness of the "brokerage fee" and the interest rate to the quantity of cash involved. The first conclusion will hold generally provided the "broker's fee" never falls below some preassigned level, e.g., it never falls below one mill per transaction, and provided the interest rate, its rate of change with C and the rate of change of the "broker's fee" all (similarly) have some upper bound, however large, at least when C is small.

9. I refer here particularly to considerations analogous to those emphasized by Duesenberry in his discussion of the relation between the consumption functions of the individual and the economy as a whole in his *Income, Saving and the Theory of Consumer Behavior* (Cambridge, Mass., 1950).

The second conclusion will not be violated persistently unless the "brokerage fee" tends to vary almost exactly in proportion with C (and it pays to hold zero cash balances) except for what may roughly be described as a limited range of values of C. Of course, it is always possible that this "exceptional range" will be the one relevant in practice. Variations in the interest rate will tend to strengthen our conclusion provided the interest rate never decreases with the quantity of cash borrowed or invested.[1]

It would perhaps not be surprising if these sufficient conditions for the more general validity of our results were usually satisfied in practice.

3. If payments are lumpy but foreseen, cash may perhaps be employed even more economically. For then it may well pay to obtain cash just before large payments fall due with little or no added cost in "brokers' fees" and considerable savings in interest payments. The extreme case would be that of a single payment during the year

---

1. For people to want to hold a positive amount of cash, the cost of cash holding must be decreasing after $C = 0$. Let b in (1) be a differentiable function of C for $C > 0$ (it will generally be discontinuous and equal to zero at $C = 0$). Then we require that the limit of the derivative of (1) be negative as C approaches zero from above, where this derivative is given by

$$\text{(i)} \quad -b\frac{T}{C^2} + \frac{T}{C}b' + \frac{i + i''C}{2}.$$

Clearly this will become negative as C approaches zero provided b is bounded from below and b', i, and i' are all bounded from above.

The second conclusion, the less than proportionate rise in minimum cost cash holdings with the volume of transactions, can be shown, with only b not constant, to hold if and only if $b - b'C + b''C^2$ is positive. This result is obtained by solving the first order minimum condition (obtained by setting (i), with the i' term omitted, equal to zero) for $\frac{T}{C}$ and noting that our conclusion is equivalent to the derivative of this ratio with respect to C being positive.

Now successive differentiation of (i) with the i' term omitted yields as our second order minimum condition $2(b - b'C) + b''C^2 > 0$ (note the resemblance to the preceding condition). Thus if our result is to be violated we must have

$$\text{(ii)} \quad b - Cb' \leqq -b''C^2 < 2(b - Cb'),$$

which at once yields $b'' \leqq 0$. Thus if b' is not to become negative (a decreasing *total* payment as the size of the withdrawal increases!) b'' must usually lie within a small neighborhood of zero, i.e., b must be approximately linear. However we know that in this case the square root formula will be (approximately) valid except in the case $b = kC$ when it will always (by (i)) pay to hold zero cash balances. Note incidentally that (ii) also yields $b - Cb' \geqq 0$ which means that our result must hold if ever the "brokerage fee" increases more than in proportion with C.

Note, finally, that if i varies with C the first order condition becomes a cubic and, provided $\infty > i' > 0$, our conclusion is strengthened, since T now tends to increase as C^2.

which would call for a zero cash balance provided the cash could be loaned out profitably at all. Cash receipts during the relevant period may have similar effects, since they can be used to make payments which happen to be due at the moment the receipts arrive. Here the extreme case involves receipts and payments always coinciding in time and amounts in which case, again, zero cash balances would be called for. Thus lumpy payments and receipts of cash, with sufficient foresight, can make for economies in the use of cash, i.e., higher velocity. This may not affect the rate of increase in transactions velocity with the level of transactions, but may nevertheless serve further to increase the effect of an injection of cash and of a cut in wages and prices. With imperfect foresight, however, the expectation that payments may be lumpy may increase the precautionary demand for cash. Moreover, the existence of a "broker's fee" which must be paid on lending or investing cash received during the period is an added inducement to keep receipts until payments fall due rather than investing, and so may further increase the demand for cash.

4. The economy in a single person's use of cash resulting from an increase in the volume of his transactions may or may not have its analogue for the economy as a whole. "External economies" may well be present if one businessman learns cash-economizing techniques from the experiences of another when both increase their transactions. On the diseconomies side it is barely conceivable that an infectious liquidity fetishism will permit a few individuals reluctant to take advantage of cash saving opportunities to block these savings for the bulk of the community. Nevertheless, at least two such possible offsets come to mind: (a) The rise in the demand for brokerage services resulting from a general increase in transactions may bring about a rise in the "brokerage fee" and thus work for an increase in average cash balances (a decreased number of visits to brokers). If cash supplies are sticky this will tend to be offset by rises in the rate of interest resulting from a rising total demand for cash, which serve to make cash more expensive to hold. (b) Widespread cash economizing might require an increase in precautionary cash holdings because in an emergency one could rely less on the ability of friends to help or creditors to be patient. This could weaken but not offset the relative reduction in cash holdings entirely, since the increase in precautionary demand is contingent on there being some relative decrease in cash holdings.

5. A priori analysis of the precautionary and the speculative demands for cash is more difficult. In particular, there seems to be

little we can say about the latter, important though it may be, except that it seems unlikely that it will work consistently in any special direction. In dealing with the precautionary demand, assumptions about probability distributions and expectations must be made.[2] It seems plausible offhand, that an increase in the volume of transactions will make for economies in the use of cash for precautionary as well as transactions purposes by permitting increased recourse to insurance principles.

Indeed, here we have a rather old argument in banking theory which does not seem to be widely known. Edgeworth,[3] and Wicksell[4] following him, suggested that a bank's precautionary cash requirements might also grow as the square root of the volume of its transactions (!). They maintained that cash demands on a bank tend to be normally distributed.[5] In this event, if it is desired to maintain a fixed probability of not running out of funds, precautionary cash requirements will be met by keeping on hand a constant multiple of the standard deviation (above the mean). But then the precautionary cash requirement of ten identical banks (with independent demands) together will be the same as that for any one of them multiplied by the square root of ten. For it is a well-known result that the standard deviation of a random sample from an infinite population increases as the square root of the size of the sample.

WILLIAM J. BAUMOL.

PRINCETON UNIVERSITY

2. See Arrow, Harris and Marschak, op. cit. for a good example of what has been done along these lines in inventory control analysis.

3. F. Y. Edgeworth, "The Mathematical Theory of Banking," Journal of the Royal Statistical Society, Vol. LI (1888), especially pp. 123–127. Fisher (loc. cit.) points out the relevance of this result for the analysis of the cash needs of the public as a whole. The result was independently rediscovered by Dr. Whitin (op. cit.) who seems to have been the first to combine it and (2) in inventory analysis.

4. K. Wicksell, Interest and Prices (London, 1936), p. 67.

5. The distribution would generally be approximately normal if its depositors were large in number, their cash demands independent and not very dissimilarly distributed. The independence assumption, of course, rules out runs on banks.

[4]

UNCERTAINTY AND THE EFFECTIVENESS OF POLICY*

By WILLIAM BRAINARD
Yale University

Economists concerned with aggregative policy spend a great deal of their time discussing the implications of various structural changes for the effectiveness of economic policy. In recent years, for example, monetary economists have debated at great length whether the rapid growth of nonbank financial intermediaries has lessened the effectiveness of conventional instruments of monetary control. Similarly, in discussions of the desirability of the addition or removal of specific financial regulations the consequences for the effectiveness of policy play an important role. One of the striking features of many of these discussions is the absence of any clear notion of what "effectiveness" is. At times it appears to be simply "bang per buck"—how large a change in some crucial variable (e.g., the long-term bond rate) results from a given change in a policy variable (e.g., open market operation). A natural question to ask is why a halving of effectiveness in this sense should not be met simply by doubling the dose of policy, with equivalent results.

It seems reasonable to suppose that the consequences of a structural change for the effectiveness of policy should be related to how it affects the policy-maker's performance in meeting his objectives. Suppose, for example, that the policy-maker wants to maximize a utility function which depends on the values of "target" variables. If, after some structural change, the policy-maker finds he is able to score higher on his utility function, then presumably the structural change has improved the effectiveness of policy and vice versa. One of the implications of the "theory of policy" in a world of certainty [6] or "certainty equivalence" [1] [3] [4] [5] is that structural changes which simply alter the magnitude of the response to policy do not alter the attainable utility level.[1] Hence such structural changes do not alter effectiveness in the above sense. Another feature of the theory of policy in a world of certainty is that a policy-maker with more instruments than targets is free to discard the excess instruments, and it makes no difference to his performance which ones he discards. These results are crucially dependent on the assumption that the response of target variables to policy in-

---

* I am indebted to Samuel Chase, Jr., Arthur Okun and James Tobin for many useful suggestions. A version of Parts I and II of this paper was presented at the Conference on Targets and Indicators of Monetary Policy held at U.C.L.A. in April, 1966.
[1] Assuming that the levels of instruments do not enter directly into the utility function.

struments is known for certain. Since it is difficult to imagine a real world policy-maker in such an enviable position, it would seem worth-while to explore the implications of relaxing that assumption. The first two sections of this paper discuss the implications of uncertainty in the response to policy actions for the selection of optimal policy. Optimal policy in the presence of this type of uncertainty is found to differ significantly from optimal policy in a world of certainty. For example, in general all instruments are used, even if there is only one target variable. Analysis of the optimality question also provides some insight into what constitutes effectiveness.

In the third section it is shown that, not surprisingly, the way a structural change alters the effectiveness of policy depends on how it affects both the expected magnitude and the predictability of response to policy actions. The third section goes on to discuss briefly some of the problems involved in assessing the consequences of structural change for the effectiveness of policy when there are several instruments and several targets, and where the structural change affects the response of the system to disturbances as well as policy instruments.

I. *One Target—One Instrument*

It is instructive to discuss the complications uncertainty creates in a world of one target and one instrument before discussing the problem of optimal use of policy instruments when there are many instruments and targets. Suppose that the policy-maker is concerned with one target variable (y). Assume that y depends linearly on a policy instrument (P)—for example, government expenditures—and various exogenous variables—for example, autonomous investment demand. For our present purposes the impact of exogenous variables may be summarized in a single variable (u).

$$(1) \qquad\qquad\qquad y = aP + u$$

where a determines the response of y to policy action.

The policy-maker faces two kinds of uncertainty. First, at the time he must make a policy decision he is uncertain about the impact of the exogenous variables (u) which affect y. This may reflect his inability to forecast perfectly either the value of exogenous variables or the response of y to them. Second, the policy-maker is uncertain about the response of y to any given policy action. He may have an estimate $\bar{a}$ of the expected value of the response coefficient a in (1) above, but he is aware that the actual response of y to policy action may differ substantially from the expected value. At the time of the 1964 tax cut, for example, there was considerable uncertainty over the magnitude of the tax multiplier.

Both types of uncertainty imply that the policy-maker cannot guarantee that y will assume its target value (y^*). But they have quite different implications for policy action. The first type of uncertainty, if present by itself, has nothing to do with the actions of the policy-maker; it is "in the system" independent of any action he takes. The assumption that all of the uncertainties are of this type is one of the reasons Theil and others [1] [3] [4] [5] are able to prescribe "certainty equivalence" behavior; that is, that the policy-maker should act on the basis of expected values as if he were certain they would actually occur. Since in this case the variance and higher moments of the distribution of y do not depend on the policy action taken, the policy-maker's actions only shift the location of y's distribution.

In the presence of uncertainty about the response of y to policy actions, however, the shape as well as the location of the distribution of y depends on the policy action. In this case the policy-maker should take into account his influence on the variability of y.[2]

We will assume that the policy-maker chooses policy on the basis of "expected utility." In particular, we will follow Theil in assuming that the policy-maker maximizes the expected value of a quadratic utility function. In the one-target case this is simply:

$$(2) \qquad\qquad U = -(y - y^*)^2$$

where y^* is the target value of y.

The assumption of the quadratic enables us to restrict our attention to the mean and variance of y and to compare our findings directly with the familiar certainty equivalence results. The assumption of a quadratic is, of course, subject to the objection that it treats positive and negative deviations from target as equally important. The use of a fancier utility function would provide additional reasons for departing from certainty equivalence.

The precise relationship between policy actions and the variance of y is not obvious. In (1) above, for example, the policy-maker may believe that the response coefficient a is a random variable depending on some unobserved variables, and that it is correlated with u. In that case the y is a random variable with a variance given by:

$$(3) \qquad\qquad \sigma_y^2 = \sigma_a^2 P^2 + \sigma_u^2 + 2\rho\sigma_a\sigma_u P$$

where σ_u^2 and σ_a^2 are the variances of u and a, respectively, and ρ is the correlation coefficient between u and a.

On the other hand, it is possible to conceive of part of the uncertainty of y as the consequence of estimation error. Even if the policy-maker

[2] Theil is of course aware that certainty equivalence behavior is not optimal in this case. In fact, he suggests that the sampling errors in the response coefficients are the most "dangerous" ones for a policy-maker who acts as if all random coefficient matrices coincide with their expectations [4, p. 74].

regards the "true" population response coefficient a as nonrandom, he may have to base his actions on an estimate of it obtained by fitting equation (1) to sample data. The estimate he uses will be a random variable, and its variance will affect the "variance" of y around its forecast value.[3]

As in the case where the population response coefficient is random, the magnitude of the policy action affects the contribution of this type of uncertainty to the variance of y. In this case, however, the contribution depends on the difference between the policy taken in the forecast period and the average level of policy pursued in the sample period used in estimating a. Assuming the u's are independent over time, a will be uncorrelated with the u for the forecast period and equation (3) may be rewritten:

$$(3') \qquad \sigma_y^2 = \sigma_a^2 (P - \bar{P})^2 + \sigma_u^2$$

where $\bar{P}$ is the average P for the sample period on which the estimate of a is based. Although we will use the first formulation to illustrate the significance of uncertainty in the response of y to policy actions, our results can be translated easily for use in the forecast error case.

Assuming the response coefficient is a random variable, we may find the expected utility associated with a given policy action by substituting (1) in (2):

$$(4) \qquad E(U) = - \left[(\bar{y} - y^*)^2 + \sigma_y^2 \right]$$

$$= - \left[(\bar{a}P + \bar{u} - y^*)^2 + \sigma_a^2 P^2 + \sigma_u^2 + 2\rho\sigma_a\sigma_u P \right]$$

where $\bar{y}$ and $\bar{u}$ are the expected values of y and u, respectively. There is no reason to suppose that $\bar{u}$ equals zero.

By differentiating (4) with respect to P and setting the derivative equal to zero, the optimal value of P is easily found to be:

$$(5) \qquad P^* = \frac{\bar{a}(y^* - \bar{u}) - \rho\sigma_a\sigma_u}{\bar{a}^2 + \sigma_a^2}$$

The optimal policy indicated by equation (5) clearly differs from the policy which would be pursued in a world of certainty or of certainty equivalence. The policy-maker should make use of more information than the expected value of the exogenous variables and of the response coefficient of a. Even when a and u are independently distributed, he

---

[3] Hooper and Zellner [2] provide a discussion of the error of forecast for multivariate regression models. In general the variance of the forecast error is $\sigma_F^2 = \sigma^2(xX1^u)[1 + x_F'^{-1}x_F]$ where x is the matrix of sample observations on the independent variables, and x_F is the vector of deviations of the independent variables from their sample means for the forecast period.

should make use of information about the variance of a as well as its mean. If a and u are not independent, he also needs to know their correlation. The assumption of a quadratic utility function does not lead to certainty equivalence except when the policy-maker is certain about the effects of his actions. Another interesting implication of (5) is that it does not in general pay to aim directly at the target. If a and u are independent, for example, equation (5) can be rewritten to show that the fraction of the expected "gap" between $\bar{u}$ and y^* which should be filled by policy action depends only on the coefficient of variation of a:

$$(5') \qquad\qquad P^* = g/(1 + V^2)$$

where $g = (y^* - \bar{u})/\bar{a}$, the expected gap, and V equals $\sigma_a/\bar{a}$, the coefficient of variation of a.[4] Only if the policy-maker is absolutely certain about a $(V = 0)$ will he close the entire gap; so long as V is finite, he will partially fill the gap.

Some care must be used in interpreting this result. The gap in this context is not the difference between what policy was "last period" and what would be required to make the expected value of y equal to y^*. In the example we have used, the gap is the difference between P equal to zero—the point where the variance of y is least—and the P required to give an expected value of y equal to y^*. If the expected value of a and u and the standard deviation of a remained unchanged for several periods, the optimal policy would also remain unchanged—the policy-maker would not reduce the gap in successive periods. In the case of "forecasting error" the gap is the difference between the average value of policy in the sample used to estimate a and the P which gives $\bar{y}$ equal to y^*. In this case, if the parameter a were reestimated each period and the expected value of u remained the same, policy would be continually revised, making the expected value of y closer and closer to y^* in successive periods.

A natural question to ask is to what extent uncertainty about a affects optimal behavior. Equation (5) indicates that "moderate" uncertainty about a may have a substantial effect. Suppose, for illustrative purposes, that the monetary authority believes that the equation $Y = aM + u$ correctly specifies the relationship between the stock of money (M), an exogenous variable (u), and money income (Y). It puts its staff to work estimating the relationship and obtains an estimate of 5 for the value of a, significant at a "t" level of 2. Further suppose that for the sample of observations on Y and M used to estimate a, the average level of M was \$100. Now suppose that for the next period the desired level of Y is \$650 and the expected value of u is taken to be \$50. In a

---

[4] (5') can be used for the estimation error case if P^* is interpreted as the deviation of optimal policy from the mean of P during the sample period, and u is defined to include $\bar{a}$ times that mean.

world of certainty M would simply be set at \$600/5 or \$120. Optimal policy in the uncertain situation confronting the policy-maker is most easily found by consulting equation (5'). If M were set at its average value during the sample period the expected value of Y would be \$550, leaving a gap of \$20 (\$100/5).

According to (5'), however, only 80 percent of this gap should be closed with a coefficient of variation of a equal to one-half. Hence it is optimal to set M at \$116 (=\$100+.8×\$20).

When a and u are not independent, the results are slightly more complicated. The policy-maker must now take into account the covariation

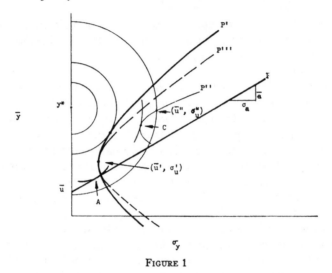

FIGURE 1

between the impact of his policy action and exogenous variables. If there is a positive correlation, it will pay him to shoot for a lower value of $\bar{y}$ than otherwise; if negative, higher. One interesting implication of this is that the fraction of the gap that the policy-maker should close will depend on which side of the target he is on. Perhaps more surprising, if a and u have sufficiently large positive correlation and there is a positive gap or sufficiently large negative correlation and there is a negative gap, it may actually pay for the policy-maker to go the "wrong" way! That is, at the initial point it may actually pay to reduce the variance of y at the expense of increasing the difference between expected y and y^*.

These results can be seen diagrammatically by consulting Figure 1 which shows the expected value of y on the vertical axis and the standard deviation of y on the horizontal axis. Indifference curves, showing various combinations of $\bar{y}$ and σ_y, which have the same expected utility, are drawn "around" y^*, the target value of y. These curves have the form $(y^* - \bar{y})^2 + \sigma_v^2 =$ constant; i.e., they are concentric circles drawn around y^*.

In order to focus on the effects of uncertainty concerning the impact of policy, let us assume for the moment that σ_u is zero. Referring to Figure 1, suppose that in the absence of policy action, y is certain to be $\bar{u}$, which is well below y^*. By increasing P by "1 unit," the policy-maker may close the expected gap between y and $\bar{y}$ by an amount $\bar{a}$, but in so doing he also increases the standard deviation of y by σ_a.[5] The line P shows the possibilities open to the policy-maker. Optimal policy corresponds to point A. Because the indifference curves are horizontal where they leave $\bar{y}$ axis, and vertical at a value of $\bar{y} = y^*$, while the slope of the line P is $\bar{a}/\sigma_a$, it always pays to do something, but it never pays to aim for y^*. It is also apparent that reductions in σ_a for a given $\bar{a}$ increase the optimal amount of policy.

These results are not altered for σ_u not equal to zero, so long as the correlation between u and a is 0. In Figure 1 the point $(\bar{u}', \sigma_{u'})$ indicates the expected value and variance of y in the absence of policy action and the line drawn through that point labeled P' indicates the opportunities available to the policy-maker. This "opportunity locus" is curved, reflecting the absence of perfect correlation between a and u. This independence guarantees that unless $\bar{u} = y^*$ it will be optimal to pursue some policy action, for the opportunity locus is vertical at the point $(\bar{u}', \sigma_{u'})$ indicating that the first little bit of policy can be undertaken without increasing the variance of y.[6]

In Figure 1 the line P'' shows the way correlation between a and u alters the opportunity locus available to the policy-maker. In the example shown, a zero level of policy would leave the economy at the point $(\bar{u}'', \sigma_{u''})$. The positive correlation between a and u tilts the locus clockwise through that point so that a small decrease in P will decrease the variance of Y. Optimal policy involves choosing point C, which in this case involves going the "wrong" way. If by chance $\bar{a}(y^* - \bar{u}) = \rho \sigma_u \sigma_a$, the policy-maker should do nothing.

Figure 2 shows the way in which the appropriate level of policy action depends on the size of the gap. For given values of $\bar{a}, \rho, \sigma_a, \sigma_u$, the larger the gap, the more the policy-maker should do. With independence of a and u this relationship is linear-homogeneous. When a and u are correlated the relationship is linear, but a zero level of policy is optimal for some nonzero gap.

[5] As a convention, the sign of policy is always chosen so that "positive" policy increases $\bar{y}$.
[6] For correlation between u and a equal to 0,

$$\frac{\partial \sigma_y}{\partial P} = \frac{\partial [(\sigma_u^2 + P^2 \sigma_a^2)^{1/2}]}{\partial P} = \left. \frac{P \sigma_a^2}{(\sigma_u^2 + P^2 \sigma_a^2)^{1/2}} \right|_{P=0} = 0$$

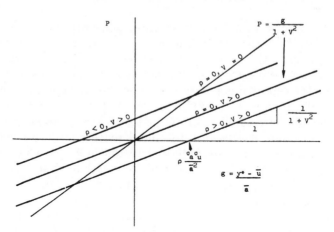

FIGURE 2

II. *Multiple Instruments*

One of the lessons of the theory of policy under certainty is that, in general, the attainment of n targets requires n instruments. If more than n instruments are available, the policy-maker is free to choose n arbitrarily in order to achieve his objectives. It should already be obvious that this rule breaks down under uncertainty. We will first show that with one target and two instruments it will generally be optimal to use some combination of both instruments.[7] It can similarly be shown that in general all instruments available should be used in pursuing one target. It follows that the addition of an objective requires some sacrifice in performance vis-à-vis objectives already being considered.

Suppose that:

$$(6) \qquad y = a_1 P_1 + a_2 P_2 + u$$

where again it is desired to maximize the expected value of the utility function given in (2). It will be convenient to define units of policy such that the $\bar{a}_i$ associated with each policy instrument is exactly 1. For simplicity let us assume that correlation between each a_i and u is 0. Then by differentiating the expected value of (2) with respect to P_1 and P_2 we find the conditions for optimal policy to be:

$$(7a) \qquad 0 = (P_1 + P_2 + \bar{u} - y^*) + P_1 \sigma_{a_1}^2 + \rho_{12}\sigma_{a_1}\sigma_{a_2}P_2$$

$$(7b) \qquad 0 = (P_1 + P_2 + \bar{u} - y^*) + P_2 \sigma_{a_2}^2 + \rho_{12}\sigma_{a_1}\sigma_{a_2}P_1$$

where ρ_{12} is the correlation between a_1 and a_2.

[7] The idea of looking at the problem of optimal policy behavior in an uncertain world as essentially a problem of portfolio choice arose in discussions with Arthur Okun around 1962.

Solving for the ratio of P_1 to total policy impact (P_1+P_2) we obtain:

(8)
$$P_1/(P_1 + P_2) = \frac{\sigma_{a_2}^2 - \rho_{12}\sigma_{a_1}\sigma_{a_2}}{(\sigma_a^2 - 2\rho_{12}\sigma_{a_1}\sigma_{a_2} + \sigma_{a_1}^2)} \quad^8$$

Equation (8) indicates the proportions in which the policy-maker should use the two policy instruments. The optimal policy portfolio as shown in (8) combines the instruments so as to minimize the coefficient of variation of their combined impact. Under the assumption of independence between the a_i's and the u, this policy portfolio can be treated as a single instrument and its optimal level determined as in Section I.

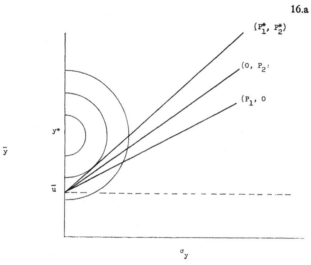

FIGURE 3

The coefficient of variation of the optimal policy package is, of course, less than or equal to the coefficient of variation of any single instrument. Figure 3 shows, for the special case where σ_u and ρ equal zero and where the ratio of the coefficient of variation of a_2 to that of a_1 is .8, the locus for the optimal combination of two policies compared to the loci available for each of the instruments used separately. Figure 3 assumes that the correlation between the impacts of the two instruments is zero. The presence of correlation between the a's complicates the computation of the optimal policy portfolio but does not alter the basic conclusion that several instruments are better than one in the pursuit of one goal.

The optimal amount of P_1 per "unit" of combined policy action

---

[8] By virtue of the normalization of a_i, of course, the standard deviations are coefficients of variation.

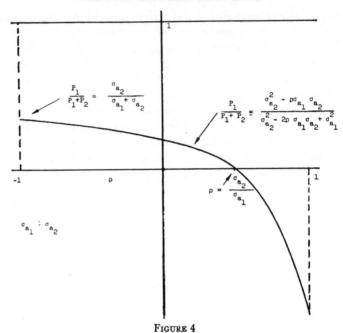

FIGURE 4

P_1+P_2 is shown in Figure 4 as a function of the correlation between a_1 and a_2. In the example shown it is assumed that the coefficient of variation of a_1 is greater than that of a_2. From Figure 4 it can be seen that for sufficiently high positive correlation it is optimal to use P_1 (the "less efficient" instrument) in the "wrong" direction.

Table 1 shows the coefficients of variation for the optimal policy

TABLE 1

COEFFICIENT OF VARIATION FOR ρ_{12} OPTIMAL POLICY PACKAGE

		−9/10	−3/4	−1/2	−1/4	0	1/4	1/2	3/4	9/10	1
	1.0	.22	.35	.50	.61	.71	.79	.87	.94	.97	1.0
	1.1	.23	.37	.52	.64	.74	.83	.90	.97	1.00	0
	1.2	.24	.39	.54	.67	.77	.86	.93	.99	.99	0
	1.6	.27	.43	.61	.74	.85	.93	.99	.98	.85	0
σ_{a_1}	2.0	.30	.47	.65	.79	.89	.97	1.00	.94	.74	0
$\overline{}$	2.4	.31	.49	.69	.82	.92	.99	1.00	.89	.67	0
σ_{a_2}	2.8	.33	.51	.71	.85	.94	.99	.99	.86	.63	0
	3.2	.34	.53	.73	.86	.95	1.00	.98	.83	.60	0
	4.0	.35	.55	.76	.89	.97	1.00	.96	.80	.56	0
	8.0	.39	.60	.81	.93	.99	.99	.92	.73	.49	0

$\sigma_{a_2}=1$.

package for various values of ρ_{12}, σ_{a_1}, σ_{a_2}. The table is constructed with the variance of a_2 normalized at one and with $\sigma a_2 < \sigma a_1$. Hence the lowest coefficient of variation of policy impact that would be obtained by using a single policy is one. The improvement realized by using both instruments rather than P_2 alone is indicated by the difference between one and the appropriate entry.

The gain from diversification of policy instruments is not a simple function of the correlation coefficient; it also depends on the ratio of coefficients of variation of the two policy instruments. As can be seen from Table 1, negative correlation between a_1 and a_2 greatly assists in reducing the variance in the impact of the policy package, the reduction being greatest for cases where the variances of the two instruments are equal. As the correlation increases, the gain from using two instruments decreases, until at some level of positive correlation none of policy P_1 is used. For correlation greater than that amount, P_1 will be used in the "wrong" direction and some reduction in variance will be realized. In the extreme cases of perfect positive or perfect negative correlation between the a's there exists a policy package with zero variance.

If there is correlation between the disturbance and the impact of either of the policy instruments, it should also be taken into account in the selection of a policy package. Other things being equal, increasing the correlation between the impact of a particular instrument and the disturbance will decrease its use relative to other instruments. The importance of such correlation depends on the size of the gap: the larger the gap, the less the relative contribution of the disturbance to the variance of y after policy action and the less important the correlation of the disturbance and instruments.

The optimal use of n instruments follows the principles illustrated with two; if the error term is independent of the policy response coefficients, the portfolio of instruments which has the lowest coefficient of variation should be chosen. In general this will involve using all of the instruments, and it may involve using some instruments the "wrong" way.

Generalization to many targets is conceptually simple but algebraically tedious. Solution of a multiple-goal problem requires specification of a multidimensional utility function which, if it is quadratic, implicitly provides weights for trading off expected values, variances, and covariances of the policy objectives. The particular solution obviously depends on the weights imbedded in the utility function. One feature of the results is perhaps worth noting: since all policy instruments would be used in pursuit of a single target, improvement in performance vis-à-vis one objective requires sacrificing other objectives—even when the number of instruments exceeds the number of objectives.

III. *Structural Change and the Effectiveness of Policy*

The evaluation of the impact of any particular structural change on the effectiveness of policy is extremely difficult.[9] For our purposes a structural change is described by the way it changes the joint distribution of the parameters a_i and u. The task of determining how the imposition of some new regulation or the emergence of some new financial market alters that distribution is obviously a major one and beyond the scope of this paper. Our relatively modest objective here is to indicate the empirical questions which the above analysis suggests are of importance.

A Single Instrument. First let us consider structural changes which affect only the impact of policy actions; i.e., which do not affect either the expected value or dispersion of the disturbance term. In addition, let us assume that the structural change in question does not alter the correlations among the policy impact coefficients and the disturbance. The effect of such a change on expected utility can be found directly by substituting the value of optimal policy (expressed in terms of $\bar{a}$, σ_a, ρ, $\bar{u}$, etc.) in the equation for expected utility (4). Alternatively, the consequences of structural change can be seen by noting how the "opportunity locus" in Figures 1 and 3 are affected. By substituting $(\bar{y}-\bar{u})/\bar{a}$ for P in equation (3) we find:

$$(9) \qquad \sigma_y = \left(\frac{\sigma_a^2}{\bar{a}^2} (\bar{y} - \bar{u})^2 + 2\rho \frac{\sigma_a}{\bar{a}} \sigma_u(\bar{y} - \bar{u}) + \sigma_u^2 \right)^{1/2}$$

It is immediately clear that a structural change which does not affect the coefficient of variation of a (nor ρ, $\bar{u}$, and σ_u) does not alter the opportunity locus and hence does not alter the expected utility derived from optimal policy. It is also clear that increasing the coefficient of variation, for ρ equal zero, results in an opportunity locus which has a larger variance for every value of $\bar{y}$ (except for zero policy). Hence increasing the coefficient of variation leads to a reduction in the effectiveness of policy. Such a shift is illustrated in Figure 1 by a movement of the opportunity locus labeled P' to the location indicated by the dotted locus labeled P'''.

One of the simplest illustrations of this result is the argument that increasing the legal reserve requirement, thereby reducing the expected response to a given sized change in reserve base, actually increases the effectiveness of monetary control. Suppose one believes that the money

---

[9] What is classified as a structural change obviously depends on the specific problem under discussion. The removal of the ceiling rate on time deposits, for example, would change the response of financial markets to open market operations; that is, it would change the structure within which the Federal Reserve conducts day-to-day policy. At the same time, however, the ceiling rate itself could be used as a policy instrument to influence target variables. While some changes in the "structure" are the direct consequence of actions by the monetary authority, others may be exogenous from their point of view.

stock is all that matters and, further, that the money stock (M) is related to the reserve base (R) by the following equation:

(10) $$M = \frac{1}{k + \epsilon} R$$

where k is the legal reserve requirement and ϵ is banks' demand for free reserves (expressed as a fraction of their deposit liabilities). Suppose further that, from the viewpoint of the monetary authority, ϵ is a random variable with a known distribution. Then it is easy to see that, for reasonable distributions of ϵ, increases in k will reduce the expected response of M to R but can reduce the standard deviation of that response more than proportionately, thereby reducing its coefficient of variation. One of the appeals of the 100 percent reserve proposal, of course, is the fact that as k approaches one, the coefficient of variation of the response of M to R goes to zero.

If the correlation between the impact of the policy instrument and u is not zero, matters are slightly more complicated. From (9) it is apparent that increases in σ_a shift the opportunity locus to the right for some values of $(\bar{y} - \bar{u})$ and to the left for others. This is illustrated for a positive ρ in Figure 5 below where the dotted locus corresponds to a higher σ_a. As indicated in Figure 5, the minimum risk that can be obtained is independent of the value of σ_a, and depends only on the value of σ_u and ρ. Hence, it is possible to get the paradoxical result that an increase in the dispersion of response can make policy more "effective" for some set

22a

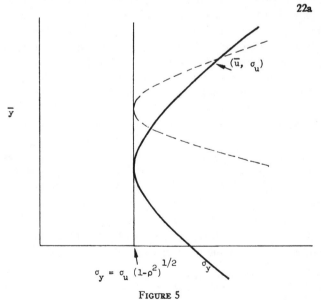

FIGURE 5

of values of $\bar{u}$ and σ_u. This peculiar result is a consequence of the fact that it is possible to reduce the variance of y below σ_u whenever μ and a are correlated. Consider, for example, the case where a and u are positively correlated, and where $\bar{\mu}$ is less than y^*. In this case a reduction in risk can be obtained for "negative" values of P; i.e., by setting $\bar{y}$ even further from y^* than $\bar{u}$. Suppose that the optimal policy initially involves going in the counterintuitive direction in order to take advantage of such risk reduction. With a larger σ_a the same reduction in risk can be obtained without pushing $\bar{y}$ as far away from y^*; hence it will result in a higher expected utility.

Multiple Instruments. The consequence of structural change when there are a number of instruments is closely analogous to the single instrument case. If the structural change does not affect the coefficient of variation for the individual instruments, their correlations, or the distribution of the disturbance, the opportunity locus is unaltered. If the coefficient of variation of an individual instrument is increased, the consequences can be analyzed in two steps.[10] First, the effect of the change on the coefficient of variation of the optimal policy package can be found. Once this is determined, its consequences for the performance of the policy-maker can be analyzed exactly as in the single instrument case.

The consequences of increasing the coefficient of variation of one instrument are illustrated in Table 1.[11] Two points illustrated in Table 1 are worthy of comment. First, so long as both instruments are used in the same direction (see Figure 4), increasing the coefficient of variation of one instrument increases the coefficient of variation of the optimal policy package. If an instrument is used in the counterintuitive direction, however, increasing its coefficient of variation improves the optimal policy package. Second, the table illustrates the obvious fact that decreasing the effectiveness of one instrument which is being used together with others has much less effect than if the instrument were being used by itself. For example, even with a correlation of $-9/10$, the consequence of increasing σ_{a_1} from 1 to 2 is to increase the coefficient of variation of the optimal policy package by less than 40 percent.

Multiple Targets. The presence of a number of target variables in the utility function greatly complicates the task of evaluating the consequences of a given structural change. It is quite unlikely that a change will affect the opportunity locus for different targets in the same way. Hence the desirability of the change will depend on the relative weights placed on the different targets in the utility function. For example, it is commonly argued that the development of the Euro-dollar market and

---

[10] Assuming the correlations between the a_i's and u are zero.

[11] Table 1 shows the effect of increasing the coefficient of variation for the less effective of the two instruments.

the general increase in international capital mobility in recent years has made monetary policy a more effective tool in stabilizing the balance of payments, while at the same time reducing its usefulness for controlling domestic economic disturbances.

Disturbances. The discussion thus far has focused on the consequences of structural change for the performance of the policy-maker when confronted with a given distribution of disturbances. A structural change which alters the response to policy actions is also likely to alter the magnitude of the problems with which he must cope. In the above example, greater capital mobility presumably increases the responsiveness of the U. S. balance of payments to disturbances; e.g., in this case to changes in the interest rates in other countries. Thus a structural change which gives the U. S. a more effective tool may also have given it a more difficult task to perform. If this is the case it is not clear that such a structural change is desirable. This can be illustrated by reference to the single instrument case with ρ equal to zero. Suppose for the moment that a structural change doubles $\bar{a}$ and σ_a, but also doubles σ_u, without altering $\bar{u}$. From Figure 1 it is clear that such a change leaves the policy-maker with a worse opportunity locus.[12] If, in addition, there is an increase in the variation of $\bar{u}$ from period to period, still greater losses result.

In the real world, evaluating the desirability of a given structural change is further complicated by the fact that a change which decreases the response of the system to one type of disturbance is likely to increase its response to another. Consider, for example, the consequences of a permanent fixed ceiling rate on time deposits. It can be argued that such a restriction on banks' competition for deposits reduces the response of the system to shifts in the demand of bank borrowers for loans. At the same time, the existence of such a ceiling may increase the destabilizing effect of shifts in depositors' preferences between the liabilities of banks and other financial intermediaries. In general, then, evaluation of some particular structural change requires an empirical judgment as to the relative importance of various kinds of disturbances.

[12] Again, when $\rho \neq 0$, it is possible to have the paradoxical result that increasing σ_u is advantageous.

REFERENCES

1. C. C. Holt, F. Modigliani, J. F. Muth and H. A. Simon, *Planning Production, Inventories, and Work Force* (Prentice-Hall, 1960).
2. John W. Hooper and Arnold Zellner, "The Error of Forecast for Multivariate Regression Models," Cowles Foundation Paper No. 171 (Cowles Found. for Res. in Econ., Yale Univ., 1962).
3. Henri Theil, *Economic Forecasts and Policy*, 2nd ed., Vol. XV of Contributions to Economic Analysis (North-Holland Pub. Co., Amsterdam, 1961).
4. ———, *Optimal Decision Rules for Government and Industry* (Rand McNally, 1964).
5. ———, "Linear Decision Rules for Macrodynamic Policy Problems," *Quantitative Planning of Economic Policy*, Bert G. Hickman, ed. (Brookings Institution, 1965), pp. 18–37.
6. J. Tinbergen, *On the Theory of Economic Policy*, 2nd ed., Vol. I of Contributions to Economic Analysis (North-Holland Pub. Co., Amsterdam, 1952).

[5]

A RE-EXAMINATION OF THE PURE CONSUMPTION LOANS MODEL

DAVID CASS AND MENAHEM E. YAARI*

Yale University

I. INTRODUCTION

PROFESSOR SAMUELSON's article (1958) on an exact consumption-loan model of interest led to an interesting controversy. At issue were the determination and properties of interest rates in a dynamic economic system with no capital. One might have thought that these exchanges, between Samuelson (1959) and Lerner (1959) on the one hand, and between Samuelson (1960) and Meckling (1960) on the other, would result, if not in a complete resolution of the disagreements, at least in the emergence of a clear picture of what the issues are and how they might be treated. Unfortunately, such was not the case. The Samuelson-Lerner and the Samuelson-Meckling dialogues leave the reader rather perplexed, as though he had just watched a New Wave film—executed with brilliance, enjoyable while in progress, but not quite clear as to what is happening and never giving one a sense of resolution.

The 1960's have brought an upsurge of interest in capital theory and, more generally, in questions of allocation over time. Now Samuelson's model, even though it has no capital, is of interest to capital theorists because it has many of the features of a model of capital accumulation with decentralized decision making. Since the 1958–60 discussions of this model by Samuelson, Lerner, and Meckling left some questions unan-

swered, we feel that a restudy of the model is in order. The following is an attempt at such a restudy.

We shall take the liberty of deviating somewhat from Samuelson's original notation.

II. THE MODEL

We shall concentrate throughout most of our discussion on the simpler of Samuelson's two models, namely, the one in which people live for two periods, earning a fixed income in the first and earning nothing in the second. In the first period of his lifetime, a person earns *one* unit of output, where "output" is something usable directly (and exclusively) in consumption, and we do not inquire wherefrom it comes.

The generation which is born at time t will be called generation t, and we shall assume that there are $(1 + n)^t$ people in it. Thus, n is the (relative) rate of growth of population, which is assumed constant. Members of generation t are thought of as being alike in all respects, so one can speak of a member of generation t without specifying the individual. Let the symbol C_t^1 stand for the first-period consumption of a member of generation t, and let C_t^2 stand for his second-period consumption. A member of generation t is assumed to value any given consumption plan (C_t^1, C_t^2) according to the value, $U(C_t^1, C_t^2)$, taken on by a "regularly shaped" utility function U at (C_t^1, C_t^2). The utility function U is assumed to be the same for all generations.

Continuing in Samuelson's footsteps,

* We are indebted to Richard Attiyeh, Herbert Scarf, and James Tobin for their comments. This essay is based on research which was supported by the National Science Foundation.

we now proceed to assume that output is non-durable and thus cannot be carried over from one period to the next. This assumption reduces the production possibilities in the model (that is, the possibilities of using output in one period in the production of output in another period) to naught. It is clear, furthermore, that the assumptions made so far are so restrictive as to rule out from the outset any possibility of trades, markets, or prices. A member of generation t who wishes to engage in a transaction cannot find anyone willing and able to participate in the transaction on the opposite side.

Given that production and trade have both been dispensed with, there remains only one other economic activity to be considered—distribution. This function is still open in our economy, for output can be taken from the young who earn it and given to the old who do not. Thus, our first task will be the examination of alternative distribution schemes. However, before proceeding with this examination, we must define the notion of "the rate of interest." Writing r_t for the rate of interest in period t, we *define:*

$$r_t = \frac{C^1_{t-1} + C^2_{t-1} - 1}{1 - C^1_{t-1}}$$

or

$$1 + r_t = \frac{C^2_{t-1}}{1 - C^1_{t-1}}.$$

Two things should be noted: (a) $1 + r_t$ is *not* a price; that is, no transactions are ever held using it as a rate of exchange. It is not even an "implicit price," in the sense of a price which emerges as a by-product of efficient allocation of resources. It is, rather, an ex post rate of exchange which is *inferred* from observation of the consumption pattern of a member of generation $t - 1$, and it has

reference neither to trade nor to efficiency.[1] (b) When $C^1_{t-1} = 1$, r_t is clearly not defined. If $C^1_{t-1} = 1$ and $C^2_{t-1} = 0$, we shall say that r_t can be any real number, and if $C^1_{t-1} = 1$ and $C^2_{t-1} > 0$, we shall say that $r_t = +\infty$.

III. DISTRIBUTION OF OUTPUT

As has already been remarked, the only economic function remaining in the model of the foregoing section is that of *distribution of output.* A pair of sequences,

$$\{C^2_t, \quad t = 0, \pm 1, \pm 2, \dots \},$$

$$\{C^1_t, \quad t = 0, \pm 1, \pm 2, \dots \},$$

with non-negative elements will be referred to as a *distribution scheme.* It specifies how much each member of any given generation shall consume in each period of his lifetime. A distribution scheme will be called *feasible* if it does not use up more output than is available in any period. In other words, the scheme $(\{C^1_t\}, \{C^2_t\})$ is feasible if and only if

$$(1 + n)^t C^1_t + (1 + n)^{t-1} C^2_{t-1} \leqq (1 + n)^t$$

or

$$C^1_t + \frac{C^2_{t-1}}{1 + n} \leqq 1$$

for all t, where the inequality arises from an assumption of free disposal.

Suppose that in period t no disposal takes place. Then,

$$C^1_t + \frac{C^2_{t-1}}{1 + n} = 1.$$

On the other hand, we have, by the definition of the rate of interest, that

$$C^1_{t-1} + \frac{C^2_{t-1}}{1 + r_t} = 1.$$

[1] Note, however, that if a member of generation $t - 1$ were to maximize utility subject to a given r_t, then $1 + r_t$ would, as usual, equal the marginal rate of substitution of second-period consumption for first-period consumption.

PURE CONSUMPTION LOANS MODEL   355

Subtracting the latter from the former, we get

$$C_t^1 - C_{t-1}^1 + \frac{r_t - n}{(1 + r_t)(1 + n)} C_{t-1}^2 = 0.$$

As an immediate consequence one now obtains that

if $C_{t-1}^1 = C_t^1 \neq 1$,   then $r_t = n$.

If $C_{t-1}^1 = C_t^1 = 1$, then r_t can be any real number, and we might as well agree once again that $r_t = n$.

This equality of r_t and n in case $C_{t-1}^1 = C_t^1$ is the manifestation in the present framework of what Samuelson (1958) calls "the biological rate of interest," which he finds "paradoxical," even "astonishing" (pp. 471 and 473, respectively) and which Meckling finds very hard to accept. The main cause for suspicion seems to be the fact that a rate of interest has been determined without any reference to impatience and time preference or, more generally, to the utility function U. Somehow, the fact that r_t is a completely mechanistic construct, having no reference to markets, seems to have become blurred.

IV. STATIONARY SCHEMES

In order to analyze the relation between the rate of interest and the rate of growth of population somewhat further, let us define a *stationary* distribution scheme by the requirement

$$\left.\begin{array}{c} C_t^1 = C^1 \\ C_t^2 = C^2 \end{array}\right\} \text{ for all } t,$$

which implies that

$$r_t = r = \frac{C^1 + C^2 - 1}{1 - C^1} \text{ for all } t.$$

We are assuming for the moment that $C^1 < 1$, so r is well defined. Now let us check the feasibility of a stationary distribution scheme. By direct substitution, we find that

$$C^1 + \frac{C^2}{1 + n} \leq 1 \quad \textit{if and only if } r \leq n.$$

Thus, the feasibility of a stationary distribution scheme is *equivalent* to the statement that the rate of interest is no greater than the rate of growth of population. Furthermore, the same algebraic operation which yielded the equivalence of the above inequalities also yields the equivalence of the strict inequality $r < n$ and the strict inequality $C^1 + C^2/(1 + n) < 1$. With a stationary distribution scheme, a rate of interest which falls short of the rate of growth of population means that some output is being discarded in every period. In other words, the inequality $r < n$ means that the distribution scheme under consideration is *inefficient* (unless consumers are satiated). This result has a familiar ring to it. In models where investment and capital accumulation are possible, we often find that, among all feasible stationary paths, the path which maximizes per capita consumption is the so-called golden-rule path, which is characterized, among other things, by the equality of the rate of interest and the rate of growth of population. Indeed, we know that a stationary path along which the (constant) rate of interest is lower than the rate of growth of population is in fact inefficient in the sense that everybody's consumption can be increased (see, for example, Phelps, 1965).

Let us recapitulate: Every stationary distribution scheme is characterized by a pair of non-negative real numbers, C^1 and C^2. The set of all feasible schemes is represented by the shaded area in Figure 1, and it corresponds precisely to the set of all schemes with a rate of interest which is no greater than the rate of growth of population. Among the latter,

D. CASS AND M. E. YAARI

only the schemes that are represented by points on the northeastern boundary line of the shaded area are *efficient.* These efficient schemes are precisely those for which the rate of interest is, in fact, *equal* to the rate of growth of population.

Note that Figure 1 actually contains part of Samuelson's (1959, p. 519) Figure 1 in his reply to Lerner. In that figure, Samuelson marks two specific schemes, represented by the points S and L, which he labels the "Samuelson plan" and the

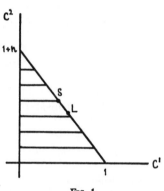

FIG. 1

"Lerner plan," respectively. Now both S and L are in fact on the efficient frontier of the shaded set and therefore both represent distribution schemes for which the rate of interest is equal to n. The discussions by both Samuelson and Lerner, in which the point L is referred to as corresponding to a *zero* rate of interest, therefore seem to be in error.[2] The only point on the efficient frontier which could possibly be taken to represent a distribution scheme with zero interest is the point $(1, 0)$, where the rate of

interest can be taken to be any real number, including zero (and also including n).

Let us turn now to the question of choosing between alternative distribution schemes. If we take all the feasible distribution schemes and ask a member of generation t which of these he prefers, he will no doubt say that the schemes which satisfy the requirement

$$C_t^1 = 1, \qquad C_t^2 = 1 + n,$$

are highest on his preference scale. These are the schemes which give generation t all the output in period t, as well as all the output in period $t + 1$ (under the assumption that *within* each generation all share alike). He will be indifferent as to which of the schemes satisfying this requirement is picked. It is obvious, therefore, that no single distribution scheme will be preferred to all other feasible schemes by all individuals. In a situation of this sort, the economist usually resorts to one of two things: Either he defines an over-all social welfare function and picks the feasible distribution scheme which maximizes it, or he restricts the choice of a scheme to a subclass of the original class of all feasible schemes, a subclass such that individual maximization over it will result in compatible choices. The subclass of all stationary distribution schemes clearly has this property, since stationarity means that everybody has the same lifetime consumption profile. Thus, if we agree to restrict the search for a distribution scheme to the class of all stationary schemes[3] (and this agreement is extraneous to the analysis, just as the

---

[2] Samuelson and Lerner both refer to the case where $n = 1$ and L is the point $(\frac{2}{3}, \frac{2}{3})$. Clearly, at that point every person foregoes $\frac{1}{3}$ units of output in the first period and receives $\frac{2}{3}$ in the second period, which corresponds to a rate of interest of 100 per cent.

[3] It seems that Lerner's concern for the equality of income distribution ought to lead him to stationarity (everybody getting the same consumption profile) and not to equality of consumption for all *within* each time period (that is, $C^1 = C^2$), which he seems to advocate in the above-cited references.

choice of a social welfare function would be) we can find one distribution which maximizes everybody's utility. We write

$$\max U(C^1, C^2)$$

subject to the constraint that the stationary scheme be feasible, that is, subject to

$$C^1 + \frac{C^2}{1+n} \leqq 1 .$$

This is indeed Samuelson's maximization problem (leading to the point S in his diagram as the solution) but stated in terms of choice among distribution schemes rather than in terms of the opportunities open to a "representative man." It should be stressed again that all the efficient points in the set over which the maximization takes place are points which correspond to a rate of interest equal to n (except the point $(1, 0)$, where the rate of interest is indeterminate).

Before leaving this part of the discussion, let us consider the problem of decentralization. It is clear that the distribution schemes discussed above (whether stationary or not) are not, in general, attainable by having each individual act on his own in a decentralized fashion. Indeed, the only distribution schemes which are attainable with each individual acting on his own through the (inactive) market are distribution schemes for which

$$\left.\begin{array}{l} C_t^1 \leqq 1 \\ C_t^2 = 0 \end{array}\right\} \text{ for all } t .$$

Among these, the only efficient scheme is given by $C_t^1 = 1$ and $C_t^2 = 0$ for all t, which also happens to be a stationary scheme. However, this is obviously not (in general) the scheme that individuals would pick, among all stationary

schemes, if they had the choice. Thus, as Samuelson points out, we have here an example in which decentralized (competitive) behavior fails to lead to an optimum. This conclusion can be sharpened considerably if one drops the assumption that output is non-durable (see Sec. VI below).

V. CONSTANT RATE OF INTEREST PATHS

In the foregoing section we have seen that the rate of interest is constant along every stationary path. We now ask whether every efficient path along which the rate of interest is constant is, in fact, stationary.

Constancy of the rate of interest means that there exists a real number r such that

$$C_t^1 + \frac{C_t^2}{1+r} = 1 \text{ for all } t .$$

Now, feasibility and efficiency of the distribution scheme mean that

$$C_t^1 + \frac{C_{t-1}^2}{1+n} = 1 \text{ for all } t .$$

Subtracting the latter from the former and rearranging leads to

$$\frac{C_t^2}{C_{t-1}^2} = \frac{1+r}{1+n} .$$

Since C_t^2 is bounded by

$$C_t^2 \leqq 1 + n \text{ for all } t ,$$

we find that the only rate of interest which can be constant for all $t = 0, \pm 1, \pm 2, \ldots$, is the rate $r = n$, which, indeed, corresponds to a stationary scheme.

However, if we only require the rate of interest to be constant from some point on, say $t = 0, 1, 2, \ldots$, then we find that $r \leqq n$ is possible, while $r > n$

358   D. CASS AND M. E. YAARI

is not.[4] If $r < n$ then as $t \to \infty$, C_t^2 tends to 0, and therefore C_t^1 tends to 1. In fact, by a straightforward calculation one can show that if there exists an $\epsilon > 0$ such that $r_t \leqq n - \epsilon$ for $t = 0, 1, 2, \ldots$, then

$$\lim_{t \to \infty} C^2 = 0 .$$

As a particular instance, this discussion applies to paths along which the rate of interest is always *zero*, which is what Lerner seems to advocate.

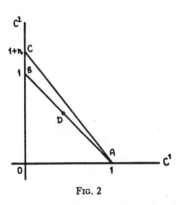

FIG. 2

VI. DURABLE OUTPUT

Now let us drop the assumption that output is completely perishable and substitute in its stead the assumption that output is completely durable.

The first thing to notice is that trades are still impossible. A member of generation t who wishes to give up a quantity of output at time t in return for a quantity of output at time $t + 1$ can never find anyone who is offering to give up a quantity of output at time $t + 1$ in return for a quantity of output at time t. On the other hand, a technology is now available to a member of generation t with which he can transform output at time t into output at time $t + 1$, unit for unit.

Suppose that with this new regime we now require our economy to proceed in an entirely decentralized fashion, each individual acting on his own. The opportunity set available to each individual is now given by the triangle OAB in Figure 2. (Recall that, when output was non-durable, the individual's opportunity set consisted only of the line segment OA.) An individual of generation t will therefore pick his consumption plan (C_t^1, C_t^2) so as to maximize $U(C_t^1, C_t^2)$ subject to $C_t^1 + C_t^2 = 1$, which will lead him to a point, say D, on the boundary of his opportunity set. Clearly, D will not in general coincide with A; that is, the individual will in general choose to consume positive amounts in both periods. Note also that the point D will be optimal for individuals of *all* generations (since we are assuming a common utility function for all) so that decentralized behavior leads, once again, to a stationary path.

Now let us look at distribution schemes which are not necessarily decentralized. Obviously, any scheme which was feasible under the assumption that output is non-durable is also feasible under the assumption that output is completely durable. Hence, the set of feasible distribution schemes in our new regime certainly contains the feasible set of the old regime. In particular, the set of all feasible stationary schemes must contain[5] the shaded set in Figure 1, which appears in Figure 2 as the triangle OAC.

A brief look at Figure 2 tells the story: While in the old regime decentralized behavior led to an efficient but (in general) non-optimal distribution scheme, in the new regime decentralization leads (in general) to an *inefficient* (to say nothing of optimality) distribution scheme.

This phenomenon, the inefficiency of

[4] Similarly, if the rate of interest is required to be constant *up to* some point, then $r \geqq n$ is possible, but $r < n$ is not.

[5] Actually, the two sets coincide.

decentralized behavior, does not disappear if we drop yet another assumption and permit capital (which in this model is in the form of inert inventories) to become productive. This has been shown recently by Diamond (1965).[6] In Diamond's model, the inefficiency appears only if people "want to save too much" (in some well-defined sense). In the present model, people in the decentralized scheme *always* want to save too much, in the sense that the efficient distribution schemes involve zero inventories at every moment of time, while the decentralized scheme (in general) involves positive inventories at every moment of time. (In Diamond's model this is not always the case because, roughly speaking, as long as inventories reproduce faster than people, it is efficient to hold them.)

VII. FINANCIAL INTERMEDIATION

Thus far, we have avoided the question of how an efficient distribution scheme might be brought about. Is there an economic agent that could be introduced into the model and whose activity would ensure efficiency? Before attempting to answer this question we must probe a little further into the nature of the inefficiency of decentralization in the model of the foregoing section.

At the heart of the inefficiency in our new model (with durable output) lies the fact that decentralization forces people to hoard output in their first period so as to be able to consume what they had hoarded in the second period. The result is that in every period a fraction of total output is put aside in the form of a savings fund, to be carried over to the next period. But when the next

[6] Note that the present model, with durable output, may be looked upon as a special case of Diamond's model, with the intensive production function (that is, the function relating output per man to capital per man) identically equal to unity.

period comes around and the older generation consumes its savings, the younger generation establishes its own savings fund and the economy ends up carrying a load of dead weight, in the form of output which is never consumed. Indeed, under the assumption of the same utility function for all, this load of dead weight keeps growing like a geometric progression, because the savings fund of generation t is $1 + n$ the size of the savings fund of generation $t - 1$.

The only way to restore efficiency to our system is to find an arrangement whereby the savings of generation t (when it is young) are used to provide for the consumption of generation $t - 1$ (when it is old). In this way, the situation in which positive amounts of real output are always being carried over, from period to period, will not arise. But this cannot be done in a decentralized manner within the present framework of assumptions. The first thing which comes to mind at this point is that maybe the trouble lies in the lack of sufficient overlap between generations, which prevents the right trades from being made.

In order to investigate this possibility, we introduce into the picture a financial intermediary of some sort (say, a banking system or a system of pension funds) which is assumed to exist concurrently with *all* generations. People are now able to save by holding the liabilities of this financial intermediary, which they will in fact prefer to do if by holding such liabilities for one period they can earn a positive rate of interest. Now, the intermediary can, in fact, offer holders of its liabilities a rate of interest of n per period simply by using the output deposited with it by generation t to redeem the liabilities which are held by generation $t - 1$. The result is that all output available in period t is in fact consumed in period t, partly by generation t and partly by generation $t - 1$. Generation $t - 1$ receives whatever generation t decides to save as payment in full (principal as well as interest) of the debt incurred to it one period earlier by the financial intermediary. There will no longer be a carryover of output from period to period and, as a result, efficiency will be restored. Indeed, optimality will be restored as well, because in response to a rate of interest of n per period people will choose to save exactly the amount which leads to the optimal distribution scheme.

The outlook seems rosy until one takes a brief look at the balance sheet of our financial intermediary, where things are rather unfortunate: The balance sheet as of the end of period t shows zero assets and liabilities of $s(1 + n)^t$, where s is the (stationary) saving ratio of people in their first period of life. This means that at the end of period t the net worth of the intermediary is given by $-s(1 + n)^t$. Now by not doing anything (that is, by shutting down) the intermediary can guarantee itself a net worth of zero, and so one might argue that it will never choose to engage in the aforementioned transactions. On the other hand, it might be argued that the intermediary should be looked upon as a social security system which is not privately owned, so that its net worth position is of no concern (or should not be of any concern). This is what Lerner seems to be saying when he decries (1959, p. 517) "those of the accountants who insist on the 'solvency' of the Social Security Administration." Later, Lerner seems to be taking a 180° turn by insisting on the very accounting practice which he had previously decried: " 'Business is fine,' said the optimistic contractor. 'It is true that I lose money on every con-

tract, but I always start a bigger one and get an advance that more than covers the loss on the old one' " (1959, p. 523).

Be that as it may, it is certainly the case that a privately owned financial intermediary will not rescue the economy from inefficiency. In other words, decentralization and competitive behavior still fail to result in efficient behavior.

VIII. LACK OF BORROWING AS A SOURCE OF INEFFICIENCY

Let x_t be the amount of output carried over by society from period t into period $t + 1$. If we restrict our attention to stationary states, then it is clear that a necessary and sufficient condition for efficiency is $x_t = 0$ for all t. However, if we wish to consider the non-stationary cases as well, the condition for efficiency becomes somewhat more complicated. For it is possible, for instance, for generation t to underconsume and for generation $t + 1$ to overconsume, with the result that x_t will be positive and yet the economy will remain efficient. More generally, the building up of inventories does not destroy efficiency so long as these inventories are eventually consumed. The exact statement in this respect is as follows: *A necessary and sufficient condition for the economy to be efficient is that there exist a subsequence* $\{x_{t_k}\}$ *of the sequence* $\{x_t\}$ *such that*

$$\lim_{k \to \infty} x_{t_k} = 0 \; .$$

The proof of this assertion will be given in the Appendix. Roughly speaking, efficiency requires that inventories return periodically to a level which is "practically zero."

From the point of view of balance sheets, x_t is clearly *net assets* (total assets minus total liabilities) in the economy at

PURE CONSUMPTION LOANS MODEL   361

the end of period t. If we concentrate our attention at the time periods t_k, we find that efficiency requires net assets at the end of these periods to be (practically) zero.[7] In other words, in order to have efficiency, it must be the case that for each outstanding asset in the economy at the end of period t_k there exists a corresponding liability outstanding at the end of period t_k. But now let us recall the time structure of our model. People live for two periods, they consume in both periods but earn income only in the first. This forces individuals to become net lenders (and never net borrowers) no matter what rate of interest prevails.[8] In particular, members of generation t_k will want to be net lenders, that is, to have an end-of-period balance sheet which shows just assets and net worth and no liabilities. But efficiency requires that aggregate net worth in the economy be zero, so there must exist someone in the economy holding liabilities in excess of assets, that is, having a negative net worth at the end of period t_k. This puts the unfavorable net worth position of the financial intermediary of Section VII in perspective. By the same token, the decentralized economy of Section VI is inefficient precisely because no one can be a net borrower while everyone wishes to be a net lender.

It is of some interest to investigate Samuelson's discussion concerning "the contrivance of money" in the light of the foregoing remarks. Clearly, if efficiency is to be attained, people must be dissuaded from holding output as a store of value and persuaded to hold another asset instead. If this other asset bears a positive rate of interest, then people will in fact make the desired shift. As Samuelson points out, the role of this other asset can very well be fulfilled by money. People would save by buying the existing money supply and dissave by selling it to next period's savers. On a stationary path, the price of money will rise by a factor of $1 + n$ in each period, which corresponds to a rate of interest of n per period, so individuals will in fact prefer holding money to holding output. Thus, at least with respect to stationary paths, the introduction of money leads to efficiency. (More precisely: Every stationary path in the money economy is efficient.) Samuelson's interpretation of this phenomenon is a philosophical one: An economy is inherently more than a mere mechanical system of particles in motion; it is, in fact, such a system *plus* something called a "Hobbes-Rousseau social contract" (Samuelson, 1958, p. 479). A physical system can operate efficiently without this added aspect, but a social system cannot.[9] Now, it seems to us that the social contract is no more involved in Samuelson's money economy than it is in any other general equilibrium model. For this reason we feel that Samuelson's discussion in this area is liable to be misleading. In general equilibrium analysis one thinks of a single market convention in which prices are announced and economic agents determine the trades and the productive activities in which they wish to engage at these prices. If the totality of all trades clears all markets, then the announced prices are said to be equilibrium prices. The question which general equilibrium theory asks is the following: Under the

---

[7] The word "practically" is intended to convey the notion that, strictly speaking, net assets at the end of period t_k might be given by some $\epsilon > 0$, but by taking k large enough, this ϵ may be taken as small as we wish. From here on, we shall neglect to remind the reader of this qualification.

[8] As long as this rate of interest exceeds -1.

[9] It is not clear whether Samuelson intends his model to constitute a *mathematical proof* of the Locke-Hobbes-Rousseau thesis.

assumption that everybody at the market convention takes prices as *given*, is there a schedule of prices which leads to the clearing of all markets? In Samuelson's money economy, commodities are time-dated output and time-dated money, and all that one asks is whether or not a given price schedule is an equilibrium price schedule. It turns out that the schedule which sets the price of output in all periods equal to 1 and the price of money in period t equal to $(1 + n)^t$ is, in fact, an equilibrium price schedule. The element of public trust in the monetary unit is reflected by the fact that a person who buys money in period t, at a price of $(1 + n)^t$, assumes that he will be able to sell it in period $t + 1$, at a price of $(1 + n)^{t+1}$. But this is precisely what is meant in general equilibrium theory by the phrase "taking prices as *given*."

At the beginning of this section, we argued that, if efficiency is to be attained, someone will have to have a balance sheet showing liabilities in excess of assets. For this reason it seems appropriate to look upon money as a liability of a monetary authority that is committed to paying one dollar to whoever presents it with one dollar. The balance sheet of this monetary authority shows only liabilities and no assets, and the value of the authority's liabilities (quantity of money multiplied by the price of money) is precisely equal to the excess of assets over liabilities in the private sector. From this point of view, Samuelson's "contrivance of money" is, in essence, no different from the financial intermediary of Section VII.

We turn now to a brief investigation of a model in which people live for *three* periods, and in which efficiency can be achieved (under some circumstances) without introducing into the economy a sector with negative net worth.

IX. A THREE-PERIOD MODEL

We have argued that in order to have efficiency there must be someone in the economy who is, at least periodically, a net borrower. Along stationary paths, this must be the case in *every* period. However, there was nothing in that argument to suggest that the net borrower must be a net borrower throughout his (or its) lifetime. Indeed, this role may well change hands over time, which was not the case with the financial intermediary of Section VII.

The prime candidate for this state of temporary net borrowership is the consumer himself. To check on this possibility, let us consider the following modification of our model: Assume that people live for three periods rather than two. In the first period of life a person grows up and is educated and therefore earns nothing; in the second period he works and earns one unit of output; in the third he is retired. Every person will now be a net borrower at the end of his first period, a net lender at the end of his second period, and he will be neither a borrower nor a lender at the end of his last period. (We are not using the terms "negative net worth" and "positive net worth" because it is not clear that they are applicable in the present context.) We shall restrict our attention to stationary paths. Along a stationary path, everybody receives the same lifetime consumption profile, say (C^1, C^2, C^3). Feasibility and efficiency now mean that the following equation holds:

$$(1 + n)C^1 + C^2 + \frac{C^3}{1 + n} = 1,$$

which is similar to the feasibility and efficiency equation in the two-period case and is derived in the same way. If we let the (constant) rate of interest along the stationary path be denoted r, then each person's budget constraint is given by

$$(1+r)C^1 + C^2 + \frac{C^3}{1+r} = 1,$$

which leads, once again, to $r = n$. In other words, the only rate of interest which can be established along an efficient stationary path is n. Each person is now viewed as maximizing the utility function $U(C^1, C^2, C^3)$ subject to the budget constraint (with n replacing r). The maximization will result in an *optimal* consumption plan, say $(\bar{C}^1, \bar{C}^2, \bar{C}^3)$. This optimal triple must be examined to see if it can be brought about by purely competitive (decentralized) trades.

The optimal consumption plan $(\bar{C}^1, \bar{C}^2, \bar{C}^3)$ will be said to be *competitively attainable* if the following equation holds:

$$\bar{C}^3 = (1+n)^2 \, \bar{C}^1 .$$

To see how this condition is obtained, consider a person of generation t. When he is young, he borrows an amount $\bar{C}^1$ from members of generation $t-1$, who are in their middle years. Next period, when he is middle-aged and generation $t-1$ is retired, he returns the loan, plus interest. In other words, he returns the amount $(1+n)\bar{C}^1$. Now aggregate borrowing by generation t (when young) is given by the amount $(1+n)^t\bar{C}^1$, and therefore total payment by generation t (when middle-aged) to generation $t-1$ (when retired) is given by $(1+n)^{t+1}\bar{C}^1$. This quantity, divided by the size of generation $t-1$, yields the per capita consumption of the retired, that is, $\bar{C}^3$. This is precisely what the foregoing equation says.

As an example, consider the utility function

$$U(C^1, C^2, C^3) = \sum_{i=1}^{3} \log C^i .$$

Maximizing it subject to the budget constraint leads to

$$(1+n)\bar{C}^1 = \bar{C}^2 = \frac{\bar{C}^3}{1+n} = \tfrac{1}{3},$$

which is clearly competitively attainable.

Why is the decentralized economy in this example efficient? Surely, it is possible to attribute this result to "the social contrivance of binding contracts." It is clearly in the interest of the middle-aged to default and ignore the debt which they have incurred when young. Even if the rules are such that a person guilty of default is denied access to the capital market as a lender (and so must lose interest on his savings), it is still true in many cases that default will result in increased consumption in all periods. Here, once again, is an opportunity to appeal to the social contract and here, once again, it would seem to be beside the point, and for very much the same reasons as before: The assumption that contracts are not defaulted upon usually goes without saying in the theory of the competitive mechanism; it does not *explain* our result, it merely *permits* it.

But our example is a very lucky one. For it is not, in general, to be expected that the optimal solution of a consumer's lifetime allocation problem will satisfy as stringent a condition as $\bar{C}^3 = (1+n)^2 \bar{C}^1$. In fact, with most utility functions this condition will not hold. If $\bar{C}^3 > (1+n)^2\bar{C}^1$ then we shall, once again, have too little borrowing in the economy and an additional agent with negative net worth would be needed in order to attain efficiency. However if $\bar{C}^3 < (1+n)^2\bar{C}^1$ then we shall have *too much* borrowing in the economy, and it will be possible to introduce a financial intermediary with *positive* net worth which will guarantee efficiency. The balance sheet of this intermediary will show I.O.U.'s of young people on the asset

D. CASS AND M. E. YAARI

side and nothing on the liabilities side. In order to see how this intermediary would operate, let us concentrate, once again, on period t. In this period, a member of generation t offers to sell a quantity $\bar{C}^1$ of I.O.U.'s. The total supply of I.O.U.'s by generation t is therefore given by $(1 + n)^t \bar{C}^1$. However, a member of generation $t - 1$ wishes to buy only $\bar{C}^3/(1 + n)$ in I.O.U.'s, so that the total quantity of I.O.U.'s demanded is $(1 + n)^{t-2}\bar{C}^3$, which falls short of the quantity supplied. The intermediary now steps in and buys the excess supply, using as payment the resources which generation $t - 1$ pays in when it redeems its own I.O.U.'s, which it sold to the intermediary in the previous period. Stationarity insures that these resources will always be precisely adequate to buy the outstanding I.O.U.'s. The result will be that physical output will not be carried over from period to period, so that efficiency will be attained. The aggregate debt of the consumer sector to the financial intermediary will grow like a geometric progression, but each consumer by himself will be balancing expenditures and receipts over his lifetime; that is, at the end of his last period of life he will have zero net worth. Under these circumstances, the intermediary may very well be thought of as a privately owned, competitive institution.

X. EFFICIENCY AND INFINITY

The possible inefficiency (or non-optimality) of the competitive mechanism, as demonstrated by Samuelson and Diamond, has given rise to a certain amount of speculation, mostly on an informal basis. Many people (including Samuelson [for example, 1958, p. 474; 1959, p. 522] and Diamond [1965, p. 1134]) seem to feel that this phenomenon has something to do with infinity. What apparently leads one to point an accusing finger at "infinity" is the fact that for the standard general equilibrium model (which is finite) we have theorems which tell us that the competitive mechanism always leads to an optimum (and, a fortiori, to efficiency). Nevertheless, the role played by "infinity" in leading the competitive mechanism astray has remained, at best, rather vague. In the present section, we wish to explore this question somewhat more systematically by trying to construct a finite model that resembles the infinite model of the foregoing discussion as closely as possible. As it turns out, inefficiency may well arise in such a finite model.

Consider an economy with m agents and m commodities (where $m > 2$). Each agent is both a consumer and a producer. Let C_i^j be the amount of commodity j *consumed* by agent i, and let Q_i^j be the amount of commodity j *produced* by agent i. Agent i (for $i = 1, 2, \ldots, m - 1$) is assumed to desire, for consumption, only two commodities: commodity i and commodity $i + 1$. (Agent m is assumed to desire commodity m and commodity 1.) Thus, agent i's utility function is given by

$$U_i = U(C_i^i, C_i^{i+1}) \qquad i = 1, \ldots, m - 1,$$

$$U_m = U(C_m^m, C_m^1),$$

where the function U is common to all. As for production possibilities, we assume that agent i can produce commodities i and $i + 1$ (with agent m producing commodities m and 1), but that he has a relative advantage in the production of commodity i. More specifically, we shall assume that agent i can produce any combination of Q_i^i and Q_i^{i+1} satisfying

$$Q_i^i \geqq 0, \qquad Q_i^{i+1} \geqq 0, \qquad Q_i^i + \frac{Q_i^{i+1}}{1 - \delta} \leqq 1,$$

where δ is some real number satisfying $0 < \delta < 1.$[10]

Recall for a moment the infinite model of Section VI (with durable output). That model is easily shown to be mathematically equivalent to a model in which population is stationary, while the storing of output is subject to *depreciation* at some constant rate, say δ. But the model which we have described in the foregoing paragraph is an exact finite analogue of this infinite model with depreciation. For, by chopping off a finite segment of the infinite model and then tying the two ends together to form a closed loop, one obtains the model that is being discussed here.

Let us, therefore, investigate the efficiency of the competitive mechanism in our finite model, to which we shall henceforth refer, for short, as the *closed-loop model*. This investigation turns on whether or not intermediation is permitted.

Case a: No intermediation.—Under the assumption that intermediation is altogether absent, it is evident that the closed-loop model is inefficient. For, without intermediation, an agent who wishes to trade, say, x units of commodity j for y units of commodity k, must find, in order to be able to make the trade, an agent who wishes to trade y units of commodity k for x units of commodity j. This is, of course, the well-known "double coincidence of wants" (see, for example, Samuelson, 1964, p. 51). Now, in the closed-loop model, things are tailored in such a way that whatever trade an agent might wish to engage in, at whatever prices, he can never find another agent wishing to engage in the same trade on the opposite

side. In other words, the double coincidence of wants never occurs. In the absence of intermediation, therefore, each agent must satisfy all his wants under complete autarky, and the doctrine of comparative advantage tells us immediately that this is inefficient. More formally, the decentralized solution of the closed-loop model in the absence of intermediation is given by

$$\left. \begin{array}{l} C_i^i \;\; = Q_i^i \\ C_i^{i+1} = Q_i^{i+1} \end{array} \right\} \text{ for } i = 1, \ldots, m,$$

where (Q_i^i, Q_i^{i+1}) is chosen so as to

$$\text{maximize } U(Q_i^i, Q_i^{i+1}),$$

$$\text{subject to } Q_i^i + \frac{Q_i^{i+1}}{1 - \delta} = 1,$$

$$Q_i^i \geqq 0, \qquad Q_i^{i+1} \geqq 0.$$

Under the assumption that $\delta > 0$, this solution is inefficient. The economy can produce more of every commodity.

Now let us go back for a moment to the model of Section VI. The inefficiency which beset the economy of that section is precisely the inefficiency which now besets our closed-loop model. All the arguments (indeed, the very words) of Section VI are applicable to the closed-loop model, with only minor changes which have to do with substituting depreciation for population growth.

Case b: The money economy.—The necessity for a double coincidence of wants disappears, as is well known, as soon as barter is abandoned in favor of the money economy. Thus, one might expect the introduction of "the contrivance of money" to cure the aforementioned inefficiency, just as it cured the inefficiency of the model of Section VI. Such, indeed, is the case. In the money economy, agent i will produce commodity i exclusively, sell some of it

---

[10] We shall, from now on, neglect to write separate expressions for the case $i = m$. Let us agree, therefore, that whenever $i = m$, $i + 1$ is simply 1.

to agent $(i - 1)$, and then use the money which he receives in return to buy some of agent $(i + 1)$'s output. More formally, let p_i be the money price of commodity i. Then, the equilibrium of the money economy is described by

$$p_i = p_j \quad \text{for all } i \text{ and } j,$$

$$Q_i^j = 0 \quad \text{if } i \neq j$$

$$= 1 \quad \text{if } i = j,$$

and (C_i^i, C_i^{i+1}) chosen so as to

$$\text{maximize } U(C_i^i, C_i^{i+1}),$$

$$\text{subject to } C_i^i + C_i^{i+1} = 1,$$

$$C_i^i \geqq 0, \quad C_i^{i+1} \geqq 0.$$

This equilibrium is efficient, and it is precisely analogous to the equilibrium in the money economy that was discussed in Section VIII. People "buy" money in return for goods which they produce, and then "sell" it for goods which they want. Basically, money here provides intermediation. Agent i sells to agent $(i - 1)$, but he is being paid in terms of output of agent $(i + 1)$.

There are several ways in which money can be introduced into the closed-loop model. The simplest is as follows: Think of agent 1 selling a promissory note to agent 2, who, in turn, proceeds to sell it to agent 3, and so on. The note travels around the loop until it reaches agent m, who redeems it from agent 1. All other agents, however, accept agent 1's note not because they are interested in agent 1's output, but simply because the note is *negotiable*. In other words, agent 1's note will assume the role of money.

Case c: The ordinary general equilibrium model.—The closed-loop model is,

after all, a finite general equilibrium model, and for the latter we have theorems concerning optimality and efficiency. What role, then, does intermediation play in the standard general equilibrium theory? The answer to this question is straightforward: In all of general equilibrium theory it is assumed (mostly implicitly) that a *central clearing house* exists, through which trades are channeled. Only with such a central clearing house is it possible to define competitive equilibrium in terms of aggregate excess demands alone. If a central clearing house were to be introduced in the closed-loop model, competitive behavior would lead to efficiency, as may be verified directly (without appealing to general theorems). But the central clearing house is obviously an intermediary. It is, in fact, precisely the analogue, in the closed-loop model, of our negative net worth intermediary of Section VII.

XI. CONCLUDING REMARK

Before closing, we would like to add a brief comment concerning the relation of the topics we have been discussing here to the Modigliani-Brumberg (1955) "life-cycle" theory of saving. Modigliani and Brumberg have postulated that aggregate saving can be explained by the interaction of individual saving for retirement and changes in the population structure. It is interesting to note that under the Modigliani-Brumberg assumptions of a zero rate of interest and an exponentially growing population, providing for old age in a way which results in positive aggregate saving is inefficient.[11]

[11] We are indebted to James Tobin for this observation.

PURE CONSUMPTION LOANS MODEL

APPENDIX

Let x_t be the level of inventories carried over by the economy from period t into period $t + 1$. In Section VIII a necessary and sufficient condition for efficiency was stated. The following is an equivalent assertion:

THEOREM: *The economy is efficient if and only if*

$$\lim_{t \to \infty} \inf x_t = 0 .$$

PROOF. (*a*) *Necessity:* Suppose $\lim \inf x_t > 0$. Then there exists an $\epsilon > 0$ and an integer T such that $x_t > \epsilon$ for $t \geqq T$. Let aggregate consumption in period T be increased by ϵ, and let consumption in all subsequent periods remain unchanged. Let the sequence of inventory levels under this new scheme be denoted $\{x'_t\}$. Clearly, $x'_t =$ x_t for $t \leqq T$ and $x'_t = x_t - \epsilon$ for $t > T$. All that must be verified to show that the new scheme is feasible is $x'_t \geqq 0$ for all t. But this follows from the hypothesis.

(*b*) *Sufficiency* is proved similarly: Assume $\lim \inf x_t = 0$. We must show that it is impossible to increase aggregate consumption in any period while keeping aggregate consumption in subsequent periods unchanged. Let aggregate consumption in period T be increased by an amount $\epsilon > 0$, where T is an arbitrary integer. Denote the new sequence of inventory levels by $\{x'_t\}$. Now for $t > T$, we have $x'_t = x_t - \epsilon$, but by hypothesis there exists a $t > T$ such that $x_t < \epsilon$. Hence x'_t would have to be negative; that is, the new scheme is not feasible.

REFERENCES

Diamond, Peter A. "National Debt in a Neoclassical Growth Model," *A.E.R.*, LV (December, 1965), 1126–50.

Lerner, Abba P. "Consumption-Loan Interest and Money" and "Rejoinder," *J.P.E.*, LXVII (October, 1959), 512–17, 523.

Meckling, W. H. "An Exact Consumption-Loan Model of Interest: A Comment" and "Rejoinder," *J.P.E.*, LXVIII (February, 1960), 72–75, 83–84.

Modigliani, F., and Brumberg, R. "Utility Analysis and the Consumption Function: An Interpretation of Cross-Section Data," in *Post-Keynesian Economics*, ed. K. K. Kurihara. London: George Allen & Unwin, 1955.

Phelps, Edmund S. "Second Essay on the Golden Rule of Accumulation," *A.E.R.*, LV (September, 1965), 793–814.

Samuelson, Paul A. "An Exact Consumption-Loan Model of Interest with or without the Contrivance of Money," *J.P.E.*, LXVI (December, 1958), 467–82.

———. "Reply," *ibid.*, LXVII (October, 1959), 518–22.

———. "Infinity, Unanimity, and Singularity: A Reply," *ibid.*, LXVIII (February, 1960), 76–82.

———. *Economics, an Introductory Analysis*. 6th ed. New York: McGraw-Hill Book Co., 1964.

[6]

Eastern Economic Journal, Volume XIV, No. 4, October–December 1988

The Barter Illusion in Classical and Neoclassical Economics

Dudley Dillard*

The veil of barter must be lifted from general economic theory if we are to have a clear and logical understanding of how our money economy behaves. Economists speak frequently of the "veil of money" and the "money illusion" but the more troublesome barter illusion is seldom acknowledged.[1] The barter illusion in classical and neoclassical economics is the subject of my paper.[2]

INTRODUCTION

Money is a problem for everyone, including professional economists. In recent years economic theorists have been seeking a way to put money into the Arrow-Debreu version of the Walrasian general equilibrium model. To quote Professor Frank Hahn of Cambridge University:

> "The most serious challenge that the existence of money poses to the theorist is this: the best developed model of the economy cannot find room for it. The best developed model is, of course, the Arrow-Debreu version of a Walrasian general equilibrium. . . . A first . . . task is to find an alternative construction without thereby sacrificing the clarity and logical coherence of Arrow-Debreu" (Hahn, 1983, p. 1).

Where does Professor Hahn propose to start searching for insights for getting money into general equilibrium? Despite misgivings about Keynes' formal economic theorizing, he confesses:

> "I none the less hold that his [Keynes] insights were several orders more profound and realistic than those of his recent critics. . . . Accordingly, in these lectures I follow various Keynesian trails in an endeavour to reach a point where theory is not so blatantly at variance with fact" (Hahn, 1983, p. xi).

Following Professor Hahn's lead, I likewise have found Keynes a useful guide in probing the relation of money to general economic theory. My problem is, however, somewhat different. Professor Hahn's problem is how to get money into economic theory; mine is how money ever got out of economic theory in the first place. To the naive mind, it must seem incredible that "the best developed model" of the economy has found no room for money. For my point of departure, I take Keynes' first draft of the *General Theory,* which he called "A Monetary Theory of Production" (Keynes, 1979, pp. 35–160/ 1973a, pp. 408–11). Also fundamental for my perspective is Keynes' response to critics in his well-known article "The General Theory of Employment" (QJE, 1937, reprinted in Keynes, 1973b, pp. 109–23).

In a monetary theory of production, the strategic condition of economic life that gives money its commanding position is the existence of great uncertainty concerning the future,

---

*Department of Economics, University of Maryland. Presidential Address, Eastern Economic Association, March 11, 1988, Boston, Mass.

especially uncertainty about the prospective yields from investing in durable capital assets. This uncertainty gives rise to a demand for money as an alternative form of holding wealth. In order to induce wealth-holders to part with their money, they must be paid (at the margin) a premium in the form of interest. The level of employment and output as a whole will shift with fluctuations in the amount of investment in capital assets. There is no automatically self-adjusting mechanism leading to full employment in a monetary theory of production, whereas in the classical and neoclassical general principles, based on neutral money, there is always a tendency toward full employment. The latter is a theory primarily about the efficiency with which given resources are employed, and not a theory about employment as such.

In its microeconomic aspect, a monetary theory of production requires a theory of business enterprise, which is the dominant economic institution of modern civilization. Money has very special meaning for business. It is both the means and the end of business activity. Keynes writes in one of his early drafts of the *General Theory:* "The firm is dealing throughout in terms of sums of money. It has no object in the world except to end up with more money than it started with. That is the essential characteristic of an entrepreneur [business] economy" (Keynes, 1979, p. 89).

Business firms advance money capital to buy materials, equipment, and to pay wages to workers. When the output of the firm is completed, it must be sold for money, that is, the output must be reconstituted as money capital if the transaction is to be deemed successful by business standards. A firm is free to produce anything it wishes, but its output has no socially recognized use value or exchange value until it is validated by sale for money. Gains by business firms are said to be "realized" by transforming output into money. What is "real" from the view of the objective of the firm is money. That is the bottom line in the actual facts of business calculation. Business firms use profit and loss statements to measure their current money gains; and balance sheets to reflect their accumulated money gains.

Among classical economists the barter illusion is reflected in their insistence that production is for consumption. This is patently wrong for a large firm in a business enterprise system. The output of a large firm has negligible consumption value for the firm, however the firm might be personified as a consumer. The output becomes a reality as a use value only upon reaching a consumer in exchange for a money purchase, corresponding to sale for money by the firm. Only in some teleological sense can it be said of a business enterprise system that the purpose of production is consumption. Consumption may be said to be the *consequence* of production, but the motivation of a firm is not consumption. A firm that can make more money by producing fewer goods is driven by its pecuniary logic to do so. The proposition that production is for consumption is one of the classical pillars that will not stand up under the scrutiny of a monetary theory of production.

"Barter Illusion" in the title of this paper refers to the view that the economic system works as if it were a barter economy. Money exists in the classical and neoclassical models but it is assumed to be no more than a refined form of barter. The principles of the theory would not be different if goods did exchange directly for goods and if wage earners bartered their labor for subsistence. Now this is an illusion because money as a store of value in a world of uncertainty does affect motives and decisions of wealth-holders and wealth-producers in a significant way. The economic system to which classical and neoclassical economics has empirical and historical reference is a money economy (Dillard, 1967, chapter 1). It has been a money economy since the sixteenth century, when mercantilism replaced feudalism.[3] A corollary of the barter illusion is that money is neutral with respect to output and employment. Economic theories resting on the barter illusion either assume away or contribute little to an understanding of many of the most troubling problems of economic life such as unemployment, general overproduction, commercial crises, and business cycles.

MERCANTILISM: MONEY AT CENTER STAGE

An explanation of the barter illusion in mainstream economics begins with Adam Smith's assault on the mercantile system. Money occupies center stage in mercantilist economics all the way from the early bullionists to the later balance-of-trade advocates. The great aberration in the history of economic analysis is not the mercantilist preoccupation with money but rather the absence of money from the principles of economics presumably applicable to the capitalist world in which classical and neoclassical economic principles were forged.

In the age of mercantilism the passions of money-making were liberated from the moral and religious restraints of medieval thought. An emphasis on acquisitive and pecuniary motives features mercantilist writing. Eli Heckscher, the historian of mercantilism, characterizes the transition from feudalism to capitalism as a shift from a hunger for goods (provisionism) to a fear of goods (Heckscher, 1936, II, p. 108). A corollary of the mercantilist fear of goods is a hunger for money. This hunger for money and aversion for goods is reflected in Thomas Mun's famous maxim for increasing the wealth and treasure of a nation by foreign trade: "Wherein wee must ever observe this rule; to sell more to strangers yearly than wee consume of theirs in value" (Monroe, 1965, p. 171). Heckscher's interpretation and Mun's maxim are consistent with Max Weber's characterization of mercantilism as, ". . . carrying the point of view of capitalistic industry into politics; the state is handled as if it consisted exclusively of capitalistic entrepreneurs" (Weber, 1961, p. 255). The idea is to sell as much as possible and buy as little as possible in order to maximize the amount of money (gold and silver) received.

The mercantilists may be said to have adumbrated a monetary theory of production. Keynes explains the similarity between his theory and the valid aspects of mercantilist thinking in terms of investment being the strategic determinant of national prosperity. A favorable balance of trade represents foreign investment, which stimulates the import of money (gold and silver); which by bringing money (gold and silver) into the economy tends to lower the domestic rate of interest and hence to stimulate domestic investment. In Keynes' theory investment is strategic because it disburses current income (effective demand) into the economy without simultaneously bringing more consumer goods onto the domestic market. The application of these principles will stimulate economic activity if there are significant amounts of unemployed labor and other productive capacity. The assumption of chronic unemployment as a normal condition is valid for the mercantilist period and seems valid throughout the history of capitalism. Economists in the age of mercantilism, including David Hume and Sir James Steuart, developed theories with elements in common with Keynes (See below). A causal relation between money and employment is fundamental to a monetary theory of production. Mercantilist doctrine rests on the premise that increases in the precious metals will stimulate economic activity.

SMITH AND THE SIN OF ADAM

What provoked Adam Smith to remove money from center stage in the principles of political economy? Clearly there is no simple answer. On a conceptual level, Smith may have viewed money as a major disturbing force in his Newtonian vision of a self-adjusting natural economic order. Non-neutral money would have posed a threat to the concept of a pre-established harmony, which is a presupposition for Smith's policy of laissez-faire.[4] In the general case, non-neutral money may be incompatible with general economic equilibrium.

Another hypothesis is that Smith was so eager to discredit mercantilist policies that he overreacted in the direction of deemphasizing money. In what Smith describes as his "very violent attack . . . upon the whole commercial system of Great Britain" (Scott, 1937, p. 283), the focus is on the place of money in mercantilism, which Smith describes as a system of political economy that represents national wealth as consisting of an abundance of gold and silver (Smith, 1937, p. 238). While Smith did not really believe the mercantilist writers were this naive,[5] he leaves no doubt of his determination to exorcise money from a prominent place in political economy. Money is reduced to impotent neutrality. This I refer to as the sin of Adam.

We shall note briefly Smith's treatment of money in three places in the *Wealth of Nations:* Book I, chapter 4, "Of the Origins and Use of Money"; Book II, chapter 2, "Of Money Considered as Part of the Great Stock of Society"; and in Book IV, chapter 1, "Of the Principles of the Commercial, or Mercantile System."

Labor is Real Wealth and Money is Nominal Wealth

Smith's chapter "Of the Origins and Use of Money" is preceded by three chapters on the division of labor and followed by three chapters on value and price. The chapter on money provides the linkage between the division of labor and terms (ratios) of exchange of goods among the specialized producers. The chapter immediately following the one on money makes the important point that labor is the real price and money only the nominal price of the things exchanged. The labor theory of value is Smith's first analytical put-down of the central role assigned to money in mercantilist economics.

Money as a Cost not a Revenue

In Book II on the accumulation of capital, Smith treats money as part of the expense of maintaining the total social capital. Money is classified as a form of circulating capital but, unlike all other forms of circulating capital, it resembles fixed capital in the sense that a deduction (depreciation) must be made before obtaining the social net revenue, or national income. Money is a cost and not a revenue in Smith's system of national accounting. The fewer the resources devoted to the maintenance of money, the greater the wealth of the nation. This is a second analytical put-down of the mercantilist doctrine that national wealth consists of money in the form of gold and silver. Money is merely the great wheel of circulation (Smith, 1937, pp. 273, 276, 280).

In this chapter Smith praises the use of paper money and bank credit because they economize on the use of resources tied up in the stock of money. The chapter discusses at length developments in Scottish banking and the issuance of paper money in the British colonies of North America and elsewhere. Smith speaks of banks converting "dead stock into active and productive stock" (1937, p. 305). Gold and silver represent the dead stock (1937, p. 305). An economy can improve its condition by exporting some of the gold and silver in exchange for something more useful.

Smith recongizes that paper money and bank credit introduce elements of potential instability into the economy, as compared to gold and silver money, but "prudent operation" of banking, with appropriate regulation of paper money can avoid "excessive multiplication" and "malicious runs" on banks (1937, p. 305).

Smith was acutely aware of financial panics. stock-jobbing tricks, bank schemes, and national disasters such as John Law's Mississippi Bubble (1937, p. 453). In his *Lectures* he covers these speculative episodes but ignores them in the *Wealth of Nations*. Despite scathing rebukes to merchants and master manufacturers—classes not to be trusted—Smith largely ignores the instability of capitalism associated with financial abuses, which even in Smith's time periodically disrupted the continuity of production.

Smith's retrogression from Steuart. Smith's retrogression into the barter illusion might have been avoided if he had taken account of the economic analysis of a contemporary Scot, Sir James Steuart, whose work, according to a recent authority, "marks a distinct turning point in the history of the theory of money" (Vickers, 1975, p. 488). Steuart's theory confronts the problem of unemployment, a widespread condition in eighteenth-century Britain, and allows a place for money and interest as instruments of policy to alleviate unemployment. The barter illusion clouded Smith's vision of the dynamics of money in relation to employment and output.

Smith ignores Hume on non-neutral money. Although Smith was well aware of the economic writings of his friend and fellow Scot, David Hume, he made no mention of Hume's analysis of the short-term benefits from increasing the quantity of money. According to Hume, in the interval between an increase in the supply of money and the subsequent rise in prices, employment and output will increase significantly (Hume, N.D., p. 170). Hume shows a clear appreciation of his contemporary mercantilists for whom money could be a positive force increasing output and employment.

In defense of Smith, it might be said that his theory is concerned with long-term equilibrium and not with short-term intervals that drew the attention of Hume and Steuart. Keynes is reported to have said that long-term equilibrium is for undergraduates, which is a corollary of his famous statement, "*In the long run* we are all dead" (Keynes, 1971, p. 65, Keynes' emphasis). Significantly for our purposes, a related but little known statement by Keynes pertains to Hume on money:

"Hume began the practice among economists of stressing the importance of the equilibrium position as compared with the ever-shifting transition towards it, though he was still enough of a mercantilist not to overlook the fact that it is in the transition that we actually have our being. 'It is only in this interval or intermediate situation, between the acquisition of money and a rise in prices, that the increasing quantity of gold and silver is favourable to industry' . . . " Keynes, 1936, p. 343n).

So Hume did see short-term advantages from increases in the supply of money, while Smith did not, or at least did not refer to it. Smith does speak of interest as "the use of money" (1937, p. 52).

Principle of the Mercantile System

In his famous chapter "Of the Principle of the Commercial or Mercantile System" Smith opens with some acute observations about the properties of money but ends weakly with money running after goods rather than goods running after money. He attributes popular misunderstandings about money to its double function as the instrument of commerce and the measure of value. "The great affair, we always find, is to get money" (1937, p. 398). Smith correctly observes that money is the socially recognized form of private wealth, which recognition is the beginning of wisdom in a monetary theory of production. "Money is the known and established instruments of commerce . . . " (1937, p. 407).

Smith notes the lower carrying costs of money as compared with goods in the hands of merchants and manufacturers. He even makes the point that goods have virtually no use value for a capitalist producer who is ". . . much more anxious to exchange his goods for money, than money for goods" (1937, p. 407). In making a shift from individual producers to the economy at large, Smith correctly stresses that goods have use value only for society at large. At this point he jumps to the conclusion: "Money, therefore, necessarily runs after goods, but goods do not always or necessarily run after money" (1937, p. 407). This seems to be saying that because goods have use value to potential consumers, that producers have no problem selling them, which begs the whole question of sufficiency of effective demand. At this point, Smith has anticipated J.B. Say's law of markets and is ensconced in a barter-like economy in which products exchange for products.

Smith fails to distinguish between use of money by consumers and the use of money capital by business firms. He writes: "The man who buys, does not always mean to sell again, but frequently to use or to consume . . . " (1937, p. 407). This is surely true for consumers, but it is not true of business firms, which buy without selling again only if they are going out of business. In the logic of a monetary theory of production, a business enterprise sells not in order to consume but in order to make money and to accumulate capital in the circular flow of money and commodities. A shortcoming of Smith and classical and neoclassical economists generally is that they have no theory of business enterprise. In a society of independent craftsmen and peasants, producers do sell in order to consume, but this is not true of large capitalist firms which are in business in order to sell for money. In defense of Smith, it might be said that he lived in an age of transition from independent craftsmen to capitalist entrepreneurs. While this excuse may hold more justification for Smith than for his successors, even by Smith's own statistics it is not correct. Smith estimates that in his time in Europe that only one craftsman in twenty was self-employed (Smith, 1973, p. 66).

J.B. SAY: CONVERTING SIN INTO DOGMA

J.B. Say occupies a central position in the development of the barter illusion. His ideas provide the transmission link from Adam Smith to David Ricardo. Whereas Smith toys with the puzzle whether goods chase money or money chases goods, in Ricardo's *Principles of Political Economy* that is no longer debatable. Money is neutralized—banned for all practical purposes—from the classical Garden of Eden. If Adam (Smith) is the original sinner, J.B. Say is the disciple who turned faith into dogma and postponed the atonement indefinitely.

Say's self-imposed task in political economy was to put order into Adam Smith's somewhat rambling discourse on the principles of political economy. This is Say's message in his long introduction to his *Treatise on Political Economy* (Say, 1971, pp. xv-lx). Undoubtedly much was lost in the process of putting the *Wealth of Nations* into a systematic treatise. Leo Rogin comments: "Say put Smith's theory in order in the same way that a cautious spouse puts her husband's trousers in order when she turns them upside down and empties them of all their valuables. So Say 'purged' Smith of 'dangerous thoughts' " (Rogin, 1956, p. 209).

Say's famous chapter on the law of markets begins in the first edition of his *Treatise* (1803) in good Smithian fashion as a refutation of mercantilist monetary fallacies. The expanded chapters of later editions focus on the question of sources of demand for products. In the English translation of the fourth edition, chapter 15 is entitled, "Of the Demand or Market for Products" (Say, 1971, pp. 132–40). Here Say states the law of markets that supply creats its own demand, because products exchange for products. The economy works as if it were a barter system with money strictly neutral with respect to output and employment.

Perhaps Say's clearest statement of his law is the following passage from chapter 15:

"... a product is no sooner created, that it, from that instant, affords a market for other products to the full extent of its own value" (Say, 1971, p. 134)

This appears to mean that if there are unemployed workers, for example, all that is required to employ them is to put them to work producing additional products because these products coming onto the market will generate sufficient demand to clear the market. No general deficiency of demand is possible because output, of the right kind,[6] will create new demand of sufficient magnitude. Involuntary unemployment is not possible in the barter-like world of J.B. Say.

With respect to money, Say continues: "For, after all, money is but the agent of the transfer of value" (1971, p. 133). A long chapter entitled "Of the Nature and Uses of Money" explains why money is a more efficient medium of exchange than actual barter; and a further chapter "Of Signs or Representatives of Money" deals with "representatives of money" such as bills of exchange, bank deposits and paper money. Thus while money provides a more efficient form of exchange than direct barter, in no sense is the use of money essentially different from barter.

Say does not distinguish between money-exchanges in an economy of self-employed producers and money exchanges in an economy of large capitalist producers. His institutional assumptions for the most part conform to those of Adam Smith. Money is used in a system of simple exchange in which producers sell in order to get money to buy the goods they need for living. Say adopts Smith's proposition that incomes not spent for consumption are nevertheless spent, because saving is a form of spending. Whether money outlays are for consumption or for investment (saving), the circular flow of sales and purchases is uninterrupted by such things as delays in purchases following sales (hoarding); or what amounts to the same thing, changes in the velocity of money, is not included in the analysis. Saving and investing, for the most part, are done by the same individual.

When the great post-Napoleonic depression swept through the nations of western Europe, Say witnessed and acknowledged the existence of general gluts, general overproduction, secular stagnation, massive unemployment, idle plants, hoarding, and the other things that are "impossible" according to his law of markets. In the first of his *Letters to Malthus* (Say, 1936), Say asks a series of sweeping questions, including: "... from whence comes that general overstock of all the markets of the universe ... ? These are the question upon which the happiness and tranquillity of nations depend" (Say, 1936, p. 2). These concessions by Say have sometimes been interpreted as a "recantation" of the law of markets (See Hollander, 1979, p. 94). However, that is not the way Say viewed either economic events or the fate of his theory. He opens his second letter to Malthus by stating: "I think I have proved in my first letter that Produce can only be bought with Produce. I still see no cause to abandon this doctrine, that it is production which opens a market for production" (Say, 1936, p. 22).

Say's staunch defense of this theory in the face of events running contrary to the theory tells us something important about the nature of economic theories. They are not a copy of the world of experience. By necessity, economic theories are highly abstract; they abstract from all but a few pertinent aspects of actual experience. One does, however, expect a theory to be realistic, meaning by realistic a theory that suggests hypotheses for understanding and for dealing effectively with insistent problems in the real world. For Say the remedies for the plight of Europe in 1821 included mainly less governmental intervention in private enterprise, lower taxes, less hoarding by banks, and more production of the right kind. Say expressed confidence that his old theory was adequate to deal with the new and wide-spread industrial fluctuations emanating from the post-Napoleonic spread of the industrial revolution. If governments and banks would behave rationally, happiness and tranquillity would return. Say remained a happy-face economist.[7]

RICARDO AND THE GOSPEL ACCORDING TO DAVID

Money in David Ricardo's *Principles of Political Economy* is rendered neutral by the heroic assumption that money in the form of gold is produced with an average composition of fixed and circulating capital. In developing his theory of distribution, Ricardo isolates money in order to focus on his labor theory of value as the "sheet anchor" of his system. As a result of the assumption that gold is produced with an average composition of capital, Ricardo says: "We shall probably possess as near an approximation to a standard measure of value as can be theoretically conceived" (Ricardo, 1951, p. 45). Having thus reduced money to an invariable unit, all changes in the price of any (other) commodity would reflect changes in its value and not a change in the monetary unit in terms of which it is measured. With this empirically unrealistic but logically potent assumption in the first chapter, money virtually disappears from the *Principles*. Such belittlement of money may seem strange for Ricardo, who attributed so much importance to money during the bullion controversy. The neutrality of money, however, is logically consistent with Ricardo's purpose, which in the *Principles* was to argue the case for repeal of the British corn laws. (See below penultimate paragraph in this section on Ricardo.)

Ricardo accepts without qualification J.B. Say's proposition that general overproduction is impossible because goods are bartered for goods. In the Preface to his *Principles* Ricardo eulogizes Say for his exposition of the principles of Adam Smith and includes a footnote explicitly praising Say's law of markets (1951, p. 7).

In his chapter on "Effects of Accumulation on Profits and Interest" Ricardo writes:

> "Productions are always bought by productions, or by services; money is only the medium by which the exchange is effected" (Ricardo, 1951, pp. 291–92).

Further, there can be no deficiency of demand because "Demand is only limited by production" (1951, p. 290). Like Say, Ricardo acknowledges there can be overproduction of particular products arising from miscalculations by producers, but these mistakes will be remedied by producers going out of business or shifting their output to other products.

Ricardo concedes "only one case" in which it is theoretically possible to have a general glut of all commodities, but the conditions for this case are so unrealistic that it occupies only one brief paragraph in the *Principles* (1951, p. 292). The one case in which a general glut might arise is that of necessaries, mostly food. If the desire to accumulate should become so strong that capitalists and others cease to consume luxuries, and only necessaries are produced, a general glut of necessaries can arise. Although wages would be abnormally high because of the intense demand for labor arising from the very rapid accumulation of capital, population cannot increase fast enough in the short run to generate a demand for all the necessaries being produced.

Such a glut could, in Ricardo's logic, be only temporary. With wages high, profits would be low (according to a Ricardian axiom), and the incentive to accumulate would be automatically checked. In the longer run, population would increase rapidly to absorb the temporarily redundant food and other necessaries. Moreover, the capitalists would be glad to produce and sell luxuries to their affluent workers (Ricardo, 1951, pp. 312–13). Thus although a general glut is theoretically imaginable, it is practicably impossible. When Malthus later confronted Ricardo with his "one possible case" on general gluts, Ricardo exclaims "Impossible" (1951b, p. 312).

There is irony in Ricardo's "one-case only" concession for a general glut. It could occur, in theory, when wages are exceptionally high. By contrast, the overproduction theories of Malthus, Sismondi, and others rest on grounds that wage-earners are so poor they cannot buy back what they produce, thus leading to general underconsumption. But in Ricardo's theoretically possible case, wage-earners are never more affluent than during the general glut.

In the famous Malthus-Ricardo controversy concerning effective demand, Malthus contends there is an optimum propensity to consume that will maximize the rate of accumulation. This is because of an organic (systematic) relation between the amount of consumer demand and the amount of capital formation needed to produce that amount of consumption. According to Malthus, the rate of accumulation can be too high in the sense that the capacity to produce will outrun the ability of society to consume. The result is overproduction and general gluts.

Ricardo argues, on the contrary, that there can never be too much capital accumulation. The rate of profit is not lowered by accumulation as such. If the profit rate falls as capital accumulates, this is only because diminishing returns in agriculture raise wages and thereby lower profits. This is the line of reasoning formulated by Ricardo in his *Essay on Profits* (1815) and reinforced in his *Principles of Political Economy* (1817) to argue for repeal of the corn laws in order that England could import cheap food and have low (Ricardian) wages, high profits, and rapid accumulation of capital to prolong England's industrial leadership. Ricardo's closely integrated theories of value, profits, wages, and rent are built into a model addressed to the burning issue of free trade in food. In scope, Ricardo's *Principles of Political Economy* is rather monographic compared to Adam Smith's *Wealth of Nations* and J.S. Mill's *Principles of Political Economy*. Ricardo's "monograph" is admirably designed to deal with the corn law problem but is not easily adapted to issues raised by the post-Napoleonic industrial depression and stagnation.

How does one account for the inability of two great economists such as Ricardo and Malthus to reconcile their differences on the issue of general overproduction? Keynes puts the answer aptly when he says: "Malthus is dealing with the money economy in which we happen to live; Ricardo with the abstraction of a neutral money economy" (Keynes, 1972, p. 97). As noted above in the case of J.B. Say, Ricardo has the problem of the appropriate level of abstraction for theorizing about general gluts. Many a broken tooth has resulted from mastication of abstractions. Ricardo's abstraction of a neutral-money economy is inappropriate for dealing with effective demand and economic depression. Time and again Ricardo responds to Malthus in terms of the illusion that the economy works as if were a barter system in which productions are bought with productions. Money makes no significant difference; effective demand cannot be deficient—that is Ricardo's false message stemming from the barter illusion.

J.S. MILL'S REASONED ANALYSIS AND CONFIRMATION OF THE FAITH

John Stuart Mill, who has been called the greatest mind of the nineteenth century, had a penchant for making statements that turned out in the fullness of time to be outrageous.[8] One of these occurs in this chapter "Of Money" in his *Principles of Political Economy:*

> "There cannot, in short, be intrinsically a more insignificant thing, in the economy of society, than money" (Mill, 1987, p 488).

The foregoing statement from the *Principles* represents Mill's mature view and is consistent with his acceptance of Say's law and the "immortal Principles" of Ricardo (Mill, 1974, p. 1). Mill was also influenced by his father, James Mill, who is sometimes credited with being the originator of the law of markets.[9]

Influence of Consumption on Production

In his momumental work on *The Economics of John Stuart Mill*. Samuel Hollander has a chapter which he suggests might be, but is not, entitled, Was Mill a Keynesian? The answer is "No," but the question suggests justifiably more flexibility in Mill than in the other classical economists. On occasions Mill seems on the verge of breaking free from the barter illusion.

In Mill's early essay "Of the Influence of Consumption on Production," written about 1830, when Mill was 24, and published in 1844 in *Essays on Some Unsettled Questions of Political Economy,* he temporarily lifts the veil of barter for a peek into the light of a money economy. In speaking of the turnover of capital, he says that in normal times a very large proportion of capital lies idle (Mill, 1974, p. 55). Periods of brisk demand are the ". . . periods of greatest production: the national capital is never called into *full employment* but at those periods" (1971, p. 67. Emphasis added).

In the 1830 essay, Mill continues in non-classical fashion to suggest that Say's law is a proposition founded on the ". . . supposition of a state of barter" (1974, p. 69). If we suppose money to be used "these propositions cease to be exactly true" (1974, p. 69).

There is a difference, says Mill, between actual barter and simple commodity exchange using money. Under pure barter, buying and selling constitute one indivisible act, whereas the use of money ". . . enables this one act of interchange to be divided into two separate acts, or operations; one of which may be performed now, and the other a year hence, or whenever it may be most convenient . . . he does not therefore necessarily add to the *immediate* demand for one commodity when he adds to the supply of another" (1974, p. 70. Mill's emphasis).

Toward the end of the 1830 essay, Mill returns to the central question of general overproduction. During periods of commercial crises Mill concedes the possibility of general overproduction of commodities and deficiency of money, assuming money is not considered to be a commodity, as Mill agrees it should not be for purposes of this analysis. In commercial or financial crises people ". . . liked better to possess money than any other commodity. Money, consequently, was in request, and other commodities were in comparative disrepute. In extreme cases, money is collected in masses, and hoarded" (1974, p. 72). This position represents a distinct departure from Say's law.

By introducing into his analysis intervals of varying length between sales for money and subsequent purchases with money, Mill takes a first step toward a monetary theory of production. Longer intervals between sales and subsequent purchases represent a propensity to hoard and at least a temporary reduction in effective demand. Even in a simple circular flow, the increased preference for money gives rise to the possibility of losses for individual sellers. This is the microcosm for MIll's acknowledgment that there can be general overproduction of commodities in commercial crises.

After this promising exploration of the sense in which it is possible to have an excess of all commodities, Mill concludes his 1830 essay with a return to the gospel of Say and Ricardo. "Nothing is more true than that it is produce which constitutes the market for produce . . ." (Mill, 1874, p. 73). Thus Mill's youthful analytical excursion "Of the Influence of Consumption on Production" fails in the end to penetrate the barter illusion.

Propositions on Capital and the Wages Fund

Through the seven editions of *Principles of Political Economy* (1848 to 1871), Mill's ideas about money seem to have changed very little. The promising analytical exercise displayed in his 1830 essay is not repeated. The veil of barter, which we have associated with the neutrality of money and the law of markets shrouds Mill's entire thousand-page treatise. He does, however, directly confront the non-neutrality of money at several points in the *Principles*. We shall note Mill's vacillation in Book I on some of his propositions on capital and the wages fund; in Book II in chapters on money and credit and in particular in the famous chapter on "Excess of Supply"; and in Book IV on the tendency of profits to fall to a minimum.

Mill's first proposition on capital is "That industry is limited by capital" (Mill, 1987, p. 63). Capital is demand for labor, and the greater the amount of capital, the greater the demand for labor. Consequently, wage earners "may always be employed in producing something" (1987, p. 66). Closely related to the first proposition is Mill's fourth proposition on capital, that "Demand for commodities is not demand for labour" (1987, p. 79). This is closely related to the wages-fund doctrine, according to which wage earners barter their labor for subsistence. The demand for labor is determined by the size of the wages fund (circulating capital.)[10] The demand for consumer goods determines the *direction* of demand and consequently the types of labor employed, but demand for labor as a whole depends on the size of the wages fund. A consumer who wishes to help wage earners as a group can do so by not spending for any commodity, but by saving and thus increasing the size of the wages fund and hence the demand for labor. Mill laments that the fourth proposition is so little understood: "It is no wonder that political economy advances slowly, when such a question as this still remains open at its very threshold" (1987, p. 80). He praises Say and Ricardo for keeping this proposition steadily in view.

The law of markets is a corollary of the wages-fund doctrine in the context of the fourth proposition on capital. If Mill had chosen to incorporate his famous 1869 recantation of the wages fund into his *Principles* of 1871, he would have been confronted with a far-reaching reconstruction of his entire treatise. At this stage of life, and in poor health, Mill was not prepared for such a task. (See Mill, 1987, p. xxxi and pp. 991–93.) He died in 1873.

Credit and Commercial Crises

Mill lifts momentarily the view of barter in discussing the impact of credit on commercial crises. In a section on "Effects of great extensions and contractions of credit. Phenomena of a commercial crisis analyzed" he describes a speculative boom initiated by expectations of large profits and fueled by trade credits, leading to sharp price increases. The rapid expansion of economic activity is followed by a major contraction and a recoil of prices from high levels. When prices fall below normal levels, credit becomes difficult to obtain from banks and other lenders even by merchants with strong credit rations.

> ". . . so now, when everybody seems to be losing, and many fail entirely, it is with difficulty that firms of known solidity can obtain even the credit to which they are accustomed . . . all dealers have engagements to fulfill . . . no one likes to part with ready money. To these rational considerations there is superadded, in extreme cases, a panic as unreasoning as the previous over-confidence; money is borrowed for short periods at almost any rate of interest, and sales of goods for immediate payment are made at almost any sacrifice" (Mill, 1987, p. 528).

Here Mill recognizes the role of credit and money in the discontinuity of production, although the emphasis is on prices rather than on output and employment. Unlike his 1830 essay, this is not just a matter of analytics; it brings into economic analysis one of the major institutional developments of the nineteenth century, the dominant position of credit.

The significance of money in commercial crises is reinforced by the credit system. In a panic or crisis, credit evaporates like snow in a blast furnace, and hard cash remains the difference between business failure and survival. Money reveals itself as the ultimate form of business wealth, the means and end of business activity. Commodities are sacrificed at almost any price in order to obtain the object of businessmen's desire, money. Crises reenact the mercantilist scenario of fear of goods and hunger for money.

Excess of Supply

Mill's chapter on "Excess of Supply" has special significance for the classical barter illusion because it contains Mill's fullest and clearest statement of the impossibility of general overproduction based on the proposition that products exchange for products. The chapter is at once docrinaire in defense of Say's law of markets and an acknowledgment of the possibility of temporary excesses of commodity supply and deficiency of money.

Mill first addresses the question whether there can be a lack of *ability*, or power, to purchase all that is produced. He asks: "What is it which constitutes the means of payment for commodities?" and replies: "It is simply commodities" (Mill, 1987, p. 557). All sellers are by definition buyers. Doubling the total output of commodities would double purchasing power. So there can be no problem. "A general over-supply, or excess of all commodities above the demand, so far as demand consists in means of payment, is thus shown to be an impossibility" (Mill, 1987, p. 558). Thus Mill reiterates the old refrain of Say's law, be it an identity, as here seems to be the case, or as an equality in equilibrium. He defines the terms to make it so.

Next Mill asks whether the *desire* to purchase may be less than the volume of output produced. This, he says, is a more plausible form of the argument for over-production. He concedes it is abstractly conceivable that this might be possible for all commodities. However, "The fact that they go on adding to the production proves that this is not *actually* the case" (1987, p. 559. Mill's emphasis). Then Mill adds the punch line: "We saw before that whoever brings additional commodities to the market, brings an additional power of purchase; we now see that he brings also an additional desire to consume; since if he had not that desire, he would not have troubled himself to produce" (1987, p. 559).

By interpreting a worker's decision to produce as an indication of his desire to produce, Mill begs the question of those wage earners who are involuntarily unemployed and do not have the opportunity to make a decision to produce. Mill does not reckon with the possibility of a failure of organization in a monetary system, that denies employment at wages more than sufficient to induce them to work.[11] Mill assumes here, as elsewhere, that production is for consumption. While there are forms of economic society based on this principle, clearly it is not true that in a system of business that the producers are also the consumers; business firms produce in order to make money on the most favorable terms. In this connection and with special reference to Mill, Keynes writes that in classical economics, ". . . money makes no real difference except frictionally and that the theory of production and employment can be worked out (like Mill's) as being based on 'real' exchange with money introduced perfunctorily in a later chapter . . ." (Keynes, 1936, pp. 19–20).

In the final section of the chapter on "Excess of Supply" Mill distinguishes cyclical and secular aspects of over-supply. He repeats his earlier acknowledgment that in commercial crises "there is really an excess of all commodities above the money demand: in other words, there is an under-supply of money" (Mill, 1987, p. 561). He reiterates that commercial crises are caused by excessive speculation, a recoil from extravagantly high prices, and the "sudden annihilation of a great mass of credit" (1987, p. 561). Reluctantly Mill concedes that such crises "may be indiscriminately called a glut of commodities or a dearth of money" (1987, p. 561).

Secular Tendency of Profits to a Minimum

Mill distinguishes cyclical phenomena such as commercial crises from conditions associated with secular tendencies for the rate of profit to fall toward a minimum with the approach of the stationary state. The tendency for the rate of profit to fall within a "hands breadth" of the minimum brings stagnation and widespread unemployment. "Establishments are shut up, or kept working without profit, hands are discharged, and numbers of persons in all ranks, being deprived of their income, and thrown for support on their savings, find themselves, after the crisis has passed away, in conditions of more or less impoverishment" (1987, p. 734). The going gets rough. These conditions of unemployment and stagnation, Mill insists, are not caused by lack of effective demand. They result rather from a profit rate fluctuating around a very low secular level and subject to revulsions that Mill describes as "almost periodical" (1987, p. 734). Mill was a keen observer of economic conditions, but he was not easily persuaded to change his theoretical model even when the facts did not seem to fit. Theories take precedence over observations.

Mill and Confirmation of the Faith

At one point, Mill pays special tribute to J.B. Say and to his father, James Mill, for proclaiming as a fundamental truth the law of markets that products exchanges for products. He declares this an issue on which economists must take a stand: "The point is fundamental; any difference of opinion on it involves radically different conceptions of Political Economy, especially in its practical aspect" (Mill, 1987, p. 562). He rebukes Malthus and Sismondi, whose "fatal misconception has spread itself like a veil between them and the more difficult portions of the subject, not suffering one ray of light to penetrate" (1987, p. 562). Mill is certainly correct when he says the acceptance or non-acceptance of the principle that products exchange for products involves radically different conceptions of political economy. He has, however, misplaced the veil; it shrouds the barter-like analysis of classical economics from the clear light of a real-world monetary economy. After penetrating into that light on some occasions, Mill's analysis falls back under the veil of barter.

NEOCLASSICAL ECONOMICS: EQUILIBRIUM WITHOUT MONEY

Thus far we have traced in some detail the barter illusion in the classical economics of Adam Smith, J.B. Say, David Ricardo, and J.S. Mill. Turning now to neoclassical theory, we find the barter illusion comfortably ensconced in a body of doctrine primarily concerned with the allocation of given resources among alternative uses in order to yield maximum satisfaction. The theory focuses on equilibrium of real satisfaction and real sacrifice, with money in a subsidiary role and typically treated, if at all, in a volume apart from the basic principles of economics. Unlike Ricardo and Mill, the neoclassical economists make no attempt to defend Say's law of markets against its critics. It is taken for granted.

Although neoclassical economics is not a homeogeneous entity, it continues the tradition of neutral money. Among the trio of founders (Jevons, Menger and Walras), its point of departure is a theory of the exchange of goods for goods among consumers who maximize satisfaction by adjusting their relative marginal utilities to proportionality with prices in a competitive market. The theory of consumer behavior is followed by a theory of the firm maximizing its profits by carrying output to the point at which marginal revenue equals marginal cost. The general message is that if consumers and producers operate rationally in purely competitive markets, the resulting equilibrium will yield maximum welfare for all concerned. The turbulence of a monetary economy does not disturb the economic tranquility because money as a store of value and an object of hoarding is largely excluded. The barter illusion is present because of assumptions that the economy works as if it were a barter system.

STANLEY JEVONS: MAXIMIZING PLEASURE THROUGH BARTER

As one of the founders of neoclassical marginalism, Stanley Jevons broke sharply with the classical tradition of Ricardo and Mill, but he was conventional and conservative on the subject of money. His marginal utility theory of value is essentially a theory of exchange based on the outcome of barter between two traders exchanging two stocks of commodities. When the bartering stops, they are said to be in equilibrium, at which point their subjective preferences (marginal utilities) correspond to objective market prices.

Money plays no part in Jevons' *Theory of Political Economy,* which is more a monograph than a general principles of the John Stuart Mill type. Jevons wrote a separate volume on *Money and the Mechanism of Exchange* (1875), which is conventional in the treatment of those topics. Jevons developed an ingenious theory of economic fluctuations in which the periodicity of business cycles is conditioned by weather conditions via the cycle of sun spots. This could hardly be called a monetary theory of cycles. Jevons accepted Say's law of markets and had no sympathy for the then current versions of underconsumption and overproduction theories.

CARL MENGER: MONEY THE MOST SALEABLE GOOD

Carl Menger differs from classical economics in more ways than Jevons, but money in Menger is no less neutral than in Jevons and the classicists. Menger's *Principles of Economics* (1950) is about a goods economy, not about a monetary economy. It is a pure theory of the value of goods, the exchange of goods for goods, including goods of a lower and higher order.

The final chapter of Menger's *Principles* is entitled "The Theory of Money." Money is a device originating among economizing individuals who seek more efficient ways of exchanging goods. The inefficiencies of direct barter are explained and illustrated. Money evolves as the most saleable of commodities from cattle-money to metallic money and coins. Money as an institution is the unintended consequence of individuals acting in their self-interest; it is not a product of social contract or of government, although government may increase the general acceptability of money by declaring it legal tender for the payment of taxes and debts.

Included in Menger's chapter of money is a discussion of money as a store of value. He recognizes that low carrying costs and durability make money an efficient form in which to accumulate wealth for future consumption. As a temporary store of value, money enables wealth-holders to postpone decisions concerning when and in what form to consume.

Menger fails to seize the opportunity to link his discussion of money as a store of value with his concern with uncertainty. He could have but did not relate his section on "Time and Error" to hoarding money as a store of value, as Keynes and Shackle do. Like the classical and neoclassical economists generally, Menger's is a theory of given resources. He makes no reference to Say's law, overproduction, unemployment, or business cycles. Money is neutral in Menger's principles of economics.

LÉON WALRAS: A THEORY OF NO UNCERTAINTY

From the point of view of the barter illusion in neoclassical economics, the case of Léon Walras is more complex than that of Jevons and Menger. All three begin their general systems with a theory of exchange without money (pure barter), but Walras proceeds to write a complete treatise on the principles of economics. He follows his theory of exchange with a theory of production and a theory of capital formation, and then a section entitled "Theory of Circulation and Money." Walras' ideas about money evolved through the four editions of the *Elements of Pure Economics*. In the preface to the fourth edition (1899) he writes: "Clearly, however, it was my theory of money that underwent the most important changes as a result of my research on the subject from 1876 to 1899" (Walras, 1954, p. 38).

Apart from the numéraire, which is present from the first edition, Walras develops money in a fuller sense as part of his general equilibrium theory. He applies his general theory of value to money. The value of money is based on the concept of a "desired cash balance" and the equality of supply (offer) and demand for money (Walras, 1954, p. 38). The "service of availability" of cash is central to his thought. Consumers and entrepreneurs have "fairly exact ideas" about their receipts and expenditures of cash needed for consumer purchases and capital outlays. Cash balances are held to meet the transactions needs of consumers and producers. Walras rules out uncertainty by assuming that the amounts and timing of these transactions are known, in which case "... we eliminate all occasion for uncertainty" (Walras, 1954, p. 318; see also p. 317). Money is held for transactions but not for speculative purposes. Walras says speculation is an aspect of applied economics (p. 310).

Despite Walras' efforts to integrate money into his model, he comes up with a system that operates as if it were a barter system. Money is neutral. In his large treatise on *Elements of Pure Economics,* Walras avoids questions of economic crises (p. 381),[12] potential overproduction, and the possibility of deficiency of effective demand. The famous controversy concerning the law of markets, which involved Ricardo and Mill on the one hand and Malthus and Sismondi on the other, is not mentioned by Walras. Involuntary unemployment is ruled out by definition. It is a theory that explains away but does not explain unemployment. Like the other neoclassical economists. Walras provides a theory of efficiency of given resources, but he does it in a more detailed and elegant manner.[13]

ALFRED MARSHALL: MONEY AS A MEASURE OF THE STRENGTH OF MOTIVES

In his *Principles of Economics* Alfred Marshall continues the classical and neoclassical tradition of neutral money, of analyzing the economy as if it were a barter system. Keynes includes Marshall among the economists who embraced Say's law of markets (Keynes, 1936, pp. 19–21), and Professor John K. Whitaker says Marshall viewed Say's law "... as an equilibrium truth of great importance" (Whitaker, 1987, p. 361).

Unlike Walras, who incorporates monetary theory into his *Elements,* Marshall makes no attempt to include monetary theory in his *Principles.* Beginning at an early date, Marshall worked out his ideas on money and presented them in separate papers and before Parliamentary committees. Only in 1923, one year before his death, did he put his work on money together into a single volume *Money, Credit and Commerce.* He developed the well-known Cambridge cash balance approach to the quantity theory of money. His theory of money and credit deals not only with price levels but also with cyclical and general unemployment, which he views as temporary departures from equilibrium resulting from disturbances in credit markets (Whitaker, 1987, p. 361).

In the *Principles* Marshall does assign to money one special and important function in economic theory that differs from that found in other treatise on economic theory. Money, says Marshall, ". . . is the centre around which economic science clusters" (Marshall, 1930, p. 22). Better than anything else, money can be used to measure approximately the strength of motives—not the motives themselves—to sacrifice and to satisfy in economic activity. On the one hand, there is a certain sum of money that will just induce an individual to undergo certain sacrifices (labor and abstinence) in production; and on the other hand, there is a certain sum of money an individual will just give up to enjoy certain satisfactions (utilities) in consumption (Marshall, 1930, pp. 14–15). Money is the common element linking Marshall's two levels of analysis, the subjective and the objective levels. At the subjective level, money measures indirectly the sacrifices of production and the satisfactions of consumption; at the objective level, money measures the expenses of production and the expenditures for consumption. Money does not, however, enter directly into the motives and decisions, as it does in a monetary theory of production. Money serves merely as the measuring rod of the force of motives. So the barter illusion dominates Marshall's economic theory in the *Principles of Economics*.[14]

SUMMARY AND CONCLUSIONS: AWAITING THE ATONEMENT

From Adam Smith to the present, money has been strangely absent from mainstream principles of economics. More precisely, money as a store of value plays no significant role in mainstream economics. Explicit in classical and implicit in neoclassical principles is the assumption that the economy operates as if it were a barter system. This I refer to as the barter illusion.

In contrast to mainstream economics with its barter illusion is a monetary theory of production in which the consequences of the essential properties of money are incorporated as part of the principles. As the perfectly liquid form of private wealth, money affects the volume of output and employment in a world of uncertainty. These effects operate mainly through the motives and decisions of business enterprise, which as the dominant institution of modern civilization, does most of the employing and most of the producing of output.

In the circular flow of converting money capital into real output and reconverting real output into money capital, the properties of money are a strategic factor. The most critical transaction in the circular flow is the sale by firms of real output for money. Every such transaction involves an incipient crisis; the transaction may fail for lack of effective demand. Profit is realized only if and when real output is converted into money on terms favorable to the firm. Mainstream economics lacks a realistic theory of business enterprise. The system of business enterprise is a monetary economy; money enters into the motives and decisions of business firms and is the measure of their success in the short run (profits) and the long run (capital accumulation). A monetary theory of production is essential for clear and coherent understanding of how a monetary economy operates.

Our theme that classical and neoclassical economics involves a barter illusion is examined by reference to four classical economists: Adam Smith, J.B. Say, David Ricardo, and J.S. Mill;

and four neoclassical economists: Stanley Jevons, Carl Menger, Leon Walras, and Alfred Marshall. Prior to Adam Smith, the mercantilists had adumbrated a monetary theory of production, which highlighted the acquisitive and pecuniary motives of the mercantile classes. Unlike his successors, Adam Smith gave full vent to the "mean and malignant expedients" (Smith, 1937, p. 577) of merchants and master manufacturers, who connived to raise prices of their customers and conspired to lower wages of their workers. Worst of all, however, they exploited the public by hoodwinking and manipulating the government in an unholy alliance to feather their mercantile nests. Smith concluded it was more important to get the commercial classes off the backs of government by a policy of laissez-faire, and to leave protection of consumers, workers, and the general public to freely competitive markets. In his assault on mercantilist policies, Smith undercut mercantilist theory by moving money from center stage to the status of a wheel of circulation. He erected a Newtonian-like natural economic order in which the disturbing force of money is absent. He purged money from economic theory. This is the sin of Adam.

J.B. Say's anti-mercantilism submerges the acquisitive and pecuniary motives of merchants and master manufacturers and converts the sin of Adam into the dogma that products exchange for products. Ricardo neutralizes money in his *Principles of Economics* and accepts Say's barter illusion as the basis for arguing against Malthus that general overproduction is impossible. John Stuart Mill, with fair and reasoned analysis, almost lifts the veil of barter, but in his final analysis confirms the faith in the barter illusion and in the immortal principles of Ricardo.

Classical economists have the virtue of arguing the cases for the barter illusion. Neoclassical economists take it for granted. In their monographic principles of economics, Jevons and Menger derive marginal utility theory from models in which individuals barter for goods until they reach an equilibrium of maximum satisfaction. Walras and Marshall develop broader treatises but do not escape the barter illusion. The significance Marshall assigns to money has nothing to do with the law of markets, which he accepts. In Marshall's *Principles of Economics* money is a device for measuring the strength of subjective sacrifices and satisfactions in production and consumption respectively.

More than any other early neoclassicist, Walras struggles to integrate money into his general equilibrium theory of prices. He does not succeed, and his general equilibrium remains a theory of refined barter. The search for Professor Hahn and others to find a way to integrate money into the Arrow-Debreu version of the Walrasian general equilibrium is evidence that the problem of getting money into general economic theory has not been resolved.

There is no guarantee that dynamic money can be conceptually reconciled with static equilibrium. Taking dynamics out of money has yielded neutral money and the barter illusion. The remaining possibility is to render equilibrium dynamic, which conceptually is not an easy task. If general equilibrium theory cannot accommodate dynamic money as a store of value under uncertainty, then general equilibrium cannot justify Professor Hahn's description as "the best developed model of the economy" (Hahn, 1983, p. 1). In that event, the logic of a monetary theory of production must prevail to the exclusion of general equilibrium. Professor Hahn would perhaps view this as throwing out the baby with the bath. Unfortunately drastic action is sometimes necessary even in economic theory.

Finally, to close on the note at which we began: General economic theorists need to lift the veil of barter from general economic theory. Only a monetary theory of production can yield a realistic and fruitful theory of our monetary economy. Atonement for the sin of Adam awaits fulfillment of this task.

NOTES

1. "Money illusion" means a failure to distinguish between real and money magnitudes, such as between real wages and money wages. "Barter illusion" is developed in the course of this paper. It refers to the misapprehension (illusion) that the economy operates *as if* it were a barter economy. Money is recognized as a medium of exchange but is neutral in relation to output and employment. "Veil of barter" is used in this paper to mean that the significance of money is obscured by the barter illusion. "Veil of money" is commonly used in the economics literature to suggest that money covers up significant real forces. The four concepts are not mutually exclusive.
2. "Classical and neoclassical economics" as used in this paper refers exclusively to the corpus of what is earlier called the "principles of political economy" and later the "principles of economics." Numerous writers developed ideas about non-neutral money, but their ideas did not become part of mainstream principles. Henry Thornton (1760–1815) is an example.
3. One of the problems with mainstream economic theory is that it has not operated with any explicit concept of an economic system. One cannot be certain whether the "principles" are intended to be universal in their application or something less than universal. Feudalism and socialism are not monetary economies in the sense the term is used in this paper, but both these system make use of money. Capitalism is a monetary economy in the sense that money is a strategic institution in the system of business enterprise. See Dillard, 1987, "Money as an Institution of Capitalism."
4. On pre-established harmony and laissez-faire, see Heckscher, 1936, esp. II, p. 318.
5. See Smith, 1937, pp. 238, 250, 626. In describing mercantilsm as a system of political economy that confused gold and silver with real wealth, Smith also pointed to the self-serving motives of merchants and master manufacturers. He said they did not necessarily know what was good for the country but it was their business to know what was good for themselves.
6. Say's output "of the right kind" fails to take account of the strategic role of investment activity in disbursing income which generates part of the demand for current output of consumer goods and services. In Keynes' theory, for example, investment is primarily a device for clearing the market for the current output of consumer goods. For Say's law to work, investment would need always to be profitable and accumulation continuous. An empirical observation of undoubted validity is that capital accumulation under capitalism has never been sustained for long periods. On analytical grounds, Say weakens his case for continuous accumulation by accepting Smith's (as contrasted with Ricardo's) view that the accumulation of capital reduces the rate of return because of increasing competition to sell output and to hire wage earners.
7. I am indebted to Professor Will Mason for this felicitous expression.
8. A well-known example of Mill's "famous last words" is, "Happily, there is nothing in the laws of value which remain (1848) for the present or any future writer to clear up; the theory of the subject is complete" (Mill, 1987, p. 436). This came on the eve of the marginal utility revolution in value theory. A lesser noticed example is Mill's "the sands of Arabia" as an example of absolutely worthless land. Mill, 1987, p. 423.
9. Hollander credits Say with the priority over James Mill on the law of markets. See Hollander, 1979, p. 95.
10. See Mill's chapter "Of Wages" for discussion of the wages-fund doctrine. See Mill, 1987, pp. 343–60.
11. See Keynes, 1979, pp. 101–2. "A state of unemployment can, I think, only be defined as . . . a failure of organization which prevents a man from producing something, the equivalent of which he would value more highly than the effort it had cost him. . . . The existence of chronic unemployment is, in itself, a proof that the classical theory is insufficiently general in its postulates."
12. Walras' only mention of crises in *Elements* is on p. 381. Crises are defined as "sudden and general disturbances of equilibrium." He argues, "The more we know about the ideal conditions of equilibrium, the better we shall be able to control or prevent crises."
13. For an interpretation of Walras that places his work in a larger perspective, with similarities to Keynes and Marx, see Morishima, 1977, esp. pp. 1–10.
14. Marshall's *Principles* includes an appendix on "Barter." See Marshall, 1930, Appendix F, pp. 791–95. Barter between two individuals exchanging limited supplies of two commodities, after the manner of Jevons' theory of exchange, will not result in a stable equilibrium because the marginal utilities of both commodities are different after each exchange. In order to reach stable equilibrium

there must be in the market ready to be exchanged a large stock of one commodity such that its marginal utility is practically constant. In the text of his *Principles* Marshall assumes the marginal utility of money to be constant for any given individual. He thus rules out the income effects of price changes. See Hicks, 1939, p. 32.
15. Arrow and Hahn tell us on p. 338 of a 369-page treatise on general equilibrium, "The economy we have been considering . . . is essentially one of barter; all acts of exchange are completed between two households exchanging one good for another." See Arrow and Hahn, 1971, p. 338. They add a final chapter on "The Keynesian Model."

REFERENCES

Arrow, Kenneth J. and F.H. Hahn. *General Competitive Analysis.* San Francisco: Holden-Day, 1971.
Dillard, Dudley. *Economic Development of the North Atlantic Community: Historical Introduction to Modern Economics.* Englewood Cliffs, N.J.: Prentice-Hall, 1967.
——————. "Money as an Institution of Capitalism," *Journal of Economic Issues,* Vol. 31 (December 1987), pp. 1623–47.
——————. "Effective Demand and the Monetary Theory of Employment," in *The Foundations of Keynesian Analysis,* edited by Alain Barrère. London: Macmillan, 1988.
Hahn, Frank. *Money and Inflation.* Cambridge: MIT Press, 1983.
Heckscher, Eli F. *Mercantilism.* two volumes. London: George Allen and Unwin, 1955.
Hicks, J.R. *Value and Capital.* Oxford: Clarendon Press, 1939.
——————. *Critical Essays in Monetary Theory.* Oxford: Clarendon Press, 1967.
Hollander, Samuel. *The Economics of David Ricardo.* Toronto: University of Toronto Press, 1979.
——————. *The Economics of John Stuart Mill.* two volumes. Toronto: University of Toronto Press, 1985.
Hume, David. *Essays: Literary, Moral and Political.* London: George Routledge and Sons, no date.
Jevons, W. Stanley. *Money and the Mechanism of Exchange.* New York: D. Appleton and Co., 1875.
——————. *The Theory of Political Economy.* London: Macmillan, 1888.
Johnson, E.A.J. *The Predecessors of Adam Smith.* New York: Prentice-Hall, 1937.
Keynes, John Maynard. *The General Theory of Employment, Interest and Money.* New York: Harcourt, Brace and Co., 1936.
——————. *A Tract on Monetary Reform.* volume 4, *The Collected Writings of John Maynard Keynes.* London: Macmillan, 1971.
——————. *Essays in Biography.* volume 10, *The Collected Writings of John Maynard Keynes.* London: Macmillan, 1972.
——————. *The General Theory and After. Part I, Preparation.* volume 13, *The Collected Writings of John Maynard Keynes.* London: Macmillan, 1973a.
——————. *The General Theory and After. Part II. Defence and Development.* volume 14, *The Collected Writings of John Maynard Keynes.* London: Macmillan, 1973b.
——————. *The General Theory and After. A Supplement.* volume 29, *The Collected Writings of John Maynard Keynes.* London: Macmillan, 1979.
Malthus, Thomas Robert. *Principles of Political Economy.* New York: Augustus M. Kelley, Inc., 1951.
Marshall, Alfred. *Money, Credit and Commerce.* London: Macmillan, 1923.
——————. *Principles of Economics.* London: Macmillan, 1930.
Menger, Carl. *Principles of Economics.* Glencoe, Ill.: Free Press, 1950.
Mill, John Stuart. *Essays of Some Unsettled Questions of Political Economy.* Clifton, N.J.: Augustus M. Kelley, Inc., 1974.
——————. *Principles of Political Economy.* Ashley edition. Fairfield, N.J.: Augustus M. Kelley, Inc., 1987.
Monroe, Arthur Eli. *Early Economic Thought.* Cambridge: Harvard University Press, 1924.
——————. *Monetary Theory before Adam Smith.* New York: Augustus M. Kelley, 1966.
Morishima, Michio. *Walras' Economics: A Pure Theory of Capital and Money.* Cambridge: Cambridge University Press, 1977.
——————. "Anti-Say's Law versus Say's Law: A Change in Paradigm," in *Evolutionary Economics: Applications of Schumpeter's Ideas.* edited by Horst Hanusch. Cambridge: Cambridge University Press, 1988.

Ricardo, David. *On the Principles of Political Economy and Taxation.* volume 1, *Works and Correspondence of David Ricardo,* edited by Piero Sraffa. Cambridge: Cambridge University Press, 1951.

————————. *Notes on Malthus's Principles of Political Economy.* volume 2, *Works and Correspondence of David Ricardo,* edited by Piero Sraffa. Cambridge: Cambridge University Press, 1951.

————————. *Papers and Pamphlets, 1815–23.* volume 4, *Works and Correspondence of David Ricardo,* edited by Piero Sraffa. Cambridge: Cambridge University Press, 1951.

Say, Jean Baptiste. *Letters to Thomas Robert Malthus on Political Economy and Stagnation of Commerce.* London: George Harding, 1936.

————————. *A Treatise on Political Economy.* New York: Augustus M. Kelley, Publishers, 1971.

Schumpeter, Joseph A. *History of Economic Analysis.* New York: Oxford University Press, 1954.

Scott, William R., *Adam Smith as Student and Professor.* Glasgow: Jackson, Son & Co., 1937.

Simmel, Georg. *The Philosophy of Money.* London: Routledge and Kegan Paul, 1978.

Skinner, Andrew S., and Thomas Wilson, editors. *Essays on Adam Smith.* Oxford: Clarendon Press, 1975.

Smith, Adam. *An Inquiry into the Nature and Causes of the Wealth of Nations.* Cannan edition. New York: Modern Library, 1937.

Steuart, Sir James. *An Inquiry into the Principles of Political Economy.* 2 volumes. Edited by Andrew S. Skinner. Chicago: University of Chicago Press, 1966.

Vickers, Douglas. *Studies in the Theory of Money, 1690–1776.* Philadelphia: Chilton, 1959.

————————. "Adam Smith and the Status of the Theory of Money," in *Essays on Adam Smith,* edited by Andrew S. Skinner and Thomas Wilson. Oxford: Clarendon Press, 1975.

Walras, Léon. *Elements of Pure Economics.* London: George Allen and Unwin, 1954.

Weber, Max. *General Economic History.* Translated by Frank H. Knight. New York: Collier Books, 1961.

Whitaker, John K. "Alfred Marshall," *The New Palgrave Dictionary of Economics.* London: Macmillan, 1987. Vol. 3, pp. 350–63.

[7]

The American Economic Review

Volume LVIII   MARCH 1968   Number 1

THE ROLE OF MONETARY POLICY*

By MILTON FRIEDMAN**

There is wide agreement about the major goals of economic policy: high employment, stable prices, and rapid growth. There is less agreement that these goals are mutually compatible or, among those who regard them as incompatible, about the terms at which they can and should be substituted for one another. There is least agreement about the role that various instruments of policy can and should play in achieving the several goals.

My topic for tonight is the role of one such instrument—monetary policy. What can it contribute? And how should it be conducted to contribute the most? Opinion on these questions has fluctuated widely. In the first flush of enthusiasm about the newly created Federal Reserve System, many observers attributed the relative stability of the 1920s to the System's capacity for fine tuning—to apply an apt modern term. It came to be widely believed that a new era had arrived in which business cycles had been rendered obsolete by advances in monetary technology. This opinion was shared by economist and layman alike, though, of course, there were some dissonant voices. The Great Contraction destroyed this naive attitude. Opinion swung to the other extreme. Monetary policy was a string. You could pull on it to stop inflation but you could not push on it to halt recession. You could lead a horse to water but you could not make him drink. Such theory by aphorism was soon replaced by Keynes' rigorous and sophisticated analysis.

Keynes offered simultaneously an explanation for the presumed impotence of monetary policy to stem the depression, a nonmonetary interpretation of the depression, and an alternative to monetary policy

* Presidential address delivered at the Eightieth Annual Meeting of the American Economic Association, Washington, D.C., December 29, 1967.

** I am indebted for helpful criticisms of earlier drafts to Armen Alchian, Gary Becker, Martin Bronfenbrenner, Arthur F. Burns, Phillip Cagan, David D. Friedman, Lawrence Harris, Harry G. Johnson, Homer Jones, Jerry Jordan, David Meiselman, Allan H. Meltzer, Theodore W. Schultz, Anna J. Schwartz, Herbert Stein, George J. Stigler, and James Tobin.

for meeting the depression and his offering was avidly accepted. If liquidity preference is absolute or nearly so—as Keynes believed likely in times of heavy unemployment—interest rates cannot be lowered by monetary measures. If investment and consumption are little affected by interest rates—as Hansen and many of Keynes' other American disciples came to believe—lower interest rates, even if they could be achieved, would do little good. Monetary policy is twice damned. The contraction, set in train, on this view, by a collapse of investment or by a shortage of investment opportunities or by stubborn thriftiness, could not, it was argued, have been stopped by monetary measures. But there was available an alternative—fiscal policy. Government spending could make up for insufficient private investment. Tax reductions could undermine stubborn thriftiness.

The wide acceptance of these views in the economics profession meant that for some two decades monetary policy was believed by all but a few reactionary souls to have been rendered obsolete by new economic knowledge. Money did not matter. Its only role was the minor one of keeping interest rates low, in order to hold down interest payments in the government budget, contribute to the "euthanasia of the rentier," and maybe, stimulate investment a bit to assist government spending in maintaining a high level of aggregate demand.

These views produced a widespread adoption of cheap money policies after the war. And they received a rude shock when these policies failed in country after country, when central bank after central bank was forced to give up the pretense that it could indefinitely keep "the" rate of interest at a low level. In this country, the public denouement came with the Federal Reserve-Treasury Accord in 1951, although the policy of pegging government bond prices was not formally abandoned until 1953. Inflation, stimulated by cheap money policies, not the widely heralded postwar depression, turned out to be the order of the day. The result was the beginning of a revival of belief in the potency of monetary policy.

This revival was strongly fostered among economists by the theoretical developments initiated by Haberler but named for Pigou that pointed out a channel—namely, changes in wealth—whereby changes in the real quantity of money can affect aggregate demand even if they do not alter interest rates. These theoretical developments did not undermine Keynes' argument against the potency of orthodox monetary measures when liquidity preference is absolute since under such circumstances the usual monetary operations involve simply substituting money for other assets without changing total wealth. But they did show how changes in the quantity of money produced in other ways could affect total spending even under such circumstances. And, more

FRIEDMAN: MONETARY POLICY 3

fundamentally, they did undermine Keynes' key theoretical proposition, namely, that even in a world of flexible prices, a position of equilibrium at full employment might not exist. Henceforth, unemployment had again to be explained by rigidities or imperfections, not as the natural outcome of a fully operative market process.

The revival of belief in the potency of monetary policy was fostered also by a re-evaluation of the role money played from 1929 to 1933. Keynes and most other economists of the time believed that the Great Contraction in the United States occurred despite aggressive expansionary policies by the monetary authorities—that they did their best but their best was not good enough.[1] Recent studies have demonstrated that the facts are precisely the reverse: the U.S. monetary authorities followed highly deflationary policies. The quantity of money in the United States fell by one-third in the course of the contraction. And it fell not because there were no willing borrowers—not because the horse would not drink. It fell because the Federal Reserve System forced or permitted a sharp reduction in the monetary base, because it failed to exercise the responsibilities assigned to it in the Federal Reserve Act to provide liquidity to the banking system. The Great Contraction is tragic testimony to the power of monetary policy—not, as Keynes and so many of his contemporaries believed, evidence of its impotence.

In the United States the revival of belief in the potency of monetary policy was strengthened also by increasing disillusionment with fiscal policy, not so much with its potential to affect aggregate demand as with the practical and political feasibility of so using it. Expenditures turned out to respond sluggishly and with long lags to attempts to adjust them to the course of economic activity, so emphasis shifted to taxes. But here political factors entered with a vengeance to prevent prompt adjustment to presumed need, as has been so graphically illustrated in the months since I wrote the first draft of this talk. "Fine tuning" is a marvelously evocative phrase in this electronic age, but it has little resemblance to what is possible in practice—not. I might add, an unmixed evil.

It is hard to realize how radical has been the change in professional opinion on the role of money. Hardly an economist today accepts views that were the common coin some two decades ago. Let me cite a few examples.

In a talk published in 1945, E. A. Goldenweiser, then Director of the Research Division of the Federal Reserve Board, described the primary objective of monetary policy as being to "maintain the value of Government bonds. . . . This country" he wrote, "will have to adjust to

---

[1] In [2], I have argued that Henry Simons shared this view with Keynes, and that it accounts for the policy changes that he recommended.

a 2½ per cent interest rate as the return on safe, long-time money, because the time has come when returns on pioneering capital can no longer be unlimited as they were in the past" [4, p. 117].

In a book on *Financing American Prosperity,* edited by Paul Homan and Fritz Machlup and published in 1945, Alvin Hansen devotes nine pages of text to the "savings-investment problem" without finding any need to use the words "interest rate" or any close facsimile thereto [5, pp. 218-27]. In his contribution to this volume, Fritz Machlup wrote, "Questions regarding the rate of interest, in particular regarding its variation or its stability, may not be among the most vital problems of the postwar economy, but they are certainly among the perplexing ones" [5, p. 466]. In his contribution, John H. Williams—not only professor at Harvard but also a long-time adviser to the New York Federal Reserve Bank—wrote, "I can see no prospect of revival of a general monetary control in the postwar period" [5, p. 383].

Another of the volumes dealing with postwar policy that appeared at this time, *Planning and Paying for Full Employment,* was edited by Abba P. Lerner and Frank D. Graham [6] and had contributors of all shades of professional opinion—from Henry Simons and Frank Graham to Abba Lerner and Hans Neisser. Yet Albert Halasi, in his excellent summary of the papers, was able to say, "Our contributors do not discuss the question of money supply. . . . The contributors make no special mention of credit policy to remedy actual depressions. . . . Inflation . . . might be fought more effectively by raising interest rates. . . . But . . . other anti-inflationary measures . . . are preferable" [6, pp. 23-24]. *A Survey of Contemporary Economics,* edited by Howard Ellis and published in 1948, was an "official" attempt to codify the state of economic thought of the time. In his contribution, Arthur Smithies wrote, "In the field of compensatory action, I believe fiscal policy must shoulder most of the load. Its chief rival, monetary policy, seems to be disqualified on institutional grounds. This country appears to be committed to something like the present low level of interest rates on a long-term basis" [1, p. 208].

These quotations suggest the flavor of professional thought some two decades ago. If you wish to go further in this humbling inquiry, I recommend that you compare the sections on money—when you can find them—in the Principles texts of the early postwar years with the lengthy sections in the current crop even, or especially, when the early and recent Principles are different editions of the same work.

The pendulum has swung far since then, if not all the way to the position of the late 1920s, at least much closer to that position than to the position of 1945. There are of course many differences between then and now, less in the potency attributed to monetary policy than in the roles assigned to it and the criteria by which the profession believes monetary policy should be guided. Then, the chief roles assigned monetary policy were to promote price stability and to preserve the gold standard; the chief criteria of monetary policy were the state of the "money market," the extent of "speculation" and the movement of gold. Today, primacy is assigned to the promotion of full employment, with the prevention of inflation a continuing but definitely secondary objective. And there is major disagreement about criteria of policy, varying from emphasis on money market conditions, interest rates, and the quantity of money to the belief that the state of employment itself should be the proximate criterion of policy.

I stress nonetheless the similarity between the views that prevailed in the late 'twenties and those that prevail today because I fear that, now as then, the pendulum may well have swung too far, that, now as then, we are in danger of assigning to monetary policy a larger role than it can perform, in danger of asking it to accomplish tasks that it cannot achieve, and, as a result, in danger of preventing it from making the contribution that it is capable of making.

Unaccustomed as I am to denigrating the importance of money, I therefore shall, as my first task, stress what monetary policy cannot do. I shall then try to outline what it can do and how it can best make its contribution, in the present state of our knowledge—or ignorance.

I. *What Monetary Policy Cannot Do*

From the infinite world of negation, I have selected two limitations of monetary policy to discuss: (1) It cannot peg interest rates for more than very limited periods; (2) It cannot peg the rate of unemployment for more than very limited periods. I select these because the contrary has been or is widely believed, because they correspond to the two main unattainable tasks that are at all likely to be assigned to monetary policy, and because essentially the same theoretical analysis covers both.

Pegging of Interest Rates

History has already persuaded many of you about the first limitation. As noted earlier, the failure of cheap money policies was a major source of the reaction against simple-minded Keynesianism. In the United States, this reaction involved widespread recognition that the wartime and postwar pegging of bond prices was a mistake, that the abandonment of this policy was a desirable and inevitable step, and that it had none of the disturbing and disastrous consequences that were so freely predicted at the time.

The limitation derives from a much misunderstood feature of the relation between money and interest rates. Let the Fed set out to keep

6   THE AMERICAN ECONOMIC REVIEW

interest rates down. How will it try to do so? By buying securities. This raises their prices and lowers their yields. In the process, it also increases the quantity of reserves available to banks, hence the amount of bank credit, and, ultimately the total quantity of money. That is why central bankers in particular, and the financial community more broadly, generally believe that an increase in the quantity of money tends to lower interest rates. Academic economists accept the same conclusion, but for different reasons. They see, in their mind's eye, a negatively sloping liquidity preference schedule. How can people be induced to hold a larger quantity of money? Only by bidding down interest rates.

Both are right, up to a point. The *initial* impact of increasing the quantity of money at a faster rate than it has been increasing is to make interest rates lower for a time than they would otherwise have been. But this is only the beginning of the process not the end. The more rapid rate of monetary growth will stimulate spending, both through the impact on investment of lower market interest rates and through the impact on other spending and thereby relative prices of higher cash balances than are desired. But one man's spending is another man's income. Rising income will raise the liquidity preference schedule and the demand for loans; it may also raise prices, which would reduce the real quantity of money. These three effects will reverse the initial downward pressure on interest rates fairly promptly, say, in something less than a year. Together they will tend, after a somewhat longer interval, say, a year or two, to return interest rates to the level they would otherwise have had. Indeed, given the tendency for the economy to overreact, they are highly likely to raise interest rates temporarily beyond that level, setting in motion a cyclical adjustment process.

A fourth effect, when and if it becomes operative, will go even farther, and definitely mean that a higher rate of monetary expansion will correspond to a higher, not lower, level of interest rates than would otherwise have prevailed. Let the higher rate of monetary growth produce rising prices, and let the public come to expect that prices will continue to rise. Borrowers will then be willing to pay and lenders will then demand higher interest rates—as Irving Fisher pointed out decades ago. This price expectation effect is slow to develop and also slow to disappear. Fisher estimated that it took several decades for a full adjustment and more recent work is consistent with his estimates.

These subsequent effects explain why every attempt to keep interest rates at a low level has forced the monetary authority to engage in successively larger and larger open market purchases. They explain why, historically, high and rising nominal interest rates have been associated with rapid growth in the quantity of money, as in Brazil or Chile or in the United States in recent years, and why low and falling interest rates have been associated with slow growth in the quantity of money, as in Switzerland now or in the United States from 1929 to 1933. As an empirical matter, low interest rates are a sign that monetary policy *has been* tight—in the sense that the quantity of money has grown slowly; high interest rates are a sign that monetary policy *has been* easy—in the sense that the quantity of money has grown rapidly. The broadest facts of experience run in precisely the opposite direction from that which the financial community and academic economists have all generally taken for granted.

Paradoxically, the monetary authority could assure low nominal rates of interest—but to do so it would have to start out in what seems like the opposite direction, by engaging in a deflationary monetary policy. Similarly, it could assure high nominal interest rates by engaging in an inflationary policy and accepting a temporary movement in interest rates in the opposite direction.

These considerations not only explain why monetary policy cannot peg interest rates; they also explain why interest rates are such a misleading indicator of whether monetary policy is "tight" or "easy." For that, it is far better to look at the rate of change of the quantity of money.[2]

Employment as a Criterion of Policy

The second limitation I wish to discuss goes more against the grain of current thinking. Monetary growth, it is widely held, will tend to stimulate employment; monetary contraction, to retard employment. Why, then, cannot the monetary authority adopt a target for employment or unemployment—say, 3 per cent unemployment; be tight when unemployment is less than the target; be easy when unemployment is higher than the target; and in this way peg unemployment at, say, 3 per cent? The reason it cannot is precisely the same as for interest rates—the difference between the immediate and the delayed consequences of such a policy.

Thanks to Wicksell, we are all acquainted with the concept of a "natural" rate of interest and the possibility of a discrepancy between the "natural" and the "market" rate. The preceding analysis of interest rates can be translated fairly directly into Wicksellian terms. The monetary authority can make the market rate less than the natural rate

[2] This is partly an empirical not theoretical judgment. In principle, "tightness" or "ease" depends on the rate of change of the quantity of money supplied compared to the rate of change of the quantity demanded excluding effects on demand from monetary policy itself. However, empirically demand is highly stable, if we exclude the effect of monetary policy, so it is generally sufficient to look at supply alone.

8   THE AMERICAN ECONOMIC REVIEW

only by inflation. It can make the market rate higher than the natural rate only by deflation. We have added only one wrinkle to Wicksell—the Irving Fisher distinction between the nominal and the real rate of interest. Let the monetary authority keep the nominal market rate for a time below the natural rate by inflation. That in turn will raise the nominal natural rate itself, once anticipations of inflation become widespread, thus requiring still more rapid inflation to hold down the market rate. Similarly, because of the Fisher effect, it will require not merely deflation but more and more rapid deflation to hold the market rate above the initial "natural" rate.

This analysis has its close counterpart in the employment market. At any moment of time, there is some level of unemployment which has the property that it is consistent with equilibrium in the structure of *real* wage rates. At that level of unemployment, real wage rates are tending on the average to rise at a "normal" secular rate, i.e., at a rate that can be indefinitely maintained so long as capital formation, technological improvements, etc., remain on their long-run trends. A lower level of unemployment is an indication that there is an excess demand for labor that will produce upward pressure on real wage rates. A higher level of unemployment is an indication that there is an excess supply of labor that will produce downward pressure on real wage rates. The "natural rate of unemployment," in other words, is the level that would be ground out by the Walrasian system of general equilibrium equations, provided there is imbedded in them the actual structural characteristics of the labor and commodity markets, including market imperfections, stochastic variability in demands and supplies, the cost of gathering information about job vacancies and labor availabilities, the costs of mobility, and so on.[8]

You will recognize the close similarity between this statement and the celebrated Phillips Curve. The similarity is not coincidental. Phillips' analysis of the relation between unemployment and wage change is deservedly celebrated as an important and original contribution. But, unfortunately, it contains a basic defect—the failure to distinguish between *nominal* wages and *real* wages—just as Wicksell's analysis failed to distinguish between *nominal* interest rates and *real* interest rates. Implicitly, Phillips wrote his article for a world in which everyone anticipated that nominal prices would be stable and in which that anticipation remained unshaken and immutable whatever happened to actual prices and wages. Suppose, by contrast, that everyone anticipates that prices will rise at a rate of more than 75 per cent a year—as, for exam-

---

[8] It is perhaps worth noting that this "natural" rate need not correspond to equality between the number unemployed and the number of job vacancies. For any given structure of the labor market, there will be some equilibrium relation between these two magnitudes, but there is no reason why it should be one of equality.

FRIEDMAN: MONETARY POLICY 9

ple, Brazilians did a few years ago. Then wages must rise at that rate simply to keep real wages unchanged. An excess supply of labor will be reflected in a less rapid rise in nominal wages than in anticipated prices,[4] not in an absolute decline in wages. When Brazil embarked on a policy to bring down the rate of price rise, and succeeded in bringing the price rise down to about 45 per cent a year, there was a sharp initial rise in unemployment because under the influence of earlier anticipations, wages kept rising at a pace that was higher than the new rate of price rise, though lower than earlier. This is the result experienced, and to be expected, of all attempts to reduce the rate of inflation below that widely anticipated.[5]

To avoid misunderstanding, let me emphasize that by using the term "natural" rate of unemployment, I do not mean to suggest that it is immutable and unchangeable. On the contrary, many of the market characteristics that determine its level are man-made and policy-made. In the United States, for example, legal minimum wage rates, the Walsh-Healy and Davis-Bacon Acts, and the strength of labor unions all make the natural rate of unemployment higher than it would otherwise be. Improvements in employment exchanges, in availability of information about job vacancies and labor supply, and so on, would tend to lower the natural rate of unemployment. I use the term "natural" for the same reason Wicksell did—to try to separate the real forces from monetary forces.

Let us assume that the monetary authority tries to peg the "market" rate of unemployment at a level below the "natural" rate. For definiteness, suppose that it takes 3 per cent as the target rate and that the "natural" rate is higher than 3 per cent. Suppose also that we start out at a time when prices have been stable and when unemployment is higher than 3 per cent. Accordingly, the authority increases the rate of monetary growth. This will be expansionary. By making nominal cash

[4] Strictly speaking, the rise in nominal wages will be less rapid than the rise in anticipated nominal wages to make allowance for any secular changes in real wages.

[5] Stated in terms of the rate of change of nominal wages, the Phillips Curve can be expected to be reasonably stable and well defined for any period for which the *average* rate of change of prices, and hence the anticipated rate, has been relatively stable. For such periods, nominal wages and "real" wages move together. Curves computed for different periods or different countries for each of which this condition has been satisfied will differ in level, the level of the curve depending on what the average rate of price change was. The higher the average rate of price change, the higher will tend to be the level of the curve. For periods or countries for which the rate of change of prices varies considerably, the Phillips Curve will not be well defined. My impression is that these statements accord reasonably well with the experience of the economists who have explored empirical Phillips Curves.

Restate Phillips' analysis in terms of the rate of change of real wages—and even more precisely, anticipated real wages—and it all falls into place. That is why students of empirical Phillips Curves have found that it helps to include the rate of change of the price level as an independent variable.

balances higher than people desire, it will tend initially to lower interest rates and in this and other ways to stimulate spending. Income and spending will start to rise.

To begin with, much or most of the rise in income will take the form of an increase in output and employment rather than in prices. People have been expecting prices to be stable, and prices and wages have been set for some time in the future on that basis. It takes time for people to adjust to a new state of demand. Producers will tend to react to the initial expansion in aggregate demand by increasing output, employees by working longer hours, and the unemployed, by taking jobs now offered at former nominal wages. This much is pretty standard doctrine.

But it describes only the initial effects. Because selling prices of products typically respond to an unanticipated rise in nominal demand faster than prices of factors of production, real wages received have gone down—though real wages anticipated by employees went up, since employees implicitly evaluated the wages offered at the earlier price level. Indeed, the simultaneous fall *ex post* in real wages to employers and rise *ex ante* in real wages to employees is what enabled employment to increase. But the decline *ex post* in real wages will soon come to affect anticipations. Employees will start to reckon on rising prices of the things they buy and to demand higher nominal wages for the future. "Market" unemployment is below the "natural" level. There is an excess demand for labor so real wages will tend to rise toward their initial level.

Even though the higher rate of monetary growth continues, the rise in real wages will reverse the decline in unemployment, and then lead to a rise, which will tend to return unemployment to its former level. In order to keep unemployment at its target level of 3 per cent, the monetary authority would have to raise monetary growth still more. As in the interest rate case, the "market" rate can be kept below the "natural" rate only by inflation. And, as in the interest rate case, too, only by accelerating inflation. Conversely, let the monetary authority choose a target rate of unemployment that is above the natural rate, and they will be led to produce a deflation, and an accelerating deflation at that.

What if the monetary authority chose the "natural" rate—either of interest or unemployment—as its target? One problem is that it cannot know what the "natural" rate is. Unfortunately, we have as yet devised no method to estimate accurately and readily the natural rate of either interest or unemployment. And the "natural" rate will itself change from time to time. But the basic problem is that even if the monetary authority knew the "natural" rate, and attempted to peg the market rate at that level, it would not be led to a determinate policy. The "market" rate will vary from the natural rate for all sorts of reasons other than monetary policy. If the monetary authority responds to these variations, it will set in train longer term effects that will make any monetary growth path it follows ultimately consistent with the rule of policy. The actual course of monetary growth will be analogous to a random walk, buffeted this way and that by the forces that produce temporary departures of the market rate from the natural rate.

To state this conclusion differently, there is always a temporary trade-off between inflation and unemployment; there is no permanent trade-off. The temporary trade-off comes not from inflation per se, but from unanticipated inflation, which generally means, from a rising rate of inflation. The widespread belief that there is a permanent trade-off is a sophisticated version of the confusion between "high" and "rising" that we all recognize in simpler forms. A rising rate of inflation may reduce unemployment, a high rate will not.

But how long, you will say, is "temporary"? For interest rates, we have some systematic evidence on how long each of the several effects takes to work itself out. For unemployment, we do not. I can at most venture a personal judgment, based on some examination of the historical evidence, that the initial effects of a higher and unanticipated rate of inflation last for something like two to five years; that this initial effect then begins to be reversed; and that a full adjustment to the new rate of inflation takes about as long for employment as for interest rates, say, a couple of decades. For both interest rates and employment, let me add a qualification. These estimates are for changes in the rate of inflation of the order of magnitude that has been experienced in the United States. For much more sizable changes, such as those experienced in South American countries, the whole adjustment process is greatly speeded up.

To state the general conclusion still differently, the monetary authority controls nominal quantities—directly, the quantity of its own liabilities. In principle, it can use this control to peg a nominal quantity—an exchange rate, the price level, the nominal level of national income, the quantity of money by one or another definition—or to peg the rate of change in a nominal quantity—the rate of inflation or deflation, the rate of growth or decline in nominal national income, the rate of growth of the quantity of money. It cannot use its control over nominal quantities to peg a real quantity—the real rate of interest, the rate of unemployment, the level of real national income, the real quantity of money, the rate of growth of real national income, or the rate of growth of the real quantity of money.

II. *What Monetary Policy Can Do*

Monetary policy cannot peg these real magnitudes at predetermined levels. But monetary policy can and does have important effects on these real magnitudes. The one is in no way inconsistent with the other.

My own studies of monetary history have made me extremely sympathetic to the oft-quoted, much reviled, and as widely misunderstood, comment by John Stuart Mill. "There cannot . . . ," he wrote, "be intrinsically a more insignificant thing, in the economy of society, than money; except in the character of a contrivance for sparing time and labour. It is a machine for doing quickly and commodiously, what would be done, though less quickly and commodiously, without it: and like many other kinds of machinery, it only exerts a distinct and independent influence of its own when it gets out of order" [7, p. 488].

True, money is only a machine, but it is an extraordinarily efficient machine. Without it, we could not have begun to attain the astounding growth in output and level of living we have experienced in the past two centuries—any more than we could have done so without those other marvelous machines that dot our countryside and enable us, for the most part, simply to do more efficiently what could be done without them at much greater cost in labor.

But money has one feature that these other machines do not share. Because it is so pervasive, when it gets out of order, it throws a monkey wrench into the operation of all the other machines. The Great Contraction is the most dramatic example but not the only one. Every other major contraction in this country has been either produced by monetary disorder or greatly exacerbated by monetary disorder. Every major inflation has been produced by monetary expansion—mostly to meet the overriding demands of war which have forced the creation of money to supplement explicit taxation.

The first and most important lesson that history teaches about what monetary policy can do—and it is a lesson of the most profound importance—is that monetary policy can prevent money itself from being a major source of economic disturbance. This sounds like a negative proposition: avoid major mistakes. In part it is. The Great Contraction might not have occurred at all, and if it had, it would have been far less severe, if the monetary authority had avoided mistakes, or if the monetary arrangements had been those of an earlier time when there was no central authority with the power to make the kinds of mistakes that the Federal Reserve System made. The past few years, to come closer to home, would have been steadier and more productive of economic well-being if the Federal Reserve had avoided drastic and erratic changes of direction, first expanding the money supply at an unduly rapid pace, then, in early 1966, stepping on the brake too hard, then, at the end of 1966, reversing itself and resuming expansion until at least November, 1967, at a more rapid pace than can long be maintained without appreciable inflation.

Even if the proposition that monetary policy can prevent money itself from being a major source of economic disturbance were a wholly negative proposition, it would be none the less important for that. As it happens, however, it is not a wholly negative proposition. The monetary machine has gotten out of order even when there has been no central authority with anything like the power now possessed by the Fed. In the United States, the 1907 episode and earlier banking panics are examples of how the monetary machine can get out of order largely on its own. There is therefore a positive and important task for the monetary authority—to suggest improvements in the machine that will reduce the chances that it will get out of order, and to use its own powers so as to keep the machine in good working order.

A second thing monetary policy can do is provide a stable background for the economy—keep the machine well oiled, to continue Mill's analogy. Accomplishing the first task will contribute to this objective, but there is more to it than that. Our economic system will work best when producers and consumers, employers and employees, can proceed with full confidence that the average level of prices will behave in a known way in the future—preferably that it will be highly stable. Under any conceivable institutional arrangements, and certainly under those that now prevail in the United States, there is only a limited amount of flexibility in prices and wages. We need to conserve this flexibility to achieve changes in relative prices and wages that are required to adjust to dynamic changes in tastes and technology. We should not dissipate it simply to achieve changes in the absolute level of prices that serve no economic function.

In an earlier era, the gold standard was relied on to provide confidence in future monetary stability. In its heyday it served that function reasonably well. It clearly no longer does, since there is scarce a country in the world that is prepared to let the gold standard reign unchecked—and there are persuasive reasons why countries should not do so. The monetary authority could operate as a surrogate for the gold standard, if it pegged exchange rates and did so exclusively by altering the quantity of money in response to balance of payment flows without "sterilizing" surpluses or deficits and without resorting to open or concealed exchange control or to changes in tariffs and quotas. But again, though many central bankers talk this way, few are in fact willing to follow this course—and again there are persuasive reasons why they should not do so. Such a policy would submit each country to the vagaries not of an impersonal and automatic gold standard but of the policies—deliberate or accidental—of other monetary authorities.

In today's world, if monetary policy is to provide a stable background for the economy it must do so by deliberately employing its powers to that end. I shall come later to how it can do so.

Finally, monetary policy can contribute to offsetting major disturbances in the economic system arising from other sources. If there is an independent secular exhilaration—as the postwar expansion was described by the proponents of secular stagnation—monetary policy can in principle help to hold it in check by a slower rate of monetary growth than would otherwise be desirable. If, as now, an explosive federal budget threatens unprecedented deficits, monetary policy can hold any inflationary dangers in check by a slower rate of monetary growth than would otherwise be desirable. This will temporarily mean higher interest rates than would otherwise prevail—to enable the government to borrow the sums needed to finance the deficit—but by preventing the speeding up of inflation, it may well mean both lower prices and lower nominal interest rates for the long pull. If the end of a substantial war offers the country an opportunity to shift resources from wartime to peacetime production, monetary policy can ease the transition by a higher rate of monetary growth than would otherwise be desirable—though experience is not very encouraging that it can do so without going too far.

I have put this point last, and stated it in qualified terms—as referring to major disturbances—because I believe that the potentiality of monetary policy in offsetting other forces making for instability is far more limited than is commonly believed. We simply do not know enough to be able to recognize minor disturbances when they occur or to be able to predict either what their effects will be with any precision or what monetary policy is required to offset their effects. We do not know enough to be able to achieve stated objectives by delicate, or even fairly coarse, changes in the mix of monetary and fiscal policy. In this area particularly the best is likely to be the enemy of the good. Experience suggests that the path of wisdom is to use monetary policy explicitly to offset other disturbances only when they offer a "clear and present danger."

III. *How Should Monetary Policy Be Conducted?*

How should monetary policy be conducted to make the contribution to our goals that it is capable of making? This is clearly not the occasion for presenting a detailed "Program for Monetary Stability"—to use the title of a book in which I tried to do so [3]. I shall restrict myself here to two major requirements for monetary policy that follow fairly directly from the preceding discussion.

The first requirement is that the monetary authority should guide itself by magnitudes that it can control, not by ones that it cannot control. If, as the authority has often done, it takes interest rates or the current unemployment percentage as the immediate criterion of policy, it will be like a space vehicle that has taken a fix on the wrong star. No matter how sensitive and sophisticated its guiding apparatus, the space vehicle will go astray. And so will the monetary authority. Of the various alternative magnitudes that it can control, the most appealing guides for policy are exchange rates, the price level as defined by some index, and the quantity of a monetary total—currency plus adjusted demand deposits, or this total plus commercial bank time deposits, or a still broader total.

For the United States in particular, exchange rates are an undesirable guide. It might be worth requiring the bulk of the economy to adjust to the tiny percentage consisting of foreign trade if that would guarantee freedom from monetary irresponsibility—as it might under a real gold standard. But it is hardly worth doing so simply to adapt to the average of whatever policies monetary authorities in the rest of the world adopt. Far better to let the market, through floating exchange rates, adjust to world conditions the 5 per cent or so of our resources devoted to international trade while reserving monetary policy to promote the effective use of the 95 per cent.

Of the three guides listed, the price level is clearly the most important in its own right. Other things the same, it would be much the best of the alternatives—as so many distinguished economists have urged in the past. But other things are not the same. The link between the policy actions of the monetary authority and the price level, while unquestionably present, is more indirect than the link between the policy actions of the authority and any of the several monetary totals. Moreover, monetary action takes a longer time to affect the price level than to affect the monetary totals and both the time lag and the magnitude of effect vary with circumstances. As a result, we cannot predict at all accurately just what effect a particular monetary action will have on the price level and, equally important, just when it will have that effect. Attempting to control directly the price level is therefore likely to make monetary policy itself a source of economic disturbance because of false stops and starts. Perhaps, as our understanding of monetary phenomena advances, the situation will change. But at the present stage of our understanding, the long way around seems the surer way to our objective. Accordingly, I believe that a monetary total is the best currently available immediate guide or criterion for monetary policy—and I believe that it matters much less which particular total is chosen than that one be chosen.

A second requirement for monetary policy is that the monetary authority avoid sharp swings in policy. In the past, monetary authorities have on occasion moved in the wrong direction—as in the episode of the Great Contraction that I have stressed. More frequently, they have moved in the right direction, albeit often too late, but have erred by moving too far. Too late and too much has been the general practice. For example, in early 1966, it was the right policy for the Federal Reserve to move in a less expansionary direction—though it should have done so at least a year earlier. But when it moved, it went too far, producing the sharpest change in the rate of monetary growth of the postwar era. Again, having gone too far, it was the right policy for the Fed to reverse course at the end of 1966. But again it went too far, not only restoring but exceeding the earlier excessive rate of monetary growth. And this episode is no exception. Time and again this has been the course followed—as in 1919 and 1920, in 1937 and 1938, in 1953 and 1954, in 1959 and 1960.

The reason for the propensity to overreact seems clear: the failure of monetary authorities to allow for the delay between their actions and the subsequent effects on the economy. They tend to determine their actions by today's conditions—but their actions will affect the economy only six or nine or twelve or fifteen months later. Hence they feel impelled to step on the brake, or the accelerator, as the case may be, too hard.

My own prescription is still that the monetary authority go all the way in avoiding such swings by adopting publicly the policy of achieving a steady rate of growth in a specified monetary total. The precise rate of growth, like the precise monetary total, is less important than the adoption of some stated and known rate. I myself have argued for a rate that would on the average achieve rough stability in the level of prices of final products, which I have estimated would call for something like a 3 to 5 per cent per year rate of growth in currency plus all commercial bank deposits or a slightly lower rate of growth in currency plus demand deposits only.[6] But it would be better to have a fixed rate that would on the average produce moderate inflation or moderate deflation, provided it was steady, than to suffer the wide and erratic perturbations we have experienced.

Short of the adoption of such a publicly stated policy of a steady rate of monetary growth, it would constitute a major improvement if the monetary authority followed the self-denying ordinance of avoiding wide swings. It is a matter of record that periods of relative stability in the rate of monetary growth have also been periods of relative stability in economic activity, both in the United States and other countries. Periods of wide swings in the rate of monetary growth have also been periods of wide swings in economic activity.

[6] In an as yet unpublished article on "The Optimum Quantity of Money," I conclude that a still lower rate of growth, something like 2 per cent for the broader definition, might be better yet in order to eliminate or reduce the difference between private and total costs of adding to real balances.

FRIEDMAN: MONETARY POLICY 17

By setting itself a steady course and keeping to it, the monetary authority could make a major contribution to promoting economic stability. By making that course one of steady but moderate growth in the quantity of money, it would make a major contribution to avoidance of either inflation or deflation of prices. Other forces would still affect the economy, require change and adjustment, and disturb the even tenor of our ways. But steady monetary growth would provide a monetary climate favorable to the effective operation of those basic forces of enterprise, ingenuity, invention, hard work, and thrift that are the true springs of economic growth. That is the most that we can ask from monetary policy at our present stage of knowledge. But that much—and it is a great deal—is clearly within our reach.

REFERENCES

1. H. S. ELLIS, ed., *A Survey of Contemporary Economics*. Philadelphia 1948.
2. MILTON FRIEDMAN, "The Monetary Theory and Policy of Henry Simons," *Jour. Law and Econ.*, Oct. 1967, *10*, 1-13.
3. ———, *A Program for Monetary Stability*. New York 1959.
4. E. A. GOLDENWEISER, "Postwar Problems and Policies," *Fed. Res. Bull.*, Feb. 1945, *31*, 112-21.
5. P. T. HOMAN AND FRITZ MACHLUP, ed., *Financing American Prosperity*. New York 1945.
6. A. P. LERNER AND F. D. GRAHAM, ed., *Planning and Paying for Full Employment*. Princeton 1946.
7. J. S. MILL, *Principles of Political Economy*, Bk. III, Ashley ed. New York 1929.

[8]

A Suggestion for Simplifying the Theory of Money[1]

By J. R. HICKS

AFTER the thunderstorms of recent years, it is with peculiar diffidence and even apprehension that one ventures to open one's mouth on the subject of money. In my own case these feelings are particularly intense, because I feel myself to be very much of a novice at the subject. My education has been mostly in the non-monetary parts of economics, and I have only come to be interested in money because I found that I could not keep it out of my non-monetary problems. Yet I am encouraged on reflection to hope that this may not prove a bad approach to the subject: that some things at least which are not very evident on direct inspection may become clearer from a cross-light of this sort.

It is of course very largely by such cross-fertilisation that economics progresses, and at least one department of non-monetary economics has hardly emerged from a very intimate affair with monetary theory. I do not, however, propose to resume this particular liaison. One understands that most economists have now read Böhm-Bawerk; yet whatever that union has bred, it has not been concord. I should prefer to seek illumination from another point of view—from a branch of economics which is more elementary, but, I think, in consequence better developed—the theory of value.

To anyone who comes over from the theory of value to the theory of money, there are a number of things which are rather startling. Chief of these is the preoccupation of monetary theorists with a certain equation, which states that the price of goods multiplied by the quantity of goods equals the amount of money which is spent on them. This equation crops up again and again, and it has all sorts of ingenious little arithmetical tricks performed on it. Sometimes it comes out

---

[1] A paper read at the Economic Club, November 1934. The reader is asked to bear in mind the fact that the paper was written to be read aloud, and to excuse certain pieces of mischief.

as $MV = PT$; and once, in its most stupendous trans-figuration, it blossomed into $P = \dfrac{E}{O} + \dfrac{I' - S}{R}$. Now we, of the theory of value, are not unfamiliar with this equation, and there was a time when we used to attach as much importance to it as monetary theorists seem to do still. This was in the middle of the last century, when we used to talk about value being " a ratio between demand and supply." Even now, we accept the equation, and work it, more or less implicitly, into our systems. But we are rather inclined to take it for granted, since it is rather tautologous, and since we have found that another equation, not alternative to the quantity equation, but complementary with it, is much more significant. This is the equation which states that the relative value of two commodities depends upon their relative marginal utility.

Now, to an *ingénu*, who comes over to monetary theory, it is extremely trying to be deprived of this sheet-anchor. It was marginal utility that really made sense of the theory of value; and to come to a branch of economics which does without marginal utility altogether! No wonder there are such difficulties and such differences! What is wanted is a " marginal revolution "!

That is my suggestion. But I know that it will meet with apparently crushing objections. I shall be told that the suggestion has been tried out before. It was tried by Wicksell, and though it led to interesting results, it did not lead to a marginal utility theory of money. It was tried by Mises, and led to the conclusion that money is a ghost of gold—because, so it appeared, money as such has no marginal utility.[1] The suggestion has a history, and its history is not encouraging.

This would be enough to frighten one off, were it not for two things. Both in the theory of value and in the theory of money there have been developments in the twenty or thirty

---

[1] A more subtle form of the same difficulty appears in the work of Marshall and his followers. They were aware that money ought to be subjected to marginal utility analysis ; but they were so dominated by the classical conception of money as a " veil " (which is valid enough at a certain level of approximation) that they persisted in regarding the demand for money as a demand for the things which money can buy— " real balances." As a result of this, their invocation of marginal utility remained little more than a pious hope. For they were unable to distinguish, on marginal utility lines, between the desire to save and the desire to hoard ; and they necessarily overlooked that indeterminateness in the " real balance " (so important in some applications of monetary theory), which occurs when the prices of consumption goods are expected to change. On the other hand, I must admit that some versions of the Marshallian theory come very close to what I am driving at. Cf. Lavington, *English Capital Market*, ch. vi.

years since Wicksell and Mises wrote. And these developments have considerably reduced the barriers that blocked their way.

In the theory of value, the work of Pareto, Wicksteed, and their successors, has broadened and deepened our whole conception of marginal utility. We now realise that the marginal utility analysis is nothing else than a general theory of choice, which is applicable whenever the choice is between alternatives that are capable of quantitative expression. Now money is obviously capable of quantitative expression, and therefore the objection that money has no marginal utility must be wrong. People do choose to have money rather than other things, and therefore, in the relevant sense, money must have a marginal utility.

But merely to call that marginal utility X, and then proceed to draw curves, would not be very helpful. Fortunately the developments in monetary theory to which I alluded come to our rescue.

Mr. Keynes' "Treatise," so far as I have been able to discover, contains at least three theories of money. One of them is the Savings and Investment theory, which, as I hinted, seems to me only a quantity theory much glorified. One of them is a Wicksellian natural rate theory. But the third is altogether much more interesting. It emerges when Mr. Keynes begins to talk about the price-level of investment goods; when he shows that this price-level depends upon the relative preference of the investor—to hold bank-deposits or to hold securities. Here at last we have something which to a value theorist looks sensible and interesting! Here at last we have a choice at the margin! And Mr. Keynes goes on to put substance into our X, by his doctrine that the relative preference depends upon the "bearishness" or "bullishness" of the public, upon their relative desire for liquidity or profit.

My suggestion may, therefore, be re-formulated. It seems to me that this third theory of Mr. Keynes really contains the most important part of his theoretical contribution; that here, at last, we have something which, on the analogy (the appropriate analogy) of value theory, does begin to offer a chance of making the whole thing easily intelligible; that it is from this point, not from velocity of circulation, natural rate of interest, or Saving and Investment, that we ought to start in constructing the theory of money. But in saying this, I am being more Keynesian than Keynes; I must endeavour to defend my position in detail.

II

The essence of the method I am proposing is that we should take the position of an individual at a particular point of time, and enquire what determines the precise quantity of money which he will desire to hold. But even to this simple formulation of the problem it is necessary to append two footnotes.

1. " Point of Time." We are dealing with an individual decision to hold money *or* something else, and such a decision is always made at a point of time. It is only by concentrating on decisions made at particular points of time that we can apply the theory of value to the problem at all. A very large amount of current controversy about money seems to me to be due to the attempt, superficially natural, but, in fact, highly inconvenient, to establish a close relation between the demand for money and *income*. Now the simple consideration that the decision to hold money is always made at a point of time shows that the connection between income and the demand for money must always be indirect. And in fact the whole conception of income is so intricate and beset by so many perplexing difficulties, that the establishment of any connection with income ought only to be hoped for at a late stage of investigation.[1]

2. " Money." What sort of money are we considering ? For the present, any sort of money. The following analysis will apply equally whether we think of money as notes, or bank deposits, or even metallic coins. It is true that with a metallic currency there is an ordinary commodity demand for the money substance to be considered, but it is relatively unimportant for most of our purposes. Perhaps it will be best if we take as our standard case that of a pure paper currency in a community where there are no banks. What follows has much wider application in reality. Only I would just ask you to keep this standard case in mind, since by using it as a basis for discussion, we may be able to save time a little.

An individual's decision to hold so much money means that he prefers to hold that amount of money, rather than either less or more. Now what are the precise contents of these displaced alternatives ? He could reduce his holding of money in three ways:

[1] Cf. Lindahl, *The Concept of Income* (Essays in honour of Gustav Cassel).

1. by spending, i.e. buying something, it does not matter what;
2. by lending money to someone else;
3. by paying off debts which he owes to someone else.

He can increase his holding of money in three corresponding ways:

1. by selling something else which he owns;
2. by borrowing from someone else;
3. by demanding repayment of money which is owed by someone else.

This classification is, I think, complete. All ways of changing one's holding of money can be reduced to one of these classes or a combination of two of them—purchase or sale, the creation of new debts or the extinction of old.

If a person decides to hold money, it is implied that he prefers to do this than to adopt any of these three alternatives. But how is such a preference possible?

A preference for holding money instead of spending it on consumption goods presents no serious difficulty, for it is obviously the ordinary case of a preference for future satisfactions over present. At any moment, an individual will not usually devote the whole of his available resources to satisfying present wants—a part will be set aside to meet the needs of the future.

The critical question arises when we look for an explanation of the preference for holding money rather than capital goods. For capital goods will ordinarily yield a positive rate of return, which money does not. What has to be explained is the decision to hold assets in the form of barren money, rather than of interest- or profit-yielding securities. And obviously just the same question arises over our second and third types of utilisation. So long as rates of interest are positive, the decision to hold money rather than lend it, or use it to pay off old debts, is apparently an unprofitable one.

This, as I see it, is really the central issue in the pure theory of money. Either we have to give an explanation of the fact that people do hold money when rates of interest are positive, or we have to evade the difficulty somehow. It is the great traditional evasions which have led to Velocities of Circulation, Natural Rates of Interest, *et id genus omne.*[1]

---

[1] I do not wish to deny that these concepts have a use in their appropriate place—that is to say, in particular applications of monetary theory. But it seems to me that

Of course, the great evaders would not have denied that there must be some explanation of the fact. But they would have put it down to "frictions," and since there was no adequate place for frictions in the rest of their economic theory, a theory of money based on frictions did not seem to them a promising field for economic analysis.

This is where I disagree. I think we have to look the frictions in the face, and see if they are really so refractory after all. This will, of course, mean that we cannot allow them to go to sleep under so vague a title.

III

The most obvious sort of friction, and undoubtedly one of the most important, is the cost of transferring assets from one form to another. This is of exactly the same character as the cost of transfer which acts as a certain impediment to change in all parts of the economic system; it doubtless comprises subjective elements as well as elements directly priced. Thus a person is deterred from investing money for short periods, partly because of brokerage charges and stamp duties, partly because it is not worth the bother.

The net advantage to be derived from investing a given quantity of money consists of the interest or profit earned less the cost of investment. It is only if this net advantage is expected to be positive (i.e. if the expected rate of interest ± capital appreciation or depreciation, is greater than the cost of investment) that it will pay to undertake the investment.

Now, since the expected interest increases both with the quantity of money to be invested and with the length of time for which it is expected that the investment will remain untouched, while the costs of investment are independent of the length of time, and (as a whole) will almost certainly increase at a diminishing rate as the quantity of money to be invested increases, it becomes clear that with any given level of costs of investment, it will not pay to invest money for less than a certain period, and in less than certain quantities. It will be profitable to hold assets for short periods, and in relatively small quantities, in monetary form.

Thus, so far as we can see at present, the amount of money a person will desire to hold depends upon three factors: the

they are a nuisance in monetary theory itself, that they offer no help in elucidating the general principles of the working of money.

dates at which he expects to make payments in the future, the cost of investment, and the expected rate of return on investment. The further ahead the future payments, the lower the cost of investment, and the higher the expected rate of return on invested capital—the lower will be the demand for money.

However, this statement is not quite accurate. For although all these factors may react on the demand for money, they may be insufficient to determine it closely. Since the quantity of available money must generally rise to some minimum before it is profitable to invest it at all, and further investment will then proceed by rather discontinuous jumps for a while, we shall expect to find the demand for money on the part of private individuals, excepting the very well-to-do, fairly insensitive to changes of this sort. But this does not mean that they are unimportant. For among those who are likely to be sensitive, we have to reckon, not only the well-to-do, but also all business men who are administering capital which is not solely their own private property. And this will give us, in total, a good deal of sensitivity.

IV

Our first list of factors influencing the demand for money—the expected rate of interest, the cost of investment, and the expected period of investment—does, therefore, isolate some factors which are really operative; but even so, it is not a complete list. For we have also to take into account the fact, which is in reality of such enormous importance, that people's expectations are never precise expectations of the kind we have been assuming. They do not say to themselves " this £100 I shall not want until June 1st " or " this investment will yield 3·7 per cent"; or, if they do, it is only a kind of shorthand. Their expectations are always, in fact, surrounded by a certain penumbra of doubt ; and the density of that penumbra is of immense importance for the problem we are considering.

The risk-factor comes into our problem in two ways : first, as affecting the expected period of investment; and second, as affecting the expected net yield of investment. There are certain differences between its ways of operation on these two lines ; but, as we shall see, the resultant effects are broadly similar.

Where risk is present, the *particular* expectation of a riskless situation is replaced by a band of possibilities, each of which is considered more or less probable. It is convenient to represent these probabilities to oneself, in statistical fashion, by a mean value, and some appropriate measure of dispersion. (No single measure will be wholly satisfactory, but here this difficulty may be overlooked.) Roughly speaking, we may assume that a change in mean value with constant dispersion has much the same sort of effect as a change in the particular expectations we have been discussing before. The peculiar problem of risk therefore reduces to an examination of the consequences of a change in dispersion. Increased dispersion means increased uncertainty.

If, therefore, our individual, instead of knowing (or thinking he knows) that he will not want his £100 till June 1st, becomes afflicted by increased uncertainty; that is to say, while still thinking that June 1st is the most likely date, he now thinks that it will be very possible that he will want it before, although it is also very possible that he will not want it till after ; what will be the effect on his conduct ? Let us suppose that when the date was certain, the investment was marginal—in the sense that the expected yield only just outweighed the cost of investment. With uncertainty introduced in the way we have described, the investment now offers a chance of larger gain, but it is offset by an equal chance of equivalent loss. In this situation, I think we are justified in assuming that he will become less willing to undertake the investment.

If this is so, uncertainty of the period for which money is free will ordinarily act as a deterrent to investment. It should be observed that uncertainty may be increased, either by a change in objective facts on which estimates are based, or in the psychology of the individual, if his temperament changes in such a way as to make him less inclined to bear risks.

To turn now to the other uncertainty—uncertainty of the yield of investment. Here again we have a penumbra; and here again we seem to be justified in assuming that spreading of the penumbra, increased dispersion of the possibilities of yield, will ordinarily be a deterrent to investment. Indeed, without assuming this to be the normal case, it would be impossible to explain some of the most obvious of the observed facts of the capital market. This sort of risk, therefore, will ordinarily be another factor tending to increase the demand for money.

V

So far the effect of risk seems fairly simple; an increase in the risk of investment will act like a fall in the expected rate of net yield; an increase in the uncertainty of future out-payments will act like a shortening of the time which is expected to elapse before those out-payments; and all will ordinarily tend to increase the demand for money. But although this is what it comes down to in the end, the detailed working of the risk-factor is not so simple; and since these further complications have an important bearing upon monetary problems, we cannot avoid discussing them here.

It is one of the peculiarities of risk that the total risk incurred when more than one risky investment is undertaken, does not bear any simple relation to the risk involved in each of the particular investments taken separately. In most cases, the " law of large numbers " comes into play (quite how, cannot be discussed here), so that the risk incurred by undertaking a number of separate risky investments will be less than that which would have been incurred if the same total capital had been invested altogether in one direction. When the number of separate investments is very large, the total risk may sometimes be reduced very low indeed.

Now in a world where cost of investment was negligible, everyone would be able to take considerable advantage of this sort of risk-reduction. By dividing up his capital into small portions, and spreading his risks, he would be able to insure himself against any large total risk on the whole amount. But in actuality, the cost of investment, making it definitely unprofitable to invest less than a certain minimum amount in any particular direction, closes the possibility of risk-reduction along these lines to all those who do not possess the command over considerable quantities of capital. This has two consequences.

On the one hand, since most people do not possess sufficient resources to enable them to take much advantage of the law of large numbers, and since even the large capitalist cannot annihilate his risks altogether in this manner, there will be a tendency to spread capital over a number of investments, not for this purpose, but for another. By investing only a proportion of total assets in risky enterprises, and investing the remainder in ways which are considered more safe, it will be possible for the individual to adjust his whole risk-situation to that which he most prefers, more closely than he could do by investing in any single enterprise. It will be possible, for example, for him to feel fairly certain that in particular unfavourable eventualities he will not lose more than a certain amount. And, since, both with an eye on future commitments with respect to debt, and future needs for consumption, large losses will lay upon him a proportionately heavier burden than small losses, this sort of adjustment to the sort of chance of loss he is prepared to stand will be very well worth while.

We shall, therefore, expect to find our representative individual distributing his assets among relatively safe and relatively risky investments; and the distribution will be governed, once again, by the objective facts upon which he bases his estimates of risk, and his subjective preference for much or little risk-bearing.

On the other hand, those persons who have command of large quantities of capital, and are able to spread their risks, are not only able to reduce the risk on their own capital fairly low—they are also able to offer very good security for the investment of an extra unit along with the rest. If, therefore, they choose to become borrowers, they are likely to be very safe borrowers. They can, therefore, provide the safe investments which their fellow-citizens need.

In the absence of such safe investments, the ordinary individual would be obliged to keep a very considerable proportion of his assets in monetary form, since money would be the only safe way of holding assets. The appearance of such safe investments will act as a substitute for money in one of its uses, and therefore diminish the demand for money.

This particular function is performed, in a modern community, not only by banks, but also by insurance companies, investment trusts, and, to a certain (perhaps small) extent, even by large concerns of other kinds, through their prior charges. And, of course, to a very large extent indeed, it is performed by government stock of various kinds.

Banks are simply the extreme case of this phenomenon ; they are enabled to go further than other concerns in the creation of money substitutes, because the security of their promises to pay is accepted generally enough for it to be possible to make payments in those promises. Bank deposits are, therefore, enabled to substitute money still further, because the cost of investment is reduced by a general belief in the absence of risk.

This is indeed a difference so great as to be properly regarded as a difference in kind ; but it is useful to observe that the creation of bank credit is not really different in its economic effects from the fundamentally similar activities of other businesses and other persons. The significant thing is that the person who deposits money with a bank does not notice any change in his liquidity position; he considers the bank deposit to be as liquid as cash. The bank, on the other hand, finds itself more liquid, if it retains the whole amount of the cash deposited; if it does not wish to be more liquid, but seeks (for example) to restore a conventional reserve ratio, it will have to increase its investments. But substantially the same sort of thing happens when anyone, whose credit is much above the average, borrows. Here the borrowing is nearly always a voluntary act on the part of the borrower, which would not be undertaken unless he was willing to become less liquid than before ; the fact that he has to pay interest on the loan means that he will be made worse off if he does not spend the proceeds. On the other hand, if the borrower's credit is good, the liquidity of the lender will not be very greatly impaired by his making the loan, so that his demand for money is likely to be at least rather less than it was before the loan was made. Thus the net effect of the loan is likely to be " inflationary," in the sense that the purchase of capital goods or securities by the borrower is likely to be a more important affair than any sale of capital goods or securities by the lender, made necessary in order for the lender to restore his liquidity position.

Does it follow that all borrowing and lending is inflationary in this sense ? I do not think so; for let us take the case when the borrower's credit is very bad, and the lender is only tempted to lend by the offer of a very high rate of interest. Then the impairment of the lender's liquidity position will be very considerable; and he may feel it necessary to sell rather less risky securities to an even greater capital sum in order to restore his liquidity position. Here the net effect would be " deflationary."

The practical conclusion of this seems to be that while *voluntary* borrowing and lending is at least a symptom of monetary expansion, and is thus likely to be accompanied by rising prices, " distress borrowing " is an exception to this rule; and it follows, further, that the sort of stimulation to lending, by persuading people to make loans which they would not have made without persuasion (which was rather a feature of certain phases of the world depression), is a dubious policy—for the lenders, perhaps without realising what they are doing, are very likely to try and restore their liquidity position, and so to offset, and perhaps more than offset, the expansive effects of the loan.

VI

It is now time for us to begin putting together the conclusions we have so far reached. Our method of analysis, it will have appeared, is simply an extension of the ordinary method of value theory. In value theory, we take a private individual's income and expenditure account; we ask which of the items in that account are under the individual's own control, and then how he will adjust these items in order to reach a most preferred position. On the production side, we make a similar analysis of the profit and loss account of the firm. My suggestion is that monetary theory needs to be based again upon a similar analysis, but this time, not of an income account, but of a capital account, a balance sheet. We have to concentrate on the forces which make assets and liabilities what they are.

So as far as banking theory is concerned, this is really the method which is currently adopted; though the essence of the problem is there somewhat obscured by the fact that banks, in their efforts to reach their " most preferred position " are hampered or assisted by the existence of conventional or legally obligatory reserve ratios. For theoretical purposes, this fact ought only to be introduced at a rather late stage; if that is done, then my suggestion can be expressed by saying that we ought to regard every individual in the community as being, on a small scale, a bank. Monetary theory becomes a sort of generalisation of banking theory.

We shall have to draw up a sort of generalised balance sheet, suitable for all individuals and institutions. It will have to be so generalised that many of the individual items will, in a great many cases, not appear. But that does not matter for our purposes. Such a generalised balance sheet will presumably run much as follows.

Assets.	*Liabilities.*
Consumption goods	
—perishable	
Consumption goods	
—durable	
Money	
Bank deposits	
Short term debts	Short term debts
Long term debts	Long term debts
Stocks and shares	
Productive equipment (in-	
cluding goods in process)	

We have been concerned up to the present with an analysis (very sketchy, I am afraid) of the equilibrium of this balance sheet. This analysis has at least shown that the relative size of the different items on this balance sheet is governed mainly by anticipation of the yield of investments and of risks.[1] It is these anticipations which play a part here corresponding to the part played by prices in value theory.[2]

Now the fact that our " equilibrium " is here determined by subjective factors like anticipations, instead of objective factors like prices, means that this purely theoretical study of money can never hope to reach results so tangible and precise as those which value theory in its more limited field can hope to attain. If I am right, the whole problem of applying monetary theory is largely one of deducing changes in antici-pations from the changes in objective data which call them forth. Obviously, this is not an easy task, and, above all, it is not one which can be performed in a mechanical fashion. It needs judgment and knowledge of business psychology much more than sustained logical reasoning. The arm-chair economist will be bad at it, but he can at least begin to realise

---

[1] As we have seen, these risks are as much a matter of the period of investment as of the yield. For certain purposes this is very important. Thus, in the case of that kind of investment which consists in the starting of actual processes of production, the yield which is expected if the process can be carried through may be considerable; but the yield if the process has to be interrupted will be large and negative. Uncertainty of the period for which resources are free will therefore have a very powerful effect in inter-rupting production. Short-run optimism will usually be enough to start a Stock Exchange boom ; but to start an industrial boom relatively long-run optimism is necessary.

[2] I am aware that too little is said in this paper about the liabilities side of the above balance sheet. A cursory examination suggests that the same forces which work through the assets side work through the liabilities side in much the same way. But this certainly requires further exploration.

B

the necessity for it, and learn to co-operate with those who can do it better than he can.

However, I am not fouling my own nest; I do not at all mean to suggest that economic theory comes here to the end of its resources. When once the connection between objective facts and anticipations has been made, theory comes again into its rights; and it will not be able to complain of a lack of opportunities.

Nevertheless, it does seem to me most important that, when considering these further questions, we should be well aware of the gap which lies behind us, and that we should bring out very clearly the assumptions which we are making about the genesis of anticipations. For this does seem to be the only way in which we can overcome the extraordinary theoretical differences of recent years, which are, I think very largely traceable to this source.

VII

Largely, but not entirely; or rather a good proportion of them seem to spring from a closely related source, which is yet not quite identical with the first. When we seek to apply to a changing world any particular sort of individual equilibrium, we need to know how the individual will respond, not only to changes in the price-stimuli, or anticipation-stimuli, but also to a change in his total wealth.[1] How will he distribute an increment (or decrement) of wealth—supposing, as we may suppose, that this wealth is measured in monetary terms ?

It may be observed that this second problem has an exact counterpart in value theory. Recent work in that field has shown the importance of considering carefully, not only how the individual reacts to price-changes, but also how he reacts to changes in his available expenditure. Total wealth, in our present problem, plays just the same part as total expenditure in the theory of value.

In the theory of money, what we particularly want to know is how the individual's demand for money will respond to a change in his total wealth—that is to say, in the value of his

[1] The amount of money demanded depends upon three groups of factors : (1) the individual's subjective preferences for holding money or other things ; (2) his wealth ; (3) his anticipations of future prices and risks. Changes in the demand for money affect present prices, but present prices affect the demand for money mainly through their effect on wealth and on price-anticipations.

net assets. Not seeing any *a priori* reason why he should react in one way rather than another, monetary theorists have often been content to make use of the simplest possible assumption—that the demand for money will be increased in the same proportion as total net assets have increased.[1] But this is a very arbitrary assumption; and it may be called in question, partly for analytical reasons, and partly because it seems to make the economic system work much too smoothly to account for observed fact. As one example of this excessive smoothness, I may instance the classical theory of international payments ; as another, Mr. Harrod's views on the " Expansion of Bank Credit " which have recently been interesting the readers of *Economica* and of the *Economist*.[2] It would hardly be too much to say that one observed fact alone is sufficient to prove that this assumption cannot be universally true (let us hope and pray that it is sometimes true, nevertheless) —the fact of the trade cycle. For if it were true, the monetary system would always exhibit a quite straightforward kind of stability; a diminished demand for money on the part of some people would raise the prices of capital goods and securities, and this would raise the demand for money on the part of the owners of those securities. Similarly an increased demand for money would lower prices, and this would lower the demand for money elsewhere. The whole thing would work out like an ordinary demand and supply diagram. But it is fairly safe to say that we do not find this straightforward stability in practice.

The analytical reason why this sort of analysis is unsatisfactory is the following: The assumption of increased wealth leading to a proportionately increased demand for money is only plausible so long as the value of assets has increased, but other things have remained equal. Now, as we have seen, the other things which are relevant to this case are not prices (as in the theory of value) but anticipations, of the yield of investment and so on. And since these anticipations must be based upon objective facts, and an unexpected increase in wealth implies a change in objective facts, of a sort very likely to be relevant to the anticipations, it is fairly safe to assume that

[1] Of course, they say " income." But in this case " income " can only be strictly interpreted as " expected income." And in most of the applications which are made, this works out in the same way as the assumption given above.

[2] The above was written before reading Mr. Harrod's rejoinder to Mr. Robertson. As I understand him, Mr. Harrod is now only maintaining that the expansion of bank credit *may* work smoothly. With that I am in no disagreement.

very many of the changes in wealth with which we are concerned will be accompanied by a change in anticipations. If
this is so, the assumption of proportionate change in the
demand for money loses most of its plausibility.

For if we assume (this is jumping over my gap, so I must
emphasise that it is only an assumption) that an increase in
wealth will very often be accompanied by an upward revision
of expectations of yield, then the change will set in motion
at least one tendency which is certain to diminish the demand
for money. Taking this into account *as well as* the direct
effect of the increase in wealth, the situation begins to look
much less clear. For it must be remembered that our provisional assumption about the direct effect was only guess-work;
there is no necessary reason why the direct effect should
increase the demand for money proportionately or even
increase it at all. So, putting the two together, it looks perfectly
possible that the demand for money may either increase or
diminish.

We are treading on thin ice; but the unpleasant possibilities
which now begin to emerge are sufficiently plausible for their
examination to be well worth while. What happens, to take a
typical case, if the demand for money is independent of changes
in wealth, so that neither an increase in wealth nor a diminu-
tion will affect the demand for money?

One can conceive of a sort of equilibrium in such a world,
but it would be a hopelessly unstable equilibrium. For if any
single person tried to increase his money holdings, and the
supply of money was not increased, prices would all fall to
zero. If any person tried to diminish his money holdings,
prices would all become infinite. In fact, of course, if demand
were so rigid, the system could only be kept going by a
continuous and meticulous adaptation of the supply of money
to the demand.

Further, in such a world, very curious results would follow
from saving. A sudden increase in saving would leave some
people (the owners of securities) with larger money balances
than they had expected; other people (the producers of consumption goods) with smaller money balances. If, in their
efforts to restore their money holdings, the owners of securities
buy more securities, and the producers of consumption goods
buy less consumption goods, a swing of prices, consumption
goods prices falling, security prices rising, would set in, and
might go on indefinitely. It could only be stopped, either by

the owners of securities buying the services of producers, or by the producers selling securities. But there is no knowing when this would happen, or where prices would finally settle; for the assumption of a rigid demand for money snaps the connecting link between money and prices.

After this, we shall be fairly inured to shocks. It will not surprise us to be told that wage-changes will avail nothing to stop either an inflation or a deflation, and we shall be able to extend the proposition for ourselves to interference with conventional or monopolistic prices of any kind, in any direction. But we shall be in a hurry to get back to business.

VIII

These exercises in the economics of an utterly unstable world give us something too mad to fit even our modern *Spätkapitalismus*; but the time which economists have spent on them will not have been wasted if they have served as a corrective to the too facile optimism engendered by the first assumption we tried. Obviously, what we want is something between the two—but not, I think, a mere splitting of the difference. This would give the assumption that an increase in wealth always raises the demand for money, but less than proportionately; if we had time, it might be profitable to work out this case in detail. It would allow for the possibility of considerable fluctuations, but they would not be such absurd and hopeless fluctuations as in the case of rigid demand.

However, I think we can do better than that. The assumption which seems to me most plausible, most consistent with the whole trend of our analysis, and at the same time to lead to results which at any rate look realistic, is one which stresses the probable differences in the reactions of different members of the community. We have already seen that a considerable proportion of a community's monetary stock is always likely to be in the hands of people who are obliged by their relative poverty to be fairly insensitive to changes in anticipations. For these people, therefore, most of the incentive to reduce their demand for money when events turn out more favourably will be missing; there seems no reason why we should not suppose that they will generally react " positively " to changes in their wealth—that an increase in wealth will raise their demand for money more or less proportionately, a fall in their wealth will diminish it. But we must also allow for the probability that other people are much more *sensitive*—that an increase in wealth is not particularly likely to increase their demand for money, and may very well diminish it.

If this is so, it would follow that where the sensitive trade together, price-fluctuations may start on very slight provocation; and once they are under way, the rather less sensitive would be enticed in. Stock exchange booms will pass over into industrial booms, if industrial entrepreneurs are also fairly sensitive; and, in exactly the same way, stock exchange depressions will pass into industrial depressions. But the insensitive are always there to act as a flywheel, defeating by their insensitivity both the exaggerated optimism and the exaggerated pessimism of the sensitive class. How this comes about I cannot attempt to explain in detail, though it would be an interesting job, for one might be able to reconcile a good many apparently divergent theories. But it would lead us too deeply into Cycle theory—I will only say that I think the period of fluctuation turns out to depend, in rather complex fashion, upon the distribution of sensitivity and the distribution of production periods between industrial units.

Instead, I may conclude with two general reflections.

If it is the insensitive people who preserve the stability of capitalism, people who are insensitive (you will remember) largely because for them the costs of transferring assets are large relatively to the amount of assets they control, then the development of capitalism, by diminishing these costs, is likely to be a direct cause of increasing fluctuations. It reduces costs in two ways: by technical devices (of which banks are only one example), and by instilling a more " capitalistic " spirit, which looks more closely to profit, and thus reduces subjective costs. In doing these things, capitalism is its own enemy, for it imperils that stability without which it breaks down.

Lastly, it seems to follow that when we are looking for policies which make for economic stability, we must not be led aside by a feeling that monetary troubles are due to " bad " economic policy, in the old sense, that all would go well if we reverted to free trade and *laisser-faire*. In so doing, we are no better than the Thebans who ascribed the plague to blood-guiltiness, or the supporters of Mr. Roosevelt who expect to reach recovery through reform. There is no reason why policies which tend to economic welfare, statically considered, should also tend to monetary stability. Indeed, the presumption is rather the other way round. A tariff, for example, may be a very good instrument of recovery on occasion, for precisely the reason which free-traders deplore; that it harms a great many people a little for the conspicuous benefit of a few. That may be just the sort of measure we want.

These will be unpalatable conclusions; but I think we must face the possibility that they are true. They offer the economist a pretty hard life, for he, at any rate, will not be able to have a clear conscience either way, over many of the alternatives he is called upon to consider. His ideals will conflict and he will not be able to seek an easy way out by sacrificing either.

[9]

MR. KEYNES AND THE "CLASSICS"; A SUGGESTED INTERPRETATION[1]

By J. R. HICKS

I

IT WILL BE ADMITTED by the least charitable reader that the entertainment value of Mr. Keynes' *General Theory of Employment* is considerably enhanced by its satiric aspect. But it is also clear that many readers have been left very bewildered by this Dunciad. Even if they are convinced by Mr. Keynes' arguments and humbly acknowledge themselves to have been "classical economists" in the past, they find it hard to remember that they believed in their unregenerate days the things Mr. Keynes says they believed. And there are no doubt others who find their historic doubts a stumbling block, which prevents them from getting as much illumination from the positive theory as they might otherwise have got.

One of the main reasons for this situation is undoubtedly to be found in the fact that Mr. Keynes takes as typical of "Classical economics" the later writings of Professor Pigou, particularly *The Theory of Unemployment*. Now *The Theory of Unemployment* is a fairly new book, and an exceedingly difficult book; so that it is safe to say that it has not yet made much impression on the ordinary teaching of economics. To most people its doctrines seem quite as strange and novel as the doctrines of Mr. Keynes himself; so that to be told that he has believed these things himself leaves the ordinary economist quite bewildered.

For example, Professor Pigou's theory runs, to a quite amazing extent, in real terms. Not only is his theory a theory of real wages and unemployment; but numbers of problems which anyone else would have preferred to investigate in money terms are investigated by Professor Pigou in terms of "wage-goods." The ordinary classical economist has no part in this *tour de force*.

But if, on behalf of the ordinary classical economist, we declare that he would have preferred to investigate many of those problems in money terms, Mr. Keynes will reply that there is no classical theory of money wages and employment. It is quite true that such a theory cannot easily be found in the textbooks. But this is only because most of the textbooks were written at a time when general changes in money wages in a closed system did not present an important problem. There can be little doubt that most economists have thought that they had

---

[1] Based on a paper which was read at the Oxford meeting of the Econometric Society (September, 1936) and which called forth an interesting discussion. It has been modified subsequently, partly in the light of that discussion, and partly as a result of further discussion in Cambridge.

a pretty fair idea of what the relation between money wages and employment actually was.

In these circumstances, it seems worth while to try to construct a typical "classical" theory, built on an earlier and cruder model than Professor Pigou's. If we can construct such a theory, and show that it does give results which have in fact been commonly taken for granted, but which do not agree with Mr. Keynes' conclusions, then we shall at last have a satisfactory basis of comparison. We may hope to be able to isolate Mr. Keynes' innovations, and so to discover what are the real issues in dispute.

Since our purpose is comparison, I shall try to set out my typical classical theory in a form similar to that in which Mr. Keynes sets out his own theory; and I shall leave out of account all secondary complications which do not bear closely upon this special question in hand. Thus I assume that I am dealing with a short period in which the quantity of physical equipment of all kinds available can be taken as fixed. I assume homogeneous labour. I assume further that depreciation can be neglected, so that the output of investment goods corresponds to new investment. This is a dangerous simplification, but the important issues raised by Mr. Keynes in his chapter on user cost are irrelevant for our purposes.

Let us begin by assuming that w, the rate of money wages per head, can be taken as given.

Let x, y, be the outputs of investment goods and consumption goods respectively, and N_x, N_y, be the numbers of men employed in producing them. Since the amount of physical equipment specialised to each industry is given, $x = f_x(N_x)$ and $y = f_y(N_y)$, where f_x, f_y, are *given* functions.

Let M be the *given* quantity of money.

It is desired to determine N_x and N_y.

First, the price-level of investment goods = their marginal cost = $w(dN_x/dx)$. And the price-level of consumption goods = their marginal cost = $w(dN_y/dy)$.

Income earned in investment trades (value of investment, or simply Investment) = $wx(dN_x/dx)$. Call this I_x.

Income earned in consumption trades = $wy(dN_y/dy)$.

Total Income = $wx(dN_x/dx) + wy(dN_y/dy)$. Call this I.

I_x is therefore a given function of N_x, I of N_x and N_y. Once I and I_x are determined, N_x and N_y can be determined.

Now let us assume the "Cambridge Quantity equation"—that there is some definite relation between Income and the demand for money. Then, approximately, and apart from the fact that the demand for money may depend not only upon total Income, but also upon its distribution between people with relatively large and relatively small demands for balances, we can write

$$M = kI.$$

As soon as k is given, total Income is therefore determined.

In order to determine I_x, we need two equations. One tells us that the amount of investment (looked at as demand for capital) depends upon the rate of interest:

$$I_x = C(i).$$

This is what becomes the marginal-efficiency-of-capital schedule in Mr. Keynes' work.

Further, Investment = Saving. And saving depends upon the rate of interest and, if you like, Income. $\therefore I_x = S(i, I)$. (Since, however, Income is already determined, we do not need to bother about inserting Income here unless we choose.)

Taking them as a system, however, we have three fundamental equations,

$$M = kI, \quad I_x = C(i), \quad I_x = S(i, I),$$

to determine three unknowns, I, I_x, i. As we have found earlier, N_x and N_y can be determined from I and I_x. Total employment, $N_x + N_y$, is therefore determined.

Let us consider some properties of this system. It follows directly from the first equation that as soon as k and M are given, I is completely determined; that is to say, total income depends directly upon the quantity of money. Total employment, however, is not necessarily determined at once from income, since it will usually depend to some extent upon the proportion of income saved, and thus upon the way production is divided between investment and consumption-goods trades. (If it so happened that the elasticities of supply were the same in each of these trades, then a shifting of demand between them would produce compensating movements in N_x and N_y, and consequently no change in total employment.)

An increase in the inducement to invest (i.e., a rightward movement of the schedule of the marginal efficiency of capital, which we have written as $C(i)$) will tend to raise the rate of interest, and so to affect saving. If the amount of saving rises, the amount of investment will rise too; labour will be employed more in the investment trades, less in the consumption trades; this will increase total employment if the elasticity of supply in the investment trades is greater than that in the consumption-goods trades—diminish it if *vice versa*.

An increase in the supply of money will necessarily raise total income, for people will increase their spending and lending until incomes have risen sufficiently to restore k to its former level. The rise in income will tend to increase employment, both in making consumption goods and in making investment goods. The total effect on employment depends upon the ratio between the expansions of these industries; and that depends upon the proportion of their increased incomes which people desire to save, which also governs the rate of interest.

So far we have assumed the rate of money wages to be given; but so long as we assume that k is independent of the level of wages, there is no difficulty about this problem either. A rise in the rate of money wages will necessarily diminish employment and raise real wages. For an unchanged money income cannot continue to buy an unchanged quantity of goods at a higher price-level; and, unless the price-level rises, the prices of goods will not cover their marginal costs. There must therefore be a fall in employment; as employment falls, marginal costs in terms of labour will diminish and therefore real wages rise. (Since a change in money wages is always accompanied by a change in real wages in the same direction, if not in the same proportion, no harm will be done, and some advantage will perhaps be secured, if one prefers to work in terms of real wages. Naturally most "classical economists" have taken this line.)

I think it will be agreed that we have here a quite reasonably consistent theory, and a theory which is also consistent with the pronouncements of a recognizable group of economists. Admittedly it follows from this theory that you may be able to increase employment by direct inflation; but whether or not you decide to favour that policy still depends upon your judgment about the probable reaction on wages, and also—in a national area—upon your views about the international standard.

Historically, this theory descends from Ricardo, though it is not actually Ricardian; it is probably more or less the theory that was held by Marshall. But with Marshall it was already beginning to be qualified in important ways; his successors have qualified it still further. What Mr. Keynes has done is to lay enormous emphasis on the qualifications, so that they almost blot out the original theory. Let us follow out this process of development.

II

When a theory like the "classical" theory we have just described is applied to the analysis of industrial fluctuations, it gets into difficulties in several ways. It is evident that total money income experiences great variations in the course of a trade cycle, and the classical theory can only explain these by variations in M or in k, or, as a third and last alternative, by changes in distribution.

(1) Variation in M is simplest and most obvious, and has been relied

on to a large extent. But the variations in M that are traceable during a trade cycle are variations that take place through the banks—they are variations in bank loans; if we are to rely on them it is urgently necessary for us to explain the connection between the supply of bank money and the rate of interest. This can be done roughly by thinking of banks as persons who are strongly inclined to pass on money by lending rather than spending it. Their action therefore tends at first to lower interest rates, and only afterwards, when the money passes into the hands of spenders, to raise prices and incomes. "The new currency, or the increase of currency, goes, not to private persons, but to the banking centers; and therefore, it increases the willingness of lenders to lend in the first instance, and lowers the rate of discount. But it afterwards raises prices; and therefore it tends to increase discount."[2] This is superficially satisfactory; but if we endeavoured to give a more precise account of this process we should soon get into difficulties. What determines the amount of money needed to produce a given fall in the rate of interest? What determines the length of time for which the low rate will last? These are not easy questions to answer.

(2) In so far as we rely upon changes in k, we can also do well enough up to a point. Changes in k can be related to changes in confidence, and it is realistic to hold that the rising prices of a boom occur because optimism encourages a reduction in balances; the fa'ling prices of a slump because pessimism and uncertainty dictate an increase. But as soon as we take this step it becomes natural to ask whether k has not abdicated its status as an independent variable, and has not become liable to be influenced by others among the variables in our fundamental equations.

(3) This last consideration is powerfully supported by another, of more purely theoretical character. On grounds of pure value theory, it is evident that the direct sacrifice made by a person who holds a stock of money is a sacrifice of interest; and it is hard to believe that the marginal principle does not operate at all in this field. As Lavington put it: "The quantity of resources which (an individual) holds in the form of money will be such that the unit of money which is just and only just worth while holding in this form yields him a return of convenience and security equal to the yield of satisfaction derived from the marginal unit spent on consumables, and equal also to the net rate of interest."[3] The demand for money depends upon the rate of interest! The stage is set for Mr. Keynes.

[2] Marshall, *Money, Credit, and Commerce*, p. 257.
[3] Lavington, *English Capital Market*, 1921, p. 30. See also Pigou, "The Exchange-value of Legal-tender Money," in *Essays in Applied Economics*, 1922, pp. 179–181.

As against the three equations of the classical theory,

$$M = kI, \quad I_x = C(i), \quad I_x = S(i, I),$$

Mr. Keynes begins with three equations,

$$M = L(i), \quad I_x = C(i), \quad I_x = S(I).$$

These differ from the classical equations in two ways. On the one hand, the demand for money is conceived as depending upon the rate of interest (Liquidity Preference). On the other hand, any possible influence of the rate of interest on the amount saved out of a given income is neglected. Although it means that the third equation becomes the multiplier equation, which performs such queer tricks, nevertheless this second amendment is a mere simplification, and ultimately insignificant.[4] It is the liquidity preference doctrine which is vital.

For it is now the rate of interest, not income, which is determined by the quantity of money. The rate of interest set against the schedule of the marginal efficiency of capital determines the value of investment; that determines income by the multiplier. Then the volume of employment (at given wage-rates) is determined by the value of investment and of income which is not saved but spent upon consumption goods.

It is this system of equations which yields the startling conclusion, that an increase in the inducement to invest, or in the propensity to consume, will not tend to raise the rate of interest, but only to increase employment. In spite of this, however, and in spite of the fact that quite a large part of the argument runs in terms of this system, and this system alone, *it is not the General Theory*. We may call it, if we like, Mr. Keynes' *special theory*. The General Theory is something appreciably more orthodox.

Like Lavington and Professor Pigou, Mr. Keynes does not in the end believe that the demand for money can be determined by one variable alone—not even the rate of interest. He lays more stress on it than they did, but neither for him nor for them can it be the only variable to be considered. The dependence of the demand for money on interest does not, in the end, do more than qualify the old de-

---

[4] This can be readily seen if we consider the equations

$$M = kI, \quad I_x = C(i), \quad I_x = S(I),$$

which embody Mr. Keynes' second amendment without his first. The third equation is already the multiplier equation, but the multiplier is shorn of his wings. For since I still depends only on M, I_x now depends only on M, and it is impossible to increase investment without increasing the willingness to save or the quantity of money. The system thus generated is therefore identical with that which, a few years ago, used to be called the "Treasury View." But Liquidity Preference transports us from the "Treasury View" to the "General Theory of Employment."

pendence on income. However much stress we lay upon the "speculative motive," the "transactions" motive must always come in as well.

Consequently we have for the General Theory

$$M = L(I, i), \quad I_x = C(i), \quad I_x = S(I).$$

With this revision, Mr. Keynes takes a big step back to Marshallian orthodoxy, and his theory becomes hard to distinguish from the revised and qualified Marshallian theories, which, as we have seen, are not new. Is there really any difference between them, or is the whole thing a sham fight? Let us have recourse to a diagram (Figure 1).

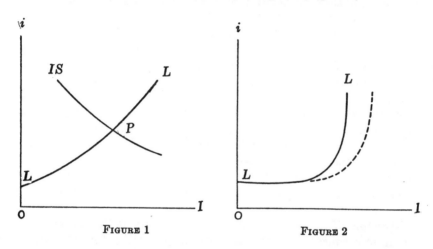

FIGURE 1   FIGURE 2

Against a given quantity of money, the first equation, $M = L(I, i)$, gives us a relation between Income (I) and the rate of interest (i). This can be drawn out as a curve (LL) which will slope upwards, since an increase in income tends to raise the demand for money, and an increase in the rate of interest tends to lower it. Further, the second two equations taken together give us another relation between Income and interest. (The marginal-efficiency-of-capital schedule determines the value of investment at any given rate of interest, and the multiplier tells us what level of income will be necessary to make savings equal to that value of investment.) The curve IS can therefore be drawn showing the relation between Income and interest which must be maintained in order to make saving equal to investment.

Income and the rate of interest are now determined together at P, the point of intersection of the curves LL and IS. They are determined together; just as price and output are determined together in the modern theory of demand and supply. Indeed, Mr. Keynes' innovation is closely parallel, in this respect, to the innovation of the marginalists.

The quantity theory tries to determine income without interest, just as the labour theory of value tried to determine price without output; each has to give place to a theory recognising a higher degree of inter-dependence.

III

But if this is the real "General Theory," how does Mr. Keynes come to make his remarks about an increase in the inducement to invest not raising the rate of interest? It would appear from our diagram that a rise in the marginal-efficiency-of-capital schedule must raise the curve IS; and, therefore, although it will raise Income and employment, it will also raise the rate of interest.

This brings us to what, from many points of view, is the most important thing in Mr. Keynes' book. It is not only possible to show that a given supply of money determines a certain relation between Income and interest (which we have expressed by the curve LL); it is also possible to say something about the shape of the curve. It will probably tend to be nearly horizontal on the left, and nearly vertical on the right. This is because there is (1) some minimum below which the rate of interest is unlikely to go, and (though Mr. Keynes does not stress this) there is (2) a maximum to the level of income which can possibly be financed with a given amount of money. If we like we can think of the curve as approaching these limits asymptotically (Figure 2).

Therefore, if the curve IS lies well to the right (either because of a strong inducement to invest or a strong propensity to consume), P will lie upon that part of the curve which is decidedly upward sloping, and the classical theory will be a good approximation, needing no more than the qualification which it has in fact received at the hands of the later Marshallians. An increase in the inducement to invest will raise the rate of interest, as in the classical theory, but it will also have some subsidiary effect in raising income, and therefore employment as well. (Mr. Keynes in 1936 is not the first Cambridge economist to have a temperate faith in Public Works.) But if the point P lies to the left of the LL curve, then the *special* form of Mr. Keynes' theory becomes valid. A rise in the schedule of the marginal efficiency of capital only increases employment, and does not raise the rate of interest at all. We are completely out of touch with the classical world.

The demonstration of this minimum is thus of central importance. It is so important that I shall venture to paraphrase the proof, setting it out in a rather different way from that adopted by Mr. Keynes.[5]

If the costs of holding money can be neglected, it will always be

---

[5] Keynes, *General Theory*, pp. 201–202.

profitable to hold money rather than lend it out, if the rate of interest is not greater than zero. Consequently the rate of interest must always be positive. In an extreme case, the shortest short-term rate may perhaps be nearly zero. But if so, the long-term rate must lie above it, for the long rate has to allow for the risk that the short rate may rise during the currency of the loan, and it should be observed that the short rate can only rise, it cannot fall.[6] This does not only mean that the long rate must be a sort of average of the probable short rates over its duration, and that this average must lie above the current short rate. There is also the more important risk to be considered, that the lender on long term may desire to have cash before the agreed date of repayment, and then, if the short rate has risen meanwhile, he may be involved in a substantial capital loss. It is this last risk which provides Mr. Keynes' "speculative motive" and which ensures that the rate for loans of indefinite duration (which he always has in mind as *the* rate of interest) cannot fall very near zero.[7]

It should be observed that this minimum to the rate of interest applies not only to one curve *LL* (drawn to correspond to a particular quantity of money) but to any such curve. If the supply of money is increased, the curve *LL* moves to the right (as the dotted curve in Figure 2), but the horizontal parts of the curve are almost the same. Therefore, again, it is this doldrum to the left of the diagram which upsets the classical theory. If *IS* lies to the right, then we can indeed increase employment by increasing the quantity of money; but if *IS* lies to the left, we cannot do so; merely monetary means will not force down the rate of interest any further.

So the General Theory of Employment is the Economics of Depression.

[6] It is just conceivable that people might become so used to the idea of very low short rates that they would not be much impressed by this risk; but it is very unlikely. For the short rate may rise, either because trade improves, and income expands; or because trade gets worse, and the desire for liquidity increases. I doubt whether a monetary system so elastic as to rule out both of these possibilities is really thinkable.

[7] Nevertheless something more than the "speculative motive" is needed to account for the system of interest rates. The shortest of all short rates must equal the relative valuation, at the margin, of money and such a bill; and the bill stands at a discount mainly because of the "convenience and security" of holding money—the inconvenience which may possibly be caused by not having cash immediately available. It is the chance that you may want to discount the bill which matters, not the chance that you will then have to discount it on unfavourable terms. The "precautionary motive," not the "speculative motive," is here dominant. But the prospective terms of rediscounting are vital, when it comes to the *difference* between short and long rates.

IV

In order to elucidate the relation between Mr. Keynes and the "Classics," we have invented a little apparatus. It does not appear that we have exhausted the uses of that apparatus, so let us conclude by giving it a little run on its own.

With that apparatus at our disposal, we are no longer obliged to make certain simplifications which Mr. Keynes makes in his exposition. We can reinsert the missing i in the third equation, and allow for any possible effect of the rate of interest upon saving; and, what is much more important, we can call in question the sole dependence of invest- ment upon the rate of interest, which looks rather suspicious in the second equation. Mathematical elegance would suggest that we ought to have I and i in all three equations, if the theory is to be really General. Why not have them there like this:

$$M = L(I, i), \quad I_z = C(I, i), \quad I_z = S(I, i)?$$

Once we raise the question of Income in the second equation, it is clear that it has a very good claim to be inserted. Mr. Keynes is in fact only enabled to leave it out at all plausibly by his device of measur- ing everything in "wage-units," which means that he allows for changes in the marginal-efficiency-of-capital schedule when there is a change in the level of money wages, but that other changes in Income are deemed not to affect the curve, or at least not in the same immediate manner. But why draw this distinction? Surely there is every reason to suppose that an increase in the demand for consumers' goods, arising from an increase in employment, will often directly stimulate an increase in investment, at least as soon as an expectation develops that the in- creased demand will continue. If this is so, we ought to include I in the second equation, though it must be confessed that the effect of I on the marginal efficiency of capital will be fitful and irregular.

The Generalized General Theory can then be set out in this way. Assume first of all a given total money Income. Draw a curve CC showing the marginal efficiency of capital (in money terms) at that given Income; a curve SS showing the supply curve of saving at that *given* Income (Figure 3). Their intersection will determine the rate of interest which makes savings equal to investment at that level of in- come. This we may call the "investment rate."

If Income rises, the curve SS will move to the right; probably CC will move to the right too. If SS moves more than CC, the investment rate of interest will fall; if CC more than SS, it will rise. (How much it rises and falls, however, depends upon the elasticities of the CC and SS curves.)

The IS curve (drawn on a separate diagram) now shows the relation between Income and the corresponding investment rate of interest. It has to be confronted (as in our earlier constructions) with an *LL* curve showing the relation between Income and the "money" rate of interest; only we can now generalise our *LL* curve a little. Instead of assuming, as before, that the supply of money is given, we can assume that there is a given monetary system—that up to a point, but only up to a point, monetary authorities will prefer to create new money rather than allow interest rates to rise. Such a generalised *LL* curve will then slope upwards only gradually—the elasticity of the curve depending on the elasticity of the monetary system (in the ordinary monetary sense).

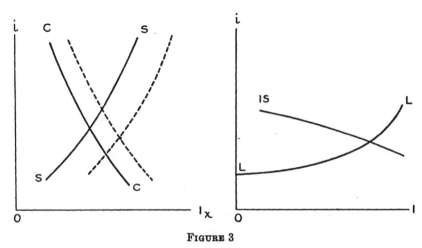

FIGURE 3

As before, Income and interest are determined where the *IS* and *LL* curves intersect—where the investment rate of interest equals the money rate. Any change in the inducement to invest or the propensity to consume will shift the *IS* curve; any change in liquidity preference or monetary policy will shift the *LL* curve. If, as the result of such a change, the investment rate is raised above the money rate, Income will tend to rise; in the opposite case, Income will tend to fall; the extent to which Income rises or falls depends on the elasticities of the curves.[8]

[8] Since $C(I, i) = S(I, i)$,
$$\frac{dI}{di} = - \frac{\partial S/\partial i - \partial C/\partial i}{\partial S/\partial I - \partial C/\partial I}.$$

The savings investment market will not be stable unless $\partial S/\partial i + (-\partial C/\partial i)$ is positive. I think we may assume that this condition is fulfilled.

If $\partial S/\partial i$ is positive, $\partial C/\partial i$ negative, $\partial S/\partial I$ and $\partial C/\partial I$ positive (the most probable state of affairs), we can say that the *IS* curve will be more elastic, the

When generalised in this way, Mr. Keynes' theory begins to look very like Wicksell's; this is of course hardly surprising.[9] There is indeed one special case where it fits Wicksell's construction absolutely. If there is "full employment" in the sense that any rise in Income immediately calls forth a rise in money wage rates; then it is *possible* that the *CC* and *SS* curves may be moved to the right to exactly the same extent, so that *IS* is horizontal. (I say possible, because it is not unlikely, in fact, that the rise in the wage level may create a presumption that wages will rise again later on; if so, *CC* will probably be shifted more than *SS*, so that *IS* will be upward sloping.) However that may be, if *IS* is horizontal, we do have a perfectly Wicksellian construction;[10] the investment rate becomes Wicksell's *natural rate* for in this case it may be thought of as determined by real causes; if there is a perfectly elastic monetary system, and the money rate is fixed below the natural rate, there is cumulative inflation; cumulative deflation if it is fixed above.

This, however, is now seen to be only one special case; we can use our construction to harbour much wider possibilities. If there is a great deal of unemployment, it is very likely that $\partial C/\partial I$ will be quite small; in that case *IS* can be relied upon to slope downwards. This is the sort of Slump Economics with which Mr. Keynes is largely concerned. But one cannot escape the impression that there may be other conditions when expectations are tinder, when a slight inflationary tendency lights them up very easily. Then $\partial C/\partial I$ may be large and an increase in Income tend to *raise* the investment rate of interest. In these circumstances, the situation is unstable at *any* given money rate; it is only an imperfectly elastic monetary system—a rising *LL* curve—that can prevent the situation getting out of hand altogether.

These, then, are a few of the things we can get out of our skeleton apparatus. But even if it may claim to be a slight extension of Mr. Keynes' similar skeleton, it remains a terribly rough and ready sort of affair. In particular, the concept of "Income" is worked monstrously hard; most of our curves are not really determinate unless something is said about the distribution of Income as well as its magnitude. Indeed, what they express is something like a relation between the price-system and the system of interest rates; and you cannot get that into a curve. Further, all sorts of questions about depreciation have been neglected; and all sorts of questions about the timing of the processes under consideration.

---

greater the elasticities of the *CC* and *SS* curves, and the larger is $\partial C/\partial I$ relatively to $\partial S/\partial I$. When $\partial C/\partial I > \partial S/\partial I$, the *IS* curve is upward sloping.

[9] Cf. Keynes, *General Theory*, p. 242.

[10] Cf. Myrdal, "Gleichgewichtsbegriff," in *Beiträge zur Geldtheorie*, ed. Hayek.

The *General Theory of Employment* is a useful book; but it is neither the beginning nor the end of Dynamic Economics.

J. R. HICKS

Gonville and Caius College
  Cambridge

[10]

INVESTMENT DECISION UNDER UNCERTAINTY: APPLICATIONS OF THE STATE-PREFERENCE APPROACH

J. HIRSHLEIFER

An earlier article [1] examined alternative approaches to the problem of investment decision under uncertainty. It was shown there that the various formulations differ essentially in specifying the *objects of choice* (commodities). Two such specifications were reviewed in detail: (1) The *mean, variability* approach — this reduces the assets or securities traded in the market to underlying objects of choice in the form of mean-return and variability-of-return measures which, it is alleged, enter into investors' preference functions.[2] (2) The *state-preference* (or, more fully, *time-state-preference*) approach — which resolves the assets or securities into distributions of dated contingent claims to income defined over the set of all possible "states of the world." [3]

The predecessor article showed that the more familiar mean, variability formulation has never been completed so as to constitute an acceptable choice-theoretic structure. If mean-return and variability-of-return are to be regarded as commodities, the analysis must go beyond the individual level of decision to show how the relative "prices" for mean-return and variability-of-return are determined in the market. There seem to be rather considerable difficulties facing theorists who attempt to fulfill this program.[4] In contrast, the state-preference approach was demonstrated to be the

1. Investment Decision Under Uncertainty: Choice-Theoretic Approaches," this *Journal*, LXXIX (Nov. 1965).
2. The most complete development is in H.M. Markowitz, *Portfolio Selection* (New York: Wiley, 1959); see also D.E. Farrar, *The Investment Decision Under Uncertainty* (Englewood Cliffs, N.J.: Prentice-Hall, 1962).
3. See K. J. Arrow, "The Role of Securities in the Optimal Allocation of Risk-Bearing," *Review of Economic Studies*, XXI (April 1964); G. Debreu, *Theory of Value* (New York: Wiley, 1959), Chap. 7; J. Hirshleifer, "Efficient Allocation of Capital in an Uncertain World," *American Economic Review*, LIV (May 1964), 77–85.
4. The furthest development to date seems to be that of W. F. Sharpe, "Capital Asset Prices: A Theory of Market Equilibrium Under Conditions of Risk," *Journal of Finance*, XIX (Sept. 1964). This may be regarded as a theory of prices for mean and variability in the "very short run," with fixed supplies of productive and financial assets.

INVESTMENT DECISION UNDER UNCERTAINTY   253

natural generalization of Fisher's theory of intertemporal choice,[5] into the domain of uncertainty. Where Fisher's objects of choice are titles to consumption as of differing dates, the generalization takes the fundamental commodities, underlying all market assets, to be contingent time-state claims — titles to consumption for speci-fied dates and states of the world. While various assets may package these underlying claims into more or less complex bundles, the "mar-ket-clearing" or "conservation" equations determine prices for the elementary time-state claims to which asset prices must conform. The idealizing assumptions, necessary for this formal theoretical structure to hold, are in some respects akin to those of standard theory in requiring a kind of precision of knowledge or belief as to preferences and opportunities that is only very approximately true of the real world. Thus, the theory that results contains uncertainty, imperfect knowledge as to the state of the world that will actually obtain in the future, but does not contain the "vagueness" we usually find psychologically associated with uncertainty.

The present article is devoted to an examination of some im-plications and applications of the time-state-preference approach, that reveal its power by casting light upon a number of unresolved controversies. These include: (1) the nature and extent of risk aversion; (2) whether there is an optimal "debt-equity mix" in financing corporate undertakings (the Modigliani-Miller problem); and (3) the "appropriate" rate of discount to employ in cost-benefit calculations for government investments not subject to the market test.

In the very simplest illustration of time-state-preference, there is one commodity ("corn"), only one possible current state (i.e., the *present* is certain), and just two possible and mutually exclusive future states. The objects of choice then can be symbolized: c_0, c_{1a}, c_{1b} — present titles to consumption of, respectively, current or time-0 corn, corn at time-1 provided that state a obtains, and corn at time-1 provided that state b obtains. Each individual has an endowment of such claims, has preference relations ordering the combinations he could possibly hold,[6] and has certain opportunities for transform-ing his endowed bundle into alternative combinations. The possible transformations can take the form of market trading ("financial opportunities") or else of physical conversions ("productive oppor-

---

5. Irving Fisher, *The Theory of Interest* (New York: Macmillan, 1930; reprinted, Augustus M. Kelley, 1955).
6. Note that he can *hold* present claims or titles to both c_{1a} and c_{1b}, although he cannot ultimately *consume* both since only one of the two states will actually obtain.

tunities") — transactions in the one case with other individuals, in
the other case with Nature.

I. State Preference, Risk Aversion, and the Utility-of-Income Function

In this section we restrict ourselves to synchronous choice among
claims to consumption in alternative future states; i.e., we are isolating the problem of risky choice from the problem of time choice.
Under these circumstances the individual's situation may be portrayed as in Figure I, which shows an indifference map and financial

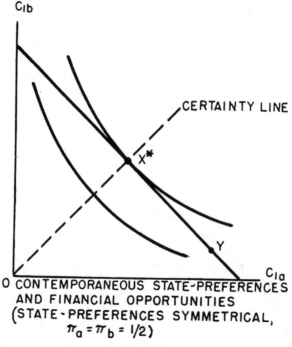

FIGURE I

or market opportunities for converting endowment Y into alternative combinations of c_{1a} and c_{1b}. The assumption here is that the
state probabilities $\pi_a = \pi_b = \frac{1}{2}$. The wealth constraint upon the
market opportunities can be written $W = P_0c_0 + P_{1a}c_{1a} + P_{1b}c_{1b}$,
where P_0, P_{1a}, and P_{1b} are the prices of the respective time-state
claims, with c_0 here taken to be a constant holding of current corn.
The wealth is in turn fixed by the value of the endowment: $W = P_0y_0$

INVESTMENT DECISION UNDER UNCERTAINTY 255

$+ P_{1a}y_{1a} + P_{1b}y_{1b}$ — where the y's represent elements of the endowment vector. The 45° "certainty line" connects combinations for which $c_{1a} = c_{1b}$.

The convexity of the indifference curves between the commodities c_{1a} and c_{1b}, which corresponds to one concept of *risk aversion*, may be justified by appeal to the general principle of diminishing marginal rate of substitution that holds for ordinary commodities. A more convincing defense, perhaps, is the observation of "non-specialization" — that individuals almost universally prefer to hedge against many contingencies rather than place all their bets on one. It is of interest to relate this formulation to the Neumann-Morgenstern utility-of-income function $v(c_1)$ that permits use of the expected-utility theorem in rationalizing risky choice.[7] It was shown in the predecessor article that a concave $v(c_1)$ function, as plotted in Figure II ("diminishing marginal utility of consumption income") is equivalent to a convex indifference map as in Figure I. In addition, the rather strong theorem was obtained that under these con-

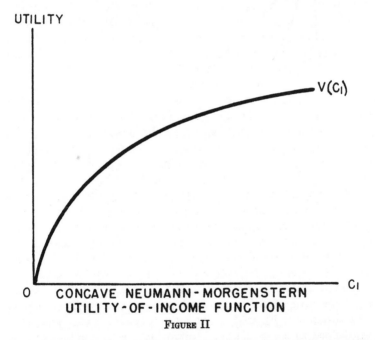

UTILITY

$v(c_1)$

O   CONCAVE NEUMANN-MORGENSTERN
     UTILITY-OF-INCOME FUNCTION
C_1

FIGURE II

7. As discussed, for example, in M. Friedman and L. J. Savage, "The Utility Analysis of Choices Involving Risk," *Journal of Political Economy,* LVI (Aug. 1948). Reprinted in American Economic Association, *Readings in Price Theory* (Homewood, Ill.: Irwin, 1952). Page references are to the latter volume.

ditions, if the probability ratio for the two states π_b/π_a is equal to the price ratio P_{1b}/P_{1a}, the individual's optimum must be on the certainty line. This is completely consistent with the Friedman-Savage formulation in terms of the Neumann-Morgenstern function, which under the same conditions leads to the conclusions that a fair gamble would not be accepted and that the individual would be willing to insure at fair odds.[8]

However, one observes in the world instances of risk-preferring behavior. Some gambles are accepted at fair, or even adverse odds. We will be considering in this section alternative explanations for this phenomenon. First, however, it is necessary to clarify one point on which error is often committed. Whether a particular contract is a *gamble* — i.e., an arrangement moving the individual farther from the 45° certainty line — or a particular asset a risky one depends not upon the terms of the contract or the nature of the asset in isolation but upon the individual's total portfolio and endowed position. While common stocks are often regarded as riskier than bonds, their purchase may stabilize an overall portfolio with respect to the hazard of inflation; i.e., may move an investor *closer* to the 45° line. Similarly, for some individuals a futures contract may be very risky, but for a hedger the same contract is "insurance" rather than a gamble. The hedger, of course, is someone who starts with a risky endowment — i.e., he has an unbalanced endowed state-distribution of income — and a contract with an *offsettingly* uneven state-distribution of return serves to bring him nearer the certainty line.

The predecessor article also showed that it was possible, by relaxing the assumption of *uniqueness* of the Neumann-Morgenstern $v(c_1)$ function, to combine convex indifference curves with solutions at fair odds that are off the 45° line (see Figure III). The assumption of a single $v(c_1)$ function implies a symmetry as to state preferences such that — adjusting for probabilities — marginal incomes, at any given level of income, are valued equivalently in all states. But since the definition of a state of the world incorporates a description of an entire world-environment, there may well be "nonpecuniary" aspects of the respective situations that would warrant biasing the pecuniary-wealth position at fair odds. There would then be a different $v(c_1)$ function for each state, as portrayed for the two-state situation in Figure IV, where the functions $v_a(c_{1a})$ and $v_b(c_{1b})$ are defined so as to continue permitting the use of the expected-utility theorem to rationalize uncertain choice. This relaxation leads to the conclusion that basically conservative behavior is still consis-

8. *Ibid.*, pp. 73–77.

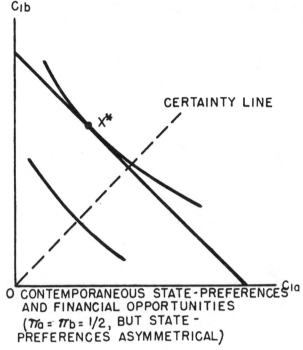

FIGURE III

tent with a certain amount of seeming risk preference — the risk preference being a kind of illusion due to looking only at the *pecuniary* income distribution. Still, this explanation hardly accounts for what we observe at Las Vegas, though it may tell us why bachelors commonly do not buy life insurance.[9]

A different explanation for the observed mixture of risk-avoiding and risk-preferring behavior has been offered by Friedman and Savage. They argue that in economic activities such as choices of occupation, business undertakings, and purchases of securities and real property, people generally prefer both low-risk and high-risk activities to moderate-risk activities. This is, assertedly, evidenced by relatively low realized average return (after allowance for unsuccessful as well as successful outcomes) on the former categories

9. While a responsible family man in his current decisions will attach considerable significance to income for his beneficiaries contingent upon his own death, a bachelor with only remote heirs has very asymmetrical state-preferences with respect to income accruing to him under the contingencies "Alive" or "Dead."

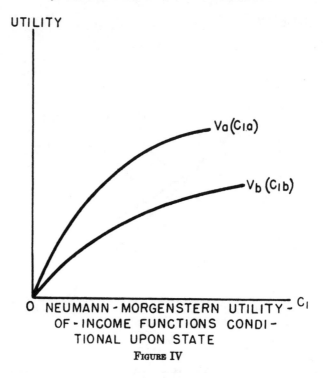

NEUMANN-MORGENSTERN UTILITY-OF-INCOME FUNCTIONS CONDITIONAL UPON STATE

FIGURE IV

as compared with the latter.[1] To explain this, and certain other observed behavior patterns — of which the most significant is the simultaneous purchase of insurance and lottery tickets by low-income individuals — Friedman and Savage construct a Neumann-Morgenstern utility-of-income function of the special shape [2] illustrated in Figure V.

This doubly-inflected curve has a concave segment at the low-income end, a convex segment for middle incomes, and finally another concave segment at the high-income end. For a lottery with only two outcomes, the relative desirability of taking or refusing the lottery is found by comparing the height along the straight line connecting the utilities of the outcomes (i.e., the expected utility of the lottery) with the height of the corresponding point along the doubly-inflected curve — the utility of the certain income alternative. If the lottery is fair, the corresponding points are vertically aligned.[3]

1. Friedman and Savage, *op. cit.*, pp. 63–66.
2. *Ibid.*, p. 85.
3. Justifications of these assertions are omitted because of their familiarity and availability in the cited source. The key to the proofs is the use of the expected-utility principle for risky outcomes.

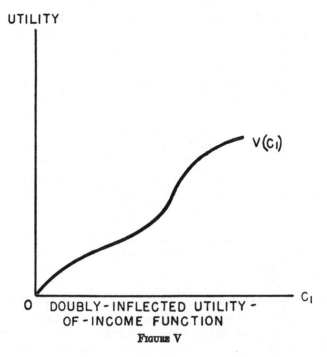

DOUBLY-INFLECTED UTILITY -
OF-INCOME FUNCTION

FIGURE V

The following may then be inferred: (1) For individuals in the middle convex segment, small-scale fair lotteries at roughly even odds (e.g., bets on heads in tosses of a coin) are preferred to certainties, become increasingly desirable as the scale of the lottery increases up to a point, after which as scale increases further the lotteries become decreasingly desirable. (2) Low-income individuals, especially if they are toward the upper end of the initial concave segment, would be inclined to buy fair "long-shot" lotteries, giving them at low cost a small chance at a relatively big prize. On the other hand, if they find themselves subject to a hazard threatening (though with low probability) a relatively large loss, they will be inclined to escape it by purchasing insurance at fair odds. (3) High-income individuals, especially if toward the lower end of their concave segment, will be inclined to bet heavily at fair odds on "short shots" (strong favorites, offering a large chance of a small gain and a small chance of a great loss) and, what amounts to the same thing, they will be inclined to avoid purchasing insurance.

Following the lead of Friedman and Savage, testable inferences can be derived if we interpret the three segments as corresponding at least roughly to three income classes. The behavior implied for the low-income class (most particularly, as we have noted, for the upper end of the low-income segment) is to some extent verified by common observation: many poor people place long-shot bets, and many purchase insurance to protect their modest sources of wealth. Actually, the data cited by Friedman-Savage [4] indicate that poorer people buy proportionately *less* insurance than other income groups; furthermore, the fraction of families purchasing insurance seems to rise smoothly with income. There is thus no indication of a risk-preferring middle segment. This evidence does not, therefore, support their position as against the alternative hypothesis of general risk aversion. The smaller purchases by poorer people may, perhaps, be explained away as due to relatively heavier transactions costs on smaller policies (leading to adverse "loading" of rates) or to possession of fewer insurable assets in proportion to income.

The behavior implied by the Friedman-Savage hypothesis for the upper-income group seems somewhat strange. Do we really see rich people failing to insure their *major* sources of wealth [5] — or, correspondingly, do we commonly observe them hazarding major sums on short-odds bets? [6] A possible defense here would be to bring in the asymmetrical income-tax treatment of gambling and casualty gains and losses, and the favorable treatment of insurance reserves — all of which combine to induce rich people to insure more and to gamble less than they otherwise would. On the other hand, it seems doubtful whether conservative behavior in these respects was really uncharacteristic of rich people even before the income tax.

But the crucial failure of the Friedman-Savage model lies in its implied behavior for the middle classes. This group, if they behaved as pictured, would be plungers of an extreme sort. They would stand ready, at any moment, to accept at fair odds a gamble of such a scale as to thrust them out of the convex segment and into (depending on the outcome) the poor-man or rich-man class. In addition, as we have remarked, it is the individual at the upper end

4. *Ibid.*, pp. 66 f.
5. Rich people would, on any risk-preference assumption, tend to self-insure (to save the transactions cost) against hazards threatening losses involving only minor fractions of their wealth. Thus we would expect to see them often foregoing the purchase of automobile collision insurance. But the Friedman-Savage assertion implies that they would omit insuring against potentially great losses such as those associated with accident liability claims, and physical disability or death of the main income-earner. Again their own evidence does not support Friedman and Savage here.
6. Occasional racetrack betting on favorites, so long as the scale is minor, means little here. The main point of the Friedman-Savage assumption is that the rich man is willing, at fair odds, to accept a hazard that (if it eventuated) would thrust him entirely out of the concave segment — out of the rich-man class! This requires betting on a scale considered pathological in our culture (see Dostoyevsky, *The Gambler*).

INVESTMENT DECISION UNDER UNCERTAINTY   261

of the low-income segment who is most inclined to take long-shot bets, and the individual at the lower end of the high-income segment who is most inclined to take short-odds bets. Thus, the model would have us believe, the solid risk-avoiders of our society are only the poorer poor, and the richer rich. Aside from the notorious lack of direct confirmation of these assertions, it is of interest to note how they conflict with observed stability patterns of the various income classes. With behavior as postulated, the middle ranks of incomes would be rapidly depopulated, the end result being a U-shaped distribution piled up at the extremes. Needless to say, this is not observed.

There is one important observation that should be considered part of the behavior that needs explaining in constructing a risk-preference model (utility-of-income function): Gambling on a scale at all likely to *impoverish* is rarely observed in middle- and upper-income groups. One way to reconcile this observation with the Friedman-Savage model would be to shrink the middle convex segment to a narrow range.[7] To do this is, however, to lose the main point of the Friedman-Savage argument, since then risk aversion would be the predominant behavior pattern after all.[8] And the problem remains of combining the risk aversion necessary for observed diversification of assets and purchase of insurance with the existence of at least a modest amount of gambling at all income levels.[9]

An easy way out of the difficulty lies in recognizing that many people take pleasure in gambling per se (i.e., as a consumption good). A modest amount of *pleasure-oriented* gambling would then not be inconsistent with risk aversion (a concave utility-of-income function) for serious *wealth-oriented* activities.[1] To make this distinction workable, however, it must be possible to distinguish observationally between pleasure-oriented and wealth-oriented gambling, the latter being defined as a deliberate attempt to change wealth

7. At one point (*op. cit.*, p. 92) Friedman and Savage do suggest that relatively few individuals are in the middle segment.

8. Substantial numbers of individuals in the middle segment are necessary to explain the alleged observation of preference for low-risk or high-risk as against moderate-risk economic activities.

9. One possible way out would be to assert that the middle segment is small and, in addition, slides up and down as the individual's income level changes — see H. Markowitz "The Utility of Wealth," *Journal of Political Economy*, LX (April 1952) — so that he is always willing to undertake a small amount of gambling from his present income level. As in the case of Ptolemy's geocentric system, when it becomes necessary to incorporate such *ad hoc* "epicycles" to save the phenomena, it is time for a new conception.

1. The following may perhaps be an illuminating analogy. Men like to live in houses on solid foundations, with square corners, and level floors. And yet they may pay money to spend a few minutes at an amusement park in a "crazy-house" with quite the reverse characteristics.

status. Fortunately, the two motives for gambling are observably distinct, because they imply radically different wagering procedures. If gambling is wealth-oriented, it will take the form of hazarding great sums (proportionate to one's endowment and hopes) on a single turn of a wheel or flip of a coin. Repetitive gambling at relatively small stakes would be absurd: the law of large numbers shrinks the variance of the overall outcome, whereas wealth-oriented gamblers are trying to achieve large changes. While repetitive small-stake gambling does not quite guarantee a final result near the mean, the likelihood of such outcomes is greatly increased; in any case, the average time required to win the desired sum (or lose the fortune hazarded) will be enormously extended. What we observe at Las Vegas is, of course, very much the repetitive, small-stake pattern. The combination of adverse odds and limited stakes assures a high probability that the final outcome for the gambler will be a modest loss — the price paid for the pleasure of gambling. All this is not to say that we never observe wealth-oriented gambling, but rather that it is not a sufficiently important phenomenon to dictate the main lines of our theory of risk.[2]

On our hypothesis, therefore, we expect to see risk aversion predominating in wealth-oriented activities at all income levels — thus explaining purchase of insurance all along the wealth scale. We also expect to see a moderate amount of pleasure-oriented gambling, again all along the wealth scale. Wealth-oriented gambling will not be a very important phenomenon, but such as exists would be concentrated among the poor.[3] This is in sharp contrast with the view of Friedman and Savage, whose theory indicates that wealth-oriented gambling will be very significant, and concentrated among

2. Some wealth-oriented gambling is based on "hunches" or "inside information" that, if true, would make the bet a lottery at *favorable* odds rather than the adverse gamble it appears — to others! Of course, given the belief in favorable odds, even a risk-avoider might gamble. There is also strictly rational wealth-oriented gambling, as in the classic case of the embezzler who plunges his remaining cash in the hope of being able to straighten out his accounts prior to an audit. Here the dollar in hand that the gambler risks is almost costless, as he cannot hope to salvage much of his illegal taking by conservative behavior. A somewhat similar argument may partially explain lower-class gambling: the floor on consumption provided by public-assistance payments — where such payments are liable to be withheld or reduced if the would-be gambler conserved his assets — permits the individual to gamble with dollars that do not fully represent sacrifices of consumption to him. Finally, there is the gambling behavior that would generally be regarded as pathological; this would be associated with subnormal or aberrant mental conditions.

3. See footnote above concerning the effect of relief payments (consumption floor) upon the propensity to gamble. Also, ill-informed believers in hunches, and subnormal or aberrant mental types, will tend to have low income status.

INVESTMENT DECISION UNDER UNCERTAINTY 263

the middle classes. We, on the contrary, would expect to find the middle classes to be the most insurance-minded. Insurance purchases by the poor would be deterred by the substantially higher transactions cost on the one hand, and the relief floor on the other. As for the rich, they are likely to possess a sufficient diversity of assets as to make self-insurance feasible (this consideration being counterbalanced somewhat by tax advantages where life insurance is concerned).

Leaving the sphere of gambling versus insurance, the most significant class of economic activity, in terms of implications for attitudes toward risk, is choice of occupation. Except in the very highest income brackets, this decision determines the nature of the major source of wealth. In addition, it is difficult to insure or diversify against certain hazards associated with occupational choice, such as cyclical unemployment and technological obsolescence. Insurance is available against physical hazards — but there will typically be penalty rates to pay for life or disability insurance in dangerous occupations. Consequently, on our hypothesis we would expect to observe relatively low returns in occupations that are highly secure in almost all respects, like teaching and civil service. In hazardous occupations such as mining, and insecure activities such as business entrepreneurship, we would expect higher average returns — even after allowing for injuries and failures. Unfortunately, the evidence available is difficult to interpret because of differences in personal qualities of individuals, nonpecuniary returns and differences of tastes with respect to them, tax and relief effects, and numerous difficulties with the data.[4]

The evidence on return to property in relation to risk is fortunately somewhat clearer. We must be careful to recollect here, however, that the "riskiness" (imbalance in the state-distribution of income) relevant for decisions is not that of particular assets in isolation. It is the variability of the state-distribution of consumption possibilities yielded by overall *portfolios* that is relevant. For some classes of assets (securities, in particular) it is relatively easy to obtain considerable diversification while holding individually

---

4. Friedman and Savage allege (*op. cit.*, pp. 63–66) that higher returns are received on (reflecting aversion to) moderate risks — and that the average returns to high-risk activities like auto-racing, piloting aircraft, business undertakings in untried fields, and the professions of law and medicine (?) are so low as to evidence an inclination in favor of bearing extreme risks. The evidence presented for these assertions is weak, to say the least. The following will illustrate one of the many problems of interpreting such data as exist: for high-risk occupations there is likely to be a selection bias (since those who overestimate the chance of success are more likely to enter) so that adverse average results are not necessarily evidence of risk preference.

risky assets. The main problem is posed by the overall swings of the business cycle, which limit the variance-minimizing effect of diversification by imposing high correlation among security returns — and, probably even more important, high correlation between overall property income and overall wage or other personal income. Consequently, and especially because of the intrinsically risky situation involved in occupational choice, the risk-aversion hypothesis would predict relatively high average return on procyclical securities and relatively low on stable or anticyclical securities. This is borne out by the historically realized yields on equities (highly procyclical in real terms).[5] Comparison of the cyclically unstable "industrial" equities with the more stable "utility" equities provides another confirmation.[6]

Thus, a combination of a risk-aversion hypothesis for wealth-oriented activities with recognition that, for many individuals, repetitive small-stake gambling (i.e., gambling guaranteed not to drastically transform the wealth level) is a pleasurable activity, serves to explain the available evidence. In contrast, the attempt to explain both insurance and gambling as reflecting a single utility-of-income function of peculiar shape leads to contradictions — in which the supposed risk-preferring group is first large and then small, first a stable and then a disappearing element, etc. — and is in conflict with more direct knowledge about the risk-seeking propensities of the various income groups.

II. OPTIMAL CAPITAL STRUCTURE

The analysis of risky investment decision in terms of state preferences may be applied in the area of corporate finance to the controversial "Proposition I" of Modigliani and Miller: "The market value of any firm is independent of its capital structure and is given by capitalizing its expected return at the rate ρ_k appropriate to its class."[7] Our main concern here will be with the first part of the proposition, the assertion that market value is independent of capital structure. Symbolically, the contention is that $D_0 + E_0 = V_0 = \overline{X}/\rho_k$, a constant — where D_0 is present (or mar-

5. H. A. Latané, "Portfolio Balance — The Demand for Money, Bonds, and Stock," *Southern Economic Journal*, XXIX (Oct. 1962).

6. Most of the difference is realized in the form of capital gains. See *Historical Statistics of the United States, Colonial Times to 1957* (Washington, 1960), p. 657.

7. F. Modigliani and M. H. Miller, "The Cost of Capital, Corporation Finance and the Theory of Investment," *American Economic Review*, XLVIII (June 1958), 268.

INVESTMENT DECISION UNDER UNCERTAINTY 265

ket) value of the debt, E_0 the value of the equity, V_0 is the assertedly constant value of the firm, and $\overline{X}$ is the firm's given operating income. The language in the second part of the proposition, and elsewhere in their paper, indicate that Modigliani and Miller were employing a mean, variability approach to risk-bearing.[8]

In the predecessor to this article, Fisher's analysis of individuals' investment decisions under certainty was generalized to include investment decisions of *firms*. The result was obtained, in equation (6‴), that the market value (wealth) of the firm under certainty equals the present value of debt repayments plus (if the firm has productive opportunities that lead to an increase of wealth) the present value of any equity increment. This looks very much like the Modigliani-Miller theorem. In fact, it is easy to extend this result, via a state-preference analysis, to decisions under uncertainty so as to validate the Modigliani-Miller theorem. The extension is based on the premise that individuals and firms form a closed system, so that all assets or claims must be held by, and only by, individuals or firms. Furthermore, looking at the situation *ex post* of the production decisions (i.e., after commitment of funds to investment), the social totals of each time-state class of assets must then be constant. What this rules out are "external drains" of which the most crucial are personal and corporate taxes. Bankruptcy penalties, transactions and underwriting costs, etc., must also be excluded.

Continuing to employ our simplifying assumption of only two time-periods (times 0 and 1), with only one present state but two future states (a and b), we first develop equations for the firm's capital input and the distribution of returns.

(1) $-q_0 = d_0 + e_0$ Capital input balance

Here q_0 is the total of corporate funds committed to investment at time 0; d_0 is the portion coming from borrowings, and e_0 the portion from equity funds.[9] (In the predecessor article we assumed $e_0 = 0$, all-debt financing being possible under certainty.)

8. In their paper the assumption is made throughout that the expected yield on equities exceeds the yield on riskless bonds; they associate the premium with "financial risk" due at least in part to variance of outcome (p. 271). Modigliani and Miller claim that their propositions do not depend upon any assumption about individual risk preferences (p. 279); this statement is correct on the level of the individual (who can maximize asset value regardless of personal risk preferences), but on the market level the existence of a premium reflects the need on balance for compensation to induce bearing of variability risk.

9. It is assumed that the firm does not consume and has null endowment. Hence all funds for investment must be obtained from outside, and also the firm has no use for funds except to invest them. While actual firms do

$$(2) \quad \begin{cases} q_{1a} = d_{1a} + e_{1a} \\ q_{1b} = d_{1b} + e_{1b} \end{cases} \quad \text{Firm's financial distributions}$$

Equations (2) say that all gross asset earnings, in either state, are fully distributed and that the only recipients are the debt and equity owners. Here d_{1a} is the gross return to debtholders if state a obtains; the other claims are defined correspondingly. If the debt is riskless, $d_{1a} = d_{1b} = d_0 (1 + r^*)$, where r^* is the promised interest rate on the bond. If the debt is risky so that in state b, let us say, $d_{1b} < d_0 (1 + r^*)$ then $e_{1b} = 0$ — since the debt is a senior claim that must be paid first before equity receives any return.

We have here three types of future time-state claims: (physical) asset claims (q_{1a} and q_{1b}), debt claims (d_{1a} and d_{1b}) and equity claims (e_{1a} and e_{1b}). Under the single-price law of markets, unit claims to the same commodity must sell at the same price. Hence, unless there are differentiations due to such features as tax status (excluded by our assumption above), the single price P_{1a} must apply to q_{1a}, d_{1a}, and e_{1a} — and correspondingly P_{1b} is the price of q_{1b}, d_{1b}, and e_{1b}. Taking c_0 as numeraire so that $P_0 = 1$, the prices for the future claims can be written in the form $P_{1a} = 1/(1 + r_{1a})$ and $P_{1b} = 1/(1 + r_{1b})$, where r_{1a} and r_{1b} are the "time-and-risk" discount rates for contingent future incomes. There is a possible source of confusion here: it might be thought that the equity claim e_{1b} is "riskier" than the debt claim d_{1b}, for example, and so should sell at a lower price. But risk has already been taken account of in the *quantification* of d_{1b} and e_{1b} — in the example given just above, if state b obtains so that d_{1b} is less than $d_0(1 + r^*)$, then the junior claim $e_{1b} = 0$. Conditionally upon the occurrence of the specified state, the various claims all become certainties.[1]

If we define present values of the firm, of the debt, and of the equity return in the natural way for this problem (*ex post* of the investment decision),[2] we obtain:

$$(3) \quad \begin{cases} V_0 = P_{1a}q_{1a} + P_{1b}q_{1b} \\ D_0 = P_{1a}d_{1a} + P_{1b}d_{1b} \\ E_0 = P_{1a}e_{1a} + P_{1b}e_{1b} \end{cases}$$

Here again there is a possible source of confusion, in that it might

make use of "internal" funds, we regard such funds as distributed to stockholders and returned to the firm for reinvestment.

1. Modigliani and Miller describe an "arbitrage" process which has the effect of enforcing this single-price law (pp. 69–71). While their argument has been the subject of controversy, it seems unexceptionable under the provisos of the model here discussed — in particular, under the assumption that the several types of claim do not diverge in tax status.

2. That is, *after* the commitment of current funds (which being "sunk," do not enter into present worth) but *before* the payout of returns to investors.

INVESTMENT DECISION UNDER UNCERTAINTY 267

seem plausible that the relative constancy of the *d*'s as compared with the *e*'s would be reflected by a kind of premium in the value D_0 as compared with E_0, given predominant risk aversion. But since each form of security is only a package of elementary claims to contingent incomes, market equilibrium requires that the value of the package equal the sum of the values of the components.[3]

The Modigliani-Miller Theorem follows immediately from (2) and (3):

(4) $$V_0 = D_0 + E_0.$$

Our formulation makes it possible to observe that the proposition in question is a special case of a Fisherian theorem. Financing operations (i.e., market conversions among claims to income) take place *within* a wealth constraint — they do not change wealth. In the familiar Fisherian analysis of choices involving time, the market value of the productive solution determines wealth; borrowing and lending can then take place to achieve a different distribution of timed income claims, but all such transformations leave wealth unchanged. In the model considered here, the productive solution determines wealth by the condition $V_0 = \overline{X}/\rho_k$; financing via alternative debt-equity ratios then represent different possible ways of distributing this wealth over time-state claims. But all the attainable distributions have the same wealth-value.

We may now examine further the significance of the "closed system" or "no external drains" proviso stated earlier. Let us suppose that there is no corporate tax, but that equity claims are given preferential treatment with respect to the external drain of the *personal* income tax on the system composed of the individuals and firms.[4] This factor, other things equal, would raise the price (lower the discounting rate) of an equity claim relative to a debt claim — and also relative to asset claims assuming these latter have to be financed by mixes of debt and equity. Then the single-price law, for claims conditioned on a given state, could not be applied, and

---

3. Consider the following analogy. Bread and butter are complements for most people, and possibly substitutes for some careful calorie-watchers — but, regardless, a package of bread and butter in competitive equilibrium must sell for the sum of the bread price and the butter price. Any divergence could only be due to a possible saving of transactions cost, but such costs are a form of "external drain" assumed away in our model. (The assumption of competitive conditions also rules out "tie-in sales" as a device for capitalizing on monopoly power.)

4. The capital gains feature applies to both debt and equity securities, though in practice equity benefits more. The unique advantage to equity is the opportunity to reinvest via "retained earnings," escaping personal tax in the process. (In our analysis, the "retention" is a mere fiction — which is not the whole story, of course.)

equations (3) and (4) would not hold. Alternatively, if we ignored the personal income tax but assumed the existence of an external drain on the corporation in the form of a *corporate* income tax, equations (2) would be modified so as to become (t_{1a} and t_{1b} indicating conditional tax liabilities):

$$(2') \quad \begin{cases} q_{1a} = d_{1a} + e_{1a} + t_{1a} \\ q_{1b} = d_{1b} + e_{1b} + t_{1b}. \end{cases}$$

Equations (2') indicate that there is an opportunity to increase wealth by tax-minimizing devices. Under the corporate income tax, debt and equity earnings are differentially treated; tax liability can be reduced by a high debt/equity fraction. The sum $d_{1a} + e_{1a}$ then, for example, would not be a constant independent of the ratio of the two — so that even though the prices (or discounting rates) for asset, debt, and (after-tax) equity earnings are identical, equation (4) would not follow.

We may conclude this section by noting that we have gone only a small step toward solving the problem of optimal capital structure in terms of a state-preference analysis. Doing so would require an integration of the personal-tax and corporate-tax effects, and consideration of other factors (such as the magnitude of bankruptcy penalties) to yield the optimal balance of debt and equity financing.[5] The limited purpose here was only to illustrate the use of a state-preference analysis in order to suggest the range of applicability and the crucial limitations of the much debated Modigliani-Miller "Proposition I."

III. Uncertainty and the Discount Rate for Public Investment

The final application to be presented here of the model of time-state-preference concerns the much controverted question: What is the "appropriate" discount rate, for use under uncertainty, in present-worth calculations evaluating government investments not subject to the market test? Many conflicting recommendations have been expressed on this question, but only two of these will be examined here for consistency with Pareto efficiency in an uncertain world.[6] Of these, the first prescribes that the government employ as

---

5. For a more complete analysis see J. Lintner, "Dividends, Earnings, Leverage, Stock Prices and the Supply of Capital to Corporations," *Review of Economics and Statistics*, XLIV (Aug. 1962). The result here differs from Lintner's in showing that uncertainty *alone* is not sufficient to negate the Modigliani-Miller theorem.

6. Among the points of view not considered here are those which reject the market evidence on time preference or time productivity in favor of a "social discount rate" excogitated from value judgments or planners' time

INVESTMENT DECISION UNDER UNCERTAINTY 269

discount rate for a public project the same rate as would be applied, in principle, by a company evaluating a "comparable" project in the private sphere. The opposing position would have the government take advantage of its power to finance exceptionally cheaply by undertaking projects that are profitable when the returns are evaluated at the government's low borrowing rate. We may think of these two as prescriptions to employ, in the first case, a *risky,* and in the second case a *riskless,* rate — to discount the mathematical expectations of the uncertain returns.

The argument for use of the risky rate runs somewhat as follows.[7] The market rate of interest is generated by an equilibrium between marginal time preferences of consumers and the marginal time productivity of resources. If neither private nor public projects involved risk, it would obviously be inefficient to depart from this equilibrium rate in evaluating intertemporal transfers of income (i.e., investments) in the public sphere. It is true that in a risky world there are many "impure" time-plus-risk interest rates rather than one pure time-rate, but the way to take this into account is to use in the public sphere the rate employed for "comparable" investments in the private sphere. Thus, if a power project would in the private sector be financed half from debt sources paying 4 per cent (this being a riskless rate, let us say) and half from equity sources requiring an expected return of 6 per cent, the government discount rate for a comparable project should be the same 5 per cent the private company must employ. Then the marginally desirable project would, in either sector, yield 5 per cent in terms of probabilistic expectation. (If corporate income tax is taken into account, the marginally desirable project in the private sphere must have an expected yield around 8.5 per cent, and so the discount rate for government investment should be correspondingly higher.) [8]

preferences. This point of view can be defended as a way of compensating for market bias due to private "myopia" or intertemporal "selfishness," but it raises issues beyond the scope of the Pareto-efficiency criterion. For discussions of this position see O. Eckstein, "A Survey of the Theory of Public Expenditure Criteria," my "Comment," and Eckstein's "Reply" in the National Bureau of Economic Research volume, *Public Finances: Needs, Sources, and Utilization* (Princeton University Press, 1961), and S. Marglin, "The Social Rate of Discount and the Optimal Rate of Investment," this *Journal,* LXXVII (Feb. 1963).

7. The argument is based on that offered in J. Hirshleifer, J. C. DeHaven, and J. W. Milliman, *Water Supply: Economics, Technology, and Policy* (University of Chicago Press, 1960), pp. 139–50.

8. It might be argued that the corporate income tax is an equalizing adjustment designed to compensate the community for certain costs imposed on it by the corporate form of business — in contrast with partnerships, proprietorships, cooperatives, government enterprises, etc. This argument raises issues which are best avoided here; the principle in contention remains the

Failure to abide by this rule leads to obviously inefficient results. If the government, merely because it can finance entirely by riskless borrowing at, say 4 per cent, employed the latter rate in its calculations, the marginally adopted project in the public sector would yield on the average but 4 per cent while private projects with higher expected yields were failing of adoption.

The opposing recommendation is based upon the contention that the higher rates required to secure funds for private investments (e.g., the 6 per cent equity yield in the illustration above) are a reflection of risk aversion — and that risk aversion is a private, not a social cost. The possibility of *pooling* independent risks is essential to this argument. A.T.&T. can pool more risks than can a small local telephone company; it will therefore, be able to finance more cheaply and so to undertake projects with a lower expected yield than the small company can. The federal government can pool risks far more effectively than A.T.&T., and so is as a practical matter quite justified in treating the expected project yield as if it were riskless. Consequently, the 4 per cent riskless discount rate is the relevant one for its calculations.[9] (It should be noted, however, that the conclusion of this argument only follows in a "second-best" sense. For, granted the premises, it would clearly be most efficient for the government to borrow in order to subsidize the higher-expected-yield private investments — a larger subsidy to the small telephone company, a smaller one to A.T.&T. — rather than for the purpose of undertaking lower-yield public investments. Only if this possibility is ruled out does it follow that lower-yielding government investments should be undertaken.)

A simple numerical illustration will indicate the incorrectness of the "pooling" argument *within the time-state model developed here*. Suppose the society consists of J identically placed individuals with identical tastes, and let the social endowment consist of $100J$ units of income (say, "corn") in time 0, $150J$ units in the time-state $1a$, and $50J$ units in time-state $1b$. Let the numeraire $P_0 = 1$. Suppose, for arithmetical convenience, that the state-probabilities $\pi_a = \pi_b = \frac{1}{2}$, and that with this distribution of consumption opportunities there is on the margin zero time preference with respect to

same, though in one case the divergence is only between 4 per cent and 5 per cent and in the other case between 4 and 8.5 per cent.
9. Many prominent theorists have repeated this argument. Among recent examples are the discussions by P. A. Samuelson and W. Vickrey at the *Principles of Efficiency* session, Papers and Proceedings of the 76th Annual Meeting, *American Economic Review*, LIV (May 1964). See also, Robert M. Solow, *Capital Theory and the Rate of Return* (Chicago: Rand-McNally, 1964), pp. 70–71.

INVESTMENT DECISION UNDER UNCERTAINTY 271

certainties: thus, the price of a unit of future certain income $P_1 = 1$ (and the riskless discount rate $r_1 = 0$ per cent) [1] where, of course, $P_1 = P_{1a} + P_{1b}$. Since by hypothesis there is risk aversion, it must be the case that the overall value of the time-1 endowment for each person — 150 (P_{1a}) + 50 (P_{1b}) — must be less than the value of the average holding as a certainty, i.e., less than $100(P_{1a}) + 100(P_{1b})$ = 100. (If the prices P_{1a} and P_{1b} were such that the average holding certain *could* be purchased within the endowment wealth constraint, it *would* be, given risk aversion.) This requires that P_{1a} be less than ½. For concreteness, let $P_{1a} = .4$, and hence P_{1b} = .6, thus determining the "impure" time-and-state discount rates $r_{1a} = 150$ per cent, and $r_{1b} = 66⅔$ per cent.[2]

Now consider various investment opportunities, all of infinitesimal scale so that we can hold the price relationships unchanged (the opportunities are infinitesimal on the social scale, but not necessarily on the individual scale). It is immediately clear that, in terms of efficiency, either a private or public project whose returns fall *exclusively* in state 1a should have these returns discounted at the rate of 150 per cent. To attempt to make a distinction between public and private here would be equivalent to charging different prices for the same commodity — c_{1a}. If the returns all fell in state 1b, the discount rate should be 66⅔ per cent. For an investment yielding returns equally in either state (i.e., an investment whose returns are certain), the 0 per cent rate would be appropriate. For a project yielding in the ratio of 3 in state 1a to 1 in state 1b (that is, in the same proportions as the private and social endowments) the appropriate discount (for application to the mathematical expectation of returns) is approximately 11.1 per cent.[3] The appropriate discount rate would be much lower if, with the same mathematical expectation of returns, the state-distribution were reversed so as to pay off more heavily in the less well-endowed state 1b (the rate to use would be *minus* 9.1 per cent, on our assumptions). In every case, of course, the "appropriate" discount rate is that which correctly distinguishes

1. Since $P_1 = 1/(1 + r_1)$.
2. Since $P_{1a} = 1/(1 + r_{1a})$, and $P_{1b} = 1/(1 + r_{1b})$.
3. This figure is derived as follows. Let x be the scale of return per dollar invested. We seek the averaged discount rate r_1^* such that the present-worth calculations in terms of r_1^* and the averaged returns lead to the same result as the explicit calculation in terms of the state-distributed returns and the corresponding r_{1a} and r_{1b}. We determine r_1^* in the equation:
$-1 + 3x/(1 + r_{1a}) + x/(1 + r_{1b}) = -1 + 2x/(1 + x_1^*)$. With $r_{1a} = 150$ per cent and $r_{1b} = 66⅔$ per cent the numerical result in the text is obtained.

efficient from inefficient projects by showing positive or negative values in a present-worth calculation.

The foregoing indicates that there is a single definite discount rate to be used, *whether a project is private or public,* in making efficiency calculations for any given state-pattern of returns. This result supports, therefore, the "risky discount rate" position on the normative issue in question. The crucial proviso is that when the recommendation is made to employ for government investments the private market discount rate for "comparable" projects, it must be understood that *"comparable" projects are those having the same proportionate time-state distribution of returns.* In particular, note that the "risky" rate might be *lower* than the riskless rate.

It is correspondingly clear that within this model the position recommending the use of the riskless discount rate with the mathematical expectation of returns must be incorrect. We have just seen that it would fail to distinguish between, on the one hand, a project paying off more heavily in the better-endowed state and, on the other hand, a project with a quantitatively identical but reversed state-pattern paying off more heavily in the more urgently desired income of the poorer-endowed state. Or, to take another example, a project yielding only a dollar in state 1*a* would have that dollar reduced to $.50 in taking the expectation, and then be discounted at the riskless rate (0 per cent here). This is equivalent to letting $r_{1a} = 100$ per cent, too lax a criterion since the correct $r_{1a} = 150$ per cent. On the other hand, if the dollar were returned in state 1*b* the recommendation would indicate too stringent a criterion, employing 100 per cent instead of the correct 66⅔ per cent. The basic reason, of course, is that the process of taking mathematical expectations considers dollars equivalent when they appertain to equally probable states — but as between two such states, the dollars in one may be much more highly-valued on the margin than in the other. In other words, dollars in distinct time-states are different commodities within the model considered here, and it is as incorrect to average them as it would be to average shoes and apples.

We may now turn to the "pooling" argument. Suppose it were possible to pool two projects, one yielding a dollar in state 1*a* and the other a dollar in state 1*b*. Since the pooled return is thus riskless, it may seem plausible to employ the riskless rate 0 per cent for the two, viewed in combination. But this is definitely incorrect. If the two projects were *necessarily* tied together, then the recommended procedure would be appropriate. But if they are really separable, they should be evaluated separately (for simplicity, we set aside

INVESTMENT DECISION UNDER UNCERTAINTY 273

complications such as possible interactions between the two). It could easily happen that the combination, if forced upon us as a combination, might be desirable — but that it might be more efficient to adopt one component and not the other, if we could separate the two. In short, the device of pooling provides no justification in efficiency terms for adopting what is incrementally a bad project, if in fact we can adopt the good one separately from the bad.[4]

Even if the "pooling" argument is rejected, it could still be maintained that the discount rate on public projects ought "usually" to be lower than those of private projects. All that is required to support this view is that government projects be "usually" (in contrast with private projects) such that they pay off in less well-endowed states. For example, a federal irrigation project pays off disproportionately when there would otherwise be a drought. Of course, some special argument is required to explain why private initiative does not exploit such opportunities. But if such opportunities are not privately exploited, then in fact the "usual" private investments would not be the *comparable* ones in the sense required by the "risky-discount-rate" position.

It may seem surprising, however, that so little can be made of "pooling" in view of the plausible arguments adduced in its favor. One can, in fact, construct a model in which the pooling argument makes more sense, and it will be instructive to compare that model with ours above. The key is to distinguish between private "states" and social "states." The idea here is related to a maxim often (rather too sweepingly) expressed in connection with life insurance calculations: "We don't know who will die next year, but we do know how many!" Similarly, the social total of endowments might be constant (thus, there is really only one social state, ignoring distribution) and yet for each individual the endowment might be uncertain.[5] For concreteness, imagine the following situation. If state *a* obtains, every odd-numbered individual has an endowment of 50 and every even-numbered individual an endowment of 150; if state *b* obtains the positions are reversed. Let us suppose, in order to make the case as strong as possible, that the investments available to even and odd classes of individuals will have returns propor-

4. Precisely this error is committed in the so-called "basin account" doctrine. This theory, put forward by proponents of certain large river basin plans, maintains that benefit-cost evaluations of component projects should be ignored so long as the overall plan shows a surplus of benefits over costs. Federal legislation has adopted this doctrine for the gigantic Missouri Basin Project. See Report of the President's Water Resources Policy Commission, Vol. 2, *Ten Rivers in America's Future* (Washington, 1950), p. 250.

5. This may have been the assumption made in Arrow's original formulation of the state-preference model. See Arrow, *op. cit.*, equation (5).

tionate to their respective endowment distributions. Then the "even" individuals will, on the basis of risk aversion, have a bias against the investments available to them, and the "odd" individuals similarly against their investments — whereas, if pooled, the investments would tend to become certainties justifying no risk discount.

Consider investments of the form requiring a time-0 input of $1, and yielding a time-1 return of $1.50 in an individual's better-endowed and $.50 in his worse-endowed state, the states again assumed equally probable. If the subjective marginal value of a dollar in an individual's better-endowed state is .4 and in his poorer-endowed state is .6 (as before), then each individual would assign a present worth of − $.10 to the investment opportunity. But if an "odd" and an "even" investment opportunity were pooled, the return would be certain; at the riskless 0 per cent rate the combination would have a zero present worth, and so be on the margin of desirability. Here pooling does not sneak in a bad project under the mantle of a good one. Rather, two projects separately bad (in terms of private calculations) may become a good project in terms of social calculations!

A model of this kind is what lies behind the usual "pooling" argument justifying the use of the riskless rate for evaluating government investments. The model diverges in two essential ways from that presented earlier justifying the employment of the risky rate. First is the assumption, already mentioned, that risk is private rather than social — i.e., that there is only one state with respect to social totals [6] but more than one state in terms of possible individual distributions within that total. Second, and this is the really critical point, is the assumption that markets are so imperfect that it is impossible for the individuals better-endowed in state a to trade claims to income in that state against the claims to income in state b that other individuals would like to sell. In short, *the single-price law of markets must be violated.*

Continuing our numerical example, the commodity c_{1a} had a subjective value equal to .4 for even-numbered individuals and .6 for odd-numbered individuals. If trade were permitted between the two classes, the two values would have to come into equality.

6. In an unpublished paper, Kenneth Arrow has employed the somewhat more general assumption of multiple social states, but where the social incomes (endowments) for the several states are *uncorrelated* with the returns from incremental investments in the private states. This also leads to the result that private risks are (on the average) socially irrelevant, and so that market rates of return reflecting private risk aversion should not influence the government's discount rate.

Holding to the assumption that a riskless future claim has unit present value ($P_{1a} + P_{1b} = 1$), P_{1a} and P_{1b} would then each have to equal .5. Then strictly private calculations, without any pooling, would show that the private investment opportunities of the example were on the margin of desirability. The discount rate for the "comparable" private investments would be 0 per cent, so that proponents of the so-called "risky discount rate" for evaluation of public investment would be led by their analysis to the correct 0 per cent rate in this case. In contrast, as we have seen, proponents of the so-called "riskless rate" — while also correct in favoring 0 per cent as the discount rate *in this case* — would be led into definite error under conditions where private risks *are* reflective of social risks.

We may conclude, therefore, that the pooling argument rests ultimately for support upon market imperfections that prevent equivalent time-state claims from selling at a uniform price, thus hindering the possibility of private movements away from risky (unbalanced with respect to state) endowments by trading. Such imperfections may, of course, be very prevalent. One important example concerns assets whose productiveness has a personal element. Such an asset may be worth much in the hands of some Mr. X, but little if traded to anyone else. It will, therefore, be difficult to reduce the riskiness associated with holding such assets.[7] Here is a case where, granted the other conditions in our illustration above, the pooling argument would have real force. But it is clear that the argument is incorrect on the level of generality at which it is usually propounded. If time-state claims can be regarded as commodities traded in perfect markets, the prescription for the use of the so-called "risky rate" — the discount rate implicit in the valuation of private projects with the *same proportionate time-state distribution of returns* — has been shown to be generally correct.

IV. CONCLUDING REMARKS

To rationalize the process of investment decision under uncertainty, and to explain the price relationships among risky assets,

---

7. The most important such asset is labor power. Riskiness might deter both a Mr. X and a Mr. Y. from investing to improve their personal labor capacities. Yet, the state-distributions of the returns from the two investments might in combination represent a certainty. This would suggest that Mr. X and Mr. Y form a partnership, so that each has 50 per cent of the certain combination (i.e., each sells the other half his claims). But, it is possible that one or both will work less productively when he only receives 50 per cent of the benefit of his personal efforts. This possibility would, therefore, inhibit such trading.

two main conceptions of the choice process have been put forward by economic theorists. Both conceptions *reduce* the observed assets traded in the marketplace into more fundamental entities — choice-objects assertedly desired by investors. Under the first and more familiar approach, the more fundamental entities are represented by mean and variability measures, μ and σ, of overall return provided by any given portfolio of assets; under the second approach, the assets are regarded as packages of more fundamental contingent claims to income at specified dates and states of the world.

In the predecessor to this article, it was shown that the state-preference formulation was the logical extension, to the world of uncertain choice, of Fisher's model of certain intertemporal choice. The various topics covered in this article were intended to serve as illustrations of the power and relevance of the state-preference approach, to show that some interesting and novel results in a number of areas can be obtained thereby. (1) As to risk aversion, under the mean vs. variability approach the investor's attitude toward risk (whether σ is for him a good or a "bad") is a personal characteristic. It remains unclear how the risk-loving or risk-avoiding propensities of individuals are composed into an overall market premium or discount for risk. In contrast, under the state-preference approach the very elementary principle of nonspecialization of choice among time-state claims, leads to the inference that in their wealth-oriented decisions, and if asset prices represent fair odds, investors seek portfolios with balanced state-distributions of income. In general, however, they will not actually achieve perfect balance (zero σ), because the endowments and productive opportunities available to society are not symmetrically distributed over all the possible states. (2) As to the unresolved question about the existence of an optimal debt-equity ratio for financing corporate investment, the state-preference formulation leads directly to a set of idealizing assumptions ("no external drains") under which all possible ratios are equivalent in market value. Where the idealized conditions do not hold, there *will* in general be an optimal ratio. (3) With regard to the appropriate discount rate for evaluating government investments, rather vaguely stated ideas concerning risk aversion as a social or a private cost can be precisely formulated in terms of time-state preferences. It was shown that the efficient discount rate, assuming perfect markets, is the market rate implicit in the valuation of private assets whose returns are "comparable" to the public investment in question — where "comparable" means having the

INVESTMENT DECISION UNDER UNCERTAINTY 277

same proportionate time-state distribution of returns. The argument often encountered, to the effect that "risk aversion is a private cost and not a social cost," was shown to be mistaken unless two restrictive conditions both hold: (a) Private risks exist, but these do not represent social risks (as when the aggregate social endowment is constant, but its distribution over the individuals varies with state). (b) Markets are imperfect, so that the single-price law of markets does not hold for contingent time-state-claims as commodities.

Going beyond the ground covered by this article, there seem to be considerable difficulties of an operational nature in more direct empirical tests employing a state-preference formulation. The mean and the variability of return embodied in a given set of assets are already only implicitly observable; when the assets are interpreted instead as packages of claims to incomes in underlying hypothetical states of the world, the fundamental choice-objects have an even higher degree of invisibility. Assets ordinarily encountered in capital markets, such as corporate bonds or equities, represent complex aggregates of claims to income in an embarrassing multiplicity of possible states of the world. Nevertheless, in some cases the interpretation may be reasonably clear. Thus, the course of stock and bond prices since 1929 has certainly reflected investors' changing views of the probabilities of more and less prosperous states of the world occurring. Here, as elsewhere, progress will depend upon the discovery of strategic simplifications that reduce seemingly intractable problems into at least partially manageable ones.[8]

UNIVERSITY OF CALIFORNIA
LOS ANGELES

8. One possible line of simplification is exemplified by the "good year/ bad year" dichotomy in H. A. Latané, "Investment Criteria: A Three Asset Portfolio Balance Model," *Review of Economics and Statistics*, XLVI (Feb. 1964).

[11]

A MODEL OF THE TRADE CYCLE

1. THE following pages do not attempt to put forward any
" new " theory of the Trade Cycle. The theory here presented
is essentially similar to all those theories which explain the Trade
Cycle as a result of the combined operation of the so-called
" multiplier " and the investment demand function as, *e.g.*, the
theories put forward in recent years by Mr. Harrod and Mr.
Kalecki.[1] The purpose of the present paper is to show, by
means of a simple diagrammatic apparatus, what are the necessary
and sufficient assumptions under which the combined operation
of these two forces inevitably gives rise to a cycle.

2. The basic principle underlying all these theories may be
sought in the proposition—a proposition that is really derived
from Mr. Keynes' *General Theory*, although not stated there in
this form—that economic activity always *tends* towards a level
where Savings and Investment are equal. Here the terms
Savings and Investment are used, of course, in a sense different
from the one according to which they are always and necessarily
equal—in the *ex-ante*, and not the *ex-post* sense. Investment
ex-ante is the value of the *designed* increments of stocks of all
kinds (*i.e.*, the value of the net addition to stocks plus the value
of the aggregate output of fixed equipment), which differs from
Investment *ex-post* by the value of the undesigned accretion (or
decumulation) of stocks. Savings *ex-ante* is the amount people
intend to save—*i.e.*, the amount they actually *would* save if they
correctly forecast their incomes. Hence *ex-ante* and *ex-post*
Saving can differ only in so far as there is an unexpected change
in the amount of income earned.

If *ex-ante* Investment exceeds *ex-ante* Saving, *either ex-post*
Investment will fall short of *ex-ante* Investment, *or ex-post* Saving
will exceed *ex-ante* Saving; and both these discrepancies will
induce an expansion in the level of activity. If *ex-ante* Investment falls short of *ex-ante* Saving *either ex-post* Investment will
exceed *ex-ante* Investment, *or ex-post* Saving will fall short of
ex-ante Saving, and both these discrepancies will induce a contraction. This must be so, because a reduction in *ex-post* Saving
as compared with *ex-ante* Saving will make consumers spend less
on consumers' goods, an excess of *ex-post* Investment over *ex-ante*.

[1] Harrod, *The Trade Cycle*; Kalecki, " A Theory of the Business Cycle,"
Review of Economic Studies, February 1937, reprinted in *Essays in Theory of
Economic Fluctuations*.

Investment (implying as it does the accretion of unwanted stocks) will cause entrepreneurs to spend less on entrepreneurial goods; while the total of activity is always determined by the sum of consumers' expenditures and entrepreneurs' expenditures. Thus a discrepancy between *ex-ante* Saving and *ex-ante* Investment must induce a change in the level of activity which proceeds until the discrepancy is removed.

3. The magnitudes of both *ex-ante* Saving and *ex-ante* Investment are themselves functions of the level of activity, and both vary positively with the level of activity. Thus if we denote the level of activity (measured in terms of employment) by x, both S and I (*ex-ante* Savings and Investment) will be single-valued functions of x [1] and both $\frac{dS}{dx}$ and $\frac{dI}{dx}$ will be positive. The first of these expresses the basic principle of the "multiplier" (that the marginal propensity to consume is less than unity),[2] and the second denotes the assumption that the demand for capital goods will be greater the greater the level of production.[3]

If we regard the $S(x)$ and $I(x)$ functions as *linear*, as in the absence of further information one is inclined to do, we have two possibilities :—

(i) $\frac{dI}{dx}$ exceeds $\frac{dS}{dx}$, in which case, as shown by Fig. 1,[4] there can be only a single position of unstable equilibrium, since above

---

[1] S and I are, of course, both functions of the rate of interest in addition to the level of activity. But the rate of interest, at any rate in the first approximation, could itself be regarded as a single valued function of the level of activity, and thus its influence incorporated in the $S(x)$ and $I(x)$ functions. (It is not necessary to assume, in order that $\frac{dI}{dx}$ should be positive, that the rates of interest —short and long term—are *constant*. We can allow for *some* variation as the rates of interest, to be associated with a change in investment and incomes, provided this variation is not large enough to prevent the change in incomes altogether. All that we are excluding here is a banking policy which so regulates interest rates as to keep the level of incomes constant.)

[2] $\frac{dS}{dx}$ is, of course, the reciprocal of Mr. Keynes' investment multiplier, which is defined as $\dfrac{1}{1 - \dfrac{dC}{dx}}$, where $\frac{dC}{dx} = 1 - \frac{dS}{dx}$.

[3] This assumption should not be confused with the "acceleration principle" (of Prof. J. M. Clark and others), which asserts that the demand for capital goods is a function of the *rate of change* of the level of activity, and not of the level of activity itself. The theory put forward below is thus not based on this "acceleration principle" (the general validity of which is questionable), but on a much simpler assumption—*i.e.*, that an increase in the current level of profits increases investment demand.

[4] In Fig. 1, as in all subsequent diagrams, the level of activity is measured along Ox and the corresponding value of *ex-ante* Investment and Saving along Oy.

the equilibrium point $I>S$, and thus activity tends to expand, below it $S>I$, and hence it tends to contract. If the S and I functions were of this character, the economic system would always be rushing either towards a state of hyper-inflation with full employment, or towards a state of complete collapse with zero employment, with no resting-place in between. Since recorded experience does not bear out such dangerous instabilities, this possibility can be dismissed.

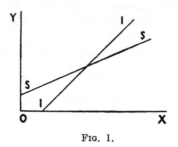

FIG. 1.

(ii) $\frac{dS}{dx}$ exceeds $\frac{dI}{dx}$, in which case, as shown in Fig. 2, there will be a single position of stable equilibrium. (This, I believe, is the assumption implied in Mr. Keynes' theory of employment.) If the economic system were of this nature, any disturbance, originating either on the investment side or on the savings side,

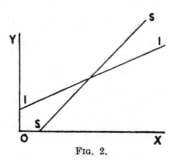

FIG. 2.

would be followed by the re-establishment of a new equilibrium, with a stable level of activity.[1] Hence this assumption fails in the opposite direction : it assumes *more* stability than the real world appears, in fact, to possess. Also, if there is any justification in the contention of the " accelerationists," the possibility of $\frac{dI}{dx}$

---

[1] Except in so far as the existence of time-lags of adjustment might prevent, on certain assumptions, the new equilibrium from being reached. Cf. Appendix below.

being greater than $\frac{dS}{dx}$, at any rate for certain values of x, cannot

be excluded. For $\frac{dI}{dx}$ could be many times greater than dx, while

$\frac{dS}{dx}$ can never be more than a fraction of dx.

4. Since thus neither of these two assumptions can be justified, we are left with the conclusion that the $I(x)$ and $S(x)$ functions cannot both be linear, at any rate over the entire range. And, in fact, on closer examination, there are good reasons for supposing that neither of them is linear.

(*a*) In the case of the investment function it is probable that $\frac{dI}{dx}$ will be *small*, both for low and for high levels of x, relatively to its " normal " level. It will be small for low levels of activity

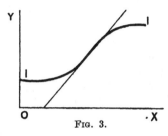

Fig. 3.

because when there is a great deal of surplus capacity, an increase in activity will not induce entrepreneurs to undertake additional construction : the rise in profits will not stimulate investment. (At the same time, the level of investment will not be zero, for there is always some investment undertaken for long-period development purposes which is independent of current activity.) But it will also be small for unusually high levels of activity, because rising costs of construction, increasing costs and increasing difficulty of borrowing will dissuade entrepreneurs from expanding still faster—at a time when they already have large commitments. Hence, given some " normal " value of $\frac{dI}{dx}$, appropriate for " normal " levels of activity, the $I(x)$ function will deviate from linearity in the manner suggested in Fig. 3.

(*b*) In the case of the savings function, the situation appears to be exactly the other way round : $\frac{dS}{dx}$ is likely to be relatively *large*, both for low and high levels of activity, as compared with its normal level. When incomes are unusually low, savings are cut

drastically, and below a certain level of income they will be
negative. When incomes are unusually high, people are likely to
save not only a higher amount, but also a larger proportion of
their income.[1] These tendencies, for society as a whole, are
likely to be reinforced by the fact that when activity is at a low
level, an increasing proportion of workers' earnings are paid out
of capital funds (in the form of unemployment benefits); while
when activity is at a high level, prices will tend to rise relatively
to wages, there will be a shift in the distribution of incomes in
favour of profits, and thus an increase in the aggregate propensity
to save.   Hence $\dfrac{dS}{dx}$ will deviate from its normal level in the
manner suggested in Fig. 4.

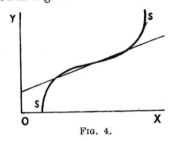

Fig. 4.

In what follows it will be assumed that the two functions
conform to these criteria. But, as the reader will note, our
analysis would remain valid even if only *one of the two* functions
behaved in the manner suggested, while the other was linear.

5. Given these assumptions about the behaviour of the savings
and investment functions, and assuming further that the *normal*
value of $\dfrac{dI}{dx}$ is greater than the normal value of $\dfrac{dS}{dx}$, the situation
will be one of multiple equilibria, as shown in Fig. 5. *A* and *B*
(in the diagram) are both stable positions, for at points below
A or *B*, $I > S$, hence activity tends to expand; above it $S > I$, hence
activity tends to contract. *C* is an unstable position in both
directions, and hence not a possible position of equilibrium. The
significance of point *C* is simply that if activity happens to be
above *C*, there will be a process of expansion which will come to a
halt at *B*; if it happens to be below *C*, there will be a process of
contraction until equilibrium is reached at *A*.

[1] Thus there is something like a " customary standard of living " based on
the " normal level " of incomes, and, corresponding to it, there is a certain normal
rate of savings. If incomes are much below it, individuals will attempt to maintain their standard of living by consuming capital; if incomes are much above it,
they will tend to save a disproportionate amount.

Hence the economic system can reach stability either at a certain high rate of activity or at a certain low rate of activity. There will be a certain depression level and a certain prosperity level at which it offers resistance to further changes in either direction. The key to the explanation of the Trade Cycle is to be found in the fact that each of these two positions is stable only *in the short period* : that as activity continues at either one of these levels, forces gradually accumulate which sooner or later will render that particular position unstable. It is to an explanation of the nature of these forces that we must now turn.

6. Both $S(x)$ and $I(x)$ are " *short-period* " functions—*i.e.*, they assume the total amount of fixed equipment in existence, and hence the amount of real income at any particular level of

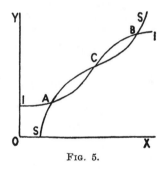

Fɪɢ. 5.

activity, as given. As these factors change in time, the S and I curves will shift their position; but according as activity is high or low (equilibrium is at B or at A) they will shift in different ways.

(i) When activity is high (equilibrium at B), the level of investment is high, the total amount of equipment gradually increases, and so, in consequence, the amount of consumers' goods produced at a given level of activity. As a result the S curve gradually shifts upwards (for there will be more consumption, and hence more saving, for any given activity); for the same reason the I curve gradually falls. (The accumulation of capital, by restricting the range of available investment opportunities, will tend to make it fall, while new inventions tend, on the whole, to make it rise. But the first of these factors is bound to be more powerful after a time.) As a result, the position of B is gradually shifted to the left and that of C to the right, thus reducing the level of activity somewhat and bringing B and C nearer to each other (see Fig. 6, " Stage II ").

The critical point is reached when, on account of these move-ments, the I and S curves become tangential and the points B and C fall together (" Stage III "). At that point equilibrium becomes unstable in a downward direction, since in the neighbour-hood of the point $S > I$ in both directions. The level of activity will now fall rapidly, on account of the excess of *ex-ante* Savings over *ex-ante* Investment, until a new equilibrium is reached at A where the position is again stable.[1, 2]

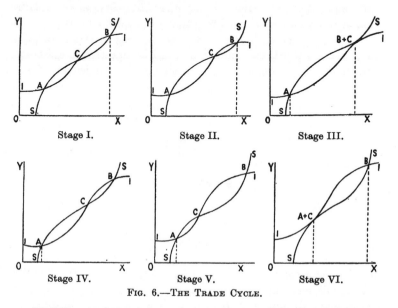

Fig. 6.—The Trade Cycle.

(ii) When activity is low, the movement of the I and S curves will tend to be in the opposite direction. For if at the level of investment corresponding to A investment is not sufficient to cover replacement, so that *net* investment in industrial plant and equipment is negative,[3] investment opportunities gradually

---

[1] The route followed in the transition from B to A might be either along the I curve or the S curve, according to whether *ex-post* Saving is adjusted to *ex-ante* Investment, or *ex-post* Investment to *ex-ante* Saving—*i.e.*, according as the disappointment of expectations occurs on the side of incomes, or in the level of entrepreneurial stocks.

[2] The fall in the rate of activity during the transition need not be very rapid, and may even take some years. This is because both entrepreneurs and con-sumers take some time to adjust their scale of purchases to their changed rate of earnings. If the process is at all prolonged, the two curves will be back at their " normal " position (as shown in Fig. 5 or " Stage IV " in Fig. 6) by the time point A is reached.

[3] It is not necessary, of course, that *total* net investment should be negative, since investment can take forms (such as armaments, etc.) whose construction does not reduce the available opportunities for the future.

accumulate and the I curve will shift upwards; and this tendency is likely to be reinforced by new inventions. For the same reason, the gradual decumulation of capital, in so far as it causes real income per unit of activity to fall, will lower the S curve.[1] These movements cause the position of A to shift to the right and that of C to shift to the left (thus separating B and C and bringing A and C nearer to each other), involving a gradual improvement in the level of activity (Stages IV and V). This will proceed until A and C fall together (the two curves again become tangential), when a new critical situation is reached; the position becomes unstable in an upward direction, since $I > S$ on either side of the equilibrium point; an upward cumulative movement will follow which can only come to rest when position B is reached (Stage VI). Thereafter the curves gradually return to the position shown in Stage I, and the cyclical movement is repeated.

7. The necessary and sufficient assumptions under which the combined operation of the saving and investment functions inevitably generate a cyclical movement which nowhere tends to come to rest, can therefore be set out as follows :—

(1) The " normal value " of $\frac{dI}{dx}$, valid for normal levels of activity, must be *greater* than the corresponding value of $\frac{dS}{dx}$.

(2) The " extreme values " of $\frac{dI}{dx}$, valid for abnormally high or abnormally low levels of activity, must be *smaller* than the corresponding values of $\frac{dS}{dx}$.

(3) The level of investment at the upper equilibrium point must be sufficiently large for the $I(x)$ function to *fall* (in time) relatively to the $S(x)$ function; and at the lower equilibrium point it must be sufficiently small for the $I(x)$ function to *rise* (in time) relatively to the $S(x)$ function. In other words, the position of zero net investment must fall within the limits set by the levels of investment ruling at $B + C$ and $A + C$, in Stage III and Stage VI, respectively.

If condition (1) did not obtain, equilibrium at C (which is in fact the " normal " equilibrium position) would be stable, instead

---

[1] It is possible that even if net investment is negative, real output per head should gradually rise in time (on account of the introduction of superior or more " capitalistic " processes of production during the depression), as a result of which S would tend to rise rather than fall. But this makes no difference so long as the I curve rises faster than the S curve.

of unstable; equilibrium would tend to get established there, and, once established, the shifts in the I and S curves, due to capital accumulation or decumulation, would merely lead to gradual changes in the level of activity until a position of stationariness is reached; they would not generate cyclical movements. If condition (2) was not satisfied (at any rate as regards *low* levels of activity) [1] the system, as we have seen, would be so unstable that capitalism could not function at all. Finally, if condition (3) did not obtain, the cyclical movements would come to a halt at some stage, owing to a cessation of the movements of the $S(x)$ and $I(x)$ functions.

This is not to suggest that in the absence of these three conditions cyclical phenomena would be altogether impossible. Only they would have to be explained with the aid of different principles; they could not be accounted for by the savings and investment functions alone.

8. In fact, conditions (1) and (2) are almost certain to be satisfied in the real world; doubt could only arise in connection with condition (3). It can be taken for granted, of course, that net investment will be *positive* while equilibrium is at position B; but it is by no means so certain that net investment will be *negative* while equilibrium is at position A.[2] It is quite possible, for example, that savings should fall rapidly at a relatively early stage of the downward movement, so that position A is reached while net investment is still positive. In that case the S and I curves will still move in the same direction as at B, with the result that the position A is gradually shifted to the left, until net investment becomes zero. At that point the movements of the I and S curves will cease; the forces making for expansion or contraction come to a standstill. Alternatively, we might assume that net investment at A is initially negative, but in the course of the gradual improvement, the position of zero net investment is reached before the forces of cumulative expansion could come into operation—*i.e.*, somewhere during Stages IV and V, and *before* the cycle reaches Stage VI. In this case, too, the cyclical movement will get into a deadlock.

---

[1] It is possible that the point B should be situated *beyond* the position of full employment—*i.e.*, that in the course of the upward movement the state of full employment should be reached before *ex-ante* Savings and Investment reach equality. In that case the upward movement would end in a state of cumulative inflation, which in turn would, sooner or later, be brought to a halt by a rise in interest rates sufficient to push the point B inside the full-employment barrier. From then onwards the cyclical movement would proceed in exactly the same manner as described.

[2] The term " net investment " here is used in the sense defined in § 6 (ii).

Hence the forces making for expansion when we start from a state of depression are not so certain in their operation as the forces making for a down-turn when we start from prosperity; the danger of chronic stagnation is greater than the danger of a chronic boom. A boom, if left to itself, is certain to come to an end; but the depression might get into a position of stationariness, and remain there until external changes (the discovery of new inventions or the opening up of new markets) come to the rescue.

9. The preceding analysis offers also certain indications regarding the determination of the period and the amplitude of the Cycle. The period of the Cycle seems to depend on two time-lags, or rather time-rates of movement : (i) on the rate at which the S and I curves shift at any particular level of investment (this, of course, will vary with the level of investment, and will be faster when investment is high or low, than in the middle); (ii) on the time taken to complete a " cumulative movement "— *i.e.*, the time required for the system to travel from $B + C$ to A or from $A + C$ to B (Stages III and VI).

The second of these factors obviously depends on the velocity with which entrepreneurs and consumers adjust their expectations and thus their buying-plans to unexpected changes in the situation. The first factor, on the other hand, seems to depend on technical data, on the construction period and durability of capital goods. The shorter the construction period, the greater will be the output of capital goods, per unit period, at a given rate of investment; the shorter the life-time of capital goods, the larger will be the percentage addition to total equipment represented by a given output of capital goods. Hence the shorter the construction-period, and the lower the durability, the faster will be the rate of shift of the S and I curves at any given rate of investment; the shorter the length of the Trade Cycle.[1]

As regards the amplitude, this depends on the *shapes* of the I and S curves, which determine the distance between A and B, at their " normal " position (*i.e.*, at Stages I and IV). The amplitude will be all the smaller the shorter the range of activity over which the " normal values " of $\frac{dI}{dx}$ and $\frac{dS}{dx}$ are operative.

[1] If the " capital intensity " of investments varies in the different phases of the Cycle in an *inverse relation* to the rate of investment (*i.e.*, is less in boom periods than in depression periods), this will tend to reduce the period of the Cycle, as compared with a situation where the capital intensity is constant, since it will increase the rate of shift of the S and I curves. Conversely, if capital intensity varied *in direct relation* with the rate of investment, this would lengthen the period. Finally, if capital intensity showed a *steady increase* throughout the Cycle, this would lengthen the boom periods and shorten the depression periods.

Variations in the amplitude of successive cycles, on the other hand, seem to depend entirely on extraneous factors, such as new inventions or secular changes in habits of saving. There appears to be no necessary reason why, in the absence of such factors, the amplitude should be gradually decreasing or vice-versa.[1]

10. Our model should also enable us to throw some light on problems of economic policy. Here I confine myself to two points. (i) It appears that measures taken to combat the depression (through public investment) have much more chance of success if taken at a relatively early stage, or at a relatively late stage, than at the bottom of the depression. If taken early, the problem is merely to prevent that gradual fall in the investment function relatively to the saving function which carries the cycle from Stage II to Stage III. But, once Stage III is passed, nothing can prevent the switch-over from the *B*-equilibrium to the *A*-equilibrium, and then the problem becomes one of raising the investment demand schedule sufficiently to lift the position to Stage VI (at which the forces of expansion come into operation). The amount of public investment required to achieve this is obviously much greater in the early phase of the depression (at Stage IV) than in the later phase (at Stage V). Thus just when the depression is at its worst the difficulty of overcoming it is the greatest. (ii) The chances of " evening out " fluctuations by " anti-cyclical " public investment appear to be remote. For if the policy is successful in preventing the downward cumulative movement, it will also succeed in keeping the level of private investment high; and for this very reason the forces making for a down-turn will continue to accumulate, thus making the need for continued public investment greater. Thus, if, on the basis of past experience, the Government Authority contemplates a four years public investment plan, in the belief that thereby it can bridge the gap between one prosperity-period and the next, it is more likely that it might succeed in *postponing* the onset of the

---

[1] At first sight one might think that this question also depends on *endogenous* factors : that the cycle will be " damped " (amplitude of successive cycles decreasing) if the point of zero net investment is so situated that there will be net capital accumulation over the cycle as a whole, and vice versa. But this is not so. If there is net accumulation over the cycle as a whole (*i.e.*, the accumulation over the boom period exceeds the decumulation during the depression), then, in the absence of extraneous changes, the position *B* at the corresponding stages of successive cycles will be situated more and more to the left; but the position *A* will also be situated more to the left, with the result that, though there will be a gradual fall in the average level of activity, there need be no decrease in the deviations around the average. The same holds, *mutatis mutandis*, if there is net decumulation over the cycle as a whole.

depression for four years than that it will prevent its occurrence altogether.[1] If the Trade Cycle is really governed by the forces analysed in this paper, the policy of internal stabilisation must be conceived along different lines.

NICHOLAS KALDOR

London School of Economics.

APPENDIX

It may be interesting to examine the relations of the model here presented to other models of the Trade Cycle based on similar principles. The one nearest to it, I think, is Mr. Kalecki's theory, given in Chap. 6 of his *Essays in the Theory of Economic Fluctuations.* The differences can best be shown by employing the same type of diagram and the same denotation as used by Mr. Kalecki. Let income be measured along OY, and the rate of investment decisions along OD. Let $D_t = \Phi e(Y_t)$ represent the rate of invest-

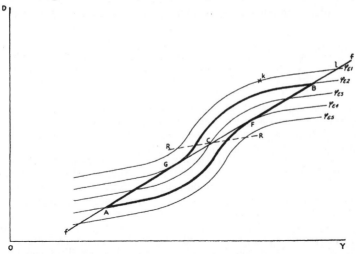

ment decisions at time t, given the quantity of equipment available. Let the family of curves Φe_1 . . . etc., represent this function for different quantities of available equipment, where e_1 represents a *smaller* quantity of equipment than e_2, and so on. Let $Y_t + \tau =$

---

[1] This argument is strictly valid only for a closed system; it is not valid in the case of a country which receives its cyclical impulses from abroad. For in that case the cyclical variations in the demand for exports can be taken as given irrespective of what the Government is doing; the chronological order of the " lean years " will not be altered by the attempt at suppressing them. Thus a policy of this type is much more likely to be successful in a small country, like Sweden, than in large countries, such as Britain or the United States, which themselves generate the cyclical forces and transmit them to others.

$f(D_t)$ be the level of income at time $t + \tau$ as a function of investment decisions at the time t. This is the same as our savings-function, which, for simplicity, and following Mr. Kalecki, we regard here as a straight line, independent of the amount of equipment. (τ represents the time lag between investment decisions and the corresponding income, which, as Mr. Kalecki has shown, depends partly on the construction-period of capital goods, and partly on the lag between income and consumption.) The meeting-points of Φe curves and the f curve are positions of short-period equilibrium, where Savings=Investment; the equilibrium is stable when the Φe curve cuts the f function from above, it is unstable when it cuts it from below. Let RR represent the locus of points on the Φe curves where the level of investment decisions corresponds to replacement so that *net* investment is zero. This curve is slightly *rising*, from left to right, since the higher the amount of equipment in existence, the greater the amount of investment needed for replacement. The point C represents the position of long period or stationary equilibrium, where Savings=Investment *and* net investment is zero.

Under our assumptions, where $\dfrac{d\Phi}{dY}$ exceeds $\dfrac{1}{\dfrac{df}{dD}}$ for certain values of Y, there must be certain levels of equipment at which the Φ curves cut the f function not once, but three times. In our diagram this will be the case if equipment is greater than e_2 and less than e_4. Given this assumption, and assuming further that the replacement level, *for the critical amounts of equipment*, falls between the limits of stability—*i.e.*, between points F and G in the diagram—the system can never settle down to a stationary equilibrium, but moves around it in a cycle. If we assume that the time-lag τ is small relatively to the time needed to reach successive Φ curves (*i.e.*, relatively to the rate at which the total quantity of equipment is increasing), so that a position of short-period equilibrium can be reached *before* significant changes occur in the amount of equipment in existence, the cyclical movement of the system will be indicated by the trajectory $AGBF$. For if we start from any arbitrary point, such as k, the cumulative forces will increase income and investment decisions until the system reaches l, and thereafter activity will move downwards (owing to the gradual accumulation of equipment) along the f line until it reaches F. At that point equilibrium becomes unstable, and a downward moving cumulative process is set up which lands the system at A. Here investment is less than replacement, and the gradual reduction in available equipment will increase activity until the system reaches G, at which the situation again becomes unstable, an upward cumulative movement follows which lands the system at B. Thus if we start from any point outside the trajectory, the system will move on to it, and the same follows if we start from any point inside. Hence, even if we started from the position of stationary long-period equilibrium (C), the unstability of the situation there must generate forces which set up a cycle.

It follows, further, that if all the fundamental data which determine the Φ and f functions—*i.e.*, tastes, technique, population, monetary policy, the elasticity of expectations, etc.—remain unchanged, the cycle would continue indefinitely with constant amplitude and period and the trend (the accumulation of capital between successive cycles) would be zero. Hence changes in the nature of successive cycles would have to be explained by dynamic changes.

In Mr. Kalecki's model $\dfrac{d\Phi}{dY}$ is supposed to be smaller than $\dfrac{1}{\dfrac{df}{dD}}$ throughout, hence all his positions of short-period equilibrium are *stable* positions. In this case, on our assumptions, no cycle would be generated at all; the system would gradually approach stationary equilibrium. He assumes, however, that the time-lag between investment decisions and the corresponding income is large relatively to the rate at which the amount of equipment is increasing—*i.e.*, the movements *along* a Φ curve and the movement *between* Φ curves are of comparable speed—in which case the movement toward a stationary equilibrium may " overshoot the mark "—*i.e.*, the rate of investment decisions can continue to fall, even after it is less than what corresponds to replacement, simply because the fall in income lags behind. Thus the introduction of the time-lag between investment decisions and the corresponding income could explain a cyclical movement even if the underlying situation is a stable one; though, in order that this cycle should not be highly damped (*i.e.*, that it should not peter out quickly in the absence of new disturbing factors), it is necessary to suppose (i) that the effect of current investment on total equipment should be relatively large, so that the equipment added during the period of the time-lag has a considerable influence on the rate or profit, and hence on investment decisions; (ii) that the angle enclosed by the f and ϕ functions should be small—*i.e.*,

that $\dfrac{1}{\dfrac{df}{dD}}$ should but slightly exceed $\dfrac{d\phi}{d\gamma}$.[1]

Previous attempts at constructing models of the Trade Cycle —such as Mr. Kalecki's or Professor Tinbergen's—have thus mostly been based on the assumption of statically stable situations, where equilibrium would persist if once reached; the existence of the cycle was explained as a result of the operation of certain time-lags which prevented the new equilibrium from being reached, once the old equilibrium, for some external cause, had been disturbed. In this sense all these theories may be regarded as being derived from the " cobweb theorem." The drawback of such explanations is that the existence of an undamped cycle can

---

[1] Hence the positions of equilibrium in Mr. Kalecki's model, though formally stable, possess only a *low* degree of stability.

be shown only as a result of a happy coincidence, of a particular constellation of the various time-lags and parameters assumed. The introduction of the assumption of unstable positions of equilibrium at and around the replacement level provides, however, as we have seen, an explanation for a cycle of *constant amplitude* irrespective of the particular values of the time-lags and parameters involved. The time-lags are only important here in determining the *period* of the cycle, they have no significance in explaining its existence.

Moreover, with the theories of the Tinbergen–Kalecki type, the amplitude of the cycle depends on the size of the initial shock. Here the amplitude is determined by endogeneous factors and the assumption of " initial shocks " is itself unnecessary.

[12]
On the concept of optimal economic growth[*]

Tjalling C. Koopmans[†]

1. Approaches in the literature

The search for a principle from which an 'optimal' rate of economic growth can be deduced holds great fascination to economists. A variety of attitudes or approaches to this problem can be discerned in the literature.

One school of thought, represented among others by Professor Bauer (1957), favors that balance between the welfare of present and future generations that is implied in the spontaneous and individual savings decisions of the present generation. A policy implementing this preference would merely seek to arrange for tax collection and other government actions affecting the economy in such a way as to distort or amend the individual savings preferences as little as possible.

Contrasting with this view is the position, expressed among others quite explicitly by Professor Allais (1947, chs VI, X), that the balancing of the interests of different generations is an ethical or political problem, in which the competitive market solution has no valid claim to moral superiority over other solutions that depend for their realization on action by the state. A more specific optimality concept is implied in the strictures of Professor Harrod (1948, p. 40) and of Frank Ramsey (1928, p. 543) against any discounting of future utilities. These authors leave little doubt that they regard only equal weights for the welfare of present and future generations as ethically defensible.

The purpose of the present paper is to do some 'logical experiments', in which various mathematical forms of the optimality criterion are confronted with a very simple model of technology and of population growth, to see what their maximization leads to. Our study is similar in purpose to Ramsey's classical paper, and to Tinbergen's recent exploration (1960) of the same problem. The underlying idea of this exploratory approach is that the problem of

[*] This research was undertaken by the Cowles Foundation for Research in Economics, under Task NR 047-006 with the Office of Naval Research, and completed under a grant from the National Science Foundation. An abbreviated version of this paper was presented at a joint session of the American Economic Association and the Econometric Society on 'Intertemporal Economic Theory' in the Boston Meetings, December 1963.
[†] I am indebted to S. Chakravarty, E.S. Phelps and H.E. Scarf for valuable comments.

optimal growth is too complicated, or at least too unfamiliar, for one to feel comfortable in making an *entirely* a priori choice of an optimality criterion before one knows the implications of alternative choices. One may wish to choose between principles on the basis of the results of their application. In order to do so, one first needs to know what these results are. This is an economic question logically prior to the ethical or political choice of a criterion.

What is a suitable mathematical formalization of the idea of an optimality criterion? The most basic notion is that of a preference ordering of growth paths. Such an ordering states for each pair of alternative growth paths whether they are equally good, and if not, which is preferred. Indifference, preference and preference-or-indifference are usually required to be transitive.

An important class of preference orderings is that representable[1] by a continuous preference function (utility function, indicator, etc.). A particular function which has been frequently used has the form

$$U = \sum_{t=1}^{\infty} x^{t-1} u(x_t)$$

for consumption paths $(x_1, x_2, \ldots)$ of infinite duration with discrete time $t = 1, 2, \ldots$. This form can be interpreted as a discounted sum of future one-period utilities $u(x_t)$ with a discount factor of x per period. This form has been derived by the present author[2] from postulates expressing, among other requirements,

(a) noncomplementarity of consumption in any three sub-periods into which the future may be partitioned;
(b) stationarity in the sense that the ordering of any two paths is not altered if both consumption sequences are postponed by one time unit and identical consumptions are inserted in the gaps so created in each path.

The utility function so obtained is 'cardinal' only in the limited sense that the simple form of a discounted sum is conserved only by *linear* transformations of the utility scale. If below we occasionally use the expressions 'utility difference', 'marginal utility', these must be interpreted as elliptic phrases referring to a preference indicator of that particularly simple form. There is no intent to claim that, even in the absence of risk or uncertainty, there is some physical or psychological significance to the comparison of utility *differences* in such a scale.

There still remains a logical gap between the derivation of the above utility function from the postulates referred to and its use in the present study: for present purposes a continuous time concept is more appropriate.

2. Plan of the present paper

We shall freely borrow from Phelps (1961) and others mentioned below the assumptions of the main model considered in Section 4, from Ramsey (1928) a device for maximizing utility over

---

1. Conditions of continuity under which a given preference ordering permits such a representation have been studied by Wold (1943) and by Debreu (1954).
2. Koopmans (1960), especially Section 14.

an infinite horizon without discounting, together with methods for applying the device, from Srinivasan (1962) and from Uzawa (1963) information about the results of maximizing a discounted sum of future consumption, and from Inagaki (1963) results about the generalization of the present problem to the case of predictable technological progress.[3] If this particular brew has not been served before, it is not put together here for any novelty of the combination. Rather, our eclectic model appears to have in it the minimum collection of elements needed to serve the two main aims of the present paper.

The first aim is to illustrate the usefulness of the tools and concepts of mathematical programming in relation to the problem of optimal economic growth.

The second aim is to argue against the complete separation of the ethical or political choice of an objective function from the investigation of the set of technologically feasible paths. Our main conclusion will be that such a separation is not workable. Ignoring realities in adopting 'principles' may lead one to search for a nonexistent optimum, or to adopt an 'optimum' that is open to unanticipated objections.

In connection with the first aim, Section 3 recalls a few results of the theory of linear and convex programming in a finite number of variables, that bear on the problem of optimum growth. The reading of this section is believed to be helpful rather than essential for what follows. Indeed, in most of its formulations, the problem of optimal growth is a special problem in mathematical programming. The main new element arises from the open-endedness of the future. If one adopts a finite time horizon, the choice of the terminal capital stock is as much a part of the problem to be solved as the choice of the path. Terminal capital, after all, represents the collection of paths beyond the horizon that it makes possible. An infinite horizon is therefore perhaps a more natural specification in many formulations of the problem of optimal growth. The mathematical complications so created are the price for the greater explicitness of long run considerations thus made possible.

Sections 4–6 analyze a model with a single producible good serving both as capital in the form of a stock, and as a consumption good in the form of a flow. It is produced under a constant technology by a labor force growing exogenously at a given exponential rate. Proofs for many of the propositions labeled (A), (B), ... in Section 4 are given under the same label in an Appendix.[4]

In Section 7 the findings of the logical experiments of Sections 5, 6 are examined. The main conclusion is that some utility functions that on a priori grounds appear quite plausible and reasonable do not permit determination of an optimal growth path even in a constant technology. Tentative and intuitive explanations for this finding are offered.

Section 8 discusses in a tentative way, and without proofs, possible extensions of the analysis to a changing technology and/or a variable rate of population growth, with none, one, or both of these regarded as policy variables.

3.   Pertinent aspects of linear and of convex programming

Let linear programming be applied to an allocation problem in terms of the quantities x_j,

---

3.   Note added in proof: A study by Pugachev (1963), which has several similarities with the present study, has been brought to my attention by J.M. Montias.

4.   Approximate equivalents of propositions (E), (F), (H), (I), (J) were obtained independently by David Cass (1963). The connection between the limiting case of a zero discount rate and the 'golden rule of accumulation' (see Section 5) is also observed and discussed in Cass's paper.

$j = 1, ..., n$ of a finite number n of commodities. Then the *feasible set* D is given by a finite number of linear inequalities

$$\sum_{j=1}^{n} a_{ij} x_j \leq b_i, \qquad i = 1, ..., m. \tag{1}$$

The objective function, or maximand, is a linear form in the x_j,

$$U = \sum_{j=1}^{n} a_j x_j. \tag{2}$$

The feasible set D is always closed, and may be bounded (as in Figure 1) or unbounded (Figure 2).

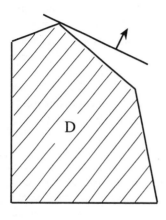

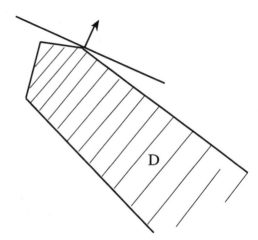

Figure 1   Figure 2

The range R of the objective function on the feasible set (the set of values assumed by the maximand on the points of the set D) is an interval. If D is bounded (contained in some hypercube), then R is necessarily also bounded. If D is unbounded, then R may still be bounded, but may also be unbounded from below, from above, or both. If R is bounded from above, an optimal point exists (Figure 2). If R is unbounded from above, no optimum exists (Figure 3). Both cases can arise on the same feasible set D through different choices of the maximand.

A highly special form of linear programming has been used by Kantorovich (1959). In this case the objective is defined by prescribing the ratios of the quantities of all *desired goods*, i.e., goods entering into the objective, and by maximizing a common scalar factor applied to these quantities (Figure 4). This problem can also be formulated in linear programming terms: One adds to the constraints (1) linear *equalities* expressing the prescribed ratios, and chooses as a maximand (2) the quantity of any one desired good, say.

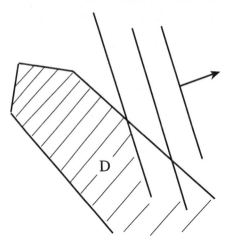

Figure 3

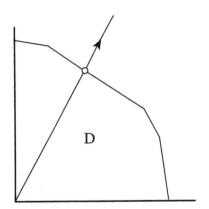

Figure 4

In convex programming the feasible set is defined by

$$g_i(x_1, \ldots, x_n) \geq 0, \qquad i = 1, \ldots, m, \tag{3}$$

where the g_i are *concave* [5] functions, and the maximand

$$U = U(x_1, \ldots, x_n) \tag{4}$$

is another concave function (Figure 5). The term *convex programming* derives from the fact that the feasible set, and each set of points on which the maximand attains or exceeds a given value, are convex.[6] Linear programming is a special case of convex programming.

---

5. A concave function $g(x_1, \ldots, x_n)$ is represented by a hypersurface $y = g(x_1, \ldots, x_n)$ in the space $\{y, x_1, \ldots, x_n\}$ that is never 'below' any of its chords (if the $+y$ direction is 'up').
6. A convex set is a set of points containing every line segment connecting two of its points.

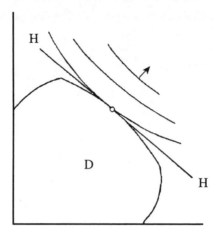

Figure 5

With any optimal point in a convex programming problem one can associate a hyperplane H through that point, which separates the feasible set from the set of points in which the maximand exceeds its value in the optimal point (H is a line in Figure 5). The direction coefficients of such a hyperplane define a vector of relative prices implicit in the optimal point. One interpretation of the implicit prices is that the opening up of an opportunity to barter unlimited amounts of commodities at those relative prices does not allow the attainment of a higher value of the maximand. Moreover, if the maximand is a differentiable utility function, one may be able, by treating utility as an additional 'commodity' and choosing its 'price' to be unity, to interpret the implicit prices of the other goods as their marginal utilities either directly in consumption, or indirectly through the extra consumption made possible by the availability of one more unit of that commodity as a factor of production.

4. A one-sector model with constant technology and steadily increasing labor force

We assume that output of the single producible commodity is a twice differentiable and concave function $F(Z, L)$, homogeneous of degree one, of the capital stock Z and the size of the labor force L. These assumptions imply full employment of labor and capital, constant returns to scale, and nonincreasing returns to an increase in only one factor of production. Since capital is treated as a stock of the single producible commodity, output is at any time t to be allocated to a positive rate of consumption X_t, and to a positive, zero, or even negative rate of net investment Y_t. Hence, if we use a continuous time concept, and denote derivatives with respect to time by dots, we have

$$X_t + Y_t = F(Z_t, L_t),$$ (5)

$$Y_t = \dot{Z}_t.$$ (6)

$F(Z, L)$ is defined for all $Z \geq 0$, $L \geq 0$. We assume further that both labor and capital are essential to production, that either factor has a positive marginal productivity, and that returns to increases in only one factor are strictly decreasing,

$$
\begin{cases}
(7a, b) & F(0, L) = 0, \qquad F(Z, 0) = 0, \\[2mm]
(7c, d) & \dfrac{\delta F}{\delta Z} > 0, \qquad\quad \dfrac{\delta F}{\delta L} > 0, \\[2mm]
(7e, f) & \dfrac{\delta^2 F}{\delta Z^2} < 0, \qquad \dfrac{\delta^2 F}{\delta L^2} < 0.
\end{cases}
\tag{7}
$$

Finally, we assume that the labor force increases at a constant positive exponential rate λ, from a given initial magnitude L_o,

$$
L_t = L_o \, e^{\lambda t}, \qquad \lambda > 0.
\tag{8a, b}
$$

The homogeneity of the production function enables us to go over to per-unit-of-labor-force concepts. Calling the unit of labor force briefly a 'worker', let x denote consumption per worker, y ditto net investment, z ditto capital stock, and

$$
f(z) = \frac{1}{L} F(Z, L) = F\!\left(\frac{Z}{L}, 1\right) = F(z, 1)
\tag{9}
$$

output per worker. Since we then have

$$
\dot{Z}_t = \frac{d}{dt}(z_t L_t) = \dot{z}_t L_t + z_t \dot{L}_t = (\dot{z}_t + \lambda z_t) L_t,
$$

the feasible set in the space of per-worker variables x_t, z_t becomes

$$
\begin{cases}
(10a) & x_t + \dot{z}_t = f(z_t) - \lambda z_t, \\[2mm]
(10b, c, d) & x_t > 0, \qquad z_t > 0, \qquad z_0 \text{ given.}
\end{cases}
\tag{10}
$$

The term λz represents the (net) investment needed if one wants merely to supply the growing labor force with capital at the existing ratio of capital per worker.

To be specific we shall call a path (x_t, z_t) satisfying (10) *attainable* (for the given z_o), and use the term *feasible* path in the wider sense of a path attainable for some $z_0 > 0$.

It is implied in (7e) that $f(z)$ is strictly concave.[7] The per-worker production function $f(z)$ is therefore represented by a curve such as is shown in Figure 6. The curve rises from the value $f(0) = 0$ with a decreasing slope. In particular, any line λz through the origin and of slope λ such that $0 < \lambda < f'(0)$ will ultimately intersect the curve and continue above it,[8]

---

7. A strictly concave function is one that is strictly 'above' all its chords.
8. To obtain (11) suppose that, for some such λ, $f(z) \geq \lambda z$ for arbitrarily large values of z. Then, by $f(0) = 0$ and the concavity of f, $f(z) \geq \lambda z$ for all $z \geq 0$. But then, for any $Z > 0$, (7b) and the continuity of $F(Z, L)$ imply the contradiction $0 = F(Z, 0) = \lim\limits_{L \to 0} F(Z, L) = \lim\limits_{L \to 0} LF\!\left(\frac{Z}{L}, 1\right) = Z \lim\limits_{Z \to \infty} \frac{1}{z} f(z) \geq Z\lambda > 0.$

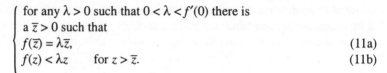

$$\begin{cases} \text{for any } \lambda > 0 \text{ such that } 0 < \lambda < f'(0) \text{ there is} \\ \text{a } \overline{z} > 0 \text{ such that} \\ f(\overline{z}) = \lambda \overline{z}, \\ f(z) < \lambda z \qquad \text{for } z > \overline{z}. \end{cases}$$

(11a)

(11b)

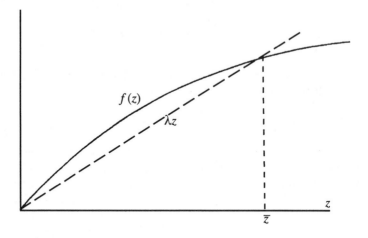

Figure 6

If λ represents the rate of growth of the labor force, $\overline{z}$ represents a capital stock per worker so large that the investment required to keep it at the same level absorbs all output, leaving nothing for consumption. If $z_0 \geq \overline{z}$, it will therefore be necessary to allow z_t to decrease at least to some level below $\overline{z}$. To avoid the uninteresting complication arising if $z_0 > \overline{z}$ we shall from here on simply define 'feasibility' so as to imply $0 < z_0 \leq \overline{z}$.

Although we have not yet defined a maximand, it may be observed that the attainable set is now defined in a space where the 'point' is a pair of positive functions x_t, z_t of time, defined for $0 \leq t < \infty$. This is an infinite–dimensional space for the double reason that we use a continuous time concept and an infinite horizon. It remains infinite-dimensional if we limit ourselves[9] to twice differentiable functions z_t and once differentiable functions x_t.

5. The path of the Golden Rule of Accumulation

To answer an important preliminary question, we first consider a Kantorovich type restriction of the problem to a one-dimensional one. The latter problem has been formulated and solved in the last few years, independently and in one form or another, by[10] Allais (1962), Desrousseaux (1961), Phelps (1961), Joan Robinson (1962), Swan (1960), Von Weizsäcker (1962).

---

9. Due to twice differentiability of the data functions $f(z)$ above and $u(x)$ below we will not be excluding any optimal paths by that requirement. However, a slightly weaker requirement will be found useful in the Appendix.
10. Dates are bibliographical only and refer to the list of references below. Some of these authors used somewhat more general models involving an exponential technological improvement factor in the production function.

Remove from the definition of the attainable set the restriction that z_0 is given, thus making initial capital a free good. Restrict the attainable set instead by an arbitrary stipulation that consumption per worker and capital per worker are to be held constant over time,

$$x_t = x, \quad z_t = z \quad \text{for all} \quad t \geq 0.$$

The new 'attainable' set then is given by

$$x = f(z) - \lambda z, \quad x > 0, \quad z > 0. \tag{12a, b, c}$$

Finally, choose z so as to maximize x, the permanent level of consumption per worker. This leads to the choice of that value $\hat{z}$ of z for which

$$f'(\hat{z}) = \lambda, \quad \text{so} \quad \hat{x} = f(\hat{z}) - \lambda \hat{z}, \tag{13a, b}$$

where $f'(z)$ denotes the derivative of $f(z)$.

Figure 7 shows the construction. Because of the essentiality of labor to production, i.e., assumption (7b) as reflected in (11), there is for any given slope λ such that $0 < \lambda < f'(0)$ a point $\hat{z}$ for which the tangent to the production function per worker has that slope. To interpret the condition (13a) note that, if we hold L fixed, then by the homogeneity of F,

$$f'(z) = \frac{\delta F(Z/L, 1)}{\delta(Z/L)} = \frac{\delta F(Z, L)}{\delta Z}.$$

Hence (13) expresses equality, at all times t, of the marginal productivity of capital (in producing capital, say) to the growth rate λ – a prescription known as the golden rule of accumulation.[11]

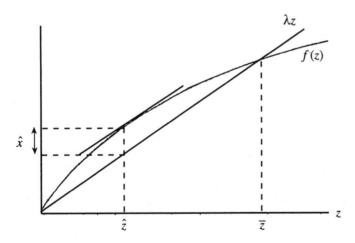

Figure 7

---

11. Phelps (1961).

6. Existence and characteristics of optimal paths

We now return to the original problem that allows x_t and z_t to vary in time and recognizes the restriction (10d) of a historically given initial capital stock, and look about for a suitable maximand. We admit to an ethical preference for neutrality as between the welfare of different generations. After some hesitation, we tentatively and arbitrarily resolve another ethical conundrum by interpreting this 'timing neutrality' in a *per capita* sense. That is, we assume first of all that labor force and population grow in proportion. Furthermore we thus imply that, starting from the golden rule path $\hat{x}$, $\hat{z}$ of the preceding section as a base line, we welcome equally a unit increase in consumption *per worker* in any one future decade, say. Mere numbers do not give one generation an edge over another in this scheme of values.

The next difficulty we face is a technical one. A previous investigation by Koopmans (1960), continued by Koopmans, Diamond and Williamson (1962), has shown that there does not exist a utility function of all consumption paths, which at the same time exhibits timing neutrality and satisfies other reasonable postulates which all utility functions used so far have agreed with. A way out of this dilemma was shown by Ramsey (1928). One can define an *eligible* set of consumption paths on which a neutral utility function can be defined. Moreover, the eligible set is a subset of the feasible set such that the remaining, *ineligible*, paths are clearly inferior to the eligible ones, in a sense still to be defined. In Ramsey's case, in which population was assumed stationary, the criterion of eligibility was a sufficiently rapid approach over time to what he called a state of *bliss*. This state was defined as either a saturation of consumers with consumption goods, or a saturation of the productive system with capital to the point where its marginal productivity has vanished – whichever state would be encountered first. We shall find that in the present case of a steady population growth the golden rule path can take the place of Ramsey's state of bliss in defining eligibility. Thus Ramsey's device can be applied to our case with what seems a lesser strain on the imagination in regard to situations outside the range of experience.

We have one more technical choice to make. For reasons of mathematical simplicity, and at some cost in 'realism', we shall model our utility function after the finite-horizon example of

$$V_T = \int_0^T u(x_t)\, dt. \tag{14}$$

As explained already in Section 1, this simple integration of an instantaneous utility flow $u(x_t)$ implies noncomplementarity between consumption in any two or more parts of the future.

We shall assume that the instantaneous utility flow is a strictly concave, increasing and twice differentiable function $u(x)$ of the instantaneous consumption flow x. This function does not change with time, and is defined for all $x > 0$. Strict concavity implies that we attribute greater weight to the marginal unit of per capita consumption of a poor generation as compared with a rich one. To assume $u(x)$ increasing rules out saturation. Finally, instead of introducing a subsistence minimum, we shall require that

$$\lim_{x \to 0} u(x) = -\infty, \tag{15}$$

a strong incentive to avoid periods of very low consumption as much as is feasible.

Let $\hat{u} = u(\hat{x})$ denote the instantaneous utility flow derived from the consumption flow per worker of the path $x_t = \hat{x}$, $z_t = \hat{z}$, of the golden rule. We shall now work with the difference between the integral (14) for any given feasible path and its value for the golden rule path, and study the behavior of this difference as T goes to infinity. The following propositions can be proved (for proofs see Appendix).

(A) *There is a number* $\bar{U}$ *such that*

$$U_T = \int_0^T (u(x_t) - \hat{u})\, dt \leq \bar{U} \tag{16}$$

for all feasible paths (x_t, z_t) *and for all horizons* T.

Thus, if utility is measured in conformity with (14), no path is 'infinitely better' than the golden rule path. In particular, no feasible path x_t can indefinitely maintain or exceed a level u of utility flow that exceeds $\hat{u}$. Thus the golden rule path continually attains the highest indefinitely maintainable utility flow.

(B) *For every feasible path, either* $\lim_{T \to \infty} U_T$ *exists (is a finite number), or* U_T *diverges to* $-\infty$ *as T tends to* ∞.

In the first case, we call the path *eligible*, in the second *ineligible*. Then (B) establishes a clear superiority of each eligible path over each ineligible one. On the eligible set we choose as the utility function

$$U = \int_0^\infty (u(x_t) - \hat{u})\, dt. \tag{17}$$

In propositions (C), (D), an *optimal* path is defined as a path maximizing U on the set of eligible and attainable paths.

It is not hard to find eligible and attainable paths for every admissible initial capital stock z_0. If $z_0 > \hat{z}$, one only needs to refrain from net investment until the capital stock $\hat{Z}_t = \hat{z}\, L_0 e^{\lambda t}$ of the golden rule path has caught up with the given initial stock $Z_0 = z_0 L_0$, and to continue along the golden rule path thereafter. If $0 < z_0 < \hat{z}$, one can through a *finite* period of tightening the belt arrive on the same path.

(C) *For any initial capital stock* z_0 *with* $0 < z_0 \leq \bar{z}$ *there exists a unique optimal path* $(\hat{x}_t, \hat{z}_t)$ *in the set of eligible and attainable paths. For* $z_0 \neq \hat{z}$, *both* $\hat{x}_t$ *and* $\hat{z}_t$ *exhibit a strictly monotonic approach to* $\hat{x}$ *and* $\hat{z}$, *respectively, from below if* $0 < z_0 < \hat{z}$, *from above if* $\hat{z} < z_0 \leq \bar{z}$. *For* $z_0 = \hat{z}$, *the optimal path is* $\hat{x}_t = \hat{x}$, $\hat{z}_t = \hat{z}$ *for all* t, *the golden rule path.*

(D) *The optimal path satisfies the condition*

$$u'(x_t)\, \dot{z}_t = \hat{u} - u(x_t) \tag{18}$$

that at any time the net increase in capital per worker multiplied by the marginal utility of consumption per worker equals the net excess of the maximum sustainable utility level over the current utility level.

This condition is similar to the Keynes–Ramsey condition (Ramsey, 1928, eq. (5)) formulated in terms of absolute amounts of consumption, and reverts to it for $\lambda = 0$. Keynes' intuitive reasoning in support of this condition carries over with only slight reinterpretation.

A number of analogous results can be obtained if the utility of a consumption path is defined as an integral over the instantaneous utility flow discounted at a *positive* instantaneous rate ρ.

(E) *The utility function*

$$V(\rho) = \int_0^\infty e^{-\rho t} u(x_t)\, dt, \text{ where } \rho > 0, \tag{19}$$

is defined for all feasible paths for which $x_t \geq \underline{x}$ *for all* t, *whenever* $\underline{x} > 0$.

Ramsey's device is therefore unnecessary in this case. We shall however obtain an economy of notation if instead of $V(\rho)$ we use the utility function

$$U(\rho) = \int_0^\infty e^{-\rho t} (u(x_t) - \hat{u})\, dt, \rho > 0, \tag{20}$$

which differs from $V(\rho)$ by a constant. As before, we shall write $U_T(\rho)$ if the integral in (20) extends from 0 to $T < \infty$.

The stipulation in (E) that keeps consumption from becoming altogether too small is necessitated by (15), merely to prevent $U_T(\rho)$ from diverging to $-\infty$ as $T \to \infty$. However, we shall for $\rho > 0$ define as the eligible-and-attainable set the set of *all* paths with the prescribed z_0 for which $V(\rho)$ exists. (E) assures us that no paths worth consideration are excluded from the eligible set. If z_0 were to be very small, we could still allow for growth by taking $\underline{x}$ correspondingly smaller.

In the following propositions (F) through (J) *optimality* is defined by maximization of (20) on the appropriate eligible-attainable set. It is assumed in propositions (F), (G), that an eligible-attainable path $(\hat{x}_t, \hat{z}_t)$ is given, which is under scrutiny for its possible optimality. The propositions associate with such a path tentative implicit prices of the consumption good and of the use of the (identical) capital good. Once optimality of the path $(\hat{x}_t, \hat{z}_t)$ is confirmed, these prices are no longer tentative, and generalize to an infinite-dimensional space the idea of a hyperplane separating attainable from better-than-optimally-attaina le programs, illustrated in Figure 5. The (dated) price of the consumption good is defined from (20) by

$$p_t = e^{-\rho t} u'(\hat{x}_t), \tag{21}$$

the present value of the marginal instantaneous utility of consumption at time *t* if the given path $(\hat{x}_t, \hat{z}_t)$ is followed. The price of the use of the capital good is similarly defined by

$$q_t = p_t\, g'(\hat{z}_t) \tag{22}$$

as the present value of the marginal productivity of capital at time t multiplied by the marginal utility of consumption at that time. Finally, we denote by

$$\hat{U}(\rho) = \hat{U}_{\infty}(\rho), \text{ where } \hat{U}_T(\rho) = \int_0^T e^{-Qt}(u(\hat{x}_t) - \hat{u}) \, dt \text{ for } T \leq \infty, \tag{23}$$

the utility of the path $(\hat{x}_t, \hat{z}_t)$ under scrutiny.

Propositions (F) and (G) hold for any eligible-attainable path $(\hat{x}_t, \hat{z}_t)$ and its corresponding prices p_t, q_t, regardless of whether that path passes the test for optimality. Propositions (H), (I) together express that test.

(F) *If $(\hat{x}_t, \hat{z}_t)$ is an eligible and attainable path, and if (x_t, z_t) is any path, feasible or not, then*

$$U_T(\rho) - \hat{U}_T(\rho) \leq \int_0^T p_t(x_t - \hat{x}_t) \, dt \tag{24}$$

for all finite T*, and for* $T = \infty$ *whenever the integral converges.*

Since both members vanish if $x_t = \hat{x}_t$ for all t, this means that both

(a) the utility $U_T(\rho)$ of the path (x_t, z_t) is maximized, subject only to the 'budget constraint'

$$\int_0^T p_t(x_t - \hat{x}_t) \, dt \leq 0,$$

if $(x_t, z_t) = (\hat{x}_t, \hat{z}_t)$, and

(b) 'consumption expenditure at implicit prices'

$$\int_0^T p_t \, x_t \, dt$$

reaches its minimum, on the set of paths with utility $U_T(\rho)$ equal to or exceeding that of the path $(\hat{x}_t, \hat{z}_t)$, if $(x_t, z_t) = (\hat{x}_t, \hat{z}_t)$.

(G) *If $(\hat{x}_t, \hat{z}_t)$, (x_t, z_t) are two eligible and attainable paths,*

$$\int_0^T p_t(x_t - \hat{x}_t) \, dt \leq \int_0^T (q_t(z_t - \hat{z}_t) - p_t(\dot{z}_t - \dot{\hat{z}}_t)) \, dt = \int (q_t + \dot{p}_t)(z_t - \hat{z}_t) \, dt - p_T(z_T - \hat{z}_T) \tag{25}$$

for all finite T*, and for* $T = \infty$ *if the integrals converge and the last term has a limit.*

Again, all three members vanish if (x_t, z_t) is itself the path $(\hat{x}_t, \hat{z}_t)$. The inequality in (25), rewritten as

$$\int_0^T p_t (x_t + \dot{z}_t - \hat{x}_t - \dot{\hat{z}}_t) \, dt - \int_0^T q_t (z_t - \hat{z}_t) \, dt \leq 0,$$

says that, at prices implicit in the path $(\hat{x}_t, \hat{z}_t)$, 'revenue' from total output minus 'rental cost of use of capital' is maximized in that path.

(24) and (25) together give rise to Propositions (H), (I), (J).

(H) *Let* $\hat{x}(\rho), \hat{z}(\rho)$ *be defined as the solution* x, z *of*

$$f'(z) = \lambda + \rho, \, f(z) - \lambda z = x, \text{ where } 0 < \lambda \leq \lambda + \rho < f'(0). \tag{26}$$

Then if $z_0 = \hat{z}(\rho)$, *the unique optimal path is* $\hat{x}_t = \hat{x}(\rho), \hat{z}_t = \hat{z}(\rho)$ *for all* t ≥ 0.

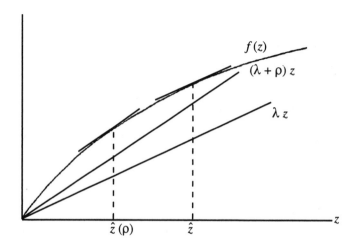

Figure 8

The determination of $z(\rho)$ is shown in Figure 8. Because of the strict concavity of $f(z), \hat{z}(\rho)$ and $\hat{x}(\rho)$ exist and are unique, and $0 < \hat{z}(\rho) < \hat{z}(\rho^*) \leq \hat{z}$ for $f'(0) - \lambda > \rho > \rho^* \geq 0$, and hence, since $f(z) - \lambda z$ increases for $0 \leq z \leq \hat{z}$,

$$\hat{x}(\rho) \equiv f(\hat{z}(\rho)) - \lambda \hat{z}(\rho) < \hat{x}(\rho^*) \leq \hat{x} \text{ for } f'(0) - \lambda > \rho > \rho^* \geq 0. \tag{27}$$

The constant optimal path made possible by the initial capital stock $z_0 = \hat{z}(\rho)$ is found to be an asymptote for the optimal paths associated with other values of z_0.

(I) *For all* z_0 *with* $0 < z_0 \leq \bar{z}$, *the unique optimal path* $(\hat{x}_t, \hat{z}_t)$ *is uniquely characterized by the two conditions*

(α) $\lim_{T \to \infty} \hat{z}_T = \hat{z}(\rho)$,

(β)   *the prices* (21), (22) *implicit in the path* $(\hat{x}_t, \hat{z}_t)$ *satisfy the differential equation*

$$q_t + \dot{p}_t = 0 \quad \text{for all} \quad t \geq 0. \tag{28}$$

To interpret condition (β), let (x_t, z_t) be a path which differs from the optimal path only slightly and only on a short open interval ζ, on which $z_t > \hat{z}_t$ (see Figure 9a). Then x_t will differ from $\hat{x}_t$ first because the slightly higher capital stock on ζ allows a slightly higher product, and secondly because acceleration of investment during the first part of ζ and deceleration during the second part leads to some postponement of consumption within ζ. In the light of (21), (22), the condition says that, for an arbitrarily small difference $z_t - \hat{z}_t$ of arbitrarily short duration, the utility effects of these two components of $x_t - \hat{x}_t$ must cancel if the path $(\hat{x}_t, \hat{z}_t)$ is to be optimal.

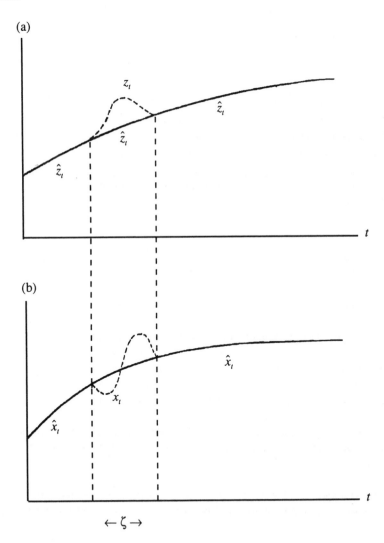

Figure 9

If condition (β) of Proposition (I) is satisfied, the inequality between the first and third members of (25) becomes

$$\int_0^T p_t (x_t - \hat{x}_t) \, dt - p_T (z_T - \hat{z}_T) \leqq 0. \tag{29}$$

The interpretation of this inequality is that, in an economy that keeps its own capital accounts (rather than renting the capital it employs), the revenue from deliveries to consumption plus the value of the capital stock at the end T of the planning horizon is maximized in the optimal path $(\hat{x}_t, \hat{z}_t)$, in comparison with all eligible-attainable paths. This is so for all finite T, and in the limit for T$\to\infty$ if such limit exists.

Finally, (24) and (29) together yield

$$U_T (\rho) - \hat{U}_T (\rho) \leq \int_0^T p_t (x_t - \hat{x}_t) \, dt \leq p_T (z_T - \hat{z}_T). \tag{30}$$

If condition (α) of Proposition (I) is also satisfied, then (21) and Proposition (J) below imply that the price p_t associated with the optimal path approaches zero as $t\to\infty$. In that case $\lim_{T\to\infty} p_T (z_T - \hat{z}_T) = 0$, and capital disappears from the accounts for an infinite horizon. The inequality between the first and last members of (30) carried to the limit for T$\to\infty$ then confirms the optimality of the path $(\hat{x}_t, \hat{z}_t)$. In the Appendix we show that the middle member of (30) also converges. We can therefore supplement statements (i), (ii), made in interpreting (F) above (with T$\to\infty$) by the statement

(iii)   Revenue from deliveries to consumption

$$\int_0^\infty p_t \, x_t \, dt$$

is maximized, on the set of eligible-attainable paths, if $(x_t, z_t) = (\hat{x}_t, \hat{z}_t)$.

Proposition (J) describes the path characterized by propositions (H), (I).

(J) *In the unique optimal path* $(\hat{x}_t, \hat{z}_t)$ *for any initial capital stock z_0 with $0 < z_0 \leqq \bar{z}$, $z_0 \neq \hat{z}(\rho)$, both $\hat{x}_t$ and $\hat{z}_t$ exhibit a monotonic and asymptotic approach to $\hat{x}(\rho)$ and $\hat{z}(\rho)$, respectively, from above if $z_0 > \hat{z}(\rho)$, from below if $z_0 < \hat{z}(\rho)$.*

For later discussion, we note from (27) that the asymptotic level $\hat{x}(\rho)$ of consumption per worker, while independent of the initial capital z_0, is reduced as the discount rate is increased. The maximum of $\hat{x}(\rho)$ for $\rho \geq 0$ is attained at $\rho = 0$. We shall not examine the cases where $\rho \geq f'(0) - \lambda$.

Finally, a word about the case where one tries to apply a negative discount factor $\rho < 0$. Writing $-\rho = \sigma$, this means looking for a utility function extending the finite-horizon example

$$V_T (-\sigma) = \int_0^T e^{\sigma t} u (x_t) \, dt$$

to an infinite horizon. This is not as far-fetched as it may seem. After all, we have so far given no weight at all to mere numbers in comparing generations. If we were to weight each generation in proportion to its number, and otherwise seek neutrality with regard to timing, the population growth parameter λ would take the place of σ above.

In order to apply Ramsey's device in the present case, one would have to find a feasible path (x_t, z_t) such that

$$W_T^*(-\sigma) = \int_0^T e^{\sigma t} \left(u(x_t^*) - u(x_t) \right) dt \tag{31}$$

is uniformly bounded from above for all feasible paths (x_t^*, z_t^*) and all values of T. The following statement says that no such path exists.

(K) *For each $\sigma > 0$, for each attainable path (x_t, z_t), where $0 < z_0 \leq \bar{z}$ and for each number $N > 0$, there exists another attainable path (x_t^*, z_t^*) and a number T^* such that*

$$W_T^*(-\sigma) > N \quad \text{for all} \quad T \geq T^*. \tag{32}$$

This says, essentially, that there is no upper bound to the range, on the attainable set, of a utility function of the type we are seeking to define. The case $\rho < 0$ is therefore analogous to the case in ordinary linear programming illustrated by Figure 4. The same difficulty was noticed and discussed by Tinbergen (1960) and by Chakravarty (1962) in connection with the case $\rho = 0$ for a model with constant returns to increases in the amount of capital alone.

In the present case, the reasons for the absence of an optimal path for $\rho < 0$ can be illustrated in terms of the path $(x_t, z_t) = (\hat{x}, \hat{z})$, optimal if $\rho = 0$ and $z_0 = \hat{z}$. From (21) we see that the implicit price of the unit of consumption good per worker, associated with this path would have to be a constant,

$$p_t = u'(\hat{x}) \quad \text{for all} \quad t.$$

This means that a sacrifice of one unit in *per capita* consumption, now made for a short period as a slight departure from this path, can be taken out by any future generation in the form of an equal augmentation of *per capita* consumption beyond that provided by the path, for a period of the same short duration. Now if either the discount rate $\rho < 0$, or if $\rho = 0$ but some weight is explicitly given to population size, it will always increase utility to delay still further the time at which the fruit of the initial sacrifice is reaped.

In the proofs of Propositions (A)–(K), given in the Appendix, one common characteristic of the problems considered is repeatedly used without explicit mention. At any time in an optimal path $(\hat{x}_t, \hat{z}_t)$, the capital stock $\hat{z}_t$ is the only link between the past and the future. This is due, on the one hand, to the utility function being an integral over time of instantaneous utilities (discounted or not). On the other hand, it arises from the fact that the feasibility constraint (10a) restricts $\dot{z}_t$ but not $\dot{x}_t$. Hence the function x_t is in principle free to vary discontinuously (even though it is found optimal for it not to do so). However, $\dot{z}_t$ is bounded by (10a, b), hence z_t can only vary continuously. The resulting property can be expressed formally as follows: If $(\hat{x}_t, \hat{z}_t)$ is an optimal path for given z_0, then, for any T, the path (x_t^*, z_t^*) defined by

$$x^*_t = \hat{x}_{T+t},\, z^*_t = \hat{z}_{T+t}$$

is optimal for $z^*_0 = \hat{z}_T$.

7. Adjusting preferences to opportunities

What have we learned from our 'logical experiments'? We have confronted a simple model of production with a utility function representing a sum of future *per capita* utilities, discounted by a positive, zero, or negative instantaneous rate of discount ρ. We have found that $\rho = 0$ is the smallest rate for which an optimal path exists.

Let us assume for the sake of argument that the present model is representative enough to be looked on as a tentative test of the applicability of the ethical principles under consideration. Then we have just managed to avoid discriminating against future generations on the basis of remoteness of the time at which they live. However, this close escape for virtue was possible only by making welfare comparisons on a *per capita* basis. If instead we should want to weight *per capita* welfare by population size, then we are forced to discriminate on the basis of historical time by positive discounting. There seems to be no way, in an indefinitely growing population, to give equal weight to all individuals living at all times in the future.

This dilemma suggests that the open-endedness of the future imposes mathematical limits on the autonomy of ethical thought. The suggestion may come as a shock to welfare economists, because no such logical obstacles have been encountered in the more fully explored problems of allocation and distribution for a finite population. It is true that the mere fact that we are considering an infinite number of people does not fully explain the dilemma. For Ramsey was able, albeit by artificial assumptions, to indicate a fair solution to the problem for the infinite future of a population of constant size. Our difficulty is therefore connected with the assumption of an indefinite growth in the population.

The following reasoning may further illuminate the reasons for the nonexistence of an optimal path with negative ρ. Assume that $0 > \rho > f'(\bar{z}) - \lambda$. (Of course, $\rho = -\lambda$ would correspond to equal weights given to the utilities of all individuals.) However, $f'(z) - \lambda > -\lambda$, and our illustration is simpler if we do keep $\hat{z}(\rho) < \bar{z}$ by taking $\rho > f'(\bar{z}) - \lambda$. Consider now an optimal path for the finite time period $0 \leqq t \leqq T$, defined by initial and terminal per-worker capital stock levels $z_0 = z_T = \hat{z}$ both equal to that level $\hat{z}$ which, *if maintained at all times*, would secure the maximum maintainable consumption per head. The analysis associated with the proofs of (H), (I), (J) in the Appendix now indicates that, if the level $\hat{z}$ is prescribed only for $t = o$ and $t = T$, the optimal path bulges out toward the level of $\hat{z}(\rho)$, as indicated in Figure 10. The interpretation is roughly as follows. The negative discount rate gives the greatest weight to the *per capita* utility of the last generation living within the planning period $[o, T]$. In response to this weighting system, the optimal path provides for a reduction in capital per worker (a 'disinvestment' in a *per capita* sense) during a terminal segment of the planning period, in order to allow for high consumption at that time. To make this possible, all preceding generations make a sacrifice. For the first generation, this takes the form of heavy investment needed to increase the capital stock more than in proportion to population growth. For the intermediate generations, it consists in approximately maintaining the capital stock – by continued proportional growth – at a *per capita* level in excess of that which would maximize *per capita* consumption.

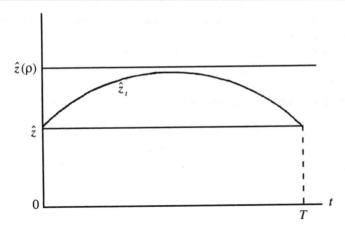

Figure 10

Now if T is increased, the benefitted generation becomes a more and more distant one. If T = ∞, there is no benefitted generation, and the limiting position of the curve in Figure 10, while mathematically well-defined, merely describes a path of indefinite and fruitless sacrifice.

The problem appears in even sharper light if technological progress is also recognized. A study by Inagaki (1963) uses a Cobb–Douglas production function

$$F(Z, L, t) = \text{const. } e^{\beta t} Z^{\alpha} L^{1-\alpha}$$

subject to exogenous technological progress at the constant proportional rate β, an instantaneous utility function

$$u(x) = \int^{x} \frac{ds}{\log s - \log \underline{x}} \tag{33}$$

exhibiting suitable behavior for large values of x, and a labor force growing exponentially at the rate λ. Among other results, Inagaki finds that, for the integral $V(\rho)$ as defined in (19) to converge on the counterpart of our path $(x_t, z_t) = (\hat{x}(\rho), \hat{z}(\rho))$, it is necessary that

$$\rho > \frac{\beta}{1 - \alpha} \tag{34}$$

Let us assume that Ramsey's device can be used also in this case, and that it would again merely result in adding the borderline value $\rho = \beta/(1 - \alpha)$ to the set of discount rates defining a utility function for which an optimal path exists. Then a predictable positive lower bound to the rate of technical progress, valid for an indefinite future period, precludes application of the ethical principle of timing neutrality in terms even of *per capita* utility – not to speak at all of weighting generations by their numbers.

Thus, if in the face of technological progress we want to hold on to the idea of maximizing a utility integral such as (33) over time, we must invent a discount rate ρ satisfying (34), or its equivalent for another production function. Such a discount rate might just have to be a pragmatic one having no basis in *a priori* ethical thought. While it might well be a result, conscious or unconscious, of political processes or decisions, it would have to be revised upward if it is estimated that technological progress will accelerate to such an extent as to 'overtake it', and could be revised downward if it is expected that progress will slow down.

One might instead conclude that the whole idea of maximizing a utility integral is not flexible enough to fit the inequality of opportunity between generations inherent in modern technology. Two alternative notions have been partially explored by the present author, using a discrete concept of time. In one of these (Koopmans, 1960; see also Koopmans *et al.*, 1964), the utility function of a consumption path x_t, $t = 1, 2, \ldots$, can be defined by a recursive relation

$$\mathrm{U}(x_1, x_2, \ldots) = \mathrm{V}(u(x_1), \mathrm{U}(x_2, x_3, \ldots))$$

in terms of a one-period utility function $u(x)$ and an aggregator function $\mathrm{V}(u, \mathrm{U})$. This formulation allows the (scale-invariant) discount factor

$$\left(\frac{\delta \mathrm{V}(u, \mathrm{U})}{\delta \mathrm{U}} \right)_{u = u(x), \ \mathrm{U} = \mathrm{U}(x, x, \ldots)}$$

associated with a constant path to increase or decrease with the level x at which the path proceeds. The second alternative (Koopmans, 1962) is an attempt to express formally the idea of a present preference for flexibility in future preferences between different commodity bundles of the same timing, or between physically the same bundles spread out differently over time, or between bundles differing in both respects. Further analysis will be needed to determine whether the first idea is sufficiently flexible to enable us to avoid the difficulties we have encountered, or, if not, whether the second idea can be made workable.

8.   Technical progress and population growth as possible policy variables

So far we have treated both technical progress and population growth as exogenously given. It should now be recognized that both variables can be, and are in many countries, influenced by public and private policies and attitudes. Technical change is furthered by government conduct or support of research and of education, by the tax treatment of depreciation and obsolescence, and by business policies with regard to research and development. Population growth is influenced by expenditures for public health, by family allowances, by government policies toward family planning, and by general cultural and religious attitudes toward the idea of population control. In addition, both variables are in part endogenously affected by the level of income.

Both possibilities of partial control raise new conceptual problems in formalizing the idea of optimal economic growth. In the middle of the scientific explosion, it is hard to assess whether technological progress can go on forever, so that also its rate can be raised or lowered forever. It is conceivable that a higher rate of discovery and invention in the present will entail a lower rate of progress at some later time when the fund of knowledge usable in production nears completion. Another consideration is that technological progress raises transition and dislocation difficulties that affect the relative welfare of different individuals within the same generation. The possibility of influencing population size raises the question of the value of population size in itself – as distinct from the question of the weight given to numbers in aggregating utility over generations, discussed above. It should be noted that all utility functions discussed in this paper imply neutrality with regard to population size as such. The question is of some importance because a different attitude might lead to a different balance between the 'value of numbers' and the loss of *per capita* income that may result from an increase in the ratio of population to land and/or other resources. This problem did not come up in the more formal analysis of the preceding section because the assumption of constant returns to proportional increases in both labor and capital precluded the recognition of resource limitations.

Appendix

A1.　*Notations*

Instantaneous discount rate . . . . . . $\rho = -\sigma$
Exponential growth rate of labor force　λ

	At time t		Integrated over time (per worker)
	Absolute	Per worker	
Consumption flow	X_t	x_t	
Capital stock	Z_t	z_t	
Labor force	L_t		
Production function	$F(Z, L)$	$f(z)$	
Utility		$u(x)$	U, V, W

Derivatives with respect to time are denoted by dots, $\dot{z}_t = \dfrac{dz_t}{dt}$,

other derivatives by dashes, $f'(z) = \dfrac{df}{dz}$, $u'(x) = \dfrac{du}{dx}$.

$\hat{}$　generally denotes optimal paths and their asymptotic levels.
$\equiv$ denotes equality by definition.

A2.　*Assumptions*

(a) = (8)　$L_t = L_0 e^{\lambda t}$ for all $t \geq 0$, where $0 < \lambda < f'(0)$,

(b) = (9)　$F(Z, L) = L f\left(\dfrac{Z}{L}\right) = L f(z)$ for all $L > 0$, $Z \geq 0$,

(c)　　　$f(0) = 0, f'(z) > 0, f''(z) < 0$ for $0 \leq z$,

(d) = (11a)　for each $\lambda > 0$ such that $0 < \lambda < f'(0)$ there is a $\bar{z}_\lambda > 0$ such that $f(\bar{z}_\lambda) = \lambda \bar{z}_\lambda$ (the subscript λ of $\bar{z}_\lambda$ is omitted in what follows),

(e) $u'(x) > 0, u''(x) < 0$ for $0 < x < \infty$, $\lim_{x \to 0} u(x) = -\infty$.

A3.   Some implications of feasibility

Given the initial stock z_0 of capital per worker, the *attainable set* of growth paths (x_t, z_t) is now given, in terms of per-worker variables, by the requirements that, for all $t \geq 0$,

$$
\left.
\begin{aligned}
&\text{(35a) } x_t > 0, z_t \geq 0, \\
&\text{(35b) } z_t \text{ is continuous,} \\
&\text{(35c) } z_t, x_t \text{ are differentiable to the right,} \\
&\text{(35d) } \dot{z}_t \text{ and } \dot{x}_t \text{ are continuous to the right,}
\end{aligned}
\right\} \tag{35}
$$

$$
x_t + \dot{z}_t = f(z_t) - \lambda z_t \equiv g(z_t), \text{ say,} \tag{36}
$$

$$
z_0 \text{ is prescribed, where } 0 < z_0 \leq \bar{z}. \tag{37}
$$

The *feasible set* is the union of all attainable sets with $0 < z_0 \leq \bar{z}$.

We note that, by Assumption (c), both the feasible set and the attainable sets are convex, and that the function $g(z)$ defined in (36) is strictly concave. Since $g(z)$ vanishes for $z = 0$ and for $z = \bar{z}$, it reaches its maximum $\hat{x}$ in a unique point $\hat{z}$, so that

$$
\left.
\begin{aligned}
&\text{(38a) } \hat{x} \equiv g(\hat{z}) > g(z) \text{ for all } z \neq \hat{z}, \text{ where } 0 < \hat{z} < \bar{z}, \\
&\text{(38b) } g'(z) > g'(\hat{z}) = 0 > g'(z^*) \text{ whenever } 0 \leq z < \hat{z} < z^* \leq \bar{z}.
\end{aligned}
\right\} \tag{38}
$$

From (35a), (36), we have

$$
\dot{z}_t < x_t + \dot{z}_t = g(z_t) \tag{39}
$$

and hence for all feasible paths, using (35a), (37), and the fact that $g(z) > 0$ only for $0 < z < \bar{z}$,

$$
0 < z_t \leq \bar{z} \text{ for all } t \geq 0. \tag{40}
$$

Here $0 = z_t$ has been ruled out because it would not allow the positive consumption $x_{t'}$ for $t' \geq t$ required by (35a).

A4.   A basic inequality and one application

The concavity Assumption (e) of $u(x)$ implies that

$$
u(x) - u(x^*) \leq u'(x^*) \cdot (x - x^*) \text{ for all } x, x^*, \tag{41}
$$

and the concavity of $g(z)$ implied in Assumption (c) and (36) that

$$
g(z) - g(z^*) \leq g'(z^*) \cdot (z - z^*) \text{ for all } z, z^*. \tag{42}
$$

We shall make many comparisons of utility integrals for feasible growth paths (x_t, z_t) and (x_t^*, z_t^*), based on (41) and on either (38) or (42). To avoid repetition we state this comparison here in its most general form, where $0 \leq T < T^* \leq \infty$, and ρ is as yet unspecified.

(43a)
$$
\begin{aligned}
{}_T U_{T^*}^*(\rho) &\equiv \int_T^{T^*} e^{-\rho t} \left(u(x_t) - u(x_t^*) \right) dt \leq \int_T^{T^*} e^{-\rho t} u'(x_t^*) (x_t - x_t^*) dt = \\
&= \int_T^{T^*} e^{-\rho t} u'(x_t^*) \left(g(z_t) - g(z_t^*) - \dot{z}_t + \dot{z}_t^* \right) dt = \\
&= \int_T^{T^*} e^{-\rho t} u'(x_t^*) \left(g(z_t) - g(z_t^*) \right) dt - \left[e^{-\rho t} u'(x_t^*) (z_t - z_t^*) \right]_T^{T^*} + \\
&\quad + \int_T^{T^*} \left[\frac{d}{dt} \left(e^{-\rho t} u'(x_t^*) \right) \right] (z_t - z_t^*) dt \leq \\
&\leq \int_T^{T^*} e^{-\rho t} \left[u'(x_t^*) (g'(z_t^*) - \rho) + u''(x_t^*) \dot{x}_t^* \right] (z_t - z_t^*) dt - \\
&\quad - \left[e^{-\rho t} u'(x_t^*) (z_t - z_t^*) \right]_T^{T^*}.
\end{aligned}
\tag{43}
$$

If $T^* = \infty$ the validity of (43) depends on convergence of the integrals involved.

One application of (43) will be used repeatedly. We define a *bulge* in a growth path (x_t, z_t) as an interval $[T, T^*]$ such that

(44a) $0 \leq T < T^* < \infty$, $z_T = z_{T^*} = z^*$, say, and

(44b) either $z^* \leq \hat{z}(\rho)$ and $z_t < z^*$ for $T < t < T^*$

or $z^* \geq \hat{z}(\rho)$ and $z_t > z^*$ for $T < t < T^*$,
$\tag{44}$

where the definition (26) of $\hat{z}(\rho)$ is extended to all values of ρ,

(45a) $\hat{z}(\rho) = \bar{z}$ for $\rho \leq g'(\bar{z})$,

(45b) $g'(\hat{z}(\rho)) = \rho$ for $g'(\bar{z}) < \rho < g'(0)$

(45c) $\hat{z}(\rho) = 0$ for $g'(0) \leq \rho$.
$\tag{45}$

Figure 11 shows z_t for a path with two bulges, both denoted $[T, T^*]$. The effect on the utility integral of 'straightening out' a bulge is found from (43) by taking $z_t^* = z^*$, $x_t^* = x^* \equiv g(z^*)$, and satisfies

$$
-\int_T^{T^*} e^{-\rho t} \left(u(x_t) - u(x^*) \right) dt \leq -u'(x^*) \left(g'(z^*) - \rho \right) \int_T^{T^*} e^{-\rho t} (z_t - z^*) dt > 0
\tag{46}
$$

if $z^* \neq \hat{z}(\rho)$, because in that case $g'(z^*) - \rho$ and $z_t - z^*$ are opposite in sign. If $z^* = z(\rho)$, and if for instance $z_t < z^*$ for $T < t < T^*$ as in the second bulge in Figure 11, we can by suitable choice of

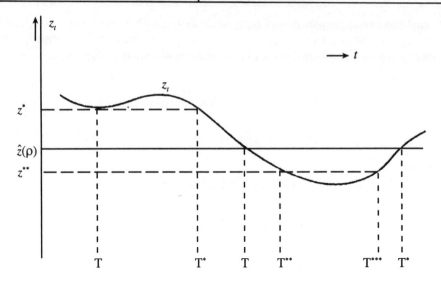

Figure 11

a number $z^{**} < \hat{z}(\rho)$ write the left-hand member of (46) as the negative sum of two such integrals, one comparing (x_i^{**}, z_i^{**}) defined by $z_i^{**} \equiv \max \{z^{**}, z_i\}$ with $(x^*, z^*) = (\hat{x}(\rho), \hat{z}(\rho))$ on $[T, T^*]$, the other comparing (x_i, z_i) with (x^{**}, z^{**}), where $x^{**} \equiv g(z^{**})$, on an interval $[T^{**}, T^{***}]$ such that $T < T^{**} < T^{***} < T^*$. Since of these integrals the former is nonpositive, the latter negative, (46) is valid also if $z^* = \hat{z}(\rho)$. We thus have

Lemma I: *For any ρ, a path (x_i, z_i) optimal on any finite or infinite time interval cannot contain a bulge.*

This conclusion, and the inequality (46) on which it is based, remain valid for $T^* = \infty$ and $\rho \geq 0$ if the definition of a bulge is extended to read '(44b) and either (44a) or (44a′)',

$$0 \leqq T < T^* = \infty, \rho \geqq 0, z_T = z^*, \text{ and if } \rho = 0 \text{ then } \lim_{t \to \infty} z_t = z^*, \qquad (44a')$$

as illustrated in Figures 12 ($\rho = 0$) and 13 ($\rho > 0$).

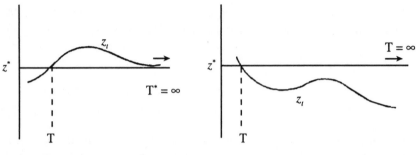

Figure 12   *Figure 13*

A5. Inferiority of indefinitely fluctuating paths if $\rho \leq 0$

We define the asymptotic range of the path (x_t, z_t) as the nonempty closed interval

$$[\underline{\zeta}, \overline{\zeta}] , \quad \underline{\zeta} \equiv \lim_{T \to \infty} \inf_{t \geq T} z_t, \quad \overline{\zeta} = \lim_{T \to \infty} \sup_{t \geq T} z_t. \tag{47}$$

A positive length $\overline{\zeta} - \underline{\zeta}$ of the asymptotic range implies that z_t continues to fluctuate between any neighborhood of $\underline{\zeta}$ and any neighborhood of $\overline{\zeta}$, infinitely often, and for arbitrarily large t.

Lemma 2: *If $\rho \leq 0$ and if $\underline{\zeta} < \overline{\zeta}$ for the attainable path (x_t, z_t), then there exists for each $N > 0$ an attainable path (x_t^*, z_t^*) and a $T_N > 0$ such that*

$$U_T^*(\rho) \equiv \int_0^T e^{-Qt} (u(x_t) - u(x_t^*)) \, dt \leq - N \text{ for all } T \geq T_N. \tag{48}$$

For the proof of Lemma 2 we must strengthen (46) to obtain a positive lower bound on the gain $_TU_{T^*}^*(\rho)$ associated with the 'straightening out' of a bulge $[T, T^*]$. For this purpose we choose an interval $[z_*, z^*]$ such that

$$\text{(a) } \underline{\zeta} < z_* < z^* < \overline{\zeta} \text{ and either (b) } \hat{z}(\rho) < z_* \text{ or (c) } z^* < \hat{z}(\rho), \tag{49}$$

which is always possible. If for definiteness we assume (49c), we have from Assumption (c) of Section A2

$$g'(z) - \rho \geq g'(z^*) - \rho \equiv \gamma > 0 \text{ for } z_* \leq z \leq z^*. \tag{50}$$

Now z_t has infinitely many bulges $[T, T^*]$ with the properties

$$z_T = z_{T^*} = z^*, z_t \leq z_* \text{ for some } t \varepsilon [T, T^*]. \tag{51}$$

Because of the continuity of z_t we can for each of these choose an interval $[\tau, \tau^*]$ such that, if we write $z^* - z_* \equiv 2 \varepsilon$,

$$T < \tau < \tau^* < T^* \text{ and } z_\tau = z_* < z_t < z_{\tau^*} = z^* - \varepsilon \text{ for } \tau < t < \tau^*. \tag{52}$$

The construction is illustrated in Figure 14. Since the *last* inequality in (46) holds also for all subintervals of $[T, T^*]$, we have from (52), (50), if $x^* \equiv g(z^*)$ and $\rho \leq 0$,

$$-_TU_{T^*}^*(\rho) \equiv - \int_T^{T^*} e^{-Qt} (u(x_t) - u(x^*)) \, dt > - u'(x^*) \gamma \int_\tau^{\tau^*} (z_t - z^*) \, dt > u'(x^*) \gamma \varepsilon (\tau^* - \tau),$$

since $\varepsilon > 0$ and $u'(x^*) \gamma > 0$. On the other hand, we have from (52), (39) with $x_t > 0$, (36) and (38a) that

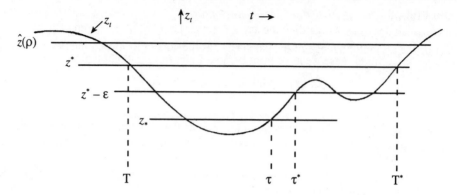

Figure 14

$$\varepsilon = \int_\tau^{\tau^*} \dot{z}_t \, dt < \int_\tau^{\tau^*} g(z_t) \, dt < (\tau^* - \tau) \, \hat{x},$$

whence $\tau^* - \tau > \varepsilon / \hat{x} > 0$ and

$$-_T U^*_{T^*} (\rho) > u'(x^*) \, \gamma \, \varepsilon^2 / \hat{x} \equiv \alpha^* > 0. \tag{53}$$

Finally, we define the feasible path (x^*_t, z^*_t) by (36) and

$$z^*_t \equiv \max \, \{z_t, z^*\} \quad \text{for} \;\; 0 \leqq t \leqq T_N, \, z^*_t = z_t \;\; \text{for} \;\; t > T_N,$$

subject to a later choice of T_N in such a way that $z_{T_N} \leqq z^*$. Then

$$-U_{T_N} (\rho) \equiv -\int_0^{T_N} e^{-\rho t} (u(x_t) - u(x^*_t)) \, dt \geqq n_{T_N} \alpha^*, \quad \text{where} \;\; \alpha^* > 0,$$

if n_T denotes the number of completed bulges in $[0, T']$. But $n_{T'} = \infty$ because there are infinitely many bulges in $[0, \overset{\lim T' \to \infty}{\infty}]$. Hence the choice of T_N such that $n_{T_N} \geqq N/\alpha^*$ establishes Lemma 2 in case (49c) holds. The proof from (49b) is similar.

A6. *Proofs for a zero discount rate ($\rho = 0$)*

PROOF OF (A)
In (43a) take $\rho = 0$, $z^*_t = \hat{z}$, so $x^*_t = \hat{x} = g(\hat{z})$. Then if we write $u(\hat{x}) \equiv \hat{u}$, $u'(\hat{x}) \equiv \hat{u}'$,

$$_T U_{T^*} \equiv \int_T^{T^*} (u(x_t) - \hat{u}) \, dt \leqq \hat{u}' \cdot (z_T - z_{T^*}) \leqq \hat{u}' \cdot \bar{z}, \tag{54}$$

by (38), (40), regardless of T, T^*, hence also for $T = 0$.

PROOF OF (B)

We distinguish three cases regarding the asymptotic range $[\underline{\zeta}, \overline{\zeta}]$ of the given path (x_t, z_t).

Case (1), $\underline{\zeta} < \overline{\zeta}$ In this case we have from Lemma 2 and from (54) applied to (x_t^*, z_t^*), for any $N > 0$,

$$U_T = \int_0^T (u(x_t) - u(x_t^*))\, dt + \int_0^T (u(x_t^*) - \hat{u})\, dt \leq -N + \hat{u}' \cdot \overline{z}$$

for all $T \geq T_N$. In this case, therefore, U_T diverges to $-\infty$ as $T \to \infty$.

Case (2), $\underline{\zeta} = \overline{\zeta} \neq \hat{z}$ For definiteness assume $\overline{\zeta} < \hat{z}$ and let $\hat{z} - \overline{\zeta} \equiv 2\varepsilon$. Then $\varepsilon > 0$ and there exists $T < \infty$ such that

$$z_t \leq \overline{\zeta} + \varepsilon = \hat{z} - \varepsilon \quad \text{for all } t \geq T. \tag{55}$$

If now in (43a) we take $\rho = 0$, $z_t^* = \hat{z}$, $x_t^* = \hat{x} = g(\hat{z})$ for all $t \geq 0$, then,

$$_TU_{T^*} \equiv \int_T^{T^*} (u(x_t) - \hat{u})\, dt \leq \hat{u}' \left[\int_T^{T^*} (g(z_t) - \hat{x})\, dt + z_T - z_{T^*} \right] \leq -\alpha\,(T^* - T) + \beta, \tag{56}$$

where by (38), (40),

$$\alpha \equiv \hat{u}' \cdot (\hat{x} - g(\hat{z} - \varepsilon)) > 0, \qquad \beta \equiv \hat{u}' \cdot \overline{z}.$$

Hence $U_{T^*} = U_T + {}_TU_{T^*}$ diverges to $-\infty$ as $T^* \to \infty$ in this case, and by similar reasoning in the case $\hat{z} < \underline{\zeta}$, hence in the entire Case (2).

Case (3), $\underline{\zeta} = \overline{\zeta} = \hat{z}$ In this case clearly

$$\lim_{T \to \infty} z_T = \hat{z}. \tag{57}$$

It follows from the third member of (54) that

$$G_T \equiv U_T + \hat{u}' \cdot z_T$$

is a nonincreasing function of T. Hence G_T either possesses a limit for $T \to \infty$ or diverges to $-\infty$. In view of (57), the same must then be true for U_T.

This completes the proof of statement (B). In addition, we have found

Lemma 3: *If $\rho = 0$, a necessary condition for eligibility of the path (x_t, z_t) is that (57) is satisfied.*

PROOF OF (C)

An optimal path $(\hat{x}_t, \hat{z}_t)$ is now defined as one that maximizes

$$U \equiv \int_0^\infty (u(x_t) - \hat{u}) \, dt \tag{58}$$

on the attainable-and-eligible set. A beautifully simple procedure used by Ramsey in his slightly different problem can be adapted to the present problem as long as $\rho = 0$.

From Lemmas 1 and 3 we conclude that, in any optimal path, $\hat{z}_t$ exhibits a nondecreasing, constant, or nonincreasing approach to $\lim_{t \to \infty} \hat{z}_t = \hat{z}$ according as $z_0 < \hat{z}, = \hat{z}$ or $> \hat{z}$. This establishes the second and third sentences of statement (C) with the term 'weakly monotonic' substituted for 'strictly monotonic'. Now consider an attainable-eligible path (x_t, z_t) for which

$$z_t = z^* \neq \hat{z} \text{ for } T \leq t \leq T^*, \text{ where } T < T^*. \tag{59}$$

Then, along the lines of (56),

$$_T U_{T^*} \equiv \int_T^{T^*} (u(x_t) - \hat{u}) \, dt \leq \hat{u}'(T^* - T) \, (g(z^*) - \hat{x}) < 0$$

by (38a). It follows that the path

$$(x_t^*, z_t^*) = \begin{cases} (x_t, z_t) & \text{for } 0 \leq t < T, \\ (x_{t+T^*-T}, z_{t+T^*-T}) & \text{for } T \leq t, \end{cases}$$

is likewise attainable, and indeed eligible and preferable to (x_t, z_t), because it achieves a utility

$$U^* = U_T^* + {}_T U^* = U_T + {}_{T^*} U > U_T + {}_T U_{T^*} + {}_{T^*} U = U.$$

Therefore (59) cannot occur in an optimal path.

It follows that, if $z_0 \neq \hat{z}$, an optimal path shows a strictly monotonic approach of $\hat{z}_t$, to the value $z_T = \hat{z}$ for $0 \leq t < T$, where $T \leq \infty$. We shall call any eligible path with that property a *superior* path. To complete the proof of the second and third sentences of (C) we only need to show that for an *optimal* path $T = \infty$. This is best obtained as a corollary of the proof of (D).

The proof of the first sentence of (C) will also be combined with that of (D).

PROOF OF (D)

For all superior paths we can now make a useful change of the variable of integration in (58) from t to z. Since, by (36), $z_t = \hat{z}$ for $t \geq T$ implies $x_t = \hat{x}$, $u(\hat{x}_t) = \hat{u}$, we have for all superior paths, using (36),

$$U = \int_{z_0}^{\hat{z}} \frac{u(x_{t(z)}) - \hat{u}}{\dot{z}_{t(z)}} \, dz = \int_{z_0}^{\hat{z}} \frac{u(x(z)) - \hat{u}}{g(z) - x(z)} \, dz. \tag{60}$$

where $t(z)$ denotes the inverse of z_t on $[0, T]$, and $x(z) \equiv x_{t(z)}$. The unknown function is now $x(z)$, defined, like $t(z)$, on the interval $z_0 \leq z < \hat{z}$, or on $\hat{z} < z \leq z_0$, as the case may be. The advantage from the change of variables lies in the fact that only $x(z)$ itself, and no derivative thereof, occur in the integrand in (60). Hence (60) is maximized on the set of superior paths if and only if $x(z)$ is given a value $\hat{x}^*(z)$ such that the integrand is maximized for almost every value of z in its domain. This requires $\hat{x}^*(z)$ for almost every z to equal the solution $x = \hat{x}(z)$ of

$$u'(x)\,(g(z) - x)) = \hat{u} - u(x). \tag{61}$$

Figure 15 shows the determination of $x = \hat{x}(z)$ for the two cases $z < \hat{z}$ and $z > \hat{z}$. It is easily seen from the diagram or analytically, using Assumptions (c), (d), (e), that a function $\hat{x}(z)$ can be uniquely determined from (61) for *all* values of z on $0 < z \leq \bar{z}$, so as to be independent of z_0, continuous and increasing for all z, and differentiable for $z \neq \hat{z}$. In particular,

$$\lim_{z \to 0} \hat{x}(z) = 0, \quad \hat{x}(\hat{z}) = \hat{x} = g(\hat{z}). \tag{62}$$

Moreover, since any feasible x_t is by (35c) continuous to the right, and since for any superior path $t(z)$ is continuous and monotonic, $\hat{x}^*(z)$ must be continuous to the right if $z_0 < \hat{z}$, to the left if $z_0 > \hat{z}$. Hence $\hat{x}^*(z) = \hat{x}(z)$ for every value of z in its domain, and the asterisk can now be omitted from $\hat{x}^*(z)$.

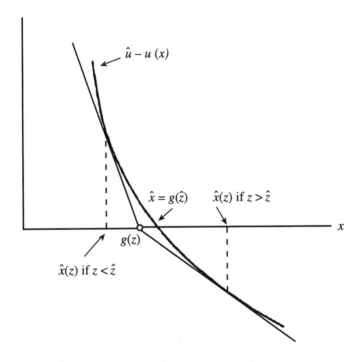

Figure 15

Once $\hat{x}(z)$ has been determined in the manner indicated, one reintroduces the time variable $t = \hat{t}(z)$ by

$$t = \int_{z_0}^{z} \frac{d\hat{t}(y)}{dy}\, dy = \int_{z_0}^{z} \frac{dy}{g(y) - \hat{x}(y)} \equiv \hat{t}(z). \tag{63}$$

The function $\hat{t}(z)$ and its inverse $\hat{z}_t$ are monotonic and differentiable with the proper range and domain in each case because, by (61) and the monotonicity of $\hat{x}(z)$,

$$g(z) - \hat{x}(z) = \frac{\hat{u} - u(\hat{x}(z))}{u'(\hat{x}(z))} \quad \begin{Bmatrix} > \\ < \end{Bmatrix}\ 0\ \text{if}\ \begin{cases} 0 < z_0 < \hat{z} \\ \hat{z} < z_0 < \overline{z} \end{cases}.$$

Hence $\hat{x}_t$ is monotonic and differentiable. In order to see that $T = \infty$ whenever $z_0 \neq \hat{z}$, one readily computes from Taylor expansions of $g(z) - g(\hat{z})$ with respect to $z - \hat{z}$, and of $g(\hat{z}(x)) - \hat{x}$ with respect to $x - \hat{x}$, that

$$\lim_{z \to \hat{z}} \frac{g(z) - \hat{x}(z)}{z - \hat{z}} = -\left(\frac{g''(\hat{z})\, u'(\hat{x})}{u''(\hat{x})} \right)^{1/2},$$

a negative real number. It follows that

$$\text{if } z_0 < \hat{z},\ \lim_{z \to \hat{z} - 0} \hat{t}(z) = \infty,\ \text{if } z_0 > \hat{z},\ \lim_{z \to \hat{z} + 0} \hat{t}(z) = \infty.$$

Therefore $T = \infty$. The proofs of (C) and (D) are thereby complete. In addition, we note that $\hat{x}(z)$ is differentiable also for $z = \hat{z}$.

A7. *Proofs for a positive discount rate $(0 < \rho < f'(0) - \lambda)$*

PROOF OF (E)

Let (x_t, z_t) be a feasible path with $x_t \geq \underline{x} > 0$ for all t. In (43) we insert $x_t^* = \underline{x}$, $z_t^* = \underline{z} < \hat{z}$ such that $g(\underline{z}) = \underline{x}$. Then, if $u(\underline{x}) \equiv \underline{u}$, $u'(\underline{x}) \equiv u'$ we have $\underline{u} \leq u(x_t)$ and hence, for $0 \leq T < T^* < \infty$,

$$0 \leq \int_{T}^{T^*} e^{-\rho t}\, (u(x_t) - \underline{u})\, dt \equiv {_T}V_{T^*}(\rho) - (\underline{u}/\rho)\, (e^{-\rho T} - e^{-\rho T^*}) \leq$$

$$\leq u' \cdot |g'(\underline{z}) - \rho| \cdot (\overline{z}/\rho)\, (e^{-\rho T} - e^{-\rho T^*}) + u'\, \overline{z}\, (e^{-\rho T} + e^{-\rho T^*}),$$

hence $\lim_{T, T^* \to \infty} {_T}V_{T^*}(\rho) = 0$ whenever $\rho > 0$.

PROOFS OF (F), (G)

These propositions express, and provide economic interpretation for, the inequalities (43) if we take $T = 0$, $T^* \to \infty$, and if the 'candidate-optimal' path $(\hat{x}_t, \hat{z}_t)$ is substituted for (x_t^*, z_t^*). This is seen by reference to the definitions (21), (22) of the implicit prices p_t, q_t of the consumption good and of the use of the same good as capital good, respectively. Proposition F represents the first inequality in (43a), which does not require feasibility of (x_t, z_t). The inequality in Proposition G is obtained from the fourth member of (43a) by using (42), the equality through integration by parts.

PROOFS OF (H), (I), (J)

Proposition (I) states two conditions (α), (β), as necessary and sufficient for the optimality of a path $(\hat{x}_t, \hat{z}_t)$. We shall first look at the implications of condition (β) in isolation. Called the *Euler condition* in the 'calculus of variations', this condition is, for a path denoted just (x_t, z_t),

$$q_t + \dot{p}_t = u'(x_t)\,(g'(z_t) - \rho) + u''(x_t) \cdot \dot{x}_t = 0 \quad \text{for all } t \geq 0. \tag{64}$$

Together with the identity (36) this condition leads to the system of differential equations

$$\left.\begin{array}{ll} (65a) & \dot{z}_t = g(z_t) - x_t \\[2mm] (65b) & \dot{x}_t = -\dfrac{u'(x_t)}{u''(x_t)}\,(g'(z_t) - \rho), \end{array}\right\} \quad t \geq 0, \tag{65}$$

for the solution of which we have a prescribed initial value z_0 of z_t, but as yet no given value of x_0. Figure 16 partitions the quadrant $x > 0$, $z \geq 0$ according to the signs of $\dot{x}_t, \dot{z}_t$ that follow from (65). Figure 17 sketches the trajectories of the point (x_t, z_t) starting from arbitrary initial values (x_0, z_0). Each trajectory is defined as the solution $x(z)$ with $x(z_0) = x_0$, or $z(x)$ with $z(x_0) = z_0$, of the corresponding differential equation

$$\frac{dz}{dx} = -\frac{u''(x)}{u'(x)} \cdot \frac{g(z) - x}{g'(z) - \rho}, \text{ or } \frac{dx}{dz} = -\frac{u'(x)}{u''(x)} \cdot \frac{g'(z) - \rho}{g(z) - x}, \tag{66}$$

respectively, obtained from (65) by elimination of t. Any segment of any trajectory defines a path optimal on a suitable time interval with prescribed initial and terminal values z_0, z_T of z_t. If we prescribe only z_0 and examine the trajectories for various x_0, we find that there is one unique value $\hat{x}_0$ of x_0 which together with z_0 identifies a trajectory (shown in the diagram as a heavier line) that meets condition (α) of Proposition (I) of an asymptotic approach, for $t \to \infty$, to $(\hat{x}(\rho), \hat{z}(\rho))$ as defined in (60), Proposition (H).

We now denote the path resulting from that particular choice $\hat{x}_0$ of x_0 by $\hat{x}_t, \hat{z}_t)$. If $z_0 < \hat{z}(\rho)$, the initial consumption flow $\hat{x}_0$ leaves room for growth in the capital stock per worker, and both $\hat{x}_t$ and $\hat{z}_t$ increase with t to approach their asymptotic values $\hat{x}(\rho)$, $\hat{z}(\rho)$, respectively, as $t \to \infty$. If $z_0 > \hat{z}$, both $\hat{x}_t, \hat{z}_t$ decrease, and approach the same asymptots from above. Finally, if $z_0 = \hat{z}(\rho)$ we must have $\hat{x}_t = \hat{x}(\rho)$, $\hat{z}_t = \hat{z}(\rho)$ for all $t \geq 0$.

Since $\hat{x}_t$ approaches the positive number $\hat{x}(\rho)$ as $t \to \infty$, p_t is by its definition (21) asymptotic to $e^{-\rho t}\,u(\hat{x}(\rho))$. Hence, in (30), $\lim\limits_{T \to \infty} p_T(z_T - \hat{z}_t) = 0$ by (40), and $(\hat{x}_t, \hat{z}_t)$ is optimal. Moreover, if (x_t, z_t) differs from $(\hat{x}_t, \hat{z}_t)$, we must have $x_t \neq \hat{x}_t$ for some t, because in the contrary case (36) and $z_0 = \hat{z}_0$ would imply $z_t = \hat{z}_t$ for all t. But then, by the attainability condition (35c), we have a strict inequality in (24) and, by (25), a strict inequality in (30), hence (x_t, z_t) is not optimal. Therefore $(\hat{x}_t, \hat{z}_t)$ is uniquely optimal for the given z_0. This completes the proof of Propositions (H), (I), (J).

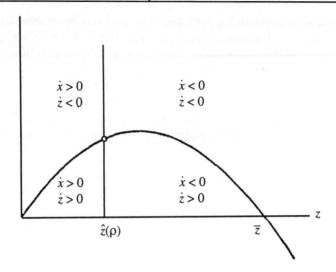

Figure 16

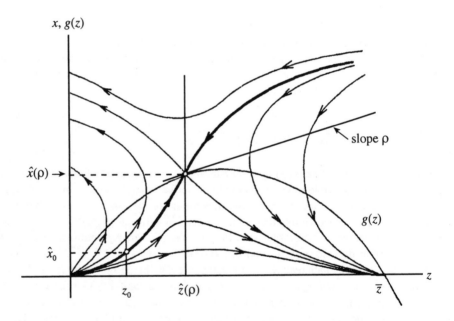

Figure 17

For completeness we consider two additional questions . If (x_t, z_t) is eligible and attainable, we have from (2)

$$\int_0^T p_t\, x_t\, dt = \int_0^T p_t\,(g(z_t) - \dot{z}_t)\, dt = \int_0^T (p_t\, g(z_t) + \dot{p}_t\, z_t)\, dt - p_T\, z_T.$$

Examining the behavior of p_t and $\dot{p}_t$ for $t \to \infty$ one finds from this formula that all the integrals occurring in statements (i), (ii), (iii) interpreting (F) and (I) converge for $T \to \infty$.

Finally, what rules out the trajectories in Figure 17 for which $x_0 \neq \hat{x}_0$? Those with $x_0 > \hat{x}$ reach the boundary $z = 0$ at some finite time, making it impossible to satisfy both (65) and (35a) for all $t \geq 0$. For each x_0^* with $0 < x_0^* < \hat{x}_0$, there is a unique attainable path (x_t^*, z_t^*) satisfying (65) for all $t \geq 0$ but in such a way that $\lim_{t \to \infty} x_t^* = 0$. This must entail either the ineligibility of (x_t^*, z_t^*), or the unboundedness of p_t^* associated with that path by (21), because otherwise (30) with (x_t^*, z_t^*, p_t^*) substituted for $(\hat{x}_t, \hat{z}_t, p_t)$ would imply the optimality of a path (x_t^*, z_t^*) already proved nonoptimal.

A8 Proofs for a negative discount rate ($\rho < 0$)

We shall need the following lemma.

Lemma 4. *If* $\varphi(x)$ *is a positive and nonincreasing function of* x *defined for all* $x > 0$, *and if* x_t *is a positive integrable function of* t *on the interval* $[T^1, T^2]$, $T^1 < T^2$, *such that*

$$\int_{T_1}^{T_2} x_t \, dt \leq (T_2 - T_1) \xi, \text{ where } \xi > 0, \tag{67}$$

then

$$\int_{T_1}^{T_2} \varphi(x_t) \, dt \geq \frac{1}{2}(T_2 - T_1) \, \varphi(2\xi) \tag{68}$$

Proof: We define

$$\mu(x) \equiv \frac{1}{T_2 - T_1} \cdot \text{measure of } \{ t \mid T_1 \leq t \leq T_2 \text{ and } x_t \leq x \}$$

Then $\mu(0) = 0$, $\mu(\infty) = 1$, and, from (67) and $x_t > 0$,

$$\xi \geq \frac{1}{T_2 - T_1} \int_{T_1}^{T_2} x_t \, dt = \int_0^\infty x \, d\mu(x) = \int_0^{2\xi} x \, d\mu(x) + \int_{2\xi}^\infty x \, d\mu(x) \geq 0 + 2\xi(1 - \mu(2\xi)), \tag{69}$$

Likewise, from the nonincreasing property of $\varphi(x)$,

$$\frac{1}{T_2 - T_1} \int_{T_1}^{T_2} \varphi(x_t) \, dt = \int_0^{2\xi} \varphi(x) \, d\mu(x) + \int_{2\xi}^\infty \varphi(x) \, d\mu(x) \geq \varphi(2\xi) \, \mu(2\xi) + 0. \tag{70}$$

Since, from (69), $\mu(2\xi) \geq \frac{1}{2}$, (70) implies (68).

PROOF OF (K)
We again distinguish the three cases with regard to the asymptotic range of z_t, used in the proof of (B).

Case (1), $\zeta < \bar{\zeta}$ In this case Proposition (K) is equivalent to Lemma 2.

Case (2), $\zeta = \bar{\zeta} \equiv \zeta \neq \hat{z}$ For definiteness assume $\zeta < \hat{z}$ and let $\hat{z} - \zeta \equiv 3\varepsilon$. Since now $\lim\limits_{t \to \infty} z_t = \zeta$ we can choose T such that

$$\hat{z} - 4\varepsilon \leq z_t \leq \hat{z} - 2\varepsilon \quad \text{for} \quad t \geq T \tag{71}$$

and at the same time large enough for there to exist an attainable path (x_t^*, z_t^*) on $[0, T]$ such that $z_T^* = z_T + \varepsilon$. For $t \geq T$ we choose (x_t^*, z_t^*) according to

$$z_t^* = z_t + \varepsilon, \quad \dot{z}_t^* = \dot{z}_t, \quad x_t^* = x_t + g(z_t^*) - g(z_t) \quad \text{for all} \quad t \geq T. \tag{72}$$

Then, (x_t^*, z_t^*) is attainable throughout, and from (42), (71), for $t \geq T$,

$$x_t^* - x_t = g(z_t^*) - g(z_t) \geq g'(z_t^*)(z_t^* - z_t) \geq g'(\hat{z} - \varepsilon) \cdot \varepsilon \equiv \eta > 0. \tag{73}$$

Hence, for $T < T^* < \infty$ and $-\rho \equiv \sigma > 0$,

$$_TW_T^*(-\sigma) \equiv \int_T^{T^*} e^{\sigma t}(u(x_t^*) - u(x_t))\, dt \geq e^{\sigma T} \int_T^{T^*} u'(x_t^*) \cdot (x_t^* - x_t)\, dt \geq \eta\, e^{\sigma T} \int_T^{T^*} u'(x_t^*)\, dt \tag{74}$$

On the other hand, by (36), (40a), (71),

$$\int_T^{T^*} x_t^*\, dt = \int_T^{T^*} g(z_t^*)\, dt + z_T^* - z_{T^*}^* \leq (T^* - T)\,\hat{x} + 2\varepsilon \leq (T^* - T)\,\xi \tag{75}$$

provided $T^* - T \geq 1$ and $\xi \equiv \hat{x} + 2\varepsilon$. It follows from (75) and Assumption (e) that x_t^* and $u'(x^*)$ when substituted for x_t and $\varphi(x)$ in Lemma 4 satisfy the premises of that lemma on the interval $[T, T^*]$. Hence, from (74), (68),

$$_TW_{T^*}(-\sigma) \geq \frac{1}{2}\eta \cdot u'(2\hat{x} + 4\varepsilon) \cdot (T^* - T)\, e^{\sigma T}$$

from which (K) follows directly. The proof for $\hat{z} < \zeta$ is similar.

Case (3), $\zeta = \bar{\zeta} = \hat{z}$ For any $\varepsilon > 0$, subject still to later choice, there now exists an integer T such that

$$\hat{z} - \varepsilon \leq z_t \leq \hat{z} + \varepsilon \quad \text{for} \quad t \geq T. \tag{76}$$

It will be useful to write $_TW_{T^*}(-\sigma)$ as the difference of two integrals

$$_TW_{T^*}(-\sigma) = \int_T^{T^*} e^{\sigma t}(u(x_t) - \hat{u})\, dt - \int_T^{T^*} e^{\sigma T}(u(x_t) - \hat{u})\, dt = {}_TU_{T^*}^*(-\sigma) - {}_TU_{T^*}(-\sigma). \tag{77}$$

Taking first the second term we have, from (43a) with $x_t^* = \hat{x}$, (36) and (38a).

$$_T U_{T^*} (-\sigma) \leq \hat{u}' \int_T^{T^*} e^{\sigma t} (g(z_t) - \hat{x} - \dot{z}_t) \, dt \leq -\hat{u}' \int_T^{T^*} e^{\sigma t} \frac{d}{dt} (z_t - \hat{z}) \, dt =$$

$$= -\hat{u}' \left[e^{\sigma T^*} (z_{T^*} - \hat{z}) - e^{\sigma T} (z_T - \hat{z}) - \sigma \int_T^{T^*} e^{\sigma t} (z_t - \hat{z}) \, dt \right] \leq$$

$$\leq \hat{u}' \varepsilon (e^{\sigma T^*} + e^{\sigma T} + (e^{\sigma T^*} - e^{\sigma T})) = 2 \, \hat{u}' \, \varepsilon \, e^{\sigma T^*} \tag{78}$$

For the first term in (77) we choose an attainable path (x_t^*, z_t^*) which for $t \geq T$ is given by

$$\left. \begin{array}{llll}
(79a) & T \leq t < T^* - 1, & z_t^* = \hat{z} + \eta, & z_t^* = 0, & x_t^* = g(\hat{z} + \eta), \\
(79b) & T^* - 1 \leq t < T^*, & z_t^* = (T^* - t)(\hat{z} + \eta) + & \dot{z}_t^* = z_{T^*} - \hat{z} - \eta, & x_t^* = g(z_t^*) - z_{T^*} \\
& & + (t - T^* + 1) z_{T^*}, & & + \hat{z} + \eta, \\
(79c) & T^* \leq t, & z_t^* = z_t, & \dot{z}_t^* = \dot{z}_t, & x_t^* = x_t,
\end{array} \right\} \tag{79}$$

where $\eta \geq 3\varepsilon$ and the number $T^* > T + 1$ are still subject to later choice. In addition, T should be sufficiently large that, besides (76), there exists an attainable path (x_t^*, z_t^*) on $[0, T]$ such that $z_T^* = \hat{z} + \eta$.

To obtain a lower bound on the first term in (77) we note that, in view of Assumption (c) and (38b), there exist numbers $\eta_0 > 0$ and $\gamma > 0$ such that, whenever $0 < \eta \leq \eta_0$,

$$|z - \hat{z}| \leq \eta \text{ implies } 0 \leq g(\hat{z}) - g(z) \leq \gamma \eta^2. \tag{80}$$

Hence, if $0 < \eta \leq \eta_0$ and $u'_0 \equiv u'(g(\hat{z} + \eta_0))$, we have from (79a) and (38b), in analogy to (78),

$$_T U_{T^* - 1}^* (-\sigma) \geq u'_0 \int_T^{T^* - 1} e^{\sigma t} (g(\hat{z} + \eta) - g(\hat{z})) \, dt \geq -u'_0 \gamma \eta^2 \sigma^{-1} (e^{\sigma(T^* - 1)} - e^{\sigma T}) >$$

$$> -u'_0 \gamma \eta^2 \sigma^{-1} e^{\sigma T^*}. \tag{81}$$

For $T^* - 1 \leq t < T^*$, x_t^* varies and must be boxed in. If $0 < \varepsilon \leq \varepsilon_0$, $0 < \eta \leq \eta_0$, we have from (79b), (38),

$$\underline{x}^* \equiv \min \{ g(\hat{z} - \varepsilon_0), g(\hat{z} + \eta_0) \} - \varepsilon_0 \leq x_t^* \leq \hat{x} + \varepsilon_0 + \eta_0 \equiv \overline{x}^*,$$

where ε_0, η_0 are chosen small enough to make $\overline{x}^* > 0$. Then, because $u'(x)$ decreases with x,

$$\overline{u}' \equiv \max \{ u'(\underline{x}^*), u'_0 \} \geq u'(x_t^*) \geq u'(\overline{x}^*) \equiv \underline{u}' > 0 \text{ for } T^* - 1 \leq t < T.$$

We therefore have from (79b), (80),

$$_{T^* - 1} U_{T^*}^* (-\sigma) \geq \int_{T^* - 1}^{T^*} e^{\sigma t} u(x_t^*) (g(z_t^*) - g(\hat{z}) - \dot{z}_t^*) \, dt \geq$$

$$\geq -\overline{u}' \gamma \eta^2 e^{\sigma T^*} + \underline{u}' \cdot (\eta - \varepsilon) e^{\sigma(T^* - 1)}. \tag{82}$$

Pulling together these inequalities we have, for any $T^{**} \geq T^{*}$, from (79c), (77), (78), (81), (82), since $\bar{u}' \geq u'_0 > \hat{u}'$,

$$_T W_{T^{**}}(-\sigma) \geq [-u'(\gamma \eta^2 (1 + \sigma^{-1}) + 2\varepsilon) + \underline{u}'(\eta - \varepsilon)e^{-\sigma}] e^{\sigma T^*} \equiv A\, e^{\sigma T^*}, \text{ say.}$$

It is now possible, within the restrictions already imposed, to choose first η and then ε small enough to make $A > 0$, next to choose T to correspond to ε according to (76), and finally, given $N > 0$, to choose T^* large enough to make

$$W_{T^{**}}(-\sigma) = W_T(-\sigma) + {_T W_{T^*}}(-\sigma) \geq W_T(-\sigma) + A e^{\sigma T^*} > N$$

for all $T^{**} \geq T^{*}$.

References

Allais, M., *Economie et Intérêt.* Imprimerie Nationale, Paris, 1947.
—— 'The Influence of Capital-Output Ratio on Real National Income'. *Econometrica*, October 1962, pp. 700–728.
Bauer, P.T., *Economic Analysis and Policy in Underdeveloped Countries.* Duke University Press, 1957, esp. pp. 112–126.
Cass, D., *Optimum Savings in an Aggregative Model of Capital Accumulation.* Technical Report No. 5, Institute for Mathematical Studies in the Social Sciences, Stanford University, 27 Nov., 1963.
Chakravarty, S., 'The Existence of an Optimum Savings Program'. *Econometrica*, January 1962, pp. 178–187.
Debreu, G., 'Representation of a Preference Ordering by a Numerical Function'. In Thrall, Coombs and Davis (eds), *Decision Processes*, John Wiley, New York, 1954, ch. XI, pp. 159–165.
Desrousseaux, J., 'Expansion stable et taux d'intérêt optimal'. *Annales des Mines*, November 1961, pp. 31–46.
Harrod, R.F., *Towards a Dynamic Economics.* Macmillan, London, 1948.
Inagaki, M., *The Golden Utility Path.* Memorandum dated 13 November 1963, Netherlands Economics Institute, Rotterdam, 31 pp., mimeo.
Kantorovich, L.V., *Ekonomicheski raschet nailuchshego ispol'zovaniia resursov* (Economic Calculation of the Best Utilization of Resources), Academy of Sciences of the USSR, Moscow, 1959 (French Translation published by Dunod, Paris, 1963).
Koopmans, T.C., 'Stationary Ordinal Utility and Impatience'. *Econometrica*, April 1960, pp. 287–309. This issue was also published separately under the title *Econometrica Essays in Honor of Ragnar Frisch.*
—— 'On Flexibility of Future Preferences'. In Bryan and Shelly (eds), *Human Judgments and Optimality*, John Wiley, New York, 1964.
—— Diamond, P.A., and Williamson, R.E., 'Stationary Utility and Time Perspective'. *Econometrica*, January–April 1964, pp. 82–100.
Phelps, E.S., 'The Golden Rule of Accumulation'. *American Economic Review*, September 1961, pp. 638–642.
Pugachev, V.F., 'O kriterii optimal'nosti ekonomiki' (Criteria of Optimality for the Economy). In *Ekonomiko-matematicheskie metody. Narodnokhoziastvennye modeli: Teoreticheskie voprosy potrebleniia*, A.L. Vainshtein, ed., Moscow, 1963.
Ramsey, F.P., 'A Mathematical Theory of Saving'. *Economic Journal*, December 1928, pp. 543–559.
Robinson, Joan, 'A Neo-Classical Theorem'. *Review of Economic Studies*, June 1962, pp. 219–226.
Srinivasan, T.N., 'On a Two-Sector Model of Growth'. *Econometrica*, July 1964, pp. 358–373.
Swan, T., *On Golden Ages and Production Functions.* Memorandum for the Round Table on Economic

Development held in April 1960 in Gamagozi, Japan, under auspices of the International Economic Association, mimeo, 18 pp.

Tinbergen, J., 'Optimum Savings and Utility Maximization over Time'. *Econometrica*, April 1960, pp. 481–489, issue also published separately as *Econometrica Essays in Honor of Ragnar Frisch*.

Uzawa, H., 'Optimal Growth in a Two-Sector Model of Capital Accumulation'. *Review of Economic Studies*, XXXI (1), 85, January 1964, pp. 1–24.

von Weizsäcker, C.C., *Wachstum, Zins und Optimale Investitonsquote*. Kyklos Verlag, Basel, 1962, pp. 96.

Wold, H., 'A Synthesis of Pure Demand Analysis', Part II. *Skandinavisk Aktuaritidskrift*, vol. 26, 1943, pp. 220–263.

Discussion

Dorfman

I feel very strongly moved to express my admiration for Prof. Koopmans' paper. As Dr. Johnson might have said, its profundity is equalled only by its ingenuity. And it reaches some remarkable and exceedingly significant conclusions.

It is important to point to two quite strong assumptions on which the conclusions rest. One of them is that Prof. Koopmans has replaced the three factors of classical economics – land, labour and capital – by a two factor model. He omits land. The technical effect of introducing land into Prof. Koopmans' model would be to change one of the essential mathematical functions. Since land is in virtually fixed supply, it would no longer be permissible to think of constant returns to scale to the two variable factors. I can only conjecture the consequences of that change, but perhaps it would strengthen the moral case for saving on the part of the present generation because they will be better endowed per capita with the third factor than future generations if population continues to grow.

The other strong assumption made by Prof. Koopmans is that capital does not depreciate. I think it was Ricardo who originally defined land to be the original and indestructible powers of the soil. We have since generalized this concept to mean the original and indestructible power of anything that we inherit. The findings of capital theory indicate that if either of those two adjectives is the more important, it is 'indestructible'. Whether a good possesses original powers or not is a matter of the past, which is now dead. From the forward looking point of view, the essential difference between capital and land or natural resources is that land does not require maintenance, but capital does, so that what Prof. Koopmans has been calling capital here might really come closer to being a kind of land or what would be from the point of view of future generations an increase in their supply of natural resources that they inherit from both their forebears and from nature itself.

Depreciation can be allowed for in this model by reinterpreting equation (10a), the basic feasibility equation on page 201. We need only think of Prof. Koopmans' λ as being composed of $\lambda_1 + \lambda_2$, where λ_1 is the rate of population growth and λ_2 is the rate of capital deterioration. With this amendment, would not this same analysis apply to an economy in which population grew and capital deteriorated?

However this may be, the fact that capital depreciates does go against the strong conclusions that Prof. Koopmans arrived at because it means that an increment to the capital stock cannot be infinitely productive because it will decay, and it may carry with it a responsibility for permanent maintenance in the face of diminishing returns and perhaps also of diminishing marginal utility in the U functions. In that case, an economy can reach a state of capital saturation in the sense that, although the utility per capita resulting from an increase in the stock of capital does not fall to zero, it falls so low that it does not exceed the social cost of maintaining it. This consideration may lead to some changes in your conclusions and help avoid some of the problems created by the infinite horizon.

Koopmans

I agree to the comments made by Prof. Dorfman that this exercise simplifies matters a great deal by ignoring land and depreciation of capital. Land would undoubtedly become a problem if population were to increase to such an extent that just space on which to exist would become very scarce, and it might actually become a problem well before that. It seems however that technology has so many possibilities for food production that are less land-intensive than the ones that are now being used, that there might be at least a temporary offset in technological progress.

As to the assumption that capital does not depreciate, I think this is a difference in degree but not in kind. As Prof. Dorfman indicates you can indeed reinterpret λ as the sum $\lambda = \lambda_1 + \lambda_2$ where λ_1 refers to population growth and λ_2 to capital depreciation.

Malinvaud

I should like to argue that Prof. Koopmans has been quite wise in these kinds of simplifications. We are certainly not living in a one commodity world in which capital would not depreciate. But some of the difficulties of intertemporal choices will appear with full clarity in very simple models. At the present stage of our research we are therefore justified to study carefully and exhaustively such simple models.

In particular it seems to me that difficulties occurring in more complex models have not been fully understood in their natures, because several sources of complications mixed their effects, and the origin of each new result was not clear. From the point of view that interests Prof. Koopmans, I do not think we should reach different qualitative conclusions if we introduce many commodities, if we assume that capital depreciates, or if we take into account the fact that land is not reproducible.

Pasinetti

I have very much enjoyed Prof. Koopmans' skilful, elegant and perspicuous analysis. Yet, I find it hard to accept his conclusions, which seem to me best summarized by the title of his Section 7 ('adjusting preferences to opportunities'). Prof. Koopmans has found that the traditional approach to optimal growth (which consists of maximizing utility over time, by accepting a certain rate of discount of utility, called ρ, as given by individual preferences) cannot always be applied. More precisely, he has found that it can be applied only when the time horizon considered is finite. When time is allowed to run from 0 to ∞, then $\rho < 0$ becomes impossible (although $\rho \geq 0$ still remains possible) because there simply would not exist a utility function to be maximized.

Thus – Prof. Koopmans concludes – the open-endedness of the future imposes limits on individual preferences. He seems to be so surprised and even so afraid of this result as to prefer, at this point, to begin to speculate on the meaning of all this.

I would suggest that the mathematical exercise should be completed, by allowing time to run from $-\infty$ to $+\infty$ (and not only from 0 to $+\infty$). I may add perhaps that to consider time as running from $-\infty$ to $+\infty$ does not mean allowing time to run in reverse. It simply means putting ourselves in a slightly different position with respect to the one Prof. Koopmans has chosen. Instead of saying, as he does: suppose we begin our process of maximization at time zero, whatever happened before; we say: suppose that optimization has been taking place since the beginning of time. (This, by the way, appears to me a more logical approach to take in the context of Prof. Koopmans' stationary society.) Now, if we allow time to run from $-\infty$ to $+\infty$, it is easy to see that, in a stationary economic system, also $\rho > 0$ becomes impossible. The only value of ρ that makes any process of utility maximization over infinity possible is $\rho = 0$.

Prof. Koopmans might be even more surprised. For, by following his arguments, we should conclude that individuals have not even a limited intertemporal preference choice: they have no choice at all.

But is it so? This conclusion – it seems to me – is fallacious, although of course the mathematical results are correct. And the fallacy stems from not bringing out explicitly the implications of the following *theorem*: on the optimum growth path (by which I mean Prof. Koopmans' 'golden rule path'), the rate of interest of the economic system is determined independently of consumers' utility functions. This theorem follows from Prof. Koopmans' own analysis. For, on the optimum path, the rate of interest must be equal to the *natural* rate of growth (which, in the particular case of a stationary economic system, is equal to zero).

But this simply means that individuals' preferences are not a determinant of the optimum rate of interest. It does not mean (as Prof. Koopmans seems to fear) that any restriction comes to be imposed on individuals' preferences. To argue otherwise would sound to me rather similar to saying, in the usual case of a one-period problem of utility maximization, that the fact that market prices are the same for all consumers imposes restrictions on individual preferences. Traditional economic theorists have solved this problem a long time ago, by referring their analysis only to what happens at the margin. Individual preferences are accepted for what they are, however different from one individual to another they may be. Yet, given these preferences, each individual will push the consumption of each commodity to the point at which the ratios of marginal utilities are equal to relative market prices. This means that we can make definite statements about ratios of *marginal* utilities, without imposing any restriction on utility functions.

Our case is similar. Consumers' preferences may be quite different at different levels of consumption, at different times, and for different individuals. Any social preference function expressing all these preferences may be equally different; and it must be accepted for what it is, without any restriction. Yet, if behaviour is to be rational, the consumption of each commodity will be distributed over time so as to equate *marginal* intertemporal rates of substitution in consumption to the externally given rate of interest. This is all we can say.

Professor Koopmans' results have been obtained because he has added something else. He has imposed on utility functions *at all levels* (and not only at the margin!) the restriction that utility always differs by ρ at any two adjacent points of time. This restriction is arbitrary, and has no justification; and I would interpret the results of his mathematical analysis as simply showing the impossibility of such an arbitrary restriction. I should conclude, therefore, that the misunderstanding has arisen from having introduced a ρ into the analysis at all. For this has meant introducing exactly what Prof. Koopmans has been afraid of, namely restrictions on consumers' preferences.

Koopmans

I do not understand the operational meaning of Prof. Pasinetti's suggestion to maximize utility over a period from $-\infty$ to $+\infty$. The following comments apply therefore to maximization from 0 to ∞, although I may thereby fail to do justice to Pasinetti's thought.

In the sentence in which Prof. Pasinetti refers to the 'golden rule path', he uses the term optimum in a sense different from mine. If an optimal path is defined as one that maximizes a utility function of the type I have discussed, the golden rule path is optimal only if both (a) the initial ratio of capital stock to labor force happens to coincide with that characteristic of the golden rule path, and (b) the chosen utility function has no discounting ($\rho = 0$). If both these conditions are satisfied, the golden rule path is optimal in my sense as well, and as Pasinetti observes the interest rate $\rho + \lambda$ equals the exogenously given growth rate λ of the labor force. However, if even only one of these conditions fails to hold, the optimal path, if one exists, differs from the golden rule path, and the interest rate differs from λ most or all of the time, and is determined by the interplay of preferences and production possibilities I have analyzed.

Finally, Prof. Pasinetti's analogy with the one-period problem of utility maximization misses the main point of my paper. In the one-period problem with a finite number of commodities, an optimal consumption choice is bound to exist if the utility function is continuous (a slight restriction on preferences!) and the opportunity set closed and bounded. In the infinite-horizon case, there is a new mathematical situation, and the existence of an optimal program is found to depend on a stronger restriction on the utility function used. To facilitate analysis, I have studied this restriction only within the class of stationary and additive per capita utility functions, expressible as a sum of future per capita utilities derived from a constant one-period utility function $u(x)$ and discounted at a constant rate ρ. Within that arbitrarily chosen class, an optimal path is found to exist if and only if $\rho \geq 0$. The question of existence of an optimal path is so far unresolved within the wider class of continuous but not necessarily stationary or additive utility functions. It is plausible to assume that within that class there will again be a subclass for which, in a given technology, no optimal path exists.

Morishima

Your argument is based on the assumption that the rate of growth of population is constant. This, together with others, implies the uniqueness of the Golden Rule path. Suppose, instead, that the rate of growth of population is an increasing function of the consumption per capita until it reaches a certain level, after which the population growth-rate will decrease. Then there are possibilities of multi-Golden Rule paths. You shall have to be concerned with the comparison between Golden Rule paths (the best Golden Rule path, the second best Golden Rule path and so on) and also with the locality of the stability of the best Golden Rule path.

You treat capital and labour in an asymmetric way: capital may be unused if too much capital is available, while labour is fully employed throughout the whole process. May I say that a certain degree of optimality has already been presupposed in your assumption of automatic maintenance of the full employment of labour? Is the full employment of labour maintained even if labour is treated in the same manner as capital, i.e. if there is a possibility of unemployment of labour?

Koopmans

I want to thank Prof. Morishima for the information he gave us for a model in which the rate of population growth is a function of consumption per head, initially increasing and thereafter decreasing. This is, I think, a realistic generalization that it is important to have.

On his second point, the asymmetry in treating capital and labour with regard to disposal, I would agree that that is something not very consistent in the paper as presented. I do not think it has affected any of the results in any of the optimal paths being considered – paths in which at all times the capital stock is fully used as much as the labour force.[1]

Mahalanobis

I am very deeply impressed by the approach and the broader results of this paper. It seems to me that although a very simple model has been used on, if you like, somewhat intuitional grounds, the conclusion seems to be extremely important from the point of view of the underdeveloped countries. The conclusion to which I am referring is that neutrality regarding timing between generations is not possible, the very nature of the process of development or of industrialization discriminates in favour of future generations. Thus I am taking to be a basic point, on page 28, the argument that accumulation of capital, permitting a higher output of consumption goods in later years must discriminate in favour of future generations. The broad conclusions may have important educative effects regarding programmes in underdeveloped countries.

I am not going into details of technical arguments, but suppose instead of the one commodity model we have three types of capital goods producing three types of consumer goods; the basket changes but there need not be any change in the total aggregation of capital goods which goes on increasing. The one-commodity model seems to me to be illustrative, and the conclusions may remain valid even if we have many commodities. This question, of course, cannot be settled without going through the full exercise of rigorous analysis.

There are three points which have been summarized in Sections 5 and 6. The point about open end I think has been clearly brought out and is logically valid.

I am repeating the question again: whether one commodity or many commodities would affect that result. Theoretically some preference functions may change. The order with which Prof. Koopmans started, that pattern of ordering, may also change. But I think Prof. Koopmans took care to point out that some kind of good ordering is all that he was keeping in mind.

A further point which is discussed on page 32, that it is likely that technological advance would continue; even if it slows down, even then, from the point of view of the present generation, the discrimination would be in favour of future generations. The question of basic decision is not whether the hundredth generation from now would be in a somewhat less

---

1. Note added after the conference: In the corrected version of the paper printed in the volume, disposal of capital use has been excluded.

favourable position; the decreasing return in terms of generations may be there even if the technological advance continued at the same rate. I do not see this as a very important consideration for present decisions.

This particular paper seems to me to be of value because of the wider implications of this Study Week. It is not a Study Week arranged by a specialist econometric society but by the Pontifical Academy of Sciences. My interest, as I have continually stressed, is in the broader implications. And from that point of view I welcome this paper as likely to have a very valuable educative effect.

It is more difficult to speak on the question of population size. It may differ from country to country. Prof. Koopmans has pointed out that where the density of population is extremely small, there may be some advantage in increasing their number, but where the density of population is high the position may be different.

Koopmans

I share the beliefs expressed by both speakers, Prof. Mahalanobis and Prof. Malinvaud, that the one-commodity study, one-commodity model does a service here in isolating just those problems that come from the open-endedness of the future. Considering those apart from other complications which arise in two- or more-commodity models, I used the term 'belief' because I do not feel that a stronger term can be used at this point. One would want to go on to two- and more-commodity models to examine whether that belief is valid but this is my present state of espectation.

On the question that Prof. Mahalanobis raised about flexibility in the ordering, that idea is merely mentioned at the end of my study. I have given some thought to the possibility of working from an ordering which has built into it the possibility of its own revision at a later time, and more particularly an ordering in which the decision maker is willing to make a present sacrifice of immediate satisfaction in order to leave open more doors in the future. He may, for instance, prefer to build a capital stock of such a nature that it can be applied to a wider range of different kinds of production, even though that kind of capital stock would not be the most economical one if the composition of production in the future were already fully specified. For somewhat longer-range planning this seems to me a matter of practical importance. My speculations on this are in a reference at the end of my paper, identified by the year 1962, and they did not carry very far. I believe that from the formal point of view it is a difficult matter to formalize this idea. I do find that the need for such an idea is strong enough to justify further formalizing effort in that direction.

Fisher

Prof. Koopmans has as always presented us with an illuminating and beautiful piece of work. I am, however, disturbed a bit at the conclusions that he wants to draw from it. He has shown that there may be severe conflicts between our ethical notions and the analysis of certain kinds of growth models. His conclusion is that we must change our ethical notions. My preference would be to say that there is something wrong with the model. In either case a good deal of further thought seems called for. More particularly, one frequently in the theory of optimization over time encounters peculiar difficulties when one uses an infinite time horizon. Now, in fact, the device of the infinite horizon was probably originally introduced because the choice of a finite horizon is an arbitrary one and because with a finite horizon one has difficulty in deciding what to do about terminal capital stock. Infinite horizons were, however, introduced primarily as a convenience. They have in several contexts now been shown to lead to difficulties all associated with divergence of the improper integral obtained in the problem. Now this suggests to me that infinite horizons are not in fact the convenience they appear. The obvious conclusion from Koopmans' paper, therefore, seems to me to be that one ought to abandon the use of infinite horizons – not that one ought to abandon certain ethical notions.

Now, of course, this may be wrong. It may turn out – and Prof. Koopmans assures me that it does – that even with a finite horizon one has similar problems which are not so severe. In that case, it may not be worth dropping infinite horizons. Still, the role of this sort of analysis is surely to tell us how one can best achieve one's ethical and social ends. In the course of analyzing that, it may turn out that such ends are unachievable. In such a case, one has to moderate one's ends. The usual circumstance, however, is that one's ends are not achievable in the sense of being contradictory whereas Prof. Koopmans has shown that our ends may be unachievable in the sense that no solution to the problem exists – that the whole analysis breaks down if one insists on certain kinds of ethical goals. This sort of circumstance does not persuade me to give up my ethical goals, but rather to refine the mode of analysis. I can understand that the end result may be that I will have to give up certain goals as unachievable, but the demonstration of that ought to be that they are unachievable and not that the problem becomes ill-defined.

Despite the fact that I am unable to agree completely with Prof. Koopmans' conclusions, however, I should like to state that his paper like that of Prof. Malinvaud is a pleasure to read and to listen to. The two papers set a standard that one wishes all the other papers and discussion in this Study Week had met.

[13]

THE VALUATION OF RISK ASSETS AND THE SELECTION OF RISKY INVESTMENTS IN STOCK PORTFOLIOS AND CAPITAL BUDGETS*

John Lintner

Introduction and Preview of Some Conclusions

THE effects of risk and uncertainty upon asset prices, upon rational decision rules for individuals and institutions to use in selecting security portfolios, and upon the proper selection of projects to include in corporate capital budgets, have increasingly engaged the attention of professional economists and other students of the capital markets and of business finance in recent years. The essential purpose of the present paper is to push back the frontiers of our knowledge of the logical structure of these related issues, albeit under idealized conditions. The immediately following text describes the contents of the paper and summarizes some of the principal results.

The first two sections of this paper deal with the *problem of selecting* optimal security portfolios by risk-averse investors who have the alternative of investing in risk-free securities with a positive return (or borrowing at the same rate of interest) and who can sell short if they wish. The first gives alternative and hopefully more transparent proofs (under these more general market conditions) for Tobin's important "separation theorem" that ". . . the proportionate composition of the non-cash assets is independent of their aggregate share of the investment balance . . . " (and hence of the optimal holding of cash) for risk averters in purely compe-

*This paper is another in a series of interrelated theoretical and statistical studies of corporate financial and investment policies being made under grants from the Rockefeller Foundation, and more recently the Ford Foundation, to the Harvard Business School. The generous support for this work is most gratefully acknowledged. The author is also much indebted to his colleagues Professors Bishop, Christenson, Kahr, Raiffa, and (especially) Schlaifer, for extensive discussion and commentary on an earlier draft of this paper; but responsibility for any errors or imperfections remains strictly his own.
[Professor Sharpe's paper, "Capital Asset Prices: A Theory of Market Equilibrium Under Conditions of Risk" (*Journal of Finance*, September 1964) appeared after this paper was in final form and on its way to the printers. My first section, which parallels the first half of his paper (with corresponding conclusions), sets the algebraic framework for sections II, III and VI, (which have no counterpart in his paper) and for section IV on the equilibrium prices of risk assets, concerning which our results differ significantly for reasons which will be explored elsewhere. Sharpe does not take up the capital budgeting problem developed in section V below.]

titive markets when utility functions are quadratic *or* rates of return are multivariate normal.[1] We then note that the same conclusion follows from an earlier theorem of Roy's [19] without dependence on quadratic utilities or normality. The second section shows that *if short sales are permitted*, the best portfolio-mix of risk assets can be determined by the solution of a single simple set of simultaneous equations without recourse to programming methods, and when covariances are zero, a still simpler ratio scheme gives the optimum, whether or not short sales are permitted. When covariances are not all zero and short sales are excluded, a single quadratic programming solution is required, but sufficient.

Following these extensions of Tobin's classic work, we concentrate on the set of risk assets held in risk averters' portfolios. In section III we develop various significant *equilibrium properties within* the risk asset portfolio. In particular, we establish conditions under which stocks will be held long (short) in optimal portfolios even when "risk premiums" are negative (positive). We also develop expressions for different combinations of expected rate of return on a given security, and its standard deviation, variance, and/or covariances which will result in the same relative holding of a stock, *ceteris paribus*. These "indifference functions" provide direct evidence on the moot issue of the appropriate functional relationships between "required rates of return" and relevant risk parameter(s) — and on the related issue of how "risk classes" of securities may best be delineated (if they are to be used).[2]

[1]Tobin [21, especially pp. 82–85]. Tobin assumed that funds are to be a allocated only over "monetary assets" (risk-free cash and default-free bonds of uncertain resale price) and allowed no short sales or borrowing. See also footnote 24 below. Other approaches are reviewed in Farrar [38].

[2]It should be noted that the classic paper by Modigliani and Miller [16] was silent on these issues. Corporations were assumed to be divided into homogeneous classes having the property that all shares of all corporations in any given class differed (at most) by a "scale factor," and hence (a) were perfectly correlated with each other and (b) were perfect substitutes for each other in perfect markets (p. 266). No comment was made on the measure of risk or uncertainty (or other attributes) relevant to the identification of different "equiva-

14 THE REVIEW OF ECONOMICS AND STATISTICS

There seems to be a general presumption among economists that relative risks are best measured by the standard deviation (or coefficient of variation) of the rate of return,[3] but in the simplest cases considered — specifically when all covariances are considered to be invariant (or zero) — the indifference functions are shown to be linear between expected rates of return and their *variance*, not standard deviation.[4] (With variances fixed, the indifference function between the ith expected rate of return and its pooled covariance with other stocks is hyperbolic.) There is no simple relation between the expected rate of return required to maintain an investor's relative holding of a stock and its standard deviation. Specifically, when covariances are non-zero and variable, the indifference functions are complex and non-linear *even if* it is assumed that the *correlations* between rates of return on different securities are invariant.

To this point we follow Tobin [21] and Markowitz [14] in assuming that current security prices are given, and that each investor acts on his own (perhaps unique) probability distribution over rates of return given these market prices. In the rest of the paper, we assume that investors' joint probability distributions pertain to dollar returns rather than rates of return[5], and for simplicity we assume that all investors assign identical sets of means, variances, and covariances to the distribution of these dollar returns. However unrealisic the latter assumption may be, it enables us, in section IV, to derive a set of (stable) equilibrium market prices which at least fully and explicitly reflect the presence of

uncertainty *per se* (as distinct from the effects of diverse expectations), and to derive further implications of such uncertainty. In particular, the aggregate market value of any company's equity is equal to the capitalization at the risk-free interest rate of a uniquely defined *certainty-equivalent* of the probability distribution of the aggregate dollar returns to all holders of its stock. For each company, this certainty equivalent is the expected value of these uncertain returns less an adjustment term which is proportional to their aggregate risk. The factor of proportionality is the *same for all companies* in equilibrium, and may be regarded as a *market price of dollar risk*. The relevant risk of each company's stock is measured, moreover, not by the standard deviation of its dollar returns, but by the *sum* of the *variance* of its own aggregate dollar returns *and* their *total covariance* with those of all other stocks.

The next section considers some of the implications of these results for the normative aspects of the capital budgeting decisions of a company whose stock is traded in the market. For simplicity, we impose further assumptions required to make capital budgeting decisions independent of decisions on how the budget is financed.[6] The capital budgeting problem becomes a quadratic programming problem analogous to that introduced earlier for the individual investor. This capital budgeting-portfolio problem is formulated, its solution is given and some of its more important properties examined. Specifically, the minimum expected return (in dollars of expected present value) required to justify the allocation of funds to a given risky project is shown to be an increasing function of each of the following factors: (*i*) the risk-free rate of return; (*ii*) the "market price of (dollar) risk"; (*iii*) the variance in the project's own present value return; (*iv*) the project's aggregate present value return-*covariance* with assets already held by the company, and (*v*) its total covariance with other projects concurrently included in the capital budget. *All five* factors are involved explicitly in the corresponding (derived) formula for the minimum acceptable *expected rate* of return on an investment project. In this model, all means

---

lent return" classes. Both Propositions I (market value of *firm* independent of capital structure) and II (the linear relation between the expected return on equity shares and the debt-equity ratio for firms within a given class) are derived from the above assumptions (and the further assumption that corporate bonds are riskless securities); they involve no inter-class comparisons, ". . . nor do they involve any assertion as to what is an adequate compensation to investors for assuming a given degree of risk. . . ." (p. 279).

[3] This is, for instance, the presumption of Hirschleifer [8, p. 113], although he was careful not to commit himself to this measure alone in a paper primarily focussed on other issues. For an inductive argument in favor of the standard deviation of the rate of return as the best measure of risk, see Gordon [5, especially pp. 69 and 76]. See also Dorfman in [3, p. 129 ff.] and Baumol [2].

[4] Except in dominantly "short" portfolios, the constant term will be larger, and the slope lower, the higher the (fixed) level of covariances of the given stocks with other stocks.

[5] The dollar return in the period is the sum of the cash dividend and the increase in market price during the period.

[6] We also assume that common stock portfolios are not "inferior goods," that the value of *all other* common stocks is invariant, and any effect of changes in capital budgets on the *covariances* between the values of different companies' *stocks* is ignored.

VALUATION OF RISK ASSETS   15

and (co)variances of present values must be calculated at the riskless rate r^*. We also show that *there can be no "risk-discount" rate* to be used in computing present values to accept or reject individual projects. In particular, the *"cost of capital"* as defined (for uncertainty) anywhere in the literature *is not the appropriate rate* to use in these decisions *even if* all new projects have the same "risk" as existing assets.

The final section of the paper briefly examines the complications introduced by institutional limits on amounts which either individuals or corporations may borrow at given rates, by rising costs of borrowed funds, and certain other "real world" complications. It is emphasized that the results of this paper are not being presented as directly applicable to practical decisions, because many of the factors which matter very siginificantly in practice have had to be ignored or assumed away. The function of these simplifying assumptions has been to permit a rigorous development of theoretical relationships and theorems which reorient much current theory (especially on capital budgeting) and provide a basis for further work.[7] More detailed conclusions will be found emphasized at numerous points in the text.

I — Portfolio Selection for an Individual Investor: The Separation Theorem

Market Assumptions

We assume that (1) *each individual* investor can invest any part of his capital in certain *risk-free assets* (e. g. deposits in insured savings accounts[8]) all of which pay interest at a common positive rate, exogeneously determined; and that (2) he can invest *any fraction* of his capital *in any* or all of a given finite set of *risky* securities which are (3) traded in a single *purely competitive market*, free of transactions costs and taxes, at given market prices,[9] which consequently do not depend on his investments or transactions. We also assume that (4) any investor may, if he wishes, borrow funds to invest in risk assets. Ex-

[7] The relation between the results of this paper and the models which were used in [11] and [12] is indicated at the end of section V.

[8] Government bonds of appropriate maturity provide another important example when their "yield" is substituted for the word "interest."

[9] Solely for convenience, we shall usually refer to all these investments as common stocks, although the analysis is of course quite general.

cept in the final section, we assume that the *interest rate paid* on such loans is the same as he would have received had he invested in risk-free savings accounts, and that there is *no limit* on the amount he can borrow at this rate. Finally (5) he makes all purchases and sales of securities and all deposits and loans at discrete points in time, so that in selecting his portfolio at any "transaction point," each investor will consider only (*i*) the cash throw-off (typically interest payments and dividends received) within the period to the next transaction point and (*ii*) changes in the market prices of stocks during this same period. The *return* on any common stock is defined to be the sum of the cash dividends received plus the change in its market price. The return on any portfolio is measured in exactly the same way, including interest received or paid.

Assumptions Regarding Investors

(1) Since we posit the existence of assets yielding *positive risk-free* returns, we assume that each investor has already decided the fraction of his total capital he wishes to hold in cash and non-interest bearing deposits for reasons of liquidity or transactions requirements.[10] Henceforth, we will speak of *an investor's capital* as the stock of funds he has available for profitable investment *after* optimal cash holdings have been deducted. We also assume that (2) each investor will have assigned a *joint probability distribution* incorporating his best judgments regarding the returns on all *individual stocks*, or at least will have specified an expected value and variance to every return and a covariance or correlation to every pair of returns. All expected values of returns are finite, all variances are non-zero and finite, and all correlations of returns are less than one in absolute value (i. e. the covariance matrix is positive-definite). The investor computes the expected value and variance of the total return on any possible *portfolio*, or mix of any specified amounts of any or all of the individual stocks, by forming the appropriately weighted average or sum of these components expected returns, variances and covariances.

[10] These latter decisions are independent of the decisions regarding the allocation of remaining funds between risk-free assets with positive return and risky stocks, which are of direct concern in this paper, because the risk-free assets with positive returns clearly dominate those with no return once liquidity and transactions requirements are satisfied at the margin.

16   THE REVIEW OF ECONOMICS AND STATISTICS

With respect to an investor's *criterion for choices* among different attainable combinations of assets, we assume that (3) if any two mixtures of assets have the *same expected return*, the investor will prefer the one having the *smaller variance* of return, and if any two mixtures of assets have the *same variance* of returns, he will prefer the one having the *greater expected value*. Tobin [21, pp. 75–76] has shown that such preferences are implied by maximization of the expected value of a von Neumann-Morgenstern utility function if *either* (*a*) the investor's *utility* function is *concave* and *quadratic or* (*b*) the investor's *utility* function is *concave, and* he has assigned probability distributions such that the *returns* on *all possible portfolios differ at most by a location and scale parameter*, (which will be the case if the joint distribution of all individual stocks is multivariate normal).

Alternative Proofs of the Separation Theorem

Since the interest rates on riskless savings bank deposits ("loans to the bank") and on borrowed funds are being assumed to be the same, we can treat borrowing as negative lending. Any portfolio can then be described in terms of (i) the *gross* amount invested in stocks, (ii) the fraction of this amount invested in each individual stock, and (iii) the *net* amount invested in loans (a negative value showing that the investor has borrowed rather than lent). But since the *total net* investment (the algebraic sum of stocks plus loans) is a given amount, the problem simply requires finding the jointly optimal values for (1) the ratio of the gross investment in stocks to the total net investment, and (2) the ratio of the gross investment in each individual stock to the total gross investment in stocks. It turns out that although the solution of (1) depends upon that of (2), in our context the latter is independent of the former. Specifically, the *separation theorem* asserts that:

Given the assumptions about borrowing, lending, and investor preferences stated earlier in this section, *the optimal proportionate composition of the stock (risk-asset) portfolio* (i.e. the solution to sub-problem 2 above) *is independent of the ratio of the gross investment in stocks to the total net investment.*

Tobin proved this important separation theorem by deriving the detailed solution for the optimal mix of risk assets *conditional* on a given gross investment in this portfolio, and then formally proving the critical invariance property stated in the theorem. Tobin used more restrictive assumptions that we do regarding the available investment opportunities and he permitted no borrowing.[11] Under our somewhat broadened assumptions in these respects, the problem fits neatly into a traditional Fisher framework, with different available combinations of expected values and standard deviations of return on alternative *stock portfolios* taking the place of the original "production opportunity" set and with the alternative investment choices being concurrent rather than between time periods. Within this framework, alternative and more transparent proofs of the separation theorem are available which do not involve the actual calculation of the best allocation in stocks over individual stock issues. As did Fisher, we shall present a simple algebraic proof[12], set out the logic of the argument leading to the theorem, and depict the essential geometry of the problem.[13]

As a preliminary step, we need to establish the relation between the investor's total investment in *any* arbitrary mixture or portfolio of individual stocks, his total net return from all his investments (including riskless assets and any borrowing), and the risk parameters of his investment position. Let the *interest rate* on riskless assets or borrowing be r^*, and the *uncertain return* (dividends plus price appreciation) *per dollar invested in the given portfolio of stocks* be r. Let w represent the *ratio* of gross investment in stocks to

[11] Tobin considered the special case where cash with no return was the only riskless asset available. While he formally required that all assets be held in non-negative quantities (thereby ruling out short sales), and that the total value of risk assets held not be greater than the investment balance available without borrowing, these non-negativity and maximum value constraints were not introduced into his formal solution of the optimal investment mix, which in turn was used in proving the invariance property stated in the theorem. Our proof of the theorem is independent of the programming constraints neglected in Tobin's proof. Later in this section we show that when short sales are properly and explicitly introduced into the set of possible portfolios, the resulting equations for the optimum portfolio mix are identical to those derived by Tobin, but that insistence on no short sales results in a somewhat more complex programming problem (when covariances are non-zero), which may however, be readily handled with computer programs now available.

[12] An alternative algebraic proof using utility functions explicitly is presented in the appendix, note I.

[13] Lockwood Rainhard, Jr. has also independently developed and presented a similar proof of the theorem in an unpublished seminar paper.

total *net* investment (stock plus riskless assets minus borrowing). Then the investor's net return per dollar of total net investment will be

(1) $\bar{y} = (1-w)r^* + w\bar{r} = r^* + w(\bar{r}-r^*); \ 0 \leq w < \infty,$

where a value of $w < 1$ indicates that the investor holds some of his capital in riskless assets and receives interest amounting to $(1-w)r^*$; while $w > 1$ indicates that the investor borrows to buy stocks on margin and pays interest amounting to the absolute value of $(1-w)r^*$. From (1) we determine the mean and variance of the net return per dollar of total net investment to be:

(2a) $\bar{y} = r^* + w(\bar{r}-r^*),$ and

(2b) $\sigma^2_y = w^2\sigma^2_r.$

Finally, after eliminating w between these two equations, we find that the direct relation between the expected value of the investor's net return per dollar of his total net investment and the risk parameters of his investment position is:

(3a) $\bar{y} = r^* + \theta\sigma_y,$ where

(3b) $\theta = (\bar{r}-r^*)/\sigma_r.$

In terms of *any* arbitrarily selected *stock* portfolio, therefore, the investor's *net* expected rate of return on his total net investment is related *linearly* to the *risk* of return on his total net investment as *measured* by *the standard deviation* of his return. Given *any* selected stock portfolio, this linear function corresponds to Fisher's "market opportunity line"; its intercept is the risk-free rate r^* and its slope is given by θ, which is determined by the parameters $\bar{r}$ and σ_r of the particular stock portfolio being considered. We also see from (2a) that, by a suitable choice of w, the investor can use *any* stock mix (and *its* associated "market opportunity line") to obtain an expected return, $\bar{y}$, as high as he likes; but that, because of (2b) and (3b), as he increases his investment w in the (tentatively chosen) mix, the standard deviation σ_y (and hence the variance σ^2_y) of the return on his total investment also becomes proportionately greater.

Now consider all possible stock portfolios. Those portfolios having the same θ value will lie on the same "market opportunity line," but those having different θ values *will offer different "market opportunity lines"* (between expected return and risk) for the investor to use. The investor's problem is to choose which stock portfolio-mix (or market opportunity line *or* θ value) to use *and* how intensively to use it (the proper

value of w). Since *any* expected return $\bar{y}$ can be obtained from *any* stock mix, an investor adhering to our choice criterion will minimize the variance of his over-all return σ^2_y associated with *any* expected return he may choose *by confining all his investment in stocks to the mix with the largest θ value. This portfolio minimizes the variance associated with any $\bar{y}$ (and hence any w value)* the investor may prefer, and *consequently, is independent* of $\bar{y}$ and w. This establishes the separation theorem[14], once we note that our assumptions regarding available portfolios[15] insure the existence of a maximum θ.

It is equally apparent that *after* determining the optimal stock portfolio (mix) by maximizing θ, the investor can complete his choice of an over-all investment position by substituting the θ of this optimal mix in (3) and decide which over-all investment position by substituting of the available ($\bar{y}$, σ_y) pairs he prefers by referring to his own utility function. Substitution of this best $\bar{y}$ value in (2a) determines a unique best value of the ratio w of gross investment in the optimal stock portfolio to his total net investment, and hence, the optimal amount of investments in riskless savings deposits or the optimal amount of borrowing as well.

This separation theorem thus has four immediate *corrolaries* which can be stated:

(*i*) *Given* the assumptions about borrowing and lending stated above, any investor whose choices maximize the expectation of any particular utility function consistent with these conditions will make *identical decisions regarding the proportionate composition of his stock* (risk-asset) *portfolio. This is true regardless of the particular utility function*[16] whose expectation he maximizes.

(*ii*) Under these assumptions, only a *single point* on the Markowitz "Efficient Frontier" *is relevant* to the investor's decision regarding his investments in *risk* assets.[17] (The next section

[14] See also the appendix, note I for a different form of proof.

[15] Specifically, that the amount invested in any stock in any stock mix is infinitely divisible, that all expected returns on individual stocks are finite, that all variances are positive and finite, and that the variance-covariance matrix is positive-definite.

[16] When probability assessments are multivariate normal, the utility function may be polynomial, exponential, etc. Even in the "non-normal" case when utility functions *are* quadratic, they may vary in its parameters. See also the reference to Roy's work in the text below.

[17] When the above conditions hold (see also final para-

shows this point can be obtained directly without calculating the remainder of the efficient set.)

Given the same assumptions, (*iii*) the parameters of the investor's particular utility within the relevant set determine *only* the ratio of his total gross investment in stocks to his total *net* investment (including riskless assets and borrowing); and (*iv*) the investor's wealth is also, consequently, relevant to determining the *absolute size* of his investment in individual stocks, but *not* to the *relative distribution* of his gross investment in stocks *among individual issues.*

The Geometry of the Separation Theorem and Its Corrolaries

The algebraic derivations given above can be represented graphically as in chart 1. Any given available stock portfolio is characterized by a pair of values $(\sigma_r, \bar{r})$ which can be represented as a point in a plane with axes σ_y and $\bar{y}$. Our assumptions insure that the points representing all available stock mixes lie in a finite region, all parts of which lie to the right of the vertical axis, and that this region is bounded by a closed curve.[18] The contours of the investor's utility function are concave upward, and any movement in a north and or west direction denotes contours of greater utility. Equation (3) shows that all the (σ_y, y) pairs attainable by combining, borrowing, or lending with *any* particular stock portfolio lie on a ray from the point $(0, r^*)$ though the point corresponding to the stock mix in question. Each possible stock portfolio thus determines a unique "market opportunity line". Given the properties of the utility function, it is obvious that shifts from one possible mix to another which *rotate* the associated market opportunity line *counter colckwise* will *move the investor to preferred positions regardless of the point on the line* he had tentatively chosen. The slope of this market-opportunity line given by (3) is θ, and the limit of the favorable rotation is given by the maximum attainable θ, which identifies the optimal mix M.[19] Once this best mix, M,

has been determined, the investor completes the optimization of his total investment position by selecting the point on the ray through M which is tangent to a utility contour in the standard manner. If his utility contours are as in the U_i set in chart 1, he uses savings accounts and does not borrow. If his utility contours are as in U_j set, he borrows in order to have a gross investment in his best stock mix greater than his net investment balance.

Risk Aversion, Normality and the Separation Theorem

The above analysis has been based on the assumptions regarding markets and investors stated at the beginning of this section. One crucial premise was investor *risk-aversion* in the form of *preference for expected return* and *preference against return-variance, ceteris paribus.* We noted that Tobin has shown that *either* concave-quadratic utility functions *or* multivariate *normality* (of probability assessments) *and any concave* utility were *sufficient* conditions to validate this premise, but they were *not* shown (or alleged) to be *necessary* conditions. This is probably fortunate because the quadratic utility of income (or wealth!) function, in spite of its popularity in theoretical work, has several undesirably restrictive and implausible properties,[20] and, despite

---

graph of this section), the modest narrowing of the relevant range of Markowitz' Efficient Set suggested by Baumol [2] is still larger than needed by a factor strictly proportionate to the number of portfolios he retains in his truncated set! This is true since the relevant set is a single portfolio under these conditions.

[18] See Markowitz [14] as cited in the appendix, note I.

[19] The analogy with the standard Fisher two-period production-opportunity case in perfect markets with equal borrowing and lending rates is clear. The optimal set of production opportunities available is found by moving along the envelope function of efficient combinations of projects onto ever higher present value lines to the highest attainable. This best set of production opportunities is independent of the investor's particular utility function which determines only whether he then lends or borrows in the market (and by how much in either case) to reach hi best over-all position. The only differences between this case and ours lie in the concurrent nature of the comparisons (instead of inter-period), and the rotation of the market opportunity lines around the common pivot of the riskless return (instead of parallel shifts in present value lines). See Fisher [4] and also Hirschlaifer [7], figure 1 and section 1a.

[20] In brief, not only does the quadratic function imply negative marginal utilities of income or wealth much "too soon" in empirical work unless the risk-aversion parameter is very small — in which case it cannot account for the degree of risk-aversion empirically found,— it also implies that, over a major part of the range of empirical data, common stocks, like potatoes in Ireland, are "inferior" goods. Offering more return at the same risk would so sate investors that they would reduce their risk-investments *because* they were more attractive. (Thereby, as Tobin [21] noted, denying the negatively sloped demand curves for *riskless* assets which are standard doctrine in "liquidity preference theory" — a conclusion which cannot, incidentally, be avoided by "limit arguments" on quadratic utilities such as he used, once borrowing and leverage are admitted.)

its mathematical convenience, multivariate normality is doubtless also suspect, especially perhaps in considering common stocks.

It is, consequently, very relevant to note that by using the Bienaymé-Tchebycheff inequality, Roy [19] has shown that investors operating on his "Safety First" principle (i.e. make risky investments so as to minimize the upper bound of the probability that the realized outcome will fall below a pre-assigned "disaster level") should maximize the ratio of the *excess* expected portfolio return (over the disaster level) to the standard deviation of the return on the portfolio[21] — which is precisely our criterion of max θ when his disaster level is equated to the risk-free rate r^*. This result, of course, does not depend on multivariate normality, and uses a different argument and form of utility function.

The *Separation Theorem*, and its Corrolaries (*i*) and (*ii*) above — and all the rest of our following analysis which depends on the maximization

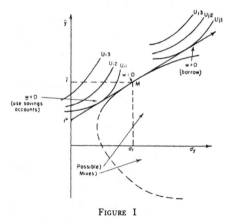

FIGURE I

This function also implausibly implies, as Pratt [17] and Arrow [1] have noted, that the insurance premiums which people would be willing to pay to hedge *given* risks *rise* progressively with wealth or income. For a related result, see Hicks [6, p. 802].

[21] Roy also notes that when judgmental distributions *are* multivariate normal, maximization of this criterion *minimizes* the probability of "disaster" (failure to do better in stocks than savings deposits or government bonds held to maturity). It should be noted, however, minimization of the probability of short falls from "disaster" levels in this "normal" case is strictly *equivalent* to expected utility maximization under *all* risk-averters' utility functions. The equivalence is *not* restricted to the utility function of the form (o, 1) (zero if "disaster" occurs, one if it doesn't), as claimed by Roy [19, p. 432] and Markowitz [14, p. 293 and following.].

of θ — is thus rigorously appropriate in the non-multivariate normal case for Safety-Firsters who minimax the stated upper bound of the chance of doing less well on portfolios including risk assets than they can do on riskless investments, just as it is for concave-expected utility maximizers in the "normal" case. On the basis of the same probability judgments, these Safety-Firsters will use the same proximate criterion function (max θ) and will choose proportionately the same risk asset portfolios as the more orothodox "utility maximizers" we have hitherto considered.

II — Portfolio Selection: The Optimal Stock Mix

Before finding the optimal stock mix — the mix which maximizes θ in (3*b*) above — it is necessary to express the return on any arbitrary mix in terms of the returns on individual stocks included in the portfolio. Although short sales are excluded by assumption in most of the writings on portfolio optimization, this restrictive assumption is arbitrary for some purposes at least, and we therefore broaden the analysis in this paper to include short sales whenever they are permitted.

Computation of Returns on a Stock Mix, When Short Sales are Permitted

We assume that there are m different stocks in the market, denoted by $i = 1, 2, \ldots, m$, and treat short sales as negative purchases. We shall use the following basic notation:

$|h_i|$ — The ratio of the gross investment in the ith stock (the market value of the amount bought *or* sold) to the gross investment in all stocks. A positive value of h_i indicates a *purchase*, while a negative value indicates a *short sale*.

$\bar{r}_i$ — The return per dollar invested in a *purchase* of the ith stock (cash dividends plus price appreciation)

$\bar{r}$ — As above, the return per dollar invested in a particular *mix* or *portfolio* of stocks.

Consider now a gross investment in the entire mix, so that the actual investment in the ith stock is equal to $|h_i|$. The returns on purchases and short sales need to be considered separately. First, we see that if $|h_i|$ is invested in a *pur-*

20   THE REVIEW OF ECONOMICS AND STATISTICS

chase ($h_i > 0$), the return will be simply $h_i\bar{r}_i$. For reasons which will be clear immediately however, we write this in the form:

(4a) $h_i\bar{r}_i = h_i(\bar{r}_i - r^*) + |h_i| r^*$.

Now suppose that $|h_i|$ is invested in a *short sale* ($h_i < o$), this gross investment being equal to the price received for the stock. (The price received must be deposited in escrow, and in addition, an amount equal to margin requirements on the current price of the stock sold must be remitted or loaned to the actual owner of the securities borrowed to effect the short sale.) In computing the *return* on a short sale, we know that the short seller must pay to the person who lends him the stock any dividends which accrue while the stock is sold short (and hence borrowed), and his capital gain (or loss) is the negative of any price appreciation during this period. In addition, the short seller will receive interest at the riskless rate r^* on the sales price placed in escrow, and he may or may not *also* receive interest at the same rate on his cash remittance to the lender of the stock. To facilitate the formal analysis, we *assume* that *both interest components* are *always received* by the short seller, and that margin requirements are 100%. In this case, the short seller's *return* per dollar of his gross investment will be ($2r^* - r_i$), and if he invests $|h_i|$ in the short sale ($h_i < o$), its contribution to his portfolio return will be:

(4b) $|h_i| (2r^* - \bar{r}_i) = h_i(\bar{r}_i - r^*) + |h_i| r^*$.

Since the right-hand sides of (4a) and (4b) are identical, the total return per dollar invested in *any* stock mix can be written as:

[22]In recent years, it has become increasingly common for the short seller to waive interest on his deposit with the lender of the security — in market parlance, for the borrowers of stock to obtain it "flat"— and when the demand for borrowing stock is large relative to the supply available for this purpose, the borrower may pay a cash premium to the lender of the stock. See Sidney M. Robbins, [18, pp. 58–59]. It will be noted that these practices reduce the expected return of short sales without changing the variance. The formal procedures developed below permit the identification of the appropriate stocks for short sale assuming the expected return is ($2r^* - \bar{r}_i$). If these stocks were to be borrowed "flat" or a premium paid, it would be *simply necessary to iterate the solution after replacing* ($\bar{r}_i - r^*$) in (4b) and (5) *for these stocks* with the value ($\bar{r}_i$) — and *if*, in addition, a premium p_i is paid, the term ($\bar{r}_i + p_i$) should be substituted (where $p_i \gtreqless o$ is the premium (if any) per dollar of sales price of the stock to be paid to lender of the stock). With equal lending and borrowing rates, changes in margin requirements will not affect the calculations. (I am indebted to Prof. Schlaifer for suggesting the use of absolute values in analyzing short sales.)

(5) $\bar{r} = \Sigma_i [h_i(\bar{r}_i - r^*) + |h_i| r^*]$
       $= r^* + \Sigma_i h_i(\bar{r}_i - r^*)$

because $\Sigma_i |h_i| = 1$ by the definition of $|h_i|$.

The expectation and variance of the return on any stock mix is consequently

(6a) $\bar{r} = r^* + \Sigma_i h_i(\bar{r}_i - r^*) = r^* + \Sigma_i h_i \bar{x}_i$,

(6b) $\bar{r} = \Sigma_{ij} h_i h_j \bar{r}_{ij} = \Sigma_{ij} h_i h_j \bar{x}_{ij}$

where $\bar{r}_{ij}$ represents the variance $\sigma_{ri}{}^2$ when $i = j$, and covariances when $i \neq j$. The notation has been further simplified in the right-hand expressions by defining:

(7) $\bar{x}_i = \bar{r}_i - r^*$,

and making appropriate substitutions in the middle expressions. The quantity θ defined in (3b) can thus be written:

(8) $\theta = \dfrac{\bar{r} - r^*}{(\bar{r})^{1/2}} = \dfrac{\bar{x}}{(\bar{x})^{1/2}} = \dfrac{\Sigma_i h_i \bar{x}_i}{(\Sigma_{ij} h_i h_j \bar{x}_{ij})^{1/2}}$.

Since h_i may be either positive or negative, equation (6a) shows that a portfolio with $\bar{r} \gtreqless r^*$ and hence with $\theta > o$ exists if there is one or more stocks with $\bar{r}_i$ not exactly equal to r^*. We assume throughout the rest of the paper that such a portfolio exists.

Determination of the Optimal Stock Portfolio

As shown in the proof of the Separation Theorem above, the optimal stock portfolio is the one which maximizes θ as defined in equation (8). We, of course, wish to maximize this value subject to the constraint

(9) $\Sigma_i |h_i| = 1$,

which follows from the definition of $|h_i|$. But we observe from equation (8) that θ is a *homogeneous function of order zero* in the h_i: the value of θ is *unchanged by any proportionate* change in all h_i. Our problem thus reduces to the simpler one of finding a vector of values yielding the *unconstrained* maximum of θ in equation (8), after which we may scale these initial solution values to satisfy the constraint.

The Optimum Portfolio When Short Sales are Permitted

We first examine the partial derivatives of (8) with respect to the h_i and find:

(10) $\dfrac{\partial \theta}{\partial h_i} = (\sigma_x)^{-1} [\bar{x}_i - \lambda(h_i \bar{x}_{ii} + \Sigma_j h_j \bar{x}_{ij})]$,

where,

(11) $\lambda = \bar{x}/\sigma_x{}^2 = \Sigma_i h_i \bar{x}_i / \Sigma_i \Sigma_j h_i h_j \bar{x}_{ij}$.

VALUATION OF RISK ASSETS

The *necessary and sufficient conditions* on the *relative* values of the h_i for a stationary *and the unique (global) maximum*[23] are obtained by setting the derivatives in (10) equal to zero, which give the set of equations

(12) $z_i \hat{x}_{ii} + \Sigma_j z_j \hat{x}_{ij} = \bar{x}_i, \quad i = 1, 2, \ldots, m;$

where we write

(13) $z_i = \lambda h_i.$

It will be noted the set of equations (12) — which are identical to those Tobin derived by a different route[24] — are *linear* in the own-*variances*, pooled *covariances*, and *excess returns* of the respective securities; and since the covariance matrix $\hat{x}$ is positive definite and hence non-singular, this system of equations has a unique solution

(14) $z_i^0 = \Sigma_j \hat{x}^{ij} \bar{x}_j$

where $\hat{x}^{ij}$ represents the ij^{th} element of $(\hat{x})^{-1}$, the inverse of the covariance matrix. Using (13), (7), and (6b), this solution may also be written in terms of the primary variables of the problem in the form

(15) $h_i^0 = (\lambda^0)^{-1} \Sigma_j \check{r}^{ij} (\bar{r}_j - r^*), \quad$ all $i.$

Moreover, since (13) implies

(16) $\Sigma_i |z_i| = \lambda \Sigma_i |h_i|,$

λ^0 may readily be evaluated, after introducing the constraint (9) as

(17) $\Sigma_i |z_i^0| = \lambda^0 \Sigma_i |h_i^0| = \lambda^0$

The optimal *relative* investments z_i^0 can consequently be scaled to the optimal proportions of the stock portfolio h_i^0, by dividing each z_i^0 by

the sum of their absolute values. A comparison of equations (16) and (11) shows further that:

(18) $\Sigma_i |z_i^0| = \lambda^0 = \bar{x}^0 / \sigma_x{}^2;$

i.e. the sum of the absolute values of the z_i^0 yields, as a byproduct, the value of the ratio of the expected excess rate of return on the optimal portfolio to the variance of the return on this best portfolio.

It is also of interest to note that if we form the corresponding λ-ratio of the expected excess return to its variance for each ith stock, we have at the optimum:

(19) $h_i^0 = (\lambda_i/\lambda^0) - \Sigma_{j \neq i} h_j^0 \bar{x}_{ij}/\bar{x}_{ii}$ where $\lambda_i = \bar{x}_i/\bar{x}_{ii}.$

The optimal fraction of each security in the best portfolio is equal to the ratio of *its* λ_i to that of the entire portfolio, *less* the ratio of its pooled covariance with other securities to its own variance. Consequently, *if* the investor were to act on the assumption that all covariances were zero, he could pick his optimal portfolio mix very simply by determining the λ_i ratio of the expected excess return $\bar{x}_i = \bar{r}_i - r^*$ of each stock to its variance $\hat{x}_{ii} = \check{r}_{ii}$, and setting each $h_i = \lambda_i/\Sigma\lambda_i$; for with no covariances,[25] $\Sigma\lambda_i = \lambda^0 = \bar{x}^0/\sigma_x{}^2$. With this simplifying assumption, the λ_i ratios of each stock suffice to determine the optimal mix by simple arithmetic;[26] in the more general case with non-zero covariances, a single set[27] of linear equations must be solved in the usual way, but no (linear or non-linear) programming is required and no more than one point on the "efficient frontier" need ever be computed, given the assumptions under which we are working.

The Optimum Portfolio When Short Sales are not Permitted

The exclusion of short sales does not complicate the above analysis *if* the investor is willing to act on an assumption of no correlations between the returns on different stocks. In this case, he finds his best portfolio of "long" holding by merely eliminating all securities whose λ_i-

---

[23]It is clear from a comparison of equations (8) and (11), showing that sgn θ = sgn λ, that only the vectors of h_i values corresponding to $\lambda > 0$ are relevant to the maximization of θ. Moreover, since θ as given in (8) and all its first partials shown in (10) are continuous functions of the h_i, it follows that when short sales are permitted, any maximum of θ must be a stationary value, and any stationary value is a maximum (rather than a minimum) when $\lambda > 0$ because θ is a convex function with a positive-definite quadratic form in its denominator. For the same reason, any maximum of θ is a unique (global) maximum.

[24]See Tobin, [21], equation (3.22), p. 83. Tobin had, however, formally required no short selling or borrowing, implying that this set of equations is valid under these constraints [so long as there is a single riskless asset (pp. 84–85)]; but the constraints were ignored in his derivation. We have shown that this set of equations *is* valid *when short sales* are properly included in the portfolio *and borrowing* is available in perfect markets in unlimited amounts. The alternative set of equilibrium conditions required when short sales are ruled out is given immediately below. The complications introduced by borrowing restrictions are examined in the final section of the paper.

[25]With no covariances, the set of equations (12) reduces to $\lambda h_i = \bar{x}_i/\hat{x}_{ii} = \lambda_i$, and after summing over all $i = 1, 2 \ldots m$, and using the constraint (9), we have immediately that $|\lambda^0| = \Sigma_i |\lambda_i|$, and $\lambda^0 > 0$ for max θ (instead of min θ).

[26]Using a more restricted market setting, Hicks [6, p. 801] has also reached an equivalent result when covariances are zero (as he assumed throughout).

[27]See, however, footnote 22, above.

ratio is negative, and investing in the remaining issues in the proportions $h_i = \lambda_i/\Sigma\lambda_i$ in accordance with the preceding paragraph.

But in the more generally realistic cases when covariances are nonzero *and* short sales are not admitted, the solution of a single bilinear or quadratic programming problem is required to determine the optimal portfolio. (All other points on the "efficient frontier," of course, continue to be irrelevant so long as there is a riskless asset and a "perfect" borrowing market.) The optimal portfolio mix is now given by the set of $h_i{}^0$ which maximize θ in equation (8) subject to the constraint that all $h_i \geqq$ o. As before, the (further) constraint that the sum of the h_i be unity (equation 9) may be ignored in the initial solution for the *relative* values of the h_i [because θ in (8) is homogeneous of order zero]. To find this optimum, we form the Lagrangian function

$$(20) \quad \phi(\underline{h}, \underline{u}) = \theta + \Sigma_i u_i h_i$$

which is to be maximized subject to $h_i \geqq$ o and $u_i \geqq$ o. Using (11), we have immediately

$$(21) \quad \frac{\partial\phi}{\partial h_i} \gtrless o \leftrightarrow \bar{x}_i - \lambda(h_i\bar{x}_{ii} + \Sigma_j h_j\bar{x}_{ij}) + \alpha u_i \gtrless o.$$

As in the previous cases, we also must have $\lambda >$ o for a maximum (rather than a minimum) of ϕ, and we shall write $z_i = \lambda h_i$ and $v_i = \alpha u_i$. The necssary and sufficient conditions for the vector of *relative* holdings $z_i{}^0$ which maximizes θ in (20) are consequently,[28] using the Kuhn-Tucker theorem [9],

[28] Equation $(22a$–$22d)$ can readily be shown to satisfy the six necessary and two further sufficient conditions of the Kuhn-Tucker theorem. Apart from the constraints $\underline{h} \geqq$ o and $\underline{u} \geqq$ o which are automatically satisfied by the computing algorithm [conditions $(22b$ and $22c)$] the four *necessary* conditions are:

1) $\left[\frac{\partial\phi}{\partial h_i}\right]^0 \leqq$ o. This condition is satisfied *as a strict equality* in our solutions by virtue of equation $(22a)$ [See equation (21)] This strict equality also shows that,

2) $h_i{}^0 \left[\frac{\partial\phi}{\partial h_i}\right]^0 =$ o, the first complementary slackness condition is also satisfied.

3) $\left[\frac{\partial\phi}{\partial u_i}\right]^0 \geqq$ o. This condition is satisfied because from equation (20), $\left[\frac{\partial\phi}{\partial u_i}\right]^0 = h_i{}^0 \geqq$ o by virtue of equation $(22b)$. This same equation shows that the second complementary slackness condition,

4) $u_i{}^0 \left[\frac{\partial\phi}{\partial u_i}\right]^0 =$ o, may be written $u_i{}^0 h_i{}^0 =$ o which is also satisfied because of equation $(22c)$ since $\alpha \neq$ o.

$$(22a) \quad z_i{}^0\bar{x}_{ii} + \Sigma_j z_j{}^0\bar{x}_{ij} - v_i{}^0 = \bar{x}_i, i = 1, 2, \ldots m;$$

where

$$(22b\text{-}d) \quad z_i{}^0 \geqq o, v_i{}^0 \geqq o, z_i{}^0 v_i{}^0 = o.$$

This system of equations can be expeditiously solved by the Wilson Simplicial Algorithm [23].

Now let m' denote the number of stocks with strictly positive holdings $z_i{}^0 >$ o in $(22b)$, and renumber the entire set of stocks so that the subset satisfying this strict inequality [and, hence also, by $(22d)$ $v_i{}^0 =$ o] are denoted 1, 2, ..., m'. *Within this* m' *subset of stocks found to belong in the optimal portfolio with positive holdings*, we consequently have, using the constraint (19),

$$(17a) \quad \Sigma_{i=1}{}^{m'} z_i{}^0 = \lambda^0 \Sigma_{i=1}{}^{m'} h_i{}^0 = \lambda^0$$

so that the *fraction* of the optimal portfolio invested in the ith stock (where $i = 1, 2 \ldots m'$) is

$$(23) \quad h_i{}^0 = z_i{}^0/\lambda^0 = z_i{}^0/\Sigma_{i=1}{}^{m'} z_i{}^0.$$

Once again, using $(17a)$ and (11), the sum of the $z_i{}^0$ within this set of stocks held yields as a by-product the ratio of the expected excess rate of return on the optimal *portfolio* to the variance of the return on this best portfolio:

$$(18a) \quad \Sigma_{i=1}{}^{m'} z_i{}^0 = \lambda^0 = \bar{x}^0/\sigma^2{}_{x^0}.$$

Moreover, since $z_i{}^0 >$ o in $(22a$ and $22b)$ strictly implies $v_i{}^0 =$ o by virtue of $(22c)$, equation $(22a)$ *for the subset of positively held stocks* $i = 1, 2 \ldots m'$ is formally identical to equation (12). We can, consequently, use these equations to bring out certain significant properties of the security portfolios which will be held by risk-averse investors trading in perfect markets.[29] *In the rest of this paper, all statements with respect to "other stocks" will refer to other stocks included within the portfolio.*

III Risk Premiums and Other Properties of Stocks Held Long or Short in Optimal Portfolios

Since the covariances between most pairs of stocks will be positive, it is clear from equation (19) that stocks held long ($h_i{}^0 >$ o) in a portfolio will generally be those whose expected

The two additional *sufficiency* conditions are of course satisfied because the variance-covariance matrix $\underline{\underline{x}}$ is positive definite, making $\phi (\underline{h}, \underline{u}^0)$ a concave function on $\underline{h}$ and $\phi (\underline{h}^0, \underline{u})$ a convex function of $\underline{u}$.

[29] More precisely, the properties of portfolios when both the investors and the markets satisfy the conditions stated at the outset of section I or, alternatively, when investors satisfy Roy's premises as noted previously.

return is enough greater than the risk-free rate to offset the disutility, so to speak, of the contribution of their variance and pooled covariance to the risk of the entire portfolio. This much is standard doctrine. Positive covariances with other securities held long in the portfolio raise the minimum level of $\bar{x}_i > 0$ which will lead to the inclusion of the ith stock as a positive holding in the optimal portfolio. But equation (19) shows that stocks whose expected returns are *less* than the riskless rate (i.e. $\bar{x}_i < 0$ or $\bar{r}_i < r^*$) will *also* be held *long* ($h_i^0 > 0$) *provided* that either (a) they are *negatively correlated* in sufficient degree with other important stocks *held long* in the portfolio, or (b) that they are *positively correlated* in sufficient degree with other important stocks *held short* in the portfolio. The precise condition for $h_i^0 > 0$ when $\bar{x}_i < 0$ is that the weighted sum of the ith covariances be sufficiently negative to satisfy

(19a) $h_i^0 > 0 \leftrightarrow |\Sigma_{j \neq i} h_j^0 \bar{x}_{ij}| > |\bar{x}_i / \lambda^0|,$

which follows from (19) since $\bar{x}_{ii} > 0$.

Since our $\bar{x}_i$ is precisely what is usually called the "risk premium" in the literature, we have just shown that the *"risk premiums" required on risky securities* (i.e. those with σ_i and $\sigma_i^2 > 0$) for them *to be held long by optimizing risk-averse investors in perfect markets need not always be positive*, as generally presumed. *They will in fact be negative* under either of the conditions stated in (a) and (b) above, summarized in (19a). The explanation is, of course, that a long holding of a security which is negatively correlated with other long holdings tends to reduce the variance of the whole portfolio by offsetting some of the variance contributed by the other securities in the portfolio, and this "variance-offsetting" effect may dominate the security's own-variance and even a negative expected excess return $\bar{x}_i < 0$.

Positive correlations with other securities held short in the portfolio have a similar variance-offsetting effect.[30]

Correspondingly, it is apparent from (19) itself that any stock with *positive* excess returns

or risk premiums ($\bar{x}_i > 0$) will be held *short* ($h_i^0 < 0$) in the portfolio *provided that either* (a) it is *positively correlated* in sufficient degree with other stocks *held long* in the portfolio, or (b) it is *negatively correlated* in sufficient degree with other stocks *held short* in the portfolio. *Positive* (negative) *risk premiums are neither a sufficient nor a necessary condition for a stock to be held long* (short).

Indifference Contours

Equation (12) (and the equivalent set (22a) restricted to stocks actually held in portfolios) also enables us to examine the *indifference contours* between expected excess returns, variances, or standard deviations and covariances of securities which will result in the *same fraction h_i^0* of the investor's portfolio being held in a given security. The general presumption in the literature, as noted in our introduction,[31] is that the market values of risk assets are adjusted in perfect markets to maintain a *linear* relation between expected rates of return (our $\bar{r}_i = \bar{x}_i + r^*$) *and risk* as measured by the *standard deviation* of return σ_i on the security in question. This presumption probably arises from the fact that this relation *is* valid for trade offs *between* a riskless security *and* a single risk asset (or a *given mix* of risk assets to be held in fixed proportions). But it can *not* be validly attributed to indifferent trade offs *between* risk assets *within* optimizing risk-asset portfolios. In point of fact, it can easily be shown that there is a *strictly linear indifference contour* between the *expected return $\bar{r}_i$* (or the expected excess return $\bar{x}_i$) *and the variance σ_i^2* (*not* the standard deviation σ_i) of the individual security, and this linear function has very straightforward properties. The assumption made in this derivation that the covariances σ_{ij} with other securities are invariant is a more reasonable one than is perhaps readily apparent.[32] Subject to the acceptability

---

[30] Stocks with negative expected excess returns or "risk premiums" ($\bar{x}_i < 0$) will, of course, enter into portfolios only as short sales (provided these are permitted) when the inequality in (19a) is reversed, i.e.

$h_i^0 < 0 \leftrightarrow \Sigma_{j \neq i} h_j^0 \bar{x}_{ij} + \bar{x}_i / \lambda^0 < 0.$ When short sales are not permitted, and (19a) is not satisfied, stocks with $\bar{x}_i < 0$ simply do not appear in the portfolio at all.

[31] See footnote 3 for references and quotations.

[32] Fixed covariances are directly implied by the assumption that every pair of ith and j^{th} stocks are related by a one-common-factor model (e.g. the general state of the economy or the general level of the stock market), so that, letting $\bar{\mu}$ represent the general exogenous factor and $\bar{\omega}$ the random outcome of endogenous factors under management's control, we have

$\bar{x}_i = a_i + b_i \bar{\mu} + \bar{\omega}_i$
$\bar{x}_j = a_j + b_j \bar{\mu} + \bar{\omega}_j$

with $\bar{\mu}$, $\bar{\omega}_i$, and $\bar{\omega}_j$ mutually independent. This model implies

$\sigma_i^2 = b_i^2 \sigma_\mu^2 + \sigma_\omega^2,$ and $\sigma_{ij} = b_i b_j \sigma_\mu^2,$

so that if management, say, varies the part under its control,

of this latter assumption, it follows that *risk classes of securities should be scaled in terms of variances* of returns rather than standard deviations (with the level of covariances reflected in the parameters of the linear function). The complexities involved when indifference contours are scaled on covariances or standard deviations are indicated below.

The conclusion that the indifference contour between $\bar{x}_i$ and the variance σ_i^2 is *linear* in the general case when all covariances σ_{ij} are held constant is established in the appendix, note II, by totally differentiating the equilibrium conditions (12) [or the equivalent set (22a) restricted to the m' stocks held in the portfolio]. But *all* pairs of values of $\bar{x}_i$ and σ_i^2 along the linear indifference coutour which holds h_i^0 fixed at some given level also rigorously imply that the proportionate mix of *all other* stocks in the portfolio is *also unchanged*. Consequently, we may proceed to derive other properties of this indifference contour by examining a simple "two security" portfolio. (The ith security is renumbered "1," and "all other" securities are called the second security.) If we then solve the equilibrium conditions[33] (12) in this two-stock case and hold $K = h_1^0/h_2^0$ constant, we have

(24) $K = h_1^0/h_2^0 = \text{constant} = (\bar{x}_1\sigma_2^2 - \bar{x}_2\sigma_{12})/(\bar{x}_2\sigma_1^2 - \bar{x}_1\sigma_{12})$

which leads to the desired explicit expression, using $\bar{r}_1 = \bar{x}_1 + r^*$,

(25) $\bar{r}_1 = r^* + W\sigma_{12} + WK\sigma_1^2$,

where

(25a) $W = \bar{x}_2/(\sigma_2^2 + K\sigma_{12})$.

Since[34] $WK = \lambda^0 h_1^0$ and $\lambda^0 > 0$, the *slope* of this indifference contour between $\bar{x}_1$ and σ_1^2 will always be positive when $h^0_1 > 0$ (as would be expected, because when σ_{12} is held constant,

increased variance requires added return to justify any given positive holding[35]); but when the first stock is held short, its expected (or excess) return and its variance along the contour vary inversely (as they should since "shorts" profit from price declines). Moreover, if we regard σ_{12} as an exogenous "shift" parameter, the *constant term* (or intercept) of this indifference contour varies directly[36] with σ_{12}, and the slope of $\bar{x}_1$ on σ_1^2 varies inversely[37] with σ_{12} in the usual case, when $\bar{x}_2 > 0$.

Now note that (25) and (25a) can be written

(25b) $\bar{r}_1 = r^* + \bar{x}_2(\sigma_{12} + K\sigma_1^2)/(\sigma_2^2 + K\sigma_{12})$,

which clearly depicts a hyperbolic (rather than linear) indifference contour on σ_{12} if σ_1^2 is regarded as fixed, and a more complex function between $\bar{r}_1$ (or x_1) and the standard deviation σ_1, which may be written (using $\sigma_{12} = \sigma_1\sigma_2\rho$),

(25b') $\bar{x}_1 = \dfrac{\bar{x}_2 K\sigma_1^2 [1 + \rho(K\sigma_1/\sigma_2)^{-1}]}{\sigma_2^2 (1 + \rho K\sigma_1/\sigma_2)}$

The *slope* of the indifference contour between $\bar{x}_1$ and σ_1 is a still more involved function, which may be written most simply as

(25c) $\dfrac{\partial \bar{x}_1}{\partial \sigma_1} = \dfrac{\bar{x}_2 [2K\sigma_1\sigma_2^2 + (K^2\sigma_1^2\sigma_2 + \sigma_2^3)\rho]}{(\sigma_2^2 + K\sigma_{12})^2}$

$= 2K\sigma_1\bar{x}_2 \dfrac{1 + (\rho/2) [(K\sigma_1/\sigma_2) + (\sigma_2/K\sigma_1)]}{\sigma^2(1 + \rho K\sigma_1/\sigma_2)^2}$.

It is true, in the usual situation with $K > 0$, $\bar{x}_2 > 0$, and $\rho > 0$, that $\bar{x}_1$ ($= \bar{r}_1 - r^*$) and $\partial x_1/\partial \sigma_1$ are necessarily positive as common doctrine presumes, *but* the complex non-linearity is evident even in this "normal case" restricted to two stocks — and the *positive risk premium* $\bar{x}_1$ *and positive slope* on σ_1, of course, *cannot be generalized*. For instance, in the admittedly less usual but important case with $\bar{x}_2 > 0$ and the intercorrelation $\rho < 0$, *both* $\bar{x}_1$ and $\partial \bar{x}_1/\partial \sigma_1$ are *alternatively negative and positive* over different ranges [38] of σ_1 for any fixed h_i^0 or $K > 0$.

$\bar{\omega}$ and σ_ω^2, the covariance will be unchanged. (This single-common-factor model is essentially the same as what Sharpe [20] calls the "diagonal" model.)

[33] The explicit solution is $z_1^0 = \lambda^0 h_1^0 = (\bar{x}_1\sigma_2^2 - \bar{x}_2\sigma_{12})/(\sigma_1^2\sigma_2^2 - \sigma_{12}^2)$; and $z_2^0 = \lambda^0 h_2^0 = (\bar{x}_2\sigma_1^2 - \bar{x}_1\sigma_{12})/(\sigma_1^2\sigma_2^2 - \sigma_{12}^2)$; where $\lambda^0 = z_1^0 + z_2^0$.

[34] Upon substituting (24) in (25) and using the preceding footnote, we have $W = \lambda^0 h_2^0 = z_2^0$, from which it follows that $WK = \lambda^0 h_2^0 h_1^0/h_2^0 = \lambda^0 h_1^0$. As noted earlier, we have $\lambda^0 > 0$ (because the investor maximizes and does not minimize θ). [It may be noted that W is used instead of z_2^0 in (25) in order to incorporate the restriction on the indifference contours that K is constant, and thereby to obtain an expression (25a) which does not contain $\bar{x}_1$ and σ_1^2 (as does z_2^0 without the constraint of constant K).]

[35] Note that this is true whether the "other security" is held long or short.

[36] Let the constant term in (25) be $C = r^* + W\sigma_{12}$. Then

$\dfrac{\partial C}{\partial \sigma_{12}} = \dfrac{(\sigma_2^2 + K\sigma_{12})\bar{x}_2 - \bar{x}_2\sigma_{12}K}{(\sigma_2^2 + K\sigma_{12})^2} = \dfrac{\bar{x}_2\sigma_2^2}{(\sigma_2^2 + K\sigma_{12})^2}$

which has the same sign as $\bar{x}_2$, independent of the sign of K, σ_{12}, or $\bar{x}_1$.

[37] We have $\partial WK/\partial \sigma_{12} = -K^2\bar{x}_2/(\sigma_2^2 + K\sigma_{12})^2$, which has a sign opposite to that of $\bar{x}_2$.

[38] With $K > 0$, $\bar{x}_2 > 0$, and $\rho < 0$, we have from (25b')
$\bar{x}_1 < 0$ if $0 < K\sigma_1/\sigma_2 < |\rho|$, and
$\bar{x}_1 > 0$ if $|\rho| < K\sigma_1/\sigma_2 < |\rho^{-1}|$.
On the other hand, from (25c) we have

Moreover, *in contrast* to the $\bar{x}_i - \sigma_1{}^2$ contour examined above, the pairs of values along the $\bar{x}_i - \sigma_i$ contour which hold $h_i{}^0$ constant do *not* imply an unchanged mix[39] of the other stocks in the optimizing portfolio when $m' > 2$; nor is λ^0 invariant along an $\bar{x}_i - \sigma_i$ contour, as it is along the $\bar{x}_1 - \sigma_1{}^2$ contour with covariances constant. For both reasons, the indifference contour between $\bar{x}_1$ and σ_1 for portfolios of $m' > 2$ stocks is very much more complex than for the two-stock case, whereas the "two-stock" contour (3) between $\bar{x}_1$ and $\sigma_1{}^2$ is exact for any number of stocks (when "all other" stocks are pooled in fixed proportions, as we have seen they can validly be). We should also observe that there does not seem to be an easy set of economically interesting assumptions which lead to *fixed correlations* as σ_1 varies (as assumed in deriving $\bar{x}_1 - \sigma_1$ indifference contours) in marked contrast to the quite interesting and plausible "single-factor" model (see footnote 32 above) which directly validates the assumption of fixed covariances used in deriving the $\bar{x}_1 - \sigma_1{}^2$ indifference contours.

In sum, we conclude that — however natural or plausible it may have seemed to relate risk premiums to standard deviations of return *within* portfolios of risk assets, and to scale risk classes of securities on this same basis — risk premiums can most simply *and* plausibly be related directly to *variances* of returns (with the level of covariances reflected in the parameters of the linear function). Since the principal function of the concept of "risk class" has been to delineate a required level of risk premium, we conclude further that risk classes should also be delineated in the same units (variances) if, indeed, the concept of risk class should be used at all.[40]

IV — Market Prices of Shares Implied by Shareholder Optimization in Purely Competitive Markets Under Idealized Uncertainty

Our analysis to this point has followed Tobin [21] and Markowitz [14] in assuming that current security prices are *exogenous data*, and that each

$$\partial \bar{x}_1 / \partial \sigma_1 < 0 \text{ if } 0 < K\sigma_1/\sigma_2 < |\rho^{-1}| - \sqrt{\rho^{-2} - 1} \ ,$$

and

$$\partial \bar{x}_1 / \partial \sigma_1 > 0 \text{ if } |\rho^{-1}| - \sqrt{\rho^{-2} - 1} < K\sigma_1/\sigma_2 < |\rho^{-1}|.$$

[39] See appendix, note 11(b).

[40] However, see below, especially the "fifth" through "seventh" points enumerated near the end of Section V.

investor acts on his own (doubtless unique) probability distribution over rates of return, *given* these market prices. I shall continue to make the same assumptions concerning markets and investors introduced in section I. In particular, it is assumed that security markets are purely competitive, transactions costs and taxes are zero, and *all* investors prefer a greater mean rate of return for a given variance and a lesser rate of return variance for any given mean return rate. But in this and the following section, I shall assume (1) that investors' joint probability distributions pertain to *dollar returns rather than rates* of return — the dollar return in the period being the sum of the cash dividend and the increase of market price during the period. Also, for simplicity, assume that (2) for *any* given set of market prices for all stocks, *all* investors assign *identical* sets of means, variances, and convariances to the joint distribution of these dollar returns (and hence for *any* set of prices, to the vector of means and the variance-covariances matrix of the rates of return $\bar{r}_i$ of all stocks), and that all correlations between stocks are < 1.

This assumption of identical probability beliefs or judgments by all investors in the market restricts the applicability of the analysis of this and the following section to what I have elsewhere characterized as *idealized uncertainty* [10, pp. 246–247]. But however unrealistic this latter assumption may be, it does enable us to derive a set of (stable) equilibrium market prices — and an important theorem concerning the properties of these prices — which at least fully and explicitly reflect the presence of uncertainty *per se* (as distinct from the effects of diverse judgmental distributions among investors).

Note first that the assumption of identical probability judgments means that (1) *the same stock mix will be optimal for every investor* (although the actual dollar gross investment in this mix — and the ratio, *w*, of gross investment in this mix to his net investment balance — will vary from one investor to the next). It consequently follows that, when the market is in equilibrium, (2) the $h_i{}^0$ given by equation (15) or (12) can be interpreted as the ratio of the *aggregate market* value of the ith stock to the total aggregate market value of all stocks, and hence, (3) *all h_i will be strictly positive.*

In order to develop further results, define

26   THE REVIEW OF ECONOMICS AND STATISTICS

V_{0i} — the aggregate market value of the ith stock at time zero,

$\check{R}_i$ — the aggregate return on the ith stock (the sum of aggregate cash dividends paid and appreciation in aggregate market value over the transaction period); and

$T \equiv \Sigma_i \, V_{0i}$, the aggregate market value of *all* stock in the market at time zero.

The original economic definitions of the variables in the portfolio optimization problem give

(26a) $h_i = V_{0i}/T$,

(26b) $\check{r}_i = \check{R}_i/V_{0i}$,

(26c) $\check{x}_i = \check{r}_i - r^* = (\check{R}_i - r^* V_{0i})/V_{0i}$,

(26d) $\check{x}_{ij} = \check{r}_{ij} = \check{R}_{ij}/V_{0i} V_{0j}$,

where $\check{R}_{ij}$ is the covariance of the aggregate dollar returns of the ith and jth stocks (and $\check{R}_{ii}$ is the ith stock's aggregate return variance). The equilibrium conditions (12) may now be written

(12a) $\dfrac{\check{R}_i - r^* V_i^0}{V_{0i}} = \lambda \dfrac{V_i^0}{T} \dfrac{\check{R}_{ii}}{(V_{0i})^2}$

     $+ \lambda \Sigma_{j \neq i} \dfrac{V_{0j}}{T} \dfrac{\check{R}_{ij}}{V_{0i} V_{0j}}$,

which reduces to

(27) $\check{R}_i - r^* V_{0i} = (\lambda/T) [\check{R}_{ii} + \Sigma_{j \neq i} \check{R}_{ij}]$

       $= (\lambda/T) \, \Sigma_j \check{R}_{ij}$.

Now $\check{R}_i - r^* V_{0i}$ represents the *expected* excess of the aggregate dollar return on the ith security over earnings at the riskless rate on its aggregate market value, and $\Sigma_j \check{R}_{ij}$ represents the aggregate risk (direct dollar return variance and total covariance) entailed in holding the stock. Equation (27) consequently establishes the following:

Theorem: Under Idealized Uncertainty, equilibrium in purely competitive markets of risk-averse investors requires that the values of all stocks will have adjusted themselves so that the *ratio* of the expected excess aggregate dollar returns of each stock to the aggregate dollar risk of holding the stock will be *the same for all* stocks (and equal to λ/T), when the risk of each stock is measured by the variance of its own dollar return and its combined covariance with that of all other stocks.

But we seek an explicit equation[41] for V_{0i}, and

to this end we note that partial summation of equation (27) over *all other* stocks gives us

(28) $\Sigma_{k \neq i} (\check{R}_k - r^* V_{0k}) = (\lambda/T) \Sigma_{k \neq i} \Sigma_j \check{R}_{kj}$.

After dividing each side of (27) by the corresponding side of (28), and solving for V_{0i}, we then find that the aggregate market value of the ith stock is related to the concurrent market values of the *other* $(m - 1)$ stocks by

(29) $V_{0i} = (\check{R}_i - W_i)/r^*$

where

(29a) $W_i = \gamma_i \Sigma_j \check{R}_{ij} = \gamma_i \, (\check{R}_{ii} + \Sigma_{j \neq i} \check{R}_{ij})$

and

(29b) $\gamma_i = \dfrac{\Sigma_{k \neq i} (\check{R}_k - r^* V_{0k})}{\Sigma_{k \neq i} \Sigma_j \check{R}_{kj}}$

       $= \dfrac{\Sigma_{k \neq i} (\check{R}_k - r^* V_{0k})}{\Sigma_{k \neq i} \Sigma_{j \neq i} \check{R}_{kj} + \Sigma_{j \neq i} \check{R}_{ij}}$.

Since (29b) *appears* to make the slope coefficient γ_i unique to each company, we must note immediately that dividing each side of (27) by its summation over *all* stocks shows that the aggregate market value of the ith stock is *also* related to the concurrent market values of all (m) stocks[42] by equation (29) when W_i is written as

(29c) $W_i = (\lambda/T) \, \Sigma_j \check{R}_{ij}$,

and

(29d) $\lambda/T = \dfrac{\Sigma_i (\check{R}_i - r^* V_{0i})}{\Sigma_i \Sigma_j \check{R}_{ij}}$.

But from equations (28) and (29b), we see that

(29e) $\gamma_i = \gamma_j = \lambda/T$,

a *common value* for *all companies in the market*. The values of W_i given by (29a) and (29c) are consequently *identical*, and *the subscripts on γ should henceforth be ignored.*

In words, equations (29) establish the following further

Theorem: Under Idealized Uncertainty, in purely competitive markets of risk-averse investors,

A) the total market value of any stock in equilibrium is equal to the *capitalization* at the *risk-free interest rate r^** of the *certainty equivalent* $(R_i - W_i)$ of its uncertain aggregate dollar return $\check{R}_i$;

B) *the difference W_i* between the expected value $\check{R}_i$ of these returns and their certainty

---

[41] I do not simply rearrange equation (27) at this point since (λ/T) includes V_{0i} as one of its terms (see equation (29d) below).

[42] Alternatively, equations (29) and (29c) follow directly from (27), and (29d) may be established by substituting (26a–d) in (11).

equivalent is *proportional* for *each* company to *its aggregate risk* represented by the *sum* $(\Sigma_j \check{R}_{ij})$ of the *variance* of these returns and their total covariance with those of all other stocks; and

C) the factor of proportionality $(\gamma = \lambda/T)$ is the *same* for *all* companies in the market.

Certain corrolaries are immediately apparent:

Corrolary I: Market values of securities are related to standard deviations of dollar returns by way of variances and covariances, *not directly* and *not linearly*.

Corrolary II: The aggregate risk $(\Sigma_j R_{ij})$ of the ith stock which is directly relevant to its aggregate market value V_{0i} is simply *its contribution* to the aggregate *variance* of the dollar returns (for *all* holders together) of *all* stocks (which is $\Sigma_i \Sigma_j \check{R}_{ij}$).

Corrolary III: The *ratio* $(\check{R}_i - W_i)/\check{R}_i$ of the *certainty-equivalent* of aggregate dollar returns to their expected value is, in general, *different for each ith* company when the market is in equilibrium;[43] but for all companies, this certainty-equivalent to expected-dollar-return ratio is the *same linear function* $\{1 - \gamma [\Sigma_j \check{R}_{ij}/\check{R}_i]\}$ of total dollar risk $(\Sigma_j \check{R}_{ij})$ attributable to the ith stock deflated by its expected dollar return $\check{R}_i$.

Several further implications also follow immediately. First, note that equation (29) can be written

$$(29') \quad V_{0i} = (\check{R}_i - W_i)/r^*$$
$$= (V_{0i} + \check{R}_i - W_i)/(1 + r^*)$$
$$= (\check{H}_i - W_i)/(1 + r^*).$$

Since $\check{R}_i$ was defined as the sum of the aggregate cash dividend and increase in value in the equity during the period, the *sum* $V_{0i} + \check{R}_i$ is equal to the expected value of the sum (denoted $\check{H}_i$) of the cash dividend and end-of-period aggregate market value of the equity, and the elements of the covariance matrix $\check{\underline{H}}$ are identical to those in $\check{\underline{R}}$. All equations (29) can consequently be validly rewritten substituting H for R throughout [and $(1 + r^*)$ for r^*], *thus explicitly determining all current values V_{0i} directly by the joint probability distributions over the end-of-period realizations*[44] $\check{H}_i$.

(The value of W_i, incidentally, is not affected by these substitutions.) Our assumption that investors hold joint probability distributions over dollar returns $\check{R}_i$ is consequently *equivalent* to an assumption that they hold distributions over end-of-period realizations, and *our analysis applies equally under either assumption.*

Moreover, after the indicated substitutions, equation $(29')$ *shows that the current aggregate value of any equity is equal to the certainty-equivalent of the sum of its prospective cash receipts (to shareholders) and total market value at the end of the period, discounted at the riskless rate r^*.* Similarly, by an extension of the same lines of analysis, the certainty equivalent of the cash dividend and market value at the end of the first period clearly may be regarded as the then-present-values using riskless discount rates of the certainty-equivalents of random receipts still further in the future. *The analysis thus justifies viewing market values as riskless-rate present values of certainty-equivalents of random future receipts,* where certainty-equivalents are related to expected values by way of variances and covariances weighted by adjustment factors γ_{it}, which may or may not be the same for each future period t.

Still another implication of equation (29) is of a more negative character. Those who like (or hope) to find a "risk" discount rate k_r with which to discount expected values under uncertainty will find from (29) that, using a subscript i for the individual firm

$$(29'') \quad V_{0i} = \frac{\check{R}_i}{k_{ri}} = \frac{\check{R}_i}{r^* (1 - W_i/\check{R}_i)^{-1}}$$
$$= \frac{\check{R}_i}{r^* (1 - \gamma \Sigma_j \check{R}_{ij}/\check{R}_i)^{-1}}$$

so that

$$(30) \quad k_{ri} = r^* (1 - \gamma \Sigma_j \check{R}_{ij}/\check{R}_i)^{-1}.$$

It is apparent that (*i*) the *appropriate "risk" discount rate k_{ri} is unique to each individual company in a competitive equilibrium* (because of the first half of corrolary III above); (*ii*) that efforts to derive it complicate rather than simplify the analysis, since (*iii*) it is a *derived* rather than a primary variable; and that (*iv*) it explicitly involves all the elements required for the determination of V_{0i} itself, and, (*v*) does so in a more

---

[43] From equations (27), (29), (29a), and (29e), this statement is true for all pairs of stocks having different aggregate market values, $V_{0i} \neq V_{0j}$.

[44] Because we are assuming only "idealized" uncertainty, the distribution of these end-of-period realizations will be independent of judgments regarding the dividend receipt and end-of-period market value separately. See Lintner [10] and Modigliani-Miller [16].

complex and non-linear fashion.[45] Having established these points, the rest of our analysis returns to the more direct and simpler relation of equation (29).

V — Corporate Capital Budgeting Under Idealized Uncertainty

Capital budgeting decisions within a corporation affect both the expected value and variances — and hence, the certainty-equivalents — of its prospective aggregate dollar returns to its owners. When the requisite conditions are satisfied, equation (29) thus provides a normative criterion for these decisions, derived from a competitive equilibrium in the securities market.

In developing these important implications of the results of the last section, I of course maintain the assumptions of idealized uncertainty in purely competitive markets of risk-averse investors with identical probability distributions, and I continue to assume, for simplicity, that there are no transactions costs or taxes. The identity of probability distributions over outcomes now covers corporate management as well as investors, and includes potential corporate investments in the capital budget as well as assets currently held by the company. Every corporate management, *ex ante*, assigns probability zero to default on its debt, and all investors also treat corporate debt as a riskless asset. I thus extend the riskless investment (or borrowing) alternative from individual investors to corporations. Each company can invest any amount of its capital budget in a perfectly safe security (savings deposit or certificate of deposit) at the riskless rate r^*, or it may borrow unlimited amounts at the *same* rate in the current or any future period.[46] I also assume that the investment opportunities available to the company in any time period are regarded as independent of the size and composition of the capital budget in any other time period.[47] I also assume there is no limited liability to corporate stock, nor any institutional or legal restriction on the investment purview of any investor, and that the riskless rate r^* is expected by everyone to remain constant over time.

Note that this set of assumptions is sufficient to validate the famous (taxless) Propositions I and II of Modigliani and Miller [15]. In particular, under these severely idealized conditions, for any given size and composition of corporate assets (investments), investors will be indifferent to the *financing* decisions of the company. Subject to these conditions, we can, consequently, derive valid decision rules for capital budgets which do not explicitly depend upon concurrent financing decisions. Moreover, these conditions make the present values of the cash flows *to any* company from its real (and financial) assets and operations equal to the total market value of investors' *claims* to these flows, i.e., to the sum of the aggregate market value of its common (and preferred) stock outstanding and its borrowings (debt)[48]. They also make any change in shareholders claims equal to the change in the present values of flows (before interest deductions) to the company less any change in debt service. The *changes* in the market value of the equity V_{0i} induced by capital budgeting decisions will consequently be precisely equal to

$$(31) \quad \Delta V_{0i} = \Delta (\bar{R}_i - W_i)/(1 + r^*)$$
$$= \Delta (\bar{H}_i - W_i)/(1 + r^*),$$

where $\Delta \bar{H}_i$ is the net change induced in the *expected* present value at the end of the first period of the cash inflows (net of interest charges) to the ith company attributable to *its assets*[49] when all present values are computed at the riskless rate r^*.

These relationships may be further simplified in a useful way by making three additional assumptions: that (*i*) the *aggregate market value*

---

[45] It may also be noted that even when *covariances* between stocks are constant, the elasticity of k_{rt} with respect to the variance $\bar{R}_{ii}$ (and *a fortiori*) to the standard deviation of return) is a unique (to the company) multiple of a hyperbolic relation of a variance-expected-return ratio:

$$(30a) \quad \frac{\bar{R}_{ii}}{k_{rt}} \cdot \frac{\partial k_{rt}}{\partial \bar{R}_{ii}} = \frac{\gamma \bar{R}_{ii}/R_i}{1 - \gamma (\Sigma_{j \neq i} \bar{R}_{ij}/R_i) - \gamma \bar{R}_{ii}/R_i}.$$

[46] The effects of removing the latter assumption are considered briefly in the final section.

[47] This simplifying assumption specifies a (stochastic) comparative static framework which rules out the complications introduced by making investor expectations of future growth in a company's investment opportunities conditional on current investment decisions. I examine the latter complications in other papers [11], and [12].

[48] See Lintner [10]. Note that in [10, especially p. 265, top 1st column] I argued that additional assumptions were needed to validate the "entity theory" under uncertainty — the last sentence of the preceding paragraph, and the stipulation that corporate bonds are riskless meet the requirement. See, however, Modigliani-Miller [16].

[49] By definition, ΔH_i is the change in the expected sum of dividend payment and market value of the equity at the end of the period. This is made equal to the statement in the text by the assumptions under which we are operating.

VALUATION OF RISK ASSETS

of *all other* stocks — and (*ii*) the *covariances* $\check{R}_{ij}$ *with* all other *stocks* are invariant to the capital budgeting decisions of the ith company; while (*iii*) the (optimal) *portfolio* of risk assets is not an "inferior good" (in the classic Slutsky-Hicks sense) *vis a vis* riskless assets. The reasonableness of (*iii*) is obvious (especially in the context of a universe of risk-averse investors!), and given (*iii*), assumption (*i*) is a convenience which only involves ignoring (generally small) second-order feedback effects (which will not reverse signs); while the plausibility of (*ii*) as a good working first approximation was indicated above (footnote 32).[60]

In this context, we now show that capital budgeting decisions by the ith firm will raise the aggregate market value of its equity V_{0i} — and hence by common agreement be in the interest of its shareholders — so long as the induced change in expected dollar return is greater than the product of the market price γ of risk and the induced variance of dollar returns, i.e.,

$$(32) \quad \Delta\check{R}_i - \gamma\Delta\check{R}_{ii} = \Delta\check{H}_i - \gamma\Delta\check{H}_{ii} > 0.$$

This assertion (or theorem) can be proved as follows. The total differential of (29) is

$$(29f) \quad r^*\Delta V_{0i} - \Delta\check{R}_i + \gamma\Delta\check{R}_{ii} + (\Sigma_j\check{R}_{ij})\Delta\gamma = 0$$

so that under the above assumptions

$$(29g) \quad \Delta\check{R}_i \gtreqless \gamma\,\Delta\check{R}_{ii} + (\Sigma_j\check{R}_{ij})d\,\gamma \to$$
$$\Delta V_{0i} \gtreqless 0 \to \Delta T \gtreqless 0.$$

But using (29e) and (29d), we have

$$(29h) \quad \Delta\gamma = (\Delta\check{R}_i - \gamma\Delta\check{R}_{ii})/\Sigma_i\Sigma_j\check{R}_{ij}$$

so that

$$(29i) \quad \Delta\check{R}_i = \gamma\Delta\check{R}_{ii} \to \Delta\gamma = 0 \to$$
$$\Delta V_{0i} = 0 \to \Delta T = 0,$$

and the first equality in (29i) defines the relevant *indifference function*.[51] Moreover, using (29h) and the fact that $\Sigma_j\check{R}_{ij} < \Sigma_i\Sigma_j\check{R}_{ij}$, we have from (29g):

$$(29j) \quad \Delta R_i \gtreqless \gamma\Delta\check{R}_{ii} \to \Delta\check{R}_i \gtreqless \gamma\Delta\check{R}_{ii} + (\Sigma_j\check{R}_{ij})\,\Delta\gamma,$$

and consequently

$$(29k) \quad \Delta\check{R}_i \gtreqless \gamma\,\Delta\check{R}_{ii} \to \Delta V_{0i} \gtreqless 0 \to \Delta T \gtreqless 0,$$

from which (32) follows immediately.

In order to explore the implications of (32)

[60] It is, however, necessary in general to redefine the variables in terms of *dollar* returns (rather than rates of return), but this seems equally reasonable.

[51] Note that this indifference function can also be derived by substituting equations (26a–d) directly into that found in section III above (equation 6b) in appendix Note II or equation (25) in the text) for the relevant case where covariances are invariant.

further, it will now be convenient to consider in more detail the capital budgeting decisions of a company whose *existing assets* have a present value computed at the rate r^* (and measured at the *end* of the first period) of $\check{H}_0^{(1)}$, a random variable with expected value $\check{H}_0^{(1)}$ and variance $\check{H}_{00}$.

The company may be provisionally holding any fraction of $\check{H}_0$ in savings deposits or CD's yielding r^*, and it may use any such funds (or borrow unlimited amounts at the *same* rate) to make new "real" investments. We assume that the company has available a set of new projects $1, 2 \ldots j \ldots n$ which respectively involve *current* investment outlays of $H_j^{(0)}$, and which have present values of the relevant incremental cash flows (valued at the *end* of the first period) of $\check{H}_j^{(1)}$. Since any diversion (or borrowing) of funds to invest in any project involves an opportunity cost of $r^* H_j^{(0)}$, we also have the "excess" dollar end-of-period present value return

$$(33) \quad \check{X}_j^{(1)} = \check{H}_j^{(1)} - r^* H_{j0}^{(0)}.$$

Finally, we shall denote the $(n+1)$'th order covariance matrix (including the existing assets $\check{H}_0$) by $\underline{\check{H}}$ or $\underline{\check{X}}$ whose corresponding elements $\check{H}_{jk} = \check{X}_{jk}$.

Determination of the Optimal Corporate Capital-Budget-Portfolio

In this simplified context, it is entirely reasonable to expect that the corporation will seek to maximize the left side of equation[52] (32) as its capital budgeting criterion. At first blush, a very complex *integer* quadratic-programming solution would seem to be required, but fortunately we can break the problem down inductively and find a valid formulation which can be solved in essentially the same manner as an individual investor's portfolio decision.

[52] Under our assumption that stock portfolios are not inferior goods, sgn ΔT = s gn $[\Delta\check{R}_i - \gamma\Delta\check{R}_{ii}]$ so that (although generally small in terms of percentages) the induced change in aggregate values of all stocks will reinforce the induced change in the *relative* value of the ith stock; the fact that $\Delta\gamma$ also has the same sign introduces a countervailing feedback, but as shown above [note especially (29g)], this latter effect is of second order and cannot reverse the sign of the criterion we use. In view of the overwhelming informational requirements of determining the maximum of a fully inclusive criterion function which allowed formula induced adjustments external to the firm, *and* the fact our criterion is a monotone rising function of this ultimate ideal, the position in the text follows.

First, we note that if a single project j is added to an existing body of assets $\bar{H}_0{}^0$, we have

$(34a)$ $\Delta \bar{R}_i - \gamma \Delta \check{R}_{ii} = \bar{H}_j{}^{(1)} - r^* H_j{}^0$
$- \gamma [H_{jj} + 2\check{H}_{j0}] = X_j{}^{(1)} - \gamma [\check{X}_{jj} + 2\check{X}_{j0}].$

Now suppose a project k is also added. The total change from j and k *together* is

$(34b)$ $(\Delta R_i - \gamma \Delta \check{R}_{ii}) = X_j{}^{(1)} + X_k{}^{(1)}$
$- \gamma [\check{X}_{jj} + \check{X}_{kk} + 2\check{X}_{j0} + 2\check{X}_{k0} + 2\check{X}_{jk}],$

while the *increment* due to adding k *with* j *already in the budget* is

$(34c)$ $(\Delta R_i - \gamma \check{R}_{ii})$
$= \check{X}_k{}^{(1)} - \gamma [\check{X}_{kk} + 2\check{X}_{k0} + 2\check{X}_{jk}].$

Given the goal of maximizing the left side of (32), the kth project should be added to the budget (already provisionally containing j) *if and only if the right* side of $(34c)$ is > 0— and if this condition is satisfied, the same test expression written for j, given inclusion of k, will show whether j should stay in. Equation $(34c)$ appropriately generalized to any number of projects, is thus a *necessary condition* to be satisfied by *each project in an optimal budget*, given the inclusion of all other projects simultaneously satisfying this condition.

The unstructured iterative or search procedure suggested by our two-project development can obviously be short-circuited by programming methods, and the integer aspect of the programming (in this situation) can conveniently be by-passed by assuming that the company may accept all or any fractional part a_j, $0 \le a_j \le 1$, of any project (since it turns out that all a_j in the final solution will take on *only* limiting values). Finally, thanks to this latter fact, the objective of maximizing the left side of (32) is equivalent[53] to maximizing

$(32')$ $Z = H_0{}^{(1)} + \Sigma_j a_j \bar{H}_j{}^{(1)} - r^* \Sigma_j a_j H_j{}^{(0)}$
$- \gamma [\Sigma_j a_j \check{H}_{jj} + 2\Sigma_j a_j \check{H}_{j0} + 2\Sigma_{j \neq k \neq 0} a_j a_k \check{H}_{jk}]$
$= \bar{H}_0{}^{(1)} + \Sigma_j a_j \bar{X}_j - \gamma [\Sigma_j a_j \check{X}_{jj} +$
$2\Sigma_j a_j \check{X}_{j0} + 2\Sigma_{j \neq k \neq 0} a_j a_k \check{X}_{jk}],$

subject to the constraints that $0 \le a_j \le 1$ for all a_j, $j = 1, 2 \ldots n$. Not only will all a_j be binary variables in the solution, but the generalized form of the necessary condition $(34c)$ will be given by the solution [see equation (37) below].

In order to maximize Z in $(32')$ subject to the

constraints on a_j, we let $q_j = 1 - a_j$ for convenience, and form the Lagrangian function

(35) $\psi(a, \mu, \eta) = Z + \Sigma_j \mu_j a_j + \Sigma_j \eta_j q_j$

which is to be maximized subject to $a_j \geqq 0$, $q_j \geqq 0$, $\mu_j \geqq 0$, and $\eta_j \geqq 0$, where μ_j and η_j are the Lagrangian multipliers associated with the respective constraints $a_j \geqq 0$ and $q_j \geqq 0$. Using (33), we have immediately

$(35')$ $\dfrac{\partial \psi}{\partial a_j} \geqq 0 \leftrightarrow \bar{X}_j - \gamma [a_j \check{X}_{jj} + 2\Sigma_j a_j \check{X}_{j0}$
$+ 2\Sigma_{k \neq 0} a_k \check{X}_{jk}] + \mu_j - \eta_j \geqq 0.$

Using the Kuhn-Tucker Theorem [9], the necessary and sufficient conditions for the optimal vector of investments $a_j{}^0$ which maximize ψ in (35) are consequently[54]

$(36a)$ $\gamma [a_j{}^0 \check{X}_{jj} + 2a_j{}^0 \check{X}_{j0} + 2\Sigma_{k \neq j \neq 0} a_k{}^0 \check{X}_{jk}]$
$- \mu_j{}^0 + \eta_j{}^0 = \bar{X}_j$
        when

$(36b, c, d, e)$ $a_j{}^0 \geqq 0$, $q_j{}^0 \geqq 0$,
        $\mu_j{}^0 \geqq 0$, $\eta_j{}^0 \geqq 0$
    and

$(36f, g)$ $\mu_j{}^0 a_j{}^0 = 0$, $\eta_j{}^0 q_j{}^0 = 0$,
            where
        $j = 1, 2 \ldots n$

in each set $(36a) - (36g)$.

Once again, these equations can be readily solved by the Wilson Simplicial Algorithm [23] on modern computing equipment. It may be observed that this formulation in terms of independent investment projects can readily be generalized to cover mutually exclusive, contingent, and compound projects[55] with no difficulty. It is also apparent that the absence of a financing constraint (due principally to our assumption

---

[53] For the reason given, the maximum of $(32')$ is the same as it would be if $(32')$ had been written in the more natural way using $a_j{}^2$ instead of a_j as the coefficient of $\check{H}_{jj}$; the use of a_j is required to make the form of $(35')$ and (37) satisfy the requirement of $(34c)$.

[54] The proof that the indicated solution satisfies the Kuhn-Tucker conditions with respect to the variables $a_j{}^0$ and $\mu_j{}^0$ is identical to that given above footnote 28 upon the substitution of $\underline{X}$ for $\underline{x}$, a_j for h_i, and μ_j for u_i, and need not be repeated. The two additional *necessary* conditions are

$(3')$ $\left[\dfrac{\partial \psi}{\partial \eta_j} \right]^0 \geqq 0$, which is satisfied, since from (35) we have

$\left[\dfrac{\partial \psi}{\partial \eta_j} \right]^0 = q_j{}^0 \geqq 0$ by virtue of $(36c)$; and this latter relation shows that the corresponding complementary slackness condition,

$(4')$ $\mu_j{}^0 \left[\dfrac{\partial \psi}{\partial \mu_j} \right]^0 = 0$, may be written $\mu_j{}^0 q_j{}^0 = 0$, and is therefore satisfied because of $(36g)$.

All three *sufficiency* conditions are also satisfied because the variance-covariance matrix $\underline{X}$ is positive definite, making $\psi(a, u^0, n^0)$ a concave function on a and $\psi(a, u^0, n^0)$ a convex function on both u and n.

[55] See Weingartner [22], 11 and 32–34.

that new riskless debt is available in unlimited amounts at a fixed rate r^*) insures that all projects will either be accepted or rejected *in toto*. All $a_j{}^0$ will be either o or 1, and the troublesome problems associated with fractional projects or recourse to integer (non-linear) programming do not arise.

Consider now the set of *accepted* projects, and denote this subset with asterisks. We then have all $a_{j*}{}^0 = a_{k*}{}^0 = 1$; the corresponding $\mu_{j*}{}^0 = \mu_{k*}{}^0 = 0$; and for any project $j*$, the corresponding $\eta_{j*}{}^0 > 0$ (i.e. *strictly positive*),[56] and the number $\eta_{j*}{}^0$ is the "dual evaluator" or "shadow price" registering the *net gain* to the company *and* its shareholders of accepting the project. Rewriting the corresponding equation from (36a), we have[57]

$$(37) \quad \eta_{j*}{}^0 = \bar{H}_{j*}{}^{(1)} - r^* H_{j*}{}^{(0)} - \gamma \,[\check{H}_{j*j*} + 2\check{H}_{j*0} + 2\Sigma_{k*\neq j*\neq 0}\check{H}_{j*k*}] > 0.$$

Several important features and implications of these results should be emphasized. First of all, note that we have shown that *even* when uncertainty is admitted in only this highly simplified way, and when any effect of changes in capital budgets on the *covariances* between returns on different companies' *stocks* is ignored, the minimum expected return (in dollars of expected present value $\bar{H}_{j*}{}^{(1)}$) required to justify the allocation of funds to a given risky project costing a given sum $H_{j*}{}^{(0)}$ is an increasing function of each of the following factors: (*i*) the risk-free rate of return r^*; (*ii*) the "market price of dollar risk", γ; (*iii*) the variance $\check{H}_{j*j*}$ in the project's own present value return; (*iv*) the project's aggregate present value return-*co*variance $\check{H}_{j*0}$ with assets already held by the company, and (*v*) its total covariance $\Sigma_{k*\neq j*\neq 0} \check{H}_{j*k*}$ with other projects concurrently included in the capital budget.

Second, it follows from this analysis that, if uncertainty is recognized to be an important fact of life, and risk-aversion is a significant property of relevant utility functions, appropriate *risk-variables* must be introduced *explicitly* into the analytical framework used in analysis, and that these risk-variables will be *essential components*

of any optimal decision rules developed. Important insights can be, and have been, derived from "certainty" models, including some *qualitative* notions of the *conditional* effects of changes in availability of funds due to fund-suppliers' reactions to uncertainty,[58] but such models ignore the decision-maker's problem of optimizing *his* investment decisions in the face of the stochastic character of the outcomes among which *he* must choose.

Third, it is clear that *stochastic considerations are a primary source of interdependencies among projects*, and these must *also enter explicitly* into optimal decision rules. In particular, note that, although own-variances are necessarily positive and subtracted in equation (37), the net gain $n_{j*}{}^0$ may still be positive and justify acceptance *even if* the expected end-of-period "excess" present-value return $(\check{X}_{j*}{}^{(1)} = \bar{H}_{j*}{}^{(1)} - r^* H_{j*}{}^{(0)})$ is negative[59]— so long as its total present-value-covariances $(\check{H}_{j*0} + \Sigma_{k*\neq j*\neq 0} \check{H}_{j*k*})$ are also negative and sufficiently large. *Sufficiently risk-reducing investments rationally belong in corporate capital budgets even at the expense of lowering expected present value returns* — an important (and realistic) feature of rational capital budgeting procedure not covered (nor even implied) in traditional analyses.

Fourth, note that, as would by now be expected, for any fixed r^* and γ, the net gain from a project is a *linear* function of its (present value) *variance* and *covariances* with existing company assets and concurrent projects. Standard deviations are not involved except as a component of (co)variances.

Fifth, the fact that the risk of a project involves all the elements in the bracketed term in (37), including covariances with other concurrent projects, indicates that in practice it will often be extremely difficult, if not impossible, to classify *projects* into respectively homogeneous "risk classes." The practice is convenient (and desirable where it does not introduce significant bias) but our analysis shows it is *not essential*, and the considerations which follow show it to be *a*

[56] We are of course here ignoring the very exceptional and coincidental case in which $\eta_{j*}{}^0 = 0$ which implies that $a_{j*}{}^0$ is indeterminate in the range $0 \leqq a_{0j} \leqq 1$, the company being *totally indifferent* whether or not all (or any part) of a project is undertaken.

[57] We use $\check{H}_{j*k*}$ to denote elements the original covariance matrix $\check{H}$ *after* all rows and columns associated with rejected projects have been removed.

[58] See Weingartner [22] and works there cited. Weingartner would of course agree with the conclusion stated here, see pp. 193–194.

[59] Indeed, in extreme cases, a project should be accepted even if the expected end-of-period present value $\bar{H}_{j*}{}^{(1)}$ is less than cost $H_{j*}{}^{(0)}$, provided negative correlations with existing assets and other concurrent investments are sufficiently strong and negative.

dangerous expedient which is positively misleading as generally employed in the literature.

Sixth, it must be emphasized that — following the requirements of the market equilibrium conditions (29) from which equations (36), (37), and (38) were derived — all means and (co)variances of present values have been calculated using the riskless rate r^*. In this connection, recall the non-linear effect on present values of varying the discount rate used in their computation. Also remember the further facts that (i) the means and variances of the distributions of present values computed at different discount rates do not vary in proportion to each other when different discount rates are applied to the same set of future stochastic cash flow data, and that (ii) the changes induced in the means and variances of the present values of different projects having different patterns and durations of future cash flows will also differ greatly as discount rates are altered. From these considerations alone, it necessarily follows that there can be no single "risk discount rate" to use in computing present values for the purpose of deciding on the acceptance or rejection of different individual projects out of a subset of projects even if all projects in the subset have the same degree of "risk."[60] The same conclusion follows a fortiori among projects with different risks.

Seventh, the preceding considerations, again a fortiori, insure that even if all new projects have the same degree of "risk" as existing assets, the "cost of capital" (as defined for uncertainty anywhere in the literature) is not the appropriate discount rate to use in accept-reject decisions on individual projects for capital budgeting.[61] This is true whether the "cost of capital" is to be used

as a "hurdle rate" (which the "expected return" must exceed) or as a discount rate in obtaining present values of net cash inflows and outflows.

Perhaps at this point the reader should be reminded of the rather heroic set of simplifying assumptions which were made at the beginning of this section. One consequence of the unreality of these assumptions is, clearly, that the results are not being presented as directly applicable to practical decisions at this stage. Too many factors that matter very significantly have been left out (or assumed away). But the very simplicity of the assumptions has enabled us to develop rigorous proofs of the above propositions which do differ substantially from current treatments of "capital budgeting under uncertainty." A little reflection should convince the reader that all the above conclusions will still hold under more realistic (complex) conditions.

Since we have shown that selection of individual projects to go in a capital budget under uncertainty by means of "risk-discount" rates (or by the so-called "cost of capital") is fundamentally in error, we should probably note that the decision criteria given by the solutions of equation (36) [and the acceptance condition (37)] — which directly involve the means and variances of present values computed at the riskless rate — do have a valid counterpart in the form of a "required expected rate of return." Specifically, if we let $[\Sigma \tilde{H}_{j*}]$ represent the entire bracket in equation (37), and divide through by the original cost of the project $H_{j*}{}^{(0)}$, we have

$$(38) \quad \bar{H}_{j*}{}^{(1)}/H_{j*}{}^{(0)} = r_{j*} > r^* + \gamma \, [\Sigma \tilde{H}_{j*}]/H_{j*}{}^{(0)}.$$

Now the ratio of the expected end-of-period present value $\bar{H}_{j*}{}^{(1)}$ to the initial cost $H_{j*}{}^{(0)}$ — i.e. the left side of (38), which we write r_{j*} — is precisely (the expected value of) what Lutz called the net short term marginal efficiency of the investment [13 p. 159]. We can thus say that the minimum acceptable expected rate of return on a project is a (positively sloped) linear function of the ratio of the project's aggregate incremental present-value-variance-covariance $(\Sigma \tilde{H}_{j*})$ to its cost $H_{j*}{}^{(0)}$. The slope coefficient is still the "market price of dollar risk", γ, and the intercept is the risk-free rate r^*. (It will be observed that our "accept-reject" rule for individual projects under uncertainty thus reduces to Lutz' rule under certainty — as it should — since with certainty the right-hand ratio term is zero.) To

---

[60] Note, as a corollary, it also follows that even if the world were simple enough that a single "as if" risk-discount rate could in principle be found, the same considerations insure that there can be no simple function relating the appropriate "risk-discount" rate to the riskless rate r^* and "degree of risk," however measured. But especially in this context, it must be emphasized that a single risk discount rate would produce non-optimal choices among projects even if (i) all projects could be assigned to meaningful risk-classes, unless it were also true that (ii) all projects had the same (actual) time-pattern of net cash flows and the same life (which is a condition having probability measure zero under uncertainty!).

[61] Note particularly that, even though we are operating under assumptions which validate Modigliani and Miller's propositions I and II, and the form of finance is not relevant to the choice of projects, we nevertheless cannot accept their use of their ρ_k — their cost of capital — as the relevant discount rate.

avoid misunderstanding and misuse of this relation, however, several further observations must
be emphasized.

a) Equation (38) — like equation (37) from
which it was derived — states a necessary condition of the (Kuhn-Tucker) optimum with respect
to the projects selected. It may validly be *used
to choose* the desirable projects out of the larger
set of *possible* projects *if the covariances among
potential projects* $\tilde{H}_{j \neq k \neq 0}$ *are all zero.*[62] *Otherwise, a programming solution of equation set* (36)
is required[63] *to find which subset of projects* H_{j*}
satisfy either (37) or (38), essentially because the
total variance of any project $[\Sigma \tilde{H}_j]$ is dependent
on *which* other projects are *concurrently included*
in the budget.

b) Although the risk-free rate $r*$ enters equation (38) *explicitly* only as the intercept [or
constant in the linear (in)equation form], it must
be emphasized again that it *also enters implicitly
as the discount rate used in computing the means
and variances of all present values which appear in*
the (in)equation. *In consequence, (i) any shift* in
the value of $r*$ *changes every term* in the function.
(ii) The changes in $\tilde{H}^{(1)}_{j*}$ and $\Sigma \tilde{H}_{j*}$ are *non-
linear and non-proportional* to each other.[64]
Since *(iii)* any shift in the value of $r*$ changes
every covariance in equation (36a) *non-proportion-
ately, (iv)* the *optimal subset of projects* $j*$ is *not
invariant* to a change in the risk-free rate $r*$.
Therefore *(v), in principal, any shift in the value
of $r*$ requires a new programming solution of the
entire set of equations* (36).

c) Even for a predetermined and fixed $r*$, and
even with respect only to *included* projects, the
condition expressed in (38) is rigorously *valid only
under the full set* of simplifying assumptions
stated at the beginning of this section. In addition, the programming solution of equation (36),
and its derivative property (38), *simultaneously
determines both the optimal composition and the
optimal size* of the capital budget *only under this
full set* of simplifying assumptions. Indeed, even

if the twin assumptions of a fixed riskless rate $r*$
and of formally unlimited borrowing opportunities at this rate are retained[65], *but* other
assumptions are (realistically) generalized —
specifically to permit expected returns on new
investments at any time to depend in part on
investments made in prior periods, and to make
the "entity value" in part a function of the
finance mix used — *then* the (set of) programming
solutions merely determines the optimal *mix or
composition* of the capital budget *conditional* on
each possible aggregate budget size and risk.[66]
Given the resulting "investment opportunity
function" — which is the three-dimensional
Markowitz-type envelope of efficient sets of
projects — the optimal capital budget size and
risk can be determined directly by market
criteria (as developed in [11] and [12])[67] but will
depend explicitly on concurrent financing decisions (e.g. retentions and leverage).[68]

VI — Some Implications of More Relaxed Assumptions

We have come a fairly long way under a
progressively larger set of restrictive assumptions. The purpose of the exercise has not been
to provide results *directly* applicable to practical
decisions at this stage — too much (other than
uncertainty *per se*) that matters greatly in prac-

---

[62] Note that covariances $\tilde{H}_{j,0}$ with *existing* assets need not
be zero since they are independent of other projects and may
be combined with the own-variance $\tilde{H}_{jj}$.

[63] In strict theory, an iterative *exhaustive* search over *all
possible* combinations *could* obviate the programming procedure, but the number of combinations would be very large
in practical problems, and economy dictates programming
methods.

[64] This statement is true *even if* the set of projects $j*$ were
invariant to a change in $r*$ which in general will not be the
case, as noted in the following text statement.

[65] If these assumptions are not retained, the position *and*
composition of the investment opportunity function (defined
immediately below in the text) are themselves dependent
on the relevant discount rate, for the reasons given in the
"sixth" point above and the preceding paragraph. (See also
Lutz [13 p. 160].) Optimization then requires the solution
of a much different and more complex set of (in)equations,
simultaneously encompassing finance-mix *and* investment mix.

[66] This stage of the analysis corresponds, in the standard
"theory of the firm," to the determination of the optimal mix
of factors for each possible scale.

[67] I should note here, however, that on the basis of the
above analysis, the correct *marginal expected* rate of return
for the investment opportunity function should be the value
of r_j* [See left side equation (38) above] for the marginally
included project at each budget size, i.e. the ratio of end-of-
period present value computed at the riskless rate $r*$ to the
project cost — rather than the different rate (generally used
by other authors) stated in [12, p. 54 top]. Correspondingly,
the relevant *average* expected return is the same ratio computed
for the budget as a whole. Correspondingly, the relevant
variance is the variance of this ratio. None of the subsequent
analysis or results of [12] are affected by this corrected specification of the inputs to the investment opportunity function.

[68] This latter solution determines the optimal point on the
investment opportunity function at which to operate. The
optimal *mix* of projects to include in the capital budget is that
which corresponds to the optimal point on the investment
opportunity function.

tice has been assumed away — but rather to develop rigorously some of the fundamental implications of uncertainty *as such* for an important class of decisions about which there has been much confusion in the theoretical literature. The more negative conclusions reached — such as, for instance, the serious distortions inherently involved in the prevalent use of a "risk-discount rate" or a "company-risk-class" "cost-of-capital" for project selection in capital budgeting — clearly will hold under more general conditions, as will the primary role under uncertainty of the *risk-free rate* (whether used to calculate *distributions* of present values *or* to form *present values of certainty-equivalents*). But others of our more affirmative results, and especially the particular equations developed, are just as clearly inherently conditional on the simplifying assumptions which have been made. While it would be out of place to undertake any exhaustive inventory here, we should nevertheless note the impact of relaxing certain key assumptions upon some of these other conclusions.

The particular formulas in sections II–V depend *inter-alia* on the *Separation Theorem* and each investor's consequent preference for the stock *mix* which maximizes θ. Recall that in proving the Separation Theorem in section I we assumed that the investor could borrow unlimited amounts at the rate r^* equal to the rate on savings deposits. Four alternatives to this assumption may be considered briefly. (1) *Borrowing Limits*: The Theorem (and the subsequent development) holds *provided* that the margin requirements turn out *not* to be binding; but if the investor's utility function is such that, given the portfolio which maximizes θ, he prefers a w greater than is permitted, *then* the Theorem does not hold and the utility function must be used explicitly to determine the optimal stock mix.[69] (2) *Borrowing rate* r^{**} *greater* than "lending rate" r^*: (a) If the max θ using r^* implies a $w < 1$, the theorem holds in original form; (b) if the max θ using r^* implies $w > 1$ *and* (upon recomputation) the max θ using r^{**} in equations (3b), (7) and (8) implies $w > 1$, the theorem also holds but r^{**}

[69] See appendix, note III.

(rather than r^*) *must be used* in sections II–V; (c) if max θ using r^* implies $w > 1$ *and* max θ using r^{**} implies $w < 1$, *then* there will be no borrowing *and* the utility function must be used explicitly to determine the optimal stock mix.[70] (3) *Borrowing rate an increasing function of leverage* $(w - 1)$: The theorem still holds under condition (2a) above, but if max θ using r^* implies $w > 1$ *then* the *optimal mix and the optimal financing* must *be determined simultaneously using the utility function* explicitly.[71] (4) The latter conclusion also follows immediately *if the borrowing rate is not independent of the stock mix*.

The *qualitative* conclusions of sections II and III hold even if the Separation Theorem does not, but the formulas would be much more complex. Similarly, the stock market equilibrium in section IV — and the parameters used for capital budgeting decisions in section V — will be altered if different investors in the market are affected differently by the "real world" considerations in the preceding paragraph (because of different utility functions, or probability assessments), or by differential tax rates. Note also that even if all our original assumptions through section IV are accepted for investors, the results in section V would have to be modified to allow for all real world complications in the cost and availability of debt and the tax treatment of debt interest versus other operating income. Finally, although explicitly ruled out in section V, it must be recalled that "limited liability," legal or other institutional restrictions or premiums, or the presence of "market risk" (as distinct from default risk) on corporate debt, *are sufficient both* to make the optimal *project mix* in the capital budget *conditional* on the finance mix (notably retentions and leverage), *and* the finance mix itself *also* something to be optimized.

Obviously, the need for further work on all these topics is great. The present paper will have succeeded in its essential purpose if it has rigorously pushed back the frontiers of theoretical understanding, and opened the doors to more fruitful theoretical and applied work.

[70] See appendix, note IV.
[71] See appendix, note V.

VALUATION OF RISK ASSETS

APPENDIX

Note I — Alternative Proof of Separation Theorem and Its Corrolaries

In this note, I present an alternative proof of the *Separation Theorem* and its corrolaries using utility functions explicity. Some readers may prefer this form, since it follows traditional theory more closely.

Let $\bar{y}$ and σ_y be the expected value and variance of the rate of return on any asset mixture and A_0 be the amount of the investor's total net investment. Given the assumptions regarding the market and the investor, stated in the text, the investor will seek to maximize the expected utility of a function which can be written in general form as

(1') $\quad E[U(A_0\bar{y}, A_0\sigma_y)] = \bar{U}(A_0\bar{y}, A_0\sigma_y),$

subject to his investment opportunities characterized by the risk-free rate r^*, at which he can invest in savings deposits or borrow any amount he desires, and by the set of all stock mixes available to him, each of which in turn is represented by a pair of values $(\bar{r}, \sigma_r)$. Our assumptions establish the following properties[72] of the utility function in (1'):

$$(1a') \quad \begin{cases} \partial\bar{U}/\partial\bar{y} = A_0\bar{U}_1 > 0; \ \partial\bar{U}/\partial\sigma_y = A_0\bar{U}_2 < 0; \\ \left.\dfrac{d\bar{y}}{d\sigma_y}\right|_{\bar{U}} = -\bar{U}_2/\bar{U}_1 > 0; \ \left.\dfrac{d^2\bar{y}}{d\sigma_y{}^2}\right|_{\bar{U}} > 0. \end{cases}$$

Also, with the assumptions we have made,[73] all available stock mixes will lie *in a finite region* all parts of which are strictly to the right of the vertical axis in the σ_r, r plane since all available mixes will have positive variance. The boundary of this region will be a closed curve[74] and the region is convex.[75] Moreover, since $\bar{U}_1 > 0$ and $\bar{U}_2 < 0$ in (1a'), all mixes within this region are dominated by those whose (σ_r, r) values lie on the part of the boundary associated with values of $\bar{r} > 0$, *and* for which changes in σ_r and $\bar{r}$ are positively associated. This is Markowitz' Efficient Set or "E–V" Frontier. We may write its equation[76] as

[72] For formal proof of these properties, see Tobin, [21], pp. 72–77.

[73] Specifically, that the amount invested in any stock mix is infinitely divisible, that all expected returns on individual stocks are finite, that all variances are positive and finite, and that the variance-covariance matrix is positive-definite.

[74] Markowitz [14] has shown that, in general, this closed curve will be made up of successive hyperbolic segments which are strictly tangent at points of overlap.

[75] Harry Markowitz, [14], chapter VII. The shape of the boundary follows from the fact that the point corresponding to any mix (in positive proportions summing to one) of any two points on the boundary lies to the left of the straight line joining those two points; and all points on and within the boundary belong to the set of available $(\sigma_r, \bar{r})$ pairs because any such point corresponds to an appropriate combination in positive proportions of at least one pair of points on the boundary.

[76] Note that the stated conditions on *the* derivatives in

(2') $\quad \bar{r} = f(\sigma_r), \ f'(\sigma_r) > 0, \ f''(\sigma_r) < 0.$

Substituting (2') in (2) and (3) in the text, we find the first order conditions for the maximization of (1) subject to (2), (3), and (2') to be given by the equalities in

(3a') $\quad \partial\bar{U}/\partial w = \bar{U}_1(\bar{r} - r^*) + \bar{U}_2\sigma_r \gtrless 0.$

(3b') $\quad \partial\bar{U}/\partial\sigma_r = \bar{U}_1 wf'(\sigma) + \bar{U}_2 w \gtrless 0.$

which immediately reduce to the two equations [using (3a) from the text]

(4') $\quad \theta = -\bar{U}_2/\bar{U}_1 = f'(\sigma_r).$

Second order conditions for a maximum are satisfied because of the concavity of (1') and (2'). The separation theorem follows immediately from (4') when we note that the equation of the first and third members $\theta = f'(\sigma)$ *is precisely the condition for the maximization*[77] of θ, since

(5a') $\quad \dfrac{\partial\theta}{\partial\sigma_r} = \dfrac{\sigma_r[f'(\sigma_r)] - [\bar{r} - r^*]}{\sigma_r{}^2} = \dfrac{f'(\sigma_r) - \theta}{\sigma_r}$

(5b') $\quad \dfrac{\partial^2\theta}{\partial(\sigma_r)^2} = \dfrac{\sigma_r f''(\sigma_r) + [f'(\sigma_r) - \theta] - [f'(\sigma_r) - \theta]}{\sigma_r{}^2}$

$\qquad\qquad = f''(\sigma_r)/\sigma_r < 0$ for all $\sigma_r > 0.$

A necessary condition for the maximization of (1') is consequently the maximization of θ (as asserted), which is independent of w. The value of $(-\bar{U}_2/\bar{U}_1)$, however, directly depends on w (for *any* given value of θ), and a second necessary condition for the maximization of $\bar{U}$ is that w be adjusted to bring this value $(-\bar{U}_2/\bar{U}_1)$ into equality with θ, thereby satisfying the usual tangency condition between utility contours and the market opportunity function (3) in the text. These two necessary conditions are also *sufficient* because of the concavity of (1') and the positive-definite property of the matrix of risk-investment opportunities. Q.E.D.

Note II

a) Indifference Contours Between x_i and σ^2_i When all σ_{ij} are Constant

The conclusion that the indifference contour between $\bar{x}_i$ and the variance σ_i^2 is *linear* in the general case when all covariances σ_{ij} are held constant can best be established by totally differentiating the equilibrium conditions (12) in the text [or the equivalent set (22a) restricted to the m' stocks held in the portfolio] which yields the set of equations

(2') hold even in the exceptional cases of discontinuity. Markowitz [14], p. 153.

[77] This conclusion clearly holds even in the exceptional cases (noted in the preceding footnote) in which the derivatives of $r = f(\sigma_r)$ are not continuous. Equation (3a') will hold as an exact equality because of the continuity of the utility function, giving $\theta = -\bar{U}_2/\bar{U}_1$. By equation (3b'), expected utility $\bar{U}$ increases with σ_r for all $f'(\sigma) \gtrless -\bar{U}_2/\bar{U}_1 = \theta$, and the max σ_r consistent with $f'(\sigma) \gtrless \theta$ maximizes θ by equation (5a').

$$\lambda^0 \sigma_{i}{}^2 dh_1{}^0 + \lambda^0 \sigma_{12} dh_2{}^0 + \ldots + \lambda^0 \sigma_{1i} dh_i{}^0 +$$
$$\ldots + \lambda^0 \sigma_{1m'} dh_{m'}{}^0 + \frac{\bar{x}_1}{\lambda^0} d\lambda^0 = 0$$

$$\vdots$$

(6) $\quad \lambda^0 \sigma_{i1}{}^0 dh_1{}^0 + \lambda^0 \sigma_{i2} dh_2{}^0 + \ldots + \lambda^0 \sigma_{i}{}^2 dh_i{}^0 +$
$$\ldots + \lambda^0 \sigma_{tm}{}' dh_{m'}{}^0 + \frac{\bar{x}_i}{\lambda^0} d\lambda^0 = dx_i - \lambda^0 h_i d\sigma_i{}^2$$

$$\vdots$$

$$\lambda^0 \sigma_{m'1} dh_1{}^0 + \lambda^0 \sigma_{m'2} dh_2{}^0 + \ldots + \lambda^0 \sigma_{m'i} dh_i{}^0 +$$
$$\ldots + \lambda^0 \sigma^2{}_m{}' dh_{m'}{}^0 + \frac{\bar{x}_{m'}}{\lambda^0} d\lambda^0 = 0$$

$$dh_1{}^0 + dh_2{}^0 + \ldots + dh_i{}^0 + \ldots + dh_{m'}{}^0 = 0$$

Denoting the coefficient matrix on the left by $\underline{H}$, and the i, j^{th} element of its inverse by H^{ij}, we have by Cramer's rule,

(6a') $\quad dh_i{}^0 = (d\bar{x}_i - \lambda^0 h_i{}^0 d\sigma_i{}^2) H^{ii}$.

Since $\underline{H}$ is non-singular, $h_i{}^0$ will be constant along an indifference contour if and only if

(6b') $\quad d\bar{x}_i = \lambda^0 h_i{}^0 d\sigma_i{}^2$.

The indifference contour is strictly linear because the slope coefficient $\lambda^0 h_i{}^0$ is invariant to the absolute levels of $\bar{x}_i$ and $\sigma_i{}^2$ when $h_i{}^0$ is constant, as may be seen by noting that

(6c') $\quad d\lambda_0{}^0 = (d\bar{x}_1 - \lambda^0 h_i{}^0 d\sigma_i{}^2) H^{i\lambda 0}$

so that

(6d') $\quad dh_i{}^0 = 0 \rightarrow d\lambda_i{}^0 = 0$,

when only $\bar{x}_i$ and $\sigma_i{}^2$ are varied. Moreover, any pair of changes $d\bar{x}_i$ and $d\sigma_i{}^2$ which hold $dh_i{}^0 = 0$ by (6a') and b') imply *no change* in the relative holding $h_j{}^0$ of *any other* security, since $dh_j{}^0 = (d\bar{x}_i - \lambda^0 h_i{}^0 d\sigma_i{}^2) H^{ij} = 0$ for all $j \neq i$ when $dh_i{}^0 = 0$. Consequently, *all* pairs of values of $\bar{x}_i$ and $\sigma_i{}^2$ along the linear indifference contour which holds $h_i{}^0$ fixed at some given level rigorously imply that the proportionate mix of *all other* stocks in the portfolio is *also unchanged* — as was also to be shown.

b) **Indifference Contours Between x_i and σ_i When ρ Constant**

If the equilibrium conditions (12) are differentiated totally to determine the indifference contours between $\bar{x}_i$ and σ_i, the left-hand side of equations (6') above will be unaffected, but the right side will be changed as follows: In the ith equation

$$d\bar{x}_i - \lambda^0 [2h_i{}^0 \sigma_i - \Sigma_{j \neq i} h_j{}^0 \sigma_j \rho_{ij}] d\sigma_i =$$
$$d\bar{x}_i - \lambda^0 (h_i{}^0 \sigma_i - \bar{x}_i/\sigma_i) d\sigma_i$$

replaces $d\bar{x}_i - \lambda^0 h_i{}^0 d\sigma_i{}^2$; the last equation is unchanged; and in all other equations $-\lambda^0 h_i{}^0 \sigma_j \rho_{ij} d\sigma_i$ replaces 0. We then have

(7a') $\quad dh_i{}^0 = [d\bar{x}_i - \lambda^0 (h_i{}^0 \sigma_i - \bar{x}_i/\sigma_i) d\sigma_i] H^{ii}$
$\quad\quad - \lambda^0 h_i{}^0 \Sigma_{j \neq i} \sigma_j \rho_{ij} H^{ij} d\sigma_i;$

(7b') $\quad dh_j{}^0 = [d\bar{x}_i - \lambda^0 (h_i{}^0 \sigma_i - \bar{x}_i/\sigma_i) d\sigma_i] H^{ij}$
$\quad\quad - \lambda^0 h_i{}^0 \Sigma_{K \neq i} \sigma_K \rho_{iK} H^{jK} d\sigma_i;$

(7c') $\quad d\lambda^0 = [d\bar{x}_i - \lambda^0 (h_i{}^0 \sigma_i - \bar{x}_i/\sigma_i) d\sigma_i] H^{i\lambda 0}$
$\quad\quad - \lambda^0 h_i \Sigma_{K \neq i} \sigma_K \rho_{iK} H^{\lambda 0K} d\sigma_i.$

Clearly, in this case, $dh_i{}^0 = 0$ does *not* imply $dh_j{}^0 = 0$, nor does it imply $d\lambda^0 = 0$.

Note III — Borrowing Limits Effective

In principle, in this case the investor must compute all the Markowitz efficient boundary segment joining M (which maximizes θ in figure 1) to the point N corresponding to the greatest attainable $\bar{r}$. Given the fixed margin w, he must then project all points on this original (unlevered) efficient set (see equation 2' above) to determine the new (levered) efficient set of $(\sigma_y, \bar{y})$ pairs attainable by using equations $(2a, b)$ in the text; and he will then choose the $(\sigma_y, \bar{y})$ pair from this latter set which maximizes utility. With concave utility functions this optimum $(\sigma_y, \bar{y})$ pair will satisfy the standard optimizing tangency conditions between the (recomputed) efficient set and the utility function. The situation is illustrated in figure 2.

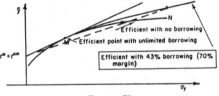

FIGURE II

Note IV — Borrowing Rate r^{**} is Higher than Lending Rate r^*

The conclusions stated in the text are obvious from the graph of this case (which incidentally is *formally* identical to Hirschleifer's treatment of the same case under certainty in [7].)

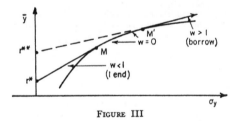

FIGURE III

The optimum depends uniquely upon the utility function if it is tangent to the efficient set with no borrowing in the range MM'.

Note V — Borrowing Rate is Dependent on Leverage

With $r^{**} = g(w)$, $g'(w) > 0$, and when the optimum $w > 1$ so that borrowing is undertaken, θ itself from equation (3) in the text becomes a function of w, which we will write $\theta(w)$. The optimizing equations, corresponding to $(3'a, b)$ above in note I, then become

VALUATION OF RISK ASSETS   37

$(6a')$ $\partial \bar{U}/\partial w = \bar{U}_1[(r - r^{**}) - wg'(w)] + \bar{U}_2\sigma_r \gtreqless 0$
$(6b')$ $\partial \bar{U}/\partial \sigma_r = \bar{U}_1 wf'(\sigma) + \bar{U}_2 w \gtreqless 0$
which reduce to the two equations
$(7')$ $\theta(w) - wg'(w)/\sigma_r = -\bar{U}_2/\bar{U}_1 = f'(\sigma)$.

The equation of the first and third members $\theta(w) - wg'(w)/\sigma_r = f'(\sigma)$ is *no longer* equal to the *maximization* of θ itself, *nor* is the solution of this equation *independent* of w which is required for the validity of the Separation Theorem. It follows that the selection of the optimal stock mix (indexed by θ) and of w *simultaneously depend upon the parameters of the utility function* (and, with normal distribution, *also* upon its *form*). Q.E.D.

[1] ARROW, KENNETH, "Comment on the Portfolio Approach to the Demand for Money and Other Assets," *The Review of Economics and Statistics, Supplement*, XLV (Feb., 1963), 24–27.

[2] BAUMOL, WILLIAM J., "An Expected Gain-Confidence Limit Criterion for Portfolio Selection," *Management Science*, X (Oct., 1963), 174–82.

[3a] DORFMAN, ROBERT, "Basic Economic and Technologic Concepts" In Arthur Maass, et. al., *Design of Water-Resource Systems* (Cambridge, Harvard University Press, 1962).

[3b] FARRAR, DONALD E., *The Investment Decision Under Uncertainty* (Englewood Cliffs, N.J., Prentice-Hall, 1962)

[4] FISHER, IRVING, *The Theory of Interest* (New York, 1930).

[5] GORDON, MYRON J., *The Investment, Financing and Valuation of the Corporation* (Homewood, Illinois: Richard D. Irwin, 1962).

[6] HICKS, J. R., "Liquidity", *The Economic Journal*, LXXII (Dec., 1962).

[7] HIRSCHLEIFER, JACK, "On the Theory of Optimal Investment Decision," *Journal of Political Economy*, LXVI (Aug., 1958).

[8] HIRSCHLEIFER, JACK, "Risk, the Discount Rate, and Investment Decisions," *American Economic Review*, LI (May, 1961).

[9] KUHN, H. W., and A. W. TUCKER, "Nonlinear Programming" in J. Neyman ed., *Proceedings of the Second Berkeley Symposium on Mathematical Statistics and Probability* (Berkeley: University of California Press, 1951), 481–492.

[10] LINTNER, JOHN, "Dividends, Earnings, Leverage, Stock Prices and the Supply of Capital to Corporations," *Review of Economics and Statistics*, XLIV (Aug., 1962).

[11] LINTNER, JOHN, "The Cost of Capital and Optimal Financing of Corporate Growth," *The Journal of Finance*, XVIII (May, 1963).

[12] LINTNER, JOHN, "Optimal Dividends and Corporate Growth Under Uncertainty," *The Quarterly Journal of Economics*, LXXVIII (Feb., 1964).

[13] LUTZ, FREDERICK and VERA, *The Theory of Investment of the Firm* (Princeton, 1951).

[14] MARKOWITZ, HARRY, *Portfolio Selection* (New York, 1959).

[15] MODIGLIANI, FRANCO and MILLER, MERTON, "The Cost of Capital, Corporation Finance and the Theory of Investment," *American Economic Review*, XLVIII (June, 1958).

[16] MODIGLIANI, FRANCO and MILLER, MERTON, "Dividend Policy, Growth and the Valuation of Shares," *Journal of Business*, XXXIV (Oct., 1961).

[17] PRATT, JOHN W., "Risk Aversion in the Small and in the Large," *Econometrica*, XXXIII (Jan.–April, 1964), 122–136.

[18] ROBBINS, SIDNEY M., *Managing Securities* (Boston: Houghton Mifflin Company, 1954).

[19] ROY, A. D., "Safety First and the Holding of Assets," *Econometrica*, XX (July, 1952), 431–449.

[20] SHARPE, WILLIAM F., "A Simplified Model for Portfolio Analysis," *Management Science*, IX (Jan., 1963), 277–293.

[21] TOBIN, JAMES, "Liquidity Preference as Behavior Toward Risk," *Review of Economic Studies*, XXVI (Feb., 1958), 65–86.

[22] WEINGARTNER, H. MARTIN, *Mathematical Programming and the Analysis of Capital Budgeting Problems* (Englewood Cliffs, New Jersey: Prentice-Hall, 1963).

[23] WILSON, ROBERT B., *A Simplicial Algorithm for Concave Programming* (unpublished D.B.A. thesis, Harvard Business School, 1963).

[14]

The Relation between Unemployment and the Rate of Change of Money Wage Rates in the United Kingdom, 1862—1957:

A Further Analysis[1]

By Richard G. Lipsey

In an earlier paper in this journal, Professor Phillips[2] has advanced the hypothesis that the percentage rate of change of money wage rates in the United Kingdom ($\dot{W}$) can be explained to a very large extent by: (i) the percentage of the labour force unemployed (U), and (ii) the *rate of change* of unemployment ($\dot{U}$). After an inspection of the data, Phillips concluded not only that there is a clearly observable relationship between these variables, but that the form of the relationship has been remarkably stable over a period of almost one hundred years. The purpose of the present paper is to reconsider Phillips' work in some detail. In particular it seemed necessary: (i) to consider the general theoretical model that is being tested; (ii) to quantify Phillips' results, determining, if possible, the proportion of the variance in money wage rates that is associated with the two variables, level of unemployment (U) and rate of change of unemployment ($\dot{U}$); (iii) to provide systematic tests of the various subsidiary hypotheses framed by Phillips during the course of his analysis; and (iv) to test hypotheses that follow from possible alternative models. The logical order in which to deal with these topics, in the absence of Phillips' paper, would be, first, to outline the phenomena which require explanation, then to develop a model which will explain the phenomena, and, finally, to test further implications of the model. Given Phillips' paper, however, a slight change of approach seems to be desirable. In the first section of this paper a report is given of the statistical analysis carried out on data for the period 1862-1913. Although the main purpose is to discover what phenomena require explanation, a rather elaborate treatment is required in order to test the hypotheses about these phenomena framed by Phillips. This is

[1] The present paper, like Professor Phillips', is a part of a wider research project financed by the Ford Foundation. The writer was assisted by Mr. Peter Lantos and Mrs. June Wickins. This paper was the subject of extended discussion at the LSE Staff Seminar on Methodology and Testing in Economics and I am indebted to all the members for many comments and suggestions; I also benefited from the discussion at the University of Manchester Advanced Economics Seminar where some of the material embodied in this paper was first presented. Mr. F. Brechling and Dr. S. F. Kaliski have given valuable criticisms and I am particularly indebted to Professor Phillips for his constant aid and encouragement.

[2] A. W. Phillips, " The Relation Between Unemployment and the Rate of Change of Money Wage Rates in the United Kingdom, 1861-1957 ", *Economica*, Nov. 1958.

A

2   ECONOMICA   [FEBRUARY

necessary in order to build up a clear picture of our explicanda. Although many of Phillips' subsidiary hypotheses are rejected, the data are shown to support Phillips' main contention that there is a significant relation between the rate of change of money wage rates and the level and the rate of change of unemployment. Having established the evidence for these relations, the second section is devoted to the construction of a theoretical model which adequately accounts for them. Phillips had given very little indication of the sort of model of market behaviour which would produce his postulated relations. The third section is devoted to an analysis of the data for the post–1918 period. The theory developed in Section II is particularly useful in interpreting the differences which occur between the relations existing in the nineteenth century and in the twentieth century.

I

The Period 1862–1913

1. *The relation between the rate of change of money wage rates* $(\dot{W})$ *and the level of unemployment* (U)[1]

The unemployment figures used by Phillips showed the percentage of the unionized labour force unemployed, while the figures for the rate of change of wage rates were calculated[2] from the Phelps Brown-Hopkins index.[3]

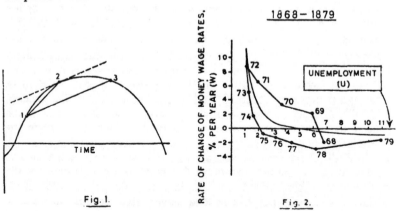

Fig. 1.

Fig. 2.

[1] Since the *level* of unemployment is uncorrelated with the *rate of change* of unemployment, as is any trend-free variable with its own rate of change, the relation between the rate of change of money wages and each of the independent variables, U and $\dot{U}$, can be considered separately. The actual r^2 for U and $\dot{U}$ is ·0002.

[2] Phillips, *ibid.*, p. 290, n. 1, took half the first central differences $(W_{t+1} - W_{t-1} \div 2)$ as the best approximation to the absolute rate of change of wages. The argument for approximating a continuous derivative by this method rather than by the more intuitively plausible method of taking the difference between this year's wage index and last year's $(W_t - W_{t-1})$ can best be explained by reference to the diagram. Fig. 1 shows a continuous time series (say one for the rate of change of wages). Only a discrete number of regularly-spaced observations are available, say those at 1, 2, and 3, and it is desired to approximate the derivative at 2 (the true value being given

1960] THE RELATION BETWEEN UNEMPLOYMENT AND WAGE RATES 3

Fig. 3 shows the data for $\dot{W}$ and U for the period under consideration. Phillips elected to describe the data by a curve of the type

$$\dot{W} = \alpha + \beta U^\gamma \dots\dots\dots\dots\dots\dots\dots\dots\dots\dots\dots \text{(1a)}$$

$$\text{or} \quad \log(\dot{W} - \alpha) = \log \beta + \gamma \log U \dots\dots\dots\dots\dots\dots \text{(1b)}$$

where $\dot{W}$ is the rate of change of money wage rates $\left(\dot{W}_i \equiv \dfrac{W_{i+1} - W_{i-1}}{2W_i} \right)$,

and U is the percentage of the labour force unemployed. This curve could not be fitted to all 52 observations because points below the asymptote ($\dot{W} < \alpha$) would require negative logarithms. Hence Phillips grouped his observations into six class intervals based on the level of unemployment[1] and found the mean values of $\dot{W}$ and U for each of the six groups. Having thus compressed his data into six points, he fitted his curve to these points, using a trial-and-error procedure, and obtained the following equation:

$$\dot{W} = -0.9 + 9.638 \, U^{-1.394}, \dots\dots\dots\dots\dots\dots\dots \text{(2)}$$

which is plotted as curve (2) in Fig. 3.

Since, for purposes of the present study, it seemed desirable to treat the data by standard statistical methods if at all possible, a new

---

by the slope of the broken line tangent to the curve at 2). Taking the rate of change to be equal to the difference between the values of the function at 2 and at 1 is equivalent to estimating the derivative at 2 to be equal to the slope of the line joining 1 and 2. But the slope of this line is typical of the value of the derivative somewhere *between* 1 and 2, so that this method gives the derivative somewhere *between* the two points of time and is thus equivalent to introducing a time lag of approximately six months into the rate-of-change series. On the other hand, taking half the first central difference is equivalent to estimating the derivative to be equal to the slope of the line joining 1 and 3. In a regular curve this latter value is likely to be closer to the true value of the derivative at 2 than is the former value. In a recent article criticising Phillips' work, Mr. Routh has argued that the actual wage rate series is too crude to make the difference between the two methods of calculating $\dot{W}$ significant. (Guy Routh, " The Relation Between Unemployment and the Rate of Change of Money Wage Rates : A Comment ", *Economica*, November, 1959.)

[3] E. H. Phelps Brown and Sheila Hopkins, " The Course of Wage Rates in Five Countries, 1860–1939 ", *Oxford Economic Papers*, June 1950. Mr. Routh (*loc. cit.*, pp. 299–305) gives a detailed study of the coverage of the wage rate and the unemployment series and argues that " . . . in the two series used by Professor Phillips, neither the weights, occupations nor the industries are a good match (p. 303) ". Routh argues, for example, that any fixed weighted index of rates will not allow for movements between areas and occupations. This is undoubtedly correct. It is, however, always possible to show that any set of statistics are not perfect or even, by some absolute standard, that they are downright bad. The relevant question is not whether the figures are perfect, but whether they are good enough for the purposes at hand. The question of whether or not the postulated relation is strong enough to show up in spite of imperfections in the data, can only be answered by the empirical results: in this case the postulated relation is strong enough. Another criticism of Phillips' article is to be found in K. G. J. C. Knowles and C. B. Winsten, " Can the Level of Unemployment Explain Changes in Wages ? ", *Bulletin of the Oxford Institute of Statistics*, May 1959.

[1] The class intervals (percentage unemployment) with the number of items contained in each class given in parentheses are: 0—2 (6), 2—3 (10), 3—4 (12), 4—5 (5), 5—7 (11), 7—11 (9) (the upper limit is included in each class).

4   ECONOMICA   [FEBRUARY

equation was adopted which could be fitted to all the 52 original observations:[1]

$$\dot{W}=a+bU^{-1}+cU^{-2}. \qquad\qquad\qquad\qquad\qquad\qquad (3)$$

It was found that, by suitable choice of the constants b and c, this curve could be made to take up a position virtually indistinguishable

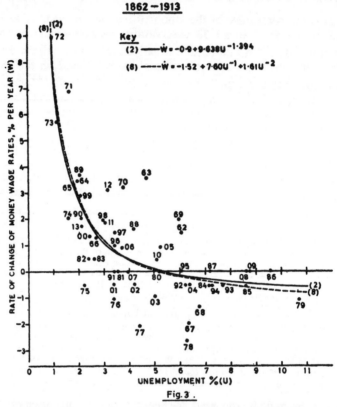

Fig. 3.

from that taken up by curve (1) for any value of γ between -1 and -2. Thus choosing between the two curves does not necessitate choosing between different hypotheses about the nature of the relation between $\dot{W}$ and U.[2]

The curve was first fitted to Phillips' six points of averages and gave the equation

$$\dot{W}=-0.44+0.023U^{-1}+12.52U^{-2}. \qquad\qquad\qquad (4)$$

[1] For purposes of the present section the shape of the relation assumed by Phillips is accepted so that the problem is merely to find an equation which takes the same shape as equation (1) but which can be fitted by least squares. In Section II the general form of the relationship between $\dot{W}$ and U is considered in some detail.

[2] When (1) and (3) are fitted to the same data, normal least squares fitting does, however, result in slightly different shapes to the two curves because in one case the sum of the squares of the residuals expressed in logarithms is minimised while, in the second case, it is the sum of the squared residuals expressed in natural numbers that is minimised.

The difference[1] between equations (2) and (4) results from the procedure of minimising the squares of the differences between the actual and the estimated values expressed in logarithms for (2) and in natural numbers for (4).[2] Next the curve was fitted to Phillips' original 52 observations for the years 1862–1913 which resulted in the following equation:

$$\dot{W} = -1.14 + 5.53U^{-1} + 3.68U^{-2}. \dotfill (5)$$

The difference between (4) and (5) indicates the distorting effect caused by fitting to points of averages rather than to the original observations.[3]

Next the Phelps Brown-Hopkins series for wage rate changes in 1881 to 1885 was replaced by the Bowley series for the same years.[4] The fitted equation then became

$$\dot{W} = -1.42 + 7.06U^{-1} + 2.31U^{-2}. \dotfill (6)$$

There is a noticeable shift in the relationship when equation (5) is replaced by equation (6) and there is room for debate as to which series for the disputed years, and thus which equation, should be used. The Bowley series conforms with the pattern seen in the other eight cycles which cover the period under consideration and thus seems to be the more plausible of the two. In the absence of any evidence favouring one series rather than the other, we cannot eliminate one merely because it does not conform with our hypothesis. Therefore, although the Bowley substitution for the years 1881–85 is used on the subjective grounds that it seems more plausible, all relations have been recalculated using the Phelps Brown-Hopkins series for the disputed years, the values for the latter being given in footnotes.

The relation specified in equation (6) gives an r^2 of 0.64, indicating that, over the period 1862–1913, 64 per cent. of the variance in money wage rates is associated with variations in the level of unemployment.[5]

2. The relation between the rate of change of wages ($\dot{W}$) and the rate of change of unemployment ($\dot{U}$)

After an inspection of his graphs Phillips noted that the relationship between $\dot{W}$ and $\dot{U}$ appeared to be important; he observed that,

[1] The different fitted relationships may be at least roughly compared by comparing the values of the asymptotes.

[2] Some of the difference is accounted for by the fact that Phillips did not fit to all six points by least squares but rather made his curve go as closely as possible to the two points representing the highest levels of unemployment and then minimised squares on the other four points.

[3] When fitting to points of averages each of the six points is given equal weight although there are considerable differences between the number of items within each class interval.

[4] The Phelps Brown-Hopkins series shows a suspicious stability in wage rates over the period 1881–85 in spite of wide variations in employment, while the Bowley series shows the usual relation with wage rates rising when unemployment falls and then falling as unemployment rises. See Phillips, *loc. cit.*, pp. 287 and 291. Routh (*loc. cit.*, p. 313) has given reasons for the stability in the Phelps Brown-Hopkins index and has argued that this index should *not* be replaced by the Bowley series for these years.

[5] Equation (5) which shows the comparable relation determined without the substitution of Bowley's index for 1881–85 gives an $r^2 = 0.64$.

compared to the value predicted by the relation between $\dot{W}$ and U, $\dot{W}$ tended to be high when unemployment was falling ($\dot{U}<O$) and low when unemployment was rising ($\dot{U}>O$). In other words, the change in money wage rates is greater than would otherwise be expected when unemployment is *falling* and less than would otherwise be expected when unemployment is *rising*. He did not, however, attempt to determine either the precise form of the relationship between $\dot{W}$ and $\dot{U}$ or its quantitative significance. Fig. 2 shows the relation between $\dot{W}$ and U for the years 1868–79 together with the curve described by equation (2). This general picture is typical of the nineteenth century cycles. The " loop " is clearly observable with the actual $\dot{W}$ being above the fitted curve when unemployment is falling and below the curve when it is rising.

It was now desired to measure this relationship which was very strongly suggested by inspection. Half the first central difference was taken as the best approximation to the rate of change of unemployment in any year.[1] Thus, a new variable was defined, $\dot{U}_t \equiv \dfrac{U_{t+1} - U_{t-1}}{2U_t} \cdot 100$, and the new regression equation became

$$\dot{W} = a + bU^{-1} + cU^{-2} + d\dot{U} \quad\dotfill\quad (7)$$

which, when fitted to the original observations, gave

$$\dot{W} = -1.52 + 7.60U^{-1} + 1.61U^{-2} - .023\dot{U} \quad\dotfill\quad (8)$$

Curve (8) in Fig. 3 shows this relation when $\dot{U}=O$. R^2 for this relationship is 0.82 while the squared partial correlation coefficients are 0.78 for U and 0.50 for $\dot{U}$. This indicates that 82 per cent. of the variance in $\dot{W}$ can be associated with variations in U and $\dot{U}$, and that $\dot{U}$ can remove 50 per cent. of the variance not already associated with U while, if $\dot{U}$ is considered first, U is associated with 78 per cent. of the residual variation in $\dot{W}$.[2]

Now that the influence of $\dot{U}$ has been measured it is possible to check quantitatively on Phillips' observation that " . . . it appears that the width of the loops obtained in each trade cycle has tended to narrow, suggesting *a reduction in the dependence of the rate of change of wage rates on the rate of change of unemployment* ".[3] This statement is taken to mean that, throughout the period, any given rate of change of unemployment was associated with a progressively diminishing rate of change of money wages (i.e., that, if it were fitted separately for

[1] See p. 2, n. 2.

[2] The relations without the Bowley substitutions 1881–85 are as follows:

$\dot{W} = -1.23 + 6.00U^{-1} + 3.05U^{-2} - .021\dot{U}$, $r^2 = 0.79$. The squared partial correlation coefficient for $\dot{U}$ of 0.41 is smaller than the one quoted in the text. As would be expected the substitution of a series without a loop for a series with a loop results in a reduction of the explanatory power of $\dot{U}$.

[3] Phillips, *loc. cit.*, p. 292, italics added. After making this observation, Phillips offers two possible explanations to account for the supposed change.

1960] THE RELATION BETWEEN UNEMPLOYMENT AND WAGE RATES 7

each cycle, the parameter d in equation (7) would diminish from cycle to cycle). In order to check this statement equation (6) was used to predict values for $\dot{W}$ and the differences between these predicted values and the observed values were plotted on a scatter diagram against $\dot{U}$.[1] A separate diagram was drawn and a straight line (i.e. $R_{(6)} = a + b\dot{U}$) was fitted for each cycle. The slope of the line is an index of the width of Phillips' loops. The values in Table 1 show that, in the cycle of 1893–1904, for example, a 100 per cent. increase in the percentage of the working force unemployed (e.g. from 3 per cent. unemployment to 6 per cent.) was associated with an observed figure for the rate of change of wage rates 2.2 per cent. below the value predicted by equation (6). The value of the r^2 indicates the importance of $\dot{U}$ as an additional explanatory variable in each cycle. An inspection of Table 1 reveals that there is considerable variation in the value of the coefficient "b" from cycle to cycle but that there is no clear

TABLE 1

STRAIGHT LINES RELATING RESIDUALS FROM EQUATION (6) TO THE RATE OF
CHANGE OF UNEMPLOYMENT

$R_6 = a + b\dot{U}$

Period([2])				b	r^2
1862–68	..	..	..	·017	·25
1868–79	..	..	..	·046	·91
1879–86	..	..	..	·015	·56
1886–93	..	..	..	·016	·91
1893–1904	..	..	..	·022	·59
1904–09	..	..	..	·011	·49

[1] Since the units in which all the variables are expressed are percentage points there is the possibility of confusion when residuals are calculated. To avoid such confusion it may be worthwhile defining all the variables and the residuals at this point:

(i) the rate of change of money wage rates at time $t \equiv$
$$\dot{W}_t \equiv \frac{W_{t+1} - W_{t-1}}{2W_t} . 100;$$

(ii) the percentage of the labour force unemployed at time $t \equiv U_t$;

(iii) the rate of change of unemployment at time $t \equiv$
$$\dot{U}_t \equiv \frac{U_{t+1} - U_{t-1}}{2U_t} . 100;$$

where W_t is the index of money wage rates. Since lagged variables are not used in this section, the time subscript t is dropped from all the variables in the equations.

(iv) the deviation of the observed value of $\dot{W}$ from the value predicted from equation $n \equiv R_n \equiv \dot{W}_o - \dot{W}_{en}$ where o stands for observed, and en for estimated, from equation n. R_n is always expressed in original units which, in the case of $\dot{W}$, are percentage points. Thus a residual of $+1$ per cent. might mean that the actual $\dot{W}$ was 3 per cent. while the estimated value was 2 per cent. R_n is always used as defined above and *never* as a proportional residual (i.e. R_n per cent. $\equiv \dfrac{\dot{W}_o - \dot{W}_{en}}{\dot{W}_{en}}$ is never used).

[2] To make the figures comparable with those of Phillips, the last year of each cycle has also been included as the first year of the subsequent cycle. The years 1910–13 are excluded because they do not constitute a complete cycle.

evidence that it becomes progressively smaller cycle by cycle. The cycle 1868–79 is unusual in that the deviations of the observed from the predicted values of $\dot{W}$ associated with any given level of $\dot{U}$ are three times as large as those associated with most other cycles. At the 5 per cent. probability level there is a significant difference between the coefficient b for the cycle 1868–79 and those for all other cycles, while the coefficients for the other cycles do not differ significantly from one another. Thus there is some evidence that the loop for 1868–79 is significantly wider than all the other loops, while there is no evidence of significant variations in widths of loop between the other cycles. A hasty comparison of the loop for the period 1868–79 with those that came afterwards may have led Phillips to the erroneous conclusion that the loops were getting progressively narrower.[1]

We must conclude therefore that there is no clear evidence in favour of the hypothesis that $\dot{U}$ is a variable whose importance was diminishing over the period. There is thus no need to attempt the sort of explanation given by Phillips.

3. *Consideration of effects of changes in the cost of living as an additional explanatory variable*

Phillips advanced the hypothesis that cost of living adjustments affect money wage rates with a threshold effect. If wage rates would have risen by X per cent. in the absence of any changes in the cost of living, then an increase of up to X per cent. in the cost of living will have no effect on wages " . . . for employers will merely be giving under the name of cost of living adjustments part of the wage increases which *they would in any case have given as a result of their competitive bidding for labour* ".[2] If, however, the cost of living rises by *more than X per cent.*, then this will also cause wages to rise by more than X per cent., i.e., by more than they otherwise would have done. This implies that the outcome of the wage bargain is unaffected by any change in the cost of living unless it actually threatens to reduce real wages, so that active and at least partially successful attempts must be made to push up money wage rates in response to price level changes that actually threaten to lower real wages. It also implies, however, either that unions passively accept any change in the price level which threatens to take away anything less than 100 per cent. of the increase in real wages that could have resulted from a rise in money wages, or that any attempts to resist such losses are totally frustrated by employers. This behaviour may seem intuitively implausible but it is necessary to see if the data provide any evidence for it.

---

[1] The same experiment was made relating $\dot{U}$ to the residuals from Phillips' own equation ($R_{(2)}$) with similar results to those given in the text. Thus the rejection of Phillips' hypothesis is not the result of the adoption of a new equation.

[2] Phillips, *loc. cit.*, p. 284, italics added. Phillips gives no reason for believing that cost-of-living adjustments operate in this manner.

1960] THE RELATION BETWEEN UNEMPLOYMENT AND WAGE RATES   9

In order to test Phillips' hypothesis two series were computed. First, the residuals $R_{(8)}$ were calculated. This series showed whether actual money wage rates had risen by more or by less than the amount associated with the existing levels of U and $\dot{U}$. The second series was the change in the real wage rate which was computed by adjusting the change in the money wage rate for the change in the retail price index.[1] A scatter diagram was then drawn relating the residuals, $R_{(8)}$, to the change in the real wage rate. The Phillips hypothesis predicts that when the real wage actually fell, the observed rise in money wage rates would be greater than the predicted rise, but it says nothing about what happens when the real wage rate rises.

In the period under consideration there were fifteen years in which the real wage fell (i.e. when the cost of living increase from the previous year to the present one was more than the increase in money wage rates). In only five of these years was the increase in money wage rates more than that predicted from the equation relating $\dot{W}$ to U and $\dot{U}$, and in none of these years was the deviation more than one half of 1 per cent.[2] In other words, of those years in which the real wage fell there was not one in which the money wage rate rose by more than one half of 1 per cent. more than was predicted by equation (8). In ten of the years in which the real wage fell the rise in money wage rates was *less* than that predicted by equation (8). Thus we must conclude that the evidence does not support Phillips' hypothesis that the cost of living affects wage rates only with a threshold effect.[3]

The rejection of Phillips' hypothesis suggests that it may be desirable to consider a simpler cost of living hypothesis. This hypothesis is that the outcome of the wage bargain is affected simply by the *change* in the cost of living, that an increase in the cost of living makes trade unions more aggressive in demanding increases and employers and arbitrators more willing to grant them, while a decrease in the cost of living acts in the reverse direction. This hypothesis predicts simply that deviations of actual wage increases from those predicted by equation (8) would be associated with the change in the cost of living index, increases in the cost of living being associated with positive deviations and decreases with negative deviations.

As a first check on this hypothesis the residuals from equation (8) were plotted against the percentage change in the cost of living index. In 37 of the 52 years under consideration the residual, R_8, was not more than 1 per cent $(-1 < R_8 < +1)$. Of the eight years in which

[1] The index used was the retail price index taken from Phelps Brown-Hopkins, *loc. cit.*

[2] The same experiment was made, using Phillips' equation (2), to estimate the values of $\dot{W}$, and the results were substantially the same as those reported in the text.

[3] One other possibility is that there might be a time lag in this process so that decreases in the real wage rate at year t would be followed by abnormally high increases in money wage rates in year $t+1$. The one year lag, however, produces results comparable to those quoted in the text.

there was a positive residual of more than 1 per cent ($R_8 > +1$), six were years in which the cost of living rose. Of the eight years in which there was a negative residual greater than 1 per cent ($R_{(8)} < -1$), seven were years in which the cost of living fell while only one was a year in which the cost of living rose. This suggested that, if there was any relation between cost of living changes and wage rate changes, it was a simple one, $\dot{W}$ being related in a straightforward manner to changes in the cost of living. The degree of scatter was, however, very large; there were, for example, eight years in which the cost of living changed by more than 2 per cent. while the actual wage rate change was within half of 1 per cent. of the value predicted by equation (8).

In order to check further on the quantitative significance of cost of living changes as an additional explanatory variable, equation (8) was amended by adding a term for the percentage change in the cost of living index. The equation then became

$$\dot{W} = a + bU^{-1} + cU^{-2} + d\dot{U} + e\dot{P} \quad \dots \dots \dots \dots \dots \dots \quad (9)$$

where $\dot{P}$ is the percentage change in the cost of living index,[1] $\dot{P}_t \equiv \dfrac{P_{t+1} - P_{t-1}}{2P_t} \cdot 100$. When fitted to the data for the years 1862 to 1913 this becomes:

$$\dot{W} = -1.21 + 6.45U^{-1} + 2.26U^{-2} - .019\,\dot{U} + .21\dot{P} \quad \dots \quad (10)$$

A comparison of equations (8) and (10) shows that the addition of a cost of living variable causes the curve relating $\dot{W}$ to U (when $\dot{U} = \dot{P} = O$) to shift upwards for levels of U greater than 3 per cent. and less than 1 per cent., while, between 1 and 3 per cent., the curve shifts slightly downwards. The (small) coefficient of $\dot{P}$ indicates that an increase of almost 5 per cent. in the cost of living is associated with an increase in money wage rates of only 1 per cent. Finally, the R^2 for this relation is 0.85 while the squared partial correlation coefficient for $\dot{P}$ is 0.17, indicating that 17 per cent. of the variance in $\dot{W}$ which remains after allowing for U and $\dot{U}$ can be removed by associating $\dot{W}$ with $\dot{P}$.[2]

---

[1] $\dot{P}_t \equiv \dfrac{P_t - P_{t-1}}{\frac{1}{2}(P_t + P_{t-1})}$ was tried as an alternative cost of living variable thus introducing a six-months' time lag on cost of living adjustments. The results were broadly similar, but the correlations slightly lower.

[2] The standard error of estimate of $\dot{W} = \cdot 86$, while standard errors for the regression coefficients are $b = 2 \cdot 12$, $c = 2 \cdot 13$, $d = \cdot 004$, $e = \cdot 07$. All of the partial correlation coefficients are significant at the 5 per cent. level and there is no evidence of significant auto-correlation in the $\dot{W}$ residuals for time lags of one to four periods at the 5 per cent. probability level. The size of the standard errors for b and c may be misleading because quite large changes can be made in these coefficients without causing large shifts in the curve relating $\dot{W}$ to U.
The comparable relations without the Bowley substitution for 1881–85 are as follows:

$$\dot{W} = -0 \cdot 94 + 4 \cdot 92U^{-1} + 3 \cdot 66U^{-2} - \cdot 016\dot{U} + 0 \cdot 20\dot{P},$$

$r^2 = 0 \cdot 82$.

Finally, it was desired to see if $\dot{P}$ could be an alternative explanatory variable to either U or $\dot{U}$. The most plausible hypothesis here seemed to be that $\dot{U}$ and $\dot{P}$ might be very highly correlated since retail prices would tend to rise on the upswing of a trade cycle and fall on the downswing. Thus the loops relating $\dot{W}$ to $\dot{U}$ might be merely a reflection of cost of living changes over the cycle. There is in fact very little relation between $\dot{U}$ and $\dot{P}$; the squared coefficient of correlation between $\dot{U}$ and $\dot{P}$ is only 0.19. In order to see which is the better explanatory variable, $\dot{U}$ or $\dot{P}$, equation (9) was amended by dropping the term for $\dot{U}$, thus producing:

$$\dot{W} = -.90 + 5.23U^{-1} + 3.20U^{-2} + .37\dot{P} \quad \dots\dots\dots\dots (11)$$

R^2 for this relation is 0.76. The squared partial correlation coefficient for $\dot{P}$ is .33, which compares with .50 for $\dot{U}$ when the effect of U is already allowed for. This indicates that $\dot{P}$ has only about two-thirds the explanatory value of $\dot{U}$ when they are considered as alternative variables to be added to the effect of U. The other possible situation would be to use $\dot{P}$ as the sole explanatory variable so that $\dot{P}$ would be an alternative for U. A linear relation between $\dot{W}$ and $\dot{P}$ produced the equation $\dot{W} = 1.14 + .55\dot{P}$ and $r^2 = 0.27$.

4. *The special explanation of 1893–96*

Phillips singled these years out for a special *ad hoc* explanation, apparently believing that the residuals were especially large or particularly significant in these years. He suggested that this could be accounted for by the growth of employers' federations in the 1890's and resistance to trade union demands from 1895 to 1897. Whatever may have been the industrial history of the period, there is no empirical evidence of *exceptional* downward pressure on wages. Estimated values for the change in money wage rates were calculated from equation (10) for the period 1894–96. The wage rate change in 1894 was actually one-third of 1 per cent. higher than the change predicted from equation (10); in 1895 it was only one-third of 1 per cent. less than that predicted by the equation, while in 1896 the actual rise (1 per cent.) was only eight-tenths of 1 per cent. less than the predicted rise (1.87 per cent.). Such very small deviations of the actual from the predicted values can hardly be regarded as significant; larger deviations than that occurring in 1896 were observed in no less than 21 of the 52 years under consideration. We must conclude, therefore, that there is no need for a special explanation of the observed events of 1893–96 which in fact conformed quite closely to the general pattern of the whole period.

5. *Conclusions*

(i) There is a significant relation between the rate of change of money wage rates on the one hand and the level of unemployment and its rate of change on the other. Over 80 per cent. of the variance in money wage rates over the period 1862–1913 can be associated with these two variables, U and $\dot{U}$. (ii) The Phillips hypothesis that the influence of the rate of change of unemployment has diminished over the period is rejected. (iii) The Phillips hypothesis that the cost of living enters with a threshold effect is rejected. There seems to be some evidence in favour of a simple (but rather weak) relation between changes in the cost of living and changes in money wage rates. (iv) There is no evidence of a *need* for any special explanation of the years 1893–96.

II

THE MODEL[1]

The analysis reported in Section I shows that there is a significant relation between $\dot{W}$, U, and $\dot{U}$, and it is now necessary to construct a theoretical model that will satisfactorily account for the relationship. It is necessary to take this step for at least three reasons. First, the relation between $\dot{W}$, U, and $\dot{U}$ is open to serious misinterpretation, and such misinterpretations can be prevented only when the model which underlies the relation is fully specified. Second, if the relation ceases to hold, or changes, and we have no model to explain it, we can only say " the relation has ceased to hold " or " the relation has changed " and we will have learned nothing more than this. If we have a model explaining the relationship, we will know the conditions under which the relation is expected to remain unchanged. Then, if a change occurs, the model will predict *why* this has happened and this prediction will give rise to further tests from which we can learn. Third, unless it is a very *ad hoc* one, the model will give rise to further testable predictions in addition to the relation between the three variables $\dot{W}$, U, and $\dot{U}$, and from the testing of these we will gain further relevant information.[2]

1. *The relation between $\dot{W}$ and U*

We shall consider this relationship, first, for a single market, and then for the whole economy, using lower-case letters to refer to the single market variables and capitals to refer to the corresponding macro-variables.

We might analyse the market for any commodity since the argument at this stage is quite general. Since, however, the subject of the

---

[1] I am particularly indebted to Mr. G. C. Archibald whose persistent criticisms of measurement without adequate theory have been to a very great extent responsible for the whole of Section II. He should in fact be regarded as joint author of part (1) of this section.

[2] The relation between $\dot{W}$, U and $\dot{U}$ is already known and the model will be specifically constructed to account for it. Thus to *test* the model against the existing observations of these variables is to conduct a " sun-rise test ", that is, to test the theory by checking some prediction which has a zero chance of being found wrong.

1960] THE RELATION BETWEEN UNEMPLOYMENT AND WAGE RATES 13

present article is the labour market we shall use the terminology appropriate to that market. The usual argument merely states that when there is excess demand, for example *ij* in Fig. 4, wage rates will rise, while, when there is excess supply, for example *mn* in Fig. 4, wage rates will fall. Nothing is said about the speed at which the adjustment takes place. We now introduce the dynamic hypothesis that the rate at which *w* changes is related to the excess demand, and specifically, the greater is the proportionate disequilibrium, the more rapidly will wages be changing.[1] Thus the hypothesis is $\dot{w} = f\left(\dfrac{d-s}{s}\right)$ which says that the speed at which wages change depends on the excess demand as a proportion of the labour force.[2] Fig. 5 illustrates a simple form of this relation, $\dot{w} = \alpha\left(\dfrac{d-s}{s} \cdot 100\right)$ according to which if we start with excess demand of, for example, $Oc\left(=\dfrac{gh}{w'g}\text{ in Fig. 4}\right)$, wages will be rising at the rate *cd*, but, if the excess demand increases to $Oa\left(=\dfrac{ij}{w''j}\text{in Figure 4}\right)$, wages will be rising at the rate *ab*.[3]

There are a number of advantages in including the relations illustrated in Fig. 5 in one's theory rather than having only the ones illustrated in Fig. 4. If it is known that both of the curves of Fig. 4 are shifting continuously (e.g. the demand curve due to cyclical variations in income, and the supply curve due to exogenous changes in the labour force), then no two price-quantity observations will lie on the same curve. It will then be difficult to discover by observation the *ceteris paribus* relations either between supply and price or between demand and price. For the relation in Fig. 5 to be observed it is necessary only that there be an unchanging *adjustment mechanism* in the market, i.e., that a given excess demand should cause a given rate of change of price *whatever the reason for the excess demand*—whether demand shift, a supply shift, or a combination of both. The rate of change of price can be observed directly and, to obtain the relation shown in Fig. 5, it is only necessary to know demand and supply *at the existing market price;* it is not necessary to know what would be demanded and supplied at other prices.

Now if excess demand for labour were directly observable there would be no need to go any further. Unfortunately, this is not the

---

[1] This is Phillips' hypothesis, *loc. cit.,* p. 283. It is also used extensively, for example, by Bent Hansen, *The Theory of Inflation,* London, 1951.

[2] If we were only concerned with a single market, the hypothesis could be expressed either in absolute or in proportional terms. Inter-market comparisons, however, require a proportionate measure. Consider the elasticity analogy. .

[3] The relationship might of course be non-linear, indicating that $\dot{w}$ increased at either an increasing or a decreasing rate as excess demand increased. The simpler linear relationship is, however, capable of explaining all of the observed phenomena and, in the absence of empirical evidence about the second derivative of $\dot{w}$, the simpler relationship is assumed.

case, at least over a large part of the period under consideration,[1] and it is necessary to relate excess demand to something that is directly observable, in this case the percentage of the labour force unemployed.

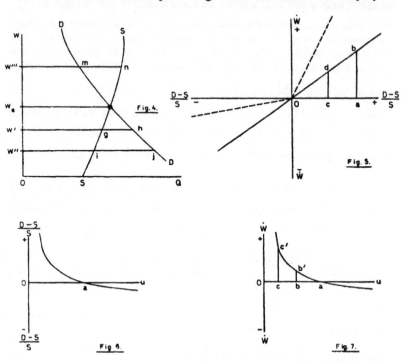

Fig.4.

Fig. 5.

Fig 6.

Fig. 7.

Fig. 6 shows the relation between $\dfrac{d-\,^{^*}s}{s}$ and the percentage of the labour force unemployed, u. When demand is equal to supply (wage rate Ow_e in Fig. 4), there will be jobs available for all those who wish to work at the going wage rate. This is *not* equivalent to saying that there will be no one unemployed, but rather that the number of unemployed will be matched by an equal number of unfilled vacancies. Given that workers change jobs for any reason whatever, and that a finite time is taken to change, zero excess demand must be accompanied by some positive amount of *frictional unemployment*. From this it follows that, when the wage rate is stable (at Ow_e in Fig. 4), there will be some quantity of unemployment (Oa in Fig. 6), the exact quantity being determined by the amount of movement and the time taken to move. Now consider points to the left of a in Fig. 6. The larger is the excess demand the easier will it be to find jobs, and the less will be the time taken in moving between jobs. Thus, unless there is a

[1] The difference between unfilled vacancies and unemployed workers might provide a reasonable direct measure of excess demand; but such data are not available for most of the period under consideration.

1960] THE RELATION BETWEEN UNEMPLOYMENT AND WAGE RATES 15

completely offsetting increase in numbers of persons moving between jobs, an increase in excess demand will cause a reduction in u. It is, however, impossible that u could be reduced below zero so that as $\dfrac{d-s}{s}$ approaches infinity, u must approach zero (or some small value >0) asymptotically.[1] Now consider points to the right of a. Any increase in excess supply brings an equal increase in the number of persons unemployed. Therefore, to the right of point a, there will be a linear relation between $\dfrac{d-s}{s}$ and u.[2]

Now in order to obtain the relation between the two observable quantities, $\dot{w}$ and u, we need merely combine Figs. 5 and 6 to obtain the relation illustrated in Fig. 7. The relation between $\dot{w}$ and $\dfrac{d-s}{s}$ (Fig. 5)

---

[1] The following is a simple model which will produce the postulated relationship:
Symbols: $L \equiv$ labour force $\equiv S$ in Fig. 4, $E \equiv$ number employed, $V \equiv$ number unemployed, $J \equiv$ total jobs available $\equiv D$ in Fig. 4, $N \equiv$ number of unemployed finding jobs, $X \equiv$ proportionate excess demand $\equiv \dfrac{J-L}{L} \equiv \dfrac{d-s}{s}$, α and β are two constants.

Assumptions: A constant proportion of those employed, αE, leave employment per unit of time; the number of unemployed who find jobs depends on the number looking for jobs and the number of jobs available: $N = \beta V (J-E)$.
A constant level of V requires: $\alpha E = \beta V (J-E)$.
But $E = L - V$, so $\alpha (L - V) = \beta V (J - L + V)$.

Expanding: $J = \dfrac{\alpha L}{\beta V} - V + L - \dfrac{\alpha}{\beta}$. But $X \equiv \dfrac{J-L}{L}$.

Eliminating J: $X = \dfrac{\alpha}{\beta V} - \dfrac{V}{L} - \dfrac{\alpha}{\beta L}$. $\quad \dots (I)$

Differentiating: $\dfrac{\partial X}{\partial V} = - \dfrac{\alpha}{\beta V^2} - \dfrac{1}{L} < 0, \dfrac{\partial^2 X}{\partial V^2} = \dfrac{\alpha}{\beta V} > 0.$

Therefore an increase in X is associated with a decrease in V but as X increases V falls at a decreasing rate and, from (I) above, as $X \to \infty$, $V \to 0$.

[2] There are some reasons for believing that, to the right of a the relation might have a slight curvature which would *increase* as u increased (i.e., $\dfrac{\partial w}{\partial u} < 0$ *and* $\dfrac{\partial^2 w}{\partial u^2} < 0$).

The excess supply of labour is $\dfrac{d-s}{s} \cdot 100$ while u is $\dfrac{d-s}{s} \cdot 100 + F$, where F is the proportion of the labour force frictionally unemployed. If F remains constant as excess supply increases, the relationship between $\dfrac{d-s}{s}$ and u will be linear. If, on the other hand, $F \to 0$ as $u \to 100$, then the line relating u to $\dfrac{d-s}{s}$ will *curve* slightly downwards, starting at $u = F$ when $\dfrac{d-s}{s} = 0$ and reaching $u = \dfrac{d-s}{s}$ when excess supply is 100 per cent. If F is small (say 5 per cent.), this curvature will be very slight. A second reason is that people in excess supply may not register as unemployed so that recorded u may not increase as fast as real excess supply. With the data used in this study it is impossible to distinguish between $\dfrac{\partial^2 \dot{w}}{\partial u^2} \lessgtr 0$ for high values of u. If, however, it were possible to demonstrate that $\dfrac{\partial^2 \dot{w}}{\partial u^2} > 0$, we should have to abandon the linear hypothesis illustrated in Fig. 5, at least for situations of excess supply.

16   ECONOMICA   [FEBRUARY

is assumed to be linear throughout. The relationship between $\dot{w}$ and u, however, is non-linear to the left of the point a because of the non-linear relation over that range between u and $\dfrac{d-s}{s}$ (Fig. 6) while the relation between w and u is linear to the right of a because of the assumed linear relation over that range between u and $\dfrac{d-s}{s}$ (Fig. 6).

The relation illustrated in Fig. 7 shows the *speed at which prices adjust to a disequilibrium* and we shall call it an *adjustment function*.

This relationship between $\dot{w}$ and u is an extremely simple one, and it holds considerable promise for empirical testing. The relation is, however, easily misinterpreted, and it may be worth considering some examples. Consider, first, a case in which a market is observed over three successive time periods at the points a, b' and c' in Fig. 7. This means that the demand and/or the supply curves have shifted over the period in such a way as to increase the disequilibrium in spite of the increase in wage rates. For example, the demand curve may have shifted so quickly to the right that the equilibrating movements in w were more than offset. Now consider a case in which the market is observed first at c', then at b' and finally at a. This is consistent with many market changes, two of which will be mentioned by way of illustration. First, both the demand and supply curves might be stable while the increase in wages restores equilibrium. Second, even though the demand curve is shifting to the right, the rate of increase in wages is fast enough to reduce the excess demand. When we observe either of these time sequences (a to b' to c' or c' to b' to a) we do not know what shifts in the curves have occurred but only that, in the first case, the shifts were such as to increase the disequilibrium in spite of equilibrating movements in w while, in the second case, any shifts that did occur either were not sufficient to offset the equilibrating changes in w or actually helped to remove the disequilibrium. If, to take a final example, the market is observed at b' over several successive periods, then we know that rightward shifts in demand and/or leftward shifts in supply were sufficient just to offset the equilibrating effects of changes in w, leaving excess demand constant.

It must be emphasised that knowledge of the shape of the adjustment function does not allow one to distinguish between *causes* of disequilibrium. Consider a market that is observed at a at time 0, at b' at $t=1$, at c' at $t=2$, at b' at $t=3$, and finally at a at $t=4$. All we know is that there was an increasing disequilibrium associated with ever faster increases in w, but that after a while the disequilibrium lessened until, at $t=4$, it is completely eliminated. Now these observations are consistent with either a rightwards shift in the demand curve, first at an increasing rate and then at a decreasing rate, or with a leftwards shift in the supply curve, indicating first a rapid withdrawal of labour supplies and then a slower withdrawal.

The relation also raises the problem of the influence of unions, but, in fact, tells us very little about their influence on the market processes. There are a number of points to notice here. First, the observation of the postulated relation is quite consistent with changes in wages caused by union-induced shifts in the labour supply curve. For, as illustrated in the previous paragraph, shifts in the supply curve would give rise to observations lying on the adjustment function. Second, unions might influence the speed of the dynamic adjustment illustrated in Fig. 5. They might, for example, cause a faster increase of wages in response to excess demand and a slower fall in response to excess supply than would otherwise occur. In other words, they might shift the adjustment function to the shape illustrated by the dotted line in Fig. 5.[1] If a completely stable relation between $\dot{w}$ and u is observed over time, all that can be said is that, whatever is the influence of the union on the market, this influence has remained *relatively stable* over that time period.

We must now consider the effect of aggregating a number of markets each with the same relation between $\dot{w}$ and u in order to obtain a relation between $\dot{W}$ (the rate of change of a national index of wage rates) and U (the percentage of the whole labour force unemployed). The main problems can be illustrated in the case of two markets, α and β, *with identical reaction functions* of the sort illustrated in Fig. 7. We assume for simplicity in exposition that the labour force is divided equally between the two markets so that

$$U = \frac{u_\alpha + u_\beta}{2} \quad \text{and} \quad \dot{W} = \frac{\dot{w}_\alpha + \dot{w}_\beta}{2}.$$

Consider, first, what would happen if both markets always had identical levels of unemployment. Since the percentage of the labour force unemployed would be the same in both markets, the national index of percentage unemployment would be the same as the figure for the two markets ($u_\alpha = u_\beta = U$). Also, since both markets would be showing identical rates of change of money wage rates, the national index would show the same rate of change ($\dot{w}_\alpha = \dot{w}_\beta = \dot{W}$). If the level of unemployment then were allowed to vary in exactly the same way in both markets (so that $u_\alpha = u_\beta$ and $\dot{w}_\alpha = \dot{w}_\beta$), it follows that the observed relation between $\dot{W}$ and U would be identical with the relation between $\dot{w}$ and u in each of the individual markets.

Consider, second, what would be observed if aggregate unemployment were held constant at say $0a$ per cent. $\left(\frac{u_\alpha + u_\beta}{2} = 0a\right)$, while the

---

[1] It is worth noting that, if they were successful in shifting the reaction function, they could be affecting the distribution of the national product even though they were completely unable to shift either the demand or supply curve and thus were unable to affect the position of *equilibrium*. By increasing the *speed of adjustment* when there is excess demand and by slowing it down when there is excess supply, they would ensure that, over any finite time period, the average wage rate would be higher than it would otherwise be.

B

distribution of this unemployment were varied as between markets (say $u_\alpha < u_\beta$). Since the relation between $\dot{w}$ and u is non-linear to the left of the point a, wages will be increasing faster in the market with excess demand (α) than they will be falling in the market with excess supply (β). Therefore the national index of wage rates will be rising $\left(\dot{W} = \dfrac{\dot{w}_\alpha + \dot{w}_\beta}{2} > 0 \right)$ in spite of the fact that the overall unemployment percentage remains unchanged at $0a$. Furthermore, as the distribution of U between the two markets is made less equal, $\dot{W}$ will take on larger and larger values since, when u_α is reduced by the same amount by which u_β is increased, $\dot{w}_\alpha$ will be increased by more than the amount by which $\dot{w}_\beta$ will be decreased.

Finally, consider what would happen if the two markets were kept in the same relation to each other (e.g. $u_\alpha = k \cdot u_\beta$, where $k < 1$) while the total level of employment $\left(\dfrac{u_\alpha + u_\beta}{2} = U \right)$ were allowed to vary. As U varies, a relation between U and $\dot{W}$ will be traced out. We will call this curve A_m for *macro-adjustment* curve and distinguish it from the curves a_i for *individual market adjustment curves*. By the reasoning in the last paragraph, this relation between $\dot{W}$ and U will lie above the individual market adjustment curves. Now consider increasing the degree of inequality between two markets (i.e. reduce the value of k). Because of the non-linearity in the individual market relations between $\dot{w}$ and u, this will increase $\dot{w}_\alpha$ by more than it will reduce $\dot{w}_\beta$. Therefore $\dot{W}$ for the whole economy will be increased. It should be noted, however, that because of the linear relation to the right of a, this upward displacement will not occur if there is excess supply in both markets (u_α and $u_\beta > 0a$).

This analysis leads to a number of important conclusions about the relation between the individual adjustment functions (the a_i's) and the macro-curve (A_m). (1) The macro-function can never lie below the individual market functions.[1] (2) The macro-function will coincide with the individual (identical) a_i's only if there is an identical percentage of the labour force unemployed in each market at all levels of aggregate unemployment. (3) Whenever there is any degree of inequality in the distribution of unemployment combined with excess demand in at least one market ($u < 0a$ for some markets), the macro-observations will lie above the individual market curves for corresponding levels of unemployment. (4) The greater is the degree of inequality between markets, the further will the macro-observations be above the individual market curves, and thus the greater will be the degree of upward displacement of the observed macro-

---

[1] If the a_i curves are not identical this conclusion reads: " The curve A_m can er lie below the " average " or typical curve a_i ".

function.[1] The macro-function relating W and U will be *linear* only if there is excess supply in all markets (i.e. if *all* markets are in the range where the relation between $\dot{w}$ and u is linear). In all other cases it will be non-linear.[2]

These conclusions have a number of interesting real-world implications: (1) If one wishes to predict the rate of change of money wage rates ($\dot{W}$), it is necessary to know not only the level of unemployment but also *its distribution between the various markets of the economy.* It follows immediately that the observed macro-function need not be accepted as immutable even if the individual functions are. The macro-relation may be shifted by a policy designed to change the degree of inequality existing between the individual markets; if the distribution of U were made more even the macro-curve would shift downwards, thus increasing the downward flexibility of the overall wage level. (2) Because of the upward displacement of the macro-observations, the observed macro-relation between $\dot{W}$ and U will always tend to overstate the upward flexibility and to understate the downward flexibility of wage rates to be found in a typical individual market. (3) Thus, given non-linear a_i's, if a stable macro-relation between $\dot{W}$ and U *is* observed over a large number of cycles, it is implied that in both the upswing and the downswing roughly the same degree of inequality of unemployment has existed as between cycles.[3] (4) Finally, great caution must be exercised in trying to infer from a statistically fitted relation between $\dot{W}$ and U what would happen to wage rates if unemployment were held constant at any level for a long time. If unemployment were held constant, we would expect the degree of inequality in its distribution between markets to change substantially. We would thus expect the macro-adjustment function to shift.[4]

2. *The relation between $\dot{W}$ and $\dot{U}$*

Phillips noted that the actual values for $\dot{W}$ tended to be above the curve relating $\dot{W}$ to U when U was falling, and below the curve when

[1] This conclusion can be upset only if the rate of response of wages to excess demand is slower than the rate of response to excess supply so that the a_i curves are kinked in the opposite way to the dotted function in Fig. 5.

[2] Thus the form of the function actually used (see equation 3) is to be understood as an approximation to the " true " curve which becomes linear (but with a negative slope) when there is excess supply in all markets. The difference between the $\frac{\partial^2 \dot{w}}{\partial u^2} = 0$ of the theory and the $\frac{\partial^2 \dot{w}}{\partial u^2} > 0$ of the fitted curve is slight over the range of u's studied, and the data is too crude to allow us to distinguish between the two.

[3] We would expect this to be true at least in some rough sense since certain sectors of the economy, e.g. the capital goods sectors, are typically hit much harder by fluctuations in the level of activity than are other sectors, e.g. the non-durable consumer goods sectors.

[4] It is an open question which way the curve would shift. It might be expected that a stable period would give time for the classical adjustment mechanism—movements of labour between markets and changes in relative prices—to reduce the degree of sectoral inequality. On the other hand, it might well be that cyclical fluctuations in employment aided the markets in adjusting to changes in demand and in techniques, and that the removal of these fluctuations would increase the average degree of inequality existing between markets.

U was rising. He therefore postulated a relation between the rate of change of wages, $\dot{W}$, and the rate of change of unemployment, $\dot{U}$, according to which $\dot{W}$ will be higher, for any given level of U, the larger is $\dot{U}$. The statistical analysis reported in Section I of this paper shows that a linear relation between $\dot{W}$ and $\dot{U}$ is capable of explaining about half of the variation in $\dot{W}$ not already associated with U alone. In the present section we must attempt a theoretical explanation of this relation.

Phillips argued that this relation was the result of a direct reaction of employers and workers to *changes* in the level of unemployment. He would seem to have had two possible reactions in mind. The first is that there will be more competitive bidding when $\dot{u}$ is negative than when it is positive, because in the former case there will be *net* hiring of labour while in the latter case there will be *net* dismissals. The second effect is the reaction of *expectations*, and hence of competitive bidding, to changes in u. Both of these explanations lead us to expect to find loops in a single labour market. It is most important to note that, to obtain a loop, it is necessary that something affect w without simultaneously affecting u. It is quite possible, however, that the factors mentioned by Phillips are unsatisfactory because they will produce changes in both $\dot{w}$ and u. We must, therefore, consider these factors carefully. Consider the first effect. When there is significant excess supply, more labour can be obtained at the going wage rate. As long as there is excess supply in a particular market throughout the period, there would seem to be no reason to expect there to be more competitive bidding on the average if excess supply falls from, say, 10 per cent. to 6 per cent., than if it rises, say, from 6 per cent. to 10 per cent. When there is significant excess demand, employers will be prepared to take on workers at the going wage rate if the labour were forthcoming. Assume that in January they are prepared to take on 10 per cent. more workers than they are employing at present but that demand steadily falls so that by December they are only prepared to take on 5 per cent. more than they are employing. There seems to be no reason to expect the situation just described to cause less competitive bidding than would occur when employers start by wanting 5 per cent. more labour in January and end by wanting 10 per cent. more in December. The second reason which Phillips apparently had in mind is that the loops might be the result of an expectation effect which makes employers bid harder when $\dot{U}$ is negative than when it is positive. Employers might vary the strength of their bidding not merely in response to present need but because of what they expect to need in the future. Assume a given demand for final goods and that the amount of labour required to produce these goods is such that 6 per cent. of the labour force would be unemployed and wages would be falling at 1 per cent. per annum. Assume, however, that the demand for goods is rising, and that employers increase their demands for labour in the expectation of needing more in the future. As a result of this change, unemployment will be lower than it otherwise would have been (say 4 per cent.) and the rate of fall of wages will be less than it otherwise would have been (say – 0.25 per cent.). There is, however, no loop; all that happens is that the point attained on the adjustment curve is different than would have been predicted solely on the basis of current demand for final goods; u is lower and w is higher than they otherwise would have been.

The difficulties encountered with these explanations in terms of a single market suggested that the origin of the loops might lie in the aggregation of the u's and the $\dot{w}$'s for a number of different labour markets each affected differently by fluctuations in the level of aggregate demand for final goods.[1]

Fig. 2 shows the observations of $\dot{W}$ and U for the twelve years 1868–79. The fitted relation between $\dot{W}$ and U lies in the middle of the observations, and this invites an interpretation of the " loops " as consisting of both positive and negative deviations from the relation $\dot{W}=f(U)$.[2] The theoretical argument of the present paper suggests, however, that this interpretation may be seriously misleading. The stable behavioural relation that we have postulated is the one between $\dot{w}$ and u in individual markets (see Fig. 7). The analysis of the previous section suggests that the macro-relation between $\dot{W}$ and U will *always be displaced upwards* from the individual market relation. The degree of upward displacement will be a function of the degree of inequality in the distribution of U between the various markets. This invites interpretation of the " loops " not as positive and negative deviations from a stable macro-relation between $\dot{W}$ and U, but as upward displacements from the stable single-market relations between w and u, the loops being produced by systematic variations in the degree of upward displacement.

In order to see how macro-observations of the type illustrated in Fig. 2 might arise, we may follow out the course of a hypothetical cycle in an economy with two imperfectly linked labour markets. Fig. 8 shows the (identical) relation between w and u in the two labour markets;[3] Arabic numerals refer to the positions at successive time periods in the two markets, while the crosses with Roman numerals show the corresponding aggregate observations that will be generated.

---

[1] The hypothesis actually offered is by no means an untestable alibi. On the contrary, it leads to a number of testable hypotheses, other than the relation between $\dot{W}$ and $\dot{U}$, that are of considerable interest. If the hypothesis stands up to these further tests it may be regarded as an interesting one. If it is refuted by these tests we shall learn from *the way in which it is refuted* much more about the conditions which must be fulfilled by its successor.

[2] Cf. Phillips, *loc. cit.*, p. 290.

[3] The assumption that the relations between w and u are identical in the two markets is relaxed later in the analysis.

22   ECONOMICA   [FEBRUARY

Assume that the economy begins in a period of depression with heavy unemployment in one market (*a*) and lighter unemployment in the second market (*b*). The cross I indicates the percentage of the total labour force unemployed and the rate of change in a national

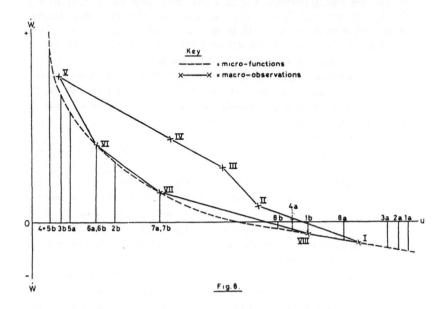

Fig. 8.

index of wage rates that will be observed. Now assume that a recovery starts, and that it is at first mainly centred in market *b*. As soon as excess demand occurs in market *b*, wage rates will begin to rise, although *U* for the whole economy is still high as a result of the heavy unemployment in market *a* (periods 2 and 3). As the excess demand in market *b* grows, the macro-observations will trace out a relation similar to that of the curve for market *b* but displaced to the right because of the influence of the heavy unemployment in market *a*. When market *a* begins to recover rapidly, *U* for the whole economy will fall rapidly but there will not be a further large increase in $\dot{W}$ until serious excess demand develops in market *a*. If both markets should reach the same level of excess demand, the macro-observations will lie on the micro-curve. Now assume a fall in activity in both markets. If U rises more or less uniformly in both markets, the observations of $\dot{W}$ in the downswing will lie near the micro-curves and, therefore, well below those for corresponding U's on the upswing. If the downswing comes before the same degree of excess demand is achieved in both markets, then the macro-observations for the down-swing will lie above what they would be if the equality of excess demand had been achieved.

The " loops " can thus be accounted for on the hypothesis that the recovery affects different markets at different times while the fall in effective demand is, at least during the early stage of the recession, more evenly distributed.[1] Another way of making the same point is to say that the hypothesis requires that time lags are greater in the upswing than in the downswing. If a fall in demand in one market causes a fall in demand in other markets with a time lag of only a few months, then all markets will be observed to decline more or less together. If, on the other hand, there is a longer time lag before an increase in demand in one market is transmitted to other markets then all markets will not recover together and there will be a greater degree of sectoral inequality in unemployment in the early upswing than in the early downswing.[2]

This analysis points a general warning against the procedure of accepting statistically fitted relations without relating them to models of *market behaviour*. We have already seen that the data is consistent with the hypothesis that there is an association between $\dot{W}$ and $\dot{U}$ but it will be noted that, if a relation $\dot{W}=f(U)$ were fitted to the macro-observations of Fig. 8, the curve would go through the centre of the loop and thus be displaced upwards from the stable micro-adjustment functions. The observed macro-curve relating $\dot{W}$ and U goes through the centre of most of the " loops " and therefore gives the average relation between $\dot{W}$ and U, *given the degrees of inequality in excess demand that have in fact been experienced*. The macro-curve will thus be useful for prediction providing that the same sort of inter-market inequalities continue to occur. Great care must be taken in using the curve to predict what would happen if the level of U were held constant for some time for, if this were done, the degree of inter-market inequality in excess demand would be expected to change considerably.[3]

---

[1] This would be true if, for example, the consumer-goods industries recovered first while the capital-goods sector did not recover until significant excess demand had developed in the consumer industries; while, on the other hand, when demand fell in one sector demand also fell in the other with less than a one year time lag.

[2] It may be objected that the assumption of identical relations between w and u greatly restricts the applicability of the model. This is not so. It has been shown in the text that varying degrees of sectoral inequalities in the distribution of unemployment (for which there is some empirical evidence) is a *sufficient* condition for the generation of the loops. If the loops are explained as a phenomena of aggregation then inequality in distribution is also a *necessary* condition. If for any level of U, u_{α} and u_{β} always bear the same relation to each other there will be unique relation between $\dot{W}$ and U for any relations: $\dot{w}_{\alpha}=f_1(u_{\alpha})$ and $\dot{w}_{\beta}=f_2(u_{\beta})$. If different reaction functions (about which we have little empirical evidence) were superimposed onto the model in the text the only difference would be a change in the *shape of the macro-loop*.

[3] This would be particularly important in the middle range of U values, where all experience has been of rapidly changing level of U, and less important at extreme values where U has more often been stable at least for two or three years at a time.

III

THE PERIOD 1919–1957

Phillips' scatter diagram relating $\dot{W}$ to U for the period 1919–57 is reproduced here as Fig. 9.[1]   The diagram reveals very little relation between the level of unemployment and the rate of change of wages. Phillips argued, however, that there was evidence of a close relation between the two variables in certain periods.   He also argued that, in the period following the second world war, the relation between $\dot{W}$ and U was substantially the same as it had been in the period 1861–1913.   In the present section we will first consider the years 1919–58 as a single period and then consider the various sub-periods dealt with by Phillips.

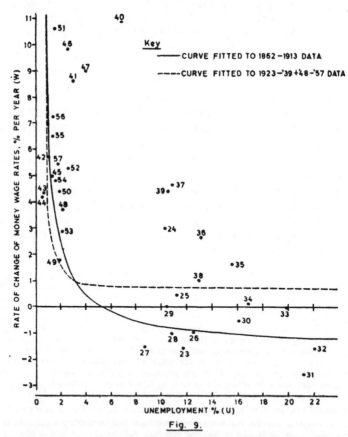

Fig. 9.

[1] The figures for the years after 1945 have been amended in an attempt to make them comparable with the earlier figures. See section (5) below. The extreme values for 1919–22, are not included as the scale would have to be drastically reduced if they were. The $\dot{W}$ values are as follows: 1919 (+28·6), 1920 (+2·5), 1921 (−25·0), 1922 (−19·1).

When considering this period there are three major hypotheses that may be worth testing: (i) that the changes in money wage rates continue to be explained mainly by changes in U, $\dot{U}$, and $\dot{P}$; (ii) that the relative explanatory power of these three independent variables is unchanged; and (iii) that the exact relation between $\dot{W}$, U, $\dot{U}$, and $\dot{P}$ is unchanged so that equation (10) which was fitted to the years 1862–1913, predicts accurately the experience of this period. The first hypothesis is in fact borne out by the data but the second and third are refuted.[1]

1. *The years 1920–39 and 1947–57*[2]

The curvilinear relation between $\dot{W}$ and U described by equation (3) was first fitted to the data for this period. R^2 for this relation is 0.28 which indicates that only a low proportion of the variance in $\dot{W}$ can be accounted for by variations in U. Next the variables $\dot{U}$ and $\dot{P}$ were added (i.e., equation 9 was fitted to this data) and the R^2 increased to 0.88. The squared partial correlation coefficients for this relation are $U=0.06$, $\dot{U}=0.05$, and $\dot{P}=0.83$ which indicate that $\dot{P}$ is the most important of the three explanatory variables while U and $\dot{U}$ add practically nothing to the explanation of $\dot{W}$. Even more startling than the high partial correlation between $\dot{W}$ and $\dot{P}$ is the magnitude of the regression coefficient for $\dot{P}$. This has a value of 1.28, indicating that on the experience of the whole period a 1 per cent. rise in prices is associated with a rise in wages of more than 1 per cent.

There are, however, a few very extreme values for $\dot{W}$ in this period and their existence poses some serious problems. The variance in $\dot{W}$ over the period under consideration is 47.2 while, if the four years 1920, 1921, 1922 and 1947 are eliminated, the variance drops to 10.2.[3] Thus 13 per cent. of the years account for 78 per cent. of the variance in $\dot{W}$, and any explanatory variable which accounts for $\dot{W}$ in these four years will necessarily produce a high R^2 for the whole period

---

[1] The model used throughout the present paper is the simplest sort of " single-equation model ". This report is a part of a larger study in which simultaneous relations will be used. The single-equation model is probably justified as a first approximation especially where it is desired to try alternative explanatory variables, alternate specification of the lags, and alternative functional forms. The single-equation model does, however, introduce some serious biases into the estimates. The most serious error is likely to be on $\dot{P}$ which is the main variable affected by other parts of the system. It is easily shown, however, that the regression coefficient of $\dot{P}$ is biased upwards. Calculations taking what appear to be reasonable specification of the dependence of prices on wages, suggest that the bias may be of the order of 0.2 to 0.3 (so that the subsequent estimate of 0.69 for the coefficient of $\dot{P}$ should probably be more like 0.40 to 0.50).

[2] The periods of the two world wars plus the first post-war year (1914–19 and 1940–46) were omitted on the argument that a period of heavy war-time controls is not an appropriate period from which to infer the relations being studied.

[3] It is probably reasonable enough to eliminate 1920 and 1947 on the argument of the previous footnote. One is less certain about the years 1921 and 1922.

*irrespective of its ability to account for variations in $\dot{W}$ over the re-
maining years.* It is also true that the regression coefficient associated
with this variable will mainly reflect the relation between it and $\dot{W}$
over these four years. There is therefore good reason to mistrust the
regression coefficients calculated from a series containing a few such
very extreme values which must dominate the whole estimation procedure. For this reason the four extreme years were dropped from
the series and the various relations recalculated.

2. *The years 1923–39 and 1948–57*

The curve fitted to this period was of the form:[1]

$$\dot{W} = a + bU^{-1} + cU^{-4} + d\dot{U} + e\dot{P} \dots\dots\dots\dots\dots\dots (12)$$

which, when fitted to the data, gives

$$\dot{W} = +0.74 + 0.43U^{-1} + 11.18U^{-4} + 0.038\dot{U} + 0.69\dot{P} \dots (13)$$

R^2 for this relation is 0.91, while the squared partial correlation coefficients are $U = 0.38$, $\dot{U} = 0.30$ and $\dot{P} = 0.76$.[2]

There are a number of interesting things to note about these results.

(i) *The General Relation*: A very high proportion of the variance in
$\dot{W}$ can be associated with these variables.[3] Thus the hypothesis that
about the same proportion of the variance in $\dot{W}$ can be associated
with U, $\dot{U}$ and $\dot{P}$ as in the earlier period is consistent with the facts.

(ii) *The Variable $\dot{P}$*: The importance of $\dot{P}$ as an explanatory variable
has greatly increased compared with the pre-war period (a squared
partial correlation coefficient of 0.76 compared to 0.17). The regression coefficient for $\dot{P}$ has also increased greatly (0.69 compared to 0.21).
This indicates a substantial movement in the direction of a one-one
relation between changes in prices and changes in wages. This is an
extremely interesting change. The face-value interpretation is that
the demand and supply model of Section II accounts for less of the
variations in wage rates in the twentieth century than it did in the
nineteenth, while more of the twentieth-century variations can be
explained in terms of wages " chasing " prices or of prices chasing
wages.

(iii) *The Variable U*: The fitted relation between $\dot{W}$ and U has
changed substantially compared with the earlier period. The curve

[1] The curvature became much sharper in this period than it was in the nineteenth
century. If Phillips' curve (2) were fitted to the data the coefficient ୪ would have
been less than minus two. Thus the fixed coefficients on U had to be changed.
The relationship described by equation (12) is the same as that described by (10)
only the curvature is more marked.

[2] The standard error of estimate for $\dot{W}$ is 0·97, standard errors for the regression
coefficients are: $b = 2·10$, $c = 6·00$, $d = ·012$, $e = 0·08$. There is no evidence of
significant auto-correlation of the residuals for lags of one to three periods at the
5 per cent. probability level. Correlation of the " independent variables " is as
follows:

$$r^2 (U, \dot{U}) = 0·003; \quad r^2 (U, \dot{P}) = 0·47; \quad r^2 (\dot{U}, \dot{P}) = 0·09$$

[3] Corrected for degrees of freedom, the R^2 is 0·89.

relating these variables has pivoted about the 3 per cent unemployment level (see Fig. 9). The new curve lies above the old one for levels of U greater than 3 per cent. and below the old one for levels of U less than 3.[1] This indicates that the post–1922 experience was of less flexibility of wages in response to excess demand, whether positive or negative, than occurred in the pre–1914 period. It will also be noted that the asymptote in equation (13) is positive. This indicates that, on the *average experience* of the 1920's and the 1930's, high levels of unemployment are not in themselves associated with a reduction in wages. Here again the theory of Section II must be recalled and the qualification " given the degree of sectoral inequality in unemployment that then existed " be emphasised.

(iv) *The Variable $\dot{U}$*: Finally, we must note the interesting changes in the relation between $\dot{W}$ and $\dot{U}$. Comparing equations (13) and (10), we see that the regression coefficient for $\dot{U}$ has changed signs. This reveals that, on the average experience of the post-1922 period, other things being equal, times of falling unemployment were associated with lower $\dot{W}$'s than were times of rising unemployment. It would appear then that Phillips' loops have changed directions. Before considering a theoretical explanation of this experience, it is necessary to check the relation between $\dot{W}$ and $\dot{U}$ in various sub-periods in order to determine exactly what it is that has to be explained. The data were broken up into three time periods and the following equation was fitted to each period[2]

$$\dot{W} = a + bU + c\dot{U} + d\dot{P} \dots \dots \dots \dots (14)$$

The coefficients for $\dot{U}$ were as follows:

$$1923\text{--}29 = +1.91, \quad 1929\text{--}39 = -6.25, \quad 1948\text{--}57 = +3.28$$

Thus we see that, taken period by period, the experience of the 1930's agreed with that of the nineteenth century while that of the 1920's and 1950's did not.

We must now ask if this experience can be explained by our theory. Feeding this data into the theory, we obtain the testable predictions that in the 1930's the upswing was associated with increasing degrees of sectoral inequalities in unemployment as some markets recovered very much more rapidly than did others. On the other hand, in the 1920's and the 1950's, downswings in activity were accompanied by increases in sectoral inequalities, while upswings were associated with decreases. Here again the theory accounts for the observations by producing hypotheses that are clearly testable. These tests, which are being conducted, are beyond the scope of the present paper.

---

[1] When the curve is fitted without a cost of living variable [$\dot{W} = f(U, \dot{U})$], it shifts upwards from its pre-1914 position over its whole range, but when $\dot{P}$ is added the curve is found to pivot as described in the text.

[2] The range of variations in U within each of the three periods is such that a linear approximation to the relation between $\dot{W}$ and U is quite adequate. A similar disaggregation for the nineteenth century is summarised in Table 1.

These considerations point to the rejection of hypotheses (ii) and (iii) listed above. Hypothesis (ii), that the variables have had the same relative importance in explaining $\dot{W}$ in the periods before and since the first world war is refuted by the fact that the partial correlation coefficients relating $\dot{W}$ to each of the independent variables have changed considerably. Hypothesis (iii) is refuted by the fact that the regression coefficients have changed markedly.

In the following sections the period under consideration is broken up into three sub-periods. By comparing the predictions of equation (10) fitted to the period 1862–1913 with those of equation (13) fitted to the present period, we seek to determine how and when these relationships have shifted.

3. *The period 1920–29*

In the years 1920 and 1921, very large decreases in both the cost of living and money wage rates were experienced. When $\dot{W}$ for these years is predicted from equation (13) the errors are extremely large (a residual of 16.8 per cent. for 1921 and of 9.8 per cent. for 1922). This shows that the relation describing the remainder of the period (equation 13) is not a good description of these two years. This is mainly because the relation between $\dot{W}$ and $\dot{P}$ seems to be stronger in these two years than it is over the rest of the period.[1] In the years 1925 to 1929 the government attempted to check aggregate demand in order to reduce the price level. Unemployment stayed at about 10 per cent., while wage rates fell on the average less than 1 per cent. per year. Phillips makes the point that the results of this experiment could have been predicted quite accurately on the basis of the experience for 1861–1913. The average annual reduction in wage rates that in fact occurred over the five years 1925–29 was 0.60 per cent. The prediction for the annual average reduction made from the equation fitted to the 1862–1913 experience (equation 10) is 1.00 per cent. We must conclude, therefore, that there was no reason to be surprised at the very slow reduction in wage rates that actually occurred, and that the experience of the late 1920's seems to provide little evidence of diminished downward flexibility of wage rates. The measurements give strong support to Phillips' statement (*loc. cit.*, p. 295) that: " The actual results obtained, given the levels of unemployment which were held, could have been predicted fairly accurately from a study of the pre-war data, if anyone had felt inclined to carry out the necessary analysis."

4. *The period 1930–39*

The equation fitted to the pre–1914 data consistently underestimates the changes in wage rates over this period. In only three years, 1936,

[1] When $\dot{W}$ is estimated from the equation fitted to the years 1920–39 and 1947–57, the residuals are only 6·8 per cent. for 1921 and 1·8 per cent. for 1922. This shows how much the estimated relation is influenced by these extreme years.

1937 and 1939, does equation (10) not predict a fall in wage rates. The average annual predicted fall over the whole period is 0.54 per cent., while the average annual error $\Sigma/R_{10}/ \div n$ was 1.67 per cent. In fact, money wage rates rose from 1934 onwards and the average annual change in wage rates over the ten-year period was +0.99 per cent. Equation (13), on the other hand, predicts this result quite accurately at 0.89 per cent. Some of the errors in individual years are, however, quite large and the average annual error over the period is 0.74 per cent. We must conclude that there is evidence that $\dot{W}$ increased faster in the 1930's than in the pre–1914 period for comparable levels of U, $\dot{U}$, and $\dot{P}$.

It should also be noted that wages rose from 1934 onwards in spite of very high levels of unemployment (never less than 10 per cent. over the entire period). There are two probable causes of this experience. First, if we accept the results of the statistical analysis as showing an increased response of wages to changes in the cost of living, much of the rise in wages in the 1930's can be explained as a response to such changes (the average annual increase in the cost of living between 1934 and 1939 was 3.15 per cent.). If, however, the increase in wages due to cost of living changes is estimated from equation (13) and this amount deducted from the actual increase, the result is still positive.[1] Something further, then, is required to explain that part of the increase in wage rates not associated with $\dot{P}$. A second reason may be found in the degree of sectoral inequality in unemployment rates. The theory produces the testable hypothesis that from 1935 onwards there was sufficient excess demand in some markets to cause an increase in the national index of wage rates in spite of extremely large excess supplies in other markets.

5. The period 1948–57[2]

The following table shows the observed and the predicted changes in wage rates over the period.[3]

It will be noted that the average annual increase predicted from equation (13) agrees very closely with the observed annual average, while the average predicted from equation (10) considerably underestimates the observed figure. Considering the predictions from

---

[1] These corrected figures for $\dot{W}$ 1934 to 1939 are:
$$-0.62, \quad +0.22, \quad +0.13, \quad +2.68, \quad +0.13, \quad -0.98.$$

[2] A detailed study of this period is to be found in L. A. Dicks-Mireaux and J. C. R. Dow, " The Determinants of Wage Inflation: United Kingdom, 1946–56 ", *The Journal of the Royal Statistical Society*, 1959. These authors obtain a coefficient of wages on prices of approximately 0.50.

[3] The figures have been changed to make them comparable with the earlier ones. The increase in coverage after the second war has been mainly in groups with very low unemployment percentages. Thus the post-war figures are not comparable with the pre-war ones. Mr. Routh (*loc. cit.*, p. 367) estimates that the figures for U must be raised by a minimum of $12\frac{1}{2}$ per cent. in order to make them comparable with the earlier figures. In the present study the figure has been increased by 20 per cent. The most accurate adjustment probably lies somewhere between these two figures.

TABLE 2

Year	Observed $\dot{W}$	Estimated $\dot{W}$ equation 13	Error	Estimated $\dot{W}$ equation 10	Error
1948 ..	3·73	2·89	0·85	4·28	−0·54
1949 ..	1·82	3·58	−1·76	3·51	−1·69
1950 ..	4·40	5·71	−1·31	4·29	0·11
1951 ..	10·61	9·95	0·66	5·57	5·04
1952 ..	5·28	5·49	−0·21	2·76	2·52
1953 ..	2·90	2·49	0·41	3·37	−0·47
1954 ..	4·88	3·76	1·12	4·53	0·35
1955 ..	6·58	7·32	−0·74	5·92	0·66
1956 ..	7·31	6·87	0·44	4·80	2·51
1957 ..	5·50	5·19	0·31	3·09	2·41
Mean ..	5·30	5·33	0·78[1]	4·21	1·63[1]

equation (13), the large errors occur in the years 1949, 1950 and 1954. 1949–50 were the years of wage restraint, and the large errors shown in Table 2 indicate that over the two years wages rose much less than would have been expected from the experience of the rest of the period 1923–57. These large errors provide a measure of the effectiveness of the wage policy. In 1954, on the other hand, the increase in wage rates was more than 1 per cent. in excess of the value predicted from equation (13). We must conclude, therefore, that except for 1949 and 1950, there is evidence of a more rapid increase in wages in response to demand and prices in the period since the second world war than in the period prior to the first world war.

       ·   ·   ·   ·

Phillips used his curve relating $\dot{W}$ to U to predict the level of unemployment that would be compatible with stable prices and a 2 per cent annual increase in productivity (a little under 2½ per cent. according to Phillips). There are at least three very serious problems involved here. (i) The estimated value can be shifted a great deal by fitting curves of different types, by including additional variables and by excluding particular years. *Thus, although it might be held with a high degree of confidence that a significant and very interesting relation had been discovered, a very low degree of confidence might be attached at this stage to a particular estimate of the parameters.*[2] (ii) The theory outlined in Section II suggests that the fitted relation may not be a very good guide to the relation between $\dot{W}$ and U if U were to

     [1] Ignoring signs.

     [2] Mr. Routh in the article already cited has constructed some alternative series to the ones used by Phillips and has done some alternative correlations. He concludes (p. 314): " I have shown that there are other equations, in some ways more valid, that would give different results." To my mind, the remarkable thing is not that Mr. Routh is able to get different results, but that the differences are so slight for all the possible variations that he suggests (see, for example, his Diagram I, p. 311). He also appears to be rather uncritical in assessing the significance of his possible variations. For example, he suggests a possible alternative to the series used by Phillips for 1948–57 and concludes " The points in Professor Phillips' Fig. ii, if row 2 (Routh's series) were substituted for row 1 (Phillips' series), would

remain substantially unchanged for a long time. (iii) A satisfactory theoretical explanation (together with independent tests) would be needed of the high correlation between $\dot{W}$ and $\dot{P}$. Until more is known about the causal links between $\dot{W}$ and $\dot{P}$ it is very dangerous to argue as if either of these variables were independent of the other.[1]

The analysis given in this paper has considerable bearing on the controversy about the causes of inflation. There are a number of points to be noted here. Phillips clearly considered a high correlation between $\dot{W}$ and U as evidence in favour of a demand-pull as against a cost-push hypothesis. This is not the occasion to state these hypotheses in sufficient detail to make them testable. However, the theory outlined in Section II suggests that there are versions of the cost-push hypothesis which are compatible with this relation.[2] The present study does, however, seem to refute the extreme version of the cost-push *spiral* which envisages an unstable situation in which wages and prices chase each other in a non-covergent cycle. This theory predicts a one-one relation between changes in prices and changes in wages, and the present coefficient of 0.69 would, if correct, refute the theory. On the other hand, it must be noted that the considerable increase in the coefficient attached to $\dot{P}$ indicates a very much closer association between changes in prices and changes in wages after the first world war than before it. Only a very much more detailed analysis than that conducted here could attempt to sort out the direction of the causation between $\dot{P}$ and $\dot{W}$. The analysis so far conducted is, however, not inconsistent with the hypothesis that there is a strong feed-back from price changes to wage changes with a great deal *but not all* of the rise in wages being attributed to wages chasing prices.

In my opinion it would be a serious mistake to try to judge between cost-push and demand-pull hypotheses solely, or even mainly, on the basis of the present paper although the material presented here is relevant evidence. The conclusions of this analysis would seem to be much more important for economic theory than for *immediate* policy issues. At this stage the numerical values of any of the parameters is not so important; what is important is the possibility of measuring and testing the type of dynamic relation used here, and of building up a theory that will, as ours already has done, suggest further hypotheses, the testing of which will in turn suggest further improvements in the theory.

The London School of Economics.

no longer ' lie closely along a smooth curve which coincides almost exactly with the curve fitted to the 1861–1913 data ' (p. 306)." This is just not correct. Consider the deviations of the two series from Phillips' curve. The standard deviation of the residuals for Routh's series are 1·6 and for Phillips 1·9, while the mean deviations are 1·4 for Routh and 1·1 for Phillips. We must conclude therefore that there is very little between the two series as far as lying on the curve is concerned.

[1] When policy decisions must be made they have, of course, to be based on the best evidence available at the moment. A premature application to policy can, however, easily discredit a hypothesis that is potentially very fruitful.

[2] See pp. 16 and 17.

[15]

ECONOMETRIC POLICY EVALUATION: A CRITIQUE

Robert E. Lucas, Jr.

1. Introduction

The fact that nominal prices and wages tend to rise more rapidly at the peak of the business cycle than they do in the trough has been well recognized from the time when the cycle was first perceived as a distinct phenomenon. The inference that permanent inflation will therefore induce a permanent economic high is no doubt equally ancient, yet it is only recently that this notion has undergone the mysterious transformation from obvious fallacy to cornerstone of the theory of economic policy.

This transformation did not arise from new developments in economic theory. On the contrary, as soon as Phelps and others made the first serious attempts to rationalize the apparent trade-off in modern theoretical terms, the zero-degree homogeneity of demand and supply functions was re-discovered in this new context (as Friedman predicted it would be) and re-named the "natural rate hypothesis".[1] It arose, instead, from the younger tradition of the econometric forecasting models, and from the commitment on the part of a large fraction of economists to the use of these models for quantitative policy evaluation. These models have implied the existence of long-run unemployment-inflation trade-offs ever since the "wage-price sectors" were first incorporated and they promise to do so in the future although the "terms" of the trade-off continue to shift.[2]

This clear-cut conflict between two rightly respected traditions — theoretical and econometric — caught those of us who viewed the two as harmoniously complementary quite by surprise. At first, it seemed that the conflict might be resolved by somewhat fancier econometric footwork. On the theoretical level, one hears talk of a "disequilibrium dynamics" which will somehow make money illusion respectable while going beyond the sterility of $\frac{dp}{dt} = k(p-p^e)$. Without underestimating the ingenuity of either econometricians or theorists, it seems to me appropriate to entertain the possibility that reconciliation along both of these lines will fail, and that one of these traditions is fundamentally in error.

The thesis of this essay is that it is the econometric tradition, or more pre-

---

[1] See Phelps et al. [31], Phelps' earlier [30] and Friedman [13].

[2] The earliest wage-price sector embodying the "trade-off" is (as far as I know) in the 1955 version of the Klein-Goldberger model [19]. It has persisted, with minimal conceptual change, into all current generation forecasting models. The subsequent shift of the "trade-off" relationship to center stage in policy discussions appears due primarily to Phillips [32] and Samuelson and Solow [33].

cisely, the "theory of economic policy" based on this tradition, which is in need of major revision. More particularly, I shall argue that the features which lead to success in short-term forecasting are unrelated to quantitative policy evaluation, that the major econometric models are (well) designed to perform the former task only, and that simulations using these models can, in principle, provide no useful information as to the actual consequences of alternative economic policies. These contentions will be based not on deviations between estimated and "true" structure prior to a policy change but on the deviations between the prior "true" structure and the "true" structure prevailing afterwards.

Before turning to details, I should like to advance two disclaimers. First, as is true with any technically difficult and novel area of science, econometric model building is subject to a great deal of ill-informed and casual criticism. Thus models are condemned as being "too big" (with equal insight, I suppose one could fault smaller models for being "too little"), too messy, too simplistic (that is, not messy enough), and, the ultimate blow, inferior to "naive" models. Surely the increasing sophistication of the "naive" alternatives to the major forecasting models is the highest of tributes to the remarkable success of the latter. I hope I can succeed in disassociating the criticism which follows from any denial of the very important advances in forecasting ability recorded by the econometric models, and of the promise they offer for advancement of comparable importance in the future.

One may well define a critique as a paper which does not fully engage the vanity of its author. In this spirit, let me offer a second disclaimer. There is little in this essay which is not implicit (and perhaps to more discerning readers, explicit) in Friedman [11], Muth [29] and, still earlier, in Knight [21]. For that matter, the criticisms I shall raise against currently popular applications of econometric theory have, for the most part, been anticipated by the major original contributors to that theory.[3] Nevertheless, the case for sustained inflation, based entirely on econometric simulations, is attended now with a seriousness it has not commanded for many decades. It may, therefore, be worthwhile to attempt to trace this case back to its foundation, and then to examine again the scientific basis of this foundation itself.

2. The Theory of Economic Policy

Virtually all quantitative macro-economic policy discussions today are conducted within a theoretical framework which I shall call "the theory of economic

---

[3]See in particular Marschak's discussion in [25] (helpfully recalled to me by T. D. Wallace) and Tinbergen's in [36], especially his discussion of "qualitative policy" in ch. 5, pp. 149-185.

policy", (following Tinbergen [35]). The essentials of this framework are so wide-ly known and subscribed to that it may be superfluous to devote space to their re-view. On the other hand, since the main theme of this paper is the inadequacy of this framework, it is probably best to have an explicit version before us.

One describes the economy in a time period t by a vector y_t of state varia-bles, a vector x_t of exogeneous forcing variables, and a vector ϵ_t of independent (through time), identically distributed random shocks. The motion of the econo-my is determined by a difference equation

$$y_{t+1} = f(y_t, x_t, \epsilon_t) \ ,$$

the distribution of ϵ_t, and a description of the temporal behavior of the forcing variables, x_t. The function f is taken to be fixed but not directly known; the task of empiricists is then to estimate f. For practical purposes, one usually thinks of estimating the values of a fixed parameter vector θ, with

$$f(y, x, \epsilon) \ \equiv \ F(y, x, \theta, \epsilon)$$

and F being specified in advance.

Mathematically, the sequence $\{x_t\}$ of forcing vectors is regarded as being "arbitrary" (that is, it is not characterized stochastically). Since the past x_t val-ues are observed, this causes no difficulty in estimating θ, and in fact simplifies the theoretical estimation problem slightly. For forecasting, one is obliged to in-sert forecasted x_t values into F.

With knowledge of the function F and θ, policy evaluation is a straight-forward matter. A _policy_ is viewed as a specification of present and future values of some components of $\{x_t\}$. With the other components somehow specified, the stochastic behavior of $\{y_t, x_t, \epsilon_t\}$ from the present on is specified, and func-tionals defined on this sequence are well-defined random variables, whose mo-ments may be calculated theoretically or obtained by numerical simulation. Sometimes, for example, one wishes to examine the mean value of a hypothetical "social objective function", such as

$$\sum_{t=o}^{\infty} \ \beta^t u(y_t, x_t, \epsilon_t)$$

under alternative policies. More usually, one is interested in the "operating char-acteristics" of the system under alternative policies. Thus, in this standard con-text, a "long-run Phillips curve" is simply a plot of average inflation – unemploy-

21

ment pairs under a range of hypothetical policies.[4]

Since one cannot treat θ as known in practice, the actual problem of policy evaluation is somewhat more complicated. The fact that θ is estimated from past sample values affects the above moment calculations for small samples; it also makes policies which promise to sharpen estimates of θ relatively more attractive. These considerations complicate without, I think, essentially altering the theory of economic policy as sketched above.

Two features of this theoretical framework deserve special comment. The first is the uneasy relationship between this theory of economic policy and traditional economic theory. The components of the vector-valued function F are behavioral relationships — demand functions; the role of theory may thus be viewed as suggesting forms for F, or in Samuelson's terms, distributing zeros throughout the Jacobian of F. This role for theory is decidedly secondary: microeconomics shows surprising power to rationalize individual econometric relationships in a variety of ways. More significantly, this micro-economic role for theory abdicates the task of describing the aggregate behavior of the system entirely to the econometrician. Theorists suggest forms for consumption, investment, price and wage setting functions separately; these suggestions, if useful, influence individual components of F. The aggregate behavior of the system then is whatever it is.[5] Surely this point of view (though I doubt if many would now endorse it in so bald a form) accounts for the demise of traditional "business cycle theory" and the widespread acceptance of a Phillips "trade-off" in the absence of any aggregative theoretical model embodying such a relationship.

Secondly, one must emphasize the intimate link between short-term forecasting and long-term simulations within this standard framework. The variance of short-term forecasts tends to zero with the variance of ϵ_t; as the latter becomes small, so also does the variance of estimated behavior of $\{y_t\}$ conditional on hypothetical policies $\{x_t\}$. Thus forecasting accuracy in the short-run implies reliability of long-term policy evaluation.

3. Adaptive Forecasting

There are many signs that practicing econometricians pay little more than lip-service to the theory outlined in the preceding section. The most striking is the indifference of econometric forecasters to data series prior to 1947. Within the theory of economic policy, more observations always sharpen parameter esti-

---

[4]See, for example, de Menil and Enzler [6], Hirsch [16] and Hymans [17].

[5]The ill-fated Brookings model project was probably the ultimate expression of this view.

mates and forecasts, and observations on "extreme" x_t values particularly so; yet even the readily available annual series from 1929-1946 are rarely used as a check on the post-war fits.

A second sign is the frequent and frequently important refitting of econometric relationships. The revisions of the wage-price sector now in progress are a good example.[6] The continuously improving precision of the estimates of θ within the fixed structure F, predicted by the theory, does not seem to be occurring in practice.

Finally, and most suggestively, is the practice of using patterns in recent residuals to revise intercept estimates for forecasting purposes. For example, if a "run" of positive residuals (predicted less actual) arises in an equation in recent periods, one revises the estimated intercept downward by their average amount. This practice accounts, for example, for the superiority of the actual Wharton forecasts as compared to forecasts based on the published version of the model.[7]

It should be emphasized that recounting these discrepancies between theory and practice is not to be taken as criticism of econometric forecasters. Certainly if new observations are better accounted for by new or modified equations, it would be foolish to continue to forecast using the old relationships. The point is simply that, econometrics textbooks not withstanding, current forecasting practice is <u>not</u> conducted within the framework of the theory of economic policy, and the unquestioned success of the forecasters should <u>not</u> be construed as evidence for the soundness or reliability of the structure proposed in that theory.

An alternative structure to that underlying the theory of economic policy has recently been proposed (in [3] and [5]) by Cooley and Prescott. The structure is of interest in the present context, since optimal forecasting within it shares many features with current forecasting practice as just described. Instead of treating the parameter vector θ as fixed, Cooley and Prescott view it as a random variable following the random walk

$$\theta_{t+1} = \theta_t + \eta_{t+1} ,$$

where $\{\eta_t\}$ is a sequence of independent, identically distributed random variables.

Maximum likelihood forecasting under this alternative framework ("adaptive regression") resembles "exponential smoothing" on the observations, with observations in the distant past receiving a small "weight" — very much as in

---

[6] See, for example, Gordon [14].

[7] A good account of this and other aspects of forecasting in theory and practice is provided by Klein [20]. A fuller treatment is available in Evans and Klein [9].

23

usual econometric practice; similarly, recent forecast errors are used to adjust the estimates. Using both artificial data and economic time series, Cooley and Prescott have shown (in [4]) that adaptive methods have good short-term forecasting properties when compared to even relatively sophisticated versions of the "fixed θ" regression model. As Klein and others have remarked, this advantage is shared by actual large-model forecasts (that is, model forecasts modified by the forecaster's judgment) over mechanical forecasts using the published versions of the model.[8]

Cooley and Prescott have proposed adaptive regression as a normative forecasting method. I am using it here in a positive sense: as an idealized "model" of the behavior of large-model forecasters. If the model is, as I believe, roughly accurate, it serves to reconcile the assertion that long-term policy evaluations based on econometric models are meaningless with the acknowledgment that the forecast accuracy of these models is good and likely to become even better. Under the adaptive structure, a small standard error of short-term forecasts is consistent with infinite variance of the long-term operating characteristics of the system.

4. Theoretical Considerations: General

To this point, I have argued simply that the standard, stable-parameter view of econometric theory and quantitative policy evaluation appears not to match several important characteristics of econometric practice, while an alternative general structure, embodying stochastic parameter drift, matches these characteristics very closely. This argument is, if accepted, sufficient to establish that the "long-run" implications of current forecasting models are without content, and that the short-term forecasting ability of these models provides no evidence of the accuracy to be expected from simulations of hypothetical policy rules.

These points are, I think, important, but their implications for the future are unclear. After all, the major econometric models are still in their first, highly successful, decade. No one, surely, expected the initial parameterizations of these models to stand forever, even under the most optimistic view of the stability of the unknown, underlying structure. Perhaps the adaptive character of this early stage of macro-economic forecasting is merely the initial groping for the true structure which, however ignored in statistical theory, all practitioners knew to be necessary. If so, the arguments of this paper are transitory debating points, obsolete soon after they are written down. Personally, I would not be sorry if this were the case, but I do not believe it is. I shall try to explain why, beginning with generalities, and then, in the following section, introducing examples.

[8]See Klein [20].

24

In section 2, we discussed an economy characterized by

$$y_{t+1} = F(y_t, x_t, \theta, \epsilon_t).$$

The function F and parameter vector θ are derived from decision rules (demand and supply functions) of agents in the economy, and these decisions are, theoretically, optimal given the situation in which each agent is placed. There is, as remarked above, no presumption that (F, θ) will be easy to discover, but it <u>is</u> the central assumption of the theory of economic policy that once they <u>are</u> (approximately) known, they will remain stable under arbitrary changes in the behavior of the forcing sequence $\{x_t\}$.

For example, suppose a reliable model (F, θ) is in hand, and one wishes to use it to assess the consequences of alternative monetary and fiscal policy rules (choices of $x_0, x_1, x_2, ...$, where $t = 0$ is "now"). According to the theory of economic policy, one then simulates the system under alternative policies (theoretically or numerically) and compares outcomes by some criterion. For such comparisons to have any meaning, it is essential that the structure (F, θ) not vary systematically with the choice of $\{x_t\}$.

<u>Everything we know about dynamic economic theory indicates that this presumption is unjustified.</u> First, the individual decision problem: "find an optimal decision rule when certain parameters (future prices, say) follow 'arbitrary' paths" is simply not well formulated. Only trivial problems in which agents can safely ignore the future can be formulated under such a vague description of market constraints. Even to obtain the decision rules underlying (F, θ) then, we have to attribute to individuals some view of the behavior of the future values of variables of concern to them. This view, in conjunction with other factors, determines their optimum decision rules. To assume stability of (F, θ) under alternative policy rules is thus to assume that agents' views about the behavior of shocks to the system are invariant under changes in the true behavior of these shocks. Without this extreme assumption, the kinds of policy simulations called for by the theory of economic policy are meaningless.

It is likely that the "drift" in θ which the adaptive models describe stochastically reflects, in part, the adaptation of the decision rules of agents to the changing character of the series they are trying to forecast.[9] Since this adaptation will be in most (though not all) cases slow, one is not surprised that adaptive

---

[9]This is not to suggest that all parameter drift is due to this source. For example, shifts in production functions due to technological change are probably well described by a random walk scheme.

methods can improve the short-term forecasting abilities of the econometric models. For longer term forecasting and policy simulations, however, ignoring the
systematic sources of drift will lead to large, unpredictable errors.

5. Theoretical Considerations: Examples

If these general theoretical observations on the likelihood of systematic
"parametric drift" in the face of variations in the structure of shocks are correct,
it should be possible to confirm them by examination of the specific decision
problems underlying the major components of aggregative models. I shall discuss
in turn consumption, investment, and the wage-price sector, or Phillips curve. In
each case, the "right hand variables" will, for simplicity, be taken as "exogenous"
(as components of $\{x_t\}$). The thought-experiments matching this assumption,
and the adaptations necessary for simultaneous equations, are too well known to
require comment.

5.1 Consumption

The easiest example to discuss with confidence is the aggregate consumption
function since, due to Friedman [11], Muth [28] and Modigliani, Brumberg and
Ando [2], [27], it has both a sound theoretical rationale and an unusually high
degree of empirical success. Adopting Friedman's formulation, permanent consumption is proportional to permanent income (an estimate of a discounted
future income stream),

$$(1) \qquad c_{pt} = k \, y_{pt} \; ;$$

actual consumption is

$$(2) \qquad c_t = c_{pt} + u_t \; ;$$

and actual, current income is

$$(3) \qquad y_t = y_{pt} + v_t \; .$$

The variables u_t, v_t are independent temporally and of each other and of y_{pt}.
An empirical "short-run" marginal propensity to consume is the sample moment corresponding to $\text{Cov}(c_t, y_t)/\text{Var}(y_t)$, or

$$k \, \frac{\text{Var}(y_{pt})}{\text{Var}(y_{pt}) + \text{Var}(v_t)} \; .$$

26

Now as long as these moments are viewed as subjective parameters in the heads of consumers, this model lacks content. Friedman, however, viewed them as true moments, known to consumers, the logical step which led to the cross-sectional tests which provided the most striking confirmation of his permanent income hypothesis.[10]

This central equating of a true probability distribution and the subjective distribution on which decisions are based was termed rational expectations by Muth, who developed its implications more generally (in [29]). In particular, in [28], Muth found the stochastic behavior of income over time under which Friedman's identification of permanent income as an exponentially weighted sum of current and lagged observations on actual income was consistent with optimal forecasting on the part of agents.[11]

To review Muth's results, we begin by recalling that permanent income is that constant flow y_{pt} which has the same value, with the subjective discount factor β, as the forecasted actual income stream:

$$(4) \qquad y_{pt} = (1-\beta) \sum_{i=0}^{\infty} \beta^i E(y_{t+i}|I_t)$$

where each expectation is conditioned on information I_t available at t.

Now let actual income y_t be a sum of three terms

$$(5) \qquad y_t = a + w_t + v_t \ ,$$

where v_t is transitory income, a is a constant, and w_t is a sum of independent increments, each with zero mean and constant variance. Muth showed that the minimum variance estimator of y_{t+i} for all i = 1,2,... is $(1-\lambda) \sum_{j=0}^{\infty} \lambda^j y_{t-j}$ where λ depends in a known way on the relative variances of w_t and v_t.[12]

---

[10]Of course, the hypothesis continues to be tested as new data sources become available, and anomalies continue to arise. (For a recent example, see Mayer [26]). Thus one may expect that, as with most "confirmed" hypotheses, it will someday be subsumed in some more general formulation.

[11]In [12], Friedman proposes an alternative view to Muth's, namely that the weight used in averaging past incomes (λ, below) is the same as the discount factor used in averaging future incomes (β, below). It is Muth's theory, rather than Friedman's of [12], which is consistent with the cross-section tests based on relative variances mentioned above.

[12]Let σ_v^2 be the variance of v_t and $\sigma_{\Delta w}^2$ be the variance of the increments of w_t, then the relationship is

$$\lambda = 1 + \frac{1}{2}\frac{\sigma_{\Delta w}^2}{\sigma_v^2} - \frac{\sigma_{\Delta w}}{\sigma_v}\sqrt{1 + \frac{1}{4}\frac{\sigma_{\Delta w}^2}{\sigma_v^2}} \ .$$

27

Inserting this estimator into (4) and summing the series gives the empirical consumption function

(6) $c_t = k(1-\beta)y_t + k\beta(1-\lambda) \sum_{j=0}^{\infty} \lambda^j y_{t-j} + u_t$.

(This formula differs slightly from Muth's because Muth implicitly assumed that c_t was determined prior to realizing y_t. The difference is not important in the sequel.)

Now let us imagine a consumer of this type, with a current income generated by an "experimenter" according to the pattern described by Muth (so that the premises of the theory of economic policy are correct for a single equation consumption function). An econometrician observing this consumer over many periods will have good success describing him by (6) whether he arrives at this equation by the Friedman-Muth reasoning, or simply hits on it by trial-and-error. Next consider <u>policies</u> taking the form of a sequence of supplements $\{x_t\}$ to this consumer's income from time T on. Whether $\{x_t\}$ is specified deterministically or by some stochastic law, whether it is announced in advance to the consumer or not, the theory of economic policy prescribes the <u>same</u> method for evaluating its consequences: add x_t to the forecasts of y_t for each $t > T$, insert into (6), and obtain the new forecasts of c_t.

If the consumer knows of the policy change in advance, it is clear that this standard method gives incorrect forecasts. For example, suppose the policy consists of a constant increase, $x_t = \overline{x}$, in income over the entire future. From (4), this leads to an increase in consumption of $k\overline{x}$. The forecast based on (6), however, is of an effect in period t of

$$(\Delta c)_t = k\overline{x} \left\{ (1-\beta) + \beta(1-\lambda) \sum_{i=0}^{t-T} \lambda^i \right\} \ .$$

Since this effect tends to the correct forecast, $k\overline{x}$, as t tends to infinity, one might conjecture that the difficulty vanishes in the "long run". To see that this conjecture is false, consider an exponentially growing supplement $x_t = \overline{x}a^t$, $1 < a < \frac{1}{\beta}$. The true effect in t-T is, from (1) and (4),

$$(\Delta c)_t = k\overline{x} \, \frac{(1-\beta)a^t}{1-a\beta} \ .$$

28

The effect as forecast by (6) is

$$(\Delta c)_t = k\bar{x} \; \{ (1-\beta) + \beta(1-\lambda) \sum_{j=0}^{t-T} (\frac{\lambda}{a})^j \} \; a^t.$$

Neither effect tends to zero, as t tends to infinity; the ratio (forecast over actual) tends to

$$(1-a\beta) \{ \; 1 \; + \; \frac{a\beta(1-\lambda)}{(1-\beta)(a-\lambda)} \; \}$$

which may lie on either side of unity.

More interesting divergences between forecasts and reality emerge when the policy is stochastic, but with characteristics known in advance. For example, let $\{x_t\}$ be a sequence of independent random variables, with zero mean and constant variance, distributed independently of u_t, v_t and w_t. This policy amounts to an increase in the variance of transitory income, lowering the weight λ in a manner given by the Muth formula. Average consumption, in fact and as forecast by (6), is not affected, but the variance of consumption is. The correct estimate of this variance effect requires revision of the weight λ; evidently the standard, fixed-parameter prediction based on (6) will again yield the wrong answer, and the error will not tend to vanish for large t.

The list of deterministic and stochastic policy changes, and their combination is inexhaustible but one need not proceed further to establish the point: for any policy change which is understood in advance, extrapolation or simulation based on (6) yields an incorrect forecast, and what is more, a correctibly incorrect forecast. What of changes in policy which are not understood in advance? As Fisher observes, "the notion that one cannot fool all of the people all of the time [need not] imply that one cannot fool all the people even some of the time."[13]

The observation is, if obvious, true enough; but it provides no support whatever for the standard forecasting method of extrapolating on the basis of (6). Our knowledge of consumption behavior is summarized in (1)-(4). For certain policy changes we can, with some confidence, guess at the permanent income recalculations consumers will go through and hope to predict their consumption responses

[13][10], p. 113.

with some accuracy. For other types of policies, particularly those involving deliberate "fooling" of consumers, it will not be at all clear how to apply (1)-(4), and hence impossible to forecast. Obviously, in such cases, there is no reason to imagine that forecasting with (6) will be accurate either.

5.2 Taxation and Investment Demand

In [15], Hall and Jorgenson provided quantitative estimates of the consequences, current and lagged, of various tax policies on the demand for producers' durable equipment. Their work is an example of the current state of the art of conditional forecasting at its best. The general method is to use econometric estimates of a Jorgensonian investment function, which captures all of the relevant tax structure in a single implicit rental price variable, to simulate the effects of alternative tax policies.

An implicit assumption in this work is that any tax change is regarded as a permanent, once-and-for-all change. Insofar as this assumption is false over the sample period, the econometric estimates are subject to bias.[14] More important for this discussion, the conditional forecasts will be valid only for tax changes believed to be permanent by taxpaying corporations.

For many issues in public finance, this obvious qualification would properly be regarded as a mere technicality. For Keynesian counter-cyclical policy, however, it is the very heart of the issue. The whole point, after all, of the investment tax credit is that it be viewed as temporary, so that it can serve as an inducement to firms to reschedule their investment projects. It should be clear that the forecasting methods used by Hall and Jorgenson (and, of course, by other econometricians) cannot be expected to yield even order-of-magnitude estimates of the effects of explicitly temporary tax adjustments.

To pursue this issue further, it will be useful to begin with an explicit version of the standard accelerator model of investment behavior. We imagine a constant returns industry in which each firm has a constant output-capital ratio λ. Using a common notation for variables at both the firm and industry level, let k_t denote capital at the beginning of year t. Output during t is λk_t. Investment during the year, i_t, affects next period's capital according to

$$k_{t+1} = i_t + (1-\delta)k_t \quad ,$$

---

[14]In particular, the low estimates of 'a' (see [15], Table 2, p. 400), which should equal capital's share in value added, are probably due to a sizeable transitory component in a variable which is treated theoretically as though it were subject to permanent changes only.

30

where δ is a constant physical rate of depreciation. Output is sold on a perfect market at a price p_t; investment goods are purchased at a constant price of unity. Profits (sales less depreciation) are taxed at the rate θ_t; there is an investment tax credit at the rate Ψ_t.

The firm is interested in maximizing the expected present value of receipts net of taxes, discounted at the constant cost of capital r. In the absence (assumed here) of adjustment costs, this involves equating the current cost of an additional unit of investment to the expected discounted net return. Assuming that the current tax bill is always large enough to cover the credit, the current <ins>cost</ins> of acquiring an additional unit of capital is $(1-\Psi_t)$, independent of the volume of investment goods purchased. Each unit of investment yields λ units of output, to be sold next period at the (unknown) price p_{t+1}. Offsetting this profit is a tax bill of $\theta_{t+1}[\lambda p_{t+1} - \delta]$. In addition, $(1-\delta)$ units of the investment good remain for use after period $t+1$; with perfect capital goods markets, these units are valued at $(1-\Psi_{t+1})$. Thus letting $E_t(\cdot)$ denote an expectation conditional on information up to period t, the expected discounted return per unit of investment in t is

$$\frac{1}{1+r} E_t[\lambda p_{t+1}(1-\theta_{t+1}) + \delta\theta_{t+1} + (1-\delta)(1-\Psi_{t+1})].$$

Since a change in next period's tax rate θ_{t+1} which is not anticipated in t is a "pure profit tax", θ_{t+1} and p_{t+1} will be uncorrelated. Hence, equating costs and returns, one equilibrium condition for the industry is

$$(7) \qquad 1-\Psi_t = \frac{1}{1+r}\{ \lambda E_t(p_{t+1})[1-E_t(\theta_{t+1})] + \delta E_t(\theta_{t+1})$$

$$+ (1-\delta)[1-E_t(\Psi_{t+1})] \}.$$

A second equilibrium condition is obtained from the assumption that the product market is cleared each period. Let industry demand be given by a linear function, with a stochastically shifting intercept a_t and a constant slope b, so that quantity demanded next period will be $a_{t+1} - bp_{t+1}$. Quantity supplied will be λ times next period's capital. Then a second equilibrium condition is

$$\lambda[i_t + (1-\delta)k_t] = a_{t+1} - bp_{t+1} .$$

31

Taking mean values of both sides,

(8) $\qquad \lambda[i_t + (1-\delta)k_t] = E_t(a_{t+1}) - bE_t(p_{t+1})$.

Since our interest is in the industry investment function, we eliminate $E_t(p_{t+1})$ between (7) and (8) to obtain:

(9) $\qquad i_t + (1-\delta)k_{t+1} = \frac{1}{\lambda} E_t(a_{t+1}) - \frac{b}{\lambda^2} [\frac{r}{1-E_t(\theta_{t+1})} + \delta]$

$\qquad + \frac{b}{\lambda^2} [\frac{(1+r)\Psi_t - (1-\delta)E_t(\Psi_{t+1})}{1 - E_t(\theta_{t+1})}]$.

Equation (9) gives the industry's "desired" stock of capital, $i_t + (1-\delta)k_t$, as a function of the expected future state of demand and the current and expected future tax structure, as well as of the cost of capital r, taken in this illustration to be constant. The second and third terms on the right are the product of the slope of the demand curve for capital, $-b\lambda^{-2}$, and the familiar Jorgensonian implicit rental price; the second term includes "interest" and depreciation costs, net of taxes; the third includes the expected capital gain (or loss) due to changes in the investment tax credit rate.

In most empirical investment studies, firms are assumed to move gradually from k_t to the desired stock given by (9), due to costs of adjustment, delivery lags, and the like. We assume here, purely for convenience, that the full adjustment occurs in a single period.

Equation (9) is operationally at the same level as equations (1) and (4) of the preceding section: it relates current behavior to unobserved expectations of future variables. To move to a testable hypothesis, one must specify the time series behavior of a_t, θ_t and Ψ_t (as was done for income in consumption theory), obtain the optimal forecasting rule, and obtain the analogue to the consumption function (6). Let us imagine that this has been accomplished, and estimates of the parameters λ and b have been obtained. How would one use these estimates to evaluate the consequences of a particular investment tax credit policy?

The method used by Hall and Jorgenson is to treat the credit as a permanent or once-and-for-all change, or implicitly to set $E_t(\Psi_{t+1})$ equal to Ψ_t. Holding

θ_t constant at θ, the effect of a change in the credit from 0 to Ψ (say) would be the same as a permanent lowering of the price of investment goods to $1-\Psi$ or, from (9), an increase in the desired capital stock of $\dfrac{b}{\lambda^2} \cdot \dfrac{r+\delta}{1-\theta}$. If the credit is in fact believed by corporations to be permanent, this forecast will be correct; otherwise it will not be.

To consider alternatives, imagine a stochastic tax credit policy which switches from 0 to a fixed number Ψ in a Markovian fashion, with transitions given by $\Pr\{\Psi_{t+1} = \Psi \mid \Psi_t = 0\} = q$ and $\Pr\{\Psi_{t+1} = \Psi \mid \Psi_t = \Psi\} = p$.[15] Then if expectations on next period's tax credit are formed rationally, conditional on the presence or absence of the credit in the current period, we have

$$E_t(\Psi_{t+1}) = \begin{cases} q\Psi & \text{if} \quad \Psi_t = 0, \\[2mm] p\Psi & \text{if} \quad \Psi_t = \Psi. \end{cases}$$

The third term on the right of (9) is then

$$\frac{b\Psi}{\lambda^2(1-\theta)} \, [-q(1-\delta)] \qquad\qquad \text{if } \Psi_t = 0,$$

$$\frac{b\Psi}{\lambda^2(1-\theta)} \, [1+r - p(1-\delta)] \qquad\qquad \text{if } \Psi_t = \Psi.$$

The difference between these terms is given by the expression

$$(10) \qquad \frac{b\Psi}{\lambda^2(1-\theta)} \, [1 + r + (q-p)(1-\delta)].$$

The expression (10) gives the increment to desired capital stock (and, with immediate adjustment, to current investment) when the tax credit is switched from zero to Ψ in an economy where the credit operates, and is known to operate, in the stochastic fashion described above. It does _not_ measure the effect of a

---

[15] A tax credit designed for stabilization would, of course, need to respond to projected movements in the shift variable a_t. In this case, the transition probabilities p and q would vary with indicators (say current and lagged a_t values) of future economic activity. Since my aim here is only to get an idea of the quantitative importance of a correct treatment of expectations, I will not pursue this design problem further.

switch in policy from a no-credit regime to the stochastic regime used here. (The difference arises because even when the credit is set at zero in the stochastic regime, the possibility of capital loss, due to the introduction of the credit in the future, increases the implicit rental on capital, relative to the situation in which the credit is expected to remain at zero forever.)

By examining extreme values of p and q one can get a good idea of the quantitative importance of expectations in measuring the effect of the credit. At one extreme, consider the case where the credit is expected almost <u>never</u> to be offered (q near 0), but once offered, it is permanent (p near 1). The effect of a switch from 0 to Ψ is, in this case, approximately

$$\frac{b\Psi}{\lambda^2(1-\theta)} \ [r + \delta],$$

using (10). This is the situation assumed, implicitly, by Hall and Jorgenson. At the other extreme, consider the case of a frequently imposed but always transitory credit (q near 1, p near 0). Applying (10), the effect of a switch in this case is approximately

$$\frac{b\Psi}{\lambda^2(1-\theta)} \ [2 + r - \delta] \ .$$

The ratio of effects is then $(2 + r - \delta)/(r + \delta)$. With r = .14 and δ = .15, this ratio is about 7.[16] We are not, then, discussing a quantitatively minor issue.

For a more realistic estimate, consider a credit which remains "off" for an average period of 5 years, and when "switched on" remains for an average of one year. These assumptions correspond to setting $p\tilde{=}0$ and $q=\frac{1}{5}$. The ratio of the effect (from (10)), under these assumptions versus those used by Hall and Jorgenson is now $[1 + r + \frac{1}{5}(1-\delta)]/(r+\delta)$. With r = .14 and δ = .15, this ratio is approximately 4.5. This ratio would probably be somewhat smaller under a more satisfactory lag structure[17], but even taking this into account, it appears likely that the <u>potential stimulus of the investment tax credit may well be several</u>

---

[16]The cost of capital of .14 and the depreciation rate of .15 (for manufacturing equipment) are annual rates from [15]. Since the ratio $(2 + r - \delta)/(r + \delta)$ is <u>not</u> time-unit free, the assumption that all movement toward the new desired stock of capital takes place in one year is crucial at this point: by defining a <u>period</u> as shorter than one year this ratio will increase, and conversely for a longer period.

[17]For the reason given in note 16.

times greater than the Hall-Jorgenson estimates would indicate.[18]

As was the case in the discussion of consumption behavior, estimation of a policy effect along the above lines presupposes a policy generated by a fixed, relatively simple rule, known by forecasters (ourselves) and by the agents subject to the policy (an assumption which is not only convenient analytically but consistent with Article 1, Section 7 of the U.S. Constitution). To go beyond the kind of order-of-magnitude calculations used here to an accurate assessment of the effects of the 1962 credit studied by Hall and Jorgenson, one would have to infer the implicit rule which generated (or was thought by corporations to generate) that policy, a task made difficult, or perhaps impossible, by the novelty of the policy at the time it was introduced. Similarly, there is no reason to hope that we can accurately forecast the effects of future ad hoc tax policies on investment behavior. On the other hand, there is every reason to believe that good quantitative assessments of counter-cyclical fiscal rules, which are built into the tax structure in a stable and well-understood way, can be obtained.

5.3   Phillips Curves

A third example is suggested by the recent controversy over the Phelps-Friedman hypothesis that permanent changes in the inflation rate will not alter the average rate of unemployment. Most of the major econometric models have been used in simulation experiments to test this proposition; the results are uniformly negative. Since expectations are involved in an essential way in labor and product market supply behavior, one would presume, on the basis of the considerations raised in section 4, that these tests are beside the point.[19] This presumption is correct, as the following example illustrates.

It will be helpful to utilize a simple, parametric model which captures the main features of the expectational view of aggregate supply – rational agents, cleared markets, incomplete information.[20] We imagine suppliers of goods to be distributed over N distinct markets i, i=1,...,N. To avoid index number problems, suppose that the same (except for location) good is traded in each market, and let y_{it} be the log of quantity supplied in market i in period t. Assume, further, that the supply y_{it} is composed of two factors

$$y_{it} = y_{it}^p + y_{it}^c \quad ,$$

---

[18]It should be noted that this conclusion reinforces the qualitative conclusion reached by Hall and Jorgenson [15], p. 413.

[19]Sargent [34] and I [23] have developed this conclusion earlier in similar contexts.

[20]This model is taken, with a few changes, from my earlier [24].

where y_{it}^p denotes normal or permanent supply, and y_{it}^c cyclical or transitory supply (both, again, in logs). We take y_{it}^p to be unresponsive to all but permanent relative price changes or, since the latter have been defined away by assuming a single good, simply unresponsive to price changes. Transitory supply y_{it}^c varies with perceived changes in the <u>relative</u> price of goods in i:

$$y_{it}^c = \beta(p_{it} - p_{it}^e) \, ,$$

where p_{it} is the log of the actual price in i at t, and p_{it}^e is the log of the general (geometric average) price level in the economy as a whole, <u>as perceived in market i</u>.[21]

Prices will vary from market to market for each t, due to the usual sources of fluctuation in relative demands. They will also fluctuate over time, due to movements in aggregate demand. We shall not explore the sources of these price movements (although this is easy enough to do) but simply postulate that the actual price in i at t consists of two components:

$$p_{it} = p_t + z_{it} \, .$$

Sellers observe the actual price p_{it}; the two components cannot be separately observed. The component p_t varies with time, but is common to all markets. Based on information obtained prior to t (call it I_{t-1}) traders in all markets take p_t to be a normally distributed random variable, with mean $\bar{p}_t$ (reflecting this past information) and variance σ^2. The component z_{it} reflects relative price variation across markets and time: z_{it} is normally distributed, independent of p_t and z_{js} (unless i=j, s=t), with mean 0 and variance τ^2.

The <u>actual</u> general price level at t is the average over markets of individual prices,

$$\frac{1}{N} \sum_{i=1}^{N} p_{it} = p_t + \frac{1}{N} \sum_{i=1}^{N} z_{it} \, .$$

We take the number of markets N to be large, so that the second term can be neglected, and p_t is the general price level. To form the supply decision, suppliers estimate p_t; assume that this estimate p_{it}^e is the mean of the true conditional

---

[21] This supply function for goods should be thought of as drawn up given a cleared labor market in i. See Lucas and Rapping [22] for an analysis of the factors underlying this function.

distribution of p_t. The latter is calculated using the observation that p_{it} is the sum of two independent normal variates, one with mean 0 and variance τ^2; one with mean $\bar{p}_t$ and variance σ^2. It follows that

$$p_{it}^e = E\{p_t \mid p_{it}, I_{t-1}\} = (1-\theta)p_{it} + \theta\bar{p}_t ,$$

where $\theta = \dfrac{\tau^2}{\sigma^2 + \tau^2}$.

Based on this unbiased but generally inaccurate estimate of the current general level of prices, suppliers in i follow

$$y_{it}^c = \beta[p_{it} - ((1-\theta)p_{it} + \theta\bar{p}_\ell)] = \theta\beta[p_{it} - \bar{p}_t] .$$

Now averaging over markets, and invoking the law of large numbers again, we have the cyclical component of <u>aggregate</u> supply:

$$y_{it}^e = \theta\beta(p_t - \bar{p}_t) .$$

Re-introducing the permanent components,

(11) $y_t = \theta\beta(p_t - \bar{p}_t) + y_{pt}$.

Though simple, (11) captures the main features of the expectational or "natural rate" view of aggregate supply. The supply of goods is viewed as following a trend path y_{pt} which is not dependent on nominal price movements. Deviations from this path are induced whenever the nominal price deviates from the level which was expected to prevail on the basis of past information. These deviations occur because agents are obliged to infer current general price movements on the basis of incomplete information.

It is worth speculating as to the sort of empirical performance one would <u>expect</u> from (11). In doing so, we ignore the trend component y_{pt}, concentrating on the determinants of p_t, β and θ. The parameter β reflects intertemporal substitution possibilities in supply: technological factors such as storability of production, and tastes for substituting labor supplied today for supply tomorrow. One would expect β to be reasonably stable over time and across economies at a similar level of development. The parameter θ is the ratio $\dfrac{\tau^2}{\sigma^2 + \tau^2}$. τ^2 reflects

37

the variability of relative prices within the economy; there is no reason to expect it to vary systematically with demand policy. σ^2 is the variance of the general price level about its expected level; it will obviously increase with increases in the volatility of demand.[22] Similarly, $\bar{p}_t$, the expected price level conditional on past information, will vary with actual, average inflation rates.

Turning to a specific example, suppose that actual prices follow the random walk

$$(12) \qquad p_t = p_{t-1} + \epsilon_t$$

where ϵ_t is normal with mean π and variance σ^2. Then $p_t = p_{t-1} + \pi$ and (11) becomes

$$(13) \qquad y_t = \theta\beta(p_t - p_{t-1}) - \theta\beta\pi + y_{pt} \ .$$

Over a sample period during which π and σ^2 remain roughly constant, and if y_{pt} can be effectively controlled for, (13) will appear to the econometrician to describe a stable trade-off between inflation and real output. The addition of lagged inflation rates will not improve the fit, or alter this conclusion in any way. Yet it is evident from (13) that a sustained increase in the inflation rate (an increase in π) will not affect real output.

This is not to say that a distributed lag version of (11) might not perform better empirically. Thus let the actual rate of inflation follow a first-order autoregressive scheme

$$\Delta p_t = \rho\Delta p_{t-1} + \epsilon_t$$

or

$$(14) \qquad p_t = (1+\rho)p_{t-1} - \rho p_{t-2} + \epsilon_t$$

where $0 < \rho < 1$ and ϵ_t is distributed as before.

Then combining (11) and (14):

$$(15) \qquad y_t = \theta\beta\Delta p_t - \theta\beta\rho\Delta p_{t-1} - \theta\beta\pi + y_{pt}.$$

---

[22] This implication that the variability in demand affects the slope of the "trade-off" is the basis for the tests of the natural rate hypothesis reported in [24], as well as those by Adie [1] and B. Klein [18].

In econometric terms, the "long-run" slope, or trade-off, would be the <u>sum</u> of the inflation coefficients, or $\theta\beta(1\text{-}\rho)$, which will not, if (14) is stable, be zero.

In short, one can imagine situations in which empirical Phillips curves exhibit long lags and situations in which there are no lagged effects. In either case, the "long-run" output-inflation relationship as calculated or simulated in the conventional way has <u>no</u> bearing on the actual consequences of pursuing a policy of inflation.

As in the consumption and investment examples, the ability to use (13) or (15) to forecast the consequences of a change in policy rests crucially on the assumption that the parameters describing the new policy (in this case π, σ^2 and ρ) are known by agents. Over periods for which this assumption is not approximately valid (obviously there have been, and will continue to be, many such periods) empirical Phillips curves will appear subject to "parameter drift," describable over the sample period, but unpredictable for all but the very near future.

6. Policy Considerations

In preceding sections, I have argued in general and by example that there are compelling empirical and theoretical reasons for believing that a structure of the form

$$y_{t+1} = F(y_t, x_t, \theta, \epsilon_t)$$

(F known, θ fixed, x_t "arbitrary") will not be of use for forecasting and policy evaluation in actual economies. For short-term forecasting, these arguments have long been anticipated in practice, and models with good (and improvable) tracking properties have been obtained by permitting and measuring "drift" in the parameter vector θ. Under adaptive models which rationalize these tracking procedures, however, long-run policy simulations are acknowledged to have infinite variance, which leaves open the question of quantitative policy evaluation.

One response to this situation, seldom defended explicitly today though in implicit form probably dominant at the most "practical" level of economic advice-giving, is simply to dismiss questions of the long-term behavior of the economy under alternative policies and focus instead on obtaining what is viewed as desirable behavior in the next few quarters. The hope is that the changes in θ induced by policy changes will occur slowly, and that conditional forecasting based on tracking models will therefore be roughly accurate for a few periods. This hope is both false and misleading. First, some policy changes induce immediate jumps in θ: for example, an explicitly temporary personal income tax surcharge will (c.f. section 5.1) induce an _immediate_ rise in propensity to consume out of disposable income and consequent errors in short-term conditional forecasts.[23] Second, even if the induced changes in θ are slow to occur, they should be counted in the short-term "objective function", yet rarely are. Thus econometric Phillips curves roughly forecast the initial phase of the current inflation, but not the "adverse" shift in the curve to which that inflation led.

What kind of structure might be at once consistent with the theoretical considerations raised in section 4 and with operational, accurate policy evaluation? One hesitates to indulge the common illusion that "general" structures are more useful than specific, empirically verified ones; nevertheless, a provisional structure, cautiously used, will facilitate the remainder of the discussion.

As observed in section 4, one cannot meaningfully discuss optimal decisions of agents under arbitrary sequences $\{x_t\}$ of future shocks. As an alternative characterization, then, let policies and other disturbances be viewed as stochastically disturbed functions of the state of the system, or (parametrically)

$$(16) \qquad x_t = G(y_t, \lambda, \eta_t)$$

where G is known, λ is a fixed parameter vector, and η_t a vector of disturbances. Then the remainder of the economy follows

$$(17) \qquad y_{t+1} = F(y_t, x_t, \theta(\lambda), \epsilon_t) \, ,$$

where, as indicated, the behavioral parameters θ vary systematically with the parameters λ governing policy and other "shocks". The econometric problem in this context is that of estimating the function $\theta(\lambda)$.

In a model of this sort, a _policy_ is viewed as a change in the parameters λ, or in the function generating the values of policy variables at particular times. A change in policy (in λ) affects the behavior of the system in two ways: first by altering the time series behavior of x_t; second by leading to modification of the behavioral parameters $\theta(\lambda)$ governing the rest of the system. Evidently, the way this latter modification can be expected to occur depends crucially on the way the policy change is carried out. If the policy change occurs by a sequence of decisions following no discussed or pre-announced pattern, it will become known to agents only gradually, and then perhaps largely as higher variance of "noise". In this case, the movement to a new $\theta(\lambda)$, if it occurs in a stable way at all, will be

---

[23]This observation has been made earlier, for exactly the reasons set out in section 5.1, by Eisner [8] and Dolde [7], p. 15.

40

unsystematic, and econometrically unpredictable. If, on the other hand, policy changes occur as fully discussed and understood changes in <u>rules,</u> there is some hope that the resulting structural changes can be forecast on the basis of estimation from past data of $\theta(\lambda)$.

It is perhaps necessary to emphasize that this point of view towards conditional forecasting, due originally to Knight and, in modern form, to Muth, does not attribute to agents unnatural powers of instantly divining the true structure of policies affecting them. More modestly, it asserts that agents' responses become predictable to outside observers only when there can be some confidence that agents and observers share a common view of the nature of the shocks which must be forecast by both.

The preference for "rules versus authority" in economic policy making suggested by this point of view, is not, as I hope is clear, based on any demonstrable optimality properties of rules-in- general (whatever that might mean). There seems to be no theoretical argument ruling out the possibility that (for example) delegating economic decision-making authority to some individual or group might not lead to superior (by some criterion) economic performance than is attainable under some, or all, hypothetical rules in the sense of (16). The point is rather that this possibility cannot <u>in principle</u> be substantiated empirically. The only <u>scientific</u> quantitative policy evaluations available to us are comparisons of the consequences of alternative policy rules.

7.   Concluding Remarks

This essay has been devoted to an exposition and elaboration of a single syllogism: given that the structure of an econometric model consists of optimal decision rules of economic agents, and that optimal decision rules vary systematically with changes in the structure of series relevant to the decision maker, it follows that any change in policy will systematically alter the structure of econometric models.

For the question of the short-term forecasting, or tracking ability of econometric models, we have seen that this conclusion is of only occasional significance. For issues involving policy evaluation, in contrast, it is fundamental; for it implies that comparisons of the effects of alternative policy rules using current macroeconometric models are invalid regardless of the performance of these models over the sample period or in ex ante short-term forecasting.

The argument is, in part, destructive: the ability to forecast the consequences of "arbitrary", unannounced sequences of policy decisions, currently claimed (at least implicitly) by the theory of economic policy, appears to be beyond the capability not only of the current-generation models, but of conceivable future models as well. On the other hand, as the consumption example shows, conditional forecasting under the alternative structure (16) and (17) is, while scientifically more demanding, entirely operational.

In short, it appears that policy makers, if they wish to forecast the response of citizens, must take the latter into their confidence. This conclusion, if ill-suited to current econometric practice, seems to accord well with a preference for democratic decision making.

42

REFERENCES

1. Adie, Douglas K., "The Importance of Expectations for the Phillips Curve Relation," Research Paper No. 133, Department of Economics, Ohio University (undated).

2. Ando, Albert and Franco Modigliani, "The Life Cycle Hypothesis of Saving; Aggregate Implications and Tests," American Economic Review, v. 53 (1963), pp. 55-84.

3. Cooley, Thomas F. and Edward C. Prescott, "An Adaptive Regression Model," International Economic Review, (June 1973), 364-71.

4. —————————, "Tests of the Adaptive Regression Model," Review of Economics and Statistics, (April 1973), 248-56.

5. —————————, "Estimation in the Presence of Sequential Parameter Variation," Econometrica, forthcoming.

6. de Menil, George and Jared J. Enzler, "Prices and Wages in the FRB-MIT-Penn Econometric Model," in Otto Eckstein, ed., The Econometrics of Price Determination Conference (Washington: Board of Governors of the Federal Reserve System and Social Science Research Council), 1972, pp. 277-308.

7. Dolde, Walter, "Capital Markets and the Relevant Horizon for Consumption Planning," Yale doctoral dissertation, 1973.

8. Eisner, Robert, "Fiscal and Monetary Policy Reconsidered," American Economic Review, v. 59 (1969), pp. 897-905.

9. Evans, Michael K. and Lawrence R. Klein, The Wharton Econometric Forecasting Model. 2nd, Enlarged Edition (Philadelphia: University of Pennsylvania Economics Research Unit), 1968.

10. Fisher, Franklin M., "Discussion" in Otto Eckstein, ed., op. cit. (reference [6]), pp. 113-115.

11. Friedman, Milton, A Theory of the Consumption Function. (Princeton: Princeton University Press), 1957.

43

12. _____, "Windfalls, the 'Horizon', and Related Concepts in the Permanent Income Hypothesis," in Carl F. Christ, et. al., eds., Measurement in Economics (Stanford: Stanford University Press), 1963, pp. 3-28.

13. _____, "The Role of Monetary Policy," American Economic Review, v. 58 (1968), pp. 1-17.

14. Gordon, Robert J., "Wage-Price Controls and the Shifting Phillips Curve," Brookings Papers on Economic Activity, 1972, no. 2, pp. 385-421.

15. Hall, Robert E. and Dale W. Jorgenson, "Tax Policy and Investment Behavior," American Economic Review, v. 57 (1967), pp. 391-414.

16. Hirsch, Albert A., "Price Simulations with the OBE Econometric Model," in Otto Eckstein, ed., op.cit. (reference [6]), pp. 237-276.

17. Hymans, Saul H., "Prices and Price Behavior in Three U.S. Econometric Models," in Otto Eckstein, ed., op. cit. (reference [6]), pp. 309-322.

18. Klein, Benjamin, "The Effect of Price Level Unpredictability on the Composition of Income Change," unpublished working paper, April, 1973.

19. Klein, Lawrence R. and Arthur S. Goldberger, An Econometric Model of the United States, 1929-1952.(Amsterdam: North Holland), 1955.

20. Klein, Lawrence R., An Essay on the Theory of Economic Prediction.(Helsinki: Yrjo Jahnsson Lectures), 1968.

21. Knight, Frank H., Risk, Uncertainty and Profit.(Boston: Houghton-Mifflin), 1921.

22. Lucas, Robert E., Jr. and Leonard A. Rapping, "Real Wages, Employment, and Inflation," Journal of Political Economy, v. 77 (1969), pp. 721-754.

23. Lucas, Robert E.,Jr., "Econometric Testing of the Natural Rate Hypothesis," in Otto Eckstein, ed., op. cit. (reference [6]), pp. 50-59.

24. _____, "Some International Evidence on Output-Inflation Trade-Offs," American Economic Review, v. 63 (1973).

25. Marschak, Jacob, "Economic Measurements for Policy and Prediction," in William C. Hood and Tjalling G. Koopmans, eds., Studies in Econometric Method, Cowles Commission Monograph 14 (New York: Wiley), 1953, pp. 1-26.

26. Mayer, Thomas, "Tests of the Permanent Income Theory with Continuous Budgets," Journal of Money, Credit, and Banking, v. 4 (1972) pp. 757-778.

27. Modigliani, Franco and Richard Brumberg, "Utility Analysis and the Consumption Function: An Interpretation of Cross-Section Data," in K. K. Kurihara, ed., Post-Keynesian Economics. (New Brunswick: Rutgers University Press), 1954.

28. Muth, John F., "Optimal Properties of Exponentially Weighted Forecasts," Journal of the American Statistical Association, v. 55 (1960), pp. 299-306.

29. _____, "Rational Expectations and the Theory of Price Movements," Econometrica, v. 29 (1961), pp. 315-335.

30. Phelps, Edmund S., "Money Wage Dynamics and Labor Market Equilibrium," Journal of Political Economy, v. 76 (1968), pp. 687-711.

31. Phelps, Edmund S., et al., The New Microeconomics in Employment and Inflation Theory. (New York: Norton), 1970.

32. Phillips, A. W., "The Relation Between Unemployment and the Rate of Change of Money Wage Rates in the United Kingdom, 1861-1957," Economica, v. 25 (1958), pp. 283-299.

33. Samuelson, Paul A. and Robert M. Solow, "Analytical Aspects of Anti-Inflation Policy," American Economic Review, v. 50 (1960), pp. 177-194.

34. Sargent, Thomas J., "A Note on the 'Accelerationist' Controversy," Journal of Money, Credit, and Banking, v. 3 (1971), pp. 721-725.

35. Tinbergen, Jan, <u>On the Theory of Economic Policy.</u> (Amsterdam: North Holland), 1952.

36. _____, <u>Economic Policy: Principles and Design.</u> (Amsterdam: North Holland), 1956.

[16]

PORTFOLIO SELECTION*

HARRY MARKOWITZ
The Rand Corporation

THE PROCESS OF SELECTING a portfolio may be divided into two stages. The first stage starts with observation and experience and ends with beliefs about the future performances of available securities. The second stage starts with the relevant beliefs about future performances and ends with the choice of portfolio. This paper is concerned with the second stage. We first consider the rule that the investor does (or should) maximize discounted expected, or anticipated, returns. This rule is rejected both as a hypothesis to explain, and as a maximum to guide investment behavior. We next consider the rule that the investor does (or should) consider expected return a desirable thing *and* variance of return an undesirable thing. This rule has many sound points, both as a maxim for, and hypothesis about, investment behavior. We illustrate geometrically relations between beliefs and choice of portfolio according to the "expected returns—variance of returns" rule.

One type of rule concerning choice of portfolio is that the investor does (or should) maximize the discounted (or capitalized) value of future returns.[1] Since the future is not known with certainty, it must be "expected" or "anticipated" returns which we discount. Variations of this type of rule can be suggested. Following Hicks, we could let "anticipated" returns include an allowance for risk.[2] Or, we could let the rate at which we capitalize the returns from particular securities vary with risk.

The hypothesis (or maxim) that the investor does (or should) maximize discounted return must be rejected. If we ignore market imperfections the foregoing rule never implies that there is a diversified portfolio which is preferable to all non-diversified portfolios. Diversification is both observed and sensible; a rule of behavior which does not imply the superiority of diversification must be rejected both as a hypothesis and as a maxim.

* This paper is based on work done by the author while at the Cowles Commission for Research in Economics and with the financial assistance of the Social Science Research Council. It will be reprinted as Cowles Commission Paper, New Series, No. 60.

1. See, for example, J. B. Williams, *The Theory of Investment Value* (Cambridge, Mass.: Harvard University Press, 1938), pp. 55–75.

2. J. R. Hicks, *Value and Capital* (New York: Oxford University Press, 1939), p. 126. Hicks applies the rule to a firm rather than a portfolio.

The foregoing rule fails to imply diversification no matter how the anticipated returns are formed; whether the same or different discount rates are used for different securities; no matter how these discount rates are decided upon or how they vary over time.[3] The hypothesis implies that the investor places all his funds in the security with the greatest discounted value. If two or more securities have the same value, then any of these or any combination of these is as good as any other.

We can see this analytically: suppose there are N securities; let r_{it} be the anticipated return (however decided upon) at time t per dollar invested in security i; let d_{it} be the rate at which the return on the ith security at time t is discounted back to the present; let X_i be the relative amount invested in security i. We exclude short sales, thus $X_i \geqslant 0$ for all i. Then the discounted anticipated return of the portfolio is

$$R = \sum_{t=1}^{\infty} \sum_{i=1}^{N} d_{it} r_{it} X_i$$

$$= \sum_{i=1}^{N} X_i \left(\sum_{t=1}^{\infty} d_{it} r_{it} \right)$$

$R_i = \sum_{t=1}^{\infty} d_{it} r_{it}$ is the discounted return of the ith security, therefore

$R = \Sigma X_i R_i$ where R_i is independent of X_i. Since $X_i \geqslant 0$ for all i and $\Sigma X_i = 1$, R is a weighted average of R_i with the X_i as non-negative weights. To maximize R, we let $X_i = 1$ for i with maximum R_i. If several Ra_a, $a = 1, \ldots, K$ are maximum then any allocation with

$$\sum_{a=1}^{K} X a_a = 1$$

maximizes R. In no case is a diversified portfolio preferred to all non-diversified portfolios.[4]

It will be convenient at this point to consider a static model. Instead of speaking of the time series of returns from the ith security $(r_{i1}, r_{i2}, \ldots, r_{it}, \ldots)$ we will speak of "the flow of returns" (r_i) from the ith security. The flow of returns from the portfolio as a whole is

3. The results depend on the assumption that the anticipated returns and discount rates are independent of the particular investor's portfolio.

4. If short sales were allowed, an infinite amount of money would be placed in the security with highest r.

$R = \Sigma X_i r_i$. As in the dynamic case if the investor wished to maximize "anticipated" return from the portfolio he would place all his funds in that security with maximum anticipated returns.

There is a rule which implies both that the investor should diversify and that he should maximize expected return. The rule states that the investor does (or should) diversify his funds among all those securities which give maximum expected return. The law of large numbers will insure that the actual yield of the portfolio will be almost the same as the expected yield.[5] This rule is a special case of the expected returns—variance of returns rule (to be presented below). It assumes that there is a portfolio which gives both maximum expected return and minimum variance, and it commends this portfolio to the investor.

This presumption, that the law of large numbers applies to a portfolio of securities, cannot be accepted. The returns from securities are too intercorrelated. Diversification cannot eliminate all variance.

The portfolio with maximum expected return is not necessarily the one with minimum variance. There is a rate at which the investor can gain expected return by taking on variance, or reduce variance by giving up expected return.

We saw that the expected returns or anticipated returns rule is inadequate. Let us now consider the expected returns—variance of returns (E-V) rule. It will be necessary to first present a few elementary concepts and results of mathematical statistics. We will then show some implications of the E-V rule. After this we will discuss its plausibility.

In our presentation we try to avoid complicated mathematical statements and proofs. As a consequence a price is paid in terms of rigor and generality. The chief limitations from this source are (1) we do not derive our results analytically for the n-security case; instead, we present them geometrically for the 3 and 4 security cases; (2) we assume static probability beliefs. In a general presentation we must recognize that the probability distribution of yields of the various securities is a function of time. The writer intends to present, in the future, the general, mathematical treatment which removes these limitations.

We will need the following elementary concepts and results of mathematical statistics:

Let Y be a random variable, i.e., a variable whose value is decided by chance. Suppose, for simplicity of exposition, that Y can take on a finite number of values $y_1, y_2, \ldots, y_N$. Let the probability that $Y =$

---

5. Williams, *op. cit.*, pp. 68, 69.

y_1, be p_1; that $Y = y_2$ be p_2 etc. The expected value (or mean) of Y is defined to be

$$E = p_1 y_1 + p_2 y_2 + \ldots + p_N y_N$$

The variance of Y is defined to be

$$V = p_1 (y_1 - E)^2 + p_2 (y_2 - E)^2 + \ldots + p_N (y_N - E)^2 .$$

V is the average squared deviation of Y from its expected value. V is a commonly used measure of dispersion. Other measures of dispersion, closely related to V are the standard deviation, $\sigma = \sqrt{V}$ and the co-efficient of variation, σ/E.

Suppose we have a number of random variables: $R_1, \ldots, R_n$. If R is a weighted sum (linear combination) of the R_i

$$R = a_1 R_1 + a_2 R_2 + \ldots + a_n R_n$$

then R is also a random variable. (For example R_1, may be the number which turns up on one die; R_2, that of another die, and R the sum of these numbers. In this case $n = 2$, $a_1 = a_2 = 1$).

It will be important for us to know how the expected value and variance of the weighted sum (R) are related to the probability distribution of the $R_1, \ldots, R_n$. We state these relations below; we refer the reader to any standard text for proof.[6]

The expected value of a weighted sum is the weighted sum of the expected values. I.e., $E(R) = a_1 E(R_1) + a_2 E(R_2) + \ldots + a_n E(R_n)$ The variance of a weighted sum is not as simple. To express it we must define "covariance." The covariance of R_1 and R_2 is

$$\sigma_{12} = E\{ [R_1 - E(R_1)] [R_2 - E(R_2)] \}$$

i.e., the expected value of [(the deviation of R_1 from its mean) times (the deviation of R_2 from its mean)]. In general we define the covariance between R_i and R_j as

$$\sigma_{ij} = E\{ [R_i - E(R_i)] [R_j - E(R_j)] \}$$

σ_{ij} may be expressed in terms of the familiar correlation coefficient (ρ_{ij}). The covariance between R_i and R_j is equal to [(their correlation) times (the standard deviation of R_i) times (the standard deviation of R_j)]:

$$\sigma_{ij} = \rho_{ij}\sigma_i\sigma_j$$

6. E.g., J. V. Uspensky, *Introduction to Mathematical Probability* (New York: McGraw-Hill, 1937), chapter 9, pp. 161–81.

The variance of a weighted sum is

$$V(R) = \sum_{i=1}^{N} a_i^2 V(X_i) + 2 \sum_{i=1}^{N} \sum_{i>1}^{N} a_i a_j \sigma_{ij}$$

If we use the fact that the variance of R_i is σ_{ii} then

$$V(R) = \sum_{i=1}^{N} \sum_{j=1}^{N} a_i a_j \sigma_{ij}$$

Let R_i be the return on the ith security. Let μ_i be the expected value of R_i; σ_{ij}, be the covariance between R_i and R_j (thus σ_{ii} is the variance of R_i). Let X_i be the percentage of the investor's assets which are allocated to the ith security. The yield (R) on the portfolio as a whole is

$$R = \sum R_i X_i$$

The R_i (and consequently R) are considered to be random variables.[7] The X_i are not random variables, but are fixed by the investor. Since the X_i are percentages we have $\Sigma X_i = 1$. In our analysis we will exclude negative values of the X_i (i.e., short sales); therefore $X_i \geqslant 0$ for all i.

The return (R) on the portfolio as a whole is a weighted sum of random variables (where the investor can choose the weights). From our discussion of such weighted sums we see that the expected return E from the portfolio as a whole is

$$E = \sum_{i=1}^{N} X_i \mu_i$$

and the variance is

$$V = \sum_{i=1}^{N} \sum_{j=1}^{N} \sigma_{ij} X_i X$$

7. I.e., we assume that the investor does (and should) act as if he had probability beliefs concerning these variables. In general we would expect that the investor could tell us, for any two events (A and B), whether he personally considered A more likely than B, B more likely than A, or both equally likely. If the investor were consistent in his opinions on such matters, he would possess a system of probability beliefs. We cannot expect the investor to be consistent in every detail. We can, however, expect his probability beliefs to be roughly consistent on important matters that have been carefully considered. We should also expect that he will base his actions upon these probability beliefs—even though they be in part subjective.

This paper does not consider the difficult question of how investors do (or should) form their probability beliefs.

For fixed probability beliefs (μ_i, σ_{ij}) the investor has a choice of various combinations of E and V depending on his choice of portfolio $X_1, \ldots, X_N$. Suppose that the set of all obtainable (E, V) combinations were as in Figure 1. The E-V rule states that the investor would (or should) want to select one of those portfolios which give rise to the (E, V) combinations indicated as efficient in the figure; i.e., those with minimum V for given E or more and maximum E for given V or less.

There are techniques by which we can compute the set of efficient portfolios and efficient (E, V) combinations associated with given μ_i

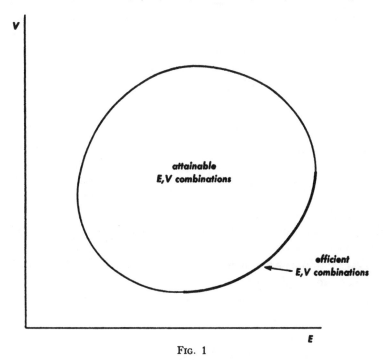

FIG. 1

and σ_{ij}. We will not present these techniques here. We will, however, illustrate geometrically the nature of the efficient surfaces for cases in which N (the number of available securities) is small.

The calculation of efficient surfaces might possibly be of practical use. Perhaps there are ways, by combining statistical techniques and the judgment of experts, to form reasonable probability beliefs (μ_i, σ_{ij}). We could use these beliefs to compute the attainable efficient combinations of (E, V). The investor, being informed of what (E, V) combinations were attainable, could state which he desired. We could then find the portfolio which gave this desired combination.

Two conditions—at least—must be satisfied before it would be practical to use efficient surfaces in the manner described above. First, the investor must desire to act according to the E-V maxim. Second, we must be able to arrive at reasonable μ_i and σ_{ij}. We will return to these matters later.

Let us consider the case of three securities. In the three security case our model reduces to

$$1) \qquad E = \sum_{i=1}^{3} X_i \mu_i$$

$$2) \qquad V = \sum_{i=1}^{3} \sum_{j=1}^{3} X_i X_j \sigma_{ij}$$

$$3) \qquad \sum_{i=1}^{3} X_i = 1$$

$$4) \qquad X_i \geqslant 0 \qquad \text{for} \qquad i = 1, 2, 3 .$$

From (3) we get

$$3') \qquad X_3 = 1 - X_1 - X_2$$

If we substitute (3') in equation (1) and (2) we get E and V as functions of X_1 and X_2. For example we find

$$1') \qquad E = \mu_3 + X_1 (\mu_1 - \mu_3) + X_2 (\mu_2 - \mu_3)$$

The exact formulas are not too important here (that of V is given below).[8] We can simply write

$$a) \qquad E = E (X_1, X_2)$$

$$b) \qquad V = V (X_1, X_2)$$

$$c) \qquad X_1 \geqslant 0, X_2 \geqslant 0, 1 - X_1 - X_2 \geqslant 0$$

By using relations (a), (b), (c), we can work with two dimensional geometry.

The attainable set of portfolios consists of all portfolios which satisfy constraints (c) and (3') (or equivalently (3) and (4)). The attainable combinations of X_1, X_2 are represented by the triangle $\overline{abc}$ in Figure 2. Any point to the left of the X_2 axis is not attainable because it violates the condition that $X_1 \geqslant 0$. Any point below the X_1 axis is not attainable because it violates the condition that $X_2 \geqslant 0$. Any

8. $V = X_1^2(\sigma_{11} - 2\sigma_{13} + \sigma_{33}) + X_2^2(\sigma_{22} - 2\sigma_{23} + \sigma_{33}) + 2X_1X_2(\sigma_{12} - \sigma_{13} - \sigma_{23} + \sigma_{33})$
$+ 2X_1 (\sigma_{13} - \sigma_{33}) + 2X_2(\sigma_{23} - \sigma_{33}) + \sigma_{33}$

point above the line $(1 - X_1 - X_2 = 0)$ is not attainable because it violates the condition that $X_3 = 1 - X_1 - X_2 \geqslant 0$.

We define an *isomean* curve to be the set of all points (portfolios) with a given expected return. Similarly an *isovariance* line is defined to be the set of all points (portfolios) with a given variance of return.

An examination of the formulae for E and V tells us the shapes of the isomean and isovariance curves. Specifically they tell us that typically[9] the isomean curves are a system of parallel straight lines; the isovariance curves are a system of concentric ellipses (see Fig. 2). For example, if $\mu_2 \neq \mu_3$ equation 1' can be written in the familiar form $X_2 = a + bX_1$; specifically (1)

$$X_2 = \frac{E - \mu_3}{\mu_2 - \mu_3} - \frac{\mu_1 - \mu_3}{\mu_2 - \mu_3} X_1.$$

Thus the slope of the isomean line associated with $E = E_0$ is $-(\mu_1 - \mu_3)/(\mu_2 - \mu_3)$ its intercept is $(E_0 - \mu_3)/(\mu_2 - \mu_3)$. If we change E we change the intercept but not the slope of the isomean line. This confirms the contention that the isomean lines form a system of parallel lines.

Similarly, by a somewhat less simple application of analytic geometry, we can confirm the contention that the isovariance lines form a family of concentric ellipses. The "center" of the system is the point which minimizes V. We will label this point X. Its expected return and variance we will label E and V. Variance increases as you move away from X. More precisely, if one isovariance curve, C_1, lies closer to X than another, C_2, then C_1 is associated with a smaller variance than C_2.

With the aid of the foregoing geometric apparatus let us seek the efficient sets.

X, the center of the system of isovariance ellipses, may fall either inside or outside the attainable set. Figure 4 illustrates a case in which X falls inside the attainable set. In this case: X is efficient. For no other portfolio has a V as low as X; therefore no portfolio can have either smaller V (with the same or greater E) or greater E with the same or smaller V. No point (portfolio) with expected return E less than E is efficient. For we have $E > E$ and $V < V$.

Consider all points with a given expected return E; i.e., all points on the isomean line associated with E. The point of the isomean line at which V takes on its least value is the point at which the isomean line

9. The isomean "curves" are as described above except when $\mu_1 = \mu_2 = \mu_3$. In the latter case all portfolios have the same expected return and the investor chooses the one with minimum variance.

As to the assumptions implicit in our description of the isovariance curves see footnote **12.**

Portfolio Selection

is tangent to an isovariance curve. We call this point $\hat{X}(E)$. If we let E vary, $\hat{X}(E)$ traces out a curve.

Algebraic considerations (which we omit here) show us that this curve is a straight line. We will call it the critical line l. The critical line passes through X for this point minimizes V for all points with $E(X_1, X_2) = E$. As we go along l in either direction from X, V increases. The segment of the critical line from X to the point where the critical line crosses

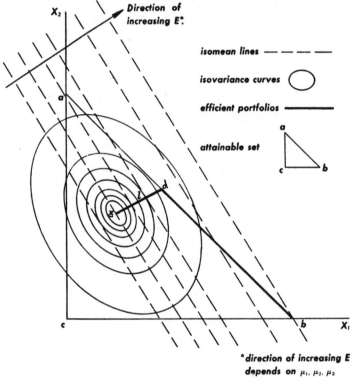

FIG. 2

the boundary of the attainable set is part of the efficient set. The rest of the efficient set is (in the case illustrated) the segment of the $\overline{ab}$ line from d to b. b is the point of maximum attainable E. In Figure 3, X lies outside the admissible area but the critical line cuts the admissible area. The efficient line begins at the attainable point with minimum variance (in this case on the $\overline{ab}$ line). It moves toward b until it intersects the critical line, moves along the critical line until it intersects a boundary and finally moves along the boundary to b. The reader may

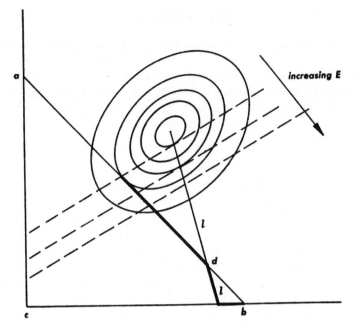

FIG. 3

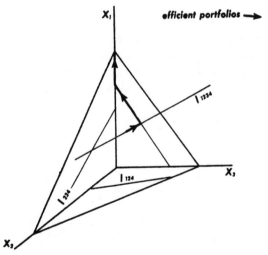

FIG. 4

Portfolio Selection   87

wish to construct and examine the following other cases: (1) X lies outside the attainable set and the critical line does not cut the attainable set. In this case there is a security which does not enter into any efficient portfolio. (2) Two securities have the same μ_i. In this case the isomean lines are parallel to a boundary line. It may happen that the efficient portfolio with maximum E is a diversified portfolio. (3) A case wherein only one portfolio is efficient.

The efficient set in the 4 security case is, as in the 3 security and also the N security case, a series of connected line segments. At one end of the efficient set is the point of minimum variance; at the other end is a point of maximum expected return[10] (see Fig. 4).

Now that we have seen the nature of the set of efficient portfolios, it is not difficult to see the nature of the set of efficient (E, V) combinations. In the three security case $E = a_0 + a_1 X_1 + a_2 X_2$ is a plane; $V = b_0 + b_1 X_1 + b_2 X_2 + b_{12} X_1 X_2 + b_{11} X_1^2 + b_{22} X_2^2$ is a paraboloid.[11] As shown in Figure 5, the section of the E-plane over the efficient portfolio set is a series of connected line segments. The section of the V-paraboloid over the efficient portfolio set is a series of connected parabola segments. If we plotted V against E for efficient portfolios we would again get a series of connected parabola segments (see Fig. 6). This result obtains for any number of securities.

Various reasons recommend the use of the expected return-variance of return rule, both as a hypothesis to explain well-established investment behavior and as a maxim to guide one's own action. The rule serves better, we will see, as an explanation of, and guide to, "investment" as distinguished from "speculative" behavior.

---

10. Just as we used the equation $\sum_{i=1}^{4} X_i = 1$ to reduce the dimensionality in the three security case, we can use it to represent the four security case in 3 dimensional space. Eliminating X_4 we get $E = E(X_1, X_2, X_3)$, $V = V(X_1, X_2, X_3)$. The attainable set is represented, in three-space, by the tetrahedron with vertices $(0, 0, 0)$, $(0, 0, 1)$, $(0, 1, 0)$, $(1, 0, 0)$, representing portfolios with, respectively, $X_4 = 1$, $X_3 = 1$, $X_2 = 1$, $X_1 = 1$.

Let s_{123} be the subspace consisting of all points with $X_4 = 0$. Similarly we can define $s_{a1}, \ldots, aa$ to be the subspace consisting of all points with $X_i = 0$, $i \neq a_1, \ldots, aa$. For each subspace $s_{a1}, \ldots, aa$ we can define a *critical line* $la_1, \ldots aa$. This line is the locus of points P where P minimizes V for all points in $s_{a1}, \ldots, aa$ with the same E as P. If a point is in $s_{a1}, \ldots, aa$ and is efficient it must be on $la_1, \ldots, aa$. The efficient set may be traced out by starting at the point of minimum available variance, moving continuously along various $la_1, \ldots, aa$ according to definite rules, ending in a point which gives maximum E. As in the two dimensional case the point with minimum available variance may be in the interior of the available set or on one of its boundaries. Typically we proceed along a given critical line until either this line intersects one of a larger subspace or meets a boundary (and simultaneously the critical line of a lower dimensional subspace). In either of these cases the efficient line turns and continues along the new line. The efficient line terminates when a point with maximum E is reached.

11. See footnote 8.

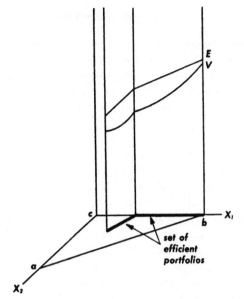

set of
efficient
portfolios

FIG. 5

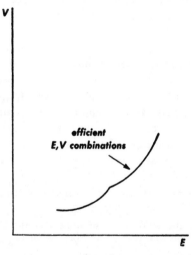

efficient
E,V combinations

FIG. 6

Portfolio Selection   89

Earlier we rejected the expected returns rule on the grounds that it never implied the superiority of diversification. The expected return-variance of return rule, on the other hand, implies diversification for a wide range of μ_i, σ_{ij}. This does not mean that the E-V rule never implies the superiority of an undiversified portfolio. It is conceivable that one security might have an extremely higher yield and lower variance than all other securities; so much so that one particular undiversified portfolio would give maximum E and minimum V. But for a large, presumably representative range of μ_i, σ_{ij} the E-V rule leads to efficient portfolios almost all of which are diversified.

Not only does the E-V hypothesis imply diversification, it implies the "right kind" of diversification for the "right reason." The adequacy of diversification is not thought by investors to depend solely on the number of different securities held. A portfolio with sixty different railway securities, for example, would not be as well diversified as the same size portfolio with some railroad, some public utility, mining, various sort of manufacturing, etc. The reason is that it is generally more likely for firms within the same industry to do poorly at the same time than for firms in dissimilar industries.

Similarly in trying to make variance small it is not enough to invest in many securities. It is necessary to avoid investing in securities with high covariances among themselves. We should diversify across industries because firms in different industries, especially industries with different economic characteristics, have lower covariances than firms within an industry.

The concepts "yield" and "risk" appear frequently in financial writings. Usually if the term "yield" were replaced by "expected yield" or "expected return," and "risk" by "variance of return," little change of apparent meaning would result.

Variance is a well-known measure of dispersion about the expected. If instead of variance the investor was concerned with standard error, $\sigma = \sqrt{V}$, or with the coefficient of dispersion, σ/E, his choice would still lie in the set of efficient portfolios.

Suppose an investor diversifies between two portfolios (i.e., if he puts some of his money in one portfolio, the rest of his money in the other. An example of diversifying among portfolios is the buying of the shares of two different investment companies). If the two original portfolios have *equal* variance then typically[12] the variance of the resulting (compound) portfolio will be less than the variance of either original port-

---

12. In no case will variance be increased. The only case in which variance will not be decreased is if the return from both portfolios are perfectly correlated. To draw the iso-variance curves as ellipses it is both necessary and sufficient to assume that no two distinct portfolios have perfectly correlated returns.

folio. This is illustrated by Figure 7. To interpret Figure 7 we note that a portfolio (P) which is built out of two portfolios $P' = (X_1', X_2')$ and $P'' = (X_1'', X_2'')$ is of the form $P = \lambda P' + (1 - \lambda)P'' = (\lambda X_1' + (1 - \lambda)X_1'', \lambda X_2' + (1 - \lambda)X_2'')$. P is on the straight line connecting P' and P''.

The E-V principle is more plausible as a rule for investment behavior as distinguished from speculative behavior. The third moment[13] M_3 of

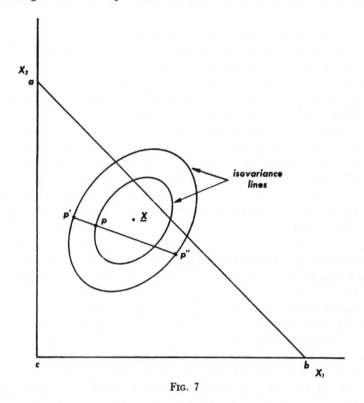

FIG. 7

the probability distribution of returns from the portfolio may be connected with a propensity to gamble. For example if the investor maximizes utility (U) which depends on E and $V (U = U(E, V), \partial U/\partial E > 0, \partial U/\partial E < 0)$ he will never accept an actuarially fair[14] bet. But if

13. If R is a random variable that takes on a finite number of values $r_1, \ldots, r_n$ with probabilities $p_1, \ldots, p_n$ respectively, and expected value E, then $M_3 = \sum_{i=1}^{n} p_i (r_i - E)^3$

14. One in which the amount gained by winning the bet times the probability of winning is equal to the amount lost by losing the bet, times the probability of losing.

$U = U(E, V, M_3)$ and if $\partial U/\partial M_3 \neq 0$ then there are some fair bets which would be accepted.

Perhaps—for a great variety of investing institutions which consider yield to be a good thing; risk, a bad thing; gambling, to be avoided—E, V efficiency is reasonable as a working hypothesis and a working maxim.

Two uses of the E-V principle suggest themselves. We might use it in theoretical analyses or we might use it in the actual selection of portfolios.

In theoretical analyses we might inquire, for example, about the various effects of a change in the beliefs generally held about a firm, or a general change in preference as to expected return versus variance of return, or a change in the supply of a security. In our analyses the X_i might represent individual securities or they might represent aggregates such as, say, bonds, stocks and real estate.[15]

To use the E-V rule in the selection of securities we must have procedures for finding reasonable μ_i and σ_{ij}. These procedures, I believe, should combine statistical techniques and the judgment of practical men. My feeling is that the statistical computations should be used to arrive at a tentative set of μ_i and σ_{ij}. Judgment should then be used in increasing or decreasing some of these μ_i and σ_{ij} on the basis of factors or nuances not taken into account by the formal computations. Using this revised set of μ_i and σ_{ij}, the set of efficient E, V combinations could be computed, the investor could select the combination he preferred, and the portfolio which gave rise to this E, V combination could be found.

One suggestion as to tentative μ_i, σ_{ij} is to use the observed μ_i, σ_{ij} for some period of the past. I believe that better methods, which take into account more information, can be found. I believe that what is needed is essentially a "probabilistic" reformulation of security analysis. I will not pursue this subject here, for this is "another story." It is a story of which I have read only the first page of the first chapter.

In this paper we have considered the second stage in the process of selecting a portfolio. This stage starts with the relevant beliefs about the securities involved and ends with the selection of a portfolio. We have not considered the first stage: the formation of the relevant beliefs on the basis of observation.

15. Care must be used in using and interpreting relations among aggregates. We cannot deal here with the problems and pitfalls of aggregation.

THE JOURNAL OF
POLITICAL ECONOMY

Volume LIX   APRIL 1951   Number 2

WEALTH, SAVING, AND THE RATE OF INTEREST

LLOYD A. METZLER

University of Chicago

I

THE fundamental thesis of classical economics, that a free-market economy has an automatic tendency to approach a state of full employment, has been a subject of heated controversy in recent decades. Indeed, after the publication of Keynes's *General Theory* there were many economists who rejected the classical thesis completely on the ground that it contained internal inconsistencies. Today, however, we are witnessing a renaissance of the classical doctrines. In part, the renaissance is attributable to world-wide economic developments since the end of the war, which have been characterized by a high level of demand and by full employment in almost all industrial countries. But the rebirth of classical theory is also attributable, in part, to attempts to reconstruct the classical doctrines along lines which make them immune to the Keynesian criticisms.

The principal architect of the reconstruction is Pigou;[1] but the basic idea of

[1] A. C. Pigou, *Employment and Equilibrium* (London, 1941), chap. vii; "The Classical Stationary State," *Economic Journal*, LIII (December, 1943), 342–51.

the remodeled classical theory can be found in the works of other economists as well, particularly in the works of Scitovszky[2] and Haberler.[3] The innovation which these economists introduced was a reconsideration, or perhaps I should say an elaboration, of the forces determining the quantity of real saving. In the classical theory the amounts of saving and investment out of a full-employment level of income were regarded as functions of the interest rate alone, and the latter was thus the primary governing force of the economic system as a whole. Equilibrium was attained, according to the classical theory, only when the interest rate was such that the quantity of real saving out of a full-employment income was equal to the quantity of real investment.[4] Scitovszky,

[2] T. Scitovszky, "Capital Accumulation, Employment and Price Rigidity," *Review of Economic Studies*, VIII (1940–41), 69–88.

[3] G. Haberler, *Prosperity and Depression* (3d ed.; Geneva, 1941), pp. 491–503.

[4] Consider, for example, the following remark of J. S. Mill: "There must be, as in other cases of value, some rate [of interest] which . . . may be called the natural rate; some rate about which the market rate oscillates, and to which it always tends to return. This rate partly depends on the amount of

Pigou, and Haberler retained this basic concept of equilibrium but argued that saving depends upon the real value of privately held wealth as well as upon the interest rate. Other things remaining the same, they said, real saving tends to be smaller and real expenditure for consumption tends to be larger, the larger is the real value of private wealth. For convenience, I shall hereafter use the expression "saving-wealth relation" to designate such a functional connection between current saving and private wealth.

The saving-wealth relation was employed by Pigou and Haberler to defend the classical theory against the criticism of Keynesian economics. In particular, the relation was employed to show that a flexible-wage economy has an automatic tendency to approach a state of full employment, as postulated in the classical theory. On account of the special purpose which it originally served, the saving-wealth relation is now widely considered to be a modification, but not a fundamental change, in the classical theory. Indeed, Haberler even suggests that some sort of functional connection between saving and wealth is implicit in works on economics which preceded the explicit recognition of the saving-wealth relation.[5]

I do not share these views. In my opinion the saving-wealth relation is more

nonclassical in its implications than any of the contributions to the subject would lead one to believe. Although the Scitovszky-Pigou-Haberler system resembles the classical system in its tendency toward a state of full employment, it is quite unlike the classical system in other respects, and these other respects have generally been overlooked. The most striking difference between the new system and the classical concerns the interest rate, and this is the subject which I wish to explore in the present paper.

The distinguishing feature of the classical theory of the interest rate is its emphasis upon so-called "real" conditions of demand and supply and its denial of the influence of monetary policy or banking policy. The classical economists believed that there exists a unique interest rate, or a unique pattern of long-term and short-term rates, at which the economic system is in equilibrium and that this unique interest rate cannot be influenced by changes in the quantity of money. The following quotation from Ricardo is representative of the classical opinion:

Interest for money . . . is not regulated by the rate at which the bank will lend, whether it be 5, 4, or 3 per cent, but by the rate of profits which can be made by the employment of capital, and which is totally independent of the quantity or of the value of money. Whether a bank lent one million, ten million, or a hundred millions, they would not permanently alter the market rate of interest; they would alter only the value of money which they thus issued. In one case, ten or twenty times more money might be required to carry on the same business than what might be required in the other.[6]

In contrast to the classical doctrine, the theory of the interest rate implicit in the Scitovszky-Pigou-Haberler system is at least partly a monetary theory, as I

accumulation going on in the hands of persons who cannot themselves attend to the employment of their savings, and partly on the comparative taste existing in the community for the active pursuits of industry, or for the leisure, ease, and independence of an annuitant" (*Principles* [5th ed.], Book III, chap. xxiii, § 1). Although Mill does not specify in this passage that the saving and investment which govern the interest rate are full-employment saving and full-employment investment, the tenor of his work strongly suggests that this is what he had in mind (see, e.g., *ibid.*, Book III, chap. xiv).

[5] *Op. cit.*, p. 499, n. 2.

[6] David Ricardo, *Principles of Political Economy* ("Everyman's ed."), p. 246.

shall demonstrate below. In this system there is no single interest rate and no single pattern of rates at which the economy is in equilibrium. Rather, there are an infinite number of different rates capable of performing the equilibrating function, and the particular rate that prevails at any given time depends to a considerable extent upon the policy of the banking authorities. Thus, in salvaging one feature of classical economics—the automatic tendency of the system to approach a state of full employment—Pigou and Haberler have destroyed another feature, namely, the real theory of the interest rate. In this respect Pigou, the archdefender of classical economics, has deserted Mill and Marshall and joined Schumpeter and Keynes![7] Although remnants of the classical, real theory of the interest rate remain, these are overshadowed, I believe, by the monetary feature which has been added. Moreover, the added feature which transforms the interest rate into a monetary rate is not liquidity preference, as in Keynesian economics, but the saving-wealth relation.

The subsequent analysis will be more understandable, I believe, if I digress from my principal theme long enough to

[7] Although Pigou is usually considered to be a defender of classical or neoclassical economic theory, his ideas concerning the interest rate were somewhat nonclassical even before the publication of his *Employment and Equilibrium*. He believed, in particular, that the banking system has a limited influence upon the equilibrium interest rate as well as upon the market rate. If the banks establish a market rate below the equilibrium rate, for example, prices and costs tend to rise, and the real expenditures of fixed-income groups are reduced. The resources thus freed are available for capital development, and the increased supply of capital reduces the equilibrium interest rate. Apart from this reservation, Pigou's earlier conception of the interest rate seems to be largely classical in its implications (see A. C. Pigou, *Industrial Fluctuations* [2d ed.; London, 1929], *passim*, but esp. p. 277).

indicate briefly the way in which the saving-wealth relation became prominent in economic theory. For this purpose consider an economic system in which the demand for investment is so low and the supply of saving so high that potential full-employment saving exceeds potential full-employment investment at all positive interest rates. In this event, there is no achievable interest rate which fulfils the classical condition of equilibrium. Whatever the interest rate may be, the demand for goods and services as a whole falls short of productive capacity. This is the Keynesian system in its simplest form. And the outcome of this situation, as envisaged by Keynes, is a cumulative reduction in output and employment, the reduction continuing until potential saving is reduced to the level of potential investment through a reduction in real income.

Suppose, however, that wages and other factor costs tend to fall when unemployment develops. To what extent will the reduction in costs stimulate output and move the system back toward full employment? Keynes argued that a general wage reduction affects output primarily through its influence on the interest rate. Any decline in wages and other costs is likely to result, he asserted, in a corresponding decline in other prices. In real terms, then, the only significant effect of the reduction in wages and other costs is an increase in the real value of money balances which tends, through liquidity preference, to reduce the interest rate. If full-employment saving exceeds full-employment investment at all possible interest rates, however, the reduction in the interest rate cannot conceivably eliminate all the deflationary gap and restore output to the full-employment level. Keynes's theory thus leads to the conclusion that wage-and-cost reductions are not an effective remedy for deficient demand.[8]

Pigou attempted to refute this Keynesian view concerning wage-and-cost reductions, and in doing so he introduced the saving-wealth relation. He suggested that, as wages and prices decline, the resulting increase in the real value of money balances will stimulate demand in a way which is independent of the change in the interest rate. Money balances constitute a part of private wealth, and the increase in the former accordingly implies an increase in the latter. As the real value of private wealth increases, the amount of saving out of a full-employment level of real income tends to decline. In this manner the excess of potential saving over potential investment which accounted for the initial unemployment is eventually eliminated. In the absence of barriers to price-and-cost reductions, the system thus has an automatic tendency to approach a state of full employment, as envisaged in the classical theory. Saving is brought into line with investment not primarily through a reduction of the interest rate but rather through a general deflation and a corresponding increase in the real value of the money supply.

I do not wish to discuss the relevance of the saving-wealth relation to the arguments frequently heard for a policy of over-all flexibility of wages and prices. Other economists have pointed out that the portion of cash balances whose real value is increased by a general deflation normally constitutes a relatively small part of total assets and that an enormous reduction of prices would therefore be required to increase the real value of a country's total wealth by any substantial amount. They have argued, further, that the general increases or decreases in prices and costs required for the successful operation of such a system might easily lead to expectations of additional price increases or decreases which would upset the stability of the whole system.[9] Such questions of economic policy, however, are not the immediate concern of this paper. I mention them here only to avoid a possible misunderstanding of what I shall say later. In what follows, I shall make the most favorable assumptions possible as to the effects of price movements upon the demand for goods and services; I shall ignore the adverse influence of fluctuating prices upon expectations and assume that there is a substantial tendency for saving to decline when the real value of private wealth rises. Given these favorable assumptions, I shall then ask how an economic system containing the saving-wealth relation is related to classical theory.

II

Before describing the theory of interest implicit in the Scitovszky-Pigou-Haberler system, I wish to say something about the meaning of a "monetary" theory of interest rates. A theory is usually regarded as a monetary theory if the economic system envisaged is one in which the equilibrium interest rate, or the equilibrium pattern of rates, can be altered by a change in the quantity of

[8] J. M. Keynes, *General Theory of Employment, Interest and Money* (New York, 1936), chap. xix. On p. 267 of this chapter, Keynes says: "There is, therefore, no ground for the belief that a flexible wage policy is capable of maintaining a state of continuous full employment; . . . The economic system cannot be made self-adjusting along these lines."

[9] M. Kalecki, "Professor Pigou on 'The Classical Stationary State,' a Comment," *Economic Journal*, LIV (April, 1944), 131–32; D. Patinkin, "Price Flexibility and Full Employment," *American Economic Review*, XXXVIII (September, 1948), 543–64.

money. Although this definition is satisfactory for most purposes, it is not sufficiently accurate to characterize an economic system containing the saving-wealth relation. It is inadequate, in particular, because it does not indicate the manner in which the quantity of money is altered. As I shall demonstrate below, the influence of a change in the quantity of money in the Scitovszky-Pigou-Haberler system depends not only upon the magnitude of the change but also upon the way in which it is brought about. Some changes in the quantity of money will alter the equilibrium interest rate while others will not.

We may distinguish, I believe, between two fundamentally different types of increase or decrease in the quantity of money. The first type is a change which takes place through open-market transactions of the central bank. The significant feature of this type of change is that it consists of an exchange of one form of asset for another. When money holdings are increased through central-bank purchase of securities, for example, holdings of securities outside the central bank are reduced by a corresponding amount. The second type of change consists of a direct increase or decrease in the money supply without any off-setting changes in private holdings of other assets. The supply of money may be reduced, for example, by a currency reform in which one unit of new money is exchanged for two units of old. Or the supply of money may be reduced by means of a governmental budgetary surplus, provided that the excess monetary receipts are impounded. In both these examples the supply of money is altered without altering private holdings of other assets, and it is this characteristic which distinguishes the second type of monetary change from the first.

I intend to show in subsequent parts of this paper that the theory of interest implicit in the Scitovszky-Pigou-Haberler system is a monetary theory if the change in the quantity of money is of the first type and a real theory if the change is of the second type. This means that open-market transactions of the central bank will have a *permanent* influence on the interest rate at which the system is in equilibrium, even after the bank has stopped its purchases or sales of securities. If the change in the quantity of money does not affect the private holdings of other assets, however, it will have no lasting influence on the interest rate. With respect to the rate of interest, the Scitovszky-Pigou-Haberler theory thus occupies an intermediate position between the classical theory and the Keynesian. The classical theory is a real theory of the interest rate from the point of view of both types of monetary change. According to the classical doctrine, neither a central-bank purchase or sale of securities nor an arbitrary increase or decrease in the quantity of money can have any effect upon the interest rate at which the economic system returns to equilibrium. As I have indicated above, the equilibrium interest rate of the classical theory is the rate at which full-employment potential saving is equal to full-employment potential investment, and this equilibrium rate is independent of both the quantity of money and the policy of the central bank. The classical theory, then, is a nonmonetary or real theory of the interest rate, regardless of whether the monetary disturbance is of the first type or the second type.

At the other extreme is Keynes's theory, which is a purely monetary theory from the point of view of either type of monetary disturbance. According to Keynes, the rate of interest is governed largely by the decisions of asset-holders concerning the proportions in which they wish to hold money and securities; that is, in Keynes's terminology, the rate is determined by liquidity preference.[10] Other things remaining unchanged, the desired ratio between money and securities tends to rise with a fall in the interest rate, and the equilibrium interest rate is the one at which the desired ratio of money to securities corresponds to the actual ratio. From this it follows that any monetary or banking policy which increases the actual quantity of money relative to the actual quantity of securities will reduce the interest rate at which the system is in equilibrium. Thus, both an arbitrary increase in the quantity of money (a disburbance of the second type) and an increase in the quantity of money through a limited and temporary purchase of securities by the central bank (a disturbance of the first type) will reduce the equilibrium interest rate in Keynes's system.

This brief and somewhat elliptical summary of the Keynesian and classical theories of the interest rate is intended to emphasize the polar positions which the two theories occupy, relative to the theory implicit in the Scitovszky-Pigou-Haberler system. The equilibrium interest rate in the classical theory is independent of monetary disturbances, regardless of whether such disturbances are of the first type or the second type. The equilibrium interest rate in Keynes's theory, on the other hand, can be permanently altered by a monetary disturbance of either type. In short, the classical theory is a real theory from the point of view of either type of disturbance, while the Keynesian theory is a monetary theory from the point of view of either type. The polar positions of the two the-

[10] Keynes, *op. cit.*, chaps. xiii, xv, and xviii.

ories explain, I believe, why no distinction has been made in the past between the two types of monetary disturbance. As I shall demonstrate below, however, the theory of the interest rate implicit in the Scitovszky-Pigou-Haberler system is intermediate between the classical theory and the Keynesian theory. It is a monetary theory from the point of view of the first type of monetary disturbance and a real theory from the point of view of the second type. But all this will, I hope, become clear as we proceed.

III

The economic system which will be investigated below is one in which the capital market is subject to three main influences: (1) the influence of current saving and investment, as in the classical or neoclassical theory; (2) the influence of decisions concerning the holding of cash or securities, as in Keynes's doctrine of liquidity preference; and (3) the influence of wealth on current saving, as in the Scitovszky-Pigou-Haberler reconstruction of the classical theory. I assume that the equilibrium rate of interest, or the equilibrium pattern of rates, is determined by the interplay of these three influences.

At the outset I wish to make a number of simplifying assumptions. Although these assumptions are somewhat unrealistic, few of them are absolutely essential, and most of them could be substantially modified without altering any of my principal results. I assume, in the first place, that the economy with which we are dealing is a closed economy with a fixed amount of labor. Second, I assume that the wage rate tends to rise whenever the demand for labor is greater than the fixed supply and to fall whenever the demand is smaller than the fixed supply. Third, I assume that all agents of production except labor are produced means of production and that all production is carried on at constant returns to scale. Under these conditions the relative prices of all commodities and services are determinate and independent of the commodity composition of the national income. We can therefore speak unambiguously of a rate of total output, or of a level of national income, at which the economy's resources are fully employed. Fourth, I assume that owners of private wealth hold such wealth in only two forms, money (including demand deposits) and common stock, and that all common stock involves approximately the same degree of risk.[11] Fifth, I assume that the central bank is legally author-

[11] Common stock has been selected as the typical security in order to avoid the difficulties associated with bonds during periods of inflation or deflation. Throughout the paper I assume that, in the absence of movements in interest rates, common-stock prices rise or fall to the same extent that other prices rise or fall, so that a general inflation or deflation does not affect the real value of securities. This means that the real value of a given quantity of securities is a function of the rate of interest alone. (See below.) Although the theory is simplified in this respect by regarding common stock as the typical security, two new problems are thereby introduced, and these must not be overlooked. Perhaps most important, when all investment is financed by issuing common stock, the idea of a functional relation between the rate of interest and the real volume of investment becomes somewhat vague. Under these circumstances businessmen do not commit themselves, as they do when they issue bonds, to the payment of fixed capital charges. Saying that investment depends upon the rate of interest when all securities are common stocks is equivalent to saying that businessmen undertake more investment when stock prices are high than when they are low.

Apart from the problem of defining an investment function, the use of common stock in our argument presents the further problem of separating risk payments from interest payments per se. I have attempted to avoid this second problem by assuming that the degree of risk is about the same for one stock as for another. I realize, however, that such an assumption does not meet the basic difficulty and that, in a more extended treatment of the subject, allowance should be made for differences in risk.

ized to buy and sell the common stock held by the owners of private wealth and that this common stock constitutes the only nonmonetary asset of the banking system.

Given these assumptions, one can readily construct a simple geometric interpretation of the forces governing the interest rate. These forces will operate in two different markets: a market for goods and services as a whole and a market for securities. Consider, first, the market for goods and services. Stability of the general price level in the goods-and-services market obviously requires that the total demand arising from a full-employment level of real income shall be equal to the economy's productive capacity; and this is equivalent to the requirement that potential saving out of a full-employment level of income shall be equal to potential investment. If potential investment at full employment exceeds potential saving, the demand for goods and services as a whole exceeds full-employment output; prices and costs accordingly tend to rise. If potential full-employment investment falls short of potential full-employment saving, on the other hand, this implies that the demand for goods and services as a whole falls short of full-employment output. Hence prices and costs tend to fall.

In the classical theory real saving and real investment were functions of a single variable—the interest rate—and the economy was assumed to be in equilibrium at only one rate. In the theory now being investigated, however, the amount of real saving at full employment is regarded as a function of two variables—the interest rate and the real value of wealth in the hands of the savers. As soon as the second variable is introduced, the concept of a single interest rate at which the goods-and-services market is in equilibrium loses its meaning. In place of the equilibrium rate of classical theory, we now have a schedule of rates, or a functional relation between the interest rate and the real value of private wealth.

In order to see how such a schedule can be derived, suppose that on a certain date the total of all privately held wealth —money and securities combined—has a certain real value. If the value of private wealth is fixed, saving may be regarded as a function of the rate of interest alone, and I shall assume that with this given saving schedule a rate of interest can be found at which full-employment saving is equal to full-employment investment. Consider, now, what would happen if the interest rate were arbitrarily increased above its equilibrium level. At the higher interest rate potential saving out of a full-employment income would exceed potential investment, which means that, other things remaining the same, the community's demand for goods and services would fall short of its capacity to produce. In other words, the increase in the rate of interest, taken by itself, would bring about a deflationary gap. But if the community's combined holdings of money and securities were increased in some manner at the same time that the rate of interest were raised, then the deflationary gap might be avoided. The increase in asset holdings would tend to reduce the amount of saving corresponding to any given rate of interest, thereby offsetting, or perhaps more than offsetting, the tendency toward excessive saving attributable to the rise in the rate of interest. The rise in the rate of interest would reduce investment, but the increase in the value of private wealth would reduce saving; and it is thus conceivable that full-employment potential saving might equal potential investment at the higher interest rate as well as at the lower rate.

Many other combinations of the interest rate and the real value of private wealth will fulfil the condition that full-employment saving equals full-employment investment, and we may accordingly conceive of a schedule or a functional relation indicating what the real value of private wealth would have to be, for many different interest rates, in order to make the community's demand for goods and services as a whole equal its capacity to produce. The real value of private wealth which fulfils this condition will be an increasing function of the rate of interest. Such a function is plotted as the line WW in Figure 1. For convenience, WW will be called the "wealth-requirements schedule." At any point on this line potential saving out of full-employment income is equal to potential investment. But, as we move upward and to the right along the line, both saving and investment decline. Investment declines because of the rise in the interest rate, while saving declines because of the increase in the real value of private wealth. Any point below WW in Figure 1 represents a point of inflationary potential. At such a point the rate of interest is too low, given the value of private wealth, to bring about an equality between full-employment saving and investment. The demand for goods and services thus exceeds capacity, and prices tend to rise. In the same way one can show that any point *above* WW represents a point of *de*flationary potential. It follows that the demand for goods and services is equal to the economy's productive capacity only for combinations of the interest rate and the value of private wealth lying on WW.

The wealth-requirements schedule has been developed, above, in terms of the real value of private wealth as a whole, and no distinction has been made between private holdings of money and private holdings of securities. Such a distinction has thus far been unnecessary because saving was assumed to be a function of *total* asset holdings and not of the *composition* of these assets. When we later discuss the securities market, however, we shall find that the division of total assets between money and securities is the decisive factor in this market. Our later task will accordingly be simplified if the wealth-requirements schedule can be broken down into its two com-

the other way round, we may say that the real value of the given common stock is inversely related to the prevailing rate of interest. The higher the rate of interest, the lower the real value of common-stock holdings and conversely. In Figure I the value of the community's security holdings is expressed as such a function of the interest rate by the line AA.

I wish to show, now, how the wealth-requirements schedule, WW, can be expressed in terms of money and interest

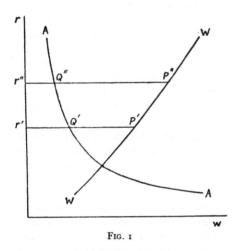

FIG. I

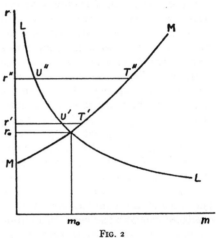

FIG. 2

ponent parts, namely, money and common stock.

If the community holds a given amount of common stock, the real value of these stock holdings will obviously depend upon the interest rate. Indeed, the interest rate itself is nothing more than the yield of the stock, and this yield, in turn, is the ratio of the income earned by the stock to its market price. In the short run the income earned by the common stock is a given amount, determined by the fixed supplies of the various agents of production; and this means that the yield, or the rate of interest, varies inversely with the real value of the stock. To put the matter

rates rather than in terms of total wealth and interest rates. For this purpose, suppose that the interest rate is temporarily set at r'' in Figure I. The wealth-requirements schedule tells us that, in order to prevent an excess or deficiency of demand from developing in the goods-and-services market at this interest rate, the community's holdings of money and securities combined will have to be $r''P''$. But the value of securities alone, at an interest rate of r'', is the distance $r''Q''$ in Figure I. If the community is to have a sufficient amount of total assets to maintain a balance between demand and supply in the goods-and-service market, its holdings of money will ·

therefore have to equal the difference between $r''P''$ and $r''Q''$, or $Q''P''$. This difference is plotted in Figure 2 as the line $r''T''$. A similar construction for a rate of interest r' carries over the distance $Q'P'$ of Figure 1 to $r'T'$ of Figure 2. The line MM of Figure 2 is the locus of all such points as T' and T''. Given the community's private holdings of securities, MM indicates the amount of money which will have to be held, at any particular interest rate, in order to keep the amount of saving out of full-employment income equal to the amount of investment. For brevity, MM will be called the "money-requirements schedule." The money-requirements schedule is thus the horizontal difference between the wealth-requirements schedule, WW, and the schedule of the real value of securities, AA.

IV

The line MM of Figure 2, like WW of Figure 1, indicates the conditions needed to maintain a balance between supply and demand in the market for currently produced goods and services. In addition to this goods-and-services market, the market for securities must also be taken into account. The entire economic system cannot be in equilibrium unless the latter market, as well as the former, has reached a balanced position. The market for *new* securities has already been allowed for, by implication, in the preceding discussion of saving and investment; in the absence of hoarding, equality between saving and investment implies equality between the supply of and the demand for new securities. But this new-securities market is usually a relatively small part of the total securities market; in many countries, indeed, the value of new securities offered on the market in a given year is an exceedingly

small fraction of the value of previously issued, or old, securities. This means that decisions of asset-holders to augment or reduce their stocks of old securities will frequently exert a much greater influence on the rate of interest than will discrepancies between current saving and current investment. The old-securities market must therefore be taken into account, along with the market for goods and services as a whole, in order to complete the description of interest rates given by Figures 1 and 2.

The existing stock of securities will influence security prices and the rate of interest only if asset-holders, on balance, decide to increase or decrease their holdings of securities, that is, only if the typical asset-holder wishes to substitute additional money for part of his security holdings or additional securities for part of his money holdings. Decisions of this sort depend largely upon the *composition* rather than the size of asset portfolios. Thus, in deciding whether to buy or sell securities, the typical asset-holder compares the existing ratio between his money holdings and his security holdings with the ratio which he regards as satisfactory under the given economic conditions. The degree of his actual liquidity, compared with a sort of optimum liquidity, governs his actions in the securities market.

I shall follow Keynes in assuming that, other things remaining the same, the typical asset-holder wishes to increase his liquidity as the rate of interest falls. Unless the banking authorities intervene, however, private asset-holders cannot, on balance, increase or decrease their holdings of old securities; as of a given moment of time, both the number of shares of stock and the quantity of money in private hands are fixed quantities. This means that, if the prevailing money-securities ratio differs from the desired ratio, security prices and the rate of interest must continue to change until the desired ratio is brought into line with the prevailing ratio; in short, the demand must be adjusted to the existing supply through appropriate movements in the rate of interest.

The influence of liquidity preference may be examined from another direction, and for present purposes this alternative point of view is more convenient. Instead of starting with a fixed amount of securities and a fixed quantity of money and asking how the rate of interest will be adjusted so that demand will equal supply, we may start with a fixed amount of securities and a fixed interest rate and ask what the total money holdings would have to be in order to satisfy the typical asset-holder with his money-securities ratio. By assuming a number of different interest rates and making similar calculations for each, a liquidity-preference schedule, or a demand-for-money schedule, can thus be built up. Suppose, for example, that, at an interest rate of r'' (Fig. 1), the typical asset-holder wishes to hold money in an amount equal to two-thirds the value of his security holdings. At this interest rate the security holdings of the community as a whole have a real value of $r''Q''$, as shown in Figure 1. It follows that asset-holders as a group will attempt to alter their security holdings and hence alter the rate of interest, unless the real value of money holdings amounts to two-thirds of $r''Q''$. Let the point U''' in Figure 2 be chosen so as to make $r''U'''$ equal to two-thirds of $r''Q''$. Suppose, now, that, when the interest rate falls to r', the typical asset-holder wishes to hold money equal to the full value of his securities. The value of total securities at an interest rate of r' is $r'Q'$ (Fig. 1), and the condition of equi-

librium in the old-securities market requires that money holdings shall equal this same amount. We may therefore select a point, U', in Figure 2 such that $r'U'$ is equal to $r'Q'$. The liquidity-preference schedule, LL, in Figure 2 is the locus of all such points as U''' and U'; it shows what the community's holdings of money would have to be, at any given interest rate, in order to create a proper balance between cash and securities.

From the construction of the diagram it is apparent that there are two reasons why the demand for money, LL (Fig. 2), tends to rise as the rate of interest falls. First, the typical asset-holder usually wants to hold a larger ratio of cash to securities at low interest rates than at high rates. And, second, the real value of securities, the denominator of the cash-securities ratio, is increased by a fall in the interest rate. In most discussions of liquidity preference only the first of these reasons is taken into account, but the second may be equally important.[12]

V

I have now discussed two different functional relations between the rate of interest and the real quantity of money; the first of these I called a money-requirements schedule, while the second is the usual liquidity-preference schedule. The money-requirements schedule represents all combinations of money balances and the rate of interest for which the community's demand for goods and services as a whole is exactly equal to its capacity to produce. At any point not on this schedule there is either an excess or a deficiency of demand and consequently

[12] The best account I have found of the second reason for the negative slope of the liquidity-preference schedule is by E. Solomon in "Money, Liquidity, and the Long-Term Rate of Interest: An Empirical Study, 1909–38" (University of Chicago dissertation, 1950).

a tendency for prices and costs to rise or fall. The money-requirements schedule, *MM*, thus indicates the possible combinations of the interest rate and the quantity of real cash balances which will maintain over-all price equilibrium in the goods-and-services market. The liquidity-preference schedule, on the other hand, describes the conditions of price equilibrium in the *securities* market. If the actual quantity of real cash balances lies on *LL*, there will be no tendency for

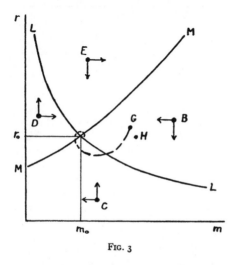

FIG. 3

asset-holders as a whole to attempt to shift from securities to cash or from cash to securities and, accordingly, no tendency for the price of securities or the rate of interest to change. At any point *not* on *LL*, however, the price of securities will either rise or fall, depending upon whether the demand for cash at the prevailing interest rate is smaller or greater than the actual amount.

From Figure 2 it is now apparent that only one combination of the interest rate and the real value of money balances will satisfy the conditions of equilibrium in both the goods-and-services market

and the securities market. I have denoted this combination by the two letters r_0 and m_0. If all prices, including wages and the costs of other agents of production, tend to rise when demand exceeds supply and to fall when supply exceeds demand, the combination r_0 and m_0 is the one toward which the economic system will gravitate. The nature of this market mechanism will be clarified, I believe, if we consider what happens to the system when the interest rate and the real value of money balances differ from the equilibrium combination r_0 and m_0.

This is done in Figure 3, where I have reproduced the essential features of Figure 2. The points B, C, D, and E in Figure 3 represent four points which do not lie on either the liquidity-preference schedule or the money-requirements schedule. Suppose, first, that the actual situation with regard to the rate of interest and the real value of cash balances at a given moment of time can be represented by the point B. What happens, in this event, to the variables of our system? The liquidity-preference schedule shows that, at the rate of interest represented by B, the community's demand for real money balances falls short of actual money holdings. Asset-holders accordingly attempt to substitute securities for their excess cash holdings, thereby forcing up security prices and reducing the rate of interest. Moreover, in the situation B the goods-and-services market as well as the securities market is out of balance. The diagram shows that, at the prevailing interest rate, money holdings are too large to bring about an equality between full-employment saving and full-employment investment. Saving is below the equilibrium level because of the excessive cash holdings, and the demand for goods and services thus exceeds the economy's capacity to produce.

As a result, prices tend to rise, and the real value of money balances is reduced. The movements in the rate of interest and in the real value of money balances are indicated by the short arrows emanating from point B.

By similar reasoning one can demonstrate that, at point C, security prices tend to fall, and the interest rate is correspondingly increased, while the prices of goods and services rise and the real value of cash balances is reduced. Likewise, at D, security prices fall, the rate of interest is increased, commodity prices and wages fall, and the real value of cash balances tends to rise. Finally, if the actual position of the variables is at E, security prices rise, the interest rate is reduced, commodity prices fall, and the real value of cash balances is thus increased. Movements of the variables in the neighborhood of the points C, D, and E have again been indicated by arrows.

Figure 3 demonstrates that when the economic system is out of balance at least one force is always operating to bring the variables of the system closer to the equilibrium point, r_0, m_0. The other force, indicated by the second of the two arrows at each of the points B, C, D, and E, operates in such a way as to impart a circular or cyclical movement to the variables. This suggests that, if the rate of interest and the quantity of real cash balances were initially at some nonequilibrium point such as G, the approach to equilibrium might be a spiral or damped cycle like the one depicted in Figure 3. Although such a damped cycle is possible, it is not inevitable, as I shall demonstrate in the Appendix. In any event, I believe it is highly unlikely that the cyclical movement implied by Figure 3 bears any close resemblance to the typical observed business cycle. Most observed cycles are cycles of output and

employment, whereas the cycle depicted in Figure 3 is largely a cycle of prices and interest rates.[13] I have presented the dynamic problem concerning the movements of prices and interest rates merely to show the tendency of the system to approach an equilibrium position and not as a contribution to the theory of business cycles.

VI

I have now shown that the market for goods and services and the market for securities can be in equilibrium simultaneously only at the point r_0, m_0 and that the economic system has an automatic tendency to approach this equilibrium. Superficially, this suggests a close analogy between the rate of interest, r_0, and the classical concept of the equilibrium rate. Like the equilibrium rate of classical theory, the rate r_0 is the only one compatible, under the assumed conditions, with equilibrium of the economic system as a whole; that is, r_0 is the only rate which satisfies both the liquidity-preference requirement and the requirement that full-employment saving shall be equal to full-employment investment. Why, then, does r_0 not have as much claim to be regarded as a real rate as does the classical concept of the real rate of interest?

Whether the rate r_0 is a real rate or a monetary rate depends, as I have indicated earlier, upon the nature of the

---

[13] Superficially, the cycle of interest rates and prices described above seems to be somewhat like the monetary part of Hicks's business-cycle theory. In reality, however, the two cyclical processes are quite different. The process envisaged by Hicks involves movements of output and employment rather than movements of prices and costs; and savings in Hicks's theory depend upon the rate of interest and real income, whereas savings in the present paper depend upon the rate of interest and the real value of private wealth (J. R. Hicks, *A Contribution to the Theory of Business Cycles* [London: Oxford University Press, 1949], chaps. 11 and 12).

monetary disturbance. If the disturbance is of the first type—that is, if it is a change in the quantity of money associated with the purchase or sale of securities by the central bank—it will alter some of the functional relations of Figure 1 and 2 and will accordingly change the equilibrium interest rate. The rate r_0 must therefore be regarded as a monetary rate from the point of view of monetary disturbances of this sort. On the other hand, if the monetary disturbance is of the second type, which consists of an increase or decrease in the quantity of money without any offsetting changes in other assets, then it will not alter the functional relations of Figures 1, 2, and 3 and will not permanently change the interest rate. The rate r_0 is thus a real rate from the point of view of monetary disturbances of the second type. Because it is simple to describe, I shall first consider a monetary disturbance of the second type.

Suppose that the economic system is initially in equilibrium at a rate of interest r_0 and a quantity of real cash balances m_0. And suppose that, while other things initially remain unchanged, the quantity of money is arbitrarily doubled by giving to each holder of money an additional quantity equal to the amount he already holds. Temporarily, the variables of the system will then be at point H of Figure 3; except for the increase in the quantity of money, nothing in the system will have changed. As I have shown above, however, there will be an automatic tendency for the variables of the system to return eventually to the former equilibrium position, r_0 and m_0. At point H both the securities market and the goods-and-services market will be out of balance, and changes will therefore occur in the interest rate and in the level of prices. The changes in prices, in

turn, will affect the real value of cash balances.

Consider, first, the securities market. After the initial monetary disturbance, the quantity of money held by the typical asset-holder is larger than he would like to hold at the prevailing interest rate, r_0. Asset-holders as a group therefore attempt to convert some of their excess cash into securities. As a result, security prices rise, which means that the interest rate falls. The fall in the interest rate increases investment, while the initial increase in the real value of cash balances reduces saving. The demand for goods and services as a whole thus exceeds productive capacity, so that commodity prices and costs begin to rise. The rise in prices tends to reduce the real value of cash balances and thereby initiates a movement of the variables back toward the original equilibrium position. The details of this dynamic process need not concern us here. Suffice it to say that the system as a whole will not be restored to equilibrium until the real value of cash balances is reduced to m_0 and the rate of interest is restored to its former level, r_0.

If the central bank does not acquire or dispose of any assets during the period of adjustment, the real value of money balances can be reduced only by an increase in the price level. Since the real value of cash balances is ultimately restored to its former level, m_0, we know that the increase in prices, in the final position of equilibrium, must be as large as the original increase in the quantity of money. In other words, doubling the nominal quantity of money must result eventually in doubling all money prices and costs, including the money prices of securities as well as the money prices of goods and services. The real variables of the system all return to their former equilibrium levels. The rate of interest, the real value of saving and investment, and the real value of securities, as well as the real value of cash balances, are all the same in the new equilibrium as before the monetary disturbance occurred. The only permanent effect of increasing the quantity of money is a proportionate increase in the general level of prices and costs.[14]

With respect to monetary disturbances of the second type, such as the one I have just described, the economic system embodying both a saving-wealth relation and a liquidity-preference schedule is evidently quite similar to the classical system. In both the classical system and the system depicted in Figure 3 the values of all real variables are independent of the quantity of money. But this is true of the system in Figure 3 only if the monetary disturbances are of the second type, whereas it is true of the classical system for both types of monetary disturbance. If the disturbance is of the first type, which consists of open-market transactions by the central bank, then the equilibrium interest rate will be altered, as I have suggested above. With respect to monetary disturbances of the first type, the equilibrium interest rate of Figure 3 is therefore a monetary rate, and in this regard it resembles the Keynesian interest rate more closely than it does the classical. In other words, by purchasing or selling securities, the banking authorities can alter not only the tem-

[14] Using a model more complex than the one I have been considering, D. Patinkin previously demonstrated that if both the saving-wealth relation and liquidity-preference are active forces, monetary disturbances of the second type will not affect the equilibrium interest rate (see "The Indeterminacy of Absolute Prices in Classical Economic Theory," *Econometrica*, XVII [January, 1949], 23–27). Patinkin did not examine the effects of monetary disturbances of the first type and accordingly concluded that the model he had constructed was closer to the classical model than to the Keynesian.

porary interest rate which prevails while the open-market transactions are taking place but also the rate at which the system will return to equilibrium after the bank's transactions in securities have ceased.

The power of the banking authorities to alter the equilibrium interest rate is attributable not to their influence upon the nominal quantity of money but to their influence upon the quantity and value of privately held securities. A central-bank purchase of securities, for example, reduces the quantity of privately held securities. This means that the AA schedule of Figure 1 is shifted to the left. And since the liquidity-preference schedule, LL, and the money-requirements schedule, MM, were both derived, in part, from the AA schedule, a shift in the latter causes the former schedules to shift as well. The system as a whole therefore comes into balance, after the securities purchases have been made, at a different rate of interest.

The effect of open-market transactions upon the equilibrium of the system can be described in terms of a ratio indicating the proportion of the total supply of securities held in private hands. Let this ratio be represented by the letter λ. Consider, first, the situation in which λ has a value of 1.0. This means that the total available supply of securities is held by private asset-holders, so that the central bank's assets consist exclusively of currency. Given the holdings of securities by private asset-holders, the rate of interest at which the system is in equilibrium can be determined, as in our earlier illustration, by the intersection of a liquidity-preference schedule, LL, and a money-requirements schedule, MM. Assuming that the value of private asset holdings when $\lambda = 1.0$ is given in Figure 4 by the solid line AA and that the wealth-requirements schedule is WW, the liquidity-preference schedule and the money-requirements schedule can be derived as in my earlier illustration. These derived schedules, for $\lambda = 1.0$, are represented in Figure 5 by the solid lines LL and MM, respectively. Under the assumed conditions with respect to security holdings, the equilibrium rate of interest is r_0, and the equilibrium value of real cash balances is m_0, as shown in Figure 5.

Suppose that this equilibrium is disturbed by a substantial purchase of se-

the real money supply. In view of our interest in the equilibrium of the system, we may pass over the dynamic problems and investigate, instead, the influence of the central bank's security purchases upon the schedules in Figures 4 and 5 which determine the ultimate resting places of our variables.

Suppose that the central bank continues to purchase securities until it has acquired one-third of the common stock available to the economy as a whole and that all transactions between asset-

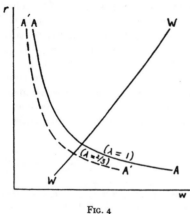

FIG. 4

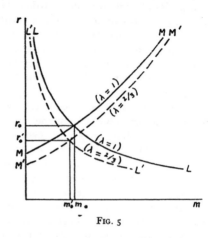

FIG. 5

curities on the part of the central bank. The dynamic process by which the economy adapts itself to such open-market transactions will probably be highly complicated. The securities will be purchased at many different prices from the various asset-holders, and this means that we cannot predict exactly how the open-market transactions will affect the cash balances of all asset-holders together. In any event, the real value of cash balances will be influenced by price movements as well as by the central bank's dealings in securities, and it is the combined effect of both influences which ultimately governs the equilibrium value of

holders and the central bank cease at this point. When the securities market and the goods-and-services market are once again in equilibrium, how will the rate of interest compare with the rate that prevailed before the open-market transactions began? According to the classical theory, the rate of interest. should return to its former level as soon as the bank's security purchases have ceased. According to the system depicted in Figures 4 and 5, however, the security purchases by the central bank will permanently *lower* the equilibrium rate of interest.

If the bank acquires one-third of all

THE RATE OF INTEREST   109

available securities, the security holdings of private asset-holders will of course be only two-thirds as large as they formerly were, so that λ will have a value of $\frac{2}{3}$. This means that at any given interest rate the real value of private security holdings will be two-thirds of its former value. The broken line $A'A'$ of Figure 4 is drawn at two-thirds of the horizontal distance of the solid line AA from the vertical axis, and $A'A'$ thus represents the real value of private security holdings, expressed again as a function of the rate of interest, after the central bank has acquired its securities. The wealth-requirements schedule, WW, depends upon preferences and upon the savings and investment schedules and presumably will be unaffected by the open-market transactions. Since the money-requirements schedule, MM, depends upon the value of private security holdings as well as upon WW, however, the MM schedule will be shifted. At any given rate of interest, the total assets—money and securities combined—needed to maintain equality between full-employment saving and full-employment investment will be the same as before. But the value of private security holdings has been reduced by the central bank's purchases, and this means that total assets cannot be maintained at the level needed for full employment unless private money holdings are increased by a corresponding amount. In short, the money-requirements schedule, MM, is moved to the right by the same amount that the securities schedule, AA, is moved to the left.[15]

[15] In describing the consequences of open-market transactions, I assume that the securities schedule, AA, is the only schedule of Figure 4 which is *directly* influenced by the central bank's purchase or sale of securities; the other schedules (i.e., the wealth-requirements schedule, the money-requirements schedule, and the liquidity-preference schedule) are assumed to be affected only in so far as they are related to, or derived from, the securities sched-

The new money-requirements schedule corresponding to $λ = \frac{2}{3}$ is shown in Figure 5 as the broken line $M'M'$.

The liquidity-preference schedule, as well as the money-requirements schedule, is affected by the central bank's purchase of securities. At any given interest rate, the proportions in which the typical asset-holder wishes to hold money and securities are presumably the same as in the old equilibrium. The value of private security holdings, however, is now only two-thirds of the former value at the same interest rate. The desired ratio between money holdings and security holdings will thus not be maintained unless the real value of money balances is reduced to two-thirds of its former value. In other words, the LL schedule in Figure 5 is shifted to the left, the relative amount of the shift being the same as the leftward shift of the securities schedule, AA. The new liquidity-preference schedule,

ule, AA. This implies that the income available to the typical asset-holder is not altered by the central bank's dealings in securities. If disposable income tended to fall or to rise with an increase or decrease in the central bank's holdings of securities, the saving and investment schedules would also be affected, and the wealth-requirements schedule, which is derived from the saving and investment schedules, would tend to shift.

Taken by themselves, however, open-market transactions may well have a slight influence on disposable income. If the central bank buys securities, for example, the income on these securities is transferred from the former owners to the bank. In the absence of offsetting transactions, the security purchases thus reduce the disposable income of private asset-holders and increase the profits of the central bank by a corresponding amount. I do not wish to discuss the complications introduced by this connection between open-market transactions and disposable income. I therefore assume throughout that any additional profits which the central bank earns by reason of its acquisition of securities are ultimately passed on to private hands in the form of reduced taxes. Under these circumstances, the security purchases by the bank will redistribute income between former asset owners and taxpayers but will not influence the total of disposable income.

for $\lambda = \frac{2}{3}$, is represented in Figure 5 by the line $L'L'$.

The combined effect of the shift in the liquidity-preference schedule and of the shift in the money-requirements schedule is a reduction in the equilibrium rate of interest from r_0 to r'_0, as indicated in Figure 5. Thus, the banking authorities by means of a limited purchase of securities have *permanently* reduced the interest rate at which the economic system is in equilibrium. The dynamic process of adjustment by which the equilibrium interest rate moves from r_0 to r'_0 will probably be highly complex, as I have indicated earlier. Nevertheless, I believe that the influence of the central bank upon the equilibrium interest rate will stand out more clearly if we consider a greatly simplified dynamic sequence.

When the central bank begins to purchase securities, the first effect is a rise in security prices and a corresponding decline in the rate of interest. The actual security transactions themselves do not alter the total value of private asset holdings but merely change the form in which assets are held. The initial result of the bank's purchases, therefore, is a rise in the value of private asset holdings (capital gains) together with a reduction in the rate of interest and a shift on the part of asset-holders from securities to money. One may presume that at the new, lower rate of interest the asset-holders have exchanged securities for cash in such a way as to satisfy their demands for liquidity; for, if this were not true, the prices of securities would continue to rise, and the interest rate to fall, until the asset-holders were willing to part with the amount of securities that the central bank wanted to buy. Although the point representing the new quantity of private money holdings and the new, temporary rate of interest will

thus lie somewhere on the liquidity-preference schedule $L'L'$, it cannot at the same time lie on the money-requirements schedule, $M'M'$, or the wealth-requirements schedule, WW. The fall in the interest rate, taken by itself, would normally lead to an excess of full-employment investment over full-employment saving and thus create an excess demand for goods and services. The inflationary pressure is further increased, however, by the capital gains, which increase the value of total private wealth holdings and thereby reduce current saving. As a result, prices and costs tend to rise, and the real value of the money supply is correspondingly reduced. The rise in prices and the reduction in the real value of private money holdings must continue until the real value of security-and-cash holdings combined is low enough to encourage a sufficient amount of saving to make full-employment saving once more equal to full-employment investment. The new equilibrium is finally achieved, as Figures 4 and 5 demonstrate, at a permanently lower rate of interest.

Now, since the new equilibrium must lie on the wealth-requirements schedule, WW, as well as on the money requirements schedule, $M'M'$, it is obvious that, when prices have finally stopped rising and the rate of interest has reached its new and lower equilibrium, the value of total private wealth must be smaller than in the old equilibrium. In short, the final result of the open-market security purchases by the central bank is a reduction in the real value of the total wealth in private hands. This reduction has occurred in two stages: the liquidity of the typical asset-holder has first been increased through the central-bank purchase of securities; and the real value of the larger liquid balances has subsequently been reduced through inflation. Thus, under a regime of flexible prices, central-bank purchase of securities is an indirect means of reducing the real value of the total assets—cash and securities combined—in private hands. The reduction in the value of privately held wealth tends, in turn, to increase saving and thereby reduces the rate of interest at which full-employment saving is equal to full-employment investment. To summarize briefly, then, we may say that the central bank is able to alter the equilibrium rate of interest through its power to alter the real value of private wealth.

VII

Assuming that saving depends upon the real value of private wealth as well as upon the interest rate, I have now demonstrated that the equilibrium interest rate is partly a real rate, as in the classical theory, and partly a monetary rate, as in Keynes's theory. Monetary disturbances of one type affect the equilibrium interest rate of the system, while disturbances of another type do not. In general, any monetary disturbance which alters the amount of securities held by the typical asset-holder tends also to affect the interest rate at which the economic system as a whole is in equilibrium. On the other hand, any monetary disturbance which does not affect private security holdings will leave the equilibrium interest rate unchanged.

The distinction which I have made between the two types of monetary disturbance suggests that the true cause of a change in the interest rate is not a change in the quantity of money per se but a change in the amount of other assets held by the typical asset-holder. This conjecture is, indeed, correct. Open-market transactions of the central bank

alter the equilibrium interest rate not because they affect the quantity of money but because they affect the quantity of privately held securities. Consider again, for example, the open-market transactions which I have described in Figures 4 and 5. In those illustrations the central bank is assumed to purchase one-third of all privately held securities. As a consequence, the level of prices is increased, the real value of private wealth declines, the propensity to save increases, and real saving finally comes into balance with real investment at a permanently lower interest rate.

Suppose, now, that the amount of privately held securities were reduced without any offsetting change in the quantity of money. Such a reduction could be brought about by a capital levy of one-third on all securities, payable only in kind. In other words, the government could require that one-third of all privately held securities be turned over to it. In what respects would the effects of such a policy differ from the effects of the open-market transactions described in Figures 4 and 5? Examination of the figures reveals that the interest rate, the volume of real investment, the real value of cash balances, and the other real variables of the system are affected in exactly the same way by a one-third levy in kind upon all securities as by a central-bank purchase of the same amount of securities. The nominal quantity of money is of course larger when the securities are acquired by purchase than when they are acquired by taxation. But the real value of bank balances is exactly the same, in the new position of equilibrium, in both cases. Thus, the only difference between the effects of the two means of acquiring the securities is a difference in the level of prices and costs. The price level is higher when the securities are acquired by purchase than when they are acquired by taxation. In all other respects the two situations are identical as far as the final results are concerned.

The foregoing example reveals the close analogy between central-bank security purchases and a capital levy on securities. In the system investigated above, a purchase of securities by the central bank is a means of reducing the real value of privately held wealth and operates just as effectively in this direction as a corresponding capital levy payable in kind. Indeed, the central bank's power to alter the equilibrium interest rate arises exclusively from its influence on the real value of privately held securities.

Through its power to change the interest rate, the central bank can also affect the rate of growth of the economy as a whole. At each different equilibrium interest rate full-employment saving is of course equal to full-employment investment, but the amount of real saving and investment varies with variations in the equilibrium interest rate. When the equilibrium rate is increased, the economic system comes into balance at a lower real value of investment and saving; and, when the equilibrium rate is reduced, the real value of saving and investment tends to increase. By purchasing securities, the central bank can reduce the real value of private wealth, thereby increasing the propensity to save and causing the system to attain a new equilibrium at a permanently lower interest rate and a permanently higher rate of capital accumulation. In a similar manner, the bank, through sales of securities, can increase the real value of private wealth, lower the propensity to save, raise the equilibrium rate of interest, and reduce the rate of capital accumulation.

Whether the bank has a substantial influence or only a negligible influence upon the rate of growth of the system depends upon its authority to buy and sell securities and upon the magnitude of the saving-wealth relation. If the saving-wealth relation is large, so that the propensity to save increases or decreases appreciably as the real value of private wealth falls or rises, and if the bank is authorized to buy and sell securities in large quantities, then the rate of growth may be affected to a considerable extent by central-bank policy. In practice, however, there will usually be an institutional barrier to the amount of securities the bank can sell; it cannot sell more securities than it owns. And this means that, when the bank has divested itself of all its securities, it has no further power to raise the equilibrium interest rate and lower the rate of growth. There may be a similar barrier to the amount of securities the bank can purchase, since only certain types of assets are eligible for the bank's portfolio. If the bank has acquired all the assets it is authorized to purchase, no further reduction of private wealth, and no further increase in private saving, can be accomplished by central-bank activity in the securities market.

In terms of the theory set out above, we may say that the central bank's power over the equilibrium interest rate and the equilibrium rate of growth will usually be determined by institutional arrangements which prevent it from purchasing more than a small fraction of private wealth or from selling more assets than it possesses. This might mean, for example, that the institutional arrangements were such that the value of λ would have to lie between 0.9 and 1.0. In most countries these institutional limits may well be so narrow that the actual power of the central bank to in-

THE RATE OF INTEREST 113

fluence the equilibrium of the system is negligible. Nevertheless, if saving depends upon the real value of private wealth as described in the saving-wealth relation, the rate of interest must be regarded as partly a monetary rate. For, if the institutional limits to central-bank action were removed or reduced, the possible variation in the equilibrium interest rate which could be brought about by the central bank would be correspondingly increased.

APPENDIX

The geometrical methods employed in the text of this paper were not sufficiently powerful to deal with some of the more difficult problems encountered, particularly the dynamic problems. I am therefore adding an analytical appendix. The symbols used in this appendix have the following meanings:

r represents the rate of interest, or the yield on common stock

m represents the real value of private money holdings

a represents the real value of all common stock, whether held by private owners or by the central bank

λ represents the proportion of the total supply of common stock held by private owners

w represents the real value of all privately held wealth, including both money and common stock

S represents the real value of current saving

I represents the real value of current investment

The amount of real saving out of a full-employment income is assumed to depend upon the real value of private wealth as well as upon the rate of interest, and we may accordingly write $S = S(r, w)$. Investment, under conditions of full employment, is assumed to depend only upon the rate of interest, and the investment function may therefore be written as follows: $I = I(r)$. If real national income under conditions of full employment is y_0, and if a proportion, c, of this consists of business profits, the real value of all common stock will be the capitalized value of these profits, thus: $a = cy_0/r$. The only remaining functional relation to be defined is the liquidity-preference function. Let $L(r)$ be such a function, indicating the proportion in which asset-holders as a group wish to hold money and common stock. With the aid of these definitions we may now write down the following system of equations:

$$\left.\begin{array}{c} S(r, w) = I(r), \\[2mm] L(r) = \dfrac{m}{\lambda a}, \\[2mm] w = \lambda a + m, \\[2mm] a = \dfrac{cy_0}{r}. \end{array}\right\} \quad (1)$$

The first of equations (1) expresses the condition that, in equilibrium, full-employment saving must equal full-employment investment. The second equation says that the rate of interest must be such that the desired proportion between money holdings and security holdings on the part of the owners of private wealth is equal to the actual proportion. The third equation is an identity, defining the real value of private wealth as the sum of private money holdings and private security holdings. Finally, the fourth of equations (1) says that the real value of all common stock is the capitalized value of business profits, where the capitalization is done at the prevailing rate of interest, r.

If the value of λ is given, equations (1) are sufficient to determine the equilibrium values of the four variables r, w, m, and a; i.e., the equations determine the rate of interest, the total real value of privately held wealth, the real value of money balances, and the real value of all common stock. The price level does not enter explicitly in equations (1), since all variables are in real terms. Nevertheless, price movements are implicitly taken into account through movements of m, the real value of the money supply. In the absence of open-market transactions, indeed, m can change only by means of general inflation or deflation.

Security purchases or sales by the central bank are indicated in equations (1) by changes in the value of λ. An increase in λ, for example, indicates a larger proportion of total securities in private hands and hence signifies security sales by the central bank. Changes in λ will obviously alter the equilibrium values of all our variables. In order to see how a central-bank sale of securities affects these equilibrium values, we may differentiate (1) with respect to λ, as follows:

$$
\left.
\begin{aligned}
(S_r - I_r)\frac{dr}{d\lambda} + S_w\frac{dw}{d\lambda} && = 0\,, \\[6pt]
-\frac{1}{\lambda a}\frac{dm}{d\lambda} + L_r\frac{dr}{d\lambda} && +\frac{m}{\lambda a^2}\frac{da}{d\lambda} = -\frac{m}{\lambda^2 a}\,, \\[6pt]
\frac{dm}{d\lambda} && -\frac{dw}{d\lambda} +\lambda\frac{da}{d\lambda} = -a \\[6pt]
-\frac{a}{r}\frac{dr}{d\lambda} && -\frac{da}{d\lambda} = 0
\end{aligned}
\right\}
\tag{2}
$$

Solving equations (2) for

$$
\frac{dr}{d\lambda},\quad \frac{dm}{d\lambda},\quad \frac{dw}{d\lambda},\quad \text{and} \quad \frac{da}{d\lambda},
$$

we find

$$
\left.
\begin{aligned}
\frac{dr}{d\lambda} &= -\frac{S_w}{\Delta}\left(\frac{1}{\lambda}+\frac{m}{\lambda^2 a}\right), \\[6pt]
\frac{dm}{d\lambda} &= \frac{1}{\Delta}\left\{(S_r - I_r)\frac{m}{\lambda^2 a} - aS_w L_r\right\}, \\[6pt]
\frac{dw}{d\lambda} &= \frac{1}{\Delta}(S_r - I_r)\left(\frac{1}{\lambda}+\frac{m}{\lambda^2 a}\right), \\[6pt]
\frac{da}{d\lambda} &= \frac{1}{\Delta}\frac{aS_w}{r}\left(\frac{1}{\lambda}+\frac{m}{\lambda^2 a}\right).
\end{aligned}
\right\}
\tag{3}
$$

The symbol Δ in equations (3) represents the basic determinant of the system, i.e.,

$$
\left.
\begin{aligned}
\Delta \equiv
\begin{vmatrix}
0 & S_r - I_r & S_w & 0 \\[4pt]
-\dfrac{1}{\lambda a} & L_r & 0 & \dfrac{m}{\lambda a^2} \\[4pt]
1 & 0 & -1 & \lambda \\[4pt]
0 & -\dfrac{a}{r} & 0 & -1
\end{vmatrix}, \\[10pt]
\equiv (S_r - I_r)\frac{1}{\lambda a} + S_w L_r - \frac{S_w}{r} - \frac{m S_w}{\lambda a r}.
\end{aligned}
\right\}
\tag{4}
$$

The subscripts in equations (3) and (4) indicate differentiation of the S, I, and L functions with respect to the variable appearing in the subscript. I assume the system is stable in the classic sense that an increase in the rate of interest creates an excess of potential saving over potential investment; this implies that $S_r - I_r$ is positive. The saving-wealth relation is represented in (3) and (4) by S_w, which is negative, indicating that an increase in the real value of private wealth reduces real saving. The slope L_r of the liquidity-preference schedule is assumed to be negative, which implies that an increase in the rate of interest reduces the desired ratio between money and securities.

With the given signs of S_r, I_r, etc., one can see from (4) that Δ is a positive determinant. Moreover, the direction of change of most of the variables of the system can be readily determined. Thus, (3) shows that $dr/d\lambda$ is positive, $dw/d\lambda$ is positive, and $da/d\lambda$ is negative. This means that open-market sales of securities have increased the rate of interest, increased the real value of private wealth (cash and securities combined), and reduced the real value of the total supply of common stock. The only change whose sign is indeterminate is $dm/d\lambda$, the change in the real value of private money holdings. The reason for this indeterminacy is not far to seek: the central-bank sales of securities have reduced private money balances, but the real value of the remaining private balances have subsequently been increased through a general deflation. The final position of real money balances thus depends upon the relative strength of these opposing forces. But whatever happens to the real value of privately held money, equations (3) show that privately held wealth as a whole has been increased by the central bank's sales of securities. The increase in the real value of private wealth has reduced the rate of saving, and it is this reduction of saving which accounts for the permanent rise in the equilibrium rate of interest.

Thus far I have investigated the stationary or equilibrium values of the system without saying anything about the dynamic process of adjustment. I shall conclude this appendix with a few remarks concerning the behavior of the variables through time, during intervals when the system is not in equilibrium.

Consider, first, the behavior of prices when total demand is different from productive capacity. The difference between demand and productive capacity is measured, of course, by the difference between potential full-employment saving and potential full-employment investment. If the former exceeds the latter, demand for goods and services falls short of productive capacity, and prices and costs accordingly tend to decline. Conversely, if full-employment investment exceeds full-employment saving, total demand exceeds capacity, and both prices and costs rise. In the absence of new borrowing or lending by the banking system, however, an increase in prices is equivalent to a fall in the real value of money balances, and the time movement of the general price level may therefore be described in terms of movements in the value of money. As a first dynamic postulate, then, I write:

$$\frac{dm}{dt} = k_1 [S(r, w) - I(r)]. \qquad (5)$$

Equation (5) says that the price level tends to fall, and the real value of money balances tends to rise, whenever potential saving exceeds potential investment. Likewise, prices rise, and the real value of money balances falls, when potential saving falls short of potential investment. The speed of the price movement, in both cases, is assumed in (5) to be proportional to the size of the inflationary or deflationary gap, and the constant, k_1, represents this speed of adjustment.

So much for the general price level in the commodity-and-service market. Consider next the movement of prices in the securities market. I assume, as I indicated in the text, that the securities market is dominated by transactions in old securities rather than by supply-and-demand conditions in the new-securities market. Specifically, I assume that security prices tend to rise whenever asset-holders on balance attempt to shift from money to securities and that security prices fall when asset-holders attempt a shift in the opposite direction. The attempted shift, in turn, depends upon whether

the actual ratio of cash to securities is higher or lower than the desired ratio, as indicated by the liquidity-preference function. Since a rise in security prices is equivalent to a fall in the rate of interest, our second dynamic postulate may be written

$$\frac{dr}{dt} = k_2 \left[L(r) - \frac{m}{\lambda a} \right]. \qquad (6)$$

In words, equation (6) says that the rate of interest rises, which means that security prices fall, when the desired ratio of money to securities exceeds the actual ratio. And, conversely, the rate of interest falls when the desired ratio is less than the actual ratio.

Equations (5) and (6) are the only equations of adjustment that we shall need. These two equations are the dynamic counterpart of the first two of equations (1). They do not form a complete system, however, since we have only two equations in four unknowns. Before we can solve our dynamic equations, we must have two more equations. The two missing equations are ·the third and fourth equations of our static system (1). These are merely definitional equations and are assumed to be satisfied at any moment of time, without lag. The third equation defines private wealth at a given moment as the sum of private security holdings and private money holdings, while the fourth equation defines the rate of interest as the yield on securities. The complete dynamic system is as follows:

$$\left.\begin{array}{l} \dfrac{dm}{dt} = k_1 [S(r, w) - I(r)], \\[2ex] \dfrac{dr}{dt} = k_2 \left[L(r) - \dfrac{m}{\lambda a} \right], \\[2ex] w = \lambda a + m \\[2ex] a = \dfrac{c y_0}{r} . \end{array}\right\} \quad (7)$$

Equations (7) cannot be explicitly solved, since we do not know the exact form of the functions S, I, and L. I shall therefore make a linear approximation of (7), which will be valid only for small deviations from the equilibrium values of the variables. If r_0, w_0, m_0, and a_0 represent the equilibrium values, we may write, as such a linear approximation,

$$\frac{dm}{dt} = \qquad k_1(S_r - I_r)(r - r_0) + k_1 S_w(w - w_0),$$

$$\frac{dr}{dt} = -k_2 \frac{1}{\lambda a}(m - m_0) + k_2 L_r(r - r_0) \qquad\qquad + k_2 \frac{m}{\lambda a^2}(a - a_0),$$

$$0 = \qquad (m - m_0) \qquad\qquad - (w - w_0) \qquad + \lambda(a - a_0),$$

$$0 = \qquad -\frac{a}{r}(r - r_0) \qquad\qquad - (a - a_0).$$

(8)

The solution of (8) takes the form

$$m = m_0 + A_1 e^{\rho_1 t} + A_2 e^{\rho_2 t},\qquad(9)$$

with similar results for r, a, and w, where A_1 and A_2 depend upon the initial values of the variables, and where ρ_1 and ρ_2 are the roots of the following equation:

$$\begin{vmatrix} -\rho & k_1(S_r - I_r) & k_1 S_w & 0 \\ -\dfrac{k_2}{\lambda a} & k_2 L_r - \rho & 0 & \dfrac{k_2 m}{\lambda a^2} \\ 1 & 0 & -1 & \lambda \\ 0 & -\dfrac{a}{r} & 0 & -1 \end{vmatrix} = 0.\qquad(10)$$

Equation (10) may be expended in powers of ρ as follows:

$$\rho^2 + \left(\frac{k_2 m}{\lambda a r} - k_2 L_r - k_1 S_w\right)\rho + k_1 k_2 \Delta = 0,\qquad(11)$$

where Δ is the basic determinant of the static system, (1).

The coefficients of the powers of ρ in equation (11) are positive, which means that the real parts of the roots of equation (11) are all negative. Thus the dynamic system is stable, for small deviations from equilibrium, regardless of the numerical values of L_r, S_w, etc. In other words, if the liquidity-preference function, the saving function, and the investment function do not alter their form or position as prices rise or fall, the dynamic system will eventually reach a stationary or static position. This does not mean, of course, that an economic system in which the saving-wealth relation is operative will always be a stable system in reality; for equations (7) and (8) have made no allowance for expectations, and such expectations may exert a strongly destabilizing influence on the system. If prices of commodities are rising, for example, consumers and producers may anticipate further price increases; if so, saving will probably decline and investment will increase, thereby widening the inflationary

gap and accelerating the price rise. Likewise, if security prices are rising, asset-holders may revise downward their estimate of what constitutes a normal ratio between money and securities; and, if they do, the resulting attempt to shift from money to securities will cause a further rise in securities prices. These possibilities suggest that equations (7) and (8) are stable only in a narrow sense.

Assuming that the system is stable, we may inquire, in conclusion, about the nature of the approach toward equilibrium. Is the solution of equation (8) cyclical or noncyclical? The answer to this question depends upon the roots of equation (10) or (11). The dynamic system will not be cyclical unless these roots are complex numbers. This means that $b^2 - 4c$ is negative, where b is the coefficient of ρ in (11) and c is the constant term. I leave it to the reader to prove the following propositions: (1) the roots of equation (11) may be either real or complex, which means that the dynamic system may or may not have a cyclical solution. (2) If k_1 and k_2, the speeds of adjustment in the commodity market and the securities market, respectively, are decidedly different in magnitude, the roots are likely to be real and the dynamic system is thus likely to be a noncyclical system. (3) If $S_r - I_r$ is large, so that a small rise in the rate of interest creates a substantial deflationary gap, the system will probably be cyclical.

[18]

A MODEL OF THE DEMAND FOR MONEY BY FIRMS *

Merton H. Miller and Daniel Orr

I. Introduction, 413. — II. A model of cash flows and the costs of cash management for business firms, 416; assumptions underlying the model, 417; optimal values of the policy parameters, 420; some properties of the solution, 423; implications for the demand for money by firms, 425; extension to allow for non-zero drift, 427. — III. The applicability of the model, 429. — Appendix, 433.

I. Introduction

Economists have long recognized the similarity between the problem of managing a cash balance and that of managing an inventory of some physical commodity. An early attempt to exploit this analogy was provided by Baumol [1] who applied to cash holdings the classical "lot size" model of inventory management that Whitin [2] had earlier brought to the attention of economists. Since that time, the analysis of the firm's control of physical stocks has been vastly extended by economists and others; but no parallel advance has occurred on the cash balance front. The Baumol model in its original or some more refined version (such as that of Tobin [3]) has remained the dominant tool for analyzing the "transactions" demand for money at the micro level.

Since the Baumol model will serve as the point of departure and of contrast for the results to be presented in this paper, it will be helpful first to summarize briefly the main assumptions and properties of that model. In essence, the decision-maker is pictured as holding two distinct types of asset: (1) an earning asset such as a savings deposit or "bond" which bears interest at given rate of, say, v per dollar per day; and (2) a noninterest bearing cash balance into which periodic receipts of income are deposited and from which a steady flow of expenditures are made at the constant rate of, say, m dollars per day.[4] Transfers of funds between the two accounts

* We wish to thank Eugene Fama, Milton Friedman, William Kruskal, Franco Modigliani, John F. Muth, Victor Niederhoffer and Lester Telser for helpful suggestions and comments. Francis Nourie set up and carried out the computations upon which Table I is based.
1. W. J. Baumol, "The Transactions Demand for Cash: An Inventory Theoretic Approach," this *Journal*, LXVI (Nov. 1952).
2. T. M. Whitin, *The Theory of Inventory Management* (Princeton University Press, 1953).
3. J. Tobin, "The Interest Elasticity of Transactions Demand for Cash," *Review of Economics and Statistics*, XXXVIII (Aug. 1956).
4. The Baumol model may also be applied to the opposite situation in

are permissible at any time, but only at a cost which, in the simplest version of the model, is taken as a constant, γ, independent of the amount transferred.[5] The precise nature of this transfer cost will vary depending on the context to which the model is being applied, but in all cases it is to be interpreted as including both the direct expenses of effecting the transfer (such as postage or bank service charges) and any opportunity costs (such as time spent waiting at the teller's window or in making and communicating decisions about purchases and sales of portfolio assets).

Given these conditions, an optimal cash management policy will call for the investment of the periodic receipts in the earning asset followed by a regularly timed sequence of security sales that transfers M dollars every $L = M/m$ days from the earning to the cash account. The operating cash balance will thus have the "sawtooth" form shown in Figure Ia. If the decision-maker assigns a

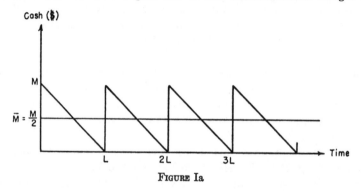

FIGURE Ia

relatively large value to M, transfers will be infrequent; but the average cash balance $\dfrac{M}{2}$ will also be high with a consequent substantial loss of interest earnings. If he assigns a low value to M, then the interest loss on idle funds is reduced, but the gains thereby realized may be eaten up by the in-and-out costs. The minimum cost solution, balancing these opposing forces, is given by the familiar "square root rule," viz., transfer $M^* = \left(\dfrac{2\gamma m}{\nu}\right)^{1/2}$ dollars every $L^* = \left(\dfrac{2\gamma}{m\nu}\right)^{1/2}$ days, implying an average cash balance (or long-run

which receipts from operations flow steadily into the cash balance at a constant rate per day subject to periodic large withdrawals for operating expenditures.

    5. Although γ represents what would ordinarily be called a "transaction cost" we shall refer to it throughout as a "transfer" cost, reserving the term "transactions" for the receipts and payments exogenous to the model.

THE DEMAND FOR MONEY BY FIRMS 415

demand for money) of $\overline{M}^* = \dfrac{M^*}{2} = \left(\dfrac{\gamma m}{2\nu}\right)^{1/2}.$[6]

Simple as it is, this inventory model of cash management, with its emphasis on the cost of putting idle cash to work, does capture the essence of one fundamental element underlying the demand for money — perhaps the single most important element in an economy such as ours with a wide variety of interest-bearing securities of very low risk and very quickly convertible to cash. Moreover, the assumptions with respect to cash flows underlying the Baumol model apply reasonably well to much of the household sector, particularly to salary-earning households. The model, however, is much less satisfactory, both from the positive and normative points of view when applied to business firms (and to entrepreneurial and professional households) who hold about half of the total money stock.

For many business firms, the typical pattern of cash management is not the simple, regular one of Figure Ia, but a more complex one which might appear as in Figure Ib. The cash balance fluctuates

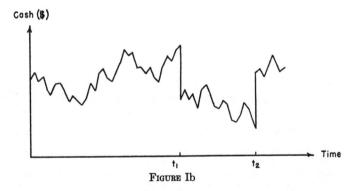

FIGURE Ib

irregularly (and to some extent unpredictably) over time in *both* directions — building up when operating receipts exceed expendi-

6. The expressions given are optimal only under the further assumption that the transfer costs under the policy are less than the interest earnings on the amounts transferred. If not, receipts should be kept entirely in cash and the average cash balance will be one-half the periodic receipt. Some additional difficulties arise with respect to the solution as developed by Baumol if the size of the periodic cash receipt is not an integer multiple of the optimal amount transferred. Tobin, *op. cit.*, presents a modified solution in which M is optimized subject to this "adding up" constraint. For further discussion and characterization of the minimum cost conditions see R. L. Teigen, "Demand and Supply Functions for Money in the United States: Some Structural Estimates," *Econometrica*, Vol. 32 (Oct. 1964) and H. G. Johnson, "Notes on the Theory of Transactions Demand for Cash," *Indian Journal of Economics*, XLIV (July 1963).

tures and falling off when the reverse is true. If the build-up is at all prolonged, a point is eventually reached (such as that indicated at t_1) at which the financial officer decides that cash holdings are excessive, and transfers a sizable quantity of funds either to the control of the portfolio staff for temporary investment or to loan retirement. In the other direction, in the face of a prolonged net drain, a level will be reached (as at t_2) at which the portfolio managers will be instructed to liquidate securities, or the firm will borrow to restore the cash balance to an "adequate working level."

The main purpose of this paper is to develop a simple, analytic model that incorporates both this "up and down" cash balance movement characteristic of business operations *and* the critical, lumpy transfer cost feature of the Baumol model. Note that we say *a* model, since for cash management as well as inventory management a wide variety of models will ultimately have to be developed by finance specialists and monetary theorists to cover all of the many important and interesting variations.[7]

II. A Model of Cash Flows and the Costs of Cash Management for Business Firms

We shall begin by listing the main assumptions underlying the model. Some of these will be recognized as mere technical simplifications. Others, however, are of a more substantive nature and will inevitably raise questions about the range of applicability of the model. Although we shall comment on certain of the substantive assumptions briefly here in passing, fuller consideration

7. In fact, there are already in the literature models that advance matters beyond the original Baumol model (such as Johnson, *op. cit.*), including some which allow for both positive and negative net changes in the cash balance. One such is the model developed by D. Patinkin in *Money, Interest, and Prices* (Evanston: Row Peterson, 1956), Chap. VII and further elaborated by Dvoretzky in the appendix to that book. It is essentially a "buffer stock" model focusing on the size of the initial cash balance needed to reduce the probability of cash run-outs during a "period" to some given, small level (transfers from other assets to cash being permitted only at the start of a period). The analysis is also restricted by the assumptions that total cash flows net out to zero in every period and that the total volume of transactions over the period is known in advance. More recently, D. Orr and W. G. Mellon have developed a model in the context of reserve holdings by banks, but otherwise similar in a number of respects to the model to be developed here, "Stochastic Reserve Losses and Expansion of Bank Credit," *American Economic Review*, LI (Sept. 1961). The main difference comes from the assumption in the Orr-Mellon model of a fixed settlement period for reserves — the Federal Reserve bi-weekly Wednesday call — which permits their problem to be treated as a series of independent, one-period decisions rather than as a single problem, continuous in time. Mention should also be made of a model for cash holdings by firms, very similar in spirit to ours, developed independently by Melvin Greenball, currently a student at the Graduate School of Business, University of Chicago.

of the matter of applicability is best postponed until Section III, after the model and its major empirical implications have been set forth.

1. The Assumptions Underlying the Model

A first group of assumptions represents the analogues and necessary extensions of those in the Baumol model. Specifically, we suppose: (1) that we continue to have a "two-asset" setting, one asset being the firm's cash balance and the other a separately managed portfolio of liquid assets (such as Treasury bills, certificates of deposit, commercial paper or other money market instruments) whose marginal and average yield is v per dollar per day; (2) that transfers between the two asset accounts may take place at any time at a given marginal cost of γ per transfer, independent of the size of the transfer, the direction of the transfer or of the time since the previous transfer;[8] and (3) that such transfers may be regarded as taking place instantaneously, i.e., that the "lead-time" involved in portfolio transfers is short enough to be ignored.

The third assumption serves, among other things, to eliminate the need for a precautionary "buffer stock" whose function in stochastic inventory problems is to protect against runouts during the lead-time. While an assumption of zero lead-time may seem quite strong at first glance, it is actually not unrealistic, at least for the larger firms with specialized staffs that monitor the cash balance and the portfolio closely. Transactions in most of the major money market instruments can be initiated by such firms merely by placing a telephone call, with delivery for the start of the next business day (and in some special cases even during the same day).[9]

---

8. Another cost component proportional to the amount transferred might be added to allow for the brokerage charges typically incurred when securities are sold before maturity. Such an extension is fairly easily handled in the context of the Baumol model. See Tobin, *op. cit.* Analytical results for the present problem, however, are much harder to obtain under that form of cost structure and would require methods different and considerably more complex than those to be used here.

9. To say that the model contains no buffer stock does not mean that we are ignoring the so-called "precautionary" motive for holding cash. While cash can be obtained instantaneously in the event of an unexpectedly large cash drain, it can only be obtained by incurring a transfer cost. Hence the possibility of such drains and consequent costs will affect the size of the optimal cash balance even though no specific part of the optimal holding can be separately identified as the precautionary balance. As for the so-called "speculative" motive, we would expect under present day conditions (where securities of very short maturity are always readily available) that most of any speculation on a fall in interest rates would take the form of shortening the maturity structure of the portfolio rather than of building up cash holdings. But the optimal cash holding might be affected indirectly by speculation, however, to the extent that the prospect of speculative gains were reflected in the value of v.

Consistent with present-day banking arrangements we shall further assume that there is a definite minimum level below which a firm's cash balance is not permitted to fall. Zero, of course, would be an absolute minimum since overdrafts are rarely allowed for business firms: even firms with open lines of credit must go through the formality (and expense) of a transfer to the cash balance before an overdrawn check will be cleared. In practice, required minimum balances are normally substantially greater than zero. The precise amount of the required minimum in any particular instance is negotiated between the parties and depends basically on the amount of banking services — mainly check processing and loan accommodation — that the firm actually uses. Since this required minimum is primarily a form of compensation to the bank in lieu of service charges we shall here regard it as completely exogenous to the problem of cash balance management and focus attention entirely on the discretionary holdings over and above the required minimum.[1] For further simplicity in notation we shall designate the required minimum level as zero.

A third group of assumptions specifies the nature of the fluctuations in the cash balance. In contrast to the completely deterministic Baumol model we shall here make the opposite extreme assumption that the net cash flows are completely stochastic; and, specfically, that they behave as if they were generated by a stationary random walk. Given this framework, it is convenient and yet sufficiently general for our purposes to suppose that the random behavior of the cash flows can be characterized as a sequence of independent Bernoulli trials. In particular, let $1/t =$ some small fraction of a working day such as 1/8, i.e., an "hour." We suppose that during any such hour the cash balance will either increase by m dollars with probability p, or decrease by m dollars with probability $q = 1-p$.[2] Over a longer interval of, say, n days, the observable

---

1. Little of importance is lost, we feel, by treating the minimum as exogenous and "suboptimizing" in terms of the "discretionary" balance only. Although a firm can certainly affect its required minimum to some extent by altering its use of bank services, the interaction of policies is likely to be extremely weak since the cost trade-offs involved and the speed with which adjustments can be made are of a very different kind in the two cases.

To the extent that a firm's required minimum balance changes over time — and it will do so periodically in response to changes in the level of activity in the account as well as to changes in the agreed interest rate used for computing the stock-equivalent of the service charge flows — we assume in effect that the whole discretionary balance is instantly and costlessly moved up or down by an appropriate transfer to or from the portfolio.

2. These increments or decrements represent only "operating" cash transactions and are to be regarded as exclusive of cash flows stemming from the portfolio, either transfers or run-offs of securities held. The proceeds of matured individual securities are assumed to be immediately reinvested.

THE DEMAND FOR MONEY BY FIRMS 419

distribution of changes in the cash balance will thus have mean $\mu_n = ntm(p - q)$ and variance $\sigma_n^2 = 4ntpqm^2$; and this distribution in turn will approach normality as n increases. Most of the subsequent discussion in the text will focus on the special symmetric or zero-drift case in which $p = q = 1/2$ (with the derivations for more complicated nonsymmetric cases relegated to the Appendix).

For this special case, $\mu_n = 0$, $\sigma_n^2 = nm^2t$ and $\sigma^2 = \dfrac{\sigma_n^2}{n} = m^2t = $ the variance of daily changes in the cash balance.

The Bernoulli process is by no means as restrictive in this context as it may appear at first glance. The properties of the Bernoulli process that are crucial for present purposes are not the implied regular timing or constant size of transaction; the critical features are rather serial independence, stationarity and the absence of discernible, regular swings in the cash balance. Any of a number of other familiar generating processes with these features might equally well have been used, all leading to the same solution as the one we present.[3]

The final set of assumptions concerns the firm's objective function. Here, following a standard practice in inventory theory we shall assume that the firm seeks to minimize the long-run average cost of managing the cash balance under some "policy of simple form."[4] In the present context, the simplest and most natural such policy is the two-parameter control-limit policy illustrated in Figure II. That is, the cash balance will be allowed to wander freely until it reaches either the lower bound, zero, or an upper bound, h, at which times a portfolio transfer will be undertaken to restore the balance to a level of z.[5] Hence, the policy implies that when the upper bound

3. That the results are not dependent on the assumed Bernoulli process can be verified by reference to a forthcoming paper by G. Antelman and I. R. Savage, "Surveillance Problems: Wiener Processes," Technical Report No. 34, University of Minnesota, Department of Statistics, Jan. 1962, on the "surveillance problem," a special case of which is very similar to and has the same solution as our cash balance problem. The Antelman-Savage paper uses a Wiener process as the generating mechanism; in an earlier paper, "Surveillance Problems," *Naval Research Logistics Quarterly*, Vol. 9 (Sept. and Dec. 1962), Savage derives the same solution for a Poisson process. Our reason for relying on the Bernoulli process here is its great simplicity, which permits the solution to be developed with only the most elementary methods.

4. For the rationalization of this approach see S. Karlin, "Steady State Solutions," Chap. XIV in Arrow, Karlin, and Scarf, *Studies in the Mathematical Theory of Inventory and Production* (Stanford University Press, 1958), esp. p. 223.

5. Such a policy is simpler and more "natural" than, say, one involving different return points after a purchase and a sale — a policy form that might be appropriate if the transfer cost were assumed to differ depending on the direction of the transfer, or if the cost of transfer were in part proportional to the size of the transfer.

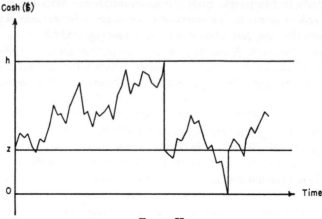

FIGURE II

is hit there will be a lump sum transfer *from* cash of $(h - z)$ dollars; and when the lower limit is triggered, a transfer *to* cash of z dollars.

Given this (h, z) policy structure, and our other assumptions, the expected cost per day of managing the firm's cash balance over any finite planning horizon of T days can be expressed formally as:

$$(1) \qquad \varepsilon(c) = \gamma \frac{\varepsilon(N)}{T} + \nu \varepsilon(M)$$

where $\varepsilon(N)$ = the expected number of portfolio transfers (in either direction) during the planning period; γ = the cost per transfer; $\varepsilon(M)$ = the average daily cash balance; and ν = the daily rate of interest earned on the portfolio.[6] The firm's objective is that of minimizing $\varepsilon(\bar{c})$ with respect to the control variables afforded by the chosen policy; the upper bound on cash holdings, h, and the intermediate return point, z.

2. *The Optimal Values of the Policy Parameters*

Turning now to the solution, consider first the term $\dfrac{\varepsilon(N)}{T}$, the expected number of transfers per day. The derivation of an expression for $\dfrac{\varepsilon(N)}{T}$ in terms of the decision variables z and h will be

---

6. The expression (1), like the loss functions in similar inventory models, is only an approximation, though normally a very close one (see G. Hadley, "A Comparison of Order Quantities Computed Using the Average Annual Cost and the Discounted Cost," *Management Science*, Vol. 10 (April 1964)) to the flow equivalent of the discounted present value of costs. The discrepancy comes from neglecting the interest on the transfer costs and on the interest itself as well as from averaging rather than integrating over the cash holdings.

THE DEMAND FOR MONEY BY FIRMS 421

performed in two parts. First the mean number of transfers will be expressed in terms of the average time interval between transfers; and then this average interval will be related to z and h.

As for the first part, suppose that the successive time intervals (measured in days) $x_1, x_2, \ldots$, between portfolio transfers are independent random drawings from a population with a well-defined probability distribution. In particular, let this distribution have mean D and finite variance. If T is a fixed planning horizon and N is a random variable denoting the number of transfers that occur during the horizon period, then (by the definition of N)

(1) $\qquad x_1 + x_2 + \ldots + x_N \leqslant T < x_1 + x_2 + \ldots + x_{N+1}.$

Or, taking expectations

$$\varepsilon(x_1 + x_2 + \ldots + x_N) \leqslant T < \varepsilon(x_1 + x_2 + \ldots + x_{N+1}).$$

Wald has proved [7] that under the assumed conditions on $\{x_i\}$

$$\varepsilon(x_1 + x_2 + \ldots + x_N) = \varepsilon(x)\,\varepsilon(N) = D\,\varepsilon(N)$$

from which the inequalities

$$D\,\varepsilon(N) \leqslant T < D\,\varepsilon(N) + D$$

are seen to hold. These in turn imply

(2) $\qquad \dfrac{1}{D} - \dfrac{1}{T} < \dfrac{\varepsilon(N)}{T} \leqslant \dfrac{1}{D}.$

Hence as T is allowed to grow unboundedly large, the ratio $\dfrac{\varepsilon(N)}{T}$,

the expected number of transfers per day, approaches $\dfrac{1}{D}$.[8]

We next seek an expression for D in terms of z and h, and here we can make direct use of classical results reviewed by Feller.[9] In particular, for a symmetric ($p = q = 1/2$) Bernoullian random walk with unit transaction "steps" originating at z and terminating at either 0 or h, Feller proves (a) that the duration of the walk is a random variable whose distribution has the properties we assumed to hold for the $\{x_i\}$; and (b) that the expected value of the duration, $D(z, h)$ is given by

(3) $\qquad D(z, h) = (z)(h - z).$

The above expression states the expected duration in terms of num-

7. A. Wald, *Sequential Analysis* (New York: Wiley, 1947), p. 52.
8. This result can be derived exactly rather than asymptotically if the cash balance changes are assumed to be generated by a continuous rather than a discrete probability mechanism. However, by maintaining a discrete framework, the stationary cash balance density, which underlies the calculation of holding cost, is far easier to derive; and since we are dealing with a steady state model, derivation of (2) as an asymptotic result is not in any sense a shortcoming.
9. W. Feller, *An Introduction to Probability Theory and Its Applications*, Vol. I (2d ed.; New York: Wiley, 1957), Chap. XIV.

ber of trials. To convert the time unit to days, we need merely divide by t, the number of operating cash transactions per day.[1] To convert z and h from unit steps to dollars we define new variables z' and h' in dollars with $z' = z \cdot m$ and $h' = h \cdot m$. Hence, the expected duration stated in days and with the bounds in dollar units is:

(4) $\qquad D(z', h') = \dfrac{(z')(h' - z')}{m^2 t}$.

Having shown that $\dfrac{\varepsilon(N)}{T}$ approaches $1/D(z, h)$ for sufficiently large T, the transfer cost term of the long-run average cost function (1.1) can thus be written as the product of γ and the reciprocal of the right-hand side of (4). (To simplify the notation we shall hereafter omit the primes on z and h in expressions based on (4) since the presence of m and t will indicate that dollar rather than transaction step units are the appropriate dimension.)

The second term of the cost function requires an expression for the long-run average cash balance in terms of z and h. This balance is simply the mean of the steady-state distribution of cash holdings. Following the usual procedure for deriving this distribution[2] the probability that the cash balance will contain precisely x units is obtained from the difference equations:

(5) $\qquad f(x) = pf(x - 1) + qf(x + 1) \qquad\qquad x \neq z$

with boundary conditions

(6) $\qquad f(z) = p[f(z - 1) + f(h - 1)] + q[f(z + 1) + f(1)]$

and

(7) $\qquad f(0) = 0, \qquad f(h) = 0$

and the density condition

(8) $\qquad \displaystyle\sum_{x=0}^{n} f(x) = 1$.

For the special case $p = q = 1/2$, the system (5) has a solution of the form

(9)
$$f(x) = A_1 + B_1 x \qquad\qquad 0 < x < z$$
$$f(x) = A_2 + B_2 (h - x) \qquad\quad z < x < h .$$

The linearity of (9) and the conditions (6) and (7) imply that the steady-state distribution of cash holdings is of discrete triangular form with base h and mode z. The mean of such a distribution is

1. Cf. above, p. 418.
2. Feller, *loc. cit.*

$$\frac{h+z}{3} \cdot {}_3$$

Combining both segments of the expected cost function, and letting $Z = h - z$, the problem can now be stated as:

$$(10) \quad \min_{Z, z} \varepsilon(c) = \frac{\gamma m^2 t}{zZ} + \frac{\nu(Z + 2z)}{3} .$$

The necessary conditions for a minimum are

$$\frac{\partial \varepsilon(c)}{\partial z} = -\frac{\gamma m^2 t}{z^2 Z} + \frac{2\nu}{3} = 0$$

$$\frac{\partial \varepsilon(c)}{\partial Z} = -\frac{\gamma m^2 t}{Z^2 z} + \frac{\nu}{3} = 0$$

which together yield the optimal values [4]

$$(11) \quad z^* = \left(\frac{3\gamma m^2 t}{4\nu}\right)^{1/3}$$

and

$$(12) \quad Z^* = 2z^*$$

or in terms of the original parameters

$$(13) \quad h^* = 3z^*.$$

3. Some Properties of the Solution

This solution has a number of interesting and in some respects quite surprising properties. Notice first that despite the symmetry of the generating process and of the cost of returning the system to z, the control rules turn out to be asymmetrical. The optimal return point lies substantially *below* the midpoint of the range over which the cash balance is permitted to wander. To put it another way, sales of portfolio assets will take place with greater average frequency and in smaller "lots" than purchases.[5] Some insight into the economic rationale of this result can be gained from Figure III in which

3. Derivations for the case $p \neq q$ are sketched in the Appendix.

4. Sufficient conditions also hold for these values.

5. Despite this asymmetry in the size and frequency of transfers, it is reassuring to note that no drift is thereby communicated to the volume of earning assets held in the firm's portfolio. This property follows directly from the probabilities of passage in a symmetric Bernoullian process; viz., Prob (first passage at 0 when process originates at z) $= \frac{h-z}{h}$ and Prob (first passage at h when process originates at z) $= 1 - \frac{h-z}{h} = \frac{z}{h}$. See Feller, *loc. cit.*

Although the portfolio has no drift, nothing in the model prevents the portfolio from becoming negative if the sales called for by the policy happen to precede or exceed the purchases over some period of time. In such cases, the firm is presumed to utilize a line of credit or some other short-term borrowing arrangement (i.e., the portfolio securities it sells are its own).

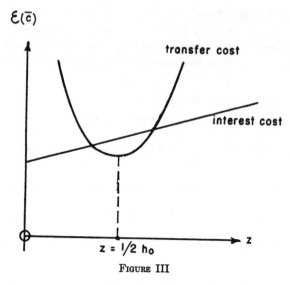

$\mathcal{E}(\bar{c})$

transfer cost

interest cost

$z = 1/2\ h_0$

z

FIGURE III

the transfer cost and the holding cost are plotted separately as functions of z for some given $h = h_0$. The transfer cost is a symmetric U-shaped function with its minimum at the midpoint, $z = 1/2\ h_0$. The idle balance cost, by contrast, is a linear increasing function of z throughout. Hence, it would obviously be uneconomical to set z greater than $h_0/2$ since both costs would be increasing in that range. But in the other direction some cost reduction can be achieved by reducing z since the transfer cost function, though rising as z moves below $1/2\ h_0$, is relatively flat in the region of its minimum.

An even more surprising aspect of the optimal solution is that z^* always lies at $1/3\ h^*$, regardless of the relative magnitudes of the cost coefficients γ and ν. Changes in these costs serve only to shrink or dilate the system as a whole with no change in the internal balance between z and h. The explanation of this result lies in the structure of the cost function (2.10). Note that z and Z enter symmetrically into the transfer cost component, but that z enters with twice as much weight as Z in the holding cost component. This means that if $Z > 2z$, we can add a small amount, $\triangle$, to z and subtract $2\triangle$ from Z with no resulting change in the holding cost term $\nu(Z + 2z)/3$. These changes, however, will transform the denominator of the transfer cost term to

$$(Z - 2\triangle)(z + \triangle) = Zz + \triangle(Z - 2z) - 2\triangle^2 > Zz$$

the last inequality necessarily holding for some small value of $\triangle$

so long as $Z > 2z$. Thus, it would pay to increase z by $\triangle$ and to reduce Z by $2\triangle$ since the higher value of the denominator implies a lower value for the transfer cost term. Similar reasoning applies to the case of $Z < 2z$ so that only if $Z = 2z$ is no such cost-reducing substitution possible.

4. *Implications for the Demand for Money by Firms*

For economists, the major interest in the solution lies in its implications for the demand for money by firms. In the present context, that demand can be identified with the average cash balance realized when operating under a policy (h, z) and hence will be given by $\dfrac{h + z}{3}$. Substituting the optimal values of h^* and z^* from (2.11) and (2.13) and recalling (from page 419 above) that $\sigma^2 = \dfrac{\sigma_n^2}{n} = m^2 t =$ the variance of the daily change in the cash balance, we obtain

$$(1) \qquad \bar{M}^* = \frac{4}{3} \left(\frac{3\gamma m^2 t}{4\nu} \right)^{1/3} = \frac{4}{3} \left(\frac{3\gamma}{4\nu} \sigma^2 \right)^{1/3}$$

as an expression for the firm's optimal average cash balance (or long-run average demand for money) in terms of the cost parameters γ and ν and the (observable) variance of daily cash flows, σ^2. As in the case of the Baumol model the demand for money is an increasing function of the cost of transferring funds to and from the earning portfolio, and a decreasing function of the interest rate or opportunity cost of the funds held in the cash balance. The novel aspect of the money demand equation (1) is the presence of σ^2, a term directly representing the variability of the cash balance, or the degree of the "lack of synchronization" between cash receipts and payments.

The fact that the variance of daily net cash flows serves as the "transactions" variable in the money demand function raises the question of how equation (1) is related to the kind of demand function typically used in empirical studies of money holdings by firms in which total sales or some closely related concept is taken as the measure of transactions. That there is a relation between total sales and the variance of changes in the cash balance is clear enough since total sales are approximately the positive changes in the cash balance summed over a time interval. But the relation is a loose one, and no precise value can be established for the elasticity of the demand for cash with respect to sales that is implied by our model. The difficulty in specifying the sales elasticity stems from the fact that even with unchanging prices sales may change in any of several ways, each with a different impact on the firm's need for cash. At one extreme, a doubling of sales may be due to a doubling of each separate receipt and expenditure invoice. In terms of the model, this is equivalent to raising the transaction step size from m to $2m$ and implies that the optimal average balance will rise by a factor of $2^{2/3}$. At the other extreme, a doubling of sales may take the form of a doubling in the frequency of transactions (i.e., a doubling of t), with the average invoice size unchanged. In this case, because of the increased opportunity for offsetting changes, the desired balance increases only by a factor of $2^{1/3}$. The range of elasticities, of course, becomes even larger when we allow for the possibility of increases in transaction magnitude accompanied by decreases in transaction frequency, or vice versa.

The existence of such a wide range for the sales elasticity in our (h, z) model is in sharp contrast to the prediction of the Baumol model where the elasticity of average cash holdings with respect to sales (assuming constant prices) is always and precisely 1/2. This uniformity of prediction is one of the most obvious weaknesses of Baumol-type models as applied to corporate cash balances. Studies of intersectoral velocities [6] show substantial differences between industries; and there is simply no convincing way of accounting for such differences in the Baumol framework. Whether our variability term provides the answer we cannot say; but it does at least offer a plausible (and testable) explanation for the observed systematic interindustry differences.

Further questions arise about the relation of our demand function (1) to the "classical" quantity theory of money and to the so-called "modern" quantity theory (running in terms of such variables as "permanent income" or wealth). As to the former, if we regard as the essence of the classical position that the demand for money in real terms be independent of the absolute price level, then equation (1) is consistent with that position. Like the Baumol model, it is homogeneous of degree one in prices, that is, it implies that a doubling of all prices (including those impounded in γ) will lead to a doubling of the quantity of money demanded. With respect to the modern quantity theory, however, the relation is much less clear. Certainly it is hard to see any direct relevance for concepts such as permanent income or wealth in the decision process at the level of the firm. But this, of course, does not rule out the possibility that

6. E.g., R. Selden, *The Postwar Rise in the Velocity of Money*, Occasional Paper 78 (New York: National Bureau of Economic Research, 1962).

aggregate permanent income or wealth might nevertheless be effective proxies for the level of transactions in macro models of the demand for money.

5. *Extension to Allow for Non-zero Drift*

Although the no-drift case is likely to be the one of greatest interest to monetary theorists, the model can be extended to incorporate systematic drift in the cash balance (in either direction).[7] The analytical expressions leading to the optimal solution values for h, z and $\overline{M}$ in the presence of drift turn out to be extremely cumbersome and hard to interpret,[8] but the main qualitative properties of

TABLE I

OPTIMAL SOLUTION VALUES AS A FUNCTION OF DRIFT

A. For $\gamma/\nu = 50$

p	z^*	h^*	$\overline{M}^*$	$|\mu|$	σ^2
1.0	1.0	11.0	5.5	1.0	0.00
0.9	1.2	10.6	5.3	0.9	0.36
0.8	1.5	10.0	5.1	0.8	0.64
0.7	1.9	9.5	4.8	0.7	0.84
0.6	2.5	9.4	4.6	0.6	0.96
0.5	3.3	10.0	4.5	0.5	1.00
0.4	4.7	11.7	4.4	0.6	0.96
0.3	6.3	13.9	4.4	0.7	0.84
0.2	7.7	16.1	4.7	0.8	0.64
0.0	11.0	—	5.5	1.0	0.00

B. For $\gamma/\nu = 500$

p	z^*	h^*	$\overline{M}^*$	$|\mu|$	σ^2
1.0	1.0	32.6	16.3	1.0	0.00
0.9	1.6	30.4	15.4	0.9	0.36
0.8	2.2	27.4	14.0	0.8	0.64
0.7	2.9	24.1	12.4	0.7	0.84
0.6	4.1	20.9	10.6	0.6	0.96
0.5	7.2	21.6	9.6	0.5	1.00
0.4	14.2	31.0	9.6	0.6	0.96
0.3	20.0	44.7	11.2	0.7	0.84
0.2	24.5	—	13.1	0.8	0.64
0.0	32.6	—	16.3	1.0	0.00

7. Drift models might be appropriate even where there was no overall net drift in the operating cash balance, but simply a heavy concentration of receipts or expenditures at regularly recurring intervals. If a firm, for example, gets 75 per cent of its monthly receipts on the tenth of the month, then the process over the remaining days might be characterized as one with $p = .25$ and $q = .75$. And similarly, in the other direction, for cases involving large, regularly recurring payments such as tax or dividend payments.

8. Cf. the Appendix.

the solutions as a function of drift can easily be seen from constructed numerical examples. Two sets of such numerical results are presented in Table I, the first for a case in which the critical cost ratio γ/ν has the extremely low value of 50; and the second for one in which it has the higher and more reasonable value of 500 (the values of m and t being taken as unity in both cases).

For extreme positive drift (the case $p = 1$) the stochastic element in the cash flow vanishes and we are, in effect, dealing with a Baumol model of the pure uniform-flow-of-receipts variety. The cash balance builds up steadily to h and then is returned to its lowest possible value (which is zero, in principle, but which we have had to set at one unit for purposes of computer calculation). As p falls, and hence as the upward drift becomes less pronounced and then changes to downward drift, the optimal "return point" z^* increases steadily in value. The behavior of the optimal upper bound, h^*, however, is somewhat surprising. As p falls, h^* first falls slowly; reaches a minimum while still in the zone of net upward drift (in the neighborhood of $p = .6$); then rises again at an increasing rate once the zone of downward drift ($p < q$) is entered. As the downward drift increases and p approaches zero, the probability of ever hitting h^* becomes microscopic, and when p reaches zero, h^* becomes entirely irrelevant to the solution. We have returned to the one-parameter Baumol model, this time of the pure uniform-flow-of-expenditures variety.

The column headed $\overline{M}^*$ in the table relates the average cash balance to drift. Starting from $p = 1$ (extreme upward drift) the optimal cash balance declines steadily with p, and is still falling in the neighborhood of the no-drift case. The minimum of $\overline{M}^*$ actually occurs somewhat beyond the no-drift point and within the zone of net downward drift (at about $p = .4$ in both panels).[9] Thereafter the optimal average balance rises again reaching the same level at $p = 0$ as obtained at $p = 1$ (which is as expected since the extreme cases are Baumol models differing only in the direction of the cash flow).

Some insight into why cash holdings are a U-shaped function of drift can be gained by relating drift to the mean and variance of the distribution of cash balance changes (shown in the last two columns of the table). In these terms, our no-drift case can be thought of as an "all variance — no mean" model; while the pure

9. The fact that the minimum occurs in both cases very near the value $p = .4$ is entirely an artifact of the particular numbers used. As successively higher values of the ratio γ/ν are used, the minimum tends to move steadily closer to the no-drift point, $p = .5$.

Baumol models for extreme drift are essentially "all mean — no variance" models. Starting near a zero value for the drift, increases in drift (in either direction) imply smaller values for the variance of daily changes in cash and this, by itself, would tend to reduce cash needs. But higher values of drift also imply larger mean daily changes in cash and this, by itself, would tend to raise average holdings. Since the mean rises faster than the variance falls; and since the responsiveness of cash holdings to the mean is greater (a square-root as opposed to a cube-root effect), the net effect of substantial amounts of drift in either direction is to increase optimal average cash balances.

III. The Applicability of the Model

Now that the model of cash management by business firms has been developed and the main properties and implications of that model have been sketched, we may turn to consider the previously postponed questions regarding the realism and empirical relevance of the model. As noted earlier, the various assumptions underlying the model fall into two categories. On the one hand are those that define the basic framework; the assumptions of a "two-asset" structure, of a lumpy component in the cost of transfers between the assets; of a negligible lead time in transfers; and, especially, of a stationary random walk for the cash flows. On the other are the special assumptions introduced primarily to simplify either the proofs or the economic interpretation of the results, such as the assumption of a constant marginal transfer cost independent of the size or direction of the transfer, or the assumption that the cash balance changes by a constant positive or negative amount at regular intervals. Insofar as the latter assumptions are concerned, many interesting variations with respect to the cost structure or the distribution of cash changes can and should be explored. Such variations will certainly lead to more complicated control rules and change other matters of detail, but the general qualitative picture is unlikely to be much altered as long as the basic framework is maintained.[1] Attention here will therefore be focused primarily on the more fundamental question of whether the framework itself constitutes a useful and meaningful way of describing the demand for money by business firms.[2]

1. This has certainly proved to be the case with the Baumol model and, in fact, with classes of inventory models generally.
2. In one sense, the single most crucial assumption in shaping the whole analysis is that substantial lump sum portfolio transfer costs exist. Here, how-

In this connection some reservations must certainly be entered with respect to the realism of the simple two-asset dichotomy. Business firms typically hold many different liquid securities in their portfolios, frequently even at the same time that they are issuing short-term claims such as commercial paper or bank loans. If this were the only problem, however, we doubt that it would constitute any very serious limitation for present purposes. In principle, it is possible to extend the model to allow for more than one portfolio asset each with its own γ and ν (and, presumably, with γ higher for those with higher yields). Analytical results for such extensions are hard to obtain, but from such limited experimentation as we have conducted with models of this type we would conjecture that the system will turn out to be very loosely coupled.

Much more serious than lumping all earning assets into a single portfolio asset is the lumping of all cash holdings into a single cash balance. Most firms do maintain an identifiable central bank balance, but they also hold many separate smaller accounts. This is particularly true of large, divisionalized firms.[3] Transfers take place not only between the field accounts and the central balance but also among the local balances and between these balances and the portfolio. For such a setting, a more appropriate inventory model might be one of the multi-stage factory-warehouse system variety — though models of the general type developed here might still be expected to govern the behavior of some of the separate components of the system. How much a multi-stage approach would affect our main conclusions is hard to say — because results to date in inventory theory with such models have been meager, and because we still have very little precise information about the relative importance of field and central balances or the cost savings that field balances permit. At the very least, however, we would expect to find smaller economies of scale than those implied under our single-balance framework.

Many will regard the assumption that the cash generating

ever, we feel that no extended defense is really necessary even though we would concede that those costs may be hard to estimate in practical applications. Their existence seems amply demonstrated by the very large minimum trading units in all the standard money market instruments (e.g., currently $100,000 for commercial bank negotiable Certificates of Deposit).

3. The results of a recent survey of cash balances practices of large corporations by W. E. Gibson, "Compensating Balance Requirements," *National Banking Review*, Vol. 2 (March 1965), indicate that the average number of separate bank balances maintained is currently about 200 per firm with some firms actually holding more than 2,300 individual accounts. Gibson's data, however, give no indication of the size distribution of the balances and many accounts undoubtedly are of only nominal size. Even so, the extent of significant multiple holding is clearly quite substantial.

mechanism is entirely stochastic as an even more serious limitation on the approach taken here. And certainly this can hardly be defended as being literally descriptive. The size and timing of many of the important individual transactions comprising the cash flow are under the direct control of the management (e.g., dividend payments). Other transactions are the foreseeable fulfillments of past commitments (such as payments on trade accounts or tax payments). Even where genuinely random changes do occur they are usually superimposed on some systematic and at least partially forecastable movements (e.g., payroll disbursements).[4] This is, however, not a very useful way of evaluating the random walk assumption or the model based on it. The decisive question is how well the assumption serves on an "as if" basis; and here the case against it is by no means an obvious one.

For normative applications, models can certainly be developed to utilize available information about local "patterns" in the cash flow. The lumpy component of transfer cost, however, may present a serious obstacle to the derivation of optimal decision rules under some kinds of programming approaches and the derivation of rules under any such approach would definitely be greatly complicated by the presence of both stochastic and deterministic elements in the cash flow. Because of these difficulties it is by no means certain here, as elsewhere in inventory theory, that the gains from exploiting more of the local information about the flows are large enough to offset the added costs of model development and implementation.

For positive applications, the usefulness of a simple stochastic model of cash management depends mainly on how closely its conditional predictions of the average frequency and size of transfer and of average cash balances correspond to those actually observed. Tolerably accurate predictions of these items are entirely possible even though firms use more complicated, *ad hoc* decision procedures based on detailed forecasts or cash budgets. In terms of operating characteristics, the main effect of such procedures and forecasts is likely to be to transform the bounds on cash holdings into zones rather than the simple limits as in our model. For example, there will be occasions when the firm will not transfer funds to the portfolio, even though current cash holdings are larger than h, because it knows or predicts that a "turnaround" will occur in the very near

---

4. To the extent that the systematic component is in the form of a simple trend then a non-zero drift model might meet the need. Even seasonal components might be incorporated by an alternating sequence of drift models, provided the seasonal movements persisted long enough relative to the mean time between transfers to avoid excessive violence to the steady-state assumptions that underlie the objective function (II. 2.10).

future. In the other direction, it may pay the firm to make a transfer even when holdings are below h if a reasonably long "quiet" period is anticipated. Because these tendencies are partially offsetting, no decisive case against a stochastic model with single-valued bounds can be established on a priori grounds.[5] Final judgment must await the results of empirical testing.

Some may argue that the empirical decision has already been rendered by recent cross-sectional studies of the corporate demand for money.[6] The failure of these studies to find any significant economies of scale in cash holdings with respect to total sales or total assets is seen as running directly counter to predictions based on inventory models either of the Baumol variety or of the (h, z) type developed here. Such a conclusion, however, would be unwarranted. Quite apart from the difficulties noted previously in the use of sales or assets as measures of transactions,[7] recall that our (h, z)

5. Another possibility that might more seriously affect the predictive power of the model would be systematic efforts to obtain closer synchronization between receipts and payments by influencing the timing of receipts and payments (e.g., by increasing discounts for early payment when interest rates rise). Such direct adjustments in timing are admittedly quite common among small firms where there is often no alternative to such brute force methods of synchronization as delaying payments to some creditors until sufficient cash receipts have been accumulated. For larger firms, however, it is unlikely to be economic to tinker with the details of the receipt and payment structure in the short run though from time to time the whole system will be re-examined (and of course, such re-examinations are likely to be made more frequently in periods of high interest rates).

6. E.g., A. H. Meltzer, "The Demand for Money: A Cross-Section Study of Business Firms," this *Journal*, LXXVII (Aug. 1963).

7. See Section II. 4, p. 425 above. On a priori grounds, one would suspect that within any given industry the variance of daily cash changes would probably tend to increase less than proportionally with sales, thus strengthening the presumption of scale economies with respect to sales under the inventory approach. The "industries" studied tend to be quite heterogeneous, however, so that it may be well to withhold judgment until some direct empirical evidence on variability in relation to size is available.

Although our concern in this paper is primarily with the demand for money by business firms it may perhaps be worth pointing out that somewhat similar problems with respect to interpreting cross-sectional elasticities arise in the case of households. In particular, it does not follow that a finding of an elasticity of money holdings with respect to *income* of unity or even greater is inconsistent with the "inventory" approach. For one thing, many (perhaps, most) households have incomes too small or too frequently received to justify moving off the "corner solution" (cf. fn. 6, p. 415) and over this range the implied income elasticity is unity. For those with incomes large enough to warrant temporary investment of idle cash, income will be the relevant "transactions" variable provided that the only portfolio purchases and sales made by the household are those transfers required by the inventory model. Where, however, the household engages in autonomous portfolio activity (such as switching in and out of investments) an additional "transactions" demand for cash balances is generated over and above that involved in spending income on current account. If the amount and frequency of such autonomous financial transactions tend to rise more than proportionally with income (which is certainly not improbable), then an income elasticity of cash holdings greater than unity might well be observed over this range even though substantial economies of scale were present with respect to total transactions.

model is intended to explain only the "discretionary" part of the firm's cash balance over and above its required minimum balance. Despite the fact that such minimum balance requirements in lieu of service charges have long been a conspicuous feature of banking arrangements for business firms in this country, little precise information is available about the absolute size of such balances or how they vary between firms and over time. As was noted earlier, however, it is at least clear that the cost-trade-offs and other strategic elements involved in determining minimum balances differ in important respects from those relating to the active transactions balances. Consequently, the empirical cross-sectional elasticities of money holdings with respect to sales represent only an average (with unknown weights) over the two very different processes.[8] In the absence of evidence, therefore, either that the negotiated minimum balances are a considerably smaller part of the total than the finance literature would lead one to believe; or that minimum balances increase substantially less than proportionally with size of firm, the issue of the validity of inventory models in representing the transactions demand for money by firms must be regarded as still very much an open one.[9]

Appendix

In general, the occupancy probabilities of a Bernoullian cash balance which drifts between 0 and h, and is returned instantly to z upon encountering either barrier, are given by the difference equation

$$f(x, t + 1) = pf(x - 1, t) + qf(x + 1, t)$$

and the boundary conditions

$$f(z, t + 1) = p[f(z - 1, t) + f(h - 1, t)] \\ + q[f(z + 1, t) + f(1, t)]$$

8. Although the functions governing the two kinds of balances are different, they are likely to have some arguments in common. In particular, our transaction-frequency variable t is closely related to the "activity" variable used in negotiating minimum balances. Both functions also contain an interest rate variable, though not necessarily the same one for the two cases.

9. For the sake of argument, we accept here the proposition that existing cross-section studies do not show significant economies of scale in cash holdings though, in fact, we have some reservations about these findings. The main one is that these studies typically fit a single money demand relation over the whole range of available size classes of firms including the very smallest sizes; whereas inventory models of the type developed here are at best applicable only for reasonably large firms. With respect to the larger size classes, the case for the existence of economies of scale does seem to be somewhat stronger (cf. Selden, *op. cit.*), though there are too few cells in the usual *Statistics of Income* or F.T.C.-S.E.C. tabulations to permit any reliable estimates of the elasticity in this range of size classes.

$$f(0, t+1) = 0$$
$$f(h, t+1) = 0$$
$$\sum_{x=0}^{h} f(x, t+1) = 1.$$

To ascertain the steady-state occupancy probabilities, we pass to the limit in time, to obtain the system

(1) $$f(x) = pf(x-1) + qf(x+1)$$

(2) $$f(z) = p[f(z-1) + f(h-1)] + q[f(z+1) + f(1)]$$

$$f(0) = f(h) = 0, \qquad \sum_{x=0}^{h} f(x) = 1.$$

The general solution for the case $p \neq q$

(3) $$\begin{aligned} f(x) &= A + B(p/q)^x & 0 \leq x \leq z \\ f(x) &= C + D(p/q)^x & z \leq x \leq h \end{aligned}$$

contains four arbitrary constants, which are evaluated via the four boundary conditions.

Since $f(0) = 0$, it follows that

(4) $$0 = A + B, \qquad B = -A.$$

Similarly,

(5) $$D = -C(p/q)^{-h}.$$

Substitution of (3), (4) and (5) in (2) yields the relation

(6) $$C = A \left[\frac{1 - (p/q)^z}{1 - (p/q)^{z-h}} \right].$$

Finally, the density condition on the summed occupancy probabilities

$$1 = \sum_{x=0}^{h} f(x) = \sum_{x=0}^{z} A[1 - (p/q)^x]$$
$$+ \sum_{x=z+1}^{h} [1 - (p/q)^{z-h}] A \left[\frac{1 - (p/q)^z}{1 - (p/q)^{z-h}} \right]$$

yields the result

(7) $$A = \frac{1 - (p/q)^{z-h}}{z[1 - (p/q)^{z-h}] + (h-z)[1 - (p/q)^z]}.$$

The values (6) and (7) may be combined to obtain a specific expression for the stationary occupancy probabilities of x, in terms of p and q.

Expression of the density permits explicit evaluation of the expected steady-state cash balance:

$$E(x) = \sum_{x=0}^{h} xf(x) = \sum_{x=0}^{z} xA[1 - (p/q)^x]$$
$$+ \sum_{x=z+1}^{h} xC[1 - (p/q)^{z-h}].$$

THE DEMAND FOR MONEY BY FIRMS 435

Use of the values (6) and (7), and resort to the identity

$$\sum_{x=1}^{h-1} x(p/q)^{x-1} \equiv d/d(p/q) \sum_{x=0}^{h} (p/q)^x$$

$$\equiv \frac{1 - h(p/q)^h - (p/q)^h - h(p/q)^{h+1}}{[1 - (p/q)]^2}$$

for $q > p$, yields the value

$$E(x) = \frac{1}{2} \left\{ \frac{1}{q-p} + h + z \right.$$
$$\left. - \frac{hz[1 - (p/q)^{z-h}]}{z[1 - (p/q)^{z-h} + (h-z)[1 - (p/q)^z]} \right\}.$$

For the other segment of the cost function, the expression for the expected duration between passages of either 0 or h is derived in Feller, *loc. cit.*: it is

$$D(z) = \frac{z}{q-p} - \frac{h}{q-p} \cdot \frac{1 - (p/q)^z}{1 - (p/q)^h} \qquad q > p.$$

GRADUATE SCHOOL OF BUSINESS, UNIVERSITY OF CHICAGO

UNIVERSITY OF CALIFORNIA, SAN DIEGO

[19]

The American Economic Review

VOLUME XLVIII   JUNE 1958   NUMBER THREE

THE COST OF CAPITAL, CORPORATION FINANCE AND THE THEORY OF INVESTMENT

By FRANCO MODIGLIANI AND MERTON H. MILLER*

What is the "cost of capital" to a firm in a world in which funds are used to acquire assets whose yields are uncertain; and in which capital can be obtained by many different media, ranging from pure debt instruments, representing money-fixed claims, to pure equity issues, giving holders only the right to a pro-rata share in the uncertain venture? This question has vexed at least three classes of economists: (1) the corporation finance specialist concerned with the techniques of financing firms so as to ensure their survival and growth; (2) the managerial economist concerned with capital budgeting; and (3) the economic theorist concerned with explaining investment behavior at both the micro and macro levels.[1]

In much of his formal analysis, the economic theorist at least has tended to side-step the essence of this cost-of-capital problem by proceeding as though physical assets—like bonds—could be regarded as yielding known, sure streams. Given this assumption, the theorist has concluded that the cost of capital to the owners of a firm is simply the rate of interest on bonds; and has derived the familiar proposition that the firm, acting rationally, will tend to push investment to the point

* The authors are, respectively, professor and associate professor of economics in the Graduate School of Industrial Administration, Carnegie Institute of Technology. This article is a revised version of a paper delivered at the annual meeting of the Econometric Society, December 1956. The authors express thanks for the comments and suggestions made at that time by the discussants of the paper, Evsey Domar, Robert Eisner and John Lintner, and subsequently by James Duesenberry. They are also greatly indebted to many of their present and former colleagues and students at Carnegie Tech who served so often and with such remarkable patience as a critical forum for the ideas here presented.

[1] The literature bearing on the cost-of-capital problem is far too extensive for listing here. Numerous references to it will be found throughout the paper though we make no claim to completeness. One phase of the problem which we do not consider explicitly, but which has a considerable literature of its own is the relation between the cost of capital and public utility rates. For a recent summary of the "cost-of-capital theory" of rate regulation and a brief discussion of some of its implications, the reader may refer to H. M. Somers [20].

where the marginal yield on physical assets is equal to the market rate of interest.[2] This proposition can be shown to follow from either of two criteria of rational decision-making which are equivalent under certainty, namely (1) the maximization of profits and (2) the maximization of market value.

According to the first criterion, a physical asset is worth acquiring if it will increase the net profit of the owners of the firm. But net profit will increase only if the expected rate of return, or yield, of the asset exceeds the rate of interest. According to the second criterion, an asset is worth acquiring if it increases the value of the owners' equity, *i.e.*, if it adds more to the market value of the firm than the costs of acquisition. But what the asset adds is given by capitalizing the stream it generates at the market rate of interest, and this capitalized value will exceed its cost if and only if the yield of the asset exceeds the rate of interest. Note that, under either formulation, the cost of capital is equal to the rate of interest on bonds, regardless of whether the funds are acquired through debt instruments or through new issues of common stock. Indeed, in a world of sure returns, the distinction between debt and equity funds reduces largely to one of terminology.

It must be acknowledged that some attempt is usually made in this type of analysis to allow for the existence of uncertainty. This attempt typically takes the form of superimposing on the results of the certainty analysis the notion of a "risk discount" to be subtracted from the expected yield (or a "risk premium" to be added to the market rate of interest). Investment decisions are then supposed to be based on a comparison of this "risk adjusted" or "certainty equivalent" yield with the market rate of interest.[3] No satisfactory explanation has yet been provided, however, as to what determines the size of the risk discount and how it varies in response to changes in other variables.

Considered as a convenient approximation, the model of the firm constructed via this certainty—or certainty-equivalent—approach has admittedly been useful in dealing with some of the grosser aspects of the processes of capital accumulation and economic fluctuations. Such a model underlies, for example, the familiar Keynesian aggregate investment function in which aggregate investment is written as a function of the rate of interest—the same riskless rate of interest which appears later in the system in the liquidity-preference equation. Yet few would maintain that this approximation is adequate. At the macroeconomic level there are ample grounds for doubting that the rate of interest has

---

[2] Or, more accurately, to the marginal cost of borrowed funds since it is customary, at least in advanced analysis, to draw the supply curve of borrowed funds to the firm as a rising one. For an advanced treatment of the certainty case, see F. and V. Lutz [13].

[3] The classic examples of the certainty-equivalent approach are found in J. R. Hicks [8] and O. Lange [11].

as large and as direct an influence on the rate of investment as this analysis would lead us to believe. At the microeconomic level the certainty model has little descriptive value and provides no real guidance to the finance specialist or managerial economist whose main problems cannot be treated in a framework which deals so cavalierly with uncertainty and ignores all forms of financing other than debt issues.[4]

Only recently have economists begun to face up seriously to the problem of the cost of capital *cum* risk. In the process they have found their interests and endeavors merging with those of the finance specialist and the managerial economist who have lived with the problem longer and more intimately. In this joint search to establish the principles which govern rational investment and financial policy in a world of uncertainty two main lines of attack can be discerned. These lines represent, in effect, attempts to extrapolate to the world of uncertainty each of the two criteria—profit maximization and market value maximization—which were seen to have equivalent implications in the special case of certainty. With the recognition of uncertainty this equivalence vanishes. In fact, the profit maximization criterion is no longer even well defined. Under uncertainty there corresponds to each decision of the firm not a unique profit outcome, but a plurality of mutually exclusive outcomes which can at best be described by a subjective probability distribution. The profit outcome, in short, has become a random variable and as such its maximization no longer has an operational meaning. Nor can this difficulty generally be disposed of by using the mathematical expectation of profits as the variable to be maximized. For decisions which affect the expected value will also tend to affect the dispersion and other characteristics of the distribution of outcomes. In particular, the use of debt rather than equity funds to finance a given venture may well increase the expected return to the owners, but only at the cost of increased dispersion of the outcomes.

Under these conditions the profit outcomes of alternative investment and financing decisions can be compared and ranked only in terms of a *subjective* "utility function" of the owners which weighs the expected yield against other characteristics of the distribution. Accordingly, the extrapolation of the profit maximization criterion of the certainty model has tended to evolve into utility maximization, sometimes explicitly, more frequently in a qualitative and heuristic form.[5]

The utility approach undoubtedly represents an advance over the certainty or certainty-equivalent approach. It does at least permit us

[4] Those who have taken a "case-method" course in finance in recent years will recall in this connection the famous Liquigas case of Hunt and Williams, [9, pp. 193–96] a case which is often used to introduce the student to the cost-of-capital problem and to poke a bit of fun at the economist's certainty-model.

[5] For an attempt at a rigorous explicit development of this line of attack, see F. Modigliani and M. Zeman [14].

to explore (within limits) some of the implications of different financing arrangements, and it does give some meaning to the "cost" of different types of funds. However, because the cost of capital has become an essentially subjective concept, the utility approach has serious drawbacks for normative as well as analytical purposes. How, for example, is management to ascertain the risk preferences of its stockholders and to compromise among their tastes? And how can the economist build a meaningful investment function in the face of the fact that any given investment opportunity might or might not be worth exploiting depending on precisely who happen to be the owners of the firm at the moment?

Fortunately, these questions do not have to be answered; for the alternative approach, based on market value maximization, can provide the basis for an operational definition of the cost of capital and a workable theory of investment. Under this approach any investment project and its concomitant financing plan must pass only the following test: Will the project, as financed, raise the market value of the firm's shares? If so, it is worth undertaking; if not, its return is less than the marginal cost of capital to the firm. Note that such a test is entirely independent of the tastes of the current owners, since market prices will reflect not only their preferences but those of all potential owners as well. If any current stockholder disagrees with management and the market over the valuation of the project, he is free to sell out and reinvest elsewhere, but will still benefit from the capital appreciation resulting from management's decision.

The potential advantages of the market-value approach have long been appreciated; yet analytical results have been meager. What appears to be keeping this line of development from achieving its promise is largely the lack of an adequate theory of the effect of financial structure on market valuations, and of how these effects can be inferred from objective market data. It is with the development of such a theory and of its implications for the cost-of-capital problem that we shall be concerned in this paper.

Our procedure will be to develop in Section I the basic theory itself and to give some brief account of its empirical relevance. In Section II, we show how the theory can be used to answer the cost-of-capital question and how it permits us to develop a theory of investment of the firm under conditions of uncertainty. Throughout these sections the approach is essentially a partial-equilibrium one focusing on the firm and "industry." Accordingly, the "prices" of certain income streams will be treated as constant and given from outside the model, just as in the standard Marshallian analysis of the firm and industry the prices of all inputs and of all other products are taken as given. We have chosen to focus at this level rather than on the economy as a whole because it is at the level of the firm and the industry that the interests of the various specialists concerned with the cost-of-capital problem come most closely together. Although the emphasis has thus been placed on partial-equilibrium analysis, the results obtained also provide the essential building blocks for a general equilibrium model which shows how those prices which are here taken as given, are themselves determined. For reasons of space, however, and because the material is of interest in its own right, the presentation of the general equilibrium model which rounds out the analysis must be deferred to a subsequent paper.

I. *The Valuation of Securities, Leverage, and the Cost of Capital*

A. *The Capitalization Rate for Uncertain Streams*

As a starting point, consider an economy in which all physical assets are owned by corporations. For the moment, assume that these corporations can finance their assets by issuing common stock only; the introduction of bond issues, or their equivalent, as a source of corporate funds is postponed until the next part of this section.

The physical assets held by each firm will yield to the owners of the firm—its stockholders—a stream of "profits" over time; but the elements of this series need not be constant and in any event are uncertain. This stream of income, and hence the stream accruing to any share of common stock, will be regarded as extending indefinitely into the future. We assume, however, that the mean value of the stream over time, or average profit per unit of time, is finite and represents a random variable subject to a (subjective) probability distribution. We shall refer to the average value over time of the stream accruing to a given share as the return of that share; and to the mathematical expectation of this average as the expected return of the share.[6] Although individual investors may have different views as to the shape of the probability distri-

---

[6] These propositions can be restated analytically as follows: The assets of the ith firm generate a stream:

$$X_i(1),\ X_i(2)\ \cdots\ X_i(T)$$

whose elements are random variables subject to the joint probability distribution:

$$\chi_i[X_i(1),\ X_i(2)\ \cdots\ X_i(t)].$$

The return to the ith firm is defined as:

$$X_i = \lim_{T\to\infty} \frac{1}{T} \sum_{t=1}^{T} X_i(t).$$

X_i is itself a random variable with a probability distribution $\Phi_i(X_i)$ whose form is determined uniquely by χ_i. The expected return $\bar{X}_i$ is defined as $\bar{X}_i = E(X_i) = \int_{X_i} X_i \Phi_i(X_i) dX_i$. If N_i is the number of shares outstanding, the return of the ith share is $x_i = (1/N)X_i$ with probability distribution $\phi_i(x_i)dx_i = \Phi_i(Nx_i)d(Nx_i)$ and expected value $\bar{x}_i = (1/N)\bar{X}_i$.

bution of the return of any share, we shall assume for simplicity that they are at least in agreement as to the expected return.[7]

This way of characterizing uncertain streams merits brief comment. Notice first that the stream is a stream of profits, not dividends. As will become clear later, as long as management is presumed to be acting in the best interests of the stockholders, retained earnings can be regarded as equivalent to a fully subscribed, pre-emptive issue of common stock. Hence, for present purposes, the division of the stream between cash dividends and retained earnings in any period is a mere detail. Notice also that the uncertainty attaches to the mean value over time of the stream of profits and should not be confused with variability over time of the successive elements of the stream. That variability and uncertainty are two totally different concepts should be clear from the fact that the elements of a stream can be variable even though known with certainty. It can be shown, furthermore, that whether the elements of a stream are sure or uncertain, the effect of variability per se on the valuation of the stream is at best a second-order one which can safely be neglected for our purposes (and indeed most others too).[8]

The next assumption plays a strategic role in the rest of the analysis. We shall assume that firms can be divided into "equivalent return" classes such that the return on the shares issued by any firm in any given class is proportional to (and hence perfectly correlated with) the return on the shares issued by any other firm in the same class. This assumption implies that the various shares within the same class differ, at most, by a "scale factor." Accordingly, if we adjust for the difference in scale, by taking the *ratio* of the return to the expected return, the probability distribution of that ratio is identical for all shares in the class. It follows that all relevant properties of a share are uniquely characterized by specifying (1) the class to which it belongs and (2) its expected return.

The significance of this assumption is that it permits us to classify firms into groups within which the shares of different firms are "homogeneous," that is, perfect substitutes for one another. We have, thus, an analogue to the familiar concept of the industry in which it is the commodity produced by the firms that is taken as homogeneous. To complete this analogy with Marshallian price theory, we shall assume in the

---

[7] To deal adequately with refinements such as differences among investors in estimates of expected returns would require extensive discussion of the theory of portfolio selection. Brief references to these and related topics will be made in the succeeding article on the general equilibrium model.

[8] The reader may convince himself of this by asking how much he would be willing to rebate to his employer for the privilege of receiving his annual salary in equal monthly installments rather than in irregular amounts over the year. See also J. M. Keynes [10, esp. pp. 53–54].

analysis to follow that the shares concerned are traded in perfect markets under conditions of atomistic competition.[9]

From our definition of homogeneous classes of stock it follows that in equilibrium in a perfect capital market the price per dollar's worth of expected return must be the same for all shares of any given class. Or, equivalently, in any given class the price of every share must be proportional to its expected return. Let us denote this factor of proportionality for any class, say the kth class, by $1/\rho_k$. Then if p_j denotes the price and $\bar{x}_j$ is the expected return per share of the jth firm in class k, we must have:

$$(1) \qquad\qquad p_j = \frac{1}{\rho_k}\,\bar{x}_j;$$

or, equivalently,

$$(2) \qquad\qquad \frac{\bar{x}_j}{p_j} = \rho_k \text{ a constant for all firms } j \text{ in class } k.$$

The constants ρ_k (one for each of the k classes) can be given several economic interpretations: (a) From (2) we see that each ρ_k is the expected rate of return of any share in class k. (b) From (1) $1/\rho_k$ is the price which an investor has to pay for a dollar's worth of expected return in the class k. (c) Again from (1), by analogy with the terminology for perpetual bonds, ρ_k can be regarded as the market rate of capitalization for the expected value of the uncertain streams of the kind generated by the kth class of firms.[10]

B. *Debt Financing and Its Effects on Security Prices*

Having developed an apparatus for dealing with uncertain streams we can now approach the heart of the cost-of-capital problem by dropping the assumption that firms cannot issue bonds. The introduction of debt-financing changes the market for shares in a very fundamental way. Because firms may have different proportions of debt in their capi-

[9] Just what our classes of stocks contain and how the different classes can be identified by outside observers are empirical questions to which we shall return later. For the present, it is sufficient to observe: (1) Our concept of a class, while not identical to that of the industry is at least closely related to it. Certainly the basic characteristics of the probability distributions of the returns on assets will depend to a significant extent on the product sold and the technology used. (2) What are the appropriate class boundaries will depend on the particular problem being studied. An economist concerned with general tendencies in the market, for example, might well be prepared to work with far wider classes than would be appropriate for an investor planning his portfolio, or a firm planning its financial strategy.

[10] We cannot, on the basis of the assumptions so far, make any statements about the relationship or spread between the various ρ's or capitalization rates. Before we could do so we would have to make further specific assumptions about the way investors believe the probability distributions vary from class to class, as well as assumptions about investors' preferences as between the characteristics of different distributions.

tal structure, shares of different companies, even in the same class, can give rise to different probability distributions of returns. In the language of finance, the shares will be subject to different degrees of financial risk or "leverage" and hence they will no longer be perfect substitutes for one another.

To exhibit the mechanism determining the relative prices of shares under these conditions, we make the following two assumptions about the nature of bonds and the bond market, though they are actually stronger than is necessary and will be relaxed later: (1) All bonds (including any debts issued by households for the purpose of carrying shares) are assumed to yield a constant income per unit of time, and this income is regarded as certain by all traders regardless of the issuer. (2) Bonds, like stocks, are traded in a perfect market, where the term perfect is to be taken in its usual sense as implying that any two commodities which are perfect substitutes for each other must sell, in equilibrium, at the same price. It follows from assumption (1) that all bonds are in fact perfect substitutes up to a scale factor. It follows from assumption (2) that they must all sell at the same price per dollar's worth of return, or what amounts to the same thing must yield the same rate of return. This rate of return will be denoted by r and referred to as the rate of interest or, equivalently, as the capitalization rate for sure streams. We now can derive the following two basic propositions with respect to the valuation of securities in companies with different capital structures:

Proposition I. Consider any company j and let $\overline{X}_j$ stand as before for the expected return on the assets owned by the company (that is, its expected profit before deduction of interest). Denote by D_j the market value of the debts of the company; by S_j the market value of its common shares; and by $V_j \equiv S_j + D_j$ the market value of all its securities or, as we shall say, the market value of the firm. Then, our Proposition I asserts that we must have in equilibrium:

(3) $$V_j \equiv (S_j + D_j) = \overline{X}_j/\rho_k, \text{ for any firm } j \text{ in class } k.$$

That is, the *market value of any firm is independent of its capital structure and is given by capitalizing its expected return at the rate ρ_k appropriate to its class.*

This proposition can be stated in an equivalent way in terms of the firm's "average cost of capital," $\overline{X}_j/V_j$, which is the ratio of its expected return to the market value of all its securities. Our proposition then is:

(4) $$\frac{\overline{X}_j}{(S_j + D_j)} \equiv \frac{\overline{X}_j}{V_j} = \rho_k, \text{ for any firm } j, \text{ in class } k.$$

That is, *the average cost of capital to any firm is completely independent of its capital structure and is equal to the capitalization rate of a pure equity stream of its class.*

To establish Proposition I we will show that as long as the relations (3) or (4) do not hold between any pair of firms in a class, arbitrage will take place and restore the stated equalities. We use the term arbitrage advisedly. For if Proposition I did not hold, an investor could buy and sell stocks and bonds in such a way as to exchange one income stream for another stream, identical in all relevant respects but selling at a lower price. The exchange would therefore be advantageous to the investor quite independently of his attitudes toward risk.[11] As investors exploit these arbitrage opportunities, the value of the overpriced shares will fall and that of the underpriced shares will rise, thereby tending to eliminate the discrepancy between the market values of the firms.

By way of proof, consider two firms in the same class and assume for simplicity only, that the expected return, $\overline{X}$, is the same for both firms. Let company 1 be financed entirely with common stock while company 2 has some debt in its capital structure. Suppose first the value of the levered firm, V_2, to be larger than that of the unlevered one, V_1. Consider an investor holding s_2 dollars' worth of the shares of company 2, representing a fraction α of the total outstanding stock, S_2. The return from this portfolio, denoted by Y_2, will be a fraction α of the income available for the stockholders of company 2, which is equal to the total return X_2 less the interest charge, rD_2. Since under our assumption of homogeneity, the anticipated total return of company 2, X_2, is, under all circumstances, the same as the anticipated total return to company 1, X_1, we can hereafter replace X_2 and X_1 by a common symbol X. Hence, the return from the initial portfolio can be written as:

$$(5) \qquad\qquad Y_2 = \alpha(X - rD_2).$$

Now suppose the investor sold his αS_2 worth of company 2 shares and acquired instead an amount $s_1 = \alpha(S_2 + D_2)$ of the shares of company 1. He could do so by utilizing the amount αS_2 realized from the sale of his initial holding and borrowing an additional amount αD_2 on his own credit, pledging his new holdings in company 1 as a collateral. He would thus secure for himself a fraction $s_1/S_1 = \alpha(S_2 + D_2)/S_1$ of the shares and earnings of company 1. Making proper allowance for the interest payments on his personal debt αD_2, the return from the new portfolio, Y_1, is given by:

---

[11] In the language of the theory of choice, the exchanges are movements from inefficient points in the interior to efficient points on the boundary of the investor's opportunity set; and not movements between efficient points along the boundary. Hence for this part of the analysis nothing is involved in the way of specific assumptions about investor attitudes or behavior other than that investors behave consistently and prefer more income to less income, *ceteris paribus*.

(6) $$Y_1 = \frac{\alpha(S_2 + D_2)}{S_1} X - r\alpha D_2 = \alpha \frac{V_2}{V_1} X - r\alpha D_2.$$

Comparing (5) with (6) we see that as long as $V_2 > V_1$ we must have $Y_1 > Y_2$, so that it pays owners of company 2's shares to sell their holdings, thereby depressing S_2 and hence V_2; and to acquire shares of company 1, thereby raising S_1 and thus V_1. We conclude therefore that levered companies cannot command a premium over unlevered companies because investors have the opportunity of putting the equivalent leverage into their portfolio directly by borrowing on personal account.

Consider now the other possibility, namely that the market value of the levered company V_2 is less than V_1. Suppose an investor holds initially an amount s_1 of shares of company 1, representing a fraction α of the total outstanding stock, S_1. His return from this holding is:

$$Y_1 = \frac{s_1}{S_1} X = \alpha X.$$

Suppose he were to exchange this initial holding for another portfolio, also worth s_1, but consisting of s_2 dollars of stock of company 2 and of d dollars of bonds, where s_2 and d are given by:

(7) $$s_2 = \frac{S_2}{V_2} s_1, \qquad d = \frac{D_2}{V_2} s_1.$$

In other words the new portfolio is to consist of stock of company 2 and of bonds in the proportions S_2/V_2 and D_2/V_2, respectively. The return from the stock in the new portfolio will be a fraction s_2/S_2 of the total return to stockholders of company 2, which is $(X - rD_2)$, and the return from the bonds will be rd. Making use of (7), the total return from the portfolio, Y_2, can be expressed as follows:

$$Y_2 = \frac{s_2}{S_2} (X - rD_2) + rd = \frac{s_1}{V_2} (X - rD_2) + r\frac{D_2}{V_2} s_1 = \frac{s_1}{V_2} X = \alpha \frac{S_1}{V_2} X$$

(since $s_1 = \alpha S_1$). Comparing Y_2 with Y_1 we see that, if $V_2 < S_1 \equiv V_1$, then Y_2 will exceed Y_1. Hence it pays the holders of company 1's shares to sell these holdings and replace them with a mixed portfolio containing an appropriate fraction of the shares of company 2.

The acquisition of a mixed portfolio of stock of a levered company j and of bonds in the proportion S_j/V_j and D_j/V_j respectively, may be regarded as an operation which "undoes" the leverage, giving access to an appropriate fraction of the unlevered return X_j. It is this possibility of undoing leverage which prevents the value of levered firms from being consistently less than those of unlevered firms, or more generally prevents the average cost of capital $\overline{X}_j/V_j$ from being systematically higher for levered than for nonlevered companies in the same class.

Since we have already shown that arbitrage will also prevent V_2 from being larger than V_1, we can conclude that in equilibrium we must have $V_2 = V_1$, as stated in Proposition I.

Proposition II. From Proposition I we can derive the following proposition concerning the rate of return on common stock in companies whose capital structure includes some debt: the expected rate of return or yield, i, on the stock of any company j belonging to the kth class is a linear function of leverage as follows:

$$(8) \qquad\qquad i_j = \rho_k + (\rho_k - r)\,D_j/S_j.$$

That is, *the expected yield of a share of stock is equal to the appropriate capitalization rate ρ_k for a pure equity stream in the class, plus a premium related to financial risk equal to the debt-to-equity ratio times the spread between ρ_k and r.* Or equivalently, the market price of any share of stock is given by capitalizing its expected return at the continuously variable rate i_j of (8).[12]

A number of writers have stated close equivalents of our Proposition I although by appealing to intuition rather than by attempting a proof and only to insist immediately that the results were not applicable to the actual capital markets.[13] Proposition II, however, so far as we have been able to discover is new.[14] To establish it we first note that, by definition, the expected rate of return, i, is given by:

$$(9) \qquad\qquad i_j \equiv \frac{\overline{X}_j - r D_j}{S_j}.$$

From Proposition I, equation (3), we know that:

$$\overline{X}_j = \rho_k(S_j + D_j).$$

Substituting in (9) and simplifying, we obtain equation (8).

---

[12] To illustrate, suppose $\overline{X} = 1000$, $D = 4000$, $r = 5$ per cent and $\rho_k = 10$ per cent. These values imply that $V = 10{,}000$ and $S = 6000$ by virtue of Proposition I. The expected yield or rate of return per share is then:

$$i = \frac{1000 - 200}{6000} = .1 + (.1 - .05)\,\frac{4000}{6000} = 13\tfrac{1}{3} \text{ per cent.}$$

[13] See, for example, J. B. Williams [21, esp. pp. 72–73]; David Durand [3]; and W. A. Morton [15]. None of these writers describe in any detail the mechanism which is supposed to keep the average cost of capital constant under changes in capital structure. They seem, however, to be visualizing the equilibrating mechanism in terms of switches by investors between stocks and bonds as the yields of each get out of line with their "riskiness." This is an argument quite different from the pure arbitrage mechanism underlying our proof, and the difference is crucial. Regarding Proposition I as resting on investors' attitudes toward risk leads inevitably to a misunderstanding of many factors influencing relative yields such as, for example, limitations on the portfolio composition of financial institutions. See below, esp. Section I.D.

[14] Morton does make reference to a linear yield function but only " . . . for the sake of simplicity and because the particular function used makes no essential difference in my conclusions" [15, p. 443, note 2].

C. *Some Qualifications and Extensions of the Basic Propositions*

The methods and results developed so far can be extended in a number of useful directions, of which we shall consider here only three: (1) allowing for a corporate profits tax under which interest payments are deductible; (2) recognizing the existence of a multiplicity of bonds and interest rates; and (3) acknowledging the presence of market imperfections which might interfere with the process of arbitrage. The first two will be examined briefly in this section with some further attention given to the tax problem in Section II. Market imperfections will be discussed in Part D of this section in the course of a comparison of our results with those of received doctrines in the field of finance.

Effects of the Present Method of Taxing Corporations. The deduction of interest in computing taxable corporate profits will prevent the arbitrage process from making the value of all firms in a given class proportional to the expected returns generated by their physical assets. Instead, it can be shown (by the same type of proof used for the original version of Proposition I) that the market values of firms in each class must be proportional in equilibrium to their expected return net of taxes (that is, to the sum of the interest paid and expected net stockholder income). This means we must replace each $\overline{X}_j$ in the original versions of Propositions I and II with a new variable $\overline{X}_j^\tau$ representing the total income net of taxes generated by the firm:

$$(10) \qquad \overline{X}_j^\tau \equiv (\overline{X}_j - rD_j)(1 - \tau) + rD_j \equiv \bar{\pi}_j^\tau + rD_j,$$

where $\bar{\pi}_j^\tau$ represents the expected net income accruing to the common stockholders and τ stands for the average rate of corporate income tax.[15]

After making these substitutions, the propositions, when adjusted for taxes, continue to have the same form as their originals. That is, Proposition I becomes:

$$(11) \qquad \frac{\overline{X}_j^\tau}{V_j} = \rho_k^\tau, \text{ for any firm in class } k,$$

and Proposition II becomes

$$(12) \qquad i_j \equiv \frac{\bar{\pi}_j^\tau}{S_j} = \rho_j^\tau + (\rho_k^\tau - r)D_j/S_j$$

where ρ_k^τ is the capitalization rate for income net of taxes in class k.

Although the form of the propositions is unaffected, certain interpretations must be changed. In particular, the after-tax capitalization rate

---

[15] For simplicity, we shall ignore throughout the tiny element of progression in our present corporate tax and treat τ as a constant independent of $(X_j - rD_j)$.

$\rho_k{}^r$ can no longer be identified with the "average cost of capital" which is $\rho_k = \overline{X}_j/V_j$. The difference between $\rho_k{}^r$ and the "true" average cost of capital, as we shall see, is a matter of some relevance in connection with investment planning within the firm (Section II). For the description of market behavior, however, which is our immediate concern here, the distinction is not essential. To simplify presentation, therefore, and to preserve continuity with the terminology in the standard literature we shall continue in this section to refer to $\rho_k{}^r$ as the average cost of capital, though strictly speaking this identification is correct only in the absence of taxes.

Effects of a Plurality of Bonds and Interest Rates. In existing capital markets we find not one, but a whole family of interest rates varying with maturity, with the technical provisions of the loan and, what is most relevant for present purposes, with the financial condition of the borrower.[16] Economic theory and market experience both suggest that the yields demanded by lenders tend to increase with the debt-equity ratio of the borrowing firm (or individual). If so, and if we can assume as a first approximation that this yield curve, $r = r(D/S)$, whatever its precise form, is the same for all borrowers, then we can readily extend our propositions to the case of a rising supply curve for borrowed funds.[17]

Proposition I is actually unaffected in form and interpretation by the fact that the rate of interest may rise with leverage; while the average cost of *borrowed* funds will tend to increase as debt rises, the average cost of funds from *all* sources will still be independent of leverage (apart from the tax effect). This conclusion follows directly from the ability of those who engage in arbitrage to undo the leverage in any financial structure by acquiring an appropriately mixed portfolio of bonds and stocks. Because of this ability, the ratio of earnings (*before* interest charges) to market value—*i.e.*, the average cost of capital from all

---

[16] We shall not consider here the extension of the analysis to encompass the time structure of interest rates. Although some of the problems posed by the time structure can be handled within our comparative statics framework, an adequate discussion would require a separate paper.

[17] We can also develop a theory of bond valuation along lines essentially parallel to those followed for the case of shares. We conjecture that the curve of bond yields as a function of leverage will turn out to be a nonlinear one in contrast to the linear function of leverage developed for common shares. However, we would also expect that the rate of increase in the yield on new issues would not be substantial in practice. This relatively slow rise would reflect the fact that interest rate increases by themselves can never be completely satisfactory to creditors as compensation for their increased risk. Such increases may simply serve to raise r so high relative to ρ that they become self-defeating by giving rise to a situation in which even normal fluctuations in earnings may force the company into bankruptcy. The difficulty of borrowing more, therefore, tends to show up in the usual case not so much in higher rates as in the form of increasingly stringent restrictions imposed on the company's management and finances by the creditors; and ultimately in a complete inability to obtain new borrowed funds, at least from the institutional investors who normally set the standards in the market for bonds.

sources—must be the same for all firms in a given class.[18] In other words, the increased cost of borrowed funds as leverage increases will tend to be offset by a corresponding reduction in the yield of common stock. This seemingly paradoxical result will be examined more closely below in connection with Proposition II.

A significant modification of Proposition I would be required only if the yield curve $r=r(D/S)$ were different for different borrowers, as might happen if creditors had marked preferences for the securities of a particular class of debtors. If, for example, corporations as a class were able to borrow at lower rates than individuals having equivalent personal leverage, then the average cost of capital to corporations might fall slightly, as leverage increased over some range, in reflection of this differential. In evaluating this possibility, however, remember that the relevant interest rate for our arbitrage operators is the rate on brokers' loans and, historically, that rate has not been noticeably higher than representative corporate rates.[19] The operations of holding companies and investment trusts which can borrow on terms comparable to operating companies represent still another force which could be expected to wipe out any marked or prolonged advantages from holding levered stocks.[20]

Although Proposition I remains unaffected as long as the yield curve is the same for all borrowers, the relation between common stock yields and leverage will no longer be the strictly linear one given by the original Proposition II. If r increases with leverage, the yield i will still tend to

[18] One normally minor qualification might be noted. Once we relax the assumption that all bonds have certain yields, our arbitrage operator faces the danger of something comparable to "gambler's ruin." That is, there is always the possibility that an otherwise sound concern—one whose long-run expected income is greater than its interest liability—might be forced into liquidation as a result of a run of temporary losses. Since reorganization generally involves costs, and because the operation of the firm may be hampered during the period of reorganization with lasting unfavorable effects on earnings prospects, we might perhaps expect heavily levered companies to sell at a slight discount relative to less heavily indebted companies of the same class.

[19] Under normal conditions, moreover, a substantial part of the arbitrage process could be expected to take the form, not of having the arbitrage operators go into debt on personal account to put the required leverage into their portfolios, but simply of having them reduce the amount of corporate bonds they already hold when they acquire underpriced unlevered stock. Margin requirements are also somewhat less of an obstacle to maintaining any desired degree of leverage in a portfolio than might be thought at first glance. Leverage could be largely restored in the face of higher margin requirements by switching to stocks having more leverage at the corporate level.

[20] An extreme form of inequality between borrowing and lending rates occurs, of course, in the case of preferred stocks, which can not be directly issued by individuals on personal account. Here again, however, we would expect that the operations of investment corporations plus the ability of arbitrage operators to sell off their holdings of preferred stocks would act to prevent the emergence of any substantial premiums (for this reason) on capital structures containing preferred stocks. Nor are preferred stocks so far removed from bonds as to make it impossible for arbitrage operators to approximate closely the risk and leverage of a corporate preferred stock by incurring a somewhat smaller debt on personal account.

rise as D/S increases, but at a decreasing rather than a constant rate. Beyond some high level of leverage, depending on the exact form of the interest function, the yield may even start to fall.[21] The relation between i and D/S could conceivably take the form indicated by the curve MD

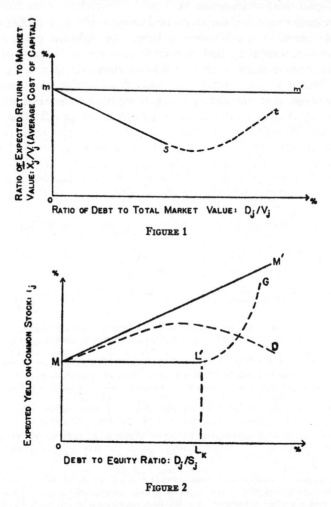

FIGURE 1

FIGURE 2

in Figure 2, although in practice the curvature would be much less pronounced. By contrast, with a constant rate of interest, the relation would be linear throughout as shown by line MM', Figure 2.

The downward sloping part of the curve MD perhaps requires some

[21] Since new lenders are unlikely to permit this much leverage (*cf*. note 17), this range of the curve is likely to be occupied by companies whose earnings prospects have fallen substantially since the time when their debts were issued.

comment since it may be hard to imagine why investors, other than those who like lotteries, would purchase stocks in this range. Remember, however, that the yield curve of Proposition II is a consequence of the more fundamental Proposition I. Should the demand by the risk-lovers prove insufficient to keep the market to the peculiar yield-curve MD, this demand would be reinforced by the action of arbitrage operators. The latter would find it profitable to own a pro-rata share of the firm as a whole by holding its stock *and* bonds, the lower yield of the shares being thus offset by the higher return on bonds.

D. *The Relation of Propositions I and II to Current Doctrines*

The propositions we have developed with respect to the valuation of firms and shares appear to be substantially at variance with current doctrines in the field of finance. The main differences between our view and the current view are summarized graphically in Figures 1 and 2. Our Proposition I [equation (4)] asserts that the average cost of capital, $\overline{X}_j^\tau/V_j$, is a constant for all firms j in class k, independently of their financial structure. This implies that, if we were to take a sample of firms in a given class, and if for each firm we were to plot the ratio of expected return to market value against some measure of leverage or financial structure, the points would tend to fall on a horizontal straight line with intercept ρ_k^τ, like the solid line mm' in Figure 1.[22] From Proposition I we derived Proposition II [equation (8)] which, taking the simplest version with r constant, asserts that, for all firms in a class, the relation between the yield on common stock and financial structure, measured by D_j/S_j, will approximate a straight line with slope $(\rho_k^\tau - r)$ and intercept ρ_k^τ. This relationship is shown as the solid line MM' in Figure 2, to which reference has been made earlier.[23]

By contrast, the conventional view among finance specialists appears to start from the proposition that, other things equal, the earnings-price ratio (or its reciprocal, the times-earnings multiplier) of a firm's common stock will normally be only slightly affected by "moderate" amounts of debt in the firm's capital structure.[24] Translated into our no-

---

[22] In Figure 1 the measure of leverage used is D_j/V_j (the ratio of debt to market value) rather than D_j/S_j (the ratio of debt to equity), the concept used in the analytical development. The D_j/V_j measure is introduced at this point because it simplifies comparison and contrast of our view with the traditional position.

[23] The line MM' in Figure 2 has been drawn with a positive slope on the assumption that $\rho_k^\tau > r$, a condition which will normally obtain. Our Proposition II as given in equation (8) would continue to be valid, of course, even in the unlikely event that $\rho_k^\tau < r$, but the slope of MM' would be negative.

[24] See, *e.g.*, Graham and Dodd [6, pp. 464–66]. Without doing violence to this position, we can bring out its implications more sharply by ignoring the qualification and treating the yield as a virtual constant over the relevant range. See in this connection the discussion in Durand [3, esp. pp. 225–37] of what he calls the "net income method" of valuation.

tation, it asserts that for any firm j in the class k,

$$(13) \qquad \frac{\overline{X}_j^r - rD_j}{S_j} \equiv \frac{\overline{\pi}_j^r}{S_j} = i_k^*, \text{ a constant for } \frac{D_j}{S_4} \leq L_k$$

or, equivalently,

$$(14) \qquad S_j = \overline{\pi}_j^r / i_k^*.$$

Here i_k^* represents the capitalization rate or earnings-price ratio on the common stock and L_k denotes some amount of leverage regarded as the maximum "reasonable" amount for firms of the class k. This assumed relationship between yield and leverage is the horizontal solid line ML' of Figure 2. Beyond L', the yield will presumably rise sharply as the market discounts "excessive" trading on the equity. This possibility of a rising range for high leverages is indicated by the broken-line segment $L'G$ in the figure.[25]

If the value of shares were really given by (14) then the over-all market value of the firm must be:

$$(16) \qquad V_j \equiv S_j + D_j = \frac{\overline{X}_j^r - rD_j}{i_k^*} + D_j = \frac{\overline{X}_j^r}{i_k^*} + \frac{(i_k^* - r)D_j}{i_k^*} .$$

That is, for any given level of expected total returns after taxes $(\overline{X}_j^r)$ and assuming, as seems natural, that $i_k^* > r$, the value of the firm must tend to *rise* with debt;[26] whereas our Proposition I asserts that the value of the firm is completely independent of the capital structure. Another way of contrasting our position with the traditional one is in terms of the cost of capital. Solving (16) for $\overline{X}_j^r / V_j$ yields:

$$(17) \qquad \overline{X}_j^r / V_j = i_k^* - (i_k^* - r)D_j / V_j.$$

According to this equation, the average cost of capital is not independent of capital structure as we have argued, but should tend to *fall* with increasing leverage, at least within the relevant range of moderate debt ratios, as shown by the line ms in Figure 1. Or to put it in more familiar terms, debt-financing should be "cheaper" than equity-financing if not carried too far.

When we also allow for the possibility of a rising range of stock yields for large values of leverage, we obtain a U-shaped curve like mst in

---

[25] To make it easier to see some of the implications of this hypothesis as well as to prepare the ground for later statistical testing, it will be helpful to assume that the notion of a critical limit on leverage beyond which yields rise rapidly, can be epitomized by a quadratic relation of the form:

$$(15) \qquad \overline{\pi}_j^r / S_j = i_k^* + \beta(D_j/S_j) + \alpha(D_j/S_j)^2, \qquad \alpha > 0.$$

[26] For a typical discussion of how a promoter can, supposedly, increase the market value of a firm by recourse to debt issues, see W. J. Eiteman [4, esp. pp. 11–13].

Figure 1.[27] That a yield-curve for stocks of the form $ML'G$ in Figure 2 implies a U-shaped cost-of-capital curve has, of course, been recognized by many writers. A natural further step has been to suggest that the capital structure corresponding to the trough of the U is an "optimal capital structure" towards which management ought to strive in the best interests of the stockholders.[28] According to our model, by contrast, no such optimal structure exists—all structures being equivalent from the point of view of the cost of capital.

Although the falling, or at least U-shaped, cost-of-capital function is in one form or another the dominant view in the literature, the ultimate rationale of that view is by no means clear. The crucial element in the position—that the expected earnings-price ratio of the stock is largely unaffected by leverage up to some conventional limit—is rarely even regarded as something which requires explanation. It is usually simply taken for granted or it is merely asserted that this is the way the market behaves.[29] To the extent that the constant earnings-price ratio has a rationale at all we suspect that it reflects in most cases the feeling that moderate amounts of debt in "sound" corporations do not really add very much to the "riskiness" of the stock. Since the extra risk is slight, it seems natural to suppose that firms will not have to pay noticeably higher yields in order to induce investors to hold the stock.[30]

A more sophisticated line of argument has been advanced by David Durand [3, pp. 231–33]. He suggests that because insurance companies and certain other important institutional investors are restricted to debt securities, nonfinancial corporations are able to borrow from them at interest rates which are lower than would be required to compensate

[27] The U-shaped nature of the cost-of-capital curve can be exhibited explicitly if the yield curve for shares as a function of leverage can be approximated by equation (15) of footnote 25. From that equation, multiplying both sides by S_j we obtain: $\bar{\pi}_j{}^\tau = \bar{X}_j{}^\tau - rD_j = i_k{}^*S_j + \beta D_j + \alpha D_j{}^2/S_j$ or, adding and subtracting $i_k{}^*D_k$ from the right-hand side and collecting terms,

$$(18) \qquad \bar{X}_j{}^\tau = i_k{}^*(S_j + D_j) + (\beta + r - i_k{}^*)D_j + \alpha D^2{}_j/S_j.$$

Dividing (18) by V_j gives an expression for the cost of capital:

$$(19) \quad \bar{X}_j{}^\tau/V_j = i_k{}^* - (i_k{}^* - r - \beta)D_j/V_j + \alpha D_j{}^2/S_jV_j = i_k{}^* - (i_k{}^* - r - \beta)D_j/V_j + \alpha(D_j/V_j)^2/(1 - D_j/V_j)$$

which is clearly U-shaped since α is supposed to be positive.

[28] For a typical statement see S. M. Robbins [16, p. 307]. See also Graham and Dodd [6, pp. 468–74].

[29] See *e.g.*, Graham and Dodd [6, p. 466].

[30] A typical statement is the following by Guthmann and Dougall [7, p. 245]: "Theoretically it might be argued that the increased hazard from using bonds and preferred stocks would counterbalance this additional income and so prevent the common stock from being more attractive than when it had a lower return but fewer prior obligations. In practice, the extra earnings from 'trading on the equity' are often regarded by investors as more than sufficient to serve as a 'premium for risk' when the proportions of the several securities are judiciously mixed."

MODIGLIANI AND MILLER: THEORY OF INVESTMENT 279

creditors in a free market. Thus, while he would presumably agree with our conclusions that stockholders could not gain from leverage in an unconstrained market, he concludes that they can gain under present institutional arrangements. This gain would arise by virtue of the "safety superpremium" which lenders are willing to pay corporations for the privilege of lending.[31]

The defective link in both the traditional and the Durand version of the argument lies in the confusion between investors' subjective risk preferences and their objective market opportunities. Our Propositions I and II, as noted earlier, do not depend for their validity on any assumption about individual risk preferences. Nor do they involve any assertion as to what is an adequate compensation to investors for assuming a given degree of risk. They rely merely on the fact that a given commodity cannot consistently sell at more than one price in the market; or more precisely that the price of a commodity representing a "bundle" of two other commodities cannot be consistently different from the weighted average of the prices of the two components (the weights being equal to the proportion of the two commodities in the bundle).

An analogy may he helpful at this point. The relations between $1/\rho_k$, the price per dollar of an unlevered stream in class k; $1/r$, the price per dollar of a sure stream, and $1/i_j$, the price per dollar of a levered stream j, in the kth class, are essentially the same as those between, respectively, the price of whole milk, the price of butter fat, and the price of milk which has been thinned out by skimming off some of the butter fat. Our Proposition I states that a firm cannot reduce the cost of capital—*i.e.*, increase the market value of the stream it generates—by securing part of its capital through the sale of bonds, even though debt money appears to be cheaper. This assertion is equivalent to the proposition that, under perfect markets, a dairy farmer cannot in general earn more for the milk he produces by skimming some of the butter fat and selling it separately, even though butter fat per unit weight, sells for more than whole milk. The advantage from skimming the milk rather than selling whole milk would be purely illusory; for what would be gained from selling the high-priced butter fat would be lost in selling the low-priced residue of thinned milk. Similarly our Proposition II—that the price per dollar of a levered stream falls as leverage increases—is an ex-

---

[31] Like Durand, Morton [15] contends "that the actual market deviates from [Proposition I] by giving a changing over-all cost of money at different points of the [leverage] scale" (p. 443, note 2, inserts ours), but the basis for this contention is nowhere clearly stated. Judging by the great emphasis given to the lack of mobility of investment funds between stocks and bonds and to the psychological and institutional pressures toward debt portfolios (see pp. 444–51 and especially his discussion of the optimal capital structure on p. 453) he would seem to be taking a position very similar to that of Durand above.

act analogue of the statement that the price per gallon of thinned milk falls continuously as more butter fat is skimmed off.[32]

It is clear that this last assertion is true as long as butter fat is worth more per unit weight than whole milk, and it holds even if, for many consumers, taking a little cream out of the milk (adding a little leverage to the stock) does not detract noticeably from the taste (does not add noticeably to the risk). Furthermore the argument remains valid even in the face of instituional limitations of the type envisaged by Durand. For suppose that a large fraction of the population habitually dines in restaurants which are required by law to serve only cream in lieu of milk (entrust their savings to institutional investors who can only buy bonds). To be sure the price of butter fat will then tend to be higher in relation to that of skimmed milk than in the absence such restrictions (the rate of interest will tend to be lower), and this will benefit people who eat at home and who like skim milk (who manage their own portfolio and are able and willing to take risk). But it will still be the case that a farmer cannot gain by skimming some of the butter fat and selling it separately (firm cannot reduce the cost of capital by recourse to borrowed funds).[33]

Our propositions can be regarded as the extension of the classical theory of markets to the particular case of the capital markets. Those who hold the current view—whether they realize it or not—must as-

[32] Let M denote the quantity of whole milk, B/M the proportion of butter fat in the whole milk, and let p_M, p_B and p_α denote, respectively, the price per unit weight of whole milk, butter fat and thinned milk from which a fraction α of the butter fat has been skimmed off. We then have the fundamental perfect market relation:

(a) $$p_\alpha(M - \alpha B) + p_B \alpha B = p_M M, \qquad 0 \leq \alpha \leq 1,$$

stating that total receipts will be the same amount $p_M M$, independently of the amount αB of butter fat that may have been sold separately. Since p_M corresponds to $1/\rho$, p_B to $1/r$, p_α to $1/i$, M to $\bar{X}$ and αB to rD, (a) is equivalent to Proposition I, $S + D = \bar{X}/\rho$. From (a) we derive:

(b) $$p_\alpha = p_M \frac{M}{M - \alpha B} - p_B \frac{\alpha B}{M - \alpha B}$$

which gives the price of thinned milk as an explicit function of the proportion of butter fat skimmed off; the function decreasing as long as $p_B > p_M$. From (a) also follows:

(c) $$1/p_\alpha = 1/p_M + (1/p_M - 1/p_B) \frac{p_B \alpha B}{p_\alpha(M - \alpha B)}$$

which is the exact analogue of Proposition II, as given by (8).

[33] The reader who likes parables will find that the analogy with interrelated commodity markets can be pushed a good deal farther than we have done in the text. For instance, the effect of changes in the market rate of interest on the over-all cost of capital is the same as the effect of a change in the price of butter on the price of whole milk. Similarly, just as the relation between the prices of skim milk and butter fat influences the kind of cows that will be reared, so the relation between i and r influences the kind of ventures that will be undertaken. If people like butter we shall have Guernseys; if they are willing to pay a high price for safety, this will encourage ventures which promise smaller but less uncertain streams per dollar of physical assets.

sume not merely that there are lags and frictions in the equilibrating process—a feeling we certainly share,[34] claiming for our propositions only that they describe the central tendency around which observations will scatter—but also that there are large and *systematic* imperfections in the market which permanently bias the outcome. This is an assumption that economists, at any rate, will instinctively eye with some skepticism.

In any event, whether such prolonged, systematic departures from equilibrium really exist or whether our propositions are better descriptions of long-run market behavior can be settled only by empirical research. Before going on to the theory of investment it may be helpful, therefore, to look at the evidence.

E. *Some Preliminary Evidence on the Basic Propositions*

Unfortunately the evidence which has been assembled so far is amazingly skimpy. Indeed, we have been able to locate only two recent studies—and these of rather limited scope—which were designed to throw light on the issue. Pending the results of more comprehensive tests which we hope will soon be available, we shall review briefly such evidence as is provided by the two studies in question: (1) an analysis of the relation between security yields and financial structure for some 43 large electric utilities by F. B. Allen [1], and (2) a parallel (unpublished) study by Robert Smith [19], for 42 oil companies designed to test whether Allen's rather striking results would be found in an industry with very different characteristics.[35] The Allen study is based on average figures for the years 1947 and 1948, while the Smith study relates to the single year 1953.

The Effect of Leverage on the Cost of Capital. According to the received view, as shown in equation (17) the average cost of capital, $\overline{X}^\tau/V$, should decline linearly with leverage as measured by the ratio D/V, at least through most of the relevant range.[36] According to Proposition I, the average cost of capital within a given class k should tend to have the same value ρ_k^τ independently of the degree of leverage. A simple test

[34] Several specific examples of the failure of the arbitrage mechanism can be found in Graham and Dodd [6, *e.g.*, pp. 646–48]. The price discrepancy described on pp. 646–47 is particularly curious since it persists even today despite the fact that a whole generation of security analysts has been brought up on this book!

[35] We wish to express our thanks to both writers for making available to us some of their original worksheets. In addition to these recent studies there is a frequently cited (but apparently seldom read) study by the Federal Communications Commission in 1938 [22] which purports to show the existence of an optimal capital structure or range of structures (in the sense defined above) for public utilities in the 1930's. By current standards for statistical investigations, however, this study cannot be regarded as having any real evidential value for the problem at hand.

[36] We shall simplify our notation in this section by dropping the subscript j used to denote a particular firm wherever this will not lead to confusion.

of the merits of the two alternative hypotheses can thus be carried out by correlating $\overline{X}^\tau/V$ with D/V. If the traditional view is correct, the correlation should be significantly negative; if our view represents a better approximation to reality, then the correlation should not be significantly different from zero.

Both studies provide information about the average value of D—the market value of bonds and preferred stock—and of V—the market value of all securities.[37] From these data we can readily compute the ratio D/V and this ratio (expressed as a percentage) is represented by the symbol d in the regression equations below. The measurement of the variable $\overline{X}^\tau/V$, however, presents serious difficulties. Strictly speaking, the numerator should measure the expected returns net of taxes, but this is a variable on which no direct information is available. As an approximation, we have followed both authors and used (1) the average value of actual net returns in 1947 and 1948 for Allen's utilities; and (2) actual net returns in 1953 for Smith's oil companies. Net return is defined in both cases as the sum of interest, preferred dividends and stockholders' income net of corporate income taxes. Although this approximation to expected returns is undoubtedly very crude, there is no reason to believe that it will systematically bias the test in so far as the sign of the regression coefficient is concerned. The roughness of the approximation, however, will tend to make for a wide scatter. Also contributing to the scatter is the crudeness of the industrial classification, since especially within the sample of oil companies, the assumption that all the firms belong to the same class in our sense, is at best only approximately valid.

Denoting by x our approximation to $\overline{X}^\tau/V$ (expressed, like d, as a percentage), the results of the tests are as follows:

Electric Utilities $x = 5.3 + .006d$ $\quad r = .12$
$$(\pm.008)$$
Oil Companies $\quad x \doteq 8.5 + .006d$ $\quad r = .04.$
$$(\pm.024)$$

The data underlying these equations are also shown in scatter diagram form in Figures 3 and 4.

The results of these tests are clearly favorable to our hypothesis.

[37] Note that for purposes of this test preferred stocks, since they represent an *expected* fixed obligation, are properly classified with bonds even though the tax status of preferred dividends is different from that of interest payments and even though preferred dividends are really fixed only as to their maximum in any year. Some difficulty of classification does arise in the case of convertible preferred stocks (and convertible bonds) selling at a substantial premium, but fortunately very few such issues were involved for the companies included in the two studies. Smith included bank loans and certain other short-term obligations (at book values) in his data on oil company debts and this treatment is perhaps open to some question. However, the amounts involved were relatively small and check computations showed that their elimination would lead to only minor differences in the test results.

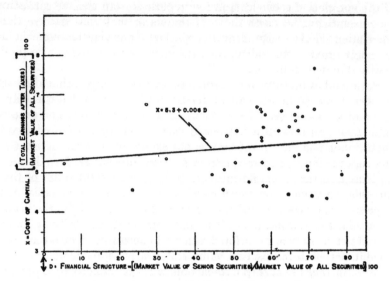

FIGURE 3. COST OF CAPITAL IN RELATION TO FINANCIAL STRUCTURE
FOR 43 ELECTRIC UTILITIES, 1947–48

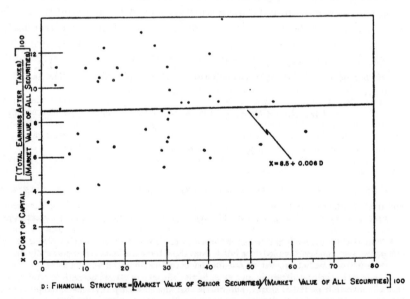

FIGURE 4. COST OF CAPITAL IN RELATION TO FINANCIAL STRUCTURE
FOR 42 OIL COMPANIES, 1953

Both correlation coefficients are very close to zero and not statistically significant. Furthermore, the implications of the traditional view fail to be supported even with respect to the sign of the correlation. The data in short provide no evidence of any tendency for the cost of capital to fall as the debt ratio increases.[38]

It should also be apparent from the scatter diagrams that there is no hint of a curvilinear, U-shaped, relation of the kind which is widely believed to hold between the cost of capital and leverage. This graphical impression was confirmed by statistical tests which showed that for both industries the curvature was not significantly different from zero, its sign actually being opposite to that hypothesized.[39]

Note also that according to our model, the constant terms of the regression equations are measures of $\rho_k{}^\tau$, the capitalization rates for unlevered streams and hence the average cost of capital in the classes in question. The estimates of 8.5 per cent for the oil companies as against 5.3 per cent for electric utilities appear to accord well with a priori expectations, both in absolute value and relative spread.

The Effect of Leverage on Common Stock Yields. According to our Proposition II—see equation 12 and Figure 2—the expected yield on common stock, $\bar{\pi}^\tau/S$, in any given class, should tend to increase with leverage as measured by the ratio D/S. The relation should tend to be linear and with positive slope through most of the relevant range (as in the curve MM' of Figure 2), though it might tend to flatten out if we move

---

[38] It may be argued that a test of the kind used is biased against the traditional view. The fact that both sides of the regression equation are divided by the variable V which may be subject to random variation might tend to impart a positive bias to the correlation. As a check on the results presented in the text, we have, therefore, carried out a supplementary test based on equation (16). This equation shows that, if the traditional view is correct, the market value of a company should, for given $\bar{X}^\tau$, increase with debt through most of the relevant range; according to our model the market value should be uncorrelated with D, given $\bar{X}^\tau$. Because of wide variations in the size of the firms included in our samples, all variables must be divided by a suitable scale factor in order to avoid spurious results in carrying out a test of equation (16). The factor we have used is the book value of the firm denoted by A. The hypothesis tested thus takes the specific form:

$$V/A = a + b(\bar{X}^\tau/A) + c(D/A)$$

and the numerator of the ratio X^τ/A is again approximated by actual net returns. The partial correlation between V/A and D/A should now be positive according to the traditional view and zero according to our model. Although division by A should, if anything, bias the results in favor of the traditional hypothesis, the partial correlation turns out to be only .03 for the oil companies and $-.28$ for the electric utilities. Neither of these coefficients is significantly different from zero and the larger one even has the wrong sign.

[39] The tests consisted of fitting to the data the equation (19) of footnote 27. As shown there, it follows from the U-shaped hypothesis that the coefficient α of the variable $(D/V)^2/(1-D/V)$, denoted hereafter by d^*, should be significant and positive. The following regression equations and partials were obtained:

Electric Utilities $x = 5.0 + .017d - .003d^*$; $r_{xd^* \cdot d} = -.15$

Oil Companies $x = 8.0 + .05d - .03d^*$; $r_{xd^* \cdot d} = -.14$.

far enough to the right (as in the curve MD'), to the extent that high leverage tends to drive up the cost of senior capital. According to the conventional view, the yield curve as a function of leverage should be a horizontal straight line (like ML') through most of the relevant range; far enough to the right, the yield may tend to rise at an increasing rate. Here again, a straight-forward correlation—in this case between $\bar{\pi}^\tau/S$ and D/S—can provide a test of the two positions. If our view is correct, the correlation should be significantly positive; if the traditional view is correct, the correlation should be negligible.

Subject to the same qualifications noted above in connection with $\bar{X}^\tau$, we can approximate $\bar{\pi}^\tau$ by actual stockholder net income.[40] Letting z denote in each case the approximation to $\bar{\pi}^\tau/S$ (expressed as a percentage) and letting h denote the ratio D/S (also in percentage terms) the following results are obtained:

$$\text{Electric Utilities} \quad z = 6.6 + .017h \qquad r = .53$$
$$(+.004)$$

$$\text{Oil Companies} \quad z = 8.9 + .051h \qquad r = .53.$$
$$(\pm.012)$$

These results are shown in scatter diagram form in Figures 5 and 6.

Here again the implications of our analysis seem to be borne out by the data. Both correlation coefficients are positive and highly significant when account is taken of the substantial sample size. Furthermore, the estimates of the coefficients of the equations seem to accord reasonably well with our hypothesis. According to equation (12) the constant term should be the value of ρ_k^τ for the given class while the slope should be $(\rho_k^\tau - r)$. From the test of Proposition I we have seen that for the oil companies the mean value of ρ_k^τ could be estimated at around 8.7. Since the average yield of senior capital during the period covered was in the order of $3\frac{1}{2}$ per cent, we should expect a constant term of about 8.7 per cent and a slope of just over 5 per cent. These values closely approximate the regression estimates of 8.9 per cent and 5.1 per cent respectively. For the electric utilities, the yield of senior capital was also on the order of $3\frac{1}{2}$ per cent during the test years, but since the estimate of the mean value of ρ_k^τ from the test of Proposition I was 5.6 per cent,

---

[40] As indicated earlier, Smith's data were for the single year 1953. Since the use of a single year's profits as a measure of expected profits might be open to objection we collected profit data for 1952 for the same companies and based the computation of $\bar{\pi}^\tau/S$ on the average of the two years. The value of $\bar{\pi}^\tau/S$ was obtained from the formula:

$$\left(\text{net earnings in 1952} \cdot \frac{\text{assets in '53}}{\text{assets in '52}} + \text{net earnings in '1953}\right) \frac{1}{2}$$
$$\div \text{ (average market value of common stock in '53).}$$

The asset adjustment was introduced as rough allowance for the effects of possible growth in the size of the firm. It might be added that the correlation computed with $\bar{\pi}^\tau/S$ based on net profits in 1953 alone was found to be only slightly smaller, namely .50.

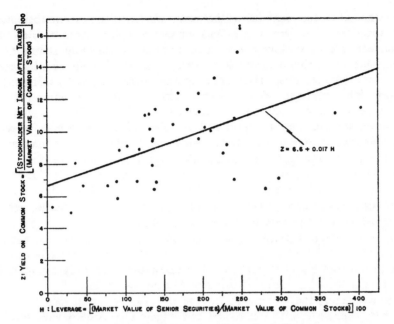

FIGURE 5. YIELD ON COMMON STOCK IN RELATION TO LEVERAGE FOR
43 ELECTRIC UTILITIES, 1947–48

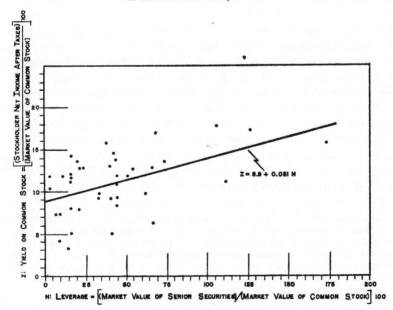

FIGURE 6. YIELD ON COMMON STOCK IN RELATION TO LEVERAGE FOR
42 OIL COMPANIES, 1952–53

the slope should be just above 2 per cent. The actual regression estimate for the slope of 1.7 per cent is thus somewhat low, but still within one standard error of its theoretical value. Because of this underestimate of the slope and because of the large mean value of leverage ($\bar{h}=160$ per cent) the regression estimate of the constant term, 6.6 per cent, is somewhat high, although not significantly different from the value of 5.6 per cent obtained in the test of Proposition I.

When we add a square term to the above equations to test for the presence and direction of curvature we obtain the following estimates:

Electric Utilities $z = 4.6 + .004h - .007h^2$

Oil Companies $\dot{}z = 8.5 + .072h - .016h^2$.

For both cases the curvature is negative. In fact, for the electric utilities, where the observations cover a wider range of leverage ratios, the negative coefficient of the square term is actually significant at the 5 per cent level. Negative curvature, as we have seen, runs directly counter to the traditional hypothesis, whereas it can be readily accounted for by our model in terms of rising cost of borrowed funds.[41]

In summary, the empirical evidence we have reviewed seems to be broadly consistent with our model and largely inconsistent with traditional views. Needless to say much more extensive testing will be required before we can firmly conclude that our theory describes market behavior. Caution is indicated especially with regard to our test of Proposition II, partly because of possible statistical pitfalls[42] and partly because not all the factors that might have a systematic effect on stock yields have been considered. In particular, no attempt was made to test the possible influence of the dividend pay-out ratio whose role has tended to receive a great deal of attention in current research and thinking. There are two reasons for this omission. First, our main objective has been to assess the prima facie tenability of *our* model, and in this model, based as it is on rational behavior by investors, dividends per se play no role. Second, in a world in which the policy of dividend stabilization is widespread, there is no simple way of disentangling the true effect of dividend payments on stock prices from their apparent effect,

[41] That the yield of senior capital tended to rise for utilities as leverage increased is clearly shown in several of the scatter diagrams presented in the published version of Allen's study. This significant negative curvature between stock yields and leverage for utilities may be partly responsible for the fact, previously noted, that the constant in the linear regression is somewhat higher and the slope somewhat lower than implied by equation (12). Note also in connection with the estimate of $\rho_k{}^\tau$ that the introduction of the quadratic term reduces the constant considerably, pushing it in fact below the a priori expectation of 5.6, though the difference is again not statistically significant.

[42] In our test, *e.g.*, the two variables z and h are both ratios with S appearing in the denominator, which may tend to impart a positive bias to the correlation (*cf.* note 38). Attempts were made to develop alternative tests, but although various possibilities were explored, we have so far been unable to find satisfactory alternatives.

the latter reflecting only the role of dividends as a proxy measure of long-term earning anticipations.[43] The difficulties just mentioned are further compounded by possible interrelations between dividend policy and leverage.[44]

II. *Implications of the Analysis for the Theory of Investment*

A. *Capital Structure and Investment Policy*

On the basis of our propositions with respect to cost of capital and financial structure (and for the moment neglecting taxes), we can derive the following simple rule for optimal investment policy by the firm:

Proposition III. If a firm in class k is acting in the best interest of the stockholders at the time of the decision, it will exploit an investment opportunity if and only if the rate of return on the investment, say ρ^*, is as large as or larger than ρ_k. That is, *the cut-off point for investment in the firm will in all cases be ρ_k and will be completely unaffected by the type of security used to finance the investment.* Equivalently, we may say that regardless of the financing used, the marginal cost of capital to a firm is equal to the average cost of capital, which is in turn equal to the capitalization rate for an unlevered stream in the class to which the firm belongs.[45]

To establish this result we will consider the three major financing alternatives open to the firm—bonds, retained earnings, and common stock issues—and show that in each case an investment is worth undertaking if, and only if, $\rho^* \geq \rho_k$.[46]

Consider first the case of an investment financed by the sale of bonds. We know from Proposition I that the market value of the firm before the investment was undertaken was:[47]

$$(20) \qquad V_0 = \overline{X}_0/\rho_k$$

[43] We suggest that failure to appreciate this difficulty is responsible for many fallacious, or at least unwarranted, conclusions about the role of dividends.

[44] In the sample of electric utilities, there is a substantial negative correlation between yields and pay-out ratios, but also between pay-out ratios and leverage, suggesting that either the association of yields and leverage or of yields and pay-out ratios may be (at least partly) spurious. These difficulties however do not arise in the case of the oil industry sample. A preliminary analysis indicates that there is here no significant relation between leverage and pay-out ratios and also no significant correlation (either gross or partial) between yields and pay-out ratios.

[45] The analysis developed in this paper is essentially a comparative-statics, not a dynamic analysis. This note of caution applies with special force to Proposition III. Such problems as those posed by expected changes in r and in ρ_k over time will not be treated here. Although they are in principle amenable to analysis within the general framework we have laid out, such an undertaking is sufficiently complex to deserve separate treatment. *Cf.* note 17.

[46] The extension of the proof to other types of financing, such as the sale of preferred stock or the issuance of stock rights is straightforward.

[47] Since no confusion is likely to arise, we have again, for simplicity, eliminated the subscripts identifying the firm in the equations to follow. Except for ρ_k, the subscripts now refer to time periods.

MODIGLIANI AND MILLER: THEORY OF INVESTMENT 289

and that the value of the common stock was:

$$(21) \qquad S_0 = V_0 - D_0.$$

If now the firm borrows I dollars to finance an investment yielding ρ^* its market value will become:

$$(22) \qquad V_1 = \frac{\overline{X}_0 + \rho^* I}{\rho_k} = V_0 + \frac{\rho^* I}{\rho_k}$$

and the value of its common stock will be:

$$(23) \qquad S_1 = V_1 - (D_0 + I) = V_0 + \frac{\rho^* I}{\rho_k} - D_0 - I$$

or using equation 21,

$$(24) \qquad S_1 = S_0 + \frac{\rho^* I}{\rho_k} - I.$$

Hence $S_1 \gtreqless S_0$ as $\rho^* \gtreqless \rho_k$.[48]

To illustrate, suppose the capitalization rate for uncertain streams in the kth class is 10 per cent and the rate of interest is 4 per cent. Then if a given company had an expected income of 1,000 and if it were financed entirely by common stock we know from Proposition I that the market value of its stock would be 10,000. Assume now that the managers of the firm discover an investment opportunity which will require an outlay of 100 and which is expected to yield 8 per cent. At first sight this might appear to be a profitable opportunity since the expected return is double the interest cost. If, however, the management borrows the necessary 100 at 4 per cent, the total expected income of the company rises to 1,008 and the market value of the firm to 10,080. But the firm now will have 100 of bonds in its capital structure so that, paradoxically, the market value of the stock must actually be reduced from 10,000 to 9,980 as a consequence of this apparently profitable investment. Or, to put it another way, the gains from being able to tap cheap, borrowed funds are more than offset for the stockholders by the market's discount-ing of the stock for the added leverage assumed.

Consider next the case of retained earnings. Suppose that in the course of its operations the firm acquired I dollars of cash (without impairing

[48] In the case of bond-financing the rate of interest on bonds does not enter explicitly into the decision (assuming the firm borrows at the market rate of interest). This is true, more-over, given the conditions outlined in Section I.C, even though interest rates may be an increasing function of debt outstanding. To the extent that the firm borrowed at a rate other than the market rate the two I's in equation (24) would no longer be identical and an additional gain or loss, as the case might be, would accrue to the shareholders. It might also be noted in passing that permitting the two I's in (24) to take on different values provides a simple method for introducing underwriting expenses into the analysis.

the earning power of its assets). If the cash is distributed as a dividend to the stockholders their wealth W_0, after the distribution will be:

$$(25) \qquad W_0 = S_0 + I = \frac{\overline{X}_0}{\rho_k} - D_0 + I$$

where $\overline{X}_0$ represents the expected return from the assets exclusive of the amount I in question. If however the funds are retained by the company and used to finance new assets whose expected rate of return is ρ^*, then the stockholders' wealth would become:

$$(26) \qquad W_1 = S_1 = \frac{\overline{X}_0 + \rho^*I}{\rho_k} - D_0 = S_0 + \frac{\rho^*I}{\rho_k}.$$

Clearly $W_1 \gtrless W_0$ as $\rho^* \gtrless \rho_k$ so that an investment financed by retained earnings raises the net worth of the owners if and only if $\rho^* > \rho_k$.[49]

Consider finally, the case of common-stock financing. Let P_0 denote the current market price per share of stock and assume, for simplicity, that this price reflects currently expected earnings only, that is, it does not reflect any future increase in earnings as a result of the investment under consideration.[50] Then if N is the original number of shares, the price per share is:

$$(27) \qquad P_0 = S_0/N$$

and the number of new shares, M, needed to finance an investment of I dollars is given by:

$$(28) \qquad M = \frac{I}{P_0}.$$

As a result of the investment the market value of the stock becomes:

$$S_1 = \frac{\overline{X}_0 + \rho^*I}{\rho_k} - D_0 = S_0 + \frac{\rho^*I}{\rho_k} = NP_0 + \frac{\rho^*I}{\rho_k}$$

and the price per share:

$$(29) \qquad P_1 = \frac{S_1}{N + M} = \frac{1}{N + M}\left[NP_0 + \frac{\rho^*I}{\rho_k}\right].$$

[49] The conclusion that ρ_k is the cut-off point for investments financed from internal funds applies not only to undistributed net profits, but to depreciation allowances (and even to the funds represented by the current sale value of any asset or collection of assets). Since the owners can earn ρ_k by investing funds elsewhere in the class, partial or total liquidating distributions should be made whenever the firm cannot achieve a marginal internal rate of return equal to ρ_k.

[50] If we assumed that the market price of the stock did reflect the expected higher future earnings (as would be the case if our original set of assumptions above were strictly followed) the analysis would differ slightly in detail, but not in essentials. The cut-off point for new investment would still be ρ_k, but where $\rho^* > \rho_k$ the gain to the original owners would be larger than if the stock price were based on the pre-investment expectations only.

MODIGLIANI AND MILLER: THEORY OF INVESTMENT 291

Since by equation (28), $I = MP_0$, we can add MP_0 and subtract I from the quantity in bracket, obtaining:

(30)
$$P_1 = \frac{1}{N + M}\left[(N + M)P_0 + \frac{\rho^* - \rho_k}{\rho_k}I\right]$$

$$= P_0 + \frac{1}{N + M}\frac{\rho^* - \rho_k}{\rho_k}I > P_0 \text{ if,}$$

and only if, $\rho^* > \rho_k$.

Thus an investment financed by common stock is advantageous to the current stockholders if and only if its yield exceeds the capitalization rate ρ_k.

Once again a numerical example may help to illustrate the result and make it clear why the relevant cut-off rate is ρ_k and not the current yield on common stock, i. Suppose that ρ_k is 10 per cent, r is 4 per cent, that the original expected income of our company is 1,000 and that management has the opportunity of investing 100 having an expected yield of 12 per cent. If the original capital structure is 50 per cent debt and 50 per cent equity, and 1,000 shares of stock are initially outstanding, then, by Proposition I, the market value of the common stock must be 5,000 or 5 per share. Furthermore, since the interest bill is $.04 \times 5,000 = 200$, the yield on common stock is $800/5,000 = 16$ per cent. It may then appear that financing the additional investment of 100 by issuing 20 shares to outsiders at 5 per share would dilute the equity of the original owners since the 100 promises to yield 12 per cent whereas the common stock is currently yielding 16 per cent. Actually, however, the income of the company would rise to 1,012; the value of the firm to 10,120; and the value of the common stock to 5,120. Since there are now 1,020 shares, each would be worth 5.02 and the wealth of the original stockholders would thus have been increased. What has happened is that the dilution in expected earnings per share (from .80 to .796) has been more than offset, in its effect upon the market price of the shares, by the decrease in leverage.

Our conclusion is, once again, at variance with conventional views,[51] so much so as to be easily misinterpreted. Read hastily, Proposition III seems to imply that the capital structure of a firm is a matter of indifference; and that, consequently, one of the core problems of corporate finance—the problem of the optimal capital structure for a firm—is no problem at all. It may be helpful, therefore, to clear up such possible misunderstandings.

[51] In the matter of investment policy under uncertainty there is no single position which represents "accepted" doctrine. For a sample of current formulations, all very different from ours, see Joel Dean [2, esp. Ch. 3], M. Gordon and E. Shapiro [5], and Harry Roberts [17].

B. *Proposition III and Financial Planning by Firms*

Misinterpretation of the scope of Proposition III can be avoided by remembering that this Proposition tells us only that the type of instrument used to finance an investment is irrelevant to the question of whether or not the investment is worth while. This does not mean that the owners (or the managers) have no grounds whatever for preferring one financing plan to another; or that there are no other policy or technical issues in finance at the level of the firm.

That grounds for preferring one type of financial structure to another will still exist within the framework of our model can readily be seen for the case of common-stock financing. In general, except for something like a widely publicized oil-strike, we would expect the market to place very heavy weight on current and recent past earnings in forming expectations as to future returns. Hence, if the owners of a firm discovered a major investment opportunity which they felt would yield much more than ρ_k, they might well prefer not to finance it via common stock at the then ruling price, because this price may fail to capitalize the new venture. A better course would be a pre-emptive issue of stock (and in this connection it should be remembered that stockholders are free to borrow and buy). Another possibility would be to finance the project initially with debt. Once the project had reflected itself in increased actual earnings, the debt could be retired either with an equity issue at much better prices or through retained earnings. Still another possibility along the same lines might be to combine the two steps by means of a convertible debenture or preferred stock, perhaps with a progressively declining conversion rate. Even such a double-stage financing plan may possibly be regarded as yielding too large a share to outsiders since the new stockholders are, in effect, being given an interest in any similar opportunities the firm may discover in the future. If there is a reasonable prospect that even larger opportunities may arise in the near future and if there is some danger that borrowing now would preclude more borrowing later, the owners might find their interests best protected by splitting off the current opportunity into a separate subsidiary with independent financing. Clearly the problems involved in making the crucial estimates and in planning the optimal financial strategy are by no means trivial, even though they should have no bearing on the basic decision to invest (as long as $\rho^* \geqq \rho_k$).[52]

Another reason why the alternatives in financial plans may not be a matter of indifference arises from the fact that managers are concerned

---

[52] Nor can we rule out the possibility that the existing owners, if unable to use a financing plan which protects their interest, may actually prefer to pass up an otherwise profitable venture rather than give outsiders an "excessive" share of the business. It is presumably in situations of this kind that we could justifiably speak of a shortage of "equity capital," though this kind of market imperfection is likely to be of significance only for small or new firms.

with more than simply furthering the interest of the owners. Such other objectives of the management—which need not be necessarily in conflict with those of the owners—are much more likely to be served by some types of financing arrangements than others. In many forms of borrowing agreements, for example, creditors are able to stipulate terms which the current management may regard as infringing on its prerogatives or restricting its freedom to maneuver. The creditors might even be able to insist on having a direct voice in the formation of policy.[53] To the extent, therefore, that financial policies have these implications for the management of the firm, something like the utility approach described in the introductory section becomes relevant to financial (as opposed to investment) decision-making. It is, however, the utility functions of the managers per se and not of the owners that are now involved.[54]

In summary, many of the specific considerations which bulk so large in traditional discussions of corporate finance can readily be superimposed on our simple framework without forcing any drastic (and certainly no systematic) alteration of the conclusion which is our principal concern, namely that for investment decisions, the marginal cost of capital is ρ_k.

C. *The Effect of the Corporate Income Tax on Investment Decisions*

In Section I it was shown that when an unintegrated corporate income tax is introduced, the original version of our Proposition I,

$$\overline{X}/V = \rho_k = \text{a constant}$$

must be rewritten as:

$$(11) \qquad \frac{(\overline{X} - rD)(1 - \tau) + rD}{V} \equiv \frac{\overline{X}^\tau}{V} = \rho_k^\tau = \text{a constant.}$$

Throughout Section I we found it convenient to refer to $\overline{X}^\tau/V$ as the cost of capital. The appropriate measure of the cost of capital relevant

---

[53] Similar considerations are involved in the matter of dividend policy. Even though the stockholders may be indifferent as to payout policy as long as investment policy is optimal, the management need not be so. Retained earnings involve far fewer threats to control than any of the alternative sources of funds and, of course, involve no underwriting expense or risk. But against these advantages management must balance the fact that sharp changes in dividend rates, which heavy reliance on retained earnings might imply, may give the impression that a firm's finances are being poorly managed, with consequent threats to the control and professional standing of the management.

[54] In principle, at least, this introduction of management's risk preferences with respect to financing methods would do much to reconcile the apparent conflict between Proposition III and such empirical findings as those of Modigliani and Zeman [14] on the close relation between interest rates and the ratio of new debt to new equity issues; or of John Lintner [12] on the considerable stability in target and actual dividend-payout ratios.

to investment decisions, however, is the ratio of the expected return *before* taxes to the market value, *i.e.*, $\overline{X}/V$. From (11) above we find:

$$(31) \qquad \frac{\overline{X}}{V} = \frac{\rho_k^{\tau} - \tau_r(D/V)}{1 - \tau} = \frac{\rho_k^{\tau}}{1 - \tau}\left[1 - \frac{\tau r D}{\rho_k^{\tau} V}\right],$$

which shows that the cost of capital now depends on the debt ratio, decreasing, as D/V rises, at the constant rate $\tau r/(1-\tau)$.[55] Thus, with a corporate income tax under which interest is a deductible expense, gains can accrue to stockholders from having debt in the capital structure, even when capital markets are perfect. The gains however are small, as can be seen from (31), and as will be shown more explicitly below.

From (31) we can develop the tax-adjusted counterpart of Proposition III by interpreting the term D/V in that equation as the proportion of debt used in any additional financing of V dollars. For example, in the case where the financing is entirely by new common stock, $D=0$ and the required rate of return ρ_k^S on a venture so financed becomes:

$$(32) \qquad \rho_k^S = \frac{\rho_k^{\tau}}{1 - \tau}.$$

For the other extreme of pure debt financing $D=V$ and the required rate of return, ρ_k^D, becomes:

$$(33) \quad \rho_k^D = \frac{\rho_k^{\tau}}{1-\tau}\left[1 - \tau\frac{r}{\rho_k^{\tau}}\right] = \rho_k^S\left[1 - \tau\frac{r}{\rho_k^{\tau}}\right] = \rho_k^S - \frac{\tau}{1-\tau}r.^{56}$$

For investments financed out of retained earnings, the problem of defining the required rate of return is more difficult since it involves a comparison of the tax consequences to the individual stockholder of receiving a dividend versus having a capital gain. Depending on the time of realization, a capital gain produced by retained earnings may be taxed either at ordinary income tax rates, 50 per cent of these rates, 25 per

[55] Equation (31) is amenable, in principle, to statistical tests similar to those described in Section I.E. However we have not made any systematic attempt to carry out such tests so far, because neither the Allen nor the Smith study provides the required information. Actually, Smith's data included a very crude estimate of tax liability, and, using this estimate, we did in fact obtain a negative relation between $\overline{X}/V$ and D/V. However, the correlation ($-.28$) turned out to be significant only at about the 10 per cent level. While this result is not conclusive, it should be remembered that, according to our theory, the slope of the regression equation should be in any event quite small. In fact, with a value of τ in the order of .5, and values of ρ_k^{τ} and r in the order of 8.5 and 3.5 per cent respectively (*cf.* Section I.E) an increase in D/V from 0 to 60 per cent (which is, approximately, the range of variation of this variable in the sample) should tend to reduce the average cost of capital only from about 17 to about 15 per cent.

[56] This conclusion does not extend to preferred stocks even though they have been classed with debt issues previously. Since preferred dividends except for a portion of those of public utilities are not in general deductible from the corporate tax, the cut-off point for new financing via preferred stock is exactly the same as that for common stock.

MODIGLIANI AND MILLER: THEORY OF INVESTMENT   295

cent, or zero, if held till death. The rate on any dividends received in the event of a distribution will also be a variable depending on the amount of other income received by the stockholder, and with the added complications introduced by the current dividend-credit provisions. If we assume that the managers proceed on the basis of reasonable estimates as to the average values of the relevant tax rates for the owners, then the required return for retained earnings $\rho_k{}^R$ can be shown to be:

$$(34) \qquad \rho_k{}^R = \rho_k{}^\tau \, \frac{1}{1-\tau} \, \frac{1-\tau_d}{1-\tau_g} = \frac{1-\tau_d}{1-\tau_g} \rho_k{}^s$$

where τ_d is the assumed rate of personal income tax on dividends and τ_g is the assumed rate of tax on capital gains.

A numerical illustration may perhaps be helpful in clarifying the relationship between these required rates of return. If we take the following round numbers as representative order-of-magnitude values under present conditions: an after-tax capitalization rate $\rho_k{}^\tau$ of 10 per cent, a rate of interest on bonds of 4 per cent, a corporate tax rate of 50 per cent, a marginal personal income tax rate on dividends of 40 per cent (corresponding to an income of about $25,000 on a joint return), and a capital gains rate of 20 per cent (one-half the marginal rate on dividends), then the required rates of return would be: (1) 20 per cent for investments financed entirely by issuance of new common shares; (2) 16 per cent for investments financed entirely by new debt; and (3) 15 per cent for investments financed wholly from internal funds.

These results would seem to have considerable significance for current discussions of the effect of the corporate income tax on financial policy and on investment. Although we cannot explore the implications of the results in any detail here, we should at least like to call attention to the remarkably small difference between the "cost" of equity funds and debt funds. With the numerical values assumed, equity money turned out to be only 25 per cent more expensive than debt money, rather than something on the order of 5 times as expensive as is commonly supposed to be the case.[57] The reason for the wide difference is that the traditional

---

[57] See *e.g.*, D. T. Smith [18]. It should also be pointed out that our tax system acts in other ways to reduce the gains from debt financing. Heavy reliance on debt in the capital structure, for example, commits a company to paying out a substantial proportion of its income in the form of interest payments taxable to the owners under the personal income tax. A debt-free company, by contrast, can reinvest in the business all of its (smaller) net income and to this extent subject the owners only to the low capital gains rate (or possibly no tax at all by virtue of the loophole at death). Thus, we should expect a high degree of leverage to be of value to the owners, even in the case of closely held corporations, primarily in cases where their firm was not expected to have much need for additional funds to expand assets and earnings in the future. To the extent that opportunities for growth were available, as they presumably would be for most successful corporations, the interest of the stockholders would tend to be better served by a structure which permitted maximum use of retained earnings.

view starts from the position that debt funds are several times cheaper than equity funds even in the absence of taxes, with taxes serving simply to magnify the cost ratio in proportion to the corporate rate. By contrast, in our model in which the repercussions of debt financing on the value of shares are taken into account, the *only* difference in cost is that due to the tax effect, and its magnitude is simply the tax on the "grossed up" interest payment. Not only is this magnitude likely to be small but our analysis yields the further paradoxical implication that the stockholders' gain from, and hence incentive to use, debt financing is actually smaller the lower the rate of interest. In the extreme case where the firm could borrow for practically nothing, the advantage of debt financing would also be practically nothing.

III. *Conclusion*

With the development of Proposition III the main objectives we outlined in our introductory discussion have been reached. We have in our Propositions I and II at least the foundations of a theory of the valuation of firms and shares in a world of uncertainty. We have shown, moreover, how this theory can lead to an operational definition of the cost of capital and how that concept can be used in turn as a basis for rational investment decision-making within the firm. Needless to say, however, much remains to be done before the cost of capital can be put away on the shelf among the solved problems. Our approach has been that of static, partial equilibrium analysis. It has assumed among other things a state of atomistic competition in the capital markets and an ease of access to those markets which only a relatively small (though important) group of firms even come close to possessing. These and other drastic simplifications have been necessary in order to come to grips with the problem at all. Having served their purpose they can now be relaxed in the direction of greater realism and relevance, a task in which we hope others interested in this area will wish to share.

REFERENCES

1. F. B. ALLEN, "Does Going into Debt Lower the 'Cost of Capital'?," *Analysts Jour.*, Aug. 1954, *10*, 57–61.
2. J. DEAN, *Capital Budgeting.* New York 1951.
3. D. DURAND, "Costs of Debt and Equity Funds for Business: Trends and Problems of Measurement" in Nat. Bur. Econ. Research, *Conference on Research in Business Finance.* New York 1952, pp. 215–47.
4. W. J. EITEMAN, "Financial Aspects of Promotion," in *Essays on Business Finance* by M. W. Waterford and W. J. Eiteman. Ann Arbor, Mich. 1952, pp. 1–17.
5. M. J. GORDON and E. SHAPIRO, "Capital Equipment Analysis: The Required Rate of Profit," *Manag. Sci.*, Oct. 1956, *3*, 102–10.

MODIGLIANI AND MILLER: THEORY OF INVESTMENT 297

6. B. Graham and L. Dodd, *Security Analysis*, 3rd ed. New York 1951.
7. G. Guthmann and H. E. Dougall, *Corporate Financial Policy*, 3rd ed. New York 1955.
8. J. R. Hicks, *Value and Capital*, 2nd ed. Oxford 1946.
9. P. Hunt and M. Williams, *Case Problems in Finance*, rev. ed. Homewood, Ill. 1954.
10. J. M. Keynes, *The General Theory of Employment, Interest and Money*. New York 1936.
11. O. Lange, *Price Flexibility and Employment*. Bloomington, Ind. 1944.
12. J. Lintner, "Distribution of Incomes of Corporations among Dividends, Retained Earnings and Taxes," *Am. Econ. Rev.*, May 1956, *46*, 97–113.
13. F. Lutz and V. Lutz, *The Theory of Investment of the Firm*. Princeton 1951.
14. F. Modigliani and M. Zeman, "The Effect of the Availability of Funds, and the Terms Thereof, on Business Investment" in Nat. Bur. Econ. Research, *Conference on Research in Business Finance*. New York 1952, pp. 263–309.
15. W. A. Morton, "The Structure of the Capital Market and the Price of Money," *Am. Econ. Rev.*, May 1954, *44*, 440–54.
16. S. M. Robbins, *Managing Securities*. Boston 1954.
17. H. V. Roberts, "Current Problems in the Economics of Capital Budgeting," *Jour. Bus.*, 1957, *30* (1), 12–16.
18. D. T. Smith, *Effects of Taxation on Corporate Financial Policy*. Boston 1952.
19. R. Smith, "Cost of Capital in the Oil Industry," (hectograph). Pittsburgh: Carnegie Inst. Tech. 1955.
20. H. M. Somers, " 'Cost of Money' as the Determinant of Public Utility Rates," *Buffalo Law Rev.*, Spring 1955, *4*, 1–28.
21. J. B. Williams, *The Theory of Investment Value*. Cambridge, Mass. 1938.
22. U. S. Federal Communications Commission, *The Problem of the "Rate of Return" in Public Utility Regulation*. Washington 1938.

[20]

LONG-RUN IMPLICATIONS OF ALTERNATIVE FISCAL POLICIES AND THE BURDEN OF THE NATIONAL DEBT[*]

BY *Franco Modigliani*

I. Introduction

The time-honored controversy over the burden of the National Debt has flared up once more.[1] The view, almost unchallenged a few years back, that the National Debt is no burden on the economy and that the real cost of government expenditure, no matter how financed, cannot be shifted to "future generations" has been on the retreat under a powerful counterattack spearheaded by the contributions of J. M. Buchanan,[2] J. E. Meade,[3] and R. A.

[*] Reprinted by permission from *The Economic Journal*, LXXI (December, 1961).

1. A number of colleagues at Massachusetts Institute of Technology and other institutions have greatly helped me with their comments on a preliminary draft of this paper. I wish particularly to acknowledge the many useful suggestions of Ralph Beals, James Buchanan, Sukhamoy Chakravarty, Margaret Hall, and Merton Miller.

2. J. M. Buchanan, *Public Principles of Public Debt* (Homewood, Illinois: Richard D. Irwin, 1958).

3. J. E. Meade, "Is the National Debt a Burden?" *Oxford Economic Papers*, X (June, 1958), 163-83, and "Is the National Debt a Burden: A Correction," *ibid.*, XI (February, 1959), 109-10.

Musgrave.[4] These authors, while relying to a considerable extent on older arguments, have significantly enriched the analysis by blending the traditional approach with the new insights provided by the Keynesian revolution. But even these most recent contributions have failed, in our view, to provide an altogether adequate framework—a failure resulting at least in part from the Keynesian tendency to emphasise flows while paying inadequate attention to stocks. It is the purpose of this paper to propose a fresh approach to this problem, and to show that, unlike its predecessors, it leads to a consistent and yet straightforward answer to all relevant questions.

Unless otherwise noted, the National Debt will be defined here as consisting of: (1) all claims against the Government held by the private sector of the economy, or by foreigners, whether interest bearing or not (and including therefore bank-held debt and government currency, if any); less (2) any claims held by the Government against the private sector and foreigners.[5]

From a methodological point of view, the central contention of our analysis is that to grasp fully the economic effects of alternative fiscal policies and of the National Debt, we must pay proper attention to stocks as well as to the usual flow variables and to the long-run as well as to the impact effects. Among the substantive implications of this line of approach, the following may be mentioned here by way of a rough summary: (1) Given the government purchase of goods and services, an increase of the (real) National Debt, whether internal or external, is generally advantageous to those present at the time of the increase (or to some subset

4. R. A. Musgrave, *The Theory of Public Finance* (McGraw-Hill, 1959), especially Chapter 23. Other recent contributions include: the reviews of Buchanan's book by A. P. Lerner, *The Journal of Political Economy*, XLVII (April, 1959), 203-6; E. R. Rolph, *The American Economic Reviews*, XLIX (March, 1959), 183-5, and A. H. Hansen, *The Review of Economics and Statistics*, XLI (June, 1959), 377-8; also "The Public Debt: A Burden on Future Generations?" by W. G. Bowen, R. G. Davis, and D. H. Kopf, *The American Economic Review*, L (September, 1960), 701-6; and the forthcoming note by A. P. Lerner, "The Burden of Debt," *The Review of Economics and Statistics*, LIV (May, 1961).

Since the completion of this paper, three comments on the Bowen, Davis, and Kopf communication by W. Vickrey, T. Scitovsky, and J. R. Elliott, and a reply by the authors have also appeared in the March, 1961, issue of *The American Economic Review*, pp. 132-43.

5. This definition implies that the National Debt could in principle be negative. Even in this case we shall refer to it by the same name, although its magnitude will be expressed by a negative number. Similarly, we refer to an operation that reduces the algebraic value of the National Debt as a "reduction," even if the debt was initially zero or negative.

thereof). (2) Such an increase will generally place a "gross burden" on those living beyond that time through a reduction in the aggregate stock of private capital, which, as long as the (net) marginal productivity of capital is positive, will in turn cause a reduction in the flow of goods and services. Furthermore, this loss (as well as the gain under (1) above) will tend to occur even when lack of effective private demand would prevent the maintenance of full employment in the absence of the deficit, though the relative size of gain and losses may be quite different in these circumstances. (3) These conclusions hold in reverse in the case of a reduction in the real National Debt. That is, such a decline is burdensome on those present at the time of the reduction and tends to generate a gross gain for those living beyond. (4) *If* the rate of interest at which the Government borrows can be taken as a good approximation to the marginal productivity of private capital, then the gross burden (or gain) to "future generations" referred to under (2) and (3) can be *measured* by the interest charges on the National Debt. (5) The gross burden may be offset in part or *in toto*, or may be even more than offset, in so far as the increase in the debt is accompanied by government expenditure which contributes to the real income of future generations, *e.g.*, through productive public capital formation.[6]

This summary is very rough indeed and is subject to numerous qualifications and amendments, many of which will be noted below. In any event, I should like to emphasise that the stress of this paper is on developing a method of analysis rather than on presenting a body of doctrines. For this reason I will try to relate my analysis to earlier points of view whenever this seems helpful in clarifying the issues involved. At the same time I will endeavor to stay clear of many traditional but somewhat sterile controversies, such as whether the analogy between private and public debt is true or false.

II. A Bird's Eye View of the Classical and Post-Keynesian No-transfer and No-burden Argument

We begin by reviewing the very persuasive arguments supporting the doctrine that the cost of the current government use of resources

---

6. The difference between the increase in the National Debt in a given interval and the Government expenditure contributing to future income corresponds roughly to the net increase in what Professor Meade has called the "deadweight" debt.

cannot be transferred to future generations and that the National Debt is no burden on them. Since these arguments have been presented many times in the last couple of centuries and have been extensively restated in recent years, we can afford to recapitulate them very briefly in terms of the three propositions presented below—at the cost of glossing over some of the fine points and of foregoing the pleasure of citing "chapter and verse."[7]

(1) Individuals or sub-groups within an economic system can, by means of borrowing, increase the current flow of goods available to them and pay for this increase out of future output. But they can do so only because their borrowing is "external," *i.e.*, matched by a lender who yields current goods in exchange for later output. But a closed community cannot dispose of more goods and services than it is currently producing. It certainly cannot increase this flow by paying with future output, for there is no way "we can dispose to-day of to-morrow's output." Hence the goods and services acquired by the Government must always be "paid for" by those present at the time in the form of a reduction in the flow of goods available to them for private use, and cannot possibly be paid for by later generations, whether the acquisition is financed by taxes or by internal borrowing. Only through external borrowing is it possible to benefit the current generation and to impose a burden on the future.

(2) Although internal borrowing will leave in its wake an obligation for future tax-payers to pay the interest on the National Debt and, possibly, to repay the principal, this obligation is not a net burden on the community as a whole, because these payments are but transfers of income between future members of the community. The loss of the tax-payers is offset in the aggregate by the gain of the beneficiary of the payment. These transfers may, of course, occur between people of different ages and hence of different "generations," and in this sense internal borrowing may cause "inter-generations transfers," but it will not cause a net loss to society.

The above two arguments, or some reasonable variant thereof, have provided the cornerstone of the no-transfer, no-burden argument over the last two centuries or so. It was left for Keynesian

7. The reader interested in establishing just who said what will find much useful material in Buchanan, *Public Principles of Public Debt*, especially Chapters 2 and 8, and in B. Griziotti, "La diversa pressione tributaria del prestito e dell'imposta" in *Studi di scienza delle finanze e diritto finanziario* (Milano: Giuffre, 1956), II, 193-273.

analysis to provide a third argument, removing thereby a potentially troublesome objection to the first two. If the cost of government expenditure always falls on the current generation, no matter how financed, why not forego altogether the painful activity of levying taxes? Yet our common sense rebels at this conclusion. A partial answer to this puzzle was provided by recognizing that taxes, even when paid back in the form of transfers, generate some "frictional loss," because most if not all feasible methods of raising tax revenue tend to interfere with the optimum allocation of resources.[8] Presumably the ever-increasing level of the National Debt resulting from full deficit financing of current expenditure would require raising through taxes an ever-growing revenue to pay the interest on the debt. Eventually the ratio of such taxes to national income plus transfers would exceed the ratio of government expenditure to national product, giving rise to frictional tax losses which could have been avoided through a balanced budget. While these considerations do provide a *prima facie* case for a balanced-budget policy, the case is not tight, for could not the interest itself be met by further borrowing?

However, we need not follow these fancy possibilities, for the Keynesian analysis has provided a much more cogent argument to support the need for an "appropriate" amount of taxation, although not necessarily for a balanced budget. This argument, which reaches its most elegant formulation in the so-called principle of "functional finance" enunciated by Lerner,[9] can be roughly summarized as follows.

(3) Given the full employment output, say $\overline{X}$, and given the share of this output which it is appropriate to allocate for government use, say $\overline{G}$, there is a maximum amount of output that is left available for the private sector, say $\overline{P} = \overline{X} - \overline{G}$. Now the private sector demand for output, say P, is a function of income and taxes, say $P = \mathcal{P}(X, T)$, with $\dfrac{\delta P}{\delta T} < 0$. Taxes are then to be set at that level, say $\overline{T}$, which satisfies the equation $\mathcal{P}(X, T) = P$. A higher

---

8. See, *e.g.*, J. E. Meade, "Mr. Lerner on 'The Economics of Control,'" *The Economic Journal*, LV (April, 1945), 47-70.

9. See, *e.g.*, "Functional Finance and the Public Debt," *Social Research*, X, No. 1, and "The Burden of the National Debt," in *Income Employment and Public Policy* (New York: W. W. Norton & Company, 1948).

level of taxes would generate unemployment and a lower level would generate inflation, both evils which it is the task of the Government to avoid. $\overline{T}$ may turn out to be larger than $\overline{G}$, calling for a surplus, or smaller than $\overline{G}$, or even perchance just equal to $\overline{G}$, implying a balanced budget. But in any event, the purpose of taxes is not to make the current members of the community pay for the government use of goods, which they will do in any event; the real reason we need to put up with the unpleasantness of taxes is to prevent the greater social evil of inflation.

III. A Bird's Eye View of the Classical and Post-Keynesian Transfer and Burden Argument

The basic contention of this school of thought, which itself has a long tradition, is that in general—though possibly with some exceptions—a debt-financed public expenditure will place no burden at all on those present at the very moment in which the expenditure takes place, and will instead place a burden on all tax-payers living thereafter. This burden may fall in part on those present at the time of the expenditure, but only insofar as they are present thereafter. The arguments which support this position have also been repeatedly stated and have been thoroughly reviewed quite recently by Buchanan. It will therefore again be sufficient to summarize them very briefly in the following two propositions:

(1) The cost of a tax-financed expenditure is borne currently, for the resources obtained by the Government come from a forcible reduction in the resources of current tax-payers. But an expenditure financed by debt, whether internal or external, as a rule places no burden on those present at the time of the expenditure in that, and insofar as, the resources acquired by the Government are surrendered in a voluntary exchange by the savers, who thereby acquire government bonds (in lieu of some other asset).

(2) The burden is imposed instead on all future tax-payers, who will have to pay taxes to service the debt. These taxes are *not* a mere transfer of income, but a net burden on society, for, in the absence of the debt-financed expenditure, the taxes would not have been levied, while the investors in bonds would have received the income just the same, directly or indirectly, from the return on the physical assets in which their savings would have been invested. This argument *does not* imply that a debt-financed expenditure will neces-

sarily affect future generations unfavorably. In order to assess the "net outcome," we must subtract from the gross burden represented by the extra taxes benefits, if any, resulting from the expenditure. Thus the net outcome might even be positive if the expenditure undertaken produced greater benefits than the private capital formation which it replaces. But the argument does imply that, through deficit financing, the expenditure of the Government is being "paid for" by future generations.

A careful application of the *reasoning* underlying (1) and (2) will reveal circumstances in which the above conclusions do not hold and the allocation of the burden may be independent of the form of financing used. There are in particular two important cases which are treated at some length by Buchanan and which bring to light the contribution of Keynesian analysis also to this side of the argument. The first is the case of debt-financed expenditure in deep depressions, when private capital formation could not, in any event, provide an adequate offset to full-employment saving. Here, according to Buchanan, not even a gross burden need result to future taxpayers, for the expenditure could in principle be financed by interest-free issuance of currency. The second exception discussed by Buchanan is that of a major war. Unfortunately, the chapter on war financing is one of the least convincing in his book, and what follows may represent more nearly my application of his framework than a faithful summary of his argument. Suppose the war effort is sufficiently severe so that the allocation of resources to various uses, and to capital formation in particular, is completely determined by war necessities. In such a situation the way in which the Government finances its expenditure cannot affect private consumption or capital formation. It would seem therefore that the burden of reduced consumption must be borne by the current generation, even if the reduction is achieved not through taxes but through a combination of rationing and voluntary increases in saving and the unspent disposable income is invested in claims against the Government. Similarly, the burden of the reduction in useful capital formation is borne by those living after the war, again independently of financing. In this case, as well as in the case of depression financing, the taxes levied to pay the interest on the increased debt would indeed seem to result in a pure transfer, for the income associated with the bonds would *not* have come to exist had the Government decided respectively to tax, or to print money, instead of borrowing.

J. E. Meade has also lately associated himself with those maintaining that the National Debt is a burden,[10] but his argument is quite different from the classical one, and bears instead all the marks of post-Keynesian analysis. He is not concerned with the differential effect of deficit versus tax financing, but asserts none the less that government debt in excess of government-owned physical capital—the so-called deadweight debt—is a burden on the economy. Unfortunately his contribution, which is so stimulating in analyzing the effects of a major capital levy, is less than convincing in its attempt to establish that the deadweight debt is a burden. For his demonstration seems to rely entirely on the proposition that elimination of the debt would be a blessing for the economy in that it would encourage saving through a "Pigou type" effect, besides reducing the frictional costs of transfers. Now the tax-friction proposition, though valid, is not new,[11] and had already been generally accepted as a second-order amendment to the no-burden argument. On the other hand, the first and central argument is rather unconvincing. For, as Meade himself recognizes, a reduction in National Debt, be it through a capital levy, budget surplus or inflation, would spur saving whether or not the debt reduced thereby was "deadweight" debt. In fact, at least the first two means would tend to increase saving, even if they were applied in a situation where the National Debt was zero to begin with, and the outcome would be that of driving the economy into a position of net indebtedness vis-à-vis the Government. Finally, Meade's analysis throws no light on whether the increase in saving following the capital levy is a permanent or a purely transitory phenomenon, nor on who, if anyone, bears the burden of a debt reduction. In spite of these apparent shortcomings, I am encouraged to think that Professor Meade's views are fundamentally quite close to those advanced here. I hope this will become gradually apparent, even without much further explicit reference to his argument.

IV. Fallacies in the No-transfer No-burden Argument

The classical argument summarized in the last section appears so far rather convincing, and if so we should be able to pinpoint the fallacies in one or more of the three propositions of Section II.

10. Meade, "Is the National Debt a Burden?"
11. See, *e.g.*, the references in footnote 8, p. 111, above, and in Buchanan, *Public Principles of Public Debt*, p. 14, footnote 8.

The fallacy in proposition (1) is not difficult to uncover. It is quite true that a closed community cannot increase its current resources by relying on tomorrow's unproduced output. None the less, the way in which we use today's resources can affect in three major ways the output that will result tomorrow from tomorrow's labor input: (i) by affecting the natural resources available to the future; (ii) by improving technological knowledge; and (iii) by affecting the stock of man-made means of production, or capital, available to future generations. Hence government expenditure, and the way it is financed, *can* affect the economy in the future if it affects any of the above three items.

The argument in (3) is also seriously inadequate, and the post-war experience has brought this home sharply. For the demand of the private sector consists of consumption C and capital formation I, and at least the latter component depends not only on income and taxes but also on monetary policy. Once we acknowledge this point, the principle of Functional Finance no longer implies a unique level of taxes. To demonstrate this point and its implications, it will be convenient—though it is not essential—to suppose that monetary policy affects P exclusively through the intermediary of the rate of interest r, *i.e.*, that $P = P(X, T, r)$ with $\dfrac{\delta P}{\delta r} < 0$; and that r in turn depends on X and the quantity of money M. But once we admit that r enters not vacuously in P we must also recognize that the equation

(1) $$P(\overline{X}, T, r) = P$$

will be satisfied not by one but by many possible values of T, each value being accompanied by the appropriate value of r, say $r(T)$. Now in most circumstances—that is, except possibly in very deep depression—there will be a range of values of T such that the corresponding $r(T)$ is achievable by an appropriate monetary policy. There is therefore not one but a whole schedule of values of T which are consistent with the maintenance of full employment and price stability, each value of T being accompanied by an appropriate monetary policy. Furthermore, within this range there will tend to be a direct connection between T and the capital formation component of $\overline{P}$. If, starting from a correct combination of T, r, and M, we lower taxes we will increase consumption, and to offset this we must reduce capital formation by appropriately tightening monetary policy. Conversely, by increasing taxes we can afford to have a larger capital formation. Thus, given the level of government expenditure, the level of taxes, and hence of budget deficit, does affect "future generations" through the stock of capital inherited by them.

Having thus brought to light the weaknesses in arguments (1) and (3), it is an easy matter to establish that, at least under certain conditions, the Keynesian framework is perfectly consistent with the classical conclusion stated in Section III. Suppose we take as a starting-point a given G, and some given combination of T and r consistent with full employment. Suppose further, as is generally assumed in Keynesian analysis, that to a first approximation consumption responds to taxes but not to interest rates. Now let the Government increase its expenditure by dG while keeping taxes constant. Then the deficit will increase precisely by $dD = dG$. What will happen to capital formation? If we are to maintain full employment without inflation we must have

$$dG + dC + dI = 0$$

and since, by assumption, taxes are constant and hence $dC = 0$, we must have

$$dG = dD = -dI$$

i.e., the debt-financed expenditure must be accompanied by an equal reduction in capital formation (with the help of the appropriate monetary policy).

This outcome is illustrated by a numerical example in Table I. Row (*a*) shows the behavior of the relevant flows in the initial situation, taken as a standard of comparison: here the budget is assumed to be balanced, although this is of no particular relevance. In row (*b*) we examine the consequence of an increase of expenditure by 100, with unchanged taxes, and hence consumption. The amount of resources available for, and hence the level of private capital formation, is cut down precisely by the amount of the deficit-financed expenditure. It is also apparent that this expenditure puts no burden on the "current" members of the community. Their (real) disposable income is unchanged by the expenditure, and consequently so is their consumption, as well as the net current addition to their personal wealth or private net worth. But because capital formation has been cut by the amount of the deficit, the community will thereafter dispose of a stock of private capital curtailed to a corresponding extent.

Thus the deficit-financed expenditure will leave in its wake an

TABLE I

A. *Effects of Government Expenditure and Financing on Private Saving and Capital Formation*

(Full Employment—All variables measured in real terms)

Method of Financing	Income, $X.$ (1)	Government Expenditure, $G.$ (2)	Taxes, $T.$ (3)	Disposable Income, $Y.$ $(X - T)$ (4)	Consumption, $C.$ $(c_0 + cY)$ $(c = 0.6)$ (5)	Saving $S = \Delta W$ $(Y - C)$ (6)	Deficit, $D.$ $(G - T)$ (7)	Private capital formation $I = \Delta K$ $(S - D)$ (8)
(a) Initial situation	2,000	300 (G_0)	300	1,700	1,500 (C_0)	200 (S_0)	0	200 (S_0)
(b) Increased expenditure— deficit financed	2,000	400 $(G_0 + dG)$	300	1,700	1,500 (C_0)	200 (S_0)	100 (dG)	100 $(S_0 - dG)$
(c) Increased expenditure— tax financed	2,000	400 $(G_0 + dG)$	400	1,600	1,440 $(C_0 - cdG)$	160 $(S_0 - sdG)$	0	160 $(S_0 - sdG)$

B. *Comparative "Burden" Effects of Alternative Budgetary Policies*

Budgetary policy.	Effect on	
	Private capital formation.	"Burden."
1. Joint effect of increased expenditure *and* deficit financing	$I(b) - I(a)^1 = (S_0 - dG) - S_0 = -dG$	$r^*(dG)$
2. Joint effect of increased expenditure and taxes	$I(c) - I(a) = (S_0 - sdG) - S_0 = -sdG$	$r^*s(dG)$
3. Differential effect of deficit financing	$I(b) - I(c) = (S_0 - dG) - (S_0 - sdG) = -(1 - s)dG = -cdG$	$r^*c(dG)$

1. $I(a)$ means investment in situation (a), and similarly for $I(b)$ and $I(c)$.

over-all burden on the economy in the form of a reduced flow of income from the reduced stock of private capital.

V. Interest Charges and the "True" Burden of Debt Financing

The analysis of the last section is seen to agree with the classical conclusion that debt financing transfers the burden of the government expenditure to those living beyond the time of the expenditure. At the same time it indicates that this burden consists in *the loss of income from capital* and not in *the taxes levied on later members to pay the interest charges*, as the classical argument contends.

In some respects this amendment to the classical burden position may be regarded as rather minor, for it can be argued that, under reasonable assumptions, the interest charges will provide a good *measure* of the true burden. Indeed, as long as the amount dD is not large in relation to the stock of capital (and the flow of saving), the loss in the future stream of output will be adequately approximated by $r^*(dD)$, where r^* denotes the marginal productivity of capital. Now if the Government borrows in a competitive market, bidding against other seekers of capital, then the (long-term) interest rate r at which it borrows will also be a reasonable approximation to r^*. Hence the annual interest charges $r(dD)$ will also be a good approximation to the true social yearly loss, or opportunity cost, $r(dD)$[12]—provided we can also establish that the initial reduction in the stock of capital will not be recouped as long as the debt is not repaid.

One can, however, think of many reasons why the interest bill might not even provide a good *measure* of the true loss. To begin with, if the government operation is of sizeable proportions it may significantly drive up interest rates, say from r_0 to r_1, since the reduction in private capital will tend to increase its marginal product. In this case the interest on the debt will overstate the true burden, which will lie somewhere between $r_0(dD)$ and $r_1(dD)$. More serious are the problems arising from various kinds of imperfections in the commodities as well as in the capital markets. In particular, the Government may succeed in borrowing at rates well below r^* by forcing banks and other intermediaries to acquire and hold bonds with yields below the market, or, as in wartime, by effectively eliminating the competition of private borrowers. In the first-mentioned

12. This is precisely the position taken by Musgrave, *The Theory of Public Finance*, p. 577.

case, *e.g.*, we should add to the interest bill the lost income accruing to the bank depositors (or at least to the bank's stockholders). There is also the rather nasty problem that, because of uncertainty, the rate of interest may not be a good measure of the productivity of physical capital. To put it very roughly, r is at best a measure of return net of a risk premium, and the actual return on capital is better thought of as a random variable whose average value is, in general, rather higher than r.[13]

Besides the relation of r to r^* there is another problem that needs to be recognized. In our discussion so far, and in our table, we have assumed that consumption, and hence private saving, were unaffected because taxes were unchanged. But once we recognize that the borrowing may increase the interest rate, we must also recognize that it may, through this route, affect consumption even with unchanged taxes. This problem might well be quickly dismissed under the principle of "*de minimis*." For, though economists may still argue as to whether an increase in interest rates will increase or decrease saving, they generally agree that the effect, if any, will be negligible.[14] But even if the rate of saving were to rise from, say, S_0 to $S_0 + e$ and the level of capital formation were accordingly reduced only by $dD - e$, one could still argue that r^*dD and not $r^*(dD - e)$ is the relevant measure of the true loss to society. This is because, as suggested by Bowen *et al.*,[15] the income generated by the extra capital formation e may be quite appropriately regarded as just necessary to offset the extra sacrifice of current consumption undertaken by those who responded to the change in r.

Thus it would appear that the classical-burden position needs to be modified to the extent of recognizing that the burden of deficit financing consists not in the increased taxes as such, but rather in the fall in income generated by the reduction in the stock of capital. But this modification would seem rather innocuous, since, admittedly, rdD will generally provide a reasonable approximate *measure* of the true burden. In fact, however, the amendment we have sug-

13. Cf. F. Modigliani and M. H. Miller, "The Cost of Capital, Corporation Finance, and the Theory of Investment," *The American Economic Review*, LVIII (June, 1958), 261-97. However, Miller has suggested to me that r may be the more relevant measure of return on capital as it deducts an appropriate allowance for the "cost" of risk bearing.

14. This is especially true if current consumption is appropriately defined to include the rental value and not the gross purchase of consumers' durables.

15. Bowen, Davis and Kopf, "The Public Debt: A Burden on Future Generations?" p. 704.

gested turns out to have rather far-reaching implications as we will show presently.

VI. Shortcomings of the Classical Transfer and Burden Argument: The Differential Effect of Deficit Versus Tax Financing

The classical conclusion that deficit financing of an expenditure places the burden on the future seems to imply that, if the expenditure were financed by taxes, there would be no burden in the future. Interestingly enough, Buchanan's book provides nowhere a systematic treatment of the temporal distribution of the burden from a tax-financed expenditure. Nor is this really surprising, for if the burden were in fact the interest of the debt, then tax financing could generate no burden on the future.[16] But if the relevant criterion is instead the loss of capital formation, then in order to find the true differential effect of debt financing versus tax financing, we must inquire about the effects of tax financing on private saving and capital formation. Only if this effect were nil or negligible would the classical conclusion be strictly valid.

Now, to an economist steeped in the Keynesian tradition, it is at once obvious that raising taxes to finance the government expenditure cannot fail to affect significantly private saving and capital formation. While tax financing will reduce disposable income by the amount of the expenditure, it will reduce consumption only by an amount $cdT = cdG$, where c is the marginal propensity to consume. The rest of the tax will be borne by a reduction in saving by sdT, where $s = 1 - c$ is the marginal propensity to save. Accordingly, if the initial position was one of full employment, as we are assuming, and inflation is to be avoided, private capital formation must itself be reduced by the amount sdD (through the appropriate monetary policy).[17] This outcome is illustrated numerically in row (c) of Table I. By comparing the outcome (a), (b), and (c) as is

16. See, however, footnote 26, p. 127, for a different explanation of Buchanan's omission.

17. The need to curtail investment when government expenditure is increased at full employment, even though it is fully tax covered, is the counterpart of the so-called multiplier effect of a balanced budget when starting from less than full utilization of resources. The tax-financed expenditure per se increases the aggregate real demand for goods and services by a dollar per dollar of expenditure. But if we start from full employment, this extra demand could only result in inflation. Hence it must be offset by a fall in investment of s dollars per dollar of expenditure, which, taking into account the multiplier effect, will reduce total demand by $s/s = 1$ dollar per dollar, as required.

done in part B of the table, we find that the differential effect of the deficit versus tax financing is to decrease capital formation by $dG - sdG = cdG$. The balance of the reduction, namely sdG, must be attributed to the expenditure as such, independently of how financed.[18] Hence, even if we are willing to regard the interest rate paid by the Government as a good approximation to r^*, the differential burden of debt financing on the future generations is not rdG but only $rcdG$.

It can readily be seen that the above result is not limited to the case we have explicitly discussed so far, in which the deficit arises from an increase in expenditure. If, for whatever reason, a portion dD of the government expenditure is not financed by taxes but by deficit, capital formation tends to be reduced by approximately $c(dD)$. This conclusion is, however, subject to one important qualification, namely that for $T = \overline{G}$, i.e., with a level of taxation balancing the budget, there exists a monetary policy capable of achieving full employment—or, in terms of our previous notation, of enforcing the required rate of interest $r(\overline{T})$. When this condition is satisfied we shall say that there is a "potentially adequate private demand," or more briefly, an "adequate demand." We shall for the moment concentrate attention on this case, reserving the task of examining the implications of a lack of adequate demand to a later point.

Our result so far, then, is that even with an adequate demand, the net or differential burden placed on the future by debt financing is not nearly as large as suggested by the classical conclusion. But note that the implied error is poor consolation for the no-transfer proponents, for they maintained that the burden is always "paid as you go." The error we have uncovered would seem to lie instead in not recognizing that a part of the burden of the expenditure is always shifted to the future. This last conclusion, however, is somewhat puzzling and disquieting. And this uneasiness can be easily increased by asking ourselves the following embarrassing question: roughly how large is the coefficient s which determines the unavoidable burden on the future? This question is embarrassing because recent empirical as well as theoretical research on the consumption function suggests that the answer depends very much on the length of time which is allowed for the adjustment. In the long run, the average propensity to save has remained pretty constant in the general order

18. This conclusion has also been reached by W. Vickrey, "The Burden of the Public Debt: Comment."

of 0.1, meaning that the marginal propensity is of the same order. But the quarterly increase in saving associated with a quarterly increase in income seems to be of a much larger order of magnitude, with estimates ranging as high as 0.5 and even higher.[19] Which is the relevant figure and why? Or does the answer depend on whether we look only at the impact effect of taxation or also at its delayed and ultimate effects? We will argue that this is indeed the case, and that insofar as we are interested in the distribution of the burden over time and between generations, the total effects are paramount.

VII. Impact Versus Total Effects of Deficit and Tax Financing

Let us come back to a comparison of rows (*b*) and (*c*) in Table I, but this time let us concentrate on the effect of taxation on the terminal net worth position of the households. We can see that if the expenditure is debt-financed this terminal position is (at least to a first approximation) the same as if the expenditure had not been undertaken. On the other hand, in the case of tax financing, in addition to the concomitant fall in consumption, we find that saving, and hence the increase in net worth, was also cut down from 200 to 160. What effect will this have on later consumption and saving behavior?

In order to answer this question we need to go beyond the standard Keynesian emphasis on current flows and try to understand why consumers wanted to add 200 to their net worth in the first place and how they will react when this goal has to be scaled down in response to higher taxes. I have elsewhere proposed some answer to these questions by advancing the hypothesis that saving (and dissaving) is not a passive reaction to income but represents instead a purposive endeavor by the households to achieve a desirable allocation of resources to consumption over their lifetime.[20] However, in what follows we do not need to rely, to any significant extent, on that model or any other specific theory of saving behavior. All that we need to keep before our eyes is the logical proposition that there are, in the final analysis, only two ways in which households can dispose of any addition to their net worth achieved through current

19. See, *e.g.*, the following two recent and as yet unpublished studies prepared for the Commission on Money and Credit: D. B. Suits, "The Determinants of Consumer Expenditure: a Review of Present Knowledge"; and E. C. Brown, R. M. Solow, A. K. Ando, and J. Kareken, "Lags in Fiscal and Monetary Policy," Part II.

20. F. Modigliani and R. Brumberg, "Utility analysis and the Consumption Function: An Interpretation of Cross-section Data," in *Post-Keynesian Economics*, K. Kurihara, ed. (Rutgers University Press, 1954).

THE AGGREGATE INVESTMENT APPROACH   123

saving: namely, either through later consumption or through a bequest to their heirs.

Now let us suppose at first that the bequest motive is small enough to be neglected and that, as a rule and on the average, each household tends to consume all of its income over its lifetime. This assumption can be conveniently restated in terms of the notion of the "over-life average propensity to consume" (*oac*), defined as the ratio of (the present value of) life consumption to (the present value of) life resources, and of the "over-life marginal propensity to consume" (*omc*), defined as the ratio of marginal increments in the same two variables. With this terminology, our current assumption is that both *omc* and *oac* are unity. It should be noted that, under reasonable hypotheses about the typical individual life cycle of earnings and consumption, an *oac* of unity for each household is consistent with a sizeable stock of aggregate assets, in the order of several times national income. With a stationary population and unchanged technology—stationary economy—this aggregate stock would tend to be constant in size, implying zero net saving in the aggregate, but it would be undergoing a continuous reshuffling of ownership from dissavers, such as retired persons, to those in the process of accumulating assets for retirement and short-run contingencies. On the other hand, with a rising population and/or technological progress, there would tend to be positive saving and a rising stock; in fact, the ratio of saving to income and of assets to income would tend to be constant in the long run if the above two forces resulted in an approximately exponential growth trend for aggregate income.[21]

Let us now consider the consequences of a non-repetitive increment in government expenditure dG, financed by a deficit, limiting ourselves at first to a stationary economy. Fig. 1 (*a*) illustrates graphically the effects of this operation on aggregate private net worth, W, and on the net stock of privately owned capital K. The horizontal dashed line AA represents the behavior of net worth in the absence of dG. It is constant by our assumption of a stationary economy, implying zero net saving, or gross saving and gross investment just sufficient to offset the wear and tear of the capital stock. If we make the further convenient assumption that there is initially no government debt (and ignore non-reproducible tangible wealth), then W coincides also with K. The incremental expenditure dG is supposed to occur in the interval t_0 to t_1 at the constant rate

21. Cf. A. K. Ando and F. Modigliani, "Growth, Fluctuations, and Stability," *The American Economic Review*, XLIX (May, 1959), 501-24.

$dG/(t_1 - t_0)$, and is financed by tapping a portion of the gross saving otherwise devoted to capital maintenance. As a result, between t_0 and t_1 K falls, as shown by the solid curve. But the net worth W remains at the same initial level as the fall in K is offset in the consumers' balance sheet by the government debt of dG. By t_1 the gap between W and K amounts to precisely dG, and thereafter the curves remain unchanged until and unless some further disturbance occurs. The final outcome is that the debt-financed expenditure, by generating a permanent wedge $dG = dD$ between W and K,[22] causes the entire cost of the expenditure to be borne by those living beyond t_1 in the form of a reduction in the stock of private capital by dG and in disposable income by $r^*(dG)$.[23] If, in addition, $r^* = r$, then before-tax income will be unaffected and the fall in disposable income will equal the tax collected to pay the interest, as claimed by the classical-burden doctrine.[24]

Consider now the effect of full tax financing of dG, illustrated in Fig. 1 (b). The line AA has the same meaning as before. The impact effect of the tax-financed expenditure—*i.e.*, the effect within the interval t_0t_1—is to reduce consumption by cdG and saving and private capital formation by sdG. Hence, as shown by the solid line, by t_1 both W and K have fallen by sdG. As we had already concluded, this fall in K partly shifts the effect of the expenditure to those living beyond t_1. However, by following up the delayed effect of the tax, we can now show that in this case: (a) the shift of the burden is only temporary, as W, and hence K, will tend to return gradually to the original pre-expenditure level, and (b) the burden transferred to the period following t_1 is borne, at least to a first approximation, entirely by those who were taxed between t_0 and t_1.

22. Permanent in the sense that it persists as long as the debt remains outstanding.

23. Actually the fall in disposable income consequent upon the fall in K is likely to give rise to a further fall in W and hence in K, but this indirect effect will tend to be of secondary magnitude. See on this point footnote 34, p. 131.

24. If the reduction in K results in a significant rise in r^* and hence r, then, as pointed out by Vickrey, "The Burden of the Public Debt: Comment," p. 135, there will tend to occur a shift in the distribution of *pre-tax* income. Labor income will tend to shrink and property income to increase—and, incidentally, this increase will tend to more than offset the fall in labor's earnings. It does not follow, however, as Vickrey has concluded, that the "primary burden of diminished future income will be felt by future wage earners." For the burden consists in the reduction of *disposable* income, and this reduction will depend on the distribution of the taxes levied to pay the interest as between property and non-property income.

THE AGGREGATE INVESTMENT APPROACH   125

FIG. 1

Effect of Deficit and Taxes on Net Worth, W, and Capital, K,
(unity over-life propensity to consume)

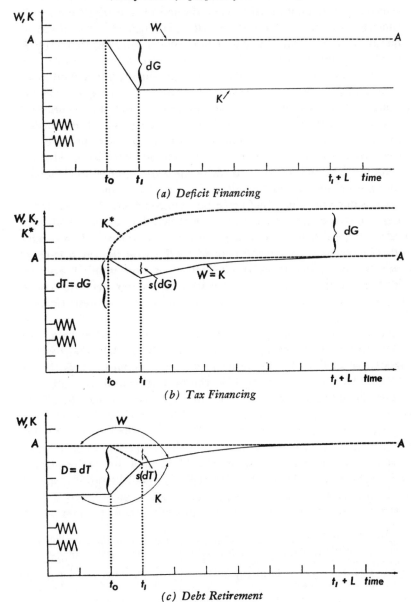

(a) Deficit Financing

(b) Tax Financing

(c) Debt Retirement

To establish this result we need only observe that since those taxed have suffered a loss of over-life (disposable) income amounting to dG as a result of the tax, they must make a commensurate reduction in over-life consumption. If the consumption is cut initially only by $c(dG)$ the balance of the tax, or $s(dG)$, is financed out of a reduction in accumulation—including possibly borrowing from other households—which at first reduces the net worth at time t_1 by $s(dG)$, but eventually must be matched by a corresponding reduction of consumption over the balance of the life span. Let L denote the length of time until the taxed generations die out. In the interval t_1 to $t_1 + L$, then, the consumption of this group will be smaller relative to its income, and hence its rate of saving will be larger, or its rate of dissaving smaller, than it would have been in the absence of the tax. On the other hand, over the same interval, the income consumption and saving of households who have entered the scene after t_1 will be basically unaffected by the operation. Hence, in the L years following t_1 there will arise some positive saving which will gradually die down as the taxed generation disappears. The precise path of aggregate saving will depend on the way the taxed generation chooses to distribute the reduction of consumption over its life. But, in any event, the cumulated net saving over the entire interval t_1 to $t_1 + L$ must come to precisely $s(dG)$, representing the required reduction of consumption relative to income of the taxed generation.[25] This cumulated saving is just sufficient to make up for the initial fall in the stock of $s(dG)$, so that by $t_1 + L$ the stock of capital (as well as W) has returned to the original level, as shown in Fig. 2 (b), and we are back in the original stationary state.

The above framework can be readily applied to analyze the effects of deficit or surplus generated under different conditions, e.g., by varying taxes, expenditure constant. Fig. 1 (c), for instance, depicts the outcome of an increase in taxes in the interval t_0 to t_1, utilized to retire the debt D outstanding at t_0. Here again the entire burden of the retirement falls on the taxed generation—although it is spread between t_0 and $t_1 + L$—and the gain accrues to those living after t_1 in the form of an increase in the stock of capital by an amount which

----

25. It may be noted that the cumulated reduction in consumption will tend to be somewhat larger than $s(dG)$ because the taxed generation will also lose some income as a result of the reduction in their wealth, amounting initially to $s(dG)$. However, the cumulated increase in saving over the interval is still $s(dG)$ because the additional loss in consumption just matches the reduction in income from this source. Actually $s(dG)$ measures essentially the *present value* as of t_1 of the required reduction in consumption.

eventually approaches the amount of debt retired and reflects the elimination of the wedge between W and K.

It is also easy to verify that our results remain valid for a growing economy, the only difference being that the dashed line AA would turn into an upward-sloping curve. With debt financing the graph of K would, from t_1 on, run at a distance dG below this line, while with tax financing the graph of $K = W$ would initially fall below it by $s(dG)$, but would tend to return to it at $t_1 + L$.

In summary, then, under unit *oac* the cost of an expenditure financed by debt, whether internal or external, tends to fall entirely on those living beyond the time of expenditure, as asserted by the classical-burden position, though it is best measured by r^*dD rather than by the incremental tax bill rdD. This burden may be eliminated at a later date by retiring the debt through a budget surplus, but thereby the full cost of the original expenditure is shifted to the later tax-payer, who financed the surplus. On the other hand, the cost of a tax-financed expenditure will tend to be borne by society as a whole, partly at the time and partly for some finite period thereafter. But the burden beyond t_1 still falls primarily on those who initially paid the tax and reflects the spreading of the burden over their lifetime.[26]

In the analysis so far we have concentrated on examining who bears the cost of the expenditure. To complete the picture we must, of course, also reckon the yield, if any, produced by dG beyond t_1. In particular, if dG results in a (permanent) addition to the stock of capital we must distinguish between W, K, and K^*, the latter denoting the total stock of private plus government-owned capital. K^* will exceed K by dG. Thus in the case of a debt-financed capital expenditure, K^* will everywhere tend to coincide with W, the

26. In a stimulating comment to a preliminary draft of this paper, Mr. Buchanan has provided an explanation for his failure to analyze the temporal distribution of the burden of a tax-financed expenditure. He points out that in line with the classic tradition, he defines the burden as the subjective loss of utility suffered by the tax-payer because of the initial loss of resources. The burden in this sense occurs entirely when the tax is levied and the later reduction of consumption cannot be separately counted as burden, as it is merely the embodiment of the original burden. I have serious reservations about the usefulness of this definition. It has, for instance, the peculiar implication that, when as a result of tax financing an heir receives a smaller inheritance or as a result of debt financing he is saddled with a larger tax bill, this cannot be counted as burden on him, as the entire burden is already accounted for in the guise of his father's grief that his heirs will enjoy a smaller net income. It is this peculiar reasoning that underlies Ricardo's famous conclusion that the cost of government expenditure is always fully borne by those present at the time.

government capital formation simply replacing the private one. For the case of tax financing, the behavior of K^* is shown by the broken line in Fig. 1 (b). Here the burden on the taxed generation results in a permanent gain for those living beyond t_1, which will gradually approach the yield on dG. In this sense one might well say that the cost of current government services can be paid for not only by the current and future generations but even by past generations.

There remains to consider how far our conclusions need to be modified if the *omc* is less than unity. Since a debt-financed expenditure does not affect the behavior of net worth, our analysis of this case basically stands, although one can conceive of some rather fancy circumstances in which modifications would be necessary.[27] In the case of tax financing, however, an *omc* of less than one implies that part of the burden of the expenditure will fall on later generations, who will receive a smaller bequest. It can be readily seen that the reduction in $K = W$ available to them will be of the order of $(oms)(dG)$, where *oms* denotes now the over-life marginal propensity to save. The differential burden of debt versus tax financing on society will correspondingly be of the order of $r(omc)(dG)$ instead of rdG.[28] In other words, the propensities to consume and save relevant to the long-run effect are precisely the over-life ones.[29] Unfortunately, these are propensities about which information is currently close to zero, both in terms of order of magnitude and stability, although some attention has begun to be devoted to this question.[30]

27. It is conceivable that, *e.g.*, the tax newly imposed to defray the interest cost might reduce the bequests. To this extent an even greater burden is placed on later generations, which will inherit a smaller K for two reasons: because of the smaller W and because of the wedge dG between W and K. An even fancier possibility is that the new tax might spur the initial generation to increase its bequests to help their heirs pay for the new tax. This would, of course, increase the burden on the current generation and decrease that on posterity.

28. Note that, regardless of the value of *omc*, the current generation must always fare at least as well, and generally better, under debt than under tax financing, even if it capitalized fully the new taxes that must be raised to pay the interest bill on the new debt. For, even in the highly unlikely event that the amount $r(dD)$ per year necessary to pay the interest bill were levied entirely on the initial generations, as long as they lived, this liability is limited by life, and hence represents a finite stream whose present value must be less than the amount dD which would have been taken away in the case of tax financing. See on this point also footnote 26 above.

29. Even with an *omc* of less than unity it is likely that the impact of the tax on bequests handed down from one generation to the next would gradually disappear so that W and K would eventually be unaffected by the tax-financed expenditure. But this is in the *very* long run indeed.

30. See, *e.g.*, J. Tobin and H. W. Guthrie, "Intergeneration Transfers of

Our analysis of the differential burden of tax versus debt financing could stand a great deal of refinement and qualifications to take proper account of the specific nature of the taxes levied to pay for dD or for the interest on the debt. But it is clear that these refinements can in principle be handled by proper application of the framework set out in this section. We shall therefore make no attempt at working out a long list of specific cases,[31] and will proceed instead to point out the implications of our framework for a somewhat different class of problems, namely where the change in debt occurs without any accompanying change either in government purchases or taxation.

VIII. *"Gratuitous" Increases in Debt, Repudiation and Inflation*

For analytical convenience we may start out by considering a case which has admittedly rather limited empirical relevance: namely, where the government debt is increased at some date t_0 by an amount dD by a "gratuitous" distribution of a corresponding amount of bonds.[32] Presumably, at least in this case, the proponents of the classical burden argument, if they apply their reasoning consistently, would have to agree with the proponents of the classical non-burden argument that the increment in the National Debt puts *no burden on the economy as a whole*, either at the time of issuance or thereafter, except for frictional transfer costs. For while it is true that from t_0 on, tax-payers are saddled with extra taxes to defray the interest bill, it is also true that the receipt of interest would not have arisen without the creation of extra debt. Note that this conclusion does not rule out the possibility that the operation may result in some transfer between generations, if by a generation we mean the set of members of the economy born at a particular date: thus the interest accruing to those receiving the gift will very likely be paid, at least partly, by a younger generation. But these are still mere income transfers involving no over-all burden.

But once we recognize that the over-all burden of the National

Wealth and The Theory of Saving," Cowles Foundation Discussion Paper No. 98 (November, 1960).

31. By so doing we are also deliberately bypassing the other major issue of fiscal policy, that of the distribution of the burden between income classes.

32. In order to avoid side issues, we will assume that the coupon rate on these bonds is such as to make their market value also equal to dD, and that no change occurs in the government purchase of goods and services, G.

Debt derives from its effects on the private stock of capital, then it becomes clear that, by and large, both classical doctrines agree with the wrong conclusion. This is indeed quite obvious in the case of a unity *oac*, a case illustrated graphically in Fig. 2 (*a*). The solid line *AA* shows as usual the behavior of $W = K$ in the absence of the gift. For the sake of variety, we deal here with a growing

FIG. 2

Effect of "Gratuitous" Changes in Debt on Net Worth, W, and Capital, K,
(unity over-life propensity to consume)

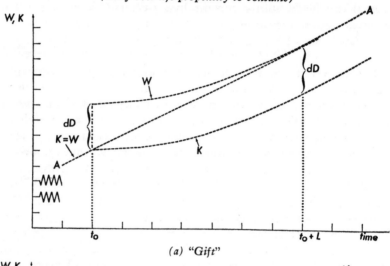

(*a*) "Gift"

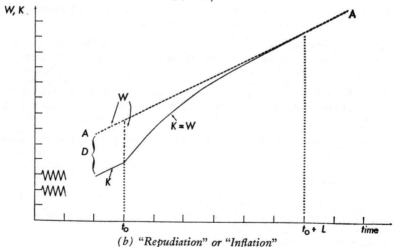

(*b*) "Repudiation" or "Inflation"

economy with positive saving and rising wealth.[33] If the gift is distributed all in one shot at point t_0, then at that point W will rise by dD, with no change in K. But now between t_0 and $t_0 + L$ the members of the generation that received the gift will gradually dispose of the bonds (or of other assets that they may have exchanged against the bonds) by selling them to current savers and using the proceeds to increase consumption over what it would have been otherwise. As this takes place, the aggregate rate of saving, and hence the accumulation of net worth and capital, is reduced. The result is that W gradually approaches the base path AA, while K, which is always lower by the wedge dD, falls below it. By $t_0 + L$ the cumulated rate of saving and physical capital formation will have been reduced by (approximately) dD, so that W will tend to coincide with AA and K to be dD lower, a position that will tend to be maintained thereafter. Thus an increase dD in the National Debt, even if it arises from a free gift, will put a burden on the economy as a whole. Under unity *oac*—after a transient period in which W is increased as a result of the gift—this burden will approach the level $r^*(dD)$, and hence approximately equal the interest on the debt.[34]

33. Just for reference, we may note that according to the Modigliani-Brumberg model, if income were growing at approximately exponential rate, W would be growing at the same rate.

34. This conclusion is strictly valid only insofar as the fall in disposable income brought about by the fall in K is matched by an equal fall in consumption. To the extent, however, that consumption falls somewhat less, cumulated saving may fall somewhat more, pushing W and K to a lower position than in our figure: but this extra adjustment will in any event tend to be of a second order of magnitude. The nature and size of this adjustment can be exhibited explicitly with reference to the Modigliani-Brumberg model of consumption behavior. As indicated earlier, this model implies that, in the long run, the aggregate net worth of consumers tends to be proportional to their (disposable) income, or (1) $W = gY$, where the proportionality constant is a decreasing function of the rate of growth of income. Suppose initially income is stationary as population and technology are both stationary. We also have the identity (2) $W = K + D$, where D denotes the National Debt. With population and technology given, the effect of capital on income can be stated by a "production function" (3) $Y = f(K)$. We have stated in the text that a gratuitous increase in D, or more generally an increase in D which does not result in government capital formation or otherwise change the production function, will tend to reduce K by dD and Y by r^*dD: *i.e.*, we have asserted $\dfrac{dK}{dD} \simeq -1$ and $\dfrac{dY}{dD} \approx -r^*$, where $r^* = \dfrac{df}{dK} = f' \simeq r$. By means of equations (1)-(3) we can now evaluate these derivatives exactly. Solving (2) for K and using (1) and (3) we have

If the *omc* is less than unity, then the burden will be smaller, tending to $(omc)(r^*dD)$, because the gift will tend to increase W "permanently" by $(oms)(dD)$ and hence K will tend to fall only by $(omc)(dD)$. As usual, this burden can be removed at any later point by taxation and retirement of the debt, but only at the cost of putting the burden on the taxed generation, which in effect will be paying for the benefits enjoyed by the beneficiaries of the gift.

Our conclusion applies directly, but for an appropriate change of "sign," to the case of a "gratuitous" one-shot reduction in the National Debt, as indicated in Fig. 2 (*b*). Such a reduction might be accomplished by repudiation, total or partial, or by a capital levy, or, much more importantly and frequently, by the simple device of (unanticipated) inflation. Thus a (once and for all) doubling of the price level is entirely equivalent to a repudiation of one-half of the National Debt at the original price level—although it has, of course, all kinds of other widespread economic effects. As far as the National Debt is concerned, this operation puts a burden on the owners of the bonds by reducing the real value of their interest income as

---

$K = gf(K) - D$. Hence $\dfrac{dK}{dD} = gf' \dfrac{dK}{dD} - 1$ or $\dfrac{dK}{dD} = \dfrac{-1}{1 - gf'} = \dfrac{-1}{1 - gr^*}$. Similarly, $\dfrac{dY}{dD} = \dfrac{-r^*}{1 - gr^*}$ and $\dfrac{dW}{dD} = \dfrac{-gr^*}{1 - gr^*}$. Thus, if $r^* \simeq r = 0.05$ and g is in the order of 4, then $\dfrac{dK}{dD}$ is $-1 \cdot 25$ instead of -1 and $\dfrac{dY}{dD}$ is $-0 \cdot 625$ instead of $-0 \cdot 05$.

I am indebted to Ralph Beals, presently a graduate student at Massachusetts Institute of Technology, for pointing out that these formulæ are not entirely general, for, within the Modigliani-Brumberg model, the second-order effect is not independent of the nature of taxes employed to defray the interest bill. In fact, the formulæ derived above are strictly valid only if the revenue is raised entirely through an income tax on non-property income. With other kinds of taxes, one obtains somewhat more complicated formulæ. For instance, if the taxes are levied on property income this will depress the net yield of wealth below r, which in turn will, in principle, affect the proportionality constant g of equation (1). However, exploration of several alternative assumptions suggests to me that the outcome is unlikely to be appreciably different from that derived above, at least in the case of direct taxes.

It can also be shown that the above formulæ will tend to hold, at least asymptotically, for an expanding economy in which population grows at an approximately constant rate and/or so does productivity as a result of technological change which is neutral in Harrod's sense, cf. *Toward a Dynamic Economics* (Macmillan, 1949), p. 23. The main features of such a growth model are discussed in Ando and Modigliani, "Growth, Fluctuations, and Stability."

well as the real value of the principal. Insofar as the first effect is concerned, we have a mere transfer from the bond-holders to the tax-payers, with no over-all effect. But the reduction in the principal generates an unmatched reduction in consumption, and hence a *transient* higher rate of saving. The resulting increase in the capital stock will benefit all those living after the inflation—provided, of course, private capital has a positive marginal product and the potentially higher rate of saving is utilized for capital formation rather than being wasted in depressed income and unemployment.

From the content of this section and the previous one it should also be apparent that our analysis basically supports Meade's conclusion concerning the burden of the deadweight debt, although this conclusion is derived by a very different line of reasoning. The deadweight debt is a burden because: (*a*) it generates a corresponding gap between aggregate net worth W and the aggregate stock of capital K^*, and (*b*) we can expect that this gap will result primarily in a fall in K^* rather than in an offsetting rise in W. Thus, if we conceive two communities A and B identical with respect to natural endowments, technical know-how and habits of private thrift, and which differ only in that A has a deadweight debt D' and B has none, community A will be poorer, roughly, by D' times the marginal productivity of capital plus frictional transfer costs.

IX. *Deficit Financing in War and in Depression*

In this concluding section we propose to apply our tools to see what light they shed on the two classical and empirically relevant issues: the pre-Keynesian problem of war financing and the post-Keynesian problem of deficit created as part of a counter-cyclical stabilization policy.

In order to face squarely the core issue of war financing, let us be concerned with the case of a major war effort of the type outlined earlier in Section III, in which the stock of capital in existence at the termination of the war is independent of the methods used to finance it. It follows immediately that, independently of financing, the war will impose a burden on postwar society as a whole to the extent that the stock of capital in existence at its termination—counting only whatever portion is useful to satisfy the postwar requirements—is less than what would have been there in the absence of war. In order to examine the residual effects, if any, of methods of financing, we must suppose that, in spite of the war's severity, we have some choice as to the extent of taxation. Also, to keep separate for the moment the possible role of inflation, we must suppose that untaxed income in excess of the predetermined consumption level is prevented from bidding up the price of goods—whether through voluntary abstention or through a fully successful system of rationing. In these conditions the unspent income must result in an increase in government debt held by the private sector, either directly or through financial intermediaries. Thus the level of taxation versus deficit financing determines essentially the size of the increment in government debt, dD. Now suppose, for the sake of the argument, that the war had been entirely financed by taxes, dD being accordingly zero. It then follows from our earlier analysis that the burden of the war will be borne almost entirely by members of the war generation. For, in addition to the sacrifice of consumption and other amenities *during* the war, they will also bear the brunt of the reduced capital stock, their accumulation of net worth being unlimited to the permitted privately financed capital formation. Thus the burden falling on society as a whole after the war will fall primarily directly on the members of the war generation (affecting others only to the extent that the reduction in the stock of capital reduces total income by more than the return on capital). They will be forced after the war to maintain a reduced level of consumption over the rest of their life, tending to save heavily in their remaining earning span and to dissave at a greatly reduced rate thereafter. This behavior in turn will produce, after the war, an abnormally large rate of aggregate saving, gradually declining with the disappearance of the war generation. As a result, by the time the war generation has disappeared, the wartime reduction in capital formation may have been substantially made up—this being more nearly true the closer the *oac* is to unity and the smaller the initial loss of capital.

If, on the other hand, through lower taxes the war generation is permitted to increase its terminal net worth by an additional amount dD, the effect, with respect to the present issue, is essentially the same as though at war's end it had been handed down gratuitously a corresponding amount of government bonds.[35] As usual, this will enable them to maintain a higher post-war consumption, reducing

35. If the bonds issued during the war carried an exceptionally low rate of interest because of the monopoly position of the Government in the market, the gift in question should be regarded, for present purposes, as represented by the market value of the bonds.

capital formation, by an extent that can range as high as dD, if the *oac* is unity. Thus the debt financing will generate both: (i) a transfer from the postwar to the war generation to the extent of taxes levied on the former to pay interest to the latter, and (ii) a permanent burden on society as a whole to the extent that the stock of capital is permanently reduced by dD—less any increase in W resulting directly from dD.[36] Insofar as in the immediate postwar period the Government, to speed up the reconstruction, pushes capital formation by raising taxes and creating a surplus, the long-run effect is eliminated. But the burden of debt financing is placed to that extent on those living in the relevant postwar period, which may again consist in part of the very same war generation.

If inflation is permitted to develop in the course of the war or immediately following it our analysis remains valid, provided the increment in the debt is measured in real, rather than money, terms. This net real increment can be expressed as $\dfrac{D_0 + dD}{1 + dP} - D_0$ where D_0 is the prewar debt and dP is the relative increase in the price level in the course of the war inflation. The above quantity, it will be noted, may even be negative if $dP > \dfrac{dD}{D_0}$, *i.e.*, if the increase in prices exceeds the relative increase in the debt. In this case the war generation will be made to carry even more than the cost of the war (unless its plight is improved by postwar transfers of income); and later generations may conceivably end up by benefiting from the war, at least following the transient period of high saving rates and rapid capital accumultaion. Perhaps the picture we have been drawing has some relevance for an understanding of the postwar experience of such countries as Germany, Italy, and Japan.

It seems hardly necessary to point out that our analysis in no way implies that in financing a war the use of debt should necessarily be minimized. Quite aside from obvious incentive considerations,

36. Note that the incremental debt dD could be regarded as a burden on society even if the economy tended to suffer from long-run stagnation, *i.e.*, a chronic tendency for a very low or zero marginal productivity of capital. For while it is true that the larger consumption bestowed on the war generation would help to sustain consumption, and thus full employment, the same result could be achieved by reducing the taxes and expanding the consumption and saving of whoever was present at the appropriate later time.

there may be perfectly good equity reasons for lightening the burden of the generation that suffered through the war by granting them a more comfortable life after the war, at the expense of later generations.

We come finally to the effects of debt generated as a counter-cyclical measure. In view of the complexity of the problem, we shall have to limit ourselves to a sketchy treatment of a limited class of situations. Our main concern is to show that, even in this case, debt financing, though quite advantageous to the current generation, will generally not be costless to future generations, at least in terms of gross burden.

Consider a situation where, in spite of the easiest possible monetary policy and with the whole structure of interest rates reduced to its lowest feasible level, the demand for private capital formation is inadequate to absorb full-employment saving with a balanced budget. But let us suppose that the situation can be counted upon to be temporary and not to recur for a long time to come. If the Government does not step in there will be a temporary contraction of employment accompanied by a contraction of consumption and of addition to net worth, which is limited to the amount of private capital formation. Suppose, on the other hand, the Government expands its expenditure to the extent needed to fill the deflationary gap, and thereby runs into a deficit dD. Let us also imagine that it succeeds in choosing its action perfectly so as to maintain full employment without inflation. Hence consumption will be kept at the full-employment level and so will the accumulation of net worth; except that this accumulation will now take the form of an addition to the National Debt to the extent dD. Thus the government action involves a current gain to society which can be measured by the income which would have been lost otherwise. What we wish to know is whether this gain places any cost on later generations (and if so, how it can be valued).

Under the assumed conditions the answer would have to be affirmative at least under unity *oac*. In this case, in fact, we can see that the cost which was spared to society would have fallen entirely on the members of the depression generation. They would have been forced over their lifetime to cut their consumption by an amount (whose present value is) equal to the lost income. This reduction would be distributed partly within the depression but partly *after* the recovery, to an extent equal to the loss in accumulation of net worth in the depression. This reduction of consumption would in turn give rise to a somewhat higher rate of capital formation after the recovery, so that by the time the depression generation disappears the stock of capital would tend to be back to where it would have been without depression. In other words, under the assumed conditions failure of the Government to act, though costly to the depression generation, tends to be costless to later generations. On the other hand, if the Government acts, the depression generation does not have to maintain a lower consumption after the recovery, and accordingly, the lost private capital formation during the depression is never made up. The creation of dD introduces again a corresponding wedge between W and K which will tend permanently to reduce the amount of physical capital available to future generations. Hence there is a loss to them to the extent that at later points of time an increment to the stock of capital would make any net positive addition to output. If the debt is never meant to be retired, then at least with well-functioning capital markets, the consol rate, being an average of anticipated future short rates, may provide at least a rough measure of the (appropriate time average) annual loss. And in this sense if the Government borrows long, the interest bill on the incremental debt may provide a rough measure of the average future (gross) burden placed on society as a whole.[37]

Once more, recognizing that the government action may involve a gross cost to future society does not imply that the action should not be taken. In the first place, because of multiplier effects the gain in income to those present is likely to be appreciably larger than the lost stock of capital which approximates the present value of the sacrificed income stream. In the second place, if the Government spends on projects which produce a yield in the future, then the gross burden will be offset by the gross yield and the net outcome may even be positive. In the third place, the gross burden can be eliminated if at some future point of time the Government runs a surplus and retires the debt. It is true that this will tend to place

37. Of course, under our present assumptions the burden as measured by the opportunity cost will be essentially zero during the period in which the debt is created, regardless of whether it takes the form of long-term debt, short-term debt, or currency creation. But in the last two cases the current interest cost will not appropriately reflect the average future burden, unless we also take into account the rate the Government will have to pay on bonds sold at later points of time to refinance the short-term debt or to reduce the money supply in order to prevent inflation.

the burden of the original deficit on those who pay the taxes financing the surplus. But if the surplus follows the deficit in short order these people will be, to a large extent, the very same ones that benefited from the original deficit; thereby the questions of inter-generation equity are minimized. The case for eradicating the deficit with a nearby surplus is, of course, strongest if the government expenditure provides nothing useful for the future, or if the deficit reflects a reduction in the tax bill, expenditure constant, resulting either from built-in flexibility arrangements or from *ad hoc* tax rebates. Thus, our analysis turns out to provide a strong case in favor of what used to be called the cyclically balanced budget.

Although we cannot pursue further here the complex issues raised by the burden aspects of counter-cyclical fiscal operations, we hope to have succeeded in showing how the tools we have developed may provide some insight into the problem. One point should be apparent even from our sketchy treatment: namely, that insofar as counter-cyclical fiscal policy is concerned, our analysis does not require any significant re-evaluation of currently accepted views. Yet, by reminding us that fiscal operations involve considerations of inter-generation equity even when used for stabilization purposes, it may help to clarify some issues. It does, for example, establish a *prima facie* case, at least with respect to *ad hoc* measures as distinguished from built-in stabilizers, for a course of action that will minimize the "deadweight" deficit and stimulate investment rather than consumption.[38] More generally, considerations of inter-generation equity suggest the desirability of a compromise between the orthodox balanced-budget principle and the principle of functional finance, which might be couched roughly as follows: as a rule, the Government should run a "deadweight" deficit only when full-employment saving exceeds the amount of capital formation consistent with the most favorable feasible monetary policy; and it should run a surplus, insofar as this is consistent with full employment, until it has wiped out previous deficits accumulated in the pursuance of this policy.

38. These considerations, *e.g.*, cast some doubt on the desirability of relying on personal tax cuts explicitly announced to be but temporary. For there is at least some ground for supposing that the temporary nature of the cut will tend to reduce the desirable impact effect on consumption and increase instead short-run saving and the (possibly) undesirable delayed consumption.

References

Bowen, William G., Richard G. Davis, and David H. Kopf. "The Burden of the Public Debt: Reply," *The American Economic Review*, LI (March, 1961), 141–43.

Bowen, William G., Richard G. Davis, and David H. Kopf. "The Public Debt: A Burden on Future Generations?" *The American Economic Review*, L (September, 1960), 701–6.

Buchanan, James M. *Public Principles of Public Debt*. Homewood, Illinois: Richard D. Irwin, Inc., 1958.

Elliott, James R. "The Burden of the Public Debt: Comment," *The American Economic Review*, LI (March, 1961), 139–41.

Hansen, Alvin H. (Review of 6, 14, and 15), "The Public Debt Reconsidered," *The Review of Economics and Statistics*, XLI (June, 1959), 370–78.

Lerner, Abba P. "The Burden of Debt," *The Review of Economics and Statistics*, XLIII (May, 1961), 139–41.

Lerner, Abba P. "The Burden of the National Debt," in Lloyd A. Metzler and others (eds.). *Income, Employment, and Public Policy: Essays in Honor of Alvin H. Hansen*. New York: W. W. Norton & Company, 1948. Pp. 255–75.

Lerner, Abba P. (Review of 6), *The Journal of Political Economy*, XLVII (April, 1959), 203–6.

Meade, James E. "Is the National Debt a Burden?" *Oxford Economic Papers*, X (June, 1958), 163–83.

Musgrave, Richard A. *The Theory of Public Finance*. New York: McGraw-Hill Book Company, Inc., 1959.

Rolph, Earl R. (Review of 6), *American Economic Review*, XLIX (March, 1959), 183–85.

Scitovsky, Tibor. "The Burden of the Public Debt: Comment," *The American Economic Review*, LI (March, 1961), 137–39.

Vickrey, William. "The Burden of the Public Debt: Comment," *The American Economic Review*, LI (March, 1961), 132–37.

[21]

CAPITAL MOBILITY AND STABILIZATION POLICY UNDER FIXED AND FLEXIBLE EXCHANGE RATES*

R. A. MUNDELL
McGill University

THE world is still a closed economy, but its regions and countries are becoming increasingly open. The trend, which has been manifested in both freer movement of goods and increased mobility of capital, has been stimulated by the dismantling of trade and exchange controls in Europe, the gradual erosion of the real burden of tariff protection, and the stability, unparalleled since 1914, of the exchange rates. The international economic climate has changed in the direction of financial integration[1] and this has important implications for economic policy.

My paper concerns the theoretical and practical implications of the increased mobility of capital. In order to present my conclusions in the simplest possible way, and to bring the implications for policy into sharpest relief, I assume the extreme degree of mobility that prevails when a country cannot maintain an interest rate different from the general level prevailing abroad. This assumption will overstate the case but it has the merit of posing a stereotype towards which international financial relations seem to be heading. At the same time it might be argued that the assumption is not far from the truth in those financial centres, of which Zurich, Amsterdam, and Brussels may be taken as examples, where the authorities already recognize their lessening ability to dominate money market conditions and insulate them from foreign influences. It should also have a high degree of relevance to a country like Canada whose financial markets are dominated to a great degree by the vast New York market.

I. METHOD OF ANALYSIS

The assumption of perfect capital mobility can be taken to mean that all securities in the system are perfect substitutes. Since different currencies are involved this implies that existing exchange rates are expected to persist indefinitely (even when the exchange rate is not pegged) and that spot and

*This paper was presented at the annual meeting of the Canadian Political Science Association in Quebec on June 6, 1963. It was written while the author was a member of the staff of the International Monetary Fund, but it does not, of course, necessarily reflect the Fund's official position.

[1]See James C. Ingram, "A Proposal for Financial Integration in the Atlantic Community," Joint Economic Committee print, Nov. 1962, for a valuable analysis of financial integration under fixed exchange rates; Harry G. Johnson, "Equilibrium under Fixed Exchange Rates," *American Economic Review*, LIII, May, 1963, 112–19, for a discussion of some of the advantages of closing the exchange rate margins; C. P. Kindleberger, "European Economic Integration and the Development of a Single Financial Center for Long-Term Capital," *Weltwirtschaftliches Archiv*, Band 90, 1963, Heft 2, 189–210, for a discussion of competition among financial centres as integration proceeds; and A. N. McLeod, "Credit Expansion in an Open Economy," *Economic Journal*, LXII, Sept., 1962, 611–40, for a theoretical discussion of related topics.

475

forward exchange rates are identical. All the complications associated with speculation, the forward market, and exchange rate margins are thereby assumed not to exist.

In order to focus attention on policies affecting the level of employment, I assume unemployed resources, constant returns to scale, and fixed money wage rates; this means that the supply of domestic output is elastic and its price level constant. I further assume that saving and taxes rise with income, that the balance of trade depends only on income and the exchange rate, that investment depends on the rate of interest, and that the demand for money depends only on income and the rate of interest. My last assumption is that the country under consideration is too small to influence foreign incomes or the world level of interest rates.

Monetary policy will be assumed to take the form of open market purchases of securities, and *fiscal policy* the form of an increase in government spending (on home goods) financed by an increase in the public debt. Floating exchange rates result when the monetary authorities do not intervene in the exchange market, and fixed exchange rates when they intervene to buy and sell international reserves at a fixed price.

TABLE I

Market\Sector	Goods		Securities		Money		International Reserves	
Government	$T-G$	+	Government Borrowing	+	Government Dishoarding	+	*1	= 0
	+		+		+		+	+
Private	$S-I$	+	Private Borrowing	+	Private Dishoarding	+	*2	= 0
	+		+		+		+	+
Foreign	$M-X$	+	Capital Outflow	+	*3	+	Increase in Reserves	= 0
	+		+		+		+	+
Banking	*4	+	Open Market Sales	+	Monetary Expansion	+	Foreign Exchange Sales	= 0
	‖		‖		‖		‖	‖
	0	+	0	+	0	+	0	= 0

*Negligible or ignored items: (1) would refer to Treasury holdings of foreign exchange; (2) to the non-bank public's holdings of foreign exchange; (3) to foreigners' holdings of domestic money (domestic currency is not a "key" currency); and (4) to the net contribution of the banking system to goods account. In the analysis government dishoarding will also be assumed zero.

Note that if the entries are defined as *ex ante* or *planned* magnitudes both the horizontal and vertical sums to zero are *equilibrium conditions*, but if they are defined as *ex post* or *realized* magnitudes the sums to zero are *identities*. Note also that the rows could be disaggregated, making special distinctions between households and firms, commercial and central banks, etc., down to each individual spending unit, just as the columns could be multiplied to distinguish between different classes of goods, money, and securities.

It will be helpful, in the following discussion, to bear in mind the distinction between conditions of *sectoral* and *market* equilibria (illustrated in the table). There is a set of sectoral restraints (described by the rows in the table) which show how expenditure in each sector of the open economy is financed: a budget deficit $(G - T)$ in the *government* sector is financed by an increase in the public debt or a reduction in government cash balances (dishoarding); an excess of investment over saving $(I - S)$ in the *private* sector is financed by net private borrowing or a reduction in privately-held money balances; a trade balance deficit ($M - X$) in the *foreign* sector[2] is financed by capital imports or a reduction in international reserves; and, finally, an excess of purchases over sales of domestic assets of the banking sector is financed by an increase in the monetary liabilities of the banking system (the money supply) or by a reduction in foreign exchange reserves. For simplicity of exposition, I shall assume that there is, initially, no lending between the sectors.

There is also a set of market restraints (described by columns in the table) which refer to the condition that demand and supply of each object of exchange be equal. The *goods and services* market is in equilibrium when the difference between investment and saving is equal to the sum of the budget surplus and the trade balance deficit. The *capital* market is in equilibrium when foreigners and domestic banks are willing to accumulate the increase in net debt of the government and the public. The *foreign exchange* market is in equilibrium when the actual increase in reserves is equal to the rate (which may be positive or negative) at which the central bank wants to buy reserves.[3] And the *money* market is in equilibrium when the community is willing to accumulate the increase in the money supply offered by the banking system. I shall also assume that, initially, each market is in equilibrium.

II. Policies under Flexible Exchange Rates

Under flexible exchange rates the central bank does not intervene to fix a given exchange rate, although this need not preclude autonomous purchases and sales of foreign exchange.

Monetary Policy. Consider the effect of an open market purchase of domestic securities in the context of a flexible exchange rate system. This results in an increase in bank reserves, a multiple expansion of money and credit, and downward pressure on the rate of interest. But the interest rate is prevented from falling by an outflow of capital, which causes a deficit in the balance of payments, and a depreciation of the exchange rate. In turn, the exchange rate depreciation (normally) improves the balance of trade and stimulates, by the multiplier process, income and employment. A new equilibrium is established when income has risen sufficiently to induce the domestic community to hold the increased stock of money created by the banking system. Since interest rates are unaltered this means that income must rise in proportion to the increase in the money supply, the factor of proportionality being the given ratio of income and money (income velocity).

In the new equilibrium private saving and taxes will have increased as a consequence of the increase in income, and this implies both net private lending and retirement of government debt. Equilibrium in the capital market then requires equality between the sum of net private lending plus debt retirement, and the rate of capital exports, which in conjunction with the

---

[2]The foreign sector refers to all the transactions of the country as a whole with respect to the outside world.

[3]For certain purposes it would be more elegant to define a separate market for foreign goods as distinct from domestic goods, but the present approach is satisfactory for the purpose on hand.

requirement of balance of payments equilibrium, implies a balance of trade surplus. Monetary policy therefore has a strong effect on the level of income and employment, not because it alters the rate of interest, but because it induces a capital outflow, depreciates the exchange rate, and causes an export surplus.[4]

It will now be shown that central bank operations in the foreign exchange market ("open market operations" in foreign exchange) can be considered an alternative form of monetary policy. Suppose the central bank buys foreign reserves (gold or foreign currency) with domestic money. This increases bank reserves, causing a multiple expansion of the money supply. The monetary expansion puts downward pressure on the interest rate and induces a capital outflow, further depreciating the exchange rate and creating an export surplus, which in turn increases, through the multiplier effect, income and employment. Eventually, when income has increased sufficiently to induce the community to hold the increased stock of money, the income-generating process ceases and all sectors are again in equilibrium, with the increased saving and taxes financing the capital outflow. This conclusion is virtually the same as the conclusion earlier reached regarding monetary policy, with the single important difference that *foreign* assets of the banks are increased in the case of foreign exchange policy while *domestic* assets are increased in the case of monetary policy. Foreign exchange policy, like monetary policy, becomes a forceful tool of stabilization policy under flexible exchange rates.

Fiscal Policy. Assume an increase in government spending financed by government borrowing. The increased spending creates an excess demand for goods and tends to raise income. But this would increase the demand for money, raise interest rates, attract a capital inflow, and appreciate the exchange rate, which in turn would have a depressing effect on income. In fact, therefore, the negative effect on income of exchange rate appreciation has to offset exactly the positive multiplier effect on income of the original increase in government spending. Income cannot change unless the money supply or interest rates change, and since the former is constant in the absence of central bank action and the latter is fixed by the world level of interest rates, income remains fixed. Since income is constant, saving and taxes are unchanged, which means, because of the condition that the goods market be in equilibrium, that the change in government spending is equal to the import surplus. In turn, the flexible exchange rate implies balance of payments equilibrium and therefore a capital inflow equal to the import surplus. Thus, both capital and goods market equilibria are assured by equality between the rate of increase in the public debt and the rate of capital imports, and between the budget deficit and the import surplus. Fiscal policy thus completely loses its force as a domestic stabilizer when the exchange rate is allowed to fluctuate and the money supply is held constant. Just as monetary policy derives its importance as a domestic stabilizer from its influence on capital flows and the exchange rate, so fiscal policy is frustrated in its effects by these same considerations.

---

[4]Richard E. Caves arrives at essentially the same result in his paper, "Flexible Exchange Rates," *American Economic Review*, LIII, May, 1963, 120–29.

III. Policies under Fixed Exchange Rates

Under fixed exchange rates the central bank intervenes in the exchange market by buying and selling reserves at the exchange parity; as already noted the exchange margins are assumed to be zero.

Monetary Policy. A central bank purchase of securities creates excess reserves and puts downward pressure on the interest rate. But a fall in the interest rate is prevented by a capital outflow, and this worsens the balance of payments. To prevent the exchange rate from falling the central bank intervenes in the market, selling foreign exchange and buying domestic money. The process continues until the accumulated foreign exchange deficit is equal to the open market purchase and the money supply is restored to its original level.

This shows that monetary policy under fixed exchange rates has no sustainable effect on the level of income. The increase in the money supply arising from open market purchases is returned to the central bank through its exchange stabilization operations. What the central bank has in fact done is to purchase securities initially for money, and then buy money with foreign exchange, the monetary effects of the combined operations cancelling. The only final effect of the open market purchase is an equivalent fall in foreign exchange reserves: the central bank has simply traded domestic assets for foreign assets.

Fiscal Policy. Assume an increase in government spending superimposed on the foreign exchange policy of pegging the exchange rate. The increased spending has a multiplier effect upon income, increasing saving, taxes, and imports. Taxes increase by less than the increase in government spending so the government supplies securities at a rate equal to the budget deficit, whereas the private sector absorbs securities at a rate equal to the increase in saving.

After the new equilibrium is established both the goods and capital markets must be in balance. In the goods market the budget deficit has as its counterpart the sum of the excess of private saving over investment and the balance of trade deficit, which implies that the induced balance of trade deficit is less than the budget deficit. In the capital market the private and foreign sectors must be willing to accumulate the new flow of government issues. But since the excess private saving is equal to the flow of private lending, and since the budget deficit equals the flow of new government issues, capital market equilibrium requires that the import deficit be exactly balanced by a capital inflow, so that there is balance of payments equilibrium after all adjustments have taken place.

There will nevertheless be a change in foreign exchange reserves. Before the flow equilibrium is established the demand for money will increase, at a constant interest rate, in proportion to the increase in income. To acquire the needed liquidity the private sector sells securities and this puts upward pressure on the interest rate, and attracts foreign capital. This improves the balance of payments temporarily, forcing the central bank to intervene by buying foreign reserves and increasing the money supply. The money supply is therefore increased indirectly through the back door of exchange rate policy. Foreign exchange reserves accumulate by the full amount of the increased cash reserves needed by the banking system to supply the increased money demanded by the public as a consequence of the increase in income.

IV. Other Policy Combinations

Other cases deserve attention in view of their prominence in policy discussions. In the following cases it is assumed that exchange rates are fixed.

Central Bank Financing of Fiscal Deficits. An important special case of combined operations of monetary, fiscal, and exchange policies is central bank financing of budget deficits under fixed exchange rates. As before, the increase in government spending yields a multiplier effect on income. In the new equilibrium there is a budget deficit, an excess of saving over investment, and a balance of trade deficit. The government issues securities at a rate equal to the budget deficit and these are (by assumption) taken up by the central bank. Capital market equilibrium therefore requires that the net flow demand for securities on the part of the private sector be equal to the net capital outflow.

It is easy to see that in the new equilibrium the balance of payments deficit and the consequent rate at which reserves are falling is exactly equal to the budget deficit and to the rate at which the central bank is buying government securities. Since the capital outflow is equal to the excess of saving over investment, and the loss of reserves is equal to the balance of payments deficit, which is the sum of the trade deficit and the capital outflow, reserves fall at a rate equal to the sum of the import deficit and the excess of saving over investment. Then since this sum equals the budget deficit, by the condition of equilibrium in the goods market, it follows that reserves fall at a rate equal to the budget deficit. The budget deficit is entirely at the expense of reserves.

There is, however, in this instance too an initial stock adjustment process. As income increases the demand for money grows, the private sector dispenses with stocks of securities, causing a capital inflow and an increase in reserves. This increase in reserves is a once-for-all inflow equal to the increase in cash reserves necessary for the banks to satisfy the increased demand for money. The rate of fall in reserves takes place, therefore, from a higher initial level.

The Special Case of Sterilization Operations. Sterilization (or neutralization) policy is a specific combination of monetary and exchange policy. When the central bank buys or sells foreign exchange the money supply increases or decreases, and the purpose of sterilization policy is to offset this effect. The mechanism is for the central bank to sell securities at the same rate that it is buying foreign exchange, and to buy securities at the same rate that it is selling foreign exchange. In reality, therefore, neutralization policy involves an exchange of foreign reserves and bonds. The exchange rate is stabilized by buying and selling reserves in exchange for securities.

Suppose the government increases spending during a time when neutralization policy is being followed. The increase in spending would normally have a multiplier effect on income. But this would increase the demand for money and put upward pressure on interest rates as the private sector dispenses with holdings of securities; this would cause a capital inflow and induce a balance of payments surplus. But now the authorities, in their rate-pegging operation, buy foreign exchange and simultaneously sell securities, thus putting added pressure on interest rates and accelerating the inflow of capital without satisfying the increased demand for money. The system has now become inconsistent, for goods market equilibrium requires an increase in income, but an increase in income can only take place if either the money supply expands or interest rates rise. The capital inflow prevents interest rates from rising and the neutralization policy inhibits the money supply from expanding. Something has to give, and it must either be the money supply or the exchange rate. If the central bank sells securities at the same rate as it is buying reserves, it cannot buy reserves at a rate fast enough to keep the exchange rate from appreciating. And if the central bank buys reserves at a rate fast enough to stabilize the exchange rate, it cannot sell securities fast enough to keep the money supply constant. Either the exchange rate appreciates or money income rises.

In a similar way it can be shown that, from an initial position of equilibrium, open market operations (monetary policy) lead to an inconsistent and overdetermined result. A purchase of securities by the central bank would cause a capital outflow, balance of payments deficit, and sales of foreign exchange by the central bank. The restrictive monetary impact of the foreign exchange sales are then offset by further open market purchases which induce further sales of foreign exchange. The process repeats itself at an accelerating speed. There is no new equilibrium because the public wants to hold just so much money, and the central bank's attempt to alter this equilibrium simply results in a fall in reserves. The sterilization procedures merely perpetuate the self-generating process until exchange reserves are exhausted, or until the world level of interest rates falls.

V. DIAGRAMMATIC ILLUSTRATION

These results can be illustrated by diagrams similar to those I have used for analysis of related problems.[5] In the top quadrant of both Figures 1 and 2,

[5]"The Appropriate Use of Monetary and Fiscal Policy for Internal and External Stability," *IMF Staff Papers*, IX, no. 1, March, 1962; "The International Disequilibrium System," *Kyklos*, XIV, no. 2, 1961, 153–72; and "Employment Policy Under Flexible Exchange Rates," this JOURNAL, XXVII, no. 4, Nov., 1961, 509–17. In the latter paper (the main purpose of which was to show that commercial policy—import restriction or export promotion—was ineffective under flexible exchange rates) it was argued that *both* monetary and fiscal policies are more effective under flexible exchange rates than under fixed exchange rates. The apparent conflict with the present analysis lies in the different definition of monetary and fiscal policy and in the extreme assumption in the present paper of perfect capital mobility. In the earlier paper fiscal policy was taken to be an increase in government spending with interest rates maintained constant by the central bank, while capital inflows were assumed to be a function of the rate of interest alone; in other words no capital inflow takes place (because the domestic interest rate is constant) while the money supply is allowed to expand in proportion to the increase in income induced by the more expansive fiscal policy. In the present paper, I have defined fiscal policy as an increase in government spending financed by government bond issues with *no* change in the money supply. In both cases the underlying model is (in essence) the same

XX plots the relation between the interest rate and income (given the exchange rate) along which there is no excess demand in the goods and services market (internal balance); LL describes a similar relation for the money market; and FF gives the external balance condition which is dominated by the world level of interest rates. Analogously in the bottom quadrants, XX plots internal balance, and FF external balance as a function of income and the exchange rate. The internal balance line in the top quadrant applies only for the given exchange rate represented by π_0 in the bottom quadrant, and the external balance schedule in the bottom quadrant applies only for the initial rate of capital imports (assumed to be zero).

Consider the effects of monetary policy (Figure 1). From Q an increase in the money supply shifts LL in the upper quadrant to L'L', implying at the original interest rate and income level (at Q) excess liquidity; this causes a capital outflow. Under flexible exchange rates FF in the lower quadrant shifts downward to F'F', and the improvement in the trade balance increases income and employment as XX in the top quadrant is pushed by the devaluation towards X'X'. The new equilibrium is at P, with an improved trade balance and greater capital outflow (or lessened inflow).

With the exchange rate fixed at $\cdot \pi_0$, however, the increase in the money supply merely creates excess liquidity, an export of capital, a balance of payments deficit, and a reduction in the money supply with no shift in XX in the top quadrant. The line L'L' returns to its original position and Q is restored as equilibrium at a lower level of reserves; Q is the only possible equilibrium consistent with both FF and XX so the money supply will adapt to it if it is allowed to. But if the increase in the money supply is accompanied by *sterilization* operations, that is, if L'L' is maintained, there can be no equilibrium. The central bank buys securities, gold flows out, and the central bank buys more securities. Since the exchange rate is maintained at π_0, XX in the top quadrant

---

and would yield the same results if the same assumptions were made about capital mobility and the same definitions were used.

It may puzzle the reader why I went to some length to alter the definitions of monetary and fiscal policy and thus to bring about a seemingly artificial difference between the conclusions based purely upon different definitions. The reason is that monetary policy cannot in any meaningful sense be defined as an alteration in the interest rate when capital is perfectly mobile, since the authorities cannot change the market rate of interest. Nor can monetary policy be defined, under conditions of perfect capital mobility, as an increase in the money supply, since the central bank has no power over the money supply either (except in transitory positions of disequilibrium) when the exchange rate is fixed. The central bank has, on the other hand, the ability to conduct an open market operation (which only temporarily changes the money supply) and that is the basis of my choice of this definition of monetary policy for the present analysis.

In an earlier paper I analysed some of the purely dynamic aspects of the adjustment process ("The Monetary Dynamics of International Adjustment Under Fixed and Flexible Exchange Rates," *Quarterly Journal of Economics*, May, 1960, 227–57) on varying assumptions regarding capital mobility, but the treatment of the perfect capital mobility case in that paper suffers from the defects I have tried to avoid in this paper by my different definition of "monetary policy." However, the basic conclusions of that paper are not vitiated by the present analysis since the basic problem posed, in the flexible exchange rate case, that "monetary policy" exerts its influence on domestic incomes only indirectly through the exchange rate, still remains, with possibilities of cyclicity and even instability depending on the adjustment speeds; in the present case it can be shown that instability at least would be ruled out if the exchange rate adapted virtually instantaneously.

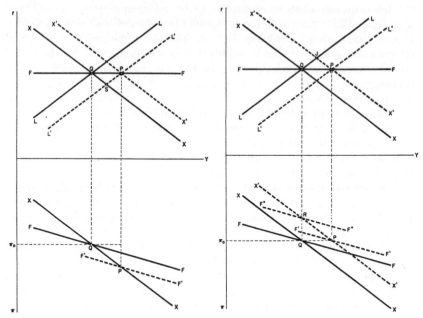

Figure 1. Monetary Policy   Figure 2. Fiscal Policy

is unaffected, as is FF. The attempt of the central bank to maintain $L'L'$ cannot satisfy both the conditions that the interest rate remains at the world level and that the new equilibrium be on XX. Either the exchange rate must change (shifting XX to $X'X'$) or the attempt to maintain $L'L'$ by sterilization operations must be abandoned.

Consider next the case of fiscal policy (Figure 2). An increase in government spending shifts XX to $X'X'$ in both quadrants. At the fixed exchange rate π_0 this increases income and increases the demand for money. Interest rates tend to rise, capital is attracted from abroad, the balance of payments improves and the money supply increases, eventually establishing $L'L'$ as the new money curve. After this instantaneous "stock adjustment," process capital is attracted from abroad sufficiently to establish $F'F'$ as the new foreign balance line, with the equilibrium P in both quadrants.

Under flexible rates, however, the money supply remains constant. The increased spending puts upward pressure on interest rates and appreciates the exchange rate. FF therefore shifts downward to $F''F''$ establishing R as the new equilibrium. At R the price of foreign exchange is lower but output and employment are unchanged.

Again, if the exchange rate is fixed *and* the authorities attempt to sterilize the initial gold inflow one of the policies must fail. This is because the new equilibrium (P) on FF and $X'X'$ in the upper quadrant is only consistent if the money supply is allowed to expand. Obviously the points J and P cannot be maintained simultaneously.

Certain qualifications or extensions to the analysis should be mentioned. The demand for money is likely to depend upon the exchange rate in addition to the interest rate and the level of income; this would slightly reduce the effectiveness of a given change in the quantity of money, and slightly increase the effectiveness of fiscal policy on income and employment under flexible exchange rates, while, of course, it has no significance in the case of fixed exchange rates.

Another possible influence is the real balance effect, but this cannot alter in any essential way the final result: income rises, under flexible exchange rates, in proportion to the increase in the money supply, whereas income remains unchanged, in the case of fixed exchange rates, because the quantity of money does not increase.

A further factor that might be considered is the negative effect of changes in the exchange rate upon the level of saving, but again there is no important alteration in the results: although the budget deficit arising from increased government spending under flexible exchange rates is then partly financed by an increase in saving of the private sector the conclusions regarding changes in the level of output and employment are unaltered.

The conclusions of course have not made any allowance for growth. Because of growth the money supply would normally be increased at a rate more or less commensurate with the actual or desired growth of the economy; my conclusions are, so to speak, superimposed on the growth situation. Moreover, many of our actual observations about the economic world are observations of disequilibrium positions; it is clearly possible to alter the money supply (under fixed exchange rates) if there is excess or deficient liquidity, although even this is in practice unnecessary since we can be assured, as we were as long ago as the days of Ricardo, that the money supply would automatically settle down to its equilibrium level. In any case these observations do not vitiate the principles I have been trying to elucidate.

CONCLUSIONS

I have demonstrated that perfect capital mobility implies different concepts of stabilization policy from those to which we have become accustomed in the post-war period. Monetary policy has no impact on employment under fixed exchange rates while fiscal policy has no effect on employment under flexible exchange rates. On the other hand, fiscal policy has a strong effect on employment under fixed exchange rates (simple Keynesian conclusions hold) while monetary policy has a strong effect on employment under flexible exchange rates (classical quantity theory conclusions hold).

A further implication of the analysis is that monetary policy under fixed exchange rates becomes a device for altering the levels of reserves, while fiscal policy under flexible exchange rates becomes a device for altering the balance of trade, both policies leaving unaffected the level of output and employment. Under fixed exchange rates, open market operations by the central bank result in equal changes in the gold stock, open market purchases causing it to decline and open market sales causing it to increase. And under flexible exchange rates, budget deficits or surpluses induced by changes in taxes or government spending cause corresponding changes in the trade balance.

Gold sterilization policies make no sense in a world of fixed exchange rates and perfect capital mobility and will ultimately lead to the breakdown of the fixed exchange system. In the absence of gold sterilization, as we have seen, an attempt of the central bank to alter the money supply is frustrated by capital outflows and automatically offsetting monetary changes through the exchange equalization operations; this is running water into a sink that is filled to the brim, causing the water to spill over the edges at the same rate that it is coming out of the tap.[6] But sterilization operations are analogous to trying to prevent the water from spilling out, even though the sink is full and water is still pouring out of the tap.

If my assumptions about capital mobility were valid in Canada,[7] it would mean that expansive fiscal policy under flexible exchange rates was of little help in increasing employment because of the ensuing inflow of capital which kept the exchange rate high and induced a balance of trade deficit: we should have observed a zero or very small multiplier. By the same token, now that Canada has adopted a fixed exchange system, we should not reason from earlier negative experience about the size of the multiplier and conclude that the multiplier is *now* low: while a reduction in the budget deficit under flexible rates would have helped the trade balance without too much damage to employment, a reduction in the budget deficit today could be expected to have a sizable impact on excess demand and unemployment.

Of course the assumption of perfect capital mobility is not literally valid; my conclusions are black and white rather than dark and light grey. To the extent that Canada can maintain an interest rate equilibrium different from that of the United States, without strong capital inflows, fiscal expansion can be expected to play *some* role in employment policy under flexible exchange rates, and monetary policy can have *some* influence on employment and output under fixed exchange rates. But if this possibility exists for us today, we can conjecture that it will exist to a lesser extent in the future.

[6]John Exter used a reservoir simile in "The Gold Losses," a speech delivered before the Economic Club of Detroit, May 7, 1962.

[7]See the accounts of the Canadian experience by Clarence Barber in his submission to the Royal Commission on Banking and Finance, April, 1962, "The Canadian Economy in Trouble," and by Harry Johnson from his speech to the Canadian Club of Toronto, November, 1962, "Canada in a Changing World." Perhaps the most complete verification of the applicability of the conclusions to the Canadian case is provided in an econometric paper by R. Rhomberg to be published in the *Journal of Political Economy*.

[22]

The Appropriate Use of Monetary and Fiscal Policy for Internal and External Stability

Robert A. Mundell *

THIS PAPER deals with the problem of achieving internal stability and balance of payments equilibrium in a country which considers it inadvisable to alter the exchange rate or to impose trade controls. It is assumed that monetary and fiscal policy can be used as independent instruments to attain the two objectives if capital flows are responsive to interest rate differentials, but it is concluded that it is a matter of extreme importance how the policies are paired with the objectives. Specifically, it is argued that monetary policy ought to be aimed at external objectives and fiscal policy at internal objectives, and that failure to follow this prescription can make the disequilibrium situation worse than before the policy changes were introduced.

The practical implication of the theory, when stabilization measures are limited to monetary policy and fiscal policy, is that a surplus country experiencing inflationary pressure should ease monetary conditions and raise taxes (or reduce government spending), and that a deficit country suffering from unemployment should tighten interest rates and lower taxes (or increase government spending).[1]

The Conditions of Equilibrium

Internal balance requires that aggregate demand for domestic output be equal to aggregate supply of domestic output at full employment. If this condition is not fulfilled, there will be inflationary pressure or recessionary potential according to whether aggregate demand exceeds

* Mr. Mundell, economist in the Special Studies Division, received his economics training at the University of British Columbia, the University of Washington, Massachusetts Institute of Technology, and the London School of Economics, and was a postdoctoral fellow at the University of Chicago. He was economist for the Royal Commission on Price Spreads of Food Products, and has taught at Boston University, the University of British Columbia, Stanford University, and the Bologna Center for The Johns Hopkins School of Advanced International Studies. He is the author of numerous articles on international trade and economic theory.

[1] This possibility has been suggested, and to a limited extent implemented, elsewhere. See, for example, De Nederlandsche Bank N.V., *Report for the Year 1960* (Amsterdam, 1961).

THE APPROPRIATE USE OF MONETARY AND FISCAL POLICY   71

or falls short of, respectively, full employment output. It will be assumed here that, during transitory periods of disequilibrium, inventories are running down, or accumulating, in excess of desired changes, according to whether the disequilibrium reflects a state of inflationary or recessionary potential.

External balance implies that the balance of trade equals (net) capital exports at the fixed exchange parity. If the balance of trade exceeds capital exports, there will be a balance of payments surplus and a tendency for the exchange rate to appreciate, which the central bank restrains by accumulating stocks of foreign exchange. And likewise, if the balance of trade falls short of capital exports, there will be a balance of payments deficit and a tendency for the exchange rate to depreciate, which the central bank prevents by dispensing with stocks of foreign exchange.

In what follows it is assumed that all foreign policies and export demand are given, that the balance of trade worsens as the level of domestic expenditure increases, and that capital flows are responsive to interest rate differentials. Then domestic expenditure can be assumed to depend only on fiscal policy (the budget surplus) and monetary policy (the interest rate) at the full employment level of output. The complete system can thus be given a geometric interpretation in the two policy variables, the interest rate and the budget surplus[2] (Diagram 1).

In the diagram, the *FF* line, which will be referred to as the "foreign-balance schedule," traces the locus of pairs of interest rates and budget surpluses (at the level of income compatible with full employment) along which the balance of payments is in equilibrium. This schedule has a negative slope because an increase in the interest rate, by reducing capital exports and lowering domestic expenditure and hence imports, improves the balance of payments; while a decrease in the budget surplus, by raising domestic expenditure and hence

---

[2] The assumptions could be made less restrictive without detracting from the generality of the conclusions. Thus, an assumption that capital imports directly affect domestic expenditure, as in theoretical transfer analysis, would tend to reinforce the conclusions. Even the (plausible) assumption that, in addition to capital flows, capital indebtedness is responsive to the rate of interest (to take account of the "stock" nature of much of international floating capital) would not change the conclusions, although it may affect the quantitative extent of the policy changes required.

Notice, however, that I have implicitly assumed away strong "Pigou" effects, speculation on international markets that is related to the size of the (positive or negative) budget surplus, forward rate movements that more than offset interest-rate–differential changes (an unlikely occurrence), and concern about the precise composition of the balance of payments; the last assumption may mean that the method of achieving equilibrium suggested below is desirable only in the short run.

DIAGRAM 1

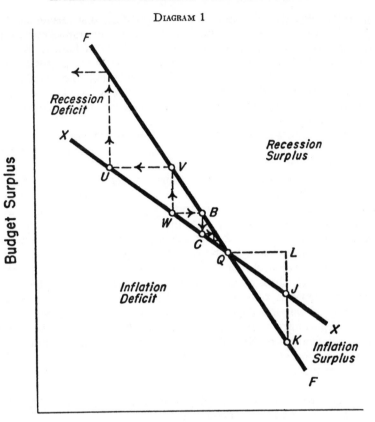

Rate of Interest

imports, worsens the balance of payments. Thus, from any point on the schedule an increase in the rate of interest would cause an external surplus, which would have to be compensated by a reduction in the budget surplus in order to restore equilibrium.. Points above and to the right of the foreign-balance schedule refer to balance of payments surpluses, while points below and to the left of the schedule represent balance of payments deficits.

A similar construction can be applied to the conditions representing internal balance. The *XX* line, or "internal-balance schedule," is the locus of pairs of interest rates and budget surpluses which permits continuing full employment equilibrium in the market for goods and services. Along this schedule, full employment output is equal to

THE APPROPRIATE USE OF MONETARY AND FISCAL POLICY   **73**

aggregate demand for output, or, what amounts to the same condition, home demand for domestic goods is equal to full employment output less exports. There is, therefore, only one level of home demand for domestic goods consistent with full employment and the given level of exports, and this implies that expenditure must be constant along XX. The internal-balance line must therefore have a negative slope, since increases in the interest rate are associated with decreases in the budget surplus, in order to maintain domestic expenditure constant.

Both the internal-balance and the foreign-balance schedules thus have negative slopes. But it is necessary also to compare the steepness of the slopes. Which of the schedules is steeper?

It can be demonstrated that FF must be steeper than XX if capital is even slightly mobile, and by an amount which depends both on the responsiveness of international capital flows to the rate of interest and on the marginal propensity to import. The absolute slope of the internal-balance schedule XX is the ratio between the responsiveness of domestic expenditure to the rate of interest and the responsiveness of domestic expenditure to the budget surplus. Now, if it is assumed for a moment that capital exports are constant, the balance of payments depends only on expenditure, since exports are assumed constant and imports depend only on expenditure. In other words, if capital exports are constant, the slope of FF also is the ratio between the responsiveness of domestic expenditure to the rate of interest and the responsiveness of such expenditure to the budget surplus. Therefore, apart from the effects of changes in capital exports, the two slopes are the same. It is then possible to see that the responsiveness of capital exports to the rate of interest makes the slope of FF greater in absolute value than the slope of XX.[3]

Consider, for example, what happens to an initial situation of over-all equilibrium at Q as this equilibrium is disturbed by an increase in the rate of interest equal to QL. Because of the higher rate of interest, there would be deflationary pressure and a balance of payments surplus at the point L. If the budget surplus is now lowered, the deflationary pressure can be eliminated at a point like J on the internal-balance schedule. But at J, expenditure is the same as it was at Q, and this means that imports, and hence the balance of *trade*, must be the same as at Q. The balance of *payments* is therefore in

[3] Both the absolute and relative values of the slopes depend on the particular fiscal policy in question. The discussion in the text applies to income tax reductions because that instrument tends to be neutral as between home and foreign spending. The conclusions would be strengthened or weakened, respectively, as the particular fiscal policy was biased toward or against home goods; the more the change in the budget surplus results from a change in spending on home goods, the greater is the difference between the slopes of XX and FF.

surplus at J because of capital imports attracted by the higher rate of interest; this makes necessary a further reduction in the budget surplus in order to bring the balance of payments again into equilibrium. It follows, then, that the point K on the foreign-balance schedule is below the point J on the internal-balance schedule, and that FF is steeper than XX. It can then also be concluded that the absolute difference in slopes is greater, the more mobile is capital (because this causes a larger external surplus at J) and the lower is the marginal propensity to import (because this necessitates a larger budget deficit to correct any given external surplus).[4]

In Diagram 1, the two schedules separate four quadrants, distinguished from one another by the conditions of internal imbalance and external disequilibrium. Only at the point where the schedules intersect are the policy variables in equilibrium.

Two Systems of Policy Response

Consider now two possible policy systems determining the behavior of fiscal policy and monetary policy when internal and external balance have not been simultaneously achieved. The government can adjust monetary policy to the requirements of internal stability, and fiscal policy to the needs of external balance, or it can use fiscal policy for purposes of internal stability and monetary policy for purposes of external balance.

It will be demonstrated first that the policy system in which the interest rate is used for internal stability, and fiscal policy is used for external equilibrium, is an unstable system. Consider, for example, a situation of full employment combined with a balance of payments deficit, represented by the point W. To correct the deficit by fiscal policy, the budget surplus must be raised from that indicated by W to that given by V. At V there will be equilibrium in the balance of

---

[4] The assumption that imports depend only on expenditure, while the latter depends partly on the rate of interest, means that imports are affected by the rate of interest, although the *share* of imports in expenditure is not. This assumption could be relaxed without fundamentally altering the results, although an exception—remote in practice but possible in theory—does arise, if import goods are highly responsive to the rate of interest while home goods are not, capital flows are only slightly responsive to the rate of interest, and the marginal propensity to buy imports is high relative to the marginal propensity to buy home goods. Under these conditions, it is possible that XX may be steeper than FF. More formally, then, it is necessary to limit the present conclusions to countries in which the ratio of the effect of budget policy on the balance of payments to its effect on domestic excess demand is less than the ratio of the effect of the interest rate on the balance of payments to its effect on excess demand.

THE APPROPRIATE USE OF MONETARY AND FISCAL POLICY   75

payments, but the increased budget surplus will have caused recessionary pressure. If now the threatening unemployment is to be prevented
by monetary policy, the rate of interest must be lowered from that
indicated by V to that described by U. But at U there is again a
balance of payments deficit, which in turn necessitates a further
increase in the budget surplus. The process continues with the interest
rate and the budget surplus moving ever further from equilibrium.[5]

To show formally that the system is unstable, it is sufficient to note
that the payments deficit at U, after the first round of policy changes,
exceeds the deficit at W. This is evident since it is known that the
balance of *trade* at U and W is the same but, because of the lower rate
of interest, the balance of *payments* at U is worse. It follows that this
type of policy reaction is unstable.

On the other hand, the opposite type of policy response is stable.
Suppose that the authorities adjust the interest rate to correspond to
the needs of external equilibrium and adjust fiscal policy to maintain
internal stability. Then from the same disequilibrium point W, the
rate of interest would be raised to B, thereby correcting the external
deficit. But the tendency toward unemployment generated by the
restrictive credit policy must now be corrected by a reduction in the
budget surplus or increase in the budget deficit. At C there is again
internal balance and a balance of payments deficit, as at W. But it is
now possible to see that the deficit at C is *less* than the deficit at W.
This follows, as before, because the balance of *trade* at C is identical
with that at W but, since the rate of interest is higher at C, the balance
of *payments* deficit must be less. The system is therefore stable.

The diagrammatic argument can be absorbed at once when it is
realized that at W—or anywhere in the quadrant representing a deficit
and recession—the interest rate is lower, and the budget surplus is
higher, than is appropriate to the over-all equilibrium at Q. The use
of fiscal policy for external balance, and monetary policy for internal
balance, drives the interest rate and budget surplus further away from
equilibrium, while the alternative system moves the instruments closer
to equilibrium.

The same argument applies to an initial disequilibrium in the
opposite quadrant, representing inflationary pressure and external
surplus. To restore equilibrium, the interest rate must be reduced,

---

[5] It need hardly be mentioned that the demonstration of instability in this
instance (or of stability in the subsequent analysis) is not dependent upon the
particular assumption that the government corrects imbalance first in one sector
and then in the other, an assumption which is made only for expositional convenience. The conclusions follow, for example, even if the authorities simultaneously
adjust fiscal and monetary policies.

and fiscal policy must be made more restrictive. Only if monetary policy is used for the external purpose, and fiscal policy for the internal purpose, will correction of the disequilibrium automatically ensue.[6]

In the other two quadrants, monetary and fiscal policies will be moving in the same direction under either system of policy response, because both tighter monetary policy and an increased budget surplus correct inflationary pressure and external deficit, and both easier monetary policy and a reduced budget surplus tend to alleviate recession and external surplus. The distinction between the two policy systems appears less important in these phases of the international trade cycle; it nevertheless remains, since inaccurate information about the exact location of the point Q could propel the situation into one of the quadrants involving either recession and deficit or inflation and surplus.[7]

Conclusions

It has been demonstrated that, in countries where employment and balance of payments policies are restricted to monetary and fiscal instruments, monetary policy should be reserved for attaining the desired level of the balance of payments, and fiscal policy for preserving internal stability under the conditions assumed here. The opposite system would lead to a progressively worsening unemployment and balance of payments situation.

The explanation can be related to what I have elsewhere called the Principle of Effective Market Classification: policies should be paired with the objectives on which they have the most influence.[8] If this principle is not followed, there will develop a tendency either for a cyclical approach to equilibrium or for instability.

[6] Even if the authorities do not wish to pair instruments and targets, they can use the information provided by the analysis to determine the relation between *actual* policies and *equilibrium* policies. Thus, situations of deficit and recession imply that the budget surplus is too high and the interest rate is too low, while situations of surplus and inflation imply the opposite. In this manner, appropriate policies can be determined by observable situations of target disequilibria.

[7] The system can be generalized for a two-country world by assuming that the other country adjusts fiscal policy to maintain internal stability. The only difference in the conclusion is that the conditions of dynamic stability of the adjustment process are slightly more restrictive, requiring that the marginal propensities to import be, *on the average*, no greater than one half; this is the usual assumption necessary to rule out any "reverse transfer" that is due to policies affecting expenditure.

[8] "The Monetary Dynamics of International Adjustment Under Fixed and Flexible Exchange Rates," *Quarterly Journal of Economics*, Vol. LXXIV (1960), pp. 249–50.

THE APPROPRIATE USE OF MONETARY AND FISCAL POLICY   **77**

The use of fiscal policy for external purposes and monetary policy for internal stability violates the principle of effective market classification, because the ratio of the effect of the rate of interest on internal stability to its effect on the balance of payments is less than the ratio of the effect of fiscal policy on internal stability to its effect on the balance of payments. And for precisely this reason the opposite set of policy responses is consistent with the principle.

On a still more general level, we have the principle that Tinbergen has made famous: that to attain a given number of independent targets there must be at least an equal number of instruments.[9] Tinbergen's Principle is concerned with the *existence* and location of a solution to the system. It does not assert that any given set of policy responses will in fact lead to that solution. To assert this, it is necessary to investigate the stability properties of a dynamic system. In this respect, the Principle of Effective Market Classification is a necessary companion to Tinbergen's Principle.

[9] J. Tinbergen, *On the Theory of Economic Policy* (Amsterdam, 1952).

[23]

Rational-Expectations-with-Misperceptions
As a Theory of the Business Cycle

Arthur M. Okun*

In my judgment, the theory of rational-expectations-with-misperceptions provides an explanation of the business cycle that: represents a constructive effort to deal with questions that sorely needed to be asked, is logically impeccable and theoretically satisfying in its response to those questions, does not identify in operational terms the specific nature of the cyclical process, and fails to account for the duration and many key features of the actual cycle.

The Micro-Macro Bridge

The centerpiece of microeconomics is the purely competitive auction market in which buyers and sellers participate atomistically as price takers and where supply and demand are equated continuously by variations in price. These individual markets aggregate into a Walrasian general equilibrium model in which aggregate output is supply-determined, changing only when production functions shift, or when stocks of capital and natural resources change, or when the flow of labor offered at a given real wage changes (because of either changes in population or changes in tastes concerning work activity). In that aggregation of perfect markets, shifts in nominal aggregate demand affect only prices and never quantities.

Macroeconomics contrasts sharply with these implications of aggregated microeconomics. It begins with the observation that output and employment display significant deviations around their supply-determined trends that are (a) serially correlated and (b) normally positively correlated with deviations around a medium-run trend of nominal spending. These fluctuations around the trend of real activity are the "business cycle" (a term that is not meant to imply strong periodicity). Clearly, the business cycle could not happen in aggregated classical microeconomics. Thus any macroeconomics that is connected to microeconomics by a solid bridge must explain how it departs from the classical micro model in its conception of the operation of markets.

*This paper was prepared for the American Enterprise Institute Seminar on Rational Expectations, held on February 1, 1980, in Washington, D.C. The views expressed are the author's and are not necessarily those of the officers, trustees, or other staff members of The Brookings Institution.

ARTHUR M. OKUN, *who was a Senior Fellow at the Brookings Institution, died on March 23, 1980.*

In fact, Keynes was explicit about the nature of his amendment. He departed from classical microeconomics *only* by modifying the labor supply function to include a wage floor. And, he offered many (indeed too many) explanations for the wage floor. But his bridge was defective; none of the explanations flowed directly from the implications of optimization by economic agents or from a specific institutional constraint. Many of the followers of Keynes operated with no bridge to microeconomics. Instead, they adopted the "fixprice method" (in Hick's terms), explicitly assuming away variations in prices and wages. And then, necessarily, nominal disturbances were found to have—purely and solely—real effects. (Indeed, this tradition began in the pre-Keynesian era, as illustrated by the accelerator theory of investment.)

The fixprice finesse may have helped economists develop a sharper focus and a better understanding of real relationships, like the consumption function, inventory and fixed investment functions, cyclical productivity relationships, and multiplier-accelerator interactions. But it had important costs. One of these was a professionally disturbing gap between macroeconomics and microeconomics. In effect, at the beginning of the macroeconomic semester, students were required to forget what they had learned in microeconomics about the equilibrating function of prices and wages. More seriously, by operating with models that took prices and wages as given for pedagogical purposes, economists tended to think of them as given for general purposes. Thus, the finesse contributed to the long lags in professional progress toward a satisfactory theory of the causes and consequences of inflation.

When the Phillips curve supplanted fixprice in the Keynesian model, it emerged as "an empirical generalization in search of a theory," as Tobin aptly put it. And the entire structure was seriously undermined when that empirical generalization collapsed.

In the last dozen years or so since that collapse, serious professional efforts have been made to construct that sorely needed macro-micro bridge. Those efforts, including the particular ones conducted by the "rational expectations school," are asking the right questions and working to provide illuminating answers.

The Misperceptions View

The particular bridge supplied by the rational expectations school amends the classical model simply and solely by assuming that buyers and sellers in any particular market may have imperfect information about prices in *other* markets. Then, even if each market passes all the standard tests of continuous clearing, complete atomism, and costless transactions, the imperfect information about other markets creates the possibility of a business cycle—of real effects from disturbances in nominal aggregate demand. And there are persuasive reasons why rational agents may have imperfect information about developments in markets in which they are not operating. Some pieces of information have costs that exceed their value. Thus, the theory is firmly grounded in the assumption of rational behavior and optimization.

In response to a generally unexpected jump in nominal aggregate demand, the aggregated classical microeconomics would predict a proportionate rise in all product and factor prices with no changes in quantities. In contrast, the rational expectations theory would envision some initial expansion of quantities resulting from misperception. A seller finding a surprisingly high price in the market for his product may respond by producing and selling a larger volume of output, because he may well not fully recognize the higher replacement costs of his inputs or the higher revenues available from alternative outputs. Some sellers in product markets may be focusing their attention on the markets in which they are operating and thus not become aware of similar price movements in factor markets and other product markets. They may then respond to a higher price for their product as though it was a higher relative price when in fact it may merely parallel the rise in the general price level.

Similarly, following the rise in nominal aggregate demand, workers encountering unexpectedly higher wages in their particular labor market may offer more work. They may respond that way for either or both of two reasons: (1) because they have a positive elasticity of supply of work effort with respect to real wages and fail to recognize the increase in consumer prices occurring in product markets; or (2) because they do not recognize that nominal wages are higher in other labor markets as well, thus raising the return from selling their labor elsewhere.

This model abandons explicitly the assumption (often implicit) of the Walrasian model that all information has zero costs. Information costs to participants in any one market about prices in *other* markets are the grains of sand thrown on the frictionless classical machinery to destroy its conclusion that nominal disturbances have only nominal effects. With that small exception this model preserves the entire apparatus of classical microeconomics. It constructs a logically and theoretically satisfactory bridge. Misperceptions about prices in other markets can account for *some* cycle in real activity.

The Nature of the Missing Information

To begin my critique of the theory, I see no way to assess the role of misperceptions about relative prices in the actually observed cycle until the rational expectations theorists give these misperceptions much more operational content than they have thus far. In general, the proponents stress the rational expectations *despite which* the cycle takes place; I wish they would focus more sharply on the misperceptions or the missing information, which are allegedly the *cause* of the cycle. In the spirit of Howard Baker, I wish to be told what the decision makers don't know, for how long they don't know it, and why they don't find out. Is there any direct empirical evidence that sellers lack timely information about other prices that are relevant to their "true" marginal costs? Are there persuasive a priori reasons why sellers are likely to lack such information in important ways for prolonged periods?

Operating on my own intuition, I find it implausible that important information is sufficiently costly to outweigh its value to rational agents on a timely basis. For one thing, by reading the newspapers, market participants obtain a virtually costless flow of information from the reporting on the monthly indices of consumer and producer prices. Even more significantly, firms and households operate in both product and factor markets at essentially the same time. How much of a communication gap or lag can rationally be maintained between the personnel manager and the sales manager of a given firm? How much of an effort is required within the family to ensure communications between the workers and the shoppers?

How long can a rational agent collect wage offers in various labor markets and still maintain a serious misperception in the face of his actual experience? Any sensible job seeker must be Bayesian. If he samples twenty labor markets and obtains twenty wage offers which all lie below his initial mean expectation of wages, he must revise that expectation downward sharply and quickly—even if he is unable to calculate that the probability of drawing such a sample is slightly less than one in a million. Is it really plausible, as econometric labor supply functions based on this model imply, that the deviation of "anticipated wages" from actual wages narrows at a rate of only 15 to 36 percent a year?

Let me raise a different question about the nature of the misperceptions and missing information. Any theory that attributes decision-making errors by private agents to missing information implies that there exists, in principle, some set of correct, timely information that would eliminate these errors. That information needs to be identified specifically. Indeed that task may have important implications for public policy. The model seems to point directly to the potential benefit from filling the critical gap of missing information that accounts for decision errors. Clearly, the production of information is subject to huge economies of scale; and, because of laws on disclosure, the government is likely to be the most efficient collector of proprietary information from businesses and households. Within the framework of this model, one must ask whether the Bureau of Labor Statistics holds the key to eliminating the cycle.

The Duration of the Cycle

More evidence about the nature of the missing information might quell my doubts and refute my tentative hypotheses. But if my suspicions are well-founded, misperceptions about relative prices are only a small first step toward accounting for a cycle of the duration and amplitude that are actually observed. And they barely begin to explain prolonged periods, like 1958–63 and 1975–77, when output and employment remained below their equilibrium values (by anyone's measure). How much of the basic profile of such periods should be attributed to consistent, repetitive overestimates by sellers of general inflation (relative to their known selling prices)? Survey data from households and business executives in those periods display no consistent pattern of overestimating inflation, so far as I am aware. Inflation forecasts made by professional economists were remarkably accurate in the early sixties and in 1976–77 as well.

Indeed, the forecasts of real activity made by economists in 1958 and 1975 (and every other recession year) accurately implied that the economy would remain in slack territory for a considerable period of time. Even an unintelligent autocorrelation equation could have rendered that verdict with a high degree of reliability in March 1958 or March 1975. What is going on at such times? When economists predict that rational decision makers will continue to restrict output below a full macroequilibrium, are we really predicting that they will continue to operate with erroneous perceptions of relative prices? And when rational private decision makers hear our voices, how can they keep ignoring valuable free information that identifies their mistake? Because private decision makers are too intelligent to make repetitive, serially correlated errors, misperceptions about relative prices can be only a small part of the story of long slack periods (and equally long boom periods like 1966–69).

When rational expectations theorists explicitly recognize the problem of persistence, they agree—and indeed insist, as an implication of their model—that the forecasting errors of private decision makers on relative prices should be serially uncorrelated over any significant time interval. But then, to account for the persistence of slack and booms, they must graft onto their cycle models lags or adjustment costs (which may be reflected in an accelerator mechanism) that maintain serially correlated movements in output and employment after the initiating relative-price misperception has disappeared. I view this search for a hybrid model as a productive and promising line of inquiry that requires and deserves much further work. It points toward a business cycle theory based on rational expectations with misperceptions and with something else. So far, that something else has been specified much more clearly in terms of the properties of difference and differential equations than in terms of economic behavior. Some of the resulting structures seem to use a Lucas-Sargent snowball to generate a Samuelson-Metzler avalanche. And, in the process, the solid macro-micro bridge of the simple model gets shaky (or at least obscured from my vision). Once misperceptions about relative prices are eliminated, what prevents that prompt restoration of a full-blown Walrasian equilibrium consistent with accurate relative-price information? Is a second type of sand being thrown on the classical machinery in such hybrid models? I look forward to further modeling in this area that should help to answer my questions.

Salient Features of the Cycle

I have raised questions and expressed doubts about the ability of the rational-expectations-with-misperceptions model to account for the duration of the cycle and especially of prolonged periods of slack that are actually observed. I would argue further that many other salient characteristics of the cycle cannot be satisfactorily explained by that model—a Walrasian system modified only by relative-price misperceptions. Obviously, any tractable theory is simplified and cannot explain or predict every feature or characteristic of experience. But it ought to have a fair degree of verisimilitude. In particular, the implications of any model for fiscal and monetary policy can be taken seriously only if its implications for other key features of the cycle stand up under empirical observation. Let me state some stylized cyclical facts which do not seem to be explicable by rational-expectations-with-misperceptions.

Inventory disequilibria. The hallmark of U.S. postwar recessions has been inventory liquidation, following a major buildup of inventories at the peak of the expansion. Standard models that assume price taking and continuous market clearing do not suggest that a disappointment about relative prices will lead traders to liquidate inventories. For example, a sudden drop in the demand for, and hence the price of, wheat that leads farmers to decrease production in the future will generally lead traders to increase stocks initially. (The price tends to fall enough currently relative to its new future expected value to provide traders with that incentive.) Why then, in the business cycle, is the aggregate cutback in production accompanied by a cutback in stocks?

Cyclical productivity patterns. Output per hour worked fluctuates in a procyclical pattern. Extant efforts to explain that phenomenon rest on disequilibria or on transactions and adjustment costs that are non-Walrasian. Can it be explained within the framework of a model that views labor markets and product markets as Walrasian?

Quits and layoffs. Quits have a procyclical pattern and are a coincident indicator at turning points. If workers lack information about wages in *other* labor markets, then they should be less likely to quit when their wages accelerate unexpectedly. According to this model, should not quits be countercyclical or at least display long lags at turning points? Layoffs display a marked countercyclical pattern. Can that (or indeed the very existence of layoffs) be explained by the model? The frequency of help-wanted signs and the volume of help-wanted advertising display strong procyclical variations. Can these be explained in the framework of the classical microeconomics adopted by this model?

Wage differentials. Pay differentials between high-wage and low-wage industries vary countercyclically. And that is the case even though cyclical fluctuations in employment tend to be greatest in the high-wage industries. Can that be explained within the framework of this model?

General pay increases in recession. During recent periods of recession and slack, like 1975–77, many nonunion firms granted general pay increases to their workers when the firms were recruiting *no* new workers at all. Why would sensible employers raise wages under such conditions at those points in time, regardless of how they expected prices or wages to move in the future?

Profits in boom years. Corporate profits (in real terms) are especially high in years of emerging excess demand. If corporations are committing decision-making errors that lead to unduly large output under such circumstances, why do their income statements look so good?

Auction markets. Prices of industrial commodities traded in organized auction markets have fallen in postwar recessions (including 1974–75); most other prices have not fallen (and rose strongly in 1974–75). Can this special behavior of auction markets be explained within the framework of a model that views all markets as auction markets?

OPEC. The record of 1974–79 makes clear that increases in the price of oil add to the price level for a given path of nominal GNP. Should that be viewed as a relative-price misperception? (Some economists invoked rational-expectations arguments to predict erroneously that oil prices could not raise the price level, given nominal GNP).

Alternative Explanations

In my judgment, rational-expectations-with-misperceptions provides a logically satisfactory but empirically unsatisfactory explanation of the business cycle. I see alternative routes to an explanation that would score much better empirically (in accounting for the duration and the salient features of the cycle) and still have a theoretically satisfactory underpinning, linked to the behavior of individual markets and resting on the rational behavior of economic agents.

I have become convinced that the most promising alternatives drop the assumption of continuous market clearing and recognize price making and wage making. They thus depart farther from the competitive, auction macro model; they are less familiar and may be fundamentally less elegant and less tractable; they show less respect for Walras and Marshall. But none of these features make them untheoretical or unsound. Without propounding my view of the cycle and the inflationary process in any detail, I do want to indicate the possibility that alternative macro views can rest on theoretically sound micro foundations.

Continuous market clearing implies the universality of organized auction markets. But, to be traded on an auction market, a product must be standardized and defined so well (at such low cost) that it can be viewed as homogeneous by a prospective buyer placing orders through a broker. Soybeans and silver meet that test; while neckties, restaurant meals, and eyeglasses clearly do not. Apparently, they cannot be homogenized or standardized at a cost that would make the auction technique efficient. And apparently from the point of view of employers, skilled workers are heterogeneous or idiosyncratic. Price tags, wage offers, shopping, and search are part of an optimal transactions mechanism for heterogeneous products. It is a tribute to the genuine efficiency of free markets that most products and nearly all types of labor are traded on markets that do not have the price-taking, quantity-making characteristics specified by so-called "efficient-markets theory."

When sellers are price makers, they necessarily act as quantity takers. And then any surprise in demand (even one that is correctly perceived as soon as it happens) must initially alter quantities and leave prices unchanged. Hence, for some very brief period, fixprice results from rational decision making by optimizing agents— and not from an institutional rigidity or from some heroic assumption to disregard market behavior.

That initial very brief period of price fixity or insensitivity is the first of a long chain of implications for optimizing by a price-tag seller. Once a firm sets prices, it must develop a method of price setting. Since that task uses resources, periodic reviews of prices and formulas for price setting can become efficient business practices. Because shopping is costly and hence potential buyers do not monitor prices continuously, sellers have incentives to inform potential buyers about prices. And that communication, to have effective value as information, may commit the seller to sell at the advertised price for a period of some substantial duration.

In general, the seller realizes that buyers extrapolate information obtained from one shopping expedition as a basis for decisions on where to shop next time. Their comparison shopping is necessarily intertemporal. The seller wants satisfied customers to extrapolate their past information and rationally tries to convey a basis for them to believe that his policy on pricing (and service as well) is consistent through time. To promote patterns of recurrent shopping or to convert buyers into regular customers, the seller has incentives to adopt a strategy that sacrifices frequent and transitory price adjustments. In exceptional cases, the seller may even find it worthwhile to assume a contractual obligation to supply his product for months or years in the future at a predetermined price, even while leaving the buyer discretion over the amount to be purchased.

Optimization by the price-tag seller thus does not consist of mimicking the absent auctioneer. Rather it establishes a variety of small and large *commitments* to price tags; and those commitments reduce the speed and magnitude of price changes in response to shifts in demand.

The considerations that lead to wage commitments in labor markets are even more obvious and more important than those that create price commitments in product markets. The costs of finding the most rewarding job are large for a worker; the costs of obtaining the most productive worker are large for the employer; and the benefits of experience on a particular job can be substantial. These considerations promote continuing relationships with substantial bilateral monopoly surpluses. In some cases, they lead to explicit contracts that fix the wage over a substantial interval, even while not fixing the amount of employment. More often, they lead to implicit contracts where the employer and the worker conduct themselves and communicate with each other in ways that help to make the continuation of the relationship worthwhile for both.

These elements can provide a theoretically sound optimization underpinning for Keynes's assumption of a money wage floor, and indeed for a generalization of that assumption. Clearly, the firm that hires a worker with a career job in mind must lead him to believe that his position will gradually improve, and certainly not worsen. Once the firm paints a bright future in order to recruit that worker, any subsequent cut in wages must be a disappointment and a source of antagonism that would jeopardize the firm's investment in that worker. Hence the firm's inhibition about reducing wages has a sound, rational basis. In fact, when money wages normally rise over time, the same inhibitions can also apply to hold-downs or even slowdowns of wages for employees who have been recruited with the expectation of moving upward absolutely and keeping up relatively.

Many so-called "rigidities" in the behavior of wages and prices are genuinely the consequences of optimizing behavior in markets with efficient transactional mechanisms for dealing with heterogeneous products and factors, which involve significant costs of information and transactions. In one sense, I am arguing that the resulting arrangements (price tags, wage offers, search, shopping, customer relations, and career jobs) proliferate the number and accentuate the separateness of "informationally distinct markets," in Lucas's terminology. Every firm becomes, in effect, a distinct labor market. And no worker can readily learn all the relevant information about the opportunities and rewards on the various jobs available elsewhere (that is, in other labor markets). As a result, prolonged and serious misperceptions about relative wages (or prices) become far more plausible in this context than in the Walrasian framework. Yet, I would stress primarily, not the misperceptions, but rather the various commitments to wages and prices that develop in such a world of heterogeneous products and factors. Because rational agents know that full information about other alternatives is costly—in other words, because they recognize their vulnerability to relative-price misperceptions—they establish patterns of behavior to minimize search and shopping costs. And those involve implicit and explicit commitments to wages and prices.

Nominal disturbances then have real effects, even when fully perceived and even when anticipated somewhat ahead of time. These real effects occur because nominal arrangements are real and lasting. Prices and wages are sticky in response to shifts in aggregate demand, basically as the result of efficient transactional mechanisms (rather than of monopoly or of government regulations).

This line of reasoning moves distinctly away from the microeconomics of Marshall and Walras. That is no virtue; but neither is it a sin. I regard it as a necessity in order to understand many macroeconomic observations that otherwise defy explanation. It is needed for fundamental monetary theory as well as for business cycle theory. As others have emphasized, supplying a rationale for money (as anything more than a numeraire) in a Walrasian framework really requires sneaking in some sort of transactions costs. If transactions were genuinely costless, any commodity sold on an auction market should be fully acceptable as a means of payment. Money really matters because the world is different from the classical microeconomic paradigm.

Despite the methodological contributions made by the model of rational-expectations-with-misperceptions, the assumption of universal auction markets has put it into a straitjacket. It offers a logical explanation of how an economy consisting entirely of markets like those observed for soybeans and silver could nonetheless experience some business cycle. The implications of that model strengthen my conviction that a soybean-silver economy would not display a business cycle with the duration or key characteristics actually observed. And I am equally convinced that the resulting guide to macro policymaking in a soybean-silver economy is fundamentally inapplicable to the actual U.S. economy.

[24]

PRICE FLEXIBILITY AND FULL EMPLOYMENT*

By DON PATINKIN

At the core of the Keynesian polemics of the past ten years and more is the relationship between price flexibility and full employment. The fundamental argument of Keynes is directed against the belief that price flexibility can be depended upon to generate full employment automatically. The defenders of the classical tradition, on the other hand, still insist upon this automaticity as a basic tenet.

During the years of continuous debate on this question, the issues at stake have been made more precise. At the same time, further material on the question of flexibility has become available. This paper is essentially an attempt to incorporate this new material, and, taking advantage of the perspective offered by time, to analyze the present state of the debate.

In Part I, the problem of price flexibility and full employment is presented from a completely static viewpoint. Part II then goes on to discuss the far more important dynamic aspects of the problem. Finally, in Part III, the implications of the discussion for the Keynesian-classical polemic are analyzed. It is shown that over the years these two camps have really come closer and closer together. It is argued that the basic issue separating them is the rapidity with which the economic system responds to price variations.

I. *Static Analysis*

1. The traditional interpretation of Keynesian economics is that it demonstrates the absence of an automatic mechanism assuring the equality of desired savings and investment at full employment. The graphical meaning of this interpretation is presented in a simplified form in Figure 1. Here desired real savings (S) and investment (I) are each assumed to depend only on the level of real income (Y). I_1, I_2, and I_3 represent three possible positions of the investment schedule. Y_0 is the full employment level of real income. If the investment desires of individuals are represented by the curve I_1, desired savings at full employment are greater than desired investment at full employment. This means that unemployment will result: the level of income will drop to Y_1, at which income desired savings and investment are equal.

* The author is assistant professor of economics at the University of Chicago. In the process of writing this paper he acknowledges having benefited from stimulating discussions with Milton Friedman, University of Chicago, and Alexander M. Henderson, University of Manchester.

Conversely, if I_3 is the investment curve, a situation of overemployment or inflation will occur: people desire to invest more at full employment than the amount of savings will permit. Only if the investment schedule happened to be I_2 would full employment desired investment and savings be equal. But since investment decisions are independent of savings decisions, there is no reason to expect the investment schedule to coincide with I_2. Hence there is no automatic assurance that full employment will result.

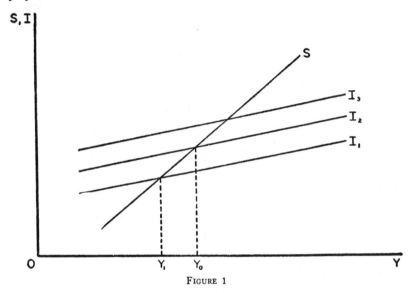

FIGURE 1

2. The classical answer to this attack is that desired savings and investment depend on the rate of interest, as well as the level of real income; and that, granted flexibility, variations in the interest rate serve as an automatic mechanism insuring full employment.

The argument can be interpreted as follows: the savings and investment functions (representing what people desire to do) are written as

$$S = \Omega\ (r,\ Y)$$
$$I = \Psi\ (r,\ Y)$$

where r represents the rate of interest.

Consider now Figure 2. On this graph there can be drawn a whole family of curves relating savings and investment to the rate of interest —one pair for each level of real income. In Figure 2, these pairs of curves are drawn for the full employment income, Y_0, and for the less than full employment income, Y_1. On the assumption that for a given rate of interest people will save and invest more at a higher level of income, the investment curve corresponding to $Y = Y_0$ is drawn above that corresponding to $Y = Y_1$; similarly for the two savings curves. The curves also reflect the assumption that, for a given level of real income, people desire to save more and invest less at higher rates of interest.

Consider now the pair of curves corresponding to the full employment income Y_0. If in Figure 2 the interest rate were r_1, then it would be true that individuals would desire to save more at full employment than they would desire to invest. But, assuming no rigidities in the interest rate, this would present no difficulties. For if the interest rate

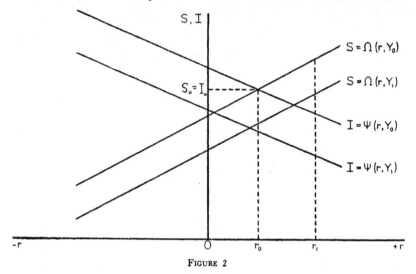

FIGURE 2

were to fall freely, savings would be discouraged, and investment stimulated until finally desired full employment savings and investment would be equated at the level $S_0 = I_0$. Similarly, if at full employment desired investment is greater than desired savings, a rise in the interest rate will prevent inflation. In this way variations in the rate of interest serve automatically to prevent any discrepancy between desired full employment investment and savings, and thus to assure full employment.

This argument can also be presented in terms of Figure 1: assume for simplicity that desired investment depends on the rate of interest as well as the level of real income, while desired savings depends only on the latter. Then downward variations in the interest rate can be counted on to raise the investment curve from, say, I_1 to I_2. That is, at any level of income people can be encouraged to invest more by a reduction in the rate of interest. Similarly, upward movements of the interest rate will shift the investment curve from, say, I_3 to I_2. Thus desired full employment savings and investment will always be equated.

3. The Keynesian answer to this classical argument is that it greatly exaggerates the importance of the interest rate. Empirical evidence has accumulated in support of the hypothesis that variations in the rate of interest have little effect on the amount of desired investment. (That savings are insensitive to the interest rate is accepted even by the classical school.) This insensitivity has been interpreted as a reflection of the presence of widespread uncertainty.[1] The possible effect of this insensitivity on the ability of the system automatically to generate full employment is analyzed in Figure 3. For simplicity the savings functions corresponding to different levels of income are reproduced from Figure 2. But the investment functions are now represented as being much less interest-sensitive than those in Figure 2. If the situation in

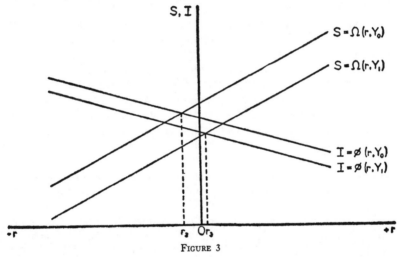

FIGURE 3

the real world were such as represented in Figure 3, it is clear that interest rate variations could never bring about full employment. For in an economy in which there are negligible costs of storing money, the interest rate can never be negative.[2] But from Figure 3 we see that the only way the interest rate can equate desired full employment savings and investment is by assuming the negative value r_2. Hence it is impossible for the full employment national income Y_0 to exist: for no

---

[1] *Cf.* Oscar Lange, *Price Flexibility and Employment* (Bloomington, Indiana, Principia Press, 1945) p. 85 and the literature cited there. For an excellent theoretical discussion of this insensitivity, *cf.* G. L. S. Shackle, "Interest Rates and the Pace of Investment," *Econ. Jour.*, Vol. LVI (1946), pp. 1-17.

[2] Note that in a dynamic world of rising prices, the effective rate of interest may become negative. But even here the *anticipated* effective rate cannot be negative. For in that event there would again be an infinite demand for money.

matter what (positive) rate of interest may prevail, the amount people want to save at full employment exceeds what they want to invest. Instead there will exist some less than full employment income (say) Y_1 for which desired savings and investment can be brought into equality at a positive rate of interest, (say) r_3 (*cf.* Figure 3).

Thus once again the automaticity of the system is thrown into question. Whether the system will generate full employment depends on whether the full employment savings and investment functions intersect at a positive rate of interest. But there is no automatic mechanism to assure that the savings and investment functions will have the proper slopes and positions to bring about such an intersection.[3]

4. Sometimes attempts are made to defend the classical position by arguing that the investment function is really higher (or the savings function lower) than represented by the Keynesians—so that desired full employment savings and investment can be equated at a positive rate of interest (*cf.* Figure 3). But this is beside the point. The fundamental reason Keynesian economics, if correct, destroys the foundations of classical economics, is that it denies the automaticity of the full employment posited by the latter. Hence a successful restatement of the classical position must demonstrate the existence of some automatic mechanism which will always bring about full employment. Thus to argue that *if* the investment or saving function is at a certain level, full employment will be brought about is irrelevant; what must be shown is that there exist forces which will *automatically* bring the investment or saving functions to the required level. In other words, the issue at stake is not the *possible,* but the *automatic,* generation of full employment.

5. In recent years Pigou has made a noteworthy attempt to remedy this deficiency in the classical theory.[4] Just as the "classics" responded to the crude Keynesian argument of § 1 by introducing a new variable —the rate of interest—into the savings function, so Pigou counters the more refined Keynesian attack of § 3 by introducing yet another variable—the absolute price level. That is, Pigou's saving schedule is a function of three variables:

$$S = \Gamma \ (r, Y, p),$$

where p represents the absolute price level.

His argument is as follows: if people would refuse to save anything

---

[3] This whole question of the contrast between the classical and the Keynesian position is discussed in much greater detail in a study which I hope to publish in the near future.

[4] A. C. Pigou, "The Classical Stationary State," *Econ. Jour.,* Vol. LIII (1943), pp. 343-51; "Economic Progress in a Stable Environment," *Economica,* n.s. XIV (1947), pp. 180-90. Although these articles deal only with a stationary state, their basic argument can readily be extended to the case in which net investment is taking place.

at negative and zero rates of interest, then the desired savings schedule would intersect the desired investment schedule at a positive rate of interest regardless of the level of income (*cf.* Figure 3). The willingness to save even without receiving interest, or even at a cost, must imply that savings are not made solely for the sake of future income (*i.e.*, interest) but also for "the desire for possession as such, conformity to tradition or custom and so on."[5] But the extent to which an individual wishes to save out of current income for reasons other than the desire of future income is inversely related to the real value of his cash balances.[6] If this is sufficiently large, all his secondary desires for saving will be fully satisfied. At this point the only reason he will con-

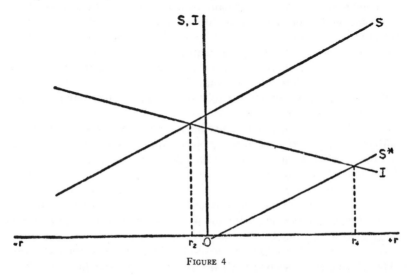

FIGURE 4

tinue to save out of current income is the primary one of anticipated future interest payments. In other words, if the real value of cash balances is sufficiently large, the savings function becomes zero at a positive rate of interest, regardless of the income level.

A graphical interpretation of this argument is presented in Figure 4. Here S and I are the full-employment savings and investment curves of Figure 3 (*i.e.*, those corresponding to $Y = Y_0$), and r_2 is again the negative rate of interest at which they are equal. Pigou then argues that by increasing the real value of cash balances, the full employment savings curve shifts to the right until it is in such a position that no

---

[5] *Ibid.*, p. 346.

[6] And all his other assets too. But the introduction of these other assets does not change Pigou's argument; while concentration on money assets brings out its (the argument's) basic aspect. *Cf.* below, § 6.

savings are desired except at positive rates of interest. This is represented by the savings curve S*, which becomes zero for a positive rate of interest. (In fact, S* shows dissaving taking place for sufficiently low rates of interest.) The full employment savings curve S* clearly intersects the full employment investment curve I at the positive rate of interest r₄. Thus by changing the real value of cash balances, desired full employment savings and investment can always be equated at a positive rate of interest.

How can we be sure that real cash balances will automatically change in the required direction and magnitude? Here Pigou brings in his assumptions of flexible wage and price levels, and a constant stock of money in circulation. If full employment saving exceeds investment, national income begins to fall, and unemployment results. If workers react to this by decreasing their money wages, then the price level will also begin to fall. As the latter continues to fall, the real value of the constant stock of money increases correspondingly. Thus, as the price level falls, the full employment saving function continuously shifts to the right until it intersects the full employment investment function at a positive rate of interest.[7]

This is the antomatic mechanism on which Pigou relies to assure full employment. It is essential to notice that it will operate regardless of the interest elasticity of the savings and investment functions—provided it is not zero.

6. The inner mechanism and distinctive characteristic of the Pigou analysis can be laid bare by considering it from a larger perspective. It is obvious that a price reduction has a stimulating effect on creditors. But, restricting ourselves to the private sector of a closed economy, to every stimulated creditor there corresponds a discouraged debtor. Hence from this viewpoint the net effect of a price reduction is likely to be in the neighborhood of zero. The neatness of the Pigou approach lies in its utilizing the fact that although the private sector considered in isolation is, on balance, neither debtor nor creditor, when considered

---

[7] The exact price level is determined when to our preceding four equations is added the liquidity preference equation $M_0 = \Lambda\,(r, p, Y)$. We then have the complete system of five equations in five variables:

$$I = \Phi\,(r, y)$$
$$S = \Gamma\,(r, p, Y)$$
$$I = S$$
$$Y = Y_0$$
$$M_0 = \Lambda\,(r, p, Y)$$

where M_0 represents the amount of money in the system. Under the Pigovian assumptions, this system possesses a consistent solution.

As will be shown in the next section, the "stock of money" (M_0) which enters in the last equation is completely different from the "stock of money" which is relevant for the Pigou analysis of the savings equation.

in its relationship to the government, it *must be* a net "creditor." This is due to the fact that the private sector always holds money, which is a (non-interest bearing) "debt" of government. If we assume that government activity is not affected by the movements of the absolute price level,[8] then the net effect of a price decline must always be stimulatory.[9] The community gains at the "expense" of a gracious government, ready, willing, and able to bear the "loss" of the increased value of its "debt" to the public.

More precisely, not every price decline need have this stimulating effect. For we must consider the effect of the price decline on the other assets held by the individual. If the decline reduces the real value of these other assets (*e.g.,* houses and other forms of consumer capital; stock shares; etc.) to an extent more than offsetting the increased value of real cash balances,[10] then the net effect will be discouraging. But the important point is that no matter what our initial position, *there exists* a price level sufficiently low so that the total real value of assets corresponding to it is greater than the original real value. Consider the extreme case in which the value of the other assets becomes arbitrarily small.[11] Clearly even here the real value of the fixed stock of money can be made as large as desired by reducing the price level sufficiently. Thus, to be rigorous, the statement in the preceding paragraph should read: "There always exists a price decline such that its effect is stimulatory." From this and the analysis of the preceding section, we can derive another statement which succinctly summarizes the results of the Pigou analysis: "In the static classical model, regardless of the position of the investment schedule, there always exists a sufficiently low price level such that full employment is generated." In any event, it is clearly sufficient to concentrate (as Pigou has done) on cash balances alone.[12]

From the preceding analysis we can also see just exactly what constitutes the "cash balance" whose increase in real value provides the stimulatory effect of the Pigou analysis. This balance clearly consists

[8] Pigou makes this assumption when he writes the investment function (which presumably also includes government expenditure) as independent of the absolute price level. *Cf.* footnote 7 above.

[9] It must be emphasized that I am abstracting here from all dynamic considerations of the effect on anticipations, etc. These will be discussed in Part II of the paper.

[10] A necessary (but not sufficient) condition for this to occur is that the price level of assets falls in a greater proportion than the general price level.

[11] I am indebted to M. Friedman for this example.

[12] *Cf.* above, footnote 6. Another possible reason for Pigou's emphasis on cash balances to the exclusion of other assets is that the relative illiquidity of the latter makes them less likely to be used as a means of satisfying the "irrational" motives of saving. Hence the inverse relationship between other assets and savings out of current income might not be so straightforward as that between real cash balances and savings.

of the net obligation of the government to the private sector of the economy. That is, it consists of the sum of interest- and non-interest-bearing government debt held outside the treasury and central bank. Thus, by excluding demand deposits and including government interest-bearing debt, it differs completely from what is usually regarded as the stock of money.

These same conclusions can be reached through a somewhat different approach. Begin with the ordinary concept of the stock of money as consisting of hand-to-hand currency and demand deposits. Consider now what changes must be made in order to arrive at the figure relevant for the Pigou analysis. Clearly, government interest-bearing debt must be added, since a price decline increases its value. Now consider money in the form of demand deposits. To the extent that it is backed by bank loans and discounts, the gains of deposit holders are offset by the losses of bank debtors.[13] Thus the net effect of a price decline on demand deposits is reduced to its effect on the excess of deposits over loans, or (approximately) on the reserves of the banks held in the form of hand-to-hand currency. Finally, hand-to-hand currency held by individuals outside the banking system is added in, and we arrive at exactly the same figure as in the preceding paragraph.

For convenience denote the stock of money relevant for the Pigou analysis by M_1. Note that this is completely different from the M_0 of footnote 7: for M_0 is defined in the usual manner as hand-to-hand currency plus demand deposits. This distinction is of fundamental importance. One of its immediate implications is that open market operations affect the economic system only through the liquidity preference equation. Since these operations merely substitute one type of government debt (currency) for another (bonds), they have no effect on M_1, and hence no direct effect on the amount of savings. We shall return to this point later.

7. How does the Pigou formulation compare with the original classical theory?[14] Although both Pigou and the "classics" stress the importance of "price flexibility," they mean completely different things. The "classics" are talking about flexibility of *relative* prices; Pigou is talking about flexibility of *absolute* prices. The classical school holds

---

[13] *Cf.* M. Kalecki, "Professor Pigou on 'The Classical Stationary State'—A Comment," *Econ. Jour.*, Vol. LIV (1944), pp. 131-32.

[14] Pigou's system, of course, assigns to the absolute price level a major role; whereas the classical system depends only on relative prices. But this difference is due to the fact that they are really concerned with different questions, since the classical analysis abstracts completely from the problem of money.

The preceding comment raises some fundamental and very complicated issues which, being somewhat extraneous to the main purpose of this essay, cannot be discussed here. *Cf.* D. Patinkin, "Relative Prices, Say's Law, and the Demand for Money," *Econometrica*, Vol. XVI (1948), pp. 135-54.

that the existence of long-run unemployment is *prima facie* evidence of rigid wages. The only way to eliminate unemployment is, then, by reducing *real* wages. (Since workers can presumably accomplish this end by reducing their money wage, this position has implicit in it the assumption of a constant price level.)[15] Pigou now recognizes that changing the relative price of labor is not enough, and that the absolute price level itself must vary. In fact, a strict interpretation of Pigou's position would indicate that unemployment can be eliminated even if real wages remain the same or even rise (namely, if the proportionate fall in prices is greater than or equal to that of wages); for in any case the effect of increased real value of cash balances is still present.[16]

The Pigou analysis differs also from the more sophisticated interpretations of the classical position. These present the effect of a wage decrease as acting through the liquidity preference equation to increase the real value of M_0 and thereby reduce the rate of interest; this in turn stimulates both consumption and investment expenditures—thus generating a higher level of national income. To this effect, Pigou now adds the direct stimulus to consumption expenditures provided by the price decline and the accompanying increase in real balances. Consequently, even if the savings and investment functions are completely insensitive to changes in the rate of interest (so that the "classical" effect through the liquidity equation is completely inoperative), a wage decrease will still be stimulatory through its effect on real balances and hence on savings.

8. Before concluding this part of the paper, one more point must be clarified. The *explicit* assumption of the Pigou analysis is that savings are directly related to the price level, and therefore inversely related to the size of real cash balances. This assumption by itself is, on *a priori* grounds, quite reasonable; but it must be emphasized that it is insufficient to bring about the conclusion desired by Pigou; for this purpose he *implicitly* makes an additional, and possibly less reasonable, assumption. Specifically, in addition to postulating explicitly the *direction* of the relationship between savings and the price level, he also implies something about its *intensity*.

The force of this distinction is illustrated by Figure 5. Here S and I are the full employment savings and investment curves of Figure 3 (*i.e.*, those corresponding to $Y = Y_0$) for a fixed price level, p_0. The other savings curves, S_1, S_2, S_3, S_4, represent the full employment

---

[15] Or at least one falling relatively less than wages.

[16] The role of real wages in Pigou's system is very ambiguous. At one point (p. 348, bottom) he assumes that reduced money wages will also decrease real wages. At another (p. 349, lines 20-38) no such assumption seems to be involved. ("As money wage-rates fall . . . prices fall and go on falling." *Ibid.*)

savings schedules corresponding to the different price levels p_1, p_2, p_3, p_4, respectively. In accordance with the Pigou assumption, as the price level falls, the savings function shifts over to the right. (That is p_1, p_2, p_3, p_4 are listed in descending order.) But it may well be that as the real value of their cash balances continues to increase, people are less and less affected by this increase. That is, for each successive increase in real balances (for each successive price level decline) the savings function moves less and less to the right, until eventually it might respond only infinitesimally, no matter how much prices fall. In graphical terms, as the price decline continues, the savings function might reach S_3 as a limiting position. That is, no matter how much the price level might fall, the savings function would never move to the right of S_3.[17] In such an event the declining price level would fail to bring about full employment. The validity of the Pigou argument thus depends on the additional assumption that the intensity of the inverse relationship between savings and real cash balances is such that it will be possible to shift over the savings function to a position where it will intercept the investment function at a positive rate of interest: say, S_4 (*cf.* Figure 5).

What is at issue here is the reaction of individuals with already large real balances to further increases in these balances. Consider an individual with a cash balance of a fixed number of dollars. As the price falls, the increased real value of these dollars must be allocated between the alternatives of an addition to either consumption and/or real balances.[18] How the individual will actually allocate the increase clearly depends on the relative marginal utilities of these two alternatives. If we are willing to assume that the marginal utility of cash balances approaches zero with sufficient rapidity relative to that of consumption, then we can ignore the possibility of the savings curve reaching a limiting position such as in Figure 5. That is, we would be maintaining the position that by increasing the individual's balances sufficiently, he will have no further incentive to add to these balances; hence he will

---

[17] Mathematically this may be stated as follows. Write the savings function as
$$S = \Gamma(r, p, Y).$$
(*Cf.* footnote 7, above.) Pigou's explicit assumption is
$$\Gamma_p(r, p, Y) > 0$$
where Γ_p is the partial derivative of S with respect to p. Yet $Y = Y_0$ represent the full employment income. Then the argument here is that the savings function, Γ, may still be of a form such that
$$\lim_{p \to 0} \Gamma(r, p, Y_0) = \Gamma^*(r, Y_0)$$
for any fixed r—where Γ^* is any curve which intersects the investment curve at a negative rate of interest. (In the argument of the text, Γ^* is taken to be S_3 in Figure 5.) Pigou tacitly assumes that the savings function approaches no such limit; or that if it does, the limiting function intersects the investment function at a positive rate of interest.

[18] I am abstracting here from the possible third alternative, investment.

spend any additional real funds on consumption, so that we can make him consume any amount desired. If, on the other hand, we admit the possibility that, for sufficiently large consumption, the decrease in the marginal utility of cash balances is accompanied by a much faster decrease in the marginal utility of consumption, then the individual will continuously use most of the additional real funds (made available by the price decline) to add to his balances. In this event, the situation of Figure 5 may well occur.

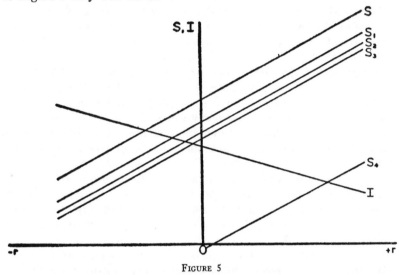

FIGURE 5

9. I do not believe we have sufficient evidence—either of an *a priori* or empirical[19] nature—to help us answer the question raised in the preceding paragraph. The empirical evidence available is consistent with the hypothesis that the effect of real balances on savings is very weak. But even granted the truth of this hypothesis, it casts no light on the question raised here. What we want to know is what happens to the effect of real balances on savings as these real balances increase in size. Even if the effect were arbitrarily small, but remained constant regardless of the size of real balances, there could be no convergence of savings functions like that pictured in Figure 5. In the face of this lack of evidence, we have to be satisfied with the conclusion that,

[19] Empirical studies on the effect of real balances on savings have been made by L. R. Klein, "The Use of Econometric Models as a Guide to Economic Policy," *Econometrica*, Vol. XV (1947), pp. 122-25. Klein's procedure was incorrect in that he used a series for M_0, instead of M_1 in fitting his equations (*cf.* last paragraph of § 6 above). However, another study, using the correct M_1 series, has been carried out by the writer in conjunction with Kenneth J. Arrow of the Cowles Commission. This study shows that the effect of cash balances on saving is at best very small.

subject to the provisos of the preceding section, Pigou has demonstrated the automaticity of full employment within the framework of the classical static model[20]—the main mechanism by which this is brought about being the effect of a price decline on cash balances.

The statement of this conclusion immediately raises the interesting question of how this set of forces, uncovered by Pigou, could have been overlooked by Keynesian economists, in general, and Keynes himself, in particular. Questions of this type can rarely be answered satisfactorily—and perhaps should not even be asked. Nevertheless, I think it is both possible and instructive to trace through the exact chain of errors in Keynes's reasoning which caused him to overlook these factors.

I submit the hypothesis that Keynes recognized the influence of assets on saving (consumption), but unfortunately thought of this influence only in terms of physical capital assets. This was his fundamental error.[21] From it immediately followed that in his main discussion of the (short-run) consumption function, where he assumed a *constant* stock of capital, the possible influence of assets was not (and could not) even be considered.[22] But as soon as Keynes discussed a period sufficiently long for noticeable capital growth, the influence of assets on savings was immediately recognized.[23] Even here Keynes could not come to the same conclusion as Pigou. For Keynes restricted himself to physical assets, and thus rightfully pointed out that it would be "an unlikely coincidence" that just the correct amount of assets should exist—*i.e.*, that amount which would push over the savings function to such a position where full employment could be generated. Compare this with the determinate process by which just exactly the "correct amount" of real cash balances is brought into existence in the Pigou analysis. (See above, § 5, paragraph 4.)

This exclusion of physical assets from the short-run consumption function was subconsciously extended to all kinds of assets. Here was the last link in the chain of errors. For later when Keynes began to examine the effects of increased real cash balances (brought about either by price declines or increases in the amount of money), he did not even consider their possible influence on consumption. Instead, he

[20] It must be re-emphasized that this conclusion holds only for static analysis. The modifications that must be introduced once dynamic factors enter are discussed in Part II.

[21] Note that there are really two distinct errors involved here. The first is the obvious one of the exclusion of monetary assets. The second is that what is relevant for the influence on saving is not the *physical* asset, but its *real* value in terms of some general price level.

[22] J. M. Keynes, *The General Theory of Employment, Interest, and Money* (New York, Harcourt, Brace, and Co., 1936), Chap. 8. See especially pp. 91-95, where Keynes considers the possible influence of other factors besides income on consumption, and does not even mention assets.

[23] *Ibid.*, p. 218, second paragraph.

concentrated exclusively on their tendency, through the liquidity function, to lower interest rates.[24] (*Cf.* above, § 7, last paragraph.)

Looking back on the nature of these errors, we cannot but be struck by the irony that they should have emanated from the man who did most to demonstrate the fundamental inseparability of the real and monetary sectors of our economy.

II. *Dynamic Analysis: The Question of Policy*

10. The Pigou analysis discussed in Part I makes two contributions. First, it uncovers a hitherto neglected set of forces at work—in its analysis of the effect of a price decline on savings through its effect on real balances. (For convenience this will be referred to as the Pigou effect.) Secondly, it proceeds to draw the implications of this new set of forces for static analysis, and summarizes its results in the following theorem (*cf.* §§ 5 and 6): *There always exists a sufficiently low price level such that, if expected to continue indefinitely,*[25] *it will generate full employment.*[26] (For convenience this will be referred to as the Pigou Theorem.) The purpose of this part of the paper is to accomplish a third objective: *viz.*, to draw the implications of the Pigou effect for dynamic analysis and policy formulation. It must be emphasized that the Pigou Theorem tells us nothing about the dynamic and policy aspects which interest us in this third objective. (This point is discussed in greater detail in § 12.)

Specifically, consider a full employment situation which is suddenly terminated by a downswing in economic activity. The question I now wish to examine is the usefulness of a policy which consists of maintaining the stock of money constant, allowing the wage and price levels to fall, and waiting for the resulting increase in real balances to restore full employment.

At the outset it must be made clear that the above policy recommendation is *not* to be attributed to Pigou. His interest is purely an intellectual one, in a purely static analysis. As he himself writes: ". . . The puzzles we have been considering . . . are academic exercises, of some slight use perhaps for clarifying thought, but with very little chance of ever being posed on the chequer board of actual life."[27]

---

[24] *Ibid.*, pp. 231-34, 266. The following passage is especially interesting: "It is, therefore, on the effect of a falling wage- and price-level on the *demand for money* that those who believe in the self-adjusting quality of the economic system must rest the weight of their argument; though I am not aware that they have done so. If the quantity of money is itself a function of the wage- and price-level, there is, indeed, nothing to hope for in this direction. But if the quantity of money is virtually fixed, it is evident that its quantity in terms of wage-units can be indefinitely increased by a sufficient reduction in money wages. . . ." (*Ibid.*, p. 266. Italics not in original.)

[25] This qualifying phrase incorporates in it the restriction of the Pigou argument to static analysis.

[26] I ignore here, as I do throughout the remainder of the paper, the difficulties raised in § 8.

[27] "Economic Progress in a Stable Environment," *Economica*, n.s. XIV (1947), p. 188.

In reality, Pigou's disavowal of a deflationary policy (contained in the paragraph from which the above quotation is taken) is not nearly as thoroughgoing as might appear on the first reading. The rejection of a price decline as a practical means of combatting unemployment may be due to: (a) the conviction that dynamic considerations invalidate its use as an immediate policy, regardless of its merits in static analysis; (b) the conviction that industrial and labor groups, sometimes with the assistance of government, prevent the price flexibility necessary for the success of a deflationary policy. A careful reading of Pigou's disclaimer indicates that he had only the second of these alternatives in mind; *i.e.*, that he felt that the policy would not work because it would not be permitted to work. What I hope to establish in this part of the essay is the first alternative: namely, that even granted full flexibility of prices, it is still highly possible that a deflationary policy will not work, due to the dynamic factors involved.

Nevertheless, nothing in this part of the paper is intended (or even relevant) as a criticism of Pigou, since the latter has clearly abstained from the problem of policy formulation. If sometimes the terms "Pigou effect" and "Pigou Theorem" are used in the following discussion, they should be understood solely as shorthand notations for the concepts previously explained.

11. The analysis of this section is based on the following two assumptions: (a) One of the prerequisites of a successful anti-depression policy is that it should be able to achieve its objective rapidly (say, within a year). (b) Prices cannot fall instantaneously; hence, the larger the price level fall necessary to bring about full employment *via* the Pigou effect, the longer the time necessary for the carrying out of the policy. (If no price fall can bring about full employment, then we can say that an infinite amount of time is necessary for the carrying out of the policy.)

There are at least two factors which act toward lengthening the period necessary to carry out a policy based on the Pigou effect. (It should be noted that none of these difficulties arises when the discussion is restricted to static analysis.) The first is the possibility that the effect of an increase in cash balances on consumption is so small, that very large increases (very great price declines) will be necessary. Certainly the burden of proof lies on those supporting a policy of absolute price flexibility to show that the economic system is sufficiently responsive to make the policy practical. So far, no one has presented the required evidence. On the contrary, whatever evidence exists indicates that the dependence of savings on cash balances is much too weak to be of any practical use (*cf.* above, footnote 19).

The second factor is a result of the price decline itself. In dynamic analysis we must give full attention to the role played by price expectations and anticipations in general. It is quite possible that the original price decline will lead to the expectation of further declines. Then purchasing decisions will be postponed, aggregate demand will fall off, and the amount of unemployment increased still more. In terms of Figures 1 and 3, the savings function will rise (consumption will be decreased) and the investment function fall, further aggravating the problem of achieving full employment. This was the point on which Keynes was so insistent.[28] Furthermore, the uncertainty about the future generated by the price decline will increase the liquidity preference of individuals. Thus if we consider an individual possessing a fixed number of dollars, and confronted with a price decline which increases the real value of these dollars, his uncertainty will make him more inclined to employ these additional real funds to increase his real balances, than to increase his expenditures.[29] In other words, the uncertainty created by the price decline might cause people to accumulate indefinitely large real cash balances, and to increase their expenditures very little, if at all.

The simultaneous interaction of this last factor with the first one will further exacerbate these difficulties. For as the period of price decline drags itself out, anticipations for the future will progressively worsen, and uncertainties further increase. The end result of letting the Pigou effect work itself out may be a disastrous deflationary spiral, continuing for several years without ever reaching any equilibrium position. Certainly our past experiences should have sensitized us to this danger.

Because of these considerations I feel that it is impractical to depend upon the Pigou effect as a means of policy: the required price decline might be either too large (factor one), or it might be the initial step of an indefinite deflationary spiral (factor two).

On this issue, it may be interesting to investigate the experience of the United States in the 1930's. In Table I, net balances are computed for the period 1929-32 according to the definition in § 6. As can be seen, although there was an 18 per cent *increase* in real balances from 1930 to 1931, real national income during this period *decreased* by 13 per cent. Even in the following year, when a further increase of 24 per cent in real balances took place, real income proceeded to fall by an additional 18 per cent. For the 1929-1932 period as a whole there was an increase in real balances of 38 per cent, and a decrease in real income of 40 per cent.

It will, of course, be objected that these data reflect the presence of "special factors," and do not indicate the real value of the Pigou effect. But the pertinent question which immediately arises is: To what extent

---

[28] See his discussion of changes in money wages, *op. cit.*, pp. 260-69, especially p. 263. *Cf.* also J. R. Hicks, *Value and Capital* (Oxford, Oxford University Press, 1939), and O. Lange, *op. cit.*

[29] *Cf.* above, § 8, last paragraph.

were these "special factors" necessary, concomitant results of the price decline itself! If the general feeling of uncertainty and adverse anticipations that marked the period is cited as one of these "special factors," the direct relationship between this and the decline in price level itself certainly cannot be overlooked. Other proposed "special factors" must be subjected to the same type of examination. The data of the preceding table are not offered as conclusive evidence. But they are certainly consistent with the previously stated hypothesis of the impracticability of using the Pigou effect as a means of policy; and they

TABLE I

Year	Money in Circulation (1)[a]	Government Debt (2)[b]	Net Balance of Individuals (3)[c]	Cost of Living Index (4)[d]	Net Real Balances of Individuals (5)[e]	Real National Income (6)[f]
1929	4.5	15.5	20.0	1.22	16.4	89.9
1930	4.2	14.3	18.5	1.19	15.5	76.3
1931	4.5	15.4	19.9	1.09	18.3	66.3
1932	5.4	16.8	22.2	.98	22.7	54.2

[a] Money in circulation as of June 30 outside the Treasury and Federal Reserve Banks, in billions of current dollars, _Banking and Monetary Statistics_, p. 408.

[b] Government interest bearing debt as of June 30, held outside government agencies and the Federal Reserve Bank, in billions of current dollars. _Ibid._, p. 512.

[c] $(3) = (1) + (2)$

[d] Bureau of Labor Statistics, cost of living index, _Survey of Current Business_, Supplement, 1942, p. 16.

[e] $(5) = (3) \div (4)$

[f] National income in billions of 1944 dollars. J. Dewhurst and Associates, _America's Needs and Resources_ (New York, The Twentieth Century Fund, 1947), p. 697.

certainly throw the burden of proof on those who argue for its practicality.

12. The argument of the preceding section requires further explanation on at least one point. In the discussion of the "second factor" there was mentioned the possibility of an indefinitely continuing spiral of deflation and unemployment. But what is the relation between this possibility and the Pigou Theorem (_cf._ § 10) established in Part I? The answer to this question may be expressed as follows:

On the downswing of the business cycle it might be interesting to know that there exists a sufficiently low price level which, if it were expected to continue existing indefinitely, would bring about full employment. Interesting, but, for policy purposes, irrelevant. For due to perverse price expectations and the dynamics of deflationary spirals, it is impossible to reach (or, once having reached, to remain at) such a position.

The implication of these remarks can be clarified by consideration of the cobweb theorem for the divergent case. Assume that a certain market can be explained in terms of the cobweb theorem. It is desired to know whether (assuming unchanged demand and supply curves) the designated market will ever reach a stationary position; that is, whether it will settle down to a unique price that will continue indefinitely to clear the market. This question is clearly divided into two parts: (a) does there exist such a price, and (b) if it does exist, will the market be able to attain it. In the case of the cobweb presented in Figure 6 it is clear that such a price does exist. For if the price p_0

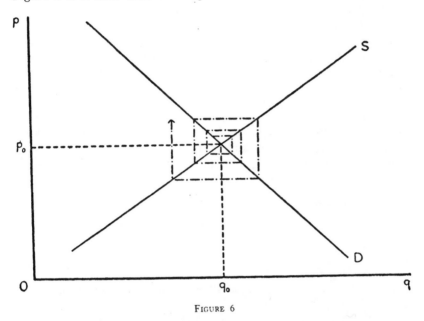

FIGURE 6

had always existed and were expected to exist indefinitely, it would continuously clear the market. But Figure 6 represents the case of a divergent cobweb; hence the market will never be able to reach the price p_0. In brief, even though p_0 exists, it is irrelevant to the workings of the market. The analogy to the argument of the preceding paragraph is obvious.[30]

III. *Conclusions*

13. The conclusions of this paper can be summarized as follows:

---

[30] The distinction of this section can be expressed in rigorous mathematical form using the dynamic system which has become familiar through the work of Samuelson and Lange (P. A. Samuelson, "The Stability of Equilibrium: Comparative Statics and Dynamics," *Econometrica*, Vol. IX [1941], pp. 97-120. Lange, *op. cit.*, pp. 91 ff.) Consider a single market and let D, S, and p represent the demand, supply and price of the particular good, respectively. Let t represent time. Then we can write this system as

in a static world with a constant stock of money,[31] price flexibility assures full employment. (I abstract here again from the difficulties raised in § 8.) But in the real dynamic world in which we live, price flexibility with a constant stock of money might generate full employment only after a long period; or might even lead to a deflationary spiral of continuous unemployment. On either of these grounds, a full employment policy based on a constant stock of money and price flexibility does not seem to be very promising.

All that this means is that our full employment policy cannot be the fairly simple one of maintaining a constant stock of money and waiting for the economic system to generate full employment automatically through price declines. Other policies will be required. One possible alternative policy can be inferred from the Pigou analysis itself: there are two ways to increase real balances. One is to keep the money stock constant and permit prices to fall. An equally effective way is to maintain the price level constant, and increase the stock of money by creating a government deficit.[32] This method of increasing real balances has the added advantage of avoiding one of the difficulties encountered previously (§ 11), for a policy of stabilizing the price

(a) $D = f(p)$ demand function

(b) $S = g(p)$ supply function

(c) $\frac{dp}{dt} = h(D-S)$ market adjusting function

The last equation has the property that

(d) $\text{sign} \frac{dp}{dt} = \text{sign} (D-S)$

i.e., price rises with excess demand and falls with excess supply. Consider now the static system identical with (a) — (c), except that it replaces (c) by

(e) $D = S$

As long as (e) is not satisfied, we see from (d) that the system will not be in stationary equilibrium, but will continue to fluctuate. Thus the existence of a solution to the static system (a), (b), (e) (*i.e.*, the consistency of (a), (b), (e) is a *necessary* condition for the existence of a stationary solution for the dynamic system (a), (b), (c). But this is not a sufficient condition. For the static system (a), (b), (e) may have a consistent solution which, if the dynamic system is not convergent, will never be reached.

Thus Pigou has completed only half the task. Setting aside the difficulties of § 8, we can accept his proof of the *consistency* of the *static* classical system. But that still leaves completely unanswered the question of whether the classical *dynamic* system will converge to this consistent solution. In this and the preceding section I have tried to show why such convergence may not occur in the real world. (I have discussed these issues in greater detail elsewhere. *Cf.* footnote 3, above.)

[31] Throughout Part III, unless otherwise indicated, "stock of money" is to be understood in the M_1 sense of the last paragraph of § 6.

[32] Considered from this perspective, the Pigou analysis presents in a rigorous fashion part of the theoretical framework implicit in the fiscal-monetary policy of the Simons-Mints position. *Cf.* the recently published collection of essays of Henry C. Simons, *Economic Policy for a Free Society* (University of Chicago Press, Chicago, 1948); and Lloyd W. Mints, "Monetary Policy," *Rev. Econ. Stat.*, Vol. XXVIII (1946), pp. 60-69.

level by increasing money stocks avoids some of the dangers of uncertainty and adverse anticipation accompanying general price declines. Nevertheless, there still remains the other difficulty—that individuals may not be very sensitive to increases in real balances. If this turned out to be true, we would have to seek still other policies.

14. We have come a long way from the crude Keynesian model of § 1. And now we can re-examine that question which has been the favorite of economists these past few years: what is the distinctive characteristic of Keynesian analysis? It certainly cannot be the claim to have demonstrated the possibility of the coexistence of underemployment equilibrium and flexible prices. This, in its day, served well as a rallying cry. But now it should be definitely recognized that this is an indefensible position. For flexibility means that the money wage falls with excess supply, and rises with excess demand; and equilibrium means that the system can continue on through time without change. Hence, by definition, a system with price flexibility cannot be in equilibrium if there is any unemployment.[33]

Nor should Keynesian economics be interpreted as asserting that just as an underemployment equilibrium is impossible, so, too, in a static system may a full-employment equilibrium be impossible. That is, the static system may be at neither an underemployment equilibrium, nor a full-employment equilibrium. In other words, the static system may be inconsistent. (This is the negative interest rate argument of § 3.) For Pigou's discussion of the effect of a declining price level on real balances shows how this inconsistency is removed. It is, of course, still possible to maintain this interpretation of Keynes on the basis of the argument of § 8. But I think this is neither necessary nor advisable. For the real significance of the Keynesian contribution can be realized only within the framework of *dynamic* economics. Whether

[33] This can be expressed mathematically in the following way: let N^S and N^D be the amounts of labor supplied and demanded, respectively; w, the money wage rate; and t, time. Then a flexible dynamic system will, by definition, contain an equation of the general type

$$\frac{dw}{dt} = f(N^D - N^S)$$

where

$$\text{sign } \frac{dw}{dt} = \text{sign } (N^D - N^S).$$

If by equilibrium is meant a situation such that

$$\frac{dw}{dt} = 0$$

then clearly this system cannot be in equilibrium unless

$$N^D - N^S = 0$$

i.e., unless there is full employment.

or not an underemployment equilibrium exists; whether or not full employment equilibrium always will be generated in a static system—all this is irrelevant. The fundamental issue raised by Keynesian economics is the *stability of the dynamic system:* its ability to return automatically to a full-employment equilibrium within a reasonable time (say, a year) if it is subjected to the customary shocks and disturbances of a peacetime economy. In other words, what Keynesian economics claims is that the economic system may be in a position of underemployment *dis*equilibrium (in the sense that wages, prices, and the amount of unemployment are continuously changing over time) for long, or even indefinite, periods of time.

But this is not sufficient to characterize the Keynesians. Everyone agrees that there exist dynamic systems which will not automatically generate full employment. What distinguishes one economic school from the other is the system (or systems) to which this lack of automaticity is attributed. If the Keynesian message is applied to an economic system with no monetary policy (if such a thing is possible to define), then it is purely trivial. For few would claim automaticity of full employment for such a system. Keynesian theory acquires meaning only when applied to systems with more intelligent monetary policies. Here an element of arbitrariness is introduced; for what is termed "Keynesian" depends entirely on the choice of the monetary policy to be used as a criterion.

On the basis of Keynes' writings, I believe it is clear that he was primarily interested in attacking the policy of assuring full employment by manipulation of the interest rate through open market operations.[34] But to Keynes, this policy was equivalent to one of wage flexibility;[35] increase the real value of the stock of money (in the M_0, not M_1, sense; *cf.* above, last paragraph of § 6) and thereby decrease the rate of for (he erroneously thought) the only effect of a wage decline was to interest—just as in open market operations. As we have pointed out above (end of §§ 6 and 7), these policies are really not equivalent. For open market operations change only M_0, whereas a wage and price decline change the real value of M_1 as well. Hence, open market operations act only through the liquidity preference equation, whereas a policy of price flexibility acts also through the savings function (*cf.* above, footnote 7 and end of § 6).

Let us now assume that even if Keynes had recognized the distinction between open market and wage flexibility policies (*i.e.*, if he had

---

[34] *Cf.* Keynes, *op. cit.*, pp. 231-34; 266-67.

[35] "There is, therefore, no ground for the belief that a flexible wage policy is capable of maintaining a state of continuous full employment;—any more than for the belief that an open market monetary policy is capable, unaided, of achieving this result. The economic system cannot be made self-adjusting along these lines." (*Ibid.*, p. 267.)

recognized the Pigou effect) he still would have continued to reject the latter as a means of assuring full employment. This is not an unreasonable assumption; for the objections cited above (§ 11) against the use of a policy based on the Pigou effect, are the very same ones that Keynes uses in arguing against open market operations.[36]

Granted this assumption, I believe it is useful to identify the Keynesian position against one which maintains that full employment can be automatically achieved *via* the Pigou effect by maintaining a constant stock of money, and providing for wage and price flexibility. It is now possible to delineate three distinct theoretical formulations of the Keynesian position—differing in varying degrees from the classical one: (a) Most opposed to the classical position is the Keynesian one which states that even if there were no problem of uncertainty and adverse anticipations (that is, even if there were a static system), and even if we were to allow an infinite amount of time for adjustment, a policy of price flexibility would still not assure the generation of full employment. (This is the negative interest rate argument of §§ 3 and 8.) (b) Then there is the position which states that, in a static world, price flexibility would always assure full employment. But in a dynamic world of uncertainty and adverse anticipations, even if we were to allow an infinite adjustment period, there is no certainty that full employment will be generated. That is, we may remain indefinitely in a position of underemployment disequilibrium. (c) Finally, there is the Keynesian position, closest to the "classics," which states that even with uncertainty full employment would eventually be generated by a policy of price flexibility; but the length of time that might be necessary for the adjustment makes the policy impractical. The ease with which each of these three positions can be defended is inversely related to its distance from the classical position.

Although these positions are quite distinct theoretically, their policy implications are very similar. (In what way would the policies of a man advocating position (a) differ from those of a man advocating (c) and stating that the adjustment would take ten years?) The policies would in general be directed at influencing the consumption and investment functions themselves, in addition to manipulating the amount of money. Thus the policies may advocate tax reductions to stimulate consumption and investment (the Simons-Mints school); or may insist on direct government investment to supplement private investment (Hansen, *et al.*). In this way we could cross-classify Keynesian positions according to their advocated policies, as well as their theoretical foundations.

---

[36] *Cf.* the passages cited in footnote 34, above.

[25]

The Golden Rule of Accumulation: A Fable for Growthmen

Once upon a time the Kingdom of Solovia was gripped by a great debate. "This is a growing economy but it can grow faster," many argued. "Sustainable growth is best," came the reply, "and that can come only from natural forces."

A few called the debate growthmanship. But most thought it would be healthy if it led to a better understanding of Solovian growth. So the King appointed a task force to learn the facts of Solovian economic life.

The committee reported that the labor force and population in Solovia grew exponentially at the rate γ. The number of working Solovians, N_t, at time t was therefore given by

$$(1) \qquad N_t = N_0 e^{\gamma t}, \qquad\qquad \gamma > 0.$$

The report expressed confidence that Solovia's supply of natural resources would remain adequate. It portrayed a competitive economy making full and efficient use of its only scarce factors, labor and capital, in the production of a single, all-satisfying commodity. Returns to scale were observed to be constant, and capital and labor were found to be so substitutable that fears of technological unemployment were dismissed.

The committee described the steady progress in Solovia's ways of production. It estimated that the efficiency of Solovian capital was increasing at the rate λ and that Solovian labor was improving at the rate μ. A continuation of these rates of technical advance was anticipated. Therefore production, P_t, at time t, was the following function of available capital, K_t, and the current labor force:

$$(2) \qquad P_t = F\,(e^{\lambda t} K_t\,,\,e^{\mu t} N_t), \qquad\qquad \lambda \geq 0, \mu \geq 0.$$

The report acknowledged further investigation of the production function might prove to be desirable.

Then the task force approached the growth issue. It doubted that technological advance could be accelerated and it took no positive stand on population increase. If γ, λ and μ were fixed parameters, then hope had to rest entirely on investment. While maintenance of the existing ratio of capital to labor would permit output per worker and per head to grow by virtue of technical progress, the report voiced the hope that higher incomes and perhaps a greater growth rate would be sought through a continuous increase in capital per worker, or what the task force called capital-deepening. It concluded by declaring the proper pace of capital-deepening to be a momentous question for Solovian political economy.

The King commended the task force for its informative and stimulating report. He invited all his subjects to join in search of an optimal investment policy. Solovian theorists considered dozens of fiscal devices for their efficiency, equity and effectiveness. Mathematicians, leading the quest for a growth strategy, grappled with extremals, functionals and Hamiltonians. Yet nothing practicable emerged.

Then a policy-maker was heard to say, "Forget grand optimality. Solovians are a simple people. We need a simple policy. Let us require that the fraction of output accumulated be fixed for all time, that is:

(3) $$\frac{dK_t}{dt} = sP_t, \text{ for all } t, 0 \leq s \leq 1.$$

If we make investment a constant proportion of output, our search for the idea investment policy reduces to finding the best value of s, the fixed investment ratio."

"It's fair," Solovians all said. The King agreed. So he established a prize for the discovery of the optimum investment ratio. The prize was to be a year abroad to learn how advanced countries had solved the growth problem.

Soon a brilliant peasant, Oiko Nomos, claimed the prize. Solovians laid down their tools, picked up pencils and pads, and converged on their capital to hear the proposed solution.

Oiko spoke. "I begin with a definition. By a *golden age* I shall mean a dynamic equilibrium in which output and capital grow exponentially at the same rate so that the capital-output ratio is stationary over time. This is precisely the pattern of growth which might emerge asymptotically from the regime contemplated for Solovia where population growth and technical progress are expected to be exponential and the investment ratio is to be fixed for all time.

"Now I am obliged to make some assumptions which I hope later researches into the exact shape of our production function will support:

"First, I assume that Solovia is capable of golden-age growth. This simply means that, corresponding to every investment ratio Solovia might adopt, there exists at least one capital-output ratio which, if established, will be exactly maintained by the dynamic equilibrium which follows from equations (1)-(3).

"Second, I assume that Solovia's golden-age growth rate is independent of its investment ratio We may call this growth rate, g, the *natural* rate of growth, in that it depends not upon our investment decisions but only upon γ, λ, μ and possibly certain parameters affecting the shape of the production function. The existence of a natural growth rate implies capital and labor are substitutable in such a way that the capital-output ratio can adjust to any value of s so as to equate the rate of capital growth,

$$\frac{sP_t}{K_t}, \text{ to the natural rate of output growth, } g.$$

"We can express the output of an economy in a golden age and having a natural growth rate by the equation:

(4) $$P_t = P_0 e^{gt}, \qquad g > 0$$

where P_0 depends upon conditions at time zero.

"We come now to a crucial notion. Consider an economy which lacks a definite beginning and which has always enjoyed golden-age growth at the natural rate. It has traveled unswervingly up a single exponential path, a path stretching back indefinitely into the past. Along this path the output rate at any specified time (though not the rate of growth) depends, in general, upon the value of the equilibrium capital-output ratio. But this ratio depends upon the investment ratio that has reigned over the golden age; we noted earlier that under conditions of natural growth the capital-output ratio is simply:

$$(5) \qquad \frac{K_t}{P_t} = \frac{s}{g}.$$

Therefore, the golden-age output rate at any time—the height of the growth path—is generally a function of the prevailing value of s. We can express this fact by replacing P_0 in (4) by the function $f(s)$. Thus:

$$(6) \qquad P_t = f(s)e^{gt}.$$

"It has been observed that a large value of s corresponds to a small ratio of output to capital. Provided that the elasticity of output with respect to capital is uniformly smaller than one, a seeming condition for stability, the smaller the ratio of output to capital, the larger must be the absolute magnitudes of both output and capital. Hence $f'(s) > 0$.

"I shall call a golden age which lacks a definite beginning a *boundless golden age*. Such an age may be endless although that is not essential for the definition; but it must be endless looking backward.

"And now, if these concepts are clear and my assumptions granted, I wish to introduce the following lemma."

"A lemma, a lemma," the crowd shouted. It was plain that the Solovians were excited by the prospect.

Oiko resumed. "The lemma: *Each generation in a boundless golden age of natural growth will prefer the same investment ratio, which is to say the same natural growth path.*

"In deciding which growth path is best from its standpoint, a generation will look only at the amount of consumption which each path offers it. Given the constancy of s, every golden-age path is associated with a consumption path on which consumption grows exponentially at the same rate as output. Under conditions of natural growth, consumption along all these paths grows at the identical rate, g, so that these time paths of consumption cannot cross. Therefore, with resources limited, there must exist some uniformly highest, feasible consumption path. This dominant consumption path offers more consumption at every point in its history than any other natural-growth consumption path. All generations in such a history will naturally prefer this path, whence its corresponding investment ratio, to any lower consumption path. A rigorous demonstration is straightforward.

"Take the consumption rate of the 'generation' in a boundless and natural golden age at time t. By (3) and (6), this is:

$$(7) \qquad C_t = (1-s)f(s)e^{gt}.$$

To find the value of s which maximizes C_t, we take the derivative with respect to s and equate it to zero. This yields:

$$(8) \qquad -f(s)e^{gt} + (1\text{-}s)\, f'(s)e^{gt} = 0.$$

"It is apparent that upon dividing (8) by e^{gt} all terms involving t vanish. The solution of equation (8) is therefore independent of the 'generation' whose consumption we choose to maximize. The s which is optimal for one generation in a natural boundless golden age is optimal for all. This proves the lemma."

Cries of "What a lemma!" resounded in the capital and Oiko was heartened by the reception. Anticipation ran high when he moved to speak again.

"And now I wish to announce a new and fundamental theorem. Theorem: *Along the optimal golden-age path, under conditions of natural growth, the rate of investment is equal to the competitive rate of profits.*

"Choosing the best value of s is simple enough in principle. A high value of s will be associated with a high golden-age output path. But too high a value of s will leave too little output available for consumption. Characterizing the exact optimum is a matter of calculus.

"Rewriting (8) in the form:

$$(8') \qquad \frac{s}{1\text{-}s} = \frac{f'(s)s}{f(s)}$$

we find that the optimal ratio of investment to consumption equals what we may call the elasticity of golden-age output at time zero with respect to the investment ratio. Looking at (6), it is obvious that, for every investment ratio, this elasticity must be the same at all points (dates) along the associated golden-age path. If this were not so, the golden-age growth rate would depend upon the investment ratio, contrary to our assumption of natural growth.

"The remaining task is to express this elasticity in explicit terms of the production function, and thus in terms of relative factor shares.[1] Now the production function indicates that $f(s) = F(K_0, N_0)$. Next we use the golden-age capital-output relation in (5) to write K_0 in the form $\dfrac{sP_0}{g}$. Upon making this substitution in the production function (2) we obtain an equation in golden-age output at time zero as function of itself, the investment ratio and the labor force:

$$(9) \qquad f(s) = F\!\left(\frac{sf(s)}{g},\, N_0 \right).$$

"Total differentiation of (9) with respect to s yields an equation in terms of $F_K(K_0, N_0)$, the marginal productivity of capital at time zero:

$$(10) \qquad f'(s) = F_K\, \frac{f(s)}{g} + F_K\, \frac{s}{g}\, f'(s).$$

[1] Oiko was seen at this point to wave gratefully to Richard Nelson for help with this proof.

Upon rearranging terms and using the capital-output relation (5) we find that

(11) $$\frac{f'(s)s}{f(s)} = \frac{a}{1-a}, \text{ where } a = \frac{F_K(K_0, N_0)K_0}{P_0}.$$

"Looking at (8') and (11) we see easily that

(12) $$s = a$$

In competitive Solovia the variable a measures capital's relative share in total output at time zero. Now we have observed that the elasticity of golden-age output with respect to the investment ratio is everywhere equal on any particular golden-age path; it follows by (11) that a, the profit-income ratio, must also be constant along any particular golden-age path. Therefore, by (12), on the optimum natural growth path the investment ratio and the profit ratio are constant and equal. This proves the theorem.

"We may call relation (12) the *golden rule of accumulation*, and with good reason. In a golden age governed by the golden rule, each generation invests on behalf of future generations that share of income which, subject to (3), it would have had past generations invest on behalf of it. We have shown that, among golden-age paths of natural growth, that golden age is best which practices the golden rule."

The Solovians were deeply impressed by Oiko and his theorems. But they were a practical people and soon full of queries. How, Oiko, does your theorem apply to Solovia? What must we do if we are not already on the golden-age, golden-rule path? Should we abide by the golden rule even when out of golden-rule equilibrium?

"Perhaps," Oiko replied. "We might attempt to approach the golden-rule path asymptotically. However I urge that we, in our lifetime, take whatever steps are required to place Solovia securely on the golden-rule path. Associated with that path is a unique capital-output ratio. If our present capital-output ratio is smaller, then our consumption must be slowed until our ratio is no longer deficient. If our present ratio exceeds the golden-rule ratio, then we must consume faster until our capital-output ratio is no longer excessive.

"Once our capital-output ratio has attained its golden-rule value, we must make a solemn compact henceforth to invest by the golden rule. If the investment ratio remains ever equal to the profit ratio, no generation in all the future of Solovia will ever wish we had chosen a different, successfully enforced investment ratio. The foundations are thus laid for a quasi-optimal social investment policy."

The crowd dispersed, happy for their Kingdom's future. But there were skeptics who reminded the King of Oiko's assumptions. They questioned Solovia's immunity from technological unemployment. They wondered whether their production function admitted of a natural growth rate. So the King named a team of econometricians to investigate the shape of the Solovian production function.

The King's econometricians were eventually satisfied that production in Solovia took place according to the Cobb-Douglas function:

(2') $$P_t = A(e^{\lambda t}K_t)^\alpha(e^{\mu t}N_t)^{1-\alpha} \qquad 0 < \alpha < 1$$

where α, a fixed parameter, was the elasticity of output with respect to the capital stock. They preferred to write it in the form:

$$(2'') \quad P_t = Ae^{\rho t} K_t^{\alpha} N_t^{1-\alpha}, \qquad \text{where} \qquad \rho = \alpha\lambda + (1-\alpha)\mu.$$

Solovians knew then they could have any capital-output ratio they desired, with full employment. The existence of a full-employment, golden-age equilibrium for every investment ratio was assured. Differentiating logarithmically, they quickly calculated from (1) and (2'') that in a golden age, capital and output would grow exponentially at the rate $\dfrac{\rho + (1-\alpha)\gamma}{1-\alpha}$, independently of the investment ratio. Thus did Solovia discover her natural rate of growth. What a triumph for Oiko. His assumptions were completely vindicated.

Joyously, the Solovians hurried to compute the golden-rule path. It did not take them long to realize that α was capital's share. On the golden-rule path, s would equal α. Next, using (5), they divided α by their natural growth rate to obtain the capital-output ratio on the golden-rule path. To their great relief, the resulting ratio exceeded their actual capital-ouput ratio by only a small factor. No wonder for they had invested most of their profits and consumed most of their wages anyway.

With Oiko's inspiring words still ringing in their ears, the Solovian people pressed the King for a program to attain the golden-rule path. So the King proclaimed golden-rule growth a national purpose and instituted special levies. Once the golden-rule path was reached, investment was continuously equated to profits and Solovians enjoyed, subject to (3), maximum social welfare ever after.

EDMUND PHELPS*

REFERENCES

1. JOAN ROBINSON, *The Accumulation of Capital*. London 1956.
2. R. M. SOLOW, "A Contribution to the Theory of Economic Growth," *Quart. Jour. Econ.*, Feb. 1956, *70*, 65-94.
3. T. W. SWAN, "Economic Growth and Capital Accumulation," *Econ. Record*, Nov. 1956, *32*, 334-61.

* The author is assistant professor of economics at Yale University.

[26]

Efficiency and Distributional Aspects of Anticipated Inflation

CHAPTERS 4 and 5 dealt with the consequences for distribution and efficiency of a change in the actual inflation rate, 'holding constant' the expected inflation rate. The subject of this chapter is the consequence for efficiency and distribution of a change in the expected inflation rate which is matched by an equal change of the actual inflation rate. It will suffice to examine, in particular, the equilibrium cases in which the actual rate of inflation is exactly equaled by the expected inflation rate. Except insofar as the government can effect a change of the expected inflation rate by announcement of its intentions or its forecasts and the like, it is of course true that the move from one equilibrium inflation rate to another will be marked by a disequilibrium transition of the sort studied in Chapters 4 and 5. Having covered disequilibrium previously, we can confine ourselves in this chapter to 'comparative statics' analysis of alternative equilibrium inflation rates.

This kind of analysis can be found in the economic literature under the heading of anticipated inflation. An inflation is said to be 'anticipated', or sometimes 'fully anticipated', if the current inflation rate is equal to the current expected inflation rate *and* if the current rate of inflation was earlier anticipated as far back in time as the age of the oldest currently existing money contracts outstanding. This year's inflation may be 'expected' this year but it may not have been anticipated in the past. Therefore an unanticipated increase of the equilibrium inflation rate, such as our comparative statics analyses will involve, will produce a wave of future price increases which will not have been anticipated. The redistributional consequences of such unanticipated losses and gains to creditors and debtors have already been covered. The distributional aspects needing attention here are only those pertaining to the rate of anticipated inflation. (We will still have to take cognizance of asset revaluations in an equilibrium shift, but for other reasons.)

After a brief introduction, the following sections discuss the consequences for allocative efficiency of the choice of the equilibrium inflation rate. The first two of these discusses the effect of inflation on the contribution of money to exchange efficiency under assumptions such that 'monetary-efficiency' is the only one of relevance. The subsequent section discusses overall monetary-fiscal efficiency in exchange from a more general and realistic point of view. The distributional consequences of the choice of the equilibrium inflation rate are taken up there. The final section brings in some other practical aspects involving the role of money as a unit of account and the associated question of the 'credibility' of the government's stabilization target when 'zero inflation' is desanctified.

6.1. *Preliminary Remarks on the Pure Theory of Money and Banking*

As is common knowledge in our society money plays four roles: as the medium of exchange, the unit of account, a store of value, and a source of anxiety.[1] Each of these roles stems from the first of these functions. Money *is* whatever has currency as the main medium of exchange. These things are well known, but a brief review may help to set the stage.

The theory of money as the principal medium of exchange, like the theory of unemployment, turns on the existence of frictions in the conduct of transactions between buyers and sellers of both goods and factor services. Fundamentally, these frictions arise from the imperfect information, and hence assurance, that each of us has that others will be able or willing to honor their credit obligations. Uncertainties about the future and the great heterogeneity of would-be borrowers and of the assets they would purchase combine to limit the amount of credit that each borrower can obtain (at terms he could afford to pay). There is a use, therefore, for some kind of money to 'keep people honest': with cash in hand, individuals can make some purchases which, while economically sound, they could not make on credit. The opportunities for trades are thus widened and markets are made less imperfect. Of course, the existence of this medium of exchange (in a limited amount) does not eliminate the extension of credit, especially to borrowers about whose credit worthiness there is good information; it may actually encourage useful extensions of credit.

---

[1] My facetious fourth function, no more obscure than that of the textbooks, calls many things to mind. The popular worry and excitement aroused by 'monetary instability' or the risk of it may indeed be a mildly productive conduit for the release of excess social tensions, or perhaps, more frequently, a counterproductive deflection of healthy social concerns. In another vein, one economist actually refers to people's concern for the safety of cash and the costs of guarding it!

It is possible to imagine, however, the development of customs in which certain liabilities (credit instruments) of some private borrowers come to be so easily exchangeable for goods at such predictable future market values that these private debts serve as money. But the prevailing wisdom for many decades has been that a laissez-faire system of private money creation 'cannot manage itself', at least not satisfactorily. What has evolved is basically a system of fiat money declared legal tender by the government and, adjoined to it, a limited system of privately created money that is guaranteed to be exchangeable at par for this fiat money and the quantity of which is limited by the central bank, that is, the Federal Reserve. There are a few credit institutions, traveler check issuers and credit card companies, whose liabilities are readily accepted as a means of payment and the quantities of which are not under government control; but the market for this private money is still sufficiently limited that these institutions do not appear to impair significantly the reliability, imperfect as it is, with which the central bank can influence the demands (money offers) of households and firms for goods.

Nevertheless there is a spectrum of private liabilities (and government obligations) that to varying degrees constitute near money. Money is what is perfectly liquid, a dollar of it being readily acceptable for an amount of a good the money price of which is quoted at a dollar. The near moneys – time deposits, some commercial and government obligations – are not perfectly liquid: a 'dollar's worth' of these near moneys cannot generally be used to buy an amount of goods the money price of which is a dollar. This is because the heterogeneous specialized nature of these assets imposes transactions costs in exchanging them for money or for one another. Finding a buyer at a specified price is risky, and if a specialist takes over that risk he charges a brokerage fee. For this same reason these near-money assets will be purchased and held by the people only if their pecuniary return is expected to be sufficiently above any pecuniary return earned by holding money to compensate for their lesser liquidity. The same is true of capital claims (equities and the rest), most of which are even less liquid. Taking for granted the convention that only money is used as payment, the demand for money to hold or the finiteness of the velocity of money is ultimately dependent, given a spread between the respective pecuniary returns, upon the presence of these transactions costs.

It is also natural that fiat money, being the most frequently traded item, should serve as the unit of account. The goods value of a unit of money is normally known with more certainty than the other-goods-value of some other good; normally the 'money price level' is more accurately estimated by people than the 'price level' of goods in general relative to some particular good that might be conceivable as a *numeraire*.

Finally, fiat money and other money exchangeable at par with it plays a role as a store of value. But the wealth represented by fiat money and other money does not necessarily make a net addition to the real value of private wealth owned by the households in the economy. The same may be said of interest-bearing public debt. It is possible that the real value of the money supply is 'backed' in part by earning assets held by the government so that the net indebtness position of the government is less than the real value of its fiat money outstanding and its interest-bearing obligations held by the public. More precisely, those assets of the government that earn user charges paid by the public (net of operating costs) or other rents paid by the private sector constitute a deduction from the addition to private wealth made by fiat money and public debt in the hands of the public in toting up net government indebtedness. Fortunately, the question of the benefit to be gained from a net contribution by the government to private wealth by debt plus fiat money creation is largely separable from the question of optimum anticipated inflation. But the extent to which money may have a comparative advantage over other assets in this function deserves some attention.

So much, by the way of preliminaries, for the theory of money in the narrow or traditional sense. We should add that in this country (as in most others) money is also involved in the theory of loan-banking and financial intermediation. The fractional reserve system on which commercial banks operate in this country places them in the role of financial intermediaries. The net amount of money created by the commercial banks has a counterpart in the loans and invest-ments undertaken by private commercial bankers. It is widely agreed that there is some gain in the efficiency of financial allocations from the existence of some funds for the disposal of loan specialists and poolers of risk such as commercial banks.

We shall need some definitions. The three kinds of fiat money – government currency, coin, and deposits at the Federal Reserve System – sum up to what may be called the quantity of outside money. This quantity is 'outside' in the sense that it is an exogenous datum for the private sector of the economy. The deposits at the central bank are not themselves money, as they are not held directly by the public.

These deposits are held by the commercial banks and serve as the base for a quantity of demand deposits at commercial banks that is larger than the base by some multiple determined by the fractional reserve ratio. It will be harmless to follow the relatively standard practice of defining these demand deposits held by the public together with their holdings of coin and currency as the total quantity of money. Then the excess of this total over the aforementioned outside quantity may be called the quantity of inside money. This last quantity is the sum lent or invested by the commercial banks – abstracting from the other loans and investments they make in connection with their time deposit business.

I have been discussing some rudiments of the pure theory of money – or more accurately, the pure theory of *some* money. This is like the pure theory of international trade that assures us that some amount of trade can be found which is superior to no trade. Some amount of 'moneyness' or liquidity is desirable as grease to overcome the frictions of imperfect information and uncertainty in the economic machine. But how much liquidity? Specifically, how does the selection of the equilibrium or expected rate of inflation affect the contribution that money makes to economic efficiency?

I begin this inquiry under the instructive yet ultimately indefensible assumption that the 'marginal social costs' of raising tax revenues and of stabilization operations are zero. The reasons why that assumption must finally be abandoned, and the ramifications of its abandonment for the answers to the above questions, are the subject of section 6.4.

6.2. *Monetary Efficiency: The Medium of Exchange*

Here I shall abstract from banking aspects of the subject, reserving this side of the question for section 6.3. Specifically, I shall suppose that the quantity of inside money is equal to zero. One can still, if he wishes, imagine the presence of demand deposits at private commercial banks, but such banks would have to be conceived as being required to keep 100 percent reserves against those deposits, thus earning whatever profits their competition allows them only through customer charges for banking services rendered.

In this rarefied setting it is fitting enough to assume that the marginal social cost of creating money and of maintaining any given real quantity of it are zero, or are at least negligible. The emphasis here is on currency. In the next section, where commercial banking is introduced, it will be important to consider various social costs of adding to the economy's liquidity.

Why should the rate of anticipated inflation have anything to do with the determination of the amount of liquidity that will prevail in macroequilibrium? The relevant concept of liquidity is the real value of the quantity of money, normalized in some way to adjust for changes in the size of the capital stock or the population of the country. If the nominal supply of money is taken as fixed, we still have to view the real value of that supply as a 'variable' in macroequilibrium with an equilibrium value corresponding to the specified macroequilibrium: then the price 'level' at any given moment of time must be such as to make the real value of that supply equal to the quantity of money demanded when expressed in real terms. If, instead, the path of the price level is taken as fixed, the supply of money must somehow be adjusted to such a level that its real value is equal to the real quantity of money demanded. In either case, macroequilibrium requires that the real quantity of money be always equal to the real quantity of money demanded. Hence, the rate of anticipated inflation, if it affects the liquidity of the economy in macroequilibrium, will do so through an effect on the real demand for money.

The principal influence of the equilibrium rate of inflation upon the real quantity of money demanded is through its effect on the opportunity cost of holding money – at least if, as asserted by the natural unemployment rate hypothesis, the volume of transactions that people would otherwise like to undertake would not be appreciably affected by the anticipated inflation rate. Given the rate of pecuniary return (if any) that is paid to holders of money, the faster the expected rate of inflation the larger each individual will perceive the opportunity cost of holding any amount of money in real terms to be. If you are holding cash and shopping now, the opportunity cost of shopping further for a better buy will be greater the more likely you think it is that those relatively better buys will be marked up in price before you find them. Under the equilibrium conditions specified here, the opportunity costs of waiting to invest in stocks or bonds will also be increased by an increase of the expected inflation rate: Share prices will on average be rising, and be expected to rise, at a rate which is increased by the same amount, and bond prices will be sufficiently down to offer a comparable increase in the nominal yields (including subsequent capital gains to maturity) expected by bond purchasers. These increased opportunity costs will induce a reduction in the real quantity of money demanded. Liquidity is thus decreased.[2]

If in fact holders of money would receive a matching increase in the pecuniary return on money when there was such an increase in the equilibrium rate of inflation, there would of course be no resulting increase in this opportunity cost of holding cash. But of course fiat money in this country pays no own-interest at all and, especially with reference to coin and currency, there are sufficient reasons why it would not be good economic policy to institute such interest payments.

One could say that the government has been somewhat exploitive, allowing itself to reap a *seigniorage* that is the difference between the zero rate, at which princes and other lucky creators of money through history have been able to 'borrow', and that at which ordinary borrowers have had to pay. Our government is not forced to pay interest on its currency or even deposits at the central bank; it has a legal monopoly on the printing of currency and it keeps the expected inflation rate low enough that no commodity money or near money can come close to rivaling its money. There are good reasons why interest ought not to be paid on at least some types of government money. It is quite impractical to make interest payments to holders of coin and currency. The costs imposed by any system of periodic registry of cash holdings with local government offices would be likely to eat up any economic gains from the resulting encouragement to greater liquidity. In addition, it is imaginable that a benevolent government might reasonably regard the nonpayment of interest on its money (or at least the underpayment) as a justifiable user tax, believing that there were more worthy uses of its scarce tax revenues. But this anticipates a portion of a subsequent section of this chapter.

We have established the notion that the smaller the anticipated inflation rate the larger, at least up to a point, the quantity of liquidity is. We have to ask now whether there exists an *ideal* quantity of liquidity and, if so, what the anticipated inflation rate must be – positive or negative, large or small – in order to achieve it in conditions of macroequilibrium.

[2] This result would at first not appear to be obtainable under the older version of the 'quantity theory of money' which makes the demand for real cash balances independent of the money rate of interest. Yet if such interest inelasticity were only the consequence of the 'income effect' of the rise in opportunity cost of liquidity, the result would still follow, because the 'compensated' demand curve for money must be negatively sloped, in the appropriate analytical setting. See Section 6.4.

Those questions can be answered meaningfully only in terms of some reasonably specific conception of the structure of the economy in question, particularly in the relevant aspects. Partly for the sake of clarity and in part because the more sophisticated analysis of the subsequent section will especially benefit by it, I shall sketch a couple of ultrasimple types of monetary economies. In these types of economies, the population is stationary as is the technology. Government expenditure (outlays of the resource-absorbing type) is confined to consumption-type goods and is also stationary over time in real terms. Taxes are imagined to be lump-sum; they are not believed by any taxpayer to be related to his taxable income and so they have no substitution effects upon the taxpayer's incentives to work or to save or to be liquid. Any transfer payments by the government, such as compensations to the disabled, are equally lump-sum in character. Thus revenue-raising and stabilization by the government are socially costless.

Throughout this section, merely to defer a complication, we exclude the government from creating money by the means of 'open-market' purchases of securities from the public. But, as the alternative to tax finance, the government can in effect print money to make its transfer and expenditure payments. In stationary equilibrium the real value of the money printed in any interval of time will be offset by equal real capital losses over that interval on existing outside money from the anticipated inflation rate corresponding to the rate of growth of the money supply.[3]

It is in this setting that the concept of the optimum rate of anticipated inflation has most often been discussed in the literature of the past decade – though, paradoxically, an optimum is somewhat less likely to exist in this situation than in the banking situation introduced in the next section. The 'optimum', here as throughout this chapter, is conceived in a static way, neglectful of any costs of

---

[3] We add some realism when we ultimately allow for the presence of government interest-bearing debt and the existence of a central bank which can buy or sell these government bonds and possible private interest-bearing liabilities or wealth claims as well. Then each stationary equilibrium will be marked by a certain constant ratio of government debt to outside money in the hands of the public. Then the budget deficit (or surplus) can more realistically be viewed as being met by government borrowing (or lending) at interest, with the central bank regularly monetizing a certain fraction of each year's government borrowing. At first we are assuming, though, that the government neither borrows nor lends at interest vis-à-vis the public directly; any budget deficit is borrowed from the central bank and any surplus is hoarded rather than invested in the private sector.

benefits accruing in the transition from one macroequilibrium (with its level of liquidity) to another macroequilibrium (with its different quantity of liquidity). In this comparative statics sense, I shall refer to the *ideal* quantity of liquidity as that degree of liquidity at which the marginal social benefit from greater liquidity equals the marginal social cost of higher liquidity. The optimum inflation rate in this idealized setting is that which produces the ideal degree of liquidity.

6.2.1. *Full Transaction Liquidity*. According to an increasingly familiar argument of recent years, there does exist such an optimum in the kind of model under discussion. In this kind of model the marginal social cost of liquidity can be taken to be zero – at least in the neighborhood where the corresponding rate of anticipated inflation imposes no calculational costs on persons of making allowances for rapidly changing trends in money wage rates and money prices. Yet there can be expected to exist a level of liquidity at which the marginal social benefit of liquidity is also zero. When liquidity has reached the point at which a further increase would not reduce further the frictional costs to individuals of exchanging goods and services with one another, the marginal social benefit of liquidity is held to be zero and there is said to be *full liquidity*. The argument is thus that, with respect to money as a medium of exchange, monetary efficiency requires that there be full liquidity.[4]

The concept of full liquidity has its origins in inventory theoretic models of the behavior and composition of an economic unit's transactions balances when, as usual, there is nonsynchronization of payments and receipts owing to the specialization of labor, the non-coincidence of wants, and so on. The periodicity of income receipts and of some expenditures causes periodic peaks in total transactions balances. These peak balances may be large enough in some households to induce them to invest a fraction in earning assets for a time when the pecuniary return on the latter, the various money rates of interest, are sufficiently above the zero pecuniary return to cash. A similar phenomenon can be expected to be found at many firms and may be quantitatively more significant. If the real yield on capital and equity claims is sufficiently large or the equilibrium rate of inflation sufficiently high, the nominal or pecuniary rates of return

---

[4] See E. S. Phelps, 'Anticipated Inflation and Economic Welfare', *Journal of Political Economy*, February 1965, and A. L. Marty, 'Money in a Theory of Finance', *Journal of Political Economy*, February 1961. Marty speaks of the satiety level of real cash balances.

available on interest-bearing assets will be large enough to encourage households to incur brokerage outlays to go in and out of earning assets, to divert their time from leisure or secondary jobs into activities such as more frequent banking to economize on cash, and to stimulate firms to divert some workers into performing financial tasks having the same purpose.

By shifting to a macroequilibrium with a sufficiently small inflation rate – perhaps a negative rate is required – the pecuniary yields on earning assets, which reflect the anticipated inflation rate, can be made small enough that there is insufficient incentive to invest any fraction of ordinary transactions balances in noncash assets. Money rates of interest on these nonmoney assets need *not* be brought to zero because of the transactions costs to each individual and firm of switching in and out of earning assets.[5] At a still lower spread in yields, the transaction demand for cash would remain at the same full-liquidity level though the quantity of cash demanded for speculative purposes would presumably be higher. Anticipated deflation is required for full liquidity if the real rates of return available on private liabilities and equity claims tend to exceed the threshold level determined by the transactions costs of switching in and out of them and by the lengths of the receipts and expenditure periods.[6]

6.2.2. *Full Precautionary Liquidity?* It is of some importance to consider the notion of ideal liquidity in terms of another motive for holding money – the precautionary motive. Cash is pictured as being held until an urgent need appears or an acceptable buying opportunity is found or presents itself. The emergence or opportunity could be a consumption act as well as an investment good.

In the above transactions demand analysis of money demand, it is

[5] This is depicted diagrammatically in Phelps, 'Anticipated Inflation'. A transactions model having this property is present in J. Tobin, 'The Interest-elasticity of transactions demand for cash', *REStat.* 38 (August 1956), pp. 241–247. Continuously variable models without set-up transactions costs miss this threshold feature.

[6] In a world of zero transactions costs, one might at first think of full liquidity as obtaining only at a zero spread, the anticipated deflation rate being matched to the real rate of return on capital so as to equate the real (nonpecuniary) yields on the two assets. All capital goods, fresh supplies as well as old capital goods and equity claims, would be willingly held as long as their real yields matched that of money, there never being a cost to switching freely from one asset to the other. But in that world where all nonmoney assets are themselves perfectly liquid, there would be no reason for money to exist.

the existence of privately owned capital and the various wealth claims to which it gives rise that provide to wealthowners their alternative to liquidity. Presumably much precautionary liquidity is likewise an alternative for households and firms to investing immediately in earning assets. I shall return in a moment to this source of precautionary demands for money

An important cause of demands by households for precautionary balances is their wish not to be unable to avail themselves of an attractive consumption purchase for lack of timely liquidity. It may be instructive to imagine, in the spirit of some modern researches into the foundations of monetary theory, that the economy produces only a polyglot of labor services, each man producing a heterogeneous consumption service unassisted by any tangible capital. Let us in fact at first exclude tangible capital and other tangible assets such as land. Money is the only store of value. Each 'producer' gropes his way through the imperfectly informed market looking for buyers of his service with the cash on hand to pay him the price he asks. As a 'consumer', he can accept (or, of course, reject) an offer to supply him with a consumption service if he has the necessary cash and he will accept occasional offers if the prices asked are low enough. The more liquid he can afford to become, the better are his chances as a consumer of not having to pass up extraordinarily attractive offers. Further, his liquidity serves him as a producer, for it saves him from having to make a drastic price reduction in the event of a distressing run of no sales. Hence, liquidity is a productive asset for the household and the more there is of it the larger the household's expectation is of 'real income' or consumption services received.[7]

In this quaint parable, liquidity is a capital good and it has a social as well as a private productivity. But it is not generally expectable that the typical household will individually be willing to make the 'apparent' consumption sacrifice necessary to accumulate liquidity to the point of maximum social benefit. Even without technological progress, 'pure time preference' may stand in the way of liquidity satiation, just as Schumpeter's savers of tangible capital leave some railroad track unstraightened. Yet if the marginal social cost of increasing liquidity can be taken to be zero, there would appear to be

[7] Correspondingly, other people's liquidity contributes to the individual's real income. The more liquid other people are the more easily will the individual be able to find buyers for his service who are liquid and so the higher his optimal relative price or rate of sales or both. On the other hand, the more liquid they are, the better they will be able to hold out for higher prices from him as a buyer of their services.

Anticipated Inflation 181

a clear gain obtainable from reducing the rate of anticipated inflation so as to instill private incentives to greater liquidity. Liquidity
saturation should be sought if, unlike capital saturation, there is no
foregone consumption cost.

But is there a full-liquidity stopping place? It is not clear that any
individual would feel there to be no further private yield to greater
liquidity at any finite liquidity level. Just as there may always be
room for a little closer straightening of rail tracks, each household
may have an insatiable want for liquidity. In this case we may say
that the social benefits from liquidity are always improvable a little
by a still closer approximation of the anticipated deflation rate to the
aforementioned pure time preference rate.[8]

Let us now acknowledge that precautionary liquidity is an alternative to investing in some immediately available earning asset. Then
the precautionary demand for idle cash balances stems partly from
the wish to be temporarily liquid as a 'precaution' against being
unable to buy an especially attractive earning asset in timely fashion
for lack of liquidity. The smaller the mean pecuniary return he
expects to find available to him on earning assets, the smaller is the
expected opportunity cost of any average fraction of his wealth held
in liquid form. The individual owning a given amount of wealth will
be likely to hold a larger fraction of it in money form on the average,
amassing larger amounts of liquidity between investments and
making his investments in larger 'lots', the smaller the opportunity
cost is to him of staying liquid.

By engineering a smaller anticipated inflation rate over some range
the government can reduce the opportunity cost of precautionary
liquidity. This can be assumed to yield some social benefit by reducing
transactions costs (as in the earlier model), that is, reducing the
average rate of turnover of the representative man's portfolio: One
would expect that the typical individual would be encouraged to
omit relatively inferior investments usually held for short-term
between longer-term placements and to make the latter investments
in larger lots.[9] But the main benefit of the increased precautionary

---

[8] In these successive approximations, liquidity and the capital gains on money
would become enormous – but so would the taxes dictated by the budget surplus
necessary to shrink the money supply for realization of the deflation. Would
such a large liquidity overhang, in fact, impose a real social cost? The answer may
better be discussed under the assumption of the coexistence of tangible capital,
as in Section 6.3.1.

[9] It is not altogether clear, however, that individuals would be encouraged to
invest for longer durations, since the opportunity cost of taking cover in liquid

liquidity would be to improve the allocative effectiveness of the market for heterogeneous capital goods. If we think of the anticipated deflation rate as being successively increased in small amounts, the pecuniary rates of return to the relatively liquid types of capital goods such as inventories will, at their initial stock levels, come to be unfavorable compared to the zero pecuniary return on money. Now while macroequilibrium requires that the existing aggregate of capital be voluntarily held, there is no requirement that each kind of capital good be held in an unvarying quantity as the opportunity cost of liquidity is successively reduced. Let us stipulate that the investment sector can transmute capital goods. Then there will result successive shifts to less liquid types of capital goods as the premium on relatively liquid capital diminishes with increased money liquidity. Full liquidity, if it exists, may be characterized as having arrived when the opportunity cost of liquidity is so small that there is no liquidity premium to any type of capital good relative to another, since liquidity is no longer scarce.[10] But at any finite spread in yields, · it is doubtful that there would be enough 'waiting' between investments such that no capital goods would exist which, owing to their extraordinary unfamiliarity and resulting thinness of the market for them, would promise a real rate of return somewhat above the norm. No finite quantity of liquidity can *perfect* the market for uncertain heterogeneous capital goods!

We can now take it as established, some might say overestablished, that the increase of liquidity associated with a decrease of the (algebraic) rate of anticipated inflation confers certain gains in monetary efficiency in terms of the present model. But a satisfactory understanding of the subject demands that we take up two loose threads much spun in the literature (one more than the other). One thread is the hypothesis that the anticipated inflation rate, in the process of altering the economy's liquidity, has an influence through its 'wealth effects' upon the rate of capital formation and hence ultimately upon the capital intensiveness of the economy. The other thread concerns the significance of inside money for the subject of monetary and financial efficiency. Both of these matters properly involve considering what scope the central bank may have for nulli-

---

money has diminished. The question of monetary 'stability' at low or negative rates of anticipated inflation will be taken up in Section 6.4. Let us attempt to abstract from this consideration here.

[10] This does not mean that there will not be *risk* premiums in rates of return.

fying or modifying certain side effects which a change of the anticipated inflation rate might otherwise have.

6.3. *Monetary Efficiency: Money, Debt, and other Stores of Value*

For centuries economists have sometimes suggested that anticipated inflation is 'good for growth' in this way: it is an inducement to greater thrift out of any given real income and hence it leads to some additional capital deepening. There is a grain of truth to this; it will be shown to be a part of a larger harvest from the more realistic analysis given below. Here I shall try to show why this conclusion does not necessarily follow in the present and more abstract setting in which these matters are usually discussed. The real objective of the present discussion is to grasp the potentialities of central bank action in the present model, and so to learn some lessons of significance for the more realistic analysis to follow.

6.3.1. *Liquidity and 'Growth'*. Early 'forced saving' analysts knew that the anticipated capital losses on fiat money implied by anticipated inflation are a subtraction from consumers' spendable income: they must set aside that much real income per unit time to maintain their sustainable consumption stream intact, other things equal. But the maintenance of the anticipated inflation implies that government taxes must fall short of the budget-balancing level by such an amount that the real value of the money freshly created by the government at each moment is just enough to replenish the real anticipated capital losses on the already existing real money supply. The saving 'forced' by the latter is offset by the government's *dis*saving represented by the former. This is for stationary equilibriums.

There now exist two modern reformulations of the old doctrine. According to one argument, the real rate of interest (or real rate of return on capital) at which households will hold a given amount of *capital* is higher the larger the real value is of the outside money which, when added to the value of the capital stock, constitutes private wealth. If this is so, the monetary economist who is bent on improving the monetary efficiency of the economy will find that, as he engineers a lower anticipated inflation rate, the 'flight' into money and the resulting increase in its real value engenders a decrease of thrift, a shift of resources to consumer goods production, and thus some rise of *real* rates of interest.[11] One would not expect this result

[11] R. A. Mundell, 'Inflation and Real Interest', *Journal of Political Economy*, June 1963.

in an economy of infinitely lived families – or their Meadean equivalents – who can be counted on to pass along all existing wealth into the future so long as its real yield does not fall short of their pure time preference rate. But one would expect to see this phenomenon in a life-cycle model of household saving where not all wealth is bequeathed in that fashion: then one would be prepared for some displacement of private capital by the enlarged social capital that is liquidity.

The second modern forced saving doctrine turns on the growth of the economy in macroequilibrium. It is postulated that the economy, if not continuously driven from macroequilibrium (i.e., from the natural unemployment rate), will exhibit a tendency to steady geometric growth rather than toward a stationary state as assumed heretofore. For simplicity we suppose that geometric population growth is the sole driving force; the economy's rate of output growth then tends toward the population rate as the 'great ratios', like capital per· head, tend to level off. In this case, real money must steadily be increased if the continuous additions to the population are to be made as liquid as the existing population. Consequently, the real value of the money created by the government to keep the real money supply constant per capita (if the growth comes only from population increase) must exceed the real capital losses on existing money from any anticipated inflation going on by an amount equal to the level of the real money supply multiplied by the steady growth rate. This is a net addition to the aggregate real spendable income to be associated with a given level of aggregate real production. One supposes that it will add something to the demand for consumption goods. The smaller the anticipated inflation rate selected, and hence the larger the real money supply, the larger this addition is. Hence, as the monetary efficiency expert 'tries' lower rates of anticipated inflation in his quest for full liquidity, one can expect that there will tend (at least eventually) to be an increase of consumption demand relative to output (at macroequilibrium) and hence a tendency for capital intensity to decline and the real rate of return to capital to find a higher level in some new balanced-growth state.[12]

[12] J. Tobin, 'Money and Growth', *Econometrica*, January 1967. See also D. Patinkin and D. Levhari, 'Money, Growth and Welfare', *American Economic Review*, September 1968. It may be noted that if the level of liquidity is far from 'full', in that neighborhood the contribution that an increment of it makes to output may for a while exceed its stimulus to consumption demand. But the former vanishes as full liquidity is approached while it is entirely reasonable to suppose that the latter does not.

Anticipated Inflation 185

There is an apparent conflict, therefore, between capital intensiveness as measured, for example, by the stock of capital per head (to
which the system tends) and liquidity as measured by the per capita
real money supply. But that conflict rests upon a questionable restriction: All money is outside money and all outside wealth is outside money. By outside wealth is meant the sum of outside money
and interest-bearing obligations of the government held by the
public net of any income-earning wealth or wealth claims held by the
government – all in real terms. It is the stock of outside wealth and
its increase that matter for consumption demand in the above
modern treatments, not the stock or increase of liquidity as such.
The link between the two can be broken as soon as we unleash the
central bank.

We now permit the treasury to run a budget deficit or surplus but
constrain it to cover such discrepancies with the issue (or retirement)
of interest-bearing obligations. We endow the central bank with the
control over the money supply – empowering it to 'monetize' all or
only a portion of the interest-bearing public debt and, if there is no
more of that left, perhaps to rediscount private wealth claims. If the
bank monetizes the entire public debt, no more and no less, we are
in the previous world where outside wealth equals outside money.
If it monetizes only a fraction of the public debt, outside wealth
exceeds outside money – by the amount of the interest-bearing
government debt held by the public rather than the bank. And if we
imagine the bank to monetize all the public debt and additionally to
make purchases of some private claims, outside wealth is then less
than outside money.

Variation of the fiscal tool – the budget deficit and hence ultimately the stock of public debt – together with the monetary tool –
open-market purchase and hence the supply of money – provide
enough control to achieve a change of liquidity without any concomitant change in thrift. The effect which an attainable increase in
the *real* money supply might otherwise have on capital intensiveness
or 'growth' can be neutralized by jointly compensatory fiscal-
monetary steps.[13] We can sketch an example:

Our hypothetical economy is initially in macroequilibrium at an

---

[13] The point is made geometrically (in too short-run a context) in Phelps,
'Anticipated Inflation'. An analysis of the choice of long-run paths available (in
the steady growth case) can be found in E. Burmeister and E. S. Phelps, 'Money,
Public Debt, Inflation and Real Interest', *Journal of Money, Credit and Banking*,
May 1971. Mention may also be made of some related work of a rather different
character by Foley, Sidrauski, Shell, Liviatan, and Sheshinski.

anticipated inflation rate of, for example, 5 percent per annum. It is also in a state of steady growth – real output, real public expenditure, capital, the real public debt (held by the central bank and the public), and the real money supply all growing at the same rate as population and the labor force, for example, 3 percent annually. Then the nominal public debt must be rising at 8 percent annually and the central bank must be monetizing an unchanging 'fraction' of that growing total (a fraction less or greater than one) so that the money supply is growing at the same rate. It follows that the annual real treasury deficit – the shortfall of taxes collected from expenditures, transfers, and interest payments to the public, all in real terms, that must be covered by borrowing – is equal to 8 percent of the real value of the public debt.[14]

Consider now that the government wishes to establish macro-equilibrium at 4 percent expected inflation and to do so without inducing any real-wealth effects upon thrift or consumption demand. Assume it were possible to reduce the expected inflation rate 'by announcement' without any interim of below-equilibrium employment and hence no unexpected 'drop' of the price 'level'. Immediately then the one-point reduction of the expected inflation rate will produce a rush from capital and capital claims (equities) into money; insofar as the public debt is not rolled over to pay the lower coupon rates of interest at which the public will now be willing to hold treasury obligations at par, there will be a rush into government interest-bearing obligations as well. Let us assume that treasury debt, to be held by the public, must promise the same real rate of return that is expected to be earned from equity holding. And let us further assume that the rate of money interest paid on the public debt is quickly adjusted downward by one percentage point so that government bonds do not appreciate relative to equities. There still remains an excess demand for money, its opportunity costs having been reduced by the one point fall of the expected inflation rate.

To shore up the demand for earning assets and hence the demand for goods – and thus to prevent an unexpected drop of the price level – the central bank need simply make whatever size open-market purchase of government debt from the public as is required to 'support' the money price of treasury obligations. Because the price level at 'time zero' is thus maintained and because the central bank

---

[14] The 'real deficit' is thus greater than the increase per unit time in the real value of the debt by the amount of the anticipated inflation rate times the real value of the debt.

pays a dollar for every dollar's worth of government debt purchased, the real value of outside wealth is consequently held constant. In this manner the central bank prevents a positive real-wealth effect that would stimulate consumption demand.

Note that with the time path of real outside wealth unchanged, the treasury must adjust its tax collections to reduce its annual real deficit to 7 percent of real outside wealth instead of 8 percent. But while the real deficit must be reduced by 1 percent of the unchanged real outside wealth, this does not necessitate an increase in real tax collections by that amount. The lower money interest to be paid on publicly held government debt automatically reduces the deficit by a fraction of the required amount equal to the fraction of outside wealth held in interest-bearing form. That leaves somehow to be accomplished a deficit reduction equal to 1 percent of outside wealth *not* in interest-bearing form; hence, 1 percent of outside money. But even this overestimates the tax increase by an amount equal to the interest payments the treasury makes on that amount of its debt which the central bank has purchased in the support operation, for this interest earned by the bank must be returned to the treasury.[15] So if the elasticity of the real value of the money supply with respect to the nominal rate of interest on earning assets is unity or greater (in absolute value), real taxes could be left alone or actually decreased while still meeting the requirement for a lower deficit. But so large an elasticity appears to be empirically quite unlikely, at least in the range of historically familiar money rates of interest. The likelihood that lower anticipated inflation requires higher rates of taxation if the volume of government expenditures and the willingness to accumulate wealth are to be left undisturbed will be a matter of major significance in the final assessment of the benefits and costs of increased anticipated inflation.

The proposition that emerges is that, over some range, the treasury and central bank can jointly control (after the necessary disequilibration) the rate of expected inflation and per capita real outside wealth; thus it can jointly determine liquidity and thrift. The point can be made another way which brings out a familiar point in

---

[15] Let C, G, Y, T, M, D, D_B, p, i, r, and x denote, respectively, real private consumption, government expenditure, income, and taxes; nominal money, government debt, and bank-held debt; money interest rate, real interest rate, and expected inflation rate. We have (1) $i - x = r$, (2) $C + G = Y$, and (3) $M = D_B$ at par values. Consumers' budget in stationary equilibrium is (4) $pC = p = pY - pT - xM + (i - x)(D - M)$. The deficit is (5) $F = pG + i(D - D_B) - pT$. Therefore, (6) $F = xD$ and (7) $pT = pG + i(D - M) - xD = pG + rD - (x + r)M$.

monetary theory which underlies it. Take the stationary case and for simplicity take the anticipated inflation rate as given; the latter determines the equal rate of growth of money and government debt outstanding. The 'levels' of money and publicly held debt at 'time zero' nevertheless remain to be determined. We know that if the levels of debt and money should each be increased equiproportionately, the macroequilibrium price 'level' will simply be increased in the same proportion, leaving real outside wealth and liquidity unaffected. If the 'level' of the money supply is increased by an open-market purchase, with no change in the existing level of the total debt, the price level must rise and so real outside wealth must fall. Liquidity in the sense of the interest spreads between earning assets is improved insofar as the decline of real outside wealth contracts

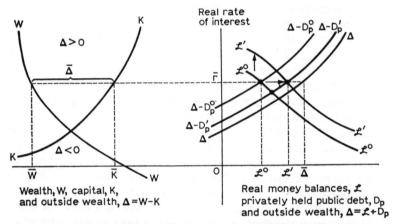

Wealth, W, capital, K, and outside wealth, $\Delta = W - K$

Real money balances, $\mathcal{L}$ privately held public debt, D_p and outside wealth, $\Delta = \mathcal{L} + D_p$

Figure 6.1 For a wealth level $\bar{W}$ and corresponding real interest rate, $\bar{r}$, the quantity of outside wealth must be $\bar{\Delta}$. Of this, the public is willing to hold $\mathcal{L}^0$ in liquid form at, for example, a zero rate of anticipated inflation. An open-market purchase, by reducing the privately held debt, for example, to D'_p, would leave an excess supply of money at $\bar{r}$ and hence cause a rise of the price level which reduces Δ. The fall of Δ would increase $\mathcal{L}$ but only insofar as it reduced r through its stimulus to deepening of capital beyond K. (The increase of $\mathcal{L}$ thus induced will moderate the fall of r by its upward shifting of the KK schedule, which shift is abstracted from.)

An appropriate simultaneous decrease of the expected inflation rate, however, can nullify the wealth effect upon capital deepening from the open-market purchase. Such a decrease shifts upward the $\mathcal{LL}$ schedule by the amount of the decrease, since the same r then corresponds to lower money rates of interest. The induced flight into money just matches the open-market purchase, $D_p^0 - D'_p$, with the result that $\mathcal{L}'$ is produced at the same $\bar{\Delta}$ and K. Without that purchase, Δ would rise, forcing K down and r up.

Anticipated Inflation 189

consumption demand and thus leads to a fall in the nominal rates of return on earning assets.[16] An appropriate increase in the supply of outstanding public debt can nullify the decline of real outside wealth, but in so doing it will erase the rise in liquidity in the above sense. There is, therefore, a certain liquidity level available for each level of real outside wealth. Additional liquidity, in the sense of the term just employed, can be purchased only at the price of reduced real outside wealth and consequent additional capital deepening – *given* the constraint that the anticipated inflation rate cannot be tampered with. But if that constraint is relaxed, the attainable liquidity level that corresponds to any prescribed level of real outside wealth and hence capital intensiveness can be improved by the 'selection' of a lower rate of anticipated inflation.[17]

An interesting observation can now be made. When the central bank was excluded and the treasury issued money rather than bonds, our earlier assumption of convenience, driving down the anticipated inflation rate toward the full-liquidity point, had the consequence of driving the real value of the money supply to infinity. This was a feature of the precautionary liquidity model in which liquidity could always be increased by a further shrinkage of the private opportunity cost of being liquid. Yet this is clearly not a necessary consequence of driving the anticipated inflation rate toward the full liquidity point once we allow open market purchases by the central bank. Given that some level of real outside wealth is to be maintained and hence also the level of capital intensiveness corresponding to it, the approach to full liquidity cannot cause the real money supply to go to infinity; the reason is that the latter cannot exceed real outside wealth by more than the real value of the claims to private capital available for purchase by the central bank and there is only a finite amount of

[16] In a celebrated paper, L. A. Metzler deduces this without there being any interest-bearing debt and hence without any real capital loss on debt left outstanding after the open-market purchase. In his analysis, the loss of ownership of equities purchased by the bank reduces real *total* private wealth if the price level should rise in proportion to the money supply. This reduction lowers consumption, reduces the interest rate, and dampens the wealth decline. See L. A. Metzler, 'Wealth, Saving and the Rate of Interest', *Journal of Political Economy*, February 1951.

[17] It is clear now, it may be noted, that we need not view, as in the earlier example, the treasury as determining the rate of anticipated inflation and the central bank as determining real outside wealth. We could equally well view the central bank as determining the anticipated inflation rate by its selection of the rate of growth of the money supply if, accordingly, we charge the treasury with maintaining a deficit policy which keeps the real value of the public debt outstanding invariant to the money growth rate.

190   *Welfare Effects and Inflation*

these (namely, the amount of capital per head that the given real outside wealth level causes to be sustained in macroequilibrium). What does go to infinity as the opportunity cost of being liquid goes to zero is the ratio of the real money supply to the capital stock *in private ownership*.

This innocent observation leads to the conclusion that (on the assumption just made of an insatiable demand for liquidity by households) full liquidity requires full intermediation by the central bank; the bank is the nation's stockholder and households hold the bank's money at a real rate of return (owing to anticipated deflation) with which equities cannot compete. It is obvious that there are strong objections to such a situation, objections involving real economic costs as well as ideological ones with which one might or might not choose to side.

We seem to have reduced the pursuit of full liquidity to a practical absurdity. In fact it will be the conclusion of this chapter that nothing like full liquidity should be sought by macroeconomic policy. But it should be understood that increases in liquidity, though not full liquidity, can be obtained by a different institutional means.

6.3.2. *'Inside' Money and Commercial Banks*. Once the anticipated inflation rate has been reduced to the point where all the public debt can be monetized without disturbing the quantity of real outside wealth, it is still possible to achieve a further increase of liquidity by the institution of private fractional reserve commercial banking. As was remarked earlier, the concept of the government-run monopoly bank in the previous setting could have been interpreted as a convenient expository device for describing the essential workings of a private banking system with 100 percent reserves under central bank control through its open-market operations. It is clearly possible for additional private assets to be monetized by reducing the fractional reserve requirement.

Assume, momentarily without questioning the assumption, that bankers are not permitted by law to pay interest on their customers' demand deposits. So there is a deposit rate ceiling at zero. It is also supposed that on the cost side there is 'free storage' of money deposits. Consequently, it is reasonable to suppose that the competition of banks with one another will prevent them from being able to 'tax' their customers' demand deposits. Then if the treasury and central bank contrive to lower the anticipated inflation rate – the operation we have been studying – there will be an increased demand for bank deposits in real terms. The private opportunity costs to households of holding bank money as well as currency will have decreased, if it is assumed that the real rate of return on earning assets is not appreciably altered. Then clearly the reduction of the fractional reserve requirement is a way that the central bank can accommodate the increased real demand for money; as before, the increase in liquidity takes place without the need for an interim period in which the price 'level' has to adjust to an inflexible money level rather than the other way around.

Now about that assumption. It is true that if the banks were permitted to pay interest and if the anticipated inflation rate were initially high enough, they would actually pay some money interest rate on money deposited with them. We might assume then that as the anticipated inflation rate is successively reduced by small amounts, this deposit rate falls by roughly the same amounts. In this case there would result no increase in the real demand for bank money, the opportunity costs of holding it not being reduced; indeed, there may be some runoff into currency. But the point is that as we are focusing in this section on ideal liquidity, we surely want to require that the opportunity costs of holding currency and holding bank money be roughly the same. This rules out achieving high liquidity in terms of bank money at the expense of currency illiquidity. Furthermore, if we are going to explore the attainment of ideal liquidity via the inside money route we can justifiably anticipate that this will entail a rate of inflation that is in the neighborhood of zero or perhaps negative. In that case, it might well be the case that the banks would not individually choose to pay interest to their depositors even if they were legally permitted to, the nominal earnings rates on their investments being so low. It is entirely appropriate in this section, therefore, to restrict ourselves to the case where deposit rates paid on bank money are zero.

We have argued that the increased demand for liquidity at a lower anticipated inflation rate can be accommodated without the necessity for central bank purchase of private liabilities or capital claims. It can be accomplished by 'inside monetization' instead of 'outside monetization'. Now the great virtue of outside monetization, developed in the previous section, is that it accommodates the increased demand for money in real terms without simultaneously allowing an increase in real outside wealth; this wealth level is the central way by which the government affects thrift and thus the room that is left, after consumption, for capital formation. So let us ask whether this inside monetization will have that same virtue.

The 'nonbank public' has sold some securities to the banks in return for an equal increase in their real holdings of bank deposits. But the owners of the banks are also people. Their assets are up in real value by the amount of the securities purchased. It is true that their liabilities are also up an equal amount, namely, by the amount of the increase in the deposits left with them. But if they do not have to pay interest on their deposits, as they do earn interest from their holdings of securities, the banks' profits are up and so is the market value of bank shares in real terms. Neglecting any increased costs from the larger scale of the banks' operations, bank shares will be increased in value by the amount of the securities purchased, which is to say by the amount of the addition to their deposits. Roughly, the real value of bank shares (in aggregate) has risen by the amount of the increase in the real money supply, and this rise in bank shares is a net addition to real private wealth.[18]

It would seem that, by the ingenious stroke of reducing the reserve requirement, the central bank has failed to accommodate the increased liquidity in such a way as to maintain the pace of capital formation. Those who were fortunate enough to own bank shares reap a windfall capital gain not matched by anyone else's capital loss, so that one would expect some increase in their consumption demand. The operation would appear to have been 'bad for growth'. This would not substantially be altered if the banks tended to compete away the increase in monopoly rents by nonprice competition for deposits that took the form of more numerous and more expensive bank branches and buildings. Capital is then diverted rather than displaced.

Yet this displacement or diversion of capital that we have deduced is a consequence of going from nothing to something. As the anticipated inflation rate is reduced further, there must come a point where bank profits fall as a result of the lower nominal interest rates earned on loans and security investments owing to the lower inflation rate. Over the range of anticipated inflation rates from 10 percent to zero, for example, it is not empirically certain whether the larger real quantity of bank-held earning assets made possible by a reduction of the anticipated inflation rate would overcome the corresponding

---

[18] If one likes, he can treat the addition to the real value of bank shares as an addition to real outside wealth on the argument that it is a rise in the capitalized value of certain government licenses.

fall of the spread between the interest rate paid on deposits and the interest rate earned on investments. It is fairly clear, I believe, that the opposition of many banks to *increased* inflation arises very largely from their unhappiness at experiencing windfall real capital losses on loans and investments contracted at nominal interest rates when the credit market was not anticipating the faster inflation. This wealth reduction is redistributive, not a net reduction.

Despite this zone of uncertainty with respect to the wealth effect, it will be instructive to finish the inside money tale. Let us first ask: If the anticipated inflation rate is further reduced toward zero and beyond, will full liquidity be approached? The accompanying decline in the nominal rates of return expected to be obtainable on earning assets will drive the public to attempt to rid themselves of an ever-larger fraction of these assets in favor of money the opportunity cost of which is correspondingly lower. This requires that reserve requirements of the commercial banks be reduced so that they can create the money deposits with which to buy these earning assets – loans, bills, and whatever other securities the banks are permitted to invest in. But like the proverbial horse led to water, the commercial banks are not thereby forced to drink down these investments. The banks themselves will have a precautionary demand for liquidity, and at a sufficiently small nominal rate of return on available earning assets the banks will prefer to hold reserves in excess of requirements. Even though the banks' depositors are insured against losses, the banks' own prudent self-interest will set a lower bound on the level to which the reserve ratio can be driven down. Because this bound is definitely above zero, full liquidity cannot be indefinitely approximated to; that is, there is some positive lower bound on the spread between the rates of return on earning assets and the zero return on money that is attributable to the incapacity of the central bank to induce the commercial banks to undertake full monetization or full intermediation.[19] Only a public agency, such as the central bank, could be so bold as to monetize the risky credit instruments and capital claims of the private sector to the point of full liquidity.

The other question we have to face is this: Are there not some

[19] Inevitably one is reminded of the 'liquidity trap'. This is not the same thing, at least as usually interpreted. Trap doctrine asserts that the real money supply goes to infinity as 'the' nominal interest rate is driven down to some positive figure. It is assumed here that the latter figure is zero. But the nominal interest rate is still bounded above zero because the real money supply has a finite upper bound so that one emerges with a conclusion that differs with respect to maximum liquidity but is the same with respect to the lowest attainable nominal interest rate.

differences in the benefits and costs from additional liquidity when it is provided by the inside money route as contrasted to the outside money route? If so, the selection of the anticipated inflation rate which offers maximum liquidity by the inside money route may not be the ideal choice, even in the highly abstract setting to which we are confining ourselves in this and the previous section. In particular, if there is a positive social cost attached to each addition to liquidity through the inside route, the ideal amount of liquidity is less than the full amount; it may also be less than the maximum inducible liquidity level.

We have already noticed one difference with respect to 'cost' of additional liquidity when generated the inside way. At sufficiently high anticipated inflation rates and correspondingly high reserve requirements, it is probable that a reduction of the inflation rate and corresponding reduction of the fractional reserve requirement will increase the real profitability for each bank of attracting an additional real dollar of deposits (at a given real cost of doing so). This increase in the profitability of expanding the scale of a bank's operation will intensify the bank's nonprice competition for deposits – whereas there will be no similar increase in the real profitability of investment in the private nonbank sector. Once liquidity has increased to the point of equilibrating the supply and demand for capital *in toto*, there is left an excess of the real rate of return to capital in the commercial bank sector over the real return still available in the other sector. This excess will be driven out by a diversion of real capital from the latter to the former sector. This shift of capital will take the form of additional bank branches and expansion of capital facilities generally in the bank sector. To some extent this shift of capital will come from nonbank financial intermediaries; this is the case if the deposit rates which these institutions pay fall by the amount (roughly) of the decline in the anticipated inflation rate and in nominal interest rates on earning assets. Here there is no cost insofar as the commercial banks take over the facilities of the non-bank intermediaries or the shift is a slow process in which each year the banks simply make the replacement investments and net investments that would otherwise have gone into the facilities of the intermediaries. But even from this 'timeless' viewpoint, there is definitely some social cost from the shift of capital away from the non-bank-non-intermediary sector.[20]

[20] An analytically disconcerting feature of this capital-cost aspect of increased inside money expansion is that once the anticipated inflation rate has been

At the lower anticipated inflation rate and correspondingly lower nominal interest rates on earning assets, households' demand for bank money will be greater, and it was of course the object of the reserve requirement reduction to supply this additional bank money. But the banks' depositors will naturally demand the kinds of services from the additional bank money that make holding more of it attractive when its opportunity costs are reduced. It is after all the availability of these services that will lead people to want to hold additional bank money rather than merely additional coin and currency. To provide the larger volume of services that goes with the increase in the size and number of deposits at the banks, more resources in the form of labor and capital will be required. Not all the increase in overall running costs of commercial banks constitutes a net cost to society, for the additional resources the banks employ for the purposes of their larger investment activities are partly offset by the reduction in the resources employed for the same purpose by nonbank financial intermediaries. However, it is the larger operating costs of the banks *qua* suppliers of liquidity that we have in mind. These are definitely net costs to society which must be set against the social benefit of the addition to liquidity that is obtained.[21]

The lesson to be drawn is that there are always positive social costs to additional liquidity (over the whole attainable range) when the increase in liquidity is produced via the inside money and banking route. They are not zero as in the parable of outside coin and currency only. At least to a degree, the same conclusion would hold if increases in liquidity were produced by a single publicly owned bank the manager of which, upon receiving the signal that the shadow price of liquidity had been marked up by the Lange-Lerner planning authorities, undertakes to hire more resources in order to produce more. Undoubtedly all the *optimum* ways by which liquidity

---

reduced moderately far, it may no longer be true that the banks will be keen to proliferate their facilities to attract additional deposits; they will begin to feel the risks of staying fully loaned up. In any case, there are other cost elements.

[21] Of course, it makes no difference to the amount of the net cost who pays for the banking services. The incidence of these costs does affect the demand for bank money however. If the reduction of the anticipated inflation rate produces an 'effective' reduction in the own-rate of interest paid to bank depositors on their deposits in the disguise of increases in service charges, the increase in the quantity of bank liquidity demanded that results from the reduction of the inflation rate will be less or even nil. The matter of deposit rates is discussed in a later section.

can be increased do impose some positive marginal social cost. This positive marginal social cost (over the whole attainable range) guarantees that the ideal quantity of liquidity – where marginal social benefit just covers marginal social cost – is smaller than the full liquidity level characterized by zero marginal social benefit.

This conclusion leaves open the question of whether the ideal level of liquidity is also smaller than the maximum amount of liquidity the commercial banks can be induced to create. I believe the answer is probably yes, especially if we introduce additional social costs, those involving risk. As the anticipated inflation rate is reduced toward the point where the banks are unwilling to expand their loans and investments, the nonbank public may possibly still gain from larger liquidity. But what of the people who own the banks? Because they are not forced to pay depositors a larger real rate of return on their deposits, while the real rates of return on earning assets are essentially unchanged, the bank owners will feel that their 'expected utility' is being decreased. Even if they grit their teeth and stay fully loaned up until the exact point of maximum liquidity is reached, it does not follow that the approach to maximum liquidity is producing a gain for them or even for society as a whole. If bank share prices are sharply down with the approach to maximum liquidity, this is some sign that intermediation and the reallocation of risk-bearing is being carried too far.

The above presumption would be strengthened if it could be shown (as is probably the case) that maximum liquidity imposes on banks the payment of a real rate of interest on money that exceeds what their free competition would drive them to pay. In fact, we know that there are some destructive side effects when banks' deposit rates reach only their 'competitive' level. Much of the support for ceilings on deposit rates, including Regulation D that forbids interest on demand deposits, comes from those who are apprehensive about 'over-banking'. They argue that there is a widespread temptation of the individual banks to offer ever higher interest rates in order to attract or retain funds. Then, in order to be able to pay out such rates, they tend to move into ever-riskier investments. In a world of perfect information, competitive market forces would prevent such situations from arising. But in our world, with its imperfect information on the part of depositors and imperfect information by bank portfolio examiners, price competition for deposits would probably entail more excessive risk-taking or more policing or both. So whether the real rate of return on deposits comes about from free competition or through reduction of the anticipated inflation rate, the social costs of the overbanking that results, or the social costs incurred to prevent its resulting, will be the same in either case.

The conclusion to be drawn from this section is the following: As fuller liquidity is sought via the inside money route – reduced anticipated inflation together with reduced reserve requirements on the commercial banks – some ideal level of liquidity is likely to be attained short of the maximum real money supply that could be achieved by this route. It is certainly not ideal, and might not be attainable if it were, to have the full monetization of illiquid assets by private commercial banks that full liquidity can be presumed to require. The anticipated inflation rate that is necessary for this ideal liquidity level may of course be negative, like that required for full liquidity, but it is possible that it is a little above zero and it will not be far from zero in either case. In all this analysis it must be remembered that we have been abstracting from the social costs of raising government revenue and the social costs of stabilization. Consequently what is 'ideal' in the way of liquidity may not, all things considered, turn out to be truly *optimum* in the world as we know it.[22]

6.3.3. *Ideal Public Indebtedness and Credit Structure.* The previous analysis of inside money gives the impression that fractional reserve commercial banking is to be thought of as a last resort for creating liquidity, real outside wealth constant or almost so, being a device that is turned to only when the central bank has run out of interest-bearing government debt to monetize. If that were the theory of fractional reserves on which the American government has operated for so many years, however, we would not see any interest-bearing public debt outstanding, or at least not so much of it. A large portion of this publicly held government debt could be monetized by the Federal Reserve without a net expansionary effect upon aggregate demand if reserve requirements were at the same time raised to 100 percent.

It is possible to say something in favor of the monetary efficiency of this arrangement; on the other hand, a complete defense, if one were possible, would have to include the argument that this is the arrangement that history has left us and that, in view of the social costs of changing it rapidly, it is best to let it evolve slowly in what one expects to be the right direction most of the time.

[22] The next section is somewhat academic and might better be omitted by readers who are in a hurry to reach the 'real world'.

Let us assume that the government is in debt, that is, that the quantity of real outside wealth is positive.[23] The question is then whether it is better invariably for the central bank to monetize this debt – as long as there is some of it left in the hands of the public and more liquidity is desired – or whether it might be preferable at some point for the central bank instead to reduce reserve requirements. The point was made earlier that inside money creation suffers from disadvantages as a way to produce liquidity compared to outside money creation – principally, the risks borne in holding the assets that are monetized would not be 'felt' by the managers of the central bank or appreciably felt by the taxpayer, while they would be felt by the owners of the private banks; and there would be some tendency (at least over certain ranges) for reserve requirement reductions coupled with reduced nominal earnings rates to lead to overreaching for return and overbanking in the form of nonprice competition. But there are some advantages to leaving some interest-bearing public debt outstanding rather than monetizing it all before turning to reduction of reserve requirements:

Even the interest-bearing debt of the federal government is relatively liquid compared to privately owned capital and most private obligations. Neglecting the costs of greater liquidity, which we have stressed adequately, the ideal situation would be one in which there are no liquidity premiums. Likewise, in traveling part of the way toward that goal, the most efficient route is one that monetizes the most illiquid assets left available. Thus the central bank may very well serve liquidity if at some point, being barred from monetizing private assets, it delegates commercial banks to monetize some of these high-yield low-liquidity assets. Nothing would be accomplished by this if the commercial banks simply monetized the government debt. Note that this redirection of some of the monetization will necessitate some rise in the interest rates paid on government debt relative to the yields earned on very illiquid assets.

There is a corollary to this in the area of ideal debt management. If the degree of illiquidity were the only attribute that distinguished one kind of government bond from another, the optimum mix of government debt outstanding would be that maturity structure which minimized illiquidity. Given the heterogeneity of financial needs within the population, it is unlikely that this precept would call for

---

[23] This raises the question of whether it is ideal for the government to maintain its indebtedness over time through deficits to keep up with real growth plus any inflation; this is discussed below.

nothing else but short-term bills; longer-term obligations would, in certain quantities, enjoy high liquidity in some segments of the financial markets. But there are other desiderata in debt management, some of which are suggested by the rest of the list of advantages to having some interest-bearing debt left in the hands of the public.

A second advantage is that in reducing reserve requirements the government shapes commercial banks into institutions that become specialized in extending credit to a part of the financial market. Of course, it might be asked why other financial institutions could not perform these services as well. One answer implicity 'discounts the future': we had commercial banks before we had the huge federal debt, and it may be wondered whether reassigning the banks' lending role to other institutions would be worth the transitional cost. But there are also zero-discount answers. Some institutional division of lending functions could be justified by the thought that if there were a single type of omnibus financial institution, there would be room for only a very few in each city or region and each such institution would enjoy an undesirable degree of monopoly power. Further, commercial banks probably enjoy greater stability in the size of their deposits, with or without central bank help, and so there seems to be some advantage in having this institution among those that extend credit; it is a good candidate for purchasing relatively illiquid credit instruments, such as the IOUs of small businesses.

Another advantage brings in stabilization policy (which will be considered more fully in the next section). The open-market purchase of government securities is a convenient instrument for stabilization policy. One merit is that the effect of stabilization on the cost and availability of credit to business borrowers may be more diffuse, though not different in total, if open-market operations are used instead of placing sole ar primary reliance on variations in reserve requirements. Another merit is that by insuring a steadier course of the required reserve ratio, the central bank may reduce somewhat the return to risk-bearing earned by the commercial banks, the incidence of which falls partly upon the types of borrowers who find it cheapest to borrow from the banks.

Finally, there may be some utility in having an interest rate visible when decisions are made by the government affecting the amount of federal borrowing. In this way the public and the legislators see a cost of government borrowing though the economist knows that it may be smaller, and sometimes greater, than the real cost. It might well be argued, however, that the public is in greater need of seeing the benefits of government borrowing, especially when economic activity is severly depressed but not only in these times.

This is a good point to take up another question that has been hovering in the background. If we are analyzing ideal financial and monetary arrangements, why should it be regarded as ideal that there should exist a positive amount of government indebtedness? First of all, we have in this country an amount of outside wealth that the most austere budgetary surpluses imaginable would take a decade or two to extinguish. By contrast, the kinds of changes in financial institutions that would be implied by inflation changes of the magnitude we have been discussing would not take nearly so long to complete. 'Selecting' the level of per capita outside wealth is really a longer-term process than selecting the equilibrium inflation rate if one is going to select zero public indebtedness.

However there are perfectly sound arguments for having a positive amount of government indebtedness. The superiority of outside liquidity over inside liquidity presents such an argument if the government is proscribed from monetizing private obligations. Then it must create outside *wealth* if it is going to create *outside* liquidity. The economics of this matter is always somewhat confusing because outside money *when backed* by government debt does double duty as source of wealth as well as liquidity. Yet distinctions can and should be made.

There is a case for some public indebtedness even if it is postulated that the central bank can monetize private tangible capital and tangible-capital claims without ill effect. One argument is that the public debt, whether held in interest-bearing form or in the form of money, offers an 'amenity' that might be called economic security. It offers fair assurance to the individual holding it that the income flow from it (the potential cash flow if only cash flow should be relevant to the individual) or its cash value will be somewhat statistically independent of the luck or misfortunes that strike the individual's holdings of human capital. Thus people may want marketable material wealth not solely because they want to sacrifice present consumption for the certainty of a greater future consumption but because they fear the risks of a loss of future earning power. Wealth will therefore be valued partly for that reason in order to be spent when emergency needs for it arise. Without the device of a budgetary deficit, the buildup of wealth would entail the sacrifice of present consumption; a deficit can create the wealth without that cost. In short, even if the central bank has created full liquidity, it has not thereby satiated the demand for economic security.[24]

There exist other arguments for the belief that the private sector would have a tendency to oversave if the government produced no outside wealth as an alternative to capital. Perhaps the public debt is the work of an equally invisible *political* hand. But there also exist reasons for thinking it possible that there is undersaving – it is possible that people overestimate or undervalue future economic benefits, saving or bequeathing less than they would really like to or ought to. As outside wealth is algebraically increased from some large negative figure, it would seem that at some point the balance of arguments would tip in favor of the undersaving contention. It is perfectly possible, perhaps probable, that this point occurs at some positive level of government indebtedness. One does not have to conclude that the present level of government indebtedness is just right. My guess is that it is too large, though this is not to say that there is enough economic security.

6.4. *Optimum Liquidity Where Taxation and Stabilization Are Costly*

We have been assuming up to now that the methods of taxation and of stabilization open to the government are not socially costly in the sense of imposing any 'deadweight loss' of consumer surplus. It will be the purpose of this section to show that when this assumption is dropped, it will be optimal to 'trade off' a certain amount of benefit from liquidity in return for some reduction in the deadweight costs of ordinary taxation and stabilization methods thereby made possible. It will be argued that the optimum quantity of liquidity, in view of this trade-off, is less than the ideal quantity of liquidity – the latter being optimum only in the 'ideal' world where it is assumed there is no such trade-off.

Even in the ideal world just visited, it was argued that the ideal monetization of capital claims and the government debt stops short of full monetization because at some point the most worthwhile increases in liquidity are too resource-absorbing. Even in the case most favorable to liquidity, where monetization is from the 'outside', there are still positive marginal social costs of increasing the

---

[24] These ideas make their appearance in A. C. Pigou, 'The Classical Stationary State', *Economic Journal*, September 1938. I have been led to the emphasis on economic security, and to the reinterpretation of Pigou, by an unpublished paper by Donald A. Nichols.

Landmark Papers in Macroeconomics

level of liquidity. If the monopoly central bank is to induce wealth-owners to hold a larger share of their wealth in the form of deposits (swapping some of their earning assets for deposits at the bank), it is likely that the social-cost-minimizing technique to do that includes offering more convenient physical facilities and customer services, not just a greater real rate of return on deposits that wealthowners can take advantage of only at positive resource costs to themselves.[25] More clear-cut is the cost of the larger investment department needed to make loan and investment decisions the greater is the degree of monetization to be achieved. If the most illiquid assets are, after allowance for appraisal costs, the first to be monetized, it may be conjectured that a level of liquidity will be reached such that the marginal social benefit from further monetization fails to cover the marginal social costs.[26]

The first step away from that idealized world has already been taken. There are political objections to the outside monetization of private obligations and capital claims; moreover, there may be economic advantages arising from 'decentralization' and 'competition' in allowing private firms, specifically commercial banks, to select the loans and investments to be made. If we accept as a datum the prohibition against central bank investment in private claims (whatever its merits), the optimum expansion of liquidity involves some inside monetization as well as outside monetization – for private obligations and capital claims are among the best candidates for monetization. But as monetization proceeds along this route toward the ideal liquidity level, we encounter the social costs of excessive risk-bearing by private commercial banks and the possibility of wasteful overbanking.

Having accepted commercial banks into the framework, it remains to accept the rest of the universe. The most conspicuous features to be reckoned with are the social costs of stabilization and the social costs of ordinary methods of taxation. Their bearing on the optimum level of liquidity in this nonideal world (however idealized in other respects) will now be considered.

6.4.1. *Stabilization Costs and Optimum Liquidity*. It was not so long ago that fiscal policy was the principal receptacle in which faith was

[25] One thinks here of post office economy and mail-order banking.

[26] Insofar as these resources which are diverted to the bank merely come from private intermediary and brokerage institutions that would otherwise have employed them, there is no net cost, but then there is presumably little or no net benefit either. I am well aware, incidentally, that the presence of positive marginal social costs does not insure against a 'corner maximum' at full monetization.

placed that the government could stabilize the economy tolerably closely around some desired equilibrium point. The central bank was assigned the more prosaic tasks of insuring orderly financial markets and desirably low nominal rates of interest. The social benefit from high liquidity is nothing new in central bank theory!

On administrative grounds and on neoclassic resource allocation grounds it came to be agreed that variations in tax rates and in the timing of certain transfer payments are preferable to variation of government expenditures and of their timing for the purposes of economic stabilization. But changes in tax rates have proven to be an inflexible instrument too. There is often legislative bickering over the distribution of the additional tax burden or tax relief. Also, legislators apparently believe that tax rates are symbols for the electorate, if not for themselves; some legislators will oppose a tax increase on the ground that it will symbolize to the executive the legislative consent to certain types of government spending; other legislators with the same antispending objectives may demand the tax increase in the hope that the wrath of the electorate will force the executive to reduce the spending.

But tax rate variations are not a perfect stabilization tool no matter how wisely they are enacted. Changes in excise tax rates often cause disturbances due to anticipatory or deferred buying (the problem of leads and lags most familiarly encountered in exchange rate and tariff rate variations). Changes in rates of income taxation, especially if believed to be temporary, may have to go so far as to produce sharp reductions in disposable incomes in order to counter the increase in employment and incomes from an expansionary disturbance, say a war or an investment boom. There is probably some zone in terms of output and the inflation rate such that the fiscal steps necessary to keep those variables inside the zone will cause more instability rather than less in terms of the success with which households are able on the average to realize their economic plans.[27]

The pendulum of opinion on methods of stabilization appears now to have swung the other way. Some economists would even give the major responsibility for economic stabilization to the monetary authorities, requiring of fiscal behavior only that major destabilizing actions be moderated where possible and that tax rates be held in reserve for use in a major disequilibrium. At the minimum, it must

---

[27] The implied criterion seems to be a sensible one if, and only if, it is the socially optimal equilibrium point that the stabilization policies are attempting to keep the economy averaging around.

be agreed that the best stabilization policy mix gives monetary policy an important stabilization role. This does not mean that the monetary authorities are not asked to keep one eye out on the long-run target inflation rate as they attempt to contain or to moderate exogenous disturbances of the economy away from the path to that target. In the same way it can be hoped that the use of temporary surtaxes will not deflect fiscal policy from tending toward its long-run stance of budgetary tightness or ease as desired for the realization of the 'growth' target. The ship's pilot circumnavigating iceberg flows and tropical storms ought not to forget the port he is paid to reach.

It is important therefore to consider the influence of the expected rate of inflation on the costs, reliability, and tasks of stabilization by monetary means. The first point to be made is that the establishment of an expected inflation rate so low as to bring about ideal liquidity, or something near it, may leave the central bank in the position of having shot its bolt. If a contractionary disturbance calls for easier money, hence additional monetization of earning assets, the central bank may find that its commandment of ideal liquidity has left it with no more government securities outstanding that it can purchase and has left the commercial banks in the position in which further reductions of the reserve requirement encourage only a small addition in their loans and investment if any addition at all. The prohibition against private investments by the central bank might then be lifted, but perhaps not without debate over the alternatives and a loss of time.

What if new methods of accomplishing the additional monetization were permitted? The central bank might be allowed to adopt a more relaxed position on rediscounting the bank's investments or, conceivably, even to monetize some private assets directly.[28] It must be conceded, though, that there are certain losses incurred when the central bank is driven to such actions compared with the less extreme steps that would be needed to accomplish the same increase in monetization when starting from less than the ideal amount of

---

[28] The possibility of a tax on the commercial banks' excess reserves at the central bank also comes to mind. If coupled with an equal tax on their holdings of currency, this could drive the banks to purchase additional earning assets to escape the tax. This is a tax on money so far as the commercial banks are concerned and one that is feasible because of the difficulty of the banks in disguising or concealing the composition of their portfolios. The feasibility of such a tax on households' money holdings is less clear. Proposals to tax money as a solution to depressions are made in A. Dahlberg, *When Capital Goes on Strike* (New York: Harper, 1938), and in S. Gesell, *The Natural Economic Order* (San Antonio, Texas: Free-Economy Publishing Co., 1934).

liquidity. These are the losses from pushing monetization beyond the ideal level. (Of course, this extreme step would be preferable to fiscal and monetary inaction that left capital and other resources idle, but that is beside the point.)

The second type of objection to the establishment of nominal interest rates low enough to secure the ideal amount of liquidity involves the reliability of monetary policy in those circumstances. This objection is often expressed by saying the demand for liquidity, when pictured as a function of the average nominal rate of interest on certain earning assets, is flatter at very low rates of interest than it is at 'medium-high' rates of interest and that, as a consequence, countercycle monetary policy is less 'effective' at very low rates of interest.[29]

A frequent counter is that if a given reduction of the nominal rate of interest must be engineered to reestablish equilibrium, the central bank need merely increase the money supply by a greater amount the flatter demand-for-money curve is. There are various answers to that at the most practical level. One of them is that it is fortunate if you can get the monetary authorities to increase the money supply at all when output and employment are falling. Just as the treasury has the tendency to think that the automatic rise of the budgetary deficit which accompanies the fall of incomes may itself be a sufficient stimulus to return the system quickly to equilibrium, the central bank may mistake the automatic fall of interest rates consequent upon the reduction in the demand for capital and credit as a sufficient countercyclical force. Another answer is that the monetary authorities may suffer from 'money interest rate illusion', thinking that it is the proportionate rate of decrease of money interest rates that matters, so that a drop from 2 percent to 1 percent appears enormous.

It is likely, however, that the most rational central bank would find its effectiveness at stabilization – for a given difficulty in the degree of instability it is confronted with – impeded by the prevalence of very low money rates of interest and high liquidity. If capital goods, equities, bonds, and money are all highly liquid, it would seem that any increase of the money supply would have a less predictable effect upon the demand for capital than would be the case if these asset types were highly complementary, held very nearly in

---

[29] One does not have to believe in a liquidity trap at a positive nominal rate of interest to agree with the flatness assumption. Note, however, that the demand for money function will not be convex everywhere, contrary to the usual textbook drawing if, as the nominal rate of interest is increased sufficiently, the demand for money approaches zero.

'fixed proportions'. The larger the increase in the money supply required to produce the mathematical expectation of the given reduction in the nominal interest rate which is assumed to be needed, therefore, the greater the risk is that the money increase will prove too little or too much. If deviations from the target have increasing marginal disutility, the policy-maker who maximizes the expectation of utility may choose an increase of the money supply having the expectation that it will be insufficient to reach the target but will compensate for this by reducing the risk of overshooting.[30] However admirably the monetary policy-maker responds to these risks, it is still true that his performance will be better on average the less chancy are the effects of the tools with which he has to operate.

The last objection to low nominal interest rates involves their effect on the strength of the destabilizing forces present in the economy. If the establishment of a low expected rate of inflation reduced the size of the tasks required of monetary stabilization policy, this might well compensate for the costs it tends to impose in the unreliability of the monetary tools available for stabilization. In fact, the establishment of a regime of low nominal interest rates corresponding to a small rate of expected inflation is likely to exacerbate the instability with which the monetary (and fiscal) authorities have to deal.

This contention depends on an assumption regarding the sensitivity of the money-market-clearing price 'level', at any given expected price trend, to exogenous disturbances in the demand for capital, particularly an increase in the expected nominal rate of return on capital, however this comes about. It can be argued on a couple of grounds that the price level which clears the market for money is more sensitive to disturbances, and hence more likely to permit a destabilizing process to develop, the higher the level of liquidity is, hence the lower nominal rates of interest are, at any initial level of real outside wealth. Once the ground has been laid for this critical assumption, we can turn to the details of the unstable process around the equilibrium inflation rate.

One basis for this argument appeals to the wealth effects on the quantity of goods demanded of a disturbance in the demand for goods. The larger the fraction of initial outside wealth that has been monetized, it may be argued, the larger is the initial rise of the price

[30] This is only one possible result of many that could occur, but it does not seem that the general point about the costs of risk will be affected by potential complexities provided the policy-maker is appropriately risk-averse. Several examples of policy-making under risk are studied in W. G. Brainard, 'Monetary Policy and Uncertainty', *American Economic Review*, May 1967.

'level' induced by an increase in the expected nominal rate of return on capital. To the extent that illiquid interest-bearing government debt is outstanding, it constitutes an extra cushion between the price level and exogenous disturbances in the demand for goods. At given nominal supplies of both money and government debt outstanding, a rise of the price level reduces the real value of both the money stock and the interest-bearing debt. But if the nominal expected return on capital has increased, interest rates will rise and the real value of the government bonds will fall further. This decline in bond prices from the rush to get into equities and physical capital itself tends to moderate the increase in the quantity of capital and consumption goods demanded and thus moderates the early rise in the price of goods. The more illiquid the outside wealth, the less liquid tinder there is to be sparked by an unanticipated increase in the attractiveness of goods as against liquidity.[31]

That thesis can be expressed in these terms: A one-point increase in the expected nominal rate of return on equities (and their close substitutes) has a larger proportionate effect on the money-market-clearing level of goods prices the more liquid is the economy – for given nominal supplies of outside money and privately held government bonds; equivalently, it results in a larger proportionate fall in the market-clearing real value of the money supply the larger the initial level of the real money supply.

Another basis for this same thesis can be built on the Keynesian liquidity effect of a rise in the expected return to capital as well as the wealth effect just examined. It is commonly believed that at very low nominal rate of interest, a given increase in the expected return on capital produces a larger proportionate decrease in the quantity of real money demanded than would be the case at moderately high money interest rates. That belief seems reasonable enough. At quite low money interest rates, monetization and intermediation have reached such heights that the demand for money is largely 'asset demand' and very volatile: Small changes in the expected nominal rates of return on capital then have large proportionate effects on the total demand for money; this compared to a situation of moderately high money interest rates.[32]

[31] This point is emphasized in D. M. Winch, 'Inflation and Resource Allocation', Queen's University Conference on Inflation and the Canadian Experience, June 22–24, 1970.

[32] Note, however, that at very high interest rates, the transaction demand for money must become highly sloped, eventually reaching the vertical zero-liquidity axis, though the asset demand is in that range nil or almost so.

208   *Welfare Effects and Inflation*

There is adequate basis, therefore, for an assumption commonly made in the neo-Keynesian analysis of instability begun in the early 1950s. That assumption is that a one-point increase of the nominal rate of interest (or return on capital) produces a larger proportionate decrease in the real quantity of money balances demanded the smaller the initial level of interest rate is. The (absolute) logarithmic slope of the 'demand curve' for real money balances is greater at very low nominal interest rates than at moderately high ones. As a consequence, the proportionate early rise of the price 'level' – and hence the initial increase of the inflation rate above the equilibrium inflation rate – that results from an increase in the expected nominal return on capital is greater the larger the initial real money supply is – equivalently, the lower the equilibrium rate of inflation is (given the real rate of return on capital). The larger the sensitivity of the actual inflation rate to such a disturbance in the demand for capital, presumably, the greater the likelihood is that expectations of greater inflation thereby induced will feed back strongly on the demand for money enough to produce a potentially unstable motion from equilibrium. The gist of these stability models, as I interpret them, can be briefly sketched.[33]

We adopt the natural-unemployment rate framework according to which a *dis*equilibrium is marked by a discrepancy between the actual and expected rates of inflation with the latter chasing the former in the adaptive-expectations manner discussed in Chapter 2. We suppose that the money supply is following some predesignated path, as is any quantity of outside wealth left unmonetized. Accordingly, a decrease in the quantity of money demanded, as from an increase in the expected pecuniary rate of return from holding capital claims, increases the quantity of equities, and ultimately, goods which are demanded and thus increases the monetary rate of inflation. This effect on the inflation rate is greater the larger the (absolute) logarithmic slope of the demand for money curve is, inasmuch as that

---

[33] The kind of mathematical model under discussion originates in two remarkable papers, W. S. Vickrey, 'Stability through Inflation', in K. K. Kurihara, ed., *Post-Keynesian Economics* (New Brunswick, N.J.: Rutgers University Press, 1954), and P. H. Cagan, 'The Monetary Dynamics of Hyperinflation', in M. Friedman, ed., *Studies in the Quantity Theory of Money* (Chicago: University of Chicago Press, 1956). Similar analyses of the stability problem, usually in a growth context, have recently been made by Sidrauski, Stein, Nagatani, and Tsiang, with much the same sort of results being obtained. 'Nonmonetary' sources of instability, ones having no obvious connection with inflation expectations, have been explored in well-known papers by Kaldor, Samuelson, Hicks, and Rose, to mention a few.

determines the size of the increased demand for goods (decreased demand for money) from the given increase in the expected nominal rate of return. The momentary increase of the inflation rate would be only temporary, the system returning to equilibrium at the expected inflation rate, if the latter did not rise by some fraction of the momentary increase in the actual inflation rate. But the induced rise of the expected inflation rate raises *pro tanto* the expected pecuniary rate of return on capital claims and goods. This feeds back upon the quantity of money demanded and hence upon the actual inflation rate produced 'next period', doing so *in proportion to* the logarithmic slope of the demand curve. The expected inflation rate is consequently increased again. Its rise can be likened to the familiar 'multiplier process' in fixed-price Keynesian models. The convergence of this process to some higher but steady expected inflation rate requires that the logarithmic slope not exceed unity by so much as to swamp the 'stabilizing' tendency of the expected inflation rate to make up only a fraction of the excess of actual or expected rates plus any other frictions one might posit which make the momentary inflation rate respond only sluggishly to each decrease in the quantity of money demanded.[34]

True, the logarithmic slope of the money demand curve will become smaller and therefore more stabilizing, according to our assumption, as nominal interest rates continue their rise. It would seem at first, therefore, that the system will stabilize after all, albeit only at some high level of the inflation rate. But if the monetary authorities do not accede to the higher-inflation equilibrium, the economy must overshoot, sending employment below the natural level into a downward spiral. Once nominal interest rates hit bottom, be that zero or some positive floor, the economy will be stuck until an 'active' fiscal policy comes to the rescue, liquidity at this point being not further augmentable by central bank efforts at monetization of the usual sort.

[34] The requirement for stability is that the 'marginal propensity to inflate with respect to the expected pecuniary return to capital' (or equivalently, the expected rate of inflation) be less than unity. In the world of Cagan and Sidrausky, this propensity is the fractional adaptive-expectations coefficient *times* the absolute value of the logarithmic slope of the money demand curve. These are continuous-time models of the simplest sort. Vickrey's discrete-time model yields a more stringent condition on the largest size of the logarithmic slope consistent for stability. It is local stability that is being analyzed and these conditions are not enough, it would appear, to guarantee global stability. I judge therefore that the problem of instability is really worse than these results show it to be when it is assumed that the money supply follows an inflexible predesignated course.

There are of course grave problems of realism in any comprehensible model of economic instability. The model has left out adaptive or discretionary monetary policy. I do not believe that it would be impossible to expect of monetary and fiscal policy that it keep the expected inflation rate averaging around some very low figure. Indeed, the central bank would get the same 'score' that it would earn in the high interest rate regime *if* it were, in the former case, to make up in a reduction of the slope of its credit *supply* the increase in the slope of the *demand* for money. But there is little reason to assume such a fully compensatory response.

The above considerations convince me that the costs incurred and the errors made in the attempt to stabilize the economy will be much greater at low rates of interest than at high rates. At low rates of inflation the trials of the stabilizers are made harder and their tools made blunter and less reliable. In a world of uncertainty, a policy of moderately high inflation in order to contain liquidity somewhere below the otherwise ideal level imposes a cost which can be viewed as the premium charged for (limited!) insurance against economic instability. Moreover it is the poor and disadvantaged who could expect to receive the largest benefits from this insurance. Some positive amount of such insurance would seem to be definitely worth buying.

6.4.2. Deadweight Costs of Ordinary Taxation. It is a familiar proposition in the theory of taxation that there are not enough fiscal tools to permit the simultaneous attainment of the many objectives that one would like to secure from the tax system. The proposition has its origin in the observation that if poll taxes are eschewed, it is open to each household to spend its time in pleasureful or ultimately productive ways that 'escape' taxation – leisure and home production being the common examples. The avoidance of poll taxes has its root in the uncertainty about the fairness that any distribution of them over households would turn out to have. The income tax, which is really many fiscal tools, one for each income bracket, exemplifies the 'imperfection' of the fiscal tools available. While it is possible over an extensive range to achieve the desired revenue for public expenditure and at the same time, by varying the progressivity, to achieve the desired distribution of after-tax income, it leaves leisure untaxed and saving twice taxed. Even if, say, saving deserves to be taxed once more (with greater or less feeling), it will be an accident if the total tax happens to produce just the right after-tax rate of return to saving. An expenditure tax, while perhaps better on the saving front, is less adaptable to the desires for tax progressivity.[35]

I shall argue here that some positive effective tax rate on liquidity, a rate which places its private opportunity cost above the marginal social benefit of liquidity at the 'ideal' level, would improve the approximation of the tax system to its various objectives. An 'inflation tax' is a useful addition to the armory of fiscal tools, no one of them being perfect by itself or even in concert. This is not quite a trivial conclusion, for the problem of fiscal inefficiency is not a matter of the paucity of tools, but rather the deleterious side effects of each tool. If one tool is merely a linear scale replica of another in use, it cannot contribute anything to fiscal efficiency. And some tax devices when used at 'positive levels' would do more harm than good, being dominated by or at least not preferred in their results to other tools. But it is very doubtful that an inflation tax falls in that immediately excludable category.

It might seem that this contention goes against an existing presumption for pricing at marginal social cost, hence production levels at the 'ideal' output rates. But that presumption fell to the ground with the development of the 'theory of second best' in the fields of tariffs and excise rates, largely in Britain, two decades ago. In fact, this attack on marginal cost pricing was only the second wave, following earlier explorations of the optimal structure of excise tax rates by Marshall, Pigou, and Ramsey.[36] In this country, the general presumption against marginal cost pricing was clearly stated by William Vickrey, a dedicated advocate of efficient resource allocation and usually associated with that pricing injunction. After speaking of various objectives that conflict with the marginal cost rule, Vickrey says:[37]

[35] See N. Kaldor, *An Expenditure Tax* (London: George Allen & Unwin, 1955), and the references to Mill, Fisher, and other writers. The latest extensive treatment of the problem of imperfect fiscal 'controllability', this one set in a dynamic context, is K. J. Arrow and M. Kurz, *Public Investment, The Rate of Return, and Optimum Fiscal Policy* (Baltimore: Johns Hopkins Press, for Resources for the Future, 1970).

[36] Much of this literature, though far from all of it, is reviewed and extended in W. J. Baumol and D. F. Bradford, 'Optimal Departures from Marginal Cost Pricing', *American Economic Review*, June 1970. See also J. S. Chipman, 'External Economies of Scale and Competitive Equilibrium', *Quarterly Journal of Economics*, August 1970. There is also the work of Meade, Little, de Graaf, Lipsey and Lancaster, Whinston and Davis, McManus, Buchanan, and others.

[37] W. S. Vickrey, 'Some Implications of Marginal Cost Pricing for Public Utilities', *American Economic Review Papers and Proceedings*, May 1955, p. 607.

By far the most important of these considerations that conflict with the strict application of marginal cost pricing is the need for revenues. Many of the more extreme advocates of marginal cost pricing for decreasing cost industries seem tacitly to assume that the Government has some perfectly costless and neutral source of revenue that is capable of very substantial expansion without ill effects. Such a state might be approached, for example, if we had an income tax free of its multiple effects, evasion proof, with no marginal cost of administration or compliance, and including in its base not only money income but all forms of direct income in kind, including an imputed value for leisure. Needless to say, this is far from the case.

The nonideal world that Vickrey describes does not yet have a presumptive pricing rule having the same wide acceptance and comprehensibility as the old marginal cost rule. Yet the following guides appear to have been established:

In a much-studied special case in consumer preferences, all taxable goods ought to be cut back if room must be made for resource-using public expenditure – and cut back roughly in the same proportion from their ideal output levels. In the general case of preferences, if good 1 has price above marginal social cost because of the need for tax revenue and good 3 has price equal to marginal social cost, because it is untaxable, for example, then there is some tax on good 2, making its price higher by some amount than its marginal social cost, that is superior to leaving it untaxed – provided this tax permits a reduction in the other tax, revenue constant. If (and only if) good 1 is more substitutable for good 3 than is good 2 at equal *ad valorem* tax rates on goods 1 and 2, there is differential pattern with a higher tax rate on good 2 and a lower one on good 1 that is superior to equal tax rates – provided each rate is in a range such that its reduction would cause a loss of tax revenue.

In all cases, the test is essentially whether the tax change will shift resources from the good or goods of which too much is consumed into the good or goods of which too little is consumed, taxes net of any (lump-sum) transfers being held constant.[38] Good 3 might be

[38] It is therefore the 'compensated elasticity of substitution' and compensated demand curves that are relevant, meaning that the representative consumer believes it could buy the same bundle of goods after the tax rate change if it wished. See W. J. Corlett and D. C. Hague, 'Complementarity and the Excess Burden of Taxation', *Review of Economic Studies*, August 1953. These results on the critical role played by separability or its absence appear also in papers by O. A. Davis and A. H. Whinston.

home-produced goods of which there is too much, given the amount of transfers or the amount of resources employed by the government the outlays for which are to be financed. If good 2 is less substitutable for leisure activities than is good 1, taxing it (good 2) more heavily will moderate the inefficient expansion of leisure that must to some extent result from the substitution effects of the taxation required for revenue.[39]

Let us now try to say something about the optimum rate of taxation of liquidity in terms of the precautionary type of liquidity model introduced above.[40] It is supposed that a given real level of after-tax transfers is to be made to the public by the government. A flat income tax rate on the cash receipts of households is one source of tax revenue for this purpose. In the normal case, an increase in the expected rate of inflation, by increasing the deficit consistent with that real outlay of transfer payments, will permit a reduction of the tax rate; the rise of the nominal interest rate (and expected inflation rate) will outweigh the induced decline in the quantity of liquidity demanded to produce a net seigniorage gain. The normal case seems certain to prevail once we are in the range of moderate nominal interest rates, whether or not it prevails very close to the ideal liquidity level. Attention will be focused on the consequences for allocative efficiency of the employment and liquidity decisions of the representative household, neglecting the effect that a change in the after-tax real rate of interest may have on the rate of total saving.

I consider two extreme cases. In the first, each household desires liquidity only for the sake of getting bargains in the things it buys, in 'getting better purchase prices'. It therefore anticipates that the portion of its outside wealth which it decides to hold in the form of interest-less real cash balances will not affect the amount of income tax it must pay. If we assume, as a rough approximation, that the before-tax real rate of interest is insensitive to the mix of taxes chosen by the government, an increase of the expected inflation rate

---

[39] This is, presumably, the slim rationale for the belief that it is best to tax most heavily those goods whose (compensated) demand curves are 'least elastic', like salt. Certainly a good whose compensated demand is highly inelastic must be highly complementary with leisure and with every other good. But some demand elasticities could be large because of the substitutability with one another, not with leisure and should not escape taxation for this reason! In the good 3 case, there does not appear to be a difference between the complementarity guide and the compensated elasticity guide. With an income tax, this is about all the goods we have in aggregative terms.

[40] The following material has benefited from lengthy discussions with Kenneth Arrow, Peter Diamond, David Levhari, and Eytan Sheshinski.

will be offset by a rise in the money interest rate on the illiquid portion of the outside wealth; the inflation tax is paid therefore primarily on the amount of wealth which the household elects to hold in liquid form.

One may think of the household's utility in this setting as being a function of the leisure it takes, its liquidity and its 'measured consumption' in the sense of its cash receipts from employment deflated by the average of prices in the market. The household's liquidity and its cash receipts combine to produce the amount of 'true consumption' that it can enjoy. For the larger its liquidity, the lower on average will the prices be of the things it purchases, given the average of the prices in the market. The household buys these three goods in amounts that depend in the usual way upon their after-tax prices or after-tax private opportunity costs. If the income tax rate is 25 percent, we may say that leisure is being subsidized at a 25 percent *ad valorem* rates. Alternatively, one is free to use the money wage as *numeraire* and to say that the after-tax price of 'measured consumption' is 33 percent; leisure from this view goes untaxed – its 'price' is still the before-tax money wage rate.

How does the income tax affect the after-tax opportunity cost of liquidity in this model? Abstracting from the expected inflation rate for a moment, an increase of the income tax rate, applied equally to interest income and to wage income, must *reduce* the after-tax opportunity cost of liquidity, whereas we saw earlier that the after-tax reward to liquidity was not touched by the income tax. Assume, for the sake of the argument, that the expected inflation rate is initially such that the before-tax money rate of interest is low enough for 'ideal' liquidity. If we recognize that the maintenance of the ideal level of liquidity imposes positive marginal social costs – the instability cost if not the other costs discussed, which are more persuasive in the mixed inside-outside money case than the pure outside money case – this money interest rate figure is definitely positive. The private opportunity cost of liquidity, however, is the after-tax money rate of interest in this case; this must be lower than the before-tax money interest rate by a fraction of the latter equal to the tax rate (one-quarter in the above example).

In this case, therefore, the income tax drives the private opportunity cost of liquidity below the marginal social cost of liquidity (equals marginal social benefit at the 'ideal' liquidity level) when, in the absence of the income tax effect, the nominal rate of interest would be appropriate for 'ideal' liquidity. If we regard measured

Anticipated Inflation 215

consumption as being untaxed, we may say that both liquidity and leisure are being subsidized to a degree because they are ways of escaping the income tax. Alternatively, we may say that while measured consumption is subject to an excise tax (33 percent in our example), leisure and liquidity are both untaxed.[41] The conclusion is that there is too little measured consumption, too little utility being produced by real consumption expenditure (using the average market price as the deflator), and too many resources being wasted in excessive leisure and liquidity. There is a lot of home production and a lot of shopping being done and not enough paid employment being undertaken.[42]

At a minimum it can then be argued that there would be an allocative gain from establishing some higher value of the expected inflation rate. There is some increase in the 'inflation tax' which will offset the implicit subsidy to liquidity coming from the income tax effect, so that the excess liquidity is eliminated, the 'ideal' level restored. This is a clear improvement at least in the normal case where there is a seigniorage gain obtained.

At this point, if we regard measured consumption as untaxed, there is still a subsidy to leisure while none on balance to liquidity. A small further increase of the inflation tax will produce only a small departure from the 'ideal' liquidity level. But in the normal case it will permit a lower income tax rate.[43] Hence it will 'buy' a reduction in the subsidy to leisure, which is well above the optimum level to begin with. This utility gain is of a greater order of magnitude than the utility loss from the first small step away from 'ideal' liquidity. Some small net tax on liquidity, producible from added expected inflation, is definitely preferable to no tax, inasmuch as it permits a reduction in the already large subsidy to leisure. This is a straightforward application of the presumptive guide sketched earlier, which

[41] The jth consumer maximizes his utility subject to a budget constraint whose first differential yields

$$dc^j + i(1-t)d\pounds^j + \phi_n^j . (1-t)dz^j = 0$$

where t is the income tax rate, c his consumption, z his leisure time, $\pounds$ his liquidity, and ϕ_n^j his marginal product. Equivalently, writing $1 + \tau = (1-t)^{-1}$, we have

$$(1 + \tau)dc^j + i . dM^j + \phi_n^j . dz^j = 0.$$

[42] S. B. Linder, *The Harried Leisure Class* (New York: Columbia University Press, 1969).

[43] This proposition might seem overqualified on the ground that going from a zero tax on liquidity to some positive tax *must* yield a positive rectangle of tax revenue net of social 'production' costs. But in principle, the tax could produce a cross effect that diminishes the income tax collected.

216					*Welfare Effects and Inflation*

says that in the normal case no taxable good should be spared some positive tax rate.

We see now that it was quite inessential to assume, realistic though it is, that at the optimum liquidity level the corresponding nominal rate of interest is positive. If the State of California could meter people for the sunshine each absorbs, even though sunning ourselves is not resource-absorbing, some small tax on basking in the sun would be a net fiscal gain, reducing the deadweight onerousness of income and sales taxes, provided only that the smallest tax on tanning does not drive us totally into the shade. Or consider the uncongested bridge that one can travel across at zero marginal social cost. Some price on crossings in excess of zero is definitely a fiscal improvement as long as the shadow price of tax revenue collected in other ways is positive. By the same analysis, the pursuit of ideal liquidity is a luxury in a world where the other sources of tax revenue impose deadweight losses of consumer surplus.

The other reference point of interest is where the net tax on liquidity is equal on an *ad valorem* basis to the tax on measured consumption, regarding leisure as being unsubsidized. The inflation tax will have reduced the income tax rate from 25 percent in our example to, for example, 20 percent, so that the new implicit excise tax rate on measured consumption is in that case 25 percent instead of 33 percent. An equal *ad valorem* rate of tax on liquidity would place its private (after tax) opportunity cost at the same 25 percent above the marginal social cost of liquidity.[44] If the marginal social cost of transforming a dollar's worth of highly illiquid assets into real cash balances is, for example, 6 percent at the second-best fiscal optimum – considering instability, overbanking, and all the rest – the household should be made to face a private opportunity cost of choosing cash instead of the illiquid asset of 7.5 percent. If breakeven

[44] At this point the reader may well ask what should be done with the special case in which the marginal social cost of liquidity is everywhere zero. Then any positive tax on liquidity would imply an infinitely high *ad valorem* rate. Yet we just convinced ourselves that free goods ought not to be exempted from taxation when costless sources of tax revenue are not available. A resolution of this puzzle consists of noting that when the 'price' of liquidity is near zero, the (compensated) elasticity of substitution between liquidity and leisure is close to zero so that, in that neighborhood, the substitutability guide to the tax differential does indicate a relatively high tax *ad valorem* on this good. The polar case, however, simply warns against the applicability of formulas that divide through by zero quantities. The literature does contain formulas in terms of 'specific' rates of tax, as the previous references show.

capital gains are untaxed, this corresponds to a before-tax nominal interest rate of nearly 9.4 percent. (A triplet of round numbers is 4.5, 6.0, and 7.5, respectively.)

But it might be guessed that liquidity is much more 'complementary' with leisure than is measured consumption. Equivalently, a differential tax on liquidity, coupled by a compensating reduction in the income tax rate in the normal case, would reduce the over-stimulation of leisure. Spending liquid assets is a principal use of unpaid household time. (It is possible that households would respond oppositely, making up for the increased liquidity tax by spending more time shopping even more carefully, being able less frequently to seize good bargains just chanced upon because they are willingly illiquid more often; but this outcome would not be my guess.) Of course, the increase of the liquidity tax encourages more 'trips to the bank', hence a reduction of paid employment and measured consumption. But the reduction of the income tax rate will reduce the encouragement of such unpaid productive activities. It is the differential effect that matters.

There is another angle (that of Ramsey, Boiteux, and Samuelson) that may produce insights into our conundrum. The optimum tax differential according to that analysis reduces measured consumption and liquidity approximately in the same proportion, the approximation being better the smaller the tax revenue to be collected. If the (compensated) demand for liquidity is more inelastic than the demand for measured consumption (money income at a given price 'level'), the higher tax rate on the former is indicated if cross-elasticities are negligible. One thinks of the demand for money as highly inelastic – the importance of being 'unimportant'! In any case, there seems to be no presumption that the net rate of tax on liquidity should be less than the tax on cash receipts. And this seems especially safe to say when one considers that the supply of saving is another allocation decision for the income tax to do damage to, alongside the employment decision, like a fiscal bull in a Pareto-ideal china shop.

The above analysis has broader applicability than might at first appear. The income tax stimulus to liquidity is a standard feature of transactions demand models of money-holding. If there are brokerage costs in moving in and out of earning assets, transactions balances are more likely to be held entirely in liquid form the higher the tax rate on interest income. Even Keynes's speculative bulls may pull in their horns more frequently the higher the government's take on any capital gain. But let us turn now to the *other* extreme case of precautionary money demand.

We shall now suppose that liquid balances are held exclusively to obtain greater average cash income over time, and this income is taxed at the flat income tax rate. The household may hold liquid assets so that it can ride out periods 'between employment' and thus obtain better selling prices for its services. By staying liquid between investments it can expect to get better asset purchase prices and hence obtain a larger interest (and rental) income on average from a given amount of wealth. In this case, the rewards from being liquid are taxed like the rewards of being illiquid. Both the reward and the private opportunity cost of being a little more liquid are reduced after income tax in the same proportion. There is no strong reason in this case for believing that the income tax has any direct stimulus on the demand for money at a given average nominal rate of interest on earning assets. Consequently it cannot in this extreme case be presumed that excess liquidity is induced by the income tax when the before-tax interest rate is set at the level of the marginal social cost of liquidity at the 'ideal' level – unlike the previous model.

Let us confine our attention to this neutral case. Then a flat tax rate on income can be viewed as a subsidy to leisure alone, employment and liquidity being affected only indirectly by this subsidy.[45] The case for levying an inflation-tax on liquidity must now rest exclusively on the premise that, in lowering the income tax rate needed and hence *its* implicit subsidy to leisure, it will induce some decline of leisure.

We have now to consider in this new context the question of differential substitutability. Would an inflation tax on liquidity, accompanied by a reduction of the income tax rate to keep revenue constant, decrease leisure? There is one fresh ground for an affirmative answer, one not applicable previously. The inflation tax might reduce between-jobs precautionary unemployment, and thus stimulate employment, by *reducing* liquidity. (The reduction of the tax rate it simultaneously permits in the normal case merely reinforces the lessening of leisure.) With liquidity more costly, there may be less shopping for jobs as well as shopping for consumer goods. We have been adhering to the notion of liquidity as capital, misallocated only

[45] If we let $\gamma(n^j, \mathcal{L}^j)$ represent our household's cash receipts, n^j being its paid employed time, the first differential of the budget equation is

$$dc^j + (1 - t)(i - \gamma_{\mathcal{L}}^j) + \gamma_n^j \cdot (1 - t)dz^j = 0,$$

but the household will equate $\gamma_{\mathcal{L}}$ to i, leaving no 'subsidy' to $\mathcal{L}^j$.

Anticipated Inflation 219

if the government injudiciously misprices it above its marginal production cost. But in a less than perfectly liquid economy of certainty
and full information, people may misuse their liquidity. Insofar as
added liquidity improves the market without greater average investment of time in 'search', there is a clear net gain. But if added
liquidity is complementary with resource-using search, the matter is
less clear.

More generally, if, at a given level of real public outlays, for
whatever reasons, a higher rate of anticipated inflation produces an
increase in the macroequilibrium level of employment – miscalculation, the symbol of money wage gains, whatever – we have an
effective answer to our differential substitutability question. In that
case, up to a point, the inflation tax will prove an allocative benefit.

It seems to me to be a sporting guess therefore that even in the
case in which all the perceived private rewards from a household's
liquidity are fully taxable at the income tax rate – surely quite an
extreme case – there is an allocative gain to be obtained from an
inflation tax on top of the income tax. In addition, there is a practical
aspect of income tax revenue collection that probably clinches the
argument. We have been abstracting from the resource-using collection costs. The administrative time required to increase tax
compliance is a positive marginal social cost of income tax revenue
collected. The administrative costs of the income tax machinery are
undoubtedly small per unit of tax revenue thus collected. But it is
surely likely that the last dollar collected imposes real resource costs.
The state may very well spend more money to collect the unpaid taxes
of the orneriest taxee than the amount of taxes he owes – though only
as an object lesson to others, and if the tax collectors optimize, they
will insure that the last dollar of their costs has a net tax yield overall.

It is just this consideration that has led many economists to support the use of a heavy inflation tax in underdeveloped countries
where the marginal administrative resource cost of income tax
revenue (and other kinds of tax revenue) must be considered substantial. In one well-known study, it was assumed that an extra
dollar of tax revenue would cost an amount of extra resources worth
10 cents. Even a small cost like that can lead to the optimality of an
enormous inflation tax.[46]

The appeal to this practical cost of income taxation does not mean

[46] M. J. Bailey, 'The Welfare Cost of Inflationary Finance', *Journal of Political
Economy*, April 1956; reprinted, with pertinent corrections, in K. J. Arrow and
T. Scitovsky, eds., *Readings in Welfare Economics* (Chicago: Irwin, for the

220   *Welfare Effects and Inflation*

that we can safely discard the subtle questions of differential substitutability and elasticity. These considerations must enter into the
calculation of an exactly optimal mix of taxes. But the marginal
administrative cost of income taxation definitely biases upward the
optimum inflation tax on liquidity. This marginal social cost, while
unquestionably much smaller in this country than in many less
developed nations, even if only 4 cents on the marginal income tax
dollar, must substantially increase the optimum tax on liquidity and,
for a given total tax revenue, decrease the optimum rate of income tax.

6.4.3. *Distribution and the Public Sector.* Only economists would
couch the analysis of the optimum liquidity tax in terms of differential
tax analysis, public expenditures and transfer payments being held
constant. It is always possible that the public and its legislators
would choose, knowingly or inadvertently, to utilize the added
'revenue' from the move to an optimal inflation tax by expanding
the public sector or, instead, by allowing that tax to cut back further
on private consumption demand so as to allow a larger share of
resources for capital formation at macroequilibrium. There may be
some who would favor a little bit of all three – lower income tax
rates, larger public expenditures and transfers, and smaller private
consumption. As I write, there is again talk among economists, as
in the years around 1960, that the public sector and capital formation both are being squeezed for want of sufficiently high taxation.
We are becoming aware that our net national product is smaller than
we thought it was if we require that the environment, like the capital
stock, be kept 'intact'. At the threshold of a major social innovation
to help the poor, the family assistance proposal, there is hesitation
and the likelihood of underfunding in any case for lack of federal
revenue. There is currently some talk of a 'housing shortage'. How
incredible it is, therefore, that at such a time it should be once again
impressed upon us how important it is to reduce expectations of
inflation, and hence repeal the inflation tax.

It was argued in Chapter 5 that windfall losses in the real value of
money holdings from unexpected inflation may very well be 'progressive' in the relevant proportional sense. It may be, however, that
when the inflation is expected, the well-to-do are better able than the
poor to hedge against that inflation, taking advantage of compen-

American Economic Association, 1969). See also A. L. Marty, 'Growth and the
Welfare Cost of Inflationary Finance', *Journal of Political Economy*, February
1967.

satory increases in the nominal rates of return on many earning assets. But if income and expenditure taxes are left unchanged in the move to an inflation tax, there may be an additional progressive influence. The government can then undertake an increased volume of public expenditures, public investments, and transfer payments without choking off private consumption, the inflation tax accommodating the expansion of these programs. This would be likely to benefit the poor proportionately more than the nonpoor. This is true if for no other reason than the fact that a dollar's worth of improvement in the environment, for example, is a larger proportion of the poor man's living standard than it is of the prosperous man's. Moreover, it is predominantly the poor, mostly crowded in cities, who derive the greatest absolute benefit from an expansion of public services and public investments designed to improve the facilities of modern, largely urban, living.

The other scenario has tax rates, real transfers, and public expenditures not directly dependent upon the increase of the inflation tax (where the interest on the public debt is calculated in the appropriate real terms). Then private consumption is constrained by the liquidity tax and some additional capital-deepening takes place in the way of private plant and equipment, industrial research, private education, and so on. How would this increase in the capital intensiveness of the economy influence the share of total socioeconomic benefit received by the poor? If one thinks of the poor as standing outside the economy and living on public assistance, the poor will have to count on larger transfers financed by the larger tax revenue from the larger output in order to stay even with the nonpoor. Conceivably, the volume of transfer payments to the poor is a 'luxury good' (income elastic), in which case there will be some logarithmic trickling down. The poor do earn income however and a larger share of their income, one assumes, comes from their wages than is the case with the nonpoor. But it is not clear that the rental to strong-back labor will thereby be increased.

Lastly, to reinforce the ideas of this section, consider that once an inflation tax has been established at high levels, it will inevitably be proposed that banks be allowed to pay interest on money. They would not be allowed presumably to compete indefinitely for deposits to such a point that the resource waste of overbanking become flagrant. But it might be proposed that the deposit-rate ceiling of zero be raised by the amount of the increase in nominal interest rates resulting from the inflation tax.

Landmark Papers in Macroeconomics

Obviously, the payment of the same own-rate of interest on every kind of money, including currency and coin, would simply undo the gain in moving to an optimal inflation tax rate. The effective tax on liquidity would thus be removed. But what would be the effect of a differentially lower effective tax on deposits alone? For the same tax revenue, either the income tax rate (or other ordinary rates of taxation) would have to be increased or else the effective rate of tax on currency would have to be increased. In the latter case, which seems the natural one, we are back to the standard question in differential tax analysis where initially two tax rates are equal and we are contemplating unequalizing them. I see no obvious case for such unequalizing of the two liquidity tax rates in terms of differential substitutability and elasticity.

There is, however, the point that it is deposits which are likely to exhibit the higher level of marginal social cost, not currency. It is the dangers of overintermediation, overbanking, and instability that impose some marginal social cost on liquidity, and these dangers refer more to deposits at banks than to coin and currency. This suggests that it is deposits that should present the higher private opportunity cost of holding, not currency. Nevertheless, it should be mentioned that one must not prohibit pecuniary interest on demand deposits, while at the same time permitting the banks to pay an effective interest on deposits held through the offering of free goods.

6.5. *Monetary Efficiency: The Unit of Account*

Probably the oldest objections to inflation involve its impairment of the efficiency of money as the principal unit of account. Before turning to these objections, we should consider briefly the proper measurement of inflation. This has not been until now a question requiring attention, for monetary efficiency with respect to liquidity alone involves only the plainly measurable levels of nominal or money interest rates, never a 'true' (or false) real rate of interest.

6.5.1. *Price Index Biases* There are many respects in which the goods that a household can buy with a fixed hoard of dollars become preferable to those purchasable previously that are not 'objectively' measurable. Greater commodity standardization, improved quality control and product reliability, cheaper acquisition of consumer information (for a given heterogeneity of the goods available), and a widening assortment of goods produced are all normal per se and have no implication for the rise of the cost of living. It has to do with the rate at which the means of living outstrips the cost of living, both properly measured. But if some of these concomitants of the growth process are neglected by the ordinary (and perfectly defensible) methods of measuring the cost of living, the rise of cost of living will be overestimated (and so too will the rate of growth).

Another unmeasured gain in the value of a hoarded dollar comes from quality improvements in the 'same' consumer good. It has been argued that undermeasurement of the quality improvements in each year's new models of consumer goods alone biases upward the Consumer Price Index by some 2 percent annually. The period since the war may on this count by itself be one of true deflation, though probably less than the average expected true deflation rate. There must be some merit in this contention. Few are the consumers who, with a fixed budget of cash to spend, would prefer to buy from the Gross National Catalog for 1950 at its listed prices than from today's catalog of superior goods even at today's much higher prices.[47]

The growing decline of amenities attributed to rising congestion and pollution does not affect the validity of the above proposition. These phenomena have to do with the economy's rate of *economic growth*, not with the algebraic decline in the purchasing power of a dollar. The decline in the (true) cost of living measures the improvement in the opportunities of a dollar, not with any improvement in the opportunities of people. The worsening of the environment does not erode the purchasing power of the dollar because the consumer who holds a dollar cannot buy an improvement in the environment *qua* consumer: if he buys tomorrow he will get increased smog tomorrow. The purchasing power of the consumer's hoarded dollar over the goods the consumption of which he can vary by purchase or nonpurchase with his dollar will still be improving at 2 percent.

When we discuss the efficiency of money as a unit of account, it is probably the *true* rate of inflation to which we should refer. It is of some interest to note that the exact choice of an index is not important insofar as liquidity is what is at stake. One's assumption about unmeasured gains in the purchasing power of a dollar cannot affect the size of the measured inflation rate that would be judged necessary for achieving the optimum amount of liquidity – *given* the way that

---

[47] The price index for a given type of good should fall by at least the decline in the price of the old model if still produced. Richard Ruggles has pointed out that this is insufficient, for the consumer's choice has been expanded since he can purchase the new model if he prefers.

inflation is measured. The real rate of return from holding a dollar is increased by the unmeasured consumption good quality improvements, given the measured ones. But the real rate of return from investment in an earning asset bearing a given nominal rate of interest will be increased by the same amount. The consumer can enjoy a superior bundle of consumer goods by waiting to consume, but money is not the only store of value available for that purpose. If the consumer hoarded for 15 years, he is able now to purchase better goods albeit at higher prices. If he invested in a government bond with 15 years to maturity and promising a nominal yield of 3 percent, he still has the option now to purchase the superior goods at the higher prices. If a nominal yield on the representative earning asset of 3 percent was deemed appropriate for optimum liquidity before it dawned on academic economists that the nation's Consumers Price Index had an upward bias, the same spread between the nominal yield on earning assets and money continues to be necessary for optimum liquidity after the scientific discovery.'

The question of what *measured* trend there should be in the measured price index for the attainment of ideal liquidity would become significant only if there were an 'inspired' insight into what *true* rate of inflation would be necessary for ideal liquidity. Ordinary economists will have to decide directly what spread in rates of nominal return between money and nonmoney assets is appropriate for optimum liquidity. Given the way the consumer price index is constructed, some measured rate of inflation will correspond to optimum liquidity, but its size and algebraic sign will be of no consequence for the determination of the optimum quality of liquidity. If the construction of the consumer price index should be reformed so as to capture previously unmeasured quality improvements, the new measured inflation rate corresponding to the same optimum liquidity level will of course be algebraically smaller. But if liquidity were the single touchstone for deciding on the rate of anticipated inflation, the price index problem could simply be ignored. All that the optimum liquidity analysis required of the consumer price index used for measuring the rate of inflation is that a reduction of the rate of inflation thus measured corresponds, real wealth constant, to a reduction in the nominal rates of return expected to be earned on capital, capital claims, and other illiquid nonmoney assets.[48]

[48] This belabors the obvious to a pulp. But what is one to do with analyses of optimum liquidity that conclude in favor of zero *true* inflation as if unmeasured quality changes had something to do with liquidity?

6.5.2. *Miscalculations* It has been argued that the higher the rate of anticipated inflation, considered as a positive quantity, the greater is the effort required by people in making purchase and sale decisions. The same contention presumably applies, with some qualification in a progressive economy, to the pace of anticipated deflation.[49]

Insofar as the argument is that rising prices present 'calculational' obstacles to the comparison of buy-now and buy-later plans, there is an obvious debating point in reply. The money rate of interest, if positive, necessitates the same sort of calculation even when the general price level is steady. But it ought to be granted that while the problem is the same in a qualitative way, it is quantitatively more difficult the faster prices are rising.

A deeper and perhaps more disturbing basis for the contention rests on the imperfectness of information on current price quotations. This same non-Walrasian feature underlies much of the theory of unemployment as the first chapter sought to show. If the various prices quoted in the market can be learned, subject to some constraint on money spent, only gradually over time and soon obsolesce, then decision-makers must to some degree base their transaction decisions upon their subjective calculations of the correction necessary to place price quotations observed in the past on a current basis. As people do not carry log tables in their heads, these calculations are onerous and some errors, random or systematic, are likely to be made. The larger the trend rates of change the greater must be the time needed and the scope for error.

It might seem that this argument points to the desirability of a zero rate of anticipated inflation, at least from the point of view of time lost in making calculations. One might wish to look into the structure of product prices, however, not simply the index. If all but one kind of product displayed uniformly falling prices at zero overall inflation, one might be inclined to favor some positive inflation so as to keep most prices constant. Stabilization of the price of the product having the median long-term rate of price change might be preferable to stabilization of the mean product price.

More important, at zero anticipated inflation, money-wage rates will be trending upward in a progressive economy. Then producers must make intertemporal calculations of the normal wage trend even at zero inflation of product prices. With a constant money wage index, product prices would be falling at the rate of productivity growth.

[49] For a discussion of this matter see, for example, H. G. Johnson, 'Monetary Efficiency', *Journal of Political Economy*, December 1968.

Does the minimum-error inflation rate lie between these two rates of price change? Or does any algebraic inflation rate in between lead to the same amount of time spent and error made: more in product markets at the deflation end and more in labor markets at the other end?

The errors made can be significant causes of allocational effects from differences in the anticipated inflation rate. A carpenter estimating what his materials will cost him may accept a job having undercompounded to the present date his past observations of the costs of those materials. A woman may resist an expensive coat not appreciating to what extent her present one and alternative new coats have gone up in price. It is likely that a higher anticipated inflation rate would produce a larger labor force participation rate and a reduced frequency of idleness of some workers, despite no change of the technological factor price relationships, because households believe they are being offered high relative wages, having failed to compound sufficiently the money-wage rate data they know about from the past.

Are such stimuli to employment and saving bad? They are not ideal instruments for the purpose. It is reasonable to regard them as imposing some social costs. Yet one may find these allocative effects from increased anticipated inflation to be a convenient handle for public policy in coping with some of the underemployment arising from market imperfections discussed in Chapter 4. As a stimulus to saving, it has the fortunate effect of not reducing employment, unlike the income tax, as a tool to keep consumption down. On account of its likely 'miscalculation effects' on employment and saving alone, therefore, the technique of anticipated inflation may well deserve a place in the mixed bag of second-best weapons that should be deployed against socially excessive unemployment in macroequilibrium.

Yet there are certainly some side costs from anticipated inflation. Another aspect to the relation of the price trend to the efficiency of money as a unit of account involves the frequency of currency reforms. Prices are not free to be chosen on the 'real line' but are rather chosen to the nearest penny. If the penny is worth a lot, half-pennies and even smaller units may be used. If all prices and nominal aggregates like the money supply should eventually double, a reform of the denominations of coin and currency would then be optimal if the mix of denominations was optimal before. Centimes may die out while more valuable units of coin and currency will be needed. Even the unit of account might be desirable to alter if prices increase manyfold. The more rapid the anticipated inflation or the anticipated deflation, the more often these currency reforms will be appropriate. While this factor is not of major importance for inflation rates in the plausible range, it is a consideration that ought not to be lost sight of. It is another factor, along with the other considerations of monetary efficiency, that makes a sufficiently rapid anticipated inflation rate too costly.

6.5.3. *Confidence in the Price Trend.* There is another consideration often argued to militate against the establishment of an inflationist regime. A level price trend is said to be unique in that only the grail of price stability can enlist the public spirit of sacrifice that the monetary authority needs on occasions if it is to keep the inflation rate under control at any reasonable figure. It may indeed be easier to impress the public with the sacredness of zero inflation than with the importance of some ill-understood target rate like 5 percent – both targets expressed in terms of the official price index its constructors chose to calculate or the price of meat and subway rides, not the true inflation rate which is unmeasurable. If the central bank is construed as having to bargain with a dissatisfied and recalcitrant mob, it may prefer the credibility of zero as its last offer, when 2 percent is demanded, to having to insist on 5 percent, when the mob is demanding 7.

A similar argument has it that inflation is like an addictive drug which is eventually overused at great expense once used at all. It might be optimal to take an occasional cigarette, even three or four a day, but it takes impossible will power not to take those cigarettes sooner and ultimately oftener.

What is the conclusion drawn? Either that inflation can be stabilized only at too high a rate or at too low a rate; or that attempts to steer a middle course will be a storm-tossed navigation. All this is bleakly pessimistic about human nature and capacities, like the choice posed of anarchy or oligarchy. Perhaps a country gets the inflation rate it deserves – relative to its advantages and abilities. It may be that we do not yet have the maturity in matters of economic policy to be able to handle the task of achieving an avowed goal of inflation at some moderate rate. Nevertheless there must by now be a good chance of doing so. It seems far-fetched to think that the kinds of personality defects and misjudgments exhibited in over-smoking, for example, would produce a serious amount of over-inflation. We do not lack for highly visible nuisance costs of inflation which the layman at present magnifies a thousand times. Moreover, at a moderate inflation rate the underlying technical power of the central bank to stabilize the economy would be enhanced, and the destabilizing impulses on the inflation rate diminished. The years since the war do not disprove that moderate inflations, in many countries at least, can proceed without leading to runaway rising inflation and with little pretense that price stability must and will be sought.

But suppose the exercise of inflation control, once unleashed from dysfunctional conventions of the fiscal and monetary past, were to be less farsighted than one would wish, leading to too high a rate. That situation would not be irreversible. And, in any case, surely libertarians who support the right of a sane adult to spend his dollars on tobacco, private schooling, and the rest should grant educated citizens the right to spend their votes for more inflation (or more unemployment) if they should wish. It is the disutility of too much inflation that should be left to limit our appetite for it, not a taboo. The method of choosing public policies should by itself be a merit of a democracy, but it is not when the people are hobbled with myths. Better to suffer from rational errors than irrational ones. Getting hold of our policy-making potentialities is as much the point as the modest though valuable economic gain that should be expected to result.

[27]

The Relation Between Unemployment and the Rate of Change of Money Wage Rates in the United Kingdom, 1861–1957[1]

By A. W. PHILLIPS

I. HYPOTHESIS

When the demand for a commodity or service is high relatively to the supply of it we expect the price to rise, the rate of rise being greater the greater the excess demand. Conversely when the demand is low relatively to the supply we expect the price to fall, the rate of fall being greater the greater the deficiency of demand. It seems plausible that this principle should operate as one of the factors determining the rate of change of money wage rates, which are the price of labour services. When the demand for labour is high and there are very few unemployed we should expect employers to bid wage rates up quite rapidly, each firm and each industry being continually tempted to offer a little above the prevailing rates to attract the most suitable labour from other firms and industries. On the other hand it appears that workers are reluctant to offer their services at less than the prevailing rates when the demand for labour is low and unemployment is high so that wage rates fall only very slowly. The relation between unemployment and the rate of change of wage rates is therefore likely to be highly non-linear.

It seems possible that a second factor influencing the rate of change of money wage rates might be the rate of change of the demand for labour, and so of unemployment. Thus in a year of rising business activity, with the demand for labour increasing and the percentage unemployment decreasing, employers will be bidding more vigorously for the services of labour than they would be in a year during which the average percentage unemployment was the same but the demand for labour was not increasing. Conversely in a year of falling business activity, with the demand for labour decreasing and the percentage unemployment increasing, employers will be less inclined to grant wage increases, and workers will be in a weaker position to press for them, than they would be in a year during which the average percentage unemployment was the same but the demand for labour was not decreasing.

A third factor which may affect the rate of change of money wage rates is the rate of change of retail prices, operating through cost of living adjustments in wage rates. It will be argued here, however, that cost of living adjustments will have little or no effect on the rate of change of money wage rates except at times when retail prices are

[1] This study is part of a wider research project financed by a grant from the Ford Foundation. The writer was assisted by Mrs. Marjory Klonarides. Thanks are due to Professor E. H. Phelps Brown, Professor J. E. Meade and Dr. R. G. Lipsey for comments on an earlier draft.

forced up by a very rapid rise in import prices (or, on rare occasions in the United Kingdom, in the prices of home-produced agricultural products). For suppose that productivity is increasing steadily at the rate of, say, 2 per cent. per annum and that aggregate demand is increasing similarly so that unemployment is remaining constant at, say, 2 per cent. Assume that with this level of unemployment and without any cost of living adjustments wage rates rise by, say, 3 per cent. per annum as the result of employers' competitive bidding for labour and that import prices and the prices of other factor services are also rising by 3 per cent. per annum. Then retail prices will be rising on average at the rate of about 1 per cent. per annum (the rate of change of factor costs minus the rate of change of productivity). Under these conditions the introduction of cost of living adjustments in wage rates will have no effect, for employers will merely be giving under the name of cost of living adjustments part of the wage increases which they would in any case have given as a result of their competitive bidding for labour.

Assuming that the value of imports is one fifth of national income, it is only at times when the annual rate of change of import prices exceeds the rate at which wage rates would rise as a result of competitive bidding by employers by more than five times the rate of increase of productivity that cost of living adjustments become an operative factor in increasing the rate of change of money wage rates. Thus in the example given above a rate of increase of import prices of more than 13 per cent. per annum would more than offset the effects of rising productivity so that retail prices would rise by more than 3 per cent. per annum. Cost of living adjustments would then lead to a greater increase in wage rates than would have occurred as a result of employers' demand for labour and this would cause a further increase in retail prices, the rapid rise in import prices thus initiating a wage-price spiral which would continue until the rate of increase of import prices dropped significantly below the critical value of about 13 per cent. per annum.

The purpose of the present study is to see whether statistical evidence supports the hypothesis that the rate of change of money wage rates in the United Kingdom can be explained by the level of unemployment and the rate of change of unemployment, except in or immediately after those years in which there was a very rapid rise in import prices, and if so to form some quantitative estimate of the relation between unemployment and the rate of change of money wage rates. The periods 1861-1913, 1913-1948 and 1948-1957 will be considered separately.

II. 1861-1913

Schlote's index of the average price of imports[1] shows an increase of 12·5 per cent. in import prices in 1862 as compared with the previous

---

[1] W. Schlote, *British Overseas Trade from 1700 to the 1930's*, Table 26.

year, an increase of 7·6 per cent. in 1900 and in 1910, and an increase of 7·0 per cent. in 1872. In no other year between 1861 and 1913 was there an increase in import prices of as much as 5 per cent. If the hypothesis stated above is correct the rise in import prices in 1862 may just have been sufficient to start up a mild wage-price spiral, but in the remainder of the period changes in import prices will have had little or no effect on the rate of change of wage rates.

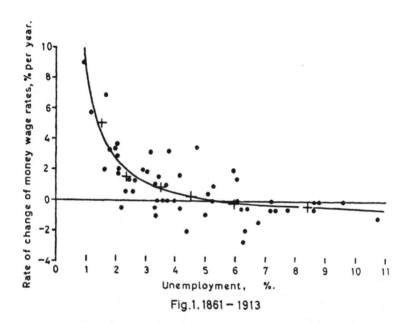

Fig.1. 1861 — 1913

A scatter diagram of the rate of change of wage rates and the percentage unemployment for the years 1861-1913 is shown in Figure 1. During this time there were 6½ fairly regular trade cycles with an average period of about 8 years. Scatter diagrams for the years of each trade cycle are shown in Figures 2 to 8. Each dot in the diagrams represents a year, the average rate of change of money wage rates during the year being given by the scale on the vertical axis and the average unemployment during the year by the scale on the horizontal axis. The rate of change of money wage rates was calculated from the index of hourly wage rates constructed by Phelps Brown and Sheila Hopkins,[1] by expressing the first central difference of the index for each year as a percentage of the index for the same year. Thus the rate of change for 1861 is taken to be half the difference between the index for 1862 and the index for 1860 expressed as a percentage of the index

---

[1] E. H. Phelps Brown and Sheila Hopkins, " The Course of Wage Rates in Five Countries, 1860-1939," *Oxford Economic Papers*, June, 1950.

286 ECONOMICA [NOVEMBER

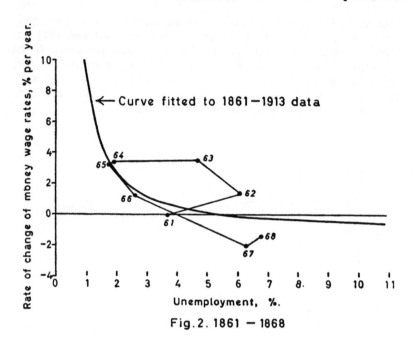

Fig. 2. 1861 — 1868

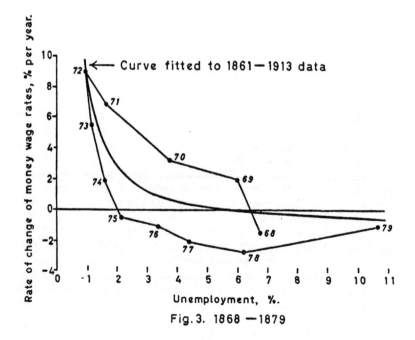

Fig. 3. 1868 —1879

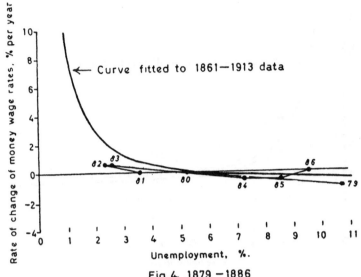

Fig.4. 1879 – 1886

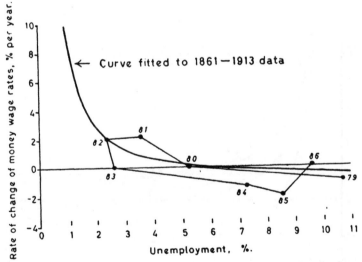

Fig.4a. 1879 – 1886, using Bowley's wage
index for the years 1881 to 1886

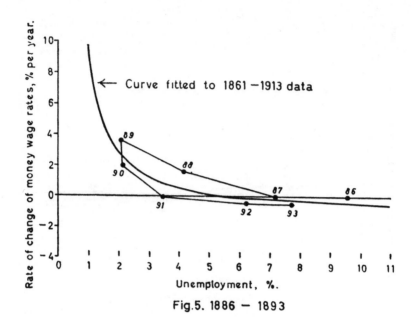

Fig.5. 1886 — 1893

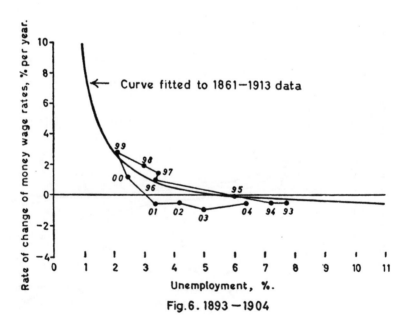

Fig.6. 1893 — 1904

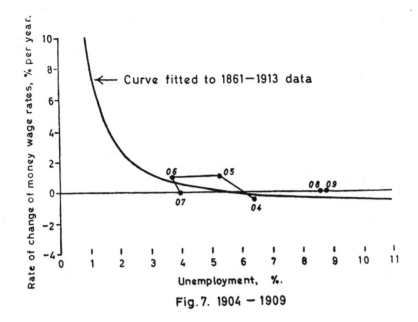

Fig.7. 1904 — 1909

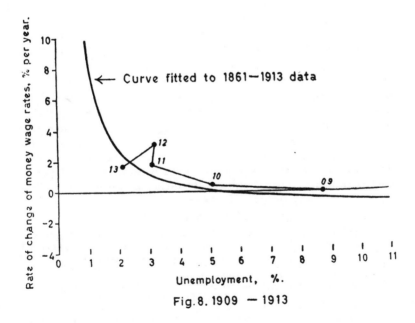

Fig.8. 1909 — 1913

for 1861, and similarly for other years.[1] The percentage unemployment figures are those calculated by the Board of Trade and the Ministry of Labour[2] from trade union returns. The corresponding percentage employment figures are quoted in Beveridge, *Full Employment in a Free Society*, Table 22.

It will be seen from Figures 2 to 8 that there is a clear tendency for the rate of change of money wage rates to be high when unemployment is low and to be low or negative when unemployment is high. There is also a clear tendency for the rate of change of money wage rates at any given level of unemployment to be above the average for that level of unemployment when unemployment is decreasing during the upswing of a trade cycle and to be below the average for that level of unemployment when unemployment is increasing during the downswing of a trade cycle.

The crosses shown in Figure 1 give the average values of the rate of change of money wage rates and of the percentage unemployment in those years in which unemployment lay between 0 and 2, 2 and 3, 3 and 4, 4 and 5, 5 and 7, and 7 and 11 per cent. respectively (the upper bound being included in each interval). Since each interval includes years in which unemployment was increasing and years in which it was decreasing the effect of changing unemployment on the rate of change of wage rates tends to be cancelled out by this averaging, so that each cross gives an approximation to the rate of change of wages which would be associated with the indicated level of unemployment if unemployment were held constant at that level.

The curve shown in Figure 1 (and repeated for comparison in later diagrams) was fitted to the crosses. The form of equation chosen was

$$y + a = bx^c$$

or
$$\log (y + a) = \log b + c \log x$$

where y is the rate of change of wage rates and x is the percentage unemployment. The constants b and c were estimated by least squares using the values of y and x corresponding to the crosses in the four intervals between 0 and 5 per cent. unemployment, the constant a being chosen by trial and error to make the curve pass as close as possible to the remaining two crosses in the intervals between 5 and 11 per cent. unemployment.[3] The equation of the fitted curve is

$$y + 0 \cdot 900 = 9 \cdot 638 x^{-1 \cdot 394}$$

or
$$\log (y + 0 \cdot 900) = 0.984 - 1 \cdot 394 \log x.$$

[1] The index is apparently intended to measure the average of wage rates during each year. The first central difference is therefore the best simple approximation to the average absolute rate of change of wage rates during a year· and the central difference expressed as a percentage of the index number is an appropriate measure of the average percentage rate of change of wage rates during the year.

[2] *Memoranda upon British and Foreign Trade and Industrial Conditions* (Second Series) (Cd. 2337), B.P.P. 1905, Vol. 84; *21st Abstract of Labour Statistics, 1919–1933* (Cd. 4625), B.P.P. 1933–34, Vol. 26.

[3] At first sight it might appear preferable to carry out a multiple regression of y on the variables x and $\frac{dx}{dt}$. However, owing to the particular form of the relation

Considering the wage changes in individual years in relation to the fitted curve, the wage increase in 1862 (see Figure 2) is definitely larger than can be accounted for by the level of unemployment and the rate of change of unemployment, and the wage increase in 1863 is also larger than would be expected. It seems that the 12·5 per cent. increase in import prices between 1861 and 1862 referred to above (and no doubt connected with the outbreak of the American civil war) was in fact sufficient to have a real effect on wage rates by causing cost of living increases in wages which were greater than the increases which would have resulted from employers' demand for labour and that the consequent wage-price spiral continued into 1863. On the other hand the increases in import prices of 7·6 per cent. between 1899 and 1900 and again between 1909 and 1910 and the increase of 7·0 per cent. between 1871 and 1872 do not seem to have had any noticeable effect on wage rates. This is consistent with the hypothesis stated above about the effect of rising import prices on wage rates.

Figure 3 and Figures 5 to 8 show a very clear relation between the rate of change of wage rates and the level and rate of change of unemployment,[1] but the relation hardly appears at all in the cycle shown in Figure 4. The wage index of Phelps Brown and Sheila Hopkins from which the changes in wage rates were calculated was based on Wood's earlier index,[2] which shows the same stability during these years. From 1880 we have also Bowley's index of wage rates.[3] If the rate of change of money wage rates for 1881 to 1886 is calculated from Bowley's index by the same method as was used before, the results shown in Figure 4a are obtained, giving the typical relation between the rate of change of wage rates and the level and rate of change of unemployment. It seems possible that some peculiarity may have occurred in the construction of Wood's index for these years. Bowley's index for the remainder of the period up to 1913 gives results which are broadly similar to those shown in Figures 5 to 8, but the pattern is

---

between y and x in the present case it is not easy to find a suitable linear multiple regression equation. An equation of the form $y + a = bxc + k\left(\frac{1}{x^m} \cdot \frac{dx}{dt}\right)$ would probably be suitable. If so the procedure which has been adopted for estimating the relation that would hold between y and x if $\frac{dx}{dt}$ were zero is satisfactory, since it can easily be shown that $\frac{1}{x^m} \cdot \frac{dx}{dt}$ is uncorrelated with x or with any power of x provided that x is, as in this case, a trend-free variable.

[1] Since the unemployment figures used are the averages of monthly percentages, the first central difference is again the best simple approximation to the average rate of change of unemployment during a year. It is obvious from an inspection of Fig. 3 and Figs. 5 to 8 that in each cycle there is a close relation between the deviations of the points from the fitted curve and the first central differences of the employment figures, though the magnitude of the relation does not seem to have remained constant over the whole period.

[2] See Phelps Brown and Sheila Hopkins, *loc. cit.*, pp. 264-5.

[3] A. L. Bowley, *Wages and Income in the United Kingdom since 1860*, Table VII, p. 30.

rather less regular than that obtained with the index of Phelps Brown and Sheila Hopkins.

From Figure 6 it can be seen that wage rates rose more slowly than usual in the upswing of business activity from 1893 to 1896 and then returned to their normal pattern of change ; but with a temporary increase in unemployment during 1897. This suggests that there may have been exceptional resistance by employers to wage increases from 1894 to 1896, culminating in industrial strife in 1897. A glance at industrial history[1] confirms this suspicion. During the 1890's there was a rapid growth of employers' federations and from 1895 to 1897 there was resistance by the employers' federations to trade union demands for the introduction of an eight-hour working day, which would have involved a rise in hourly wage rates. This resulted in a strike by the Amalgamated Society of Engineers, countered by the Employers' Federation with a lock-out which lasted until January 1898.

From Figure 8 it can be seen that the relation between wage changes and unemployment was again disturbed in 1912. From the monthly figures of percentage unemployment in trade unions[2] we find that unemployment rose from 2·8 per cent. in February 1912 to 11.3 per cent. in March, falling back to 3·6 per cent. in April and 2·7 per cent. in May, as the result of a general stoppage of work in coal mining. If an adjustment is made to eliminate the effect of the strike on unemployment the figure for the average percentage unemployment during 1912 would be reduced by about 0·8 per cent., restoring the typical pattern of the relation between the rate of change of wage rates and the level and rate of change of unemployment.

From a comparison of Figures 2 to 8 it appears that the width of loops obtained in each trade cycle has tended to narrow, suggesting a reduction in the dependence of the rate of change of wage rates on the rate of change of unemployment. There seem to be two possible explanations of this. First, in the coal and steel industries before the first world war sliding scale adjustments were common, by which wage rates were linked to the prices of the products.[3] Given the tendency of product prices to rise with an increase in business activity and fall with a decrease in business activity, these agreements may have strengthened the relation between changes in wage rates and changes in unemployment in these industries. During the earlier years of the period these industries would have fairly large weights in the wage index, but with the greater coverage of the statistical material available in later years the weights of these industries in the index would be reduced. Second, it is possible that the decrease in the width of the loops resulted not so much from a reduction in the dependence of wage

[1] See B. C. Roberts, *The Trades Union Congress, 1868-1921*, Chapter IV, especially pp. 158-162.
[2] *21st Abstract of Labour Statistics, 1919–1933, loc. cit.*
[3] I am indebted to Professor Phelps Brown for pointing this out to me.

changes on changes in unemployment as from the introduction of a time lag in the response of wage changes to changes in the level of unemployment, caused by the extension of collective bargaining and particularly by the growth of arbitration and conciliation procedures. If such a time lag existed in the later years of the period the wage change in any year should be related, not to average unemployment during that year, but to the average unemployment lagged by, perhaps, several months. This would have the effect of moving each point in the diagrams horizontally part of the way towards the point of the preceding year and it can easily be seen that this would widen the loops in the diagrams. This fact makes it difficult to discriminate at all closely between the effect of time lags and the effect of dependence of wage changes on the rate of change of unemployment.

III. 1913-1948

A scatter diagram of the rate of change of wage rates and percentage unemployment for the years 1913-1948 is shown in Figure 9. From 1913 to 1920 the series used are a continuation of those used for the period 1861-1913. From 1921 to 1948 the Ministry of Labour's index of hourly wage rates at the end of December of each year[1] has been used, the percentage change in the index each year being taken as a measure of the average rate of change of wage rates during that year. The Ministry of Labour's figures for the percentage unemployment in the United Kingdom[2] have been used for the years 1921-1945. For the years 1946-1948 the unemployment figures were taken from the *Statistical Yearbooks* of the International Labour Organisation.

It will be seen from Figure 9 that there was an increase in unemployment in 1914 (mainly due to a sharp rise in the three months following the commencement of the war). From 1915 to 1918 unemployment was low and wage rates rose rapidly. The cost of living was also rising rapidly and formal agreements for automatic cost of living adjustments in wage rates became widespread, but it is not clear whether the cost of living adjustments were a real factor in increasing wage rates or whether they merely replaced increases which would in any case have occurred as a result of the high demand for labour. Demobilisation brought increased unemployment in 1919 but wage rates continued to rise rapidly until 1920, probably as a result of the rapidly rising import prices, which reached their peak in 1920, and consequent cost of living adjustments in wage rates. There was then a sharp increase in unemployment from 2·6 per cent. in 1920 to 17·0 per cent. in 1921, accompanied by a fall of 22·2 per cent. in wage rates in 1921. Part of the fall can be explained by the extremely rapid increase in unemployment, but a fall of 12·8 per cent. in the cost of living, largely a result of falling import prices, was no doubt also a major factor. In 1922 unemployment was 14·3 per cent. and wage rates fell by 19·1 per cent. Although

[1] *Ministry of Labour Gazette*, April, 1958, p. 133.
[2] *Ibid.*, January, 1940 and subsequent issues.

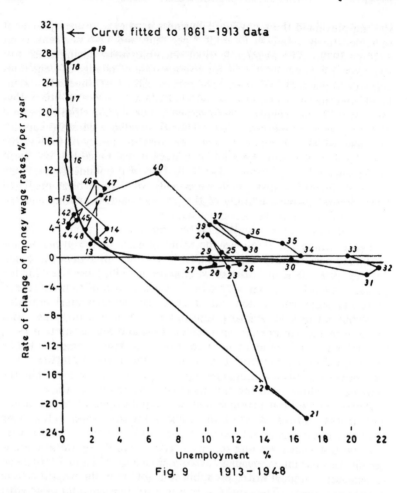

Fig. 9   1913 – 1948

unemployment was high in this year it was decreasing, and the major part of the large fall in wage rates must be explained by the fall of 17·5 per cent. in the cost of living index between 1921 and 1922. After this experience trade unions became less enthusiastic about agreements for automatic cost of living adjustments and the number of these agreements declined.

From 1923 to 1929 there were only small changes in import prices and in the cost of living. In 1923 and 1924 unemployment was high but decreasing. Wage rates fell slightly in 1923 and rose by 3·1 per cent. in 1924. It seems likely that if business activity had continued to improve after 1924 the changes in wage rates would have shown the usual pattern of the recovery phase of earlier trade cycles. However, the decision to check demand in an attempt to force the price level down in order to restore the gold standard at the pre-war parity of sterling prevented the recovery of business activity and unemployment remained fairly steady between 9·7 per cent. and 12·5 per cent. from 1925 to 1929. The average level of unemployment during these five years was 10·94 per cent. and the average rate of change of wage rates was − 0·60 per cent. per year. The rate of change of wage rates calculated from the curve fitted to the 1861-1913 data for a level of unemployment of 10·94 per cent. is − 0·56 per cent. per year, in close agreement with the average observed value. Thus the evidence does not support the view, which is sometimes expressed, that the policy of forcing the price level down failed because of increased resistance to downward movements of wage rates. The actual results obtained, given the levels of unemployment which were held, could have been predicted fairly accura ely from a study of the pre-war data, if anyone had felt inclined to carry out the necessary analysis.

The relation between wage changes and unemployment during the 1929-1937 trade cycle follows the usual pattern of the cycles in the 1861-1913 period except for the higher level of unemployment throughout the cycle. The increases in wage rates in 1935, 1936 and 1937 are perhaps rather larger than would be expected to result from the rate of change of employment alone and part of the increases must probably be attributed to cost of living adjustments. The cost of living index rose 3·1 per cent. in 1935, 3·0 per cent. in 1936 and 5·2 per cent. in 1937, the major part of the increase in each of these years being due to the rise in the food component of the index. Only in 1937 can the rise in food prices be fully accounted for by rising import prices; in 1935 and 1936 it seems likely that the policies introduced to raise prices of home-produced agricultural produce played a significant part in increasing food prices and so the cost of living index and wage rates. The extremely uneven geographical distribution of unemployment may also have been a factor tending to increase the rapidity of wage changes during the upswing of business activity between 1934 and 1937.

Increases in import prices probably contributed to the wage increases in 1940 and 1941. The points in Figure 9 for the remaining war years show the effectiveness of the economic controls introduced. After an increase in unemployment in 1946 due to demobilisation and in 1947 due to the coal crisis, we return in 1948 almost exactly to the fitted relation between unemployment and wage changes.

IV.   1948-1957

A scatter diagram for the years 1948-1957 is shown in Figure 10. The unemployment percentages shown are averages of the monthly unemployment percentages in Great Britain during the calendar years indicated, taken from the *Ministry of Labour Gazette*. The Ministry of Labour does not regularly publish figures of the percentage unemployment in the United Kingdom ; but from data published in the *Statistical Yearbooks* of the International Labour Organisation it appears that unemployment in the United Kingdom was fairly consistently about 0·1 per cent. higher than that in Great Britain throughout this period. The wage index used was the index of weekly wage rates, published monthly in the *Ministry of Labour Gazette*, the percentage change during each calendar year being taken as a measure of the average rate of change of money wage rates during the year. The Ministry does not regularly publish an index of hourly wage rates ;[1] but an index of normal weekly hours published in the *Ministry of Labour*

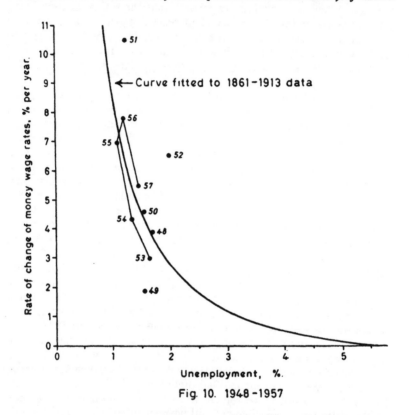

Fig. 10. 1948 – 1957

Gazette of September 1957 shows a reduction of 0·2 per cent. in 1948 and in 1949 and an average annual reduction of approximately 0·04 per cent. from 1950 to 1957. The percentage changes in hourly rates would therefore be greater than the percentage changes in weekly rates by these amounts.

It will be argued later that a rapid rise in import prices during 1947 led to a sharp increase in retail prices in 1948 which tended to stimulate wage increases during 1948, but that this tendency was offset by the

[1] An index of hourly wage rates covering the years considered in this section is, however, given in the *Ministry of Labour Gazette* of April, 1958.

policy of wage restraint introduced by Sir Stafford Cripps in the spring
of 1948 ; that wage increases during 1949 were exceptionally low as a
result of the policy of wage restraint ; that a rapid rise in import prices
during 1950 and 1951 led to a rapid rise in retail prices during 1951
and 1952 which caused cost of living increases in wage rates in excess
of the increases that would have occurred as a result of the demand for
labour, but that there were no special factors of wage restraint or
rapidly rising import prices to affect the wage increases in 1950 or in

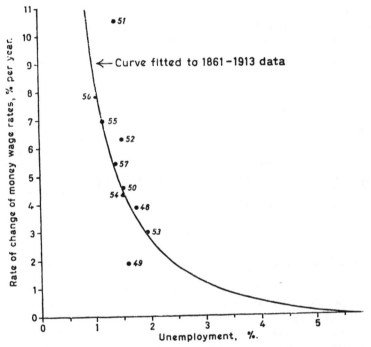

Fig. 11. 1948–1957, with unemployment
lagged 7 months

the five years from 1953 to 1957. It can be seen from Figure 10 that
the point for 1950 lies very close to the curve fitted to the 1861-1913
data and that the points for 1953 to 1957 lie on a narrow loop around
this curve, the direction of the loop being the reverse of the direction
of the loops shown in Figures 2 to 8. A loop in this direction could
result from a time lag in the adjustment of wage rates. If the rate of
change of wage rates during each calendar year is related to unemployment lagged seven months, i.e. to the average of the monthly percentages of unemployment from June of the preceding year to May of
that year, the scatter diagram shown in Figure 11 is obtained. The
loop has now disappeared and the points for the years 1950 and 1953

to 1957 lie closely along a smooth curve which coincides almost exactly with the curve fitted to the 1861-1913 data.

In Table 1 below the percentage changes in money wage rates during the years 1948-1957 are shown in column (1). The figures in column (2) are the percentage changes in wage rates calculated from the curve fitted to the 1861-1913 data corresponding to the unemployment percentages shown in Figure 11, i.e. the average percentages of unemployment lagged seven months. On the hypothesis that has been used in this paper, these figures represent the percentages by which wage rates would be expected to rise, given the level of employment for each year, as a result of employers' competitive bidding for labour, i.e. they represent the " demand pull " element in wage adjustments.

TABLE 1

	(1) Change in wage rates	(2) Demand pull	(3) Cost push	(4) Change in import prices
1947	..	..	..	20·1
1948	3·9	3·5	7·1	10·6
1949	1·9	4·1	2·9	4·1
1950	4·6	4·4	3·0	26·5
1951	10·5	5·2	9·0	23·3
1952	6·4	4·5	9·3	−11·7
1953	3·0	3·0	3·0	− 4·8
1954	4·4	4·5	1·9	5·0
1955	6·9	6·8	4·6	1·9
1956	7·9	8·0	4·9	3·8
1957	5·4	5·2	3·8	− 7·3

The relevant figure on the cost side in wage negotiations is the percentage increase shown by the retail price index in the month in which the negotiations are proceeding over the index of the corresponding month of the previous year. The average of these monthly percentages for each calendar year is an appropriate measure of the " cost push " element in wage adjustments, and these averages[1] are given in column (3). The percentage change in the index of import prices[2] during each year is given in column (4).

From Table 1 we see that in 1948 the cost push element was considerably greater than the demand pull element, as a result of the lagged effect on retail prices of the rapid rise in import prices during the previous year, and the change in wage rates was a little greater than could be accounted for by the demand pull element. It would probably have been considerably greater but for the co-operation of the trade unions in Sir Stafford Cripps' policy of wage restraint. In 1949 the cost element was less than the demand element and the actual change in

[1] Calculated from the retail price index published in the *Monthly Digest of Statistics*. The figure for 1948 is the average of the last seven months of the year.
[2] *Board of Trade Journal.*

wage rates was also much less, no doubt as a result of the policy of wage restraint which is generally acknowledged to have been effective in 1949. In 1950 the cost element was lower than the demand element and the actual wage change was approximately equal to the demand element.

Import prices rose very rapidly during 1950 and 1951 as a result of the devaluation of sterling in September 1949 and the outbreak of the Korean War in 1950. In consequence the retail price index rose rapidly during 1951 and 1952 so that the cost element in wage negotiations considerably exceeded the demand element. The actual wage increase in each year also considerably exceeded the demand element so that these two years provide a clear case of cost inflation.

In 1953 the cost element was equal to the demand element and in the years 1954 to 1957 it was well below the demand element. In each of these years the actual wage increase was almost exactly equal to the demand element. Thus in these five years, and also in 1950, there seems to have been pure demand inflation.

V. CONCLUSIONS

The statistical evidence in Sections II to IV above seems in general to support the hypothesis stated in Section I, that the rate of change of money wage rates can be explained by the level of unemployment and the rate of change of unemployment, except in or immediately after those years in which there is a sufficiently rapid rise in import prices to offset the tendency for increasing productivity to reduce the cost of living.

Ignoring years in which import prices rise rapidly enough to initiate a wage-price spiral, which seem to occur very rarely except as a result of war, and assuming an increase in productivity of 2 per cent. per year, it seems from the relation fitted to the data that if aggregate demand were kept at a value which would maintain a stable level of product prices the associated level of unemployment would be a little under $2\frac{1}{2}$ per cent. If, as is sometimes recommended, demand were kept at a value which would maintain stable wage rates the associated level of unemployment would be about $5\frac{1}{2}$ per cent.

Because of the strong curvature of the fitted relation in the region of low percentage unemployment, there will be a lower average rate of increase of wage rates if unemployment is held constant at a given level than there will be if unemployment is allowed to fluctuate about that level.

These conclusions are of course tentative. There is need for much more detailed research into the relations between unemployment, wage rates, prices and productivity.

The London School of Economics.

[28]

Economic
Progress in a Stable Environment

By A. C. PIGOU

I

IN actual life the process of economic change is dominated by technical developments resulting from scientific discoveries and is closely associated with changes in the size of the population of working age. In what follows I shall rule both these things out of account. I shall assume, moreover, that the stock of money circulating outside the banks is fixed and that the Government does not attempt to control investment with a view to regulating employment. Finally, I shall assume that the State nowhere intervenes by fixing maximum prices below, or minimum prices above, those which would rule in a free market. This implies that at the ruling prices there are no unsatisfied demands or unwanted supplies; in other words that markets are everywhere cleared, or, if we will, that all parts of the economic system are always in market equilibrium—to be sharply distinguished from what I shall call in a moment thorough-going equilibrium.

The theme I propose is this. Let us imagine ourselves situated in an initial year in which some investment is taking place, and let us ask what thereafter, subject to the conditions set out in the last paragraph, will happen. The enquiry is most conveniently conducted in two divisions; first on the assumption that people make net savings —I use this term as equivalent to net investment—solely on account of the material returns which they expect them presently to yield, so that, if these expected returns were nil, there would be no net saving; and, secondly, on the more realistic assumption that saving is partly motivated by a desire to hold capital wealth as such as a source of prestige, individual security and so on. On the first assumption the analysis is straightforward, but on the second some awkward puzzles may—not must—present themselves.

II

In Frank Ramsey's well known article, " A mathematical theory of saving,"[1] the first of these two assumptions is implicitly adopted. On this basis Ramsey observes that, for the economic system in any closed community to be in thorough-going equilibrium, the rate of return obtainable from the marginal unit of capital must be equal to the representative man's rate of time preference. So long as there

[1] *Economic Journal*, Dec. 1928.

is any difference between these two things, that will constitute a continuing stimulus towards net investment or towards net disinvestment ; so that the state of the economic system is continually changing. When there is net investment or disinvestment there cannot be thorough-going equilibrium ; when there is thorough-going equilibrium there cannot be net investment or net disinvestment. Here we are supposing that in our initial year some net investment is taking place, so that we have to do with a forward, not a backward, movement. What are the characteristics of this movement ?

There is one preliminary complication to be cleared out of the way. We may properly, for the present purpose, disregard cyclical fluctuations in the proportion of available work-people actually employed, but we must not exclude the possibility of a trend of change in this proportion. The monetary authorities being assumed to hold the stock of money circulating outside the banks constant, if the income velocity of money·varies, its variations cannot be offset by compensating variations in this stock. As we shall see in a moment, the gradual expansion in the stock of capital will entail a gradual fall in the rate of interest in terms of consumption goods. This may be expected to entail a gradual fall in the income velocity of money and, therefore, in money income, or effective demand. Other things being equal, this should set up a downward pressure on money wage rates, which, so far as it is resisted, will promote unemployment. The pressure will diminish as the rate at which the rate of interest is falling decreases. Hence the proportion of productive resources out of employment might be expected to become smaller and the proportion actually employed larger as the years pass. This movement can, however, hardly be other than slow and weak ; and in any case, so far as it is realised, should reinforce rather than counteract the broad tendencies I am about to describe. We need not, therefore, trouble ourselves about it. What then are these broad tendencies ?

First, under the pressure of the excess of the rate of interest in terms of consumption goods over the representative man's rate of time preference, new investment will be continuously taking place, the stock of capital in existence will continuously grow, and, therefore, in the conditions we are supposing, the stock of capital actually at work will continuously grow.

Secondly, with the stock of capital at work increasing and the stock of labour (as we are supposing) constant, the rate of return to investment, and so the rate of interest in terms of consumption goods—a slightly ambiguous concept—will, in the absence of technical change, become continuously smaller.

Thirdly, there will be a reaction on the size of real income. Since we are supposing the population of working age to be constant, the aggregate stock of resources, capital *plus* labour, available for work must be continuously increasing. Granted that the percentage of employment is not decreasing, real output or income is bound continuously to expand unless the effective length of the working day is being contemporaneously cut down fast enough to offset this tendency.

By the effective length of the working day, whether for labour or for capital, is meant the proportion of the twenty-four hours in which work of standard efficiency is being done ; so that a twelve hours' actual day is not 50 per cent. longer than, but of the same length as, an eight hours' day if work in the shorter day is 50 per cent. more efficient. It should be noted that for capital the effective length of the working day is not necessarily the same as it is for labour ; since it is possible to operate the same equipment with one, two or three shifts of labour per day ; and, the shorter the working day for labour is, the more inducement employers have to introduce multiple shifts. So far as they succeed in doing this, reductions in the effective length of the working day for labour will be associated with expansions for capital. That, however, is a secondary matter and we may ignore it. What may be expected to happen to the effective length of the working day for labour ?

The more capital there is the greater is the capacity of the community to produce real income ; and people may be expected to take out some part of their more favourable conjuncture in extra leisure. This is not, indeed, *necessary*. The effort-cost of producing a given quantity of consumers' goods having diminished, people *might* decide, in consequence, to increase the amount of their effort. In fact, however, the progressive growth of capital, which has taken place in modern times, has been accompanied by a downward trend in the hours of labour. Moreover, it is well known that wealthier countries on the whole enjoy shorter working hours than poorer countries. These considerations suggest, though, of course, they do not prove, that enlargements in the stock of capital are likely, as a rule, to entail contractions in the effective length of the working day for labour.

Now the size of a community's real income or output depends, in given conditions of technique and so on, on the size of the stocks of capital and labour in existence, the proportions of these stocks actually engaged in work and the effective length of the working day. We have seen that, as the years pass, the stock of capital will be increasing while, we are supposing, the stock of labour and the proportions of both stocks actually at work, will at worst be constant. These conditions in combination make for an increase in real income. True, a third factor, the accompanying decrease in the effective length of the working day, will cause real income to increase less fast than it would do otherwise. But, except in a practically impossible limiting case, it cannot cancel the *whole* of the increase that would have occurred apart from it. Hence real income must continuously grow.

Thus as the years pass, with the population of working age constant and no alteration in technique, three major developments must take place ; a continuing increase in the stock of capital both in existence and actually at work ; a continuing fall in the rate of interest in terms of consumption goods ; and a continuing increase in real income. There remains the question what will happen to the volume of annual investment. Since the economic system is moving towards a goal at which, if it is ultimately attained, this will be nothing, it must at *some* stage enter upon a decreasing phase. It need not, indeed, enter upon that phase immediately or even soon after our initial year is left behind. For, while the fall in the rate of interest, taken by itself, tends to make the rate of investment fall, the associated increase in real income, taken by itself, tends to make it grow. Still, eventually, whether before, in or after our initial year, it is bound to start downwards on a final movement towards nothing.

The general nature of the process—if we like to be pompous, the ' dynamic process '—that I have been describing is plain enough. What of the goal towards which it is moving ? We cannot suppose that the representative man's rate of time preference is ever negative, no matter how large an income he has. Hence there can be no question of the rate of interest in terms of consumption goods falling to zero, in consequence of the expansion in the stock of capital, *before* it has come to equality with this rate of time preference. It does not strictly follow from this that there must be some stock of capital in respect of which the rate of interest and the rate of time preference would have equal positive values. For conceivably the two rates, one or both of them always falling, might approach each other asymptotically without actually coinciding in respect of any finite stock of capital. We may, however, I think, disregard this possibility—it is a mathematical toy—and conceive that there *is* a goal with a finite stock of capital, a nil rate of investment and a positive rate of interest, in terms of consumption goods, such that, *if* the economic system hit it, in the absence of technical or population change it would stay there in the thorough-going equilibrium of a stationary state. Indeed there *may* (not, of course, must) be several alternative goals—positions of thorough-going equilibrium—at which the economic system would come to rest if it once got there. But this is a trivial point ; because, since we suppose ourselves to start with a state of things in which some investment is taking place, the first point of intersection between the rate of interest curve and the rate of time preference curve (in respect of stationary states) at which the system arrives must be a stable one, and, even though other points of stable equilibrium also exist, there are no means, in the conditions we are supposing, by which the economic system can get to them. Thus for practical purposes there is only one goal in which we need interest ourselves.

The question still remains whether the economic system need ever hit that goal ; whether it might not, after coming close to it, overshoot the mark and thereafter, with alternating investment and disinvestment, oscillate about it for ever. We need not, I think,

B

trouble ourselves unduly about this suggestion. For, as the goal is approached, the force impelling to movement, in this case the gap between the rate of interest and the rate of time preference, becomes progressively weaker and advances are made by smaller and smaller steps—a quite different state of affairs from that illustrated by the celebrated pig cycle. As the first hero struggles panting up the final slope of Mount Everest, it is exceedingly unlikely that he will overshoot his mark and thereafter step backwards and forwards across it for ever. He will sit down; and, for so long as he dare, stay sat down. This, too, then is a toy. On the assumption we have so far been making the economic system will eventually reach and stay at what we may call, if we like, the Ramseyan thorough-going equilibrium— the classical stationary state.

III

So far we have built our analysis on the first of the two assumptions distinguished above, namely that people save merely for the sake of the material return that they expect presently to receive—for the sake, that is to say, of the rate of interest in terms of consumption goods—so that, if this rate were nil, there would be no net saving. We now turn to the other and more realistic assumption. People are led to save in part by a desire actually to hold wealth for the amenity, so to speak, derived from holding it; the representative man with an income not too small would almost certainly save some-thing—be ready to supply some resources for investment—even if the rate of interest were nil. This greatly complicates our problem. For now a thorough-going equilibrium requires, not that the rate of interest in terms of consumption goods shall be equal to the rate of time preference, but that it shall be less than the rate of time preference by some quantity that represents the rate of amenity return from marginal saving. The rate at which *borrowings and lendings* take place is, indeed, the rate of interest alone without any amenity allowance. The reason is that, when a man borrows resources from another man, no addition is made to his net capital assets, because what he receives is exactly offset by the capital debt created against it. In like manner, when a man lends to another man, no deduction is made from his net capital assets. Therefore what he borrows carries no increment of amenity, and no such element enters into what he pays for loans. But the rate of interest plus the amenity allowance is what the representative man, who in the last resort is both demander and supplier, balances in his mind against the burden he suffers in withdrawing from consumption and supplying (to himself) for investment the marginal apple so supplied. This fact opens up a possibility excluded on our previous assumption, namely that the rate of interest in terms of consumption goods may fall to nothing *before* the stock of capital has become large enough for this rate of interest plus this amenity value to have come to equality with the rate of time preference. This possibility need not, of course, be realised. It may quite well happen that the rate of interest plus our amenity value comes to equality with the rate of time preference while the rate of interest is still positive. In that case everything happens just as it would do in the conditions described in the last section. But it is no longer *necessary* for thorough-going equilibrium to be attained with a stock of capital in respect of which the rate of interest in terms of consumption goods is still positive. If thorough-going equilibrium is *not* attained while that is still so, while the earlier stages of the movement forward from our initial year are as we found them to be on our first assumption, presently a critical point is reached, and we are confronted with a new kind of situation.

The essential fact is this. Since money can be held without appreciable cost it is impossible for the money rate of interest to be less than nothing. Further, since in a thorough-going equilibrium there can be no expectation of a change in relative values, all commodity rates of interest must be the same as the money rate. It follows that no sort of rate of interest can be less than nothing. Hence, in the conditions we are supposing, it may be impossible for the economic system to attain its goal—an equilibrium in which the rate of interest in terms of consumption goods plus the amenity value of marginal saving is equal to, that is to say, is as small as, the rate of time preference. What then will happen?

This is where Lord Keynes comes on the scene. His argument is broadly this. People still want to save. This follows from the fact that the rate of interest plus the amenity value of marginal saving is greater than the rate of time preference. But they will not save by making new real investment at negative interest because it is open to them to hold money at nil interest. Consequently, the representative man will progressively draw money out of the circulation into savings deposits, so that, in the absence of new creations of money, money income must progressively fall or—another way of saying the same thing—money income must fall through the income velocity of money being reduced. Now in these circumstances, if the rate of money wages is held rigid in spite of growing unemployment, unemployment must grow; the proportion of available resources at work contracting roughly in proportion to the contraction in money income. But this process will not go on for ever. The representative man's rate of time preference is sure to be substantially larger for small real incomes than for large, because with a smaller real income he is under stronger pressure to focus attention on the present moment. The contraction of employment entailing, as it does, a corresponding contraction of real income, carries with it, therefore, an increase in this rate. Presently the rate rises so far that it reaches equality with the rate of interest plus the money measure of the amenity value of marginal savings proper to the stock of capital that has been attained. At this point the economic system comes into equilibrium. People no longer desire to save anything, and, therefore, money income no longer contracts. The stock of capital is the same as it was when the rate of interest became nothing; but employment, and therewith real income, is smaller—maybe much smaller. The situation thus reached, provided that money wage rates are still maintained, is one of stable equilibrium—the low level equilibrium that I have sometimes called Lord Keynes's Day of Judgment. Whether real income then is lower, not merely than it was at the critical moment when the rate of time preference became nothing, but than it was in our initial year, depends, of course, on how far distant from that critical moment our initial year was.

This solution is clearly valid provided that the money wage rate is in fact rigidly maintained in the face of heavy and growing unemployment. It is, however, very hard to believe that, in given conditions of technique and so on, the proportion of available resources at work will be determined permanently, as this solution requires, by such superficial things as the money and price situation. In the Keynesian equilibrium wage earners, having infinite time at their disposal, are surely bound to see through the money façade to the realities behind. There must, it would seem, be *some* proportion of employment, not necessarily, of course, "full" employment, to the attainment of which they would set themselves irrespective of the monetary situation. If this is in fact so, the position proper to Lord Keynes's Day of Judgment will not be attained or even approached. Money wage rates will continually fall to prevent employment from falling; but the income velocity of money and money income will also continuously fall. Thus money wage rates, money income and money prices will all move downwards for ever, while employment and real income remain fairly stable and fairly good. With money wage rates free to vary to any extent, this and not the Keynesian Day of Judgment appears *prima facie* to be the goal of the economic process.

But this appearance is deceptive. As the money rate of wages falls the money price of consumption goods falls also. This entails that the value in terms of consumption goods of the stock of money, and, along with this, that of other sorts of non-instrumental property, such as Old Masters, which are specially attractive as receptacles for, or embodiments of, savings, expands. This means that the total stock of property, as valued in consumption goods, which is held by the public becomes progressively larger and larger. It must be remembered, indeed, that not all the stock of money held by the public constitutes a net asset to them. Part of it is offset by debts from them to the banks in respect of advances and discounts. In 1938, the last full pre-war year, these amounted to 1,200 millions as against 2,160 millions of deposits; while the note circulation was 485 millions. Thus of the public's aggregate money holdings, notes and deposits together, only some 1,400 millions out of a total of 2,600 millions constituted a net element in their holding of property. Hence the addition made to this holding of property as valued in consumption goods when prices fall is smaller than it might perhaps be thought to be at first sight. None the less, it is likely to be substantial. Now the amenity value in terms of satisfaction derived from holding an additional unit of property evidently becomes smaller the more units of property (as measured in consumption goods) that there are ; while, with a given real income, the value of a unit of satisfaction in terms of consumption goods is, of course, given. Hence, with employment the same as it was when the rate of interest first became nothing, the marginal amenity yield of savings expressed in consumption goods must become smaller and smaller as money income contracts, until finally, it plus the rate of interest coincides with the rate of time preference and a genuine equilibrium is established. Henceforward the stock of capital, employment and real income remain for ever what they were at the critical moment when the rate of interest first became nothing. That rate itself continues for ever at nothing ; the rate of time preference continues for ever at that level above nothing at which it stood then ; and the marginal amenity yield of (nil) new savings is for ever equal to the excess of the rate of time preference above nothing. Real income, being the same as it was at the critical moment, is obviously larger than it was in our initial year.

To sum up then. If, as the years pass and capital accumulates, the rate of interest in terms of consumption goods plus the marginal amenity yield of savings becomes equal to the representative man's rate of time preference before the rate of interest falls to nothing, thorough-going equilibrium will be then and there established and there are no complications. But, if, before this equality can be achieved, the rate of interest has fallen to nothing, the upshot is uncertain. If money wage rates are rigidly maintained, at this point the economic engine will be put into reverse until a new low level equilibrium is established with a lower, perhaps a much lower, level of employment and real income. If, on the other hand, money wage rates move downward freely, equilibrium will ultimately be established with the stock of capital, employment, real income, the rate of interest and the rate of time preference standing as they stood when the rate of interest first reached nil level, but with the marginal amenity yield of nil new savings so far contracted that this plus the rate of interest is no longer greater than, but is equal to, the rate of time preference.

IV

The foregoing analysis holds good, of course, only on the basis of the assumptions set out at the beginning of this article. It is extremely improbable that these assumptions will ever be satisfied in practice.

For, even if we allow the population of working age to be stable and the faculty of invention to disappear, it is ridiculous to suppose that the public authorities would stand passive in the case of catastrophic disturbances. If a situation arose in which money income was being driven inexorably downwards in the way contemplated in the last section, no government would allow money wage rates to rush downwards very far ; legal minimum rates would inevitably be established. This would very likely be done soon enough to prevent the type of final equilibrium described on page 187 from emerging. But, equally, no government could allow the movement towards the Keynesian equilibrium, with its massive unemployment, to proceed very far. It would be bound to intervene by itself undertaking on behalf of the community investment at negative rates of interest or by adopting some other means to arrest the downrush of money income. Thus the puzzles we have been considering in the last section are academic exercises, of some slight use perhaps for clarifying thought, but with very little chance of ever being posed on the chequer board of actual life.

[29]

OPTIMAL CHOICE OF MONETARY POLICY INSTRUMENTS IN A SIMPLE STOCHASTIC MACRO MODEL *

WILLIAM POOLE

I. INTRODUCTION

In this paper a solution to the "instrument problem" — more commonly known as the "target problem" — is determined within the context of the Hicksian *IS-LM* model. Baldly stated, the problem arises as a result of the fact that the monetary authorities may operate through either interest rate changes or money stock changes, but not through both independently, and therefore must decide whether to use the interest rate or the money stock as the policy instrument. The analysis produces two major findings. First, for some values of the parameters an interest rate policy is superior to a money stock policy while for other values of the parameters the reverse is true. Second, it is possible to define a combination policy in which the interest rate and money stock are maintained in a certain relationship to each other — the nature of the relationship depending on the values of the parameters — and to show that the optimal combination policy is as good as or superior to either the interest rate or money stock policies no matter what the values of the parameters.

The remainder of this section will be spent in clarifying some terminological questions connected with the words "instrument" and "target." Then in Section II the nature of the instrument problem will be discussed more carefully and an intuitive solution to the problem will be presented. In Section III the intuitive solution is made precise by applying the theory of optimal decision making under uncertainty to a formal model. In Section IV it is shown that the "either-or" solution to the instrument problem can be improved

* An earlier version of this paper was presented at the December 1967 meetings of the Econometric Society, and I am indebted to my discussant at the meetings, Donald P. Tucker, for many useful comments. I am also indebted to Carl F. Christ, Jurg Niehans, William H. Oakland, and the referees of this journal for their valuable comments. Unfortunately, I am unable to pass off responsibility for any remaining errors to the above-named individuals.

upon by adopting a combination policy in which the interest rate and money stock are maintained in a constant relationship to each other. The analysis is extended in Section V to a dynamic model. Finally, in Section VI appear concluding remarks and suggestions for further research.

Before analyzing the nature of the instrument problem it may be helpful to comment on terminology. A considerable literature exists in which economic policy is discussed in terms of the adjustment of policy instruments in order to influence variables termed "target" or "goal" variables. However, recent monetary policy literature has sometimes departed from this framework by introducing the concept of "proximate" or "intermediate" targets which lie between the instruments (or "tools") of monetary policy (e.g., open market operations, discount rate, and so on) and goals of policy. The rationale for introducing the proximate target concept would seem to be the notion that a close and systematic relationship exists between proximate targets and goals, the relationship holding over time and space, while the relationship between the tools of monetary policy and the proximate targets depends heavily on institutional factors which are stable neither over time nor over space. However, if as assumed throughout this paper the money stock can be set at exactly the desired level, then the money stock may as well be called an instrument of monetary policy rather than a proximate target.

The definition of an instrument as a policy-controlled variable which can be set exactly for all practical purposes is, of course, not very precise since people may disagree as to what "practical purposes" are. Nevertheless, such an approach promotes a fruitful evolution of research since at a given state of knowledge failures to reach desired levels of goal variables may be largely due to factors other than errors in reaching desired values of instruments. With advances in knowledge it becomes increasingly important to account for errors in reaching desired values of instruments, and the analysis can then shift the definition of "instruments" to more precisely controllable variables. It is, for example, a straightforward matter to use the approach of this paper to treat the monetary base as an instrument and the money stock as a stochastic function of the monetary base.

In the analysis of this paper policy variables assumed to be controlled without error will be called instruments, and no use will be made of the proximate target concept. It is to the nature of the instrument problem that we now turn.

II. The Instrument Problem

The proper choice of monetary policy instruments is a topic which has been hotly debated in recent years. Three major positions in the debate may be identified. First, there are those who argue that monetary policy should set the money stock while letting the interest rate fluctuate as it will. In one variant of this position the authorities should simply achieve a constant rate of growth of the money stock; in another variant the authorities should adjust the growth in the money stock in response to the current state of the economy, causing the money stock to grow more rapidly in recession and less rapidly in boom.

The second major position in the debate is held by those who favor using money market conditions as the monetary policy instrument. The more precise proponents of this general position would argue that the authorities should push interest rates up in times of boom and down in times of recession, while the money supply is allowed to fluctuate as it will. Others, while conceding the importance of interest rates, would also tend to think in terms of the level of free reserves in the banking system, the rate of growth of bank credit with one or more components of bank credit being specially emphasized, or the overall "tone" of the money markets. Most proponents of this position would probably agree that the short-term interest rate is the best single variable to represent money market conditions if a single variable must be selected for analytical purposes.

The third major position is taken by the fence-sitters who argue that the monetary authorities should use both the money stock and the interest rate as instruments. It is, of course, recognized that the money stock and the interest rate cannot be set independently, but the idea seems to be to maintain some sort of relationship between the two instruments. The trouble with this position is that it usually amounts to nothing more than a plea for wise behavior by the authorities since it is never explained how the instruments should be adjusted according to economic conditions. However, as shown in Section IV, this position can be made precise within the context of a well-defined model.

The very existence of the instrument problem may puzzle those who are used to thinking of policy formulation in terms of a deterministic macro model. In such a model, assuming that it is possible to reach full employment through monetary policy, the policy prescription may be in terms of either the interest rate or the money stock; it makes no difference which instrument is selected. This point may be demonstrated within the context of a Hicksian *IS-LM* type model.

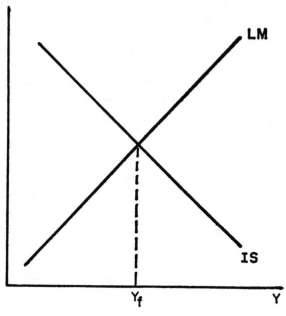

Figure I

Figure I shows the familiar *IS-LM* diagram in which the price level is assumed constant. The monetary policy problem is viewed as setting the money stock at the level such that the *LM* function will cut the *IS* function at the full employment level of income, Y_f. Alternatively, the policy problem could be viewed as in Figure II with the monetary authorities setting the interest rate at r^*,[1] thereby making the *LM* function horizontal.[2] In the deterministic model it obviously makes no difference whatsoever whether the policy prescription is in terms of setting the interest rate at r^* or in terms of setting the money stock at the level, say M^*, that makes the *LM* function cut the *IS* function at Y_f.

But now consider Figure III, in which the *IS* function is ran-

---

1. The interest rate could be set through a bond-pegging program such as practiced by the United States during World War II. Of course, the level of the peg could be altered from time to time.

2. The *LM* function is ordinarily defined in terms of a constant money stock. However, a logical extension is to treat the money supply as interest-elastic as a result of the activities of the commercial banking system or, in the present context, of the monetary authorities. A pegged interest rate, of course, is a polar case in terms of interest elasticity of supply.

OPTIMAL CHOICE OF MONETARY POLICY   **201**

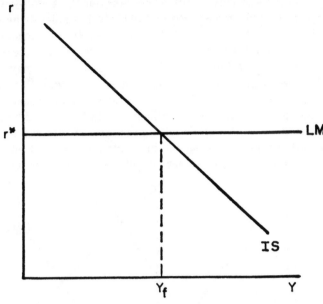

FIGURE II

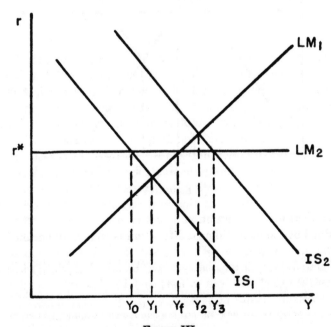

FIGURE III

domly shocked and may lie anywhere between IS_1 and IS_2. On the assumption that the money demand function is stable, if the money stock is set at M^* the LM function will be LM_1 and income may end up anywhere between Y_1 and Y_2. However, if the interest rate is set at r^*, the LM function will be LM_2, and income may end up anywhere between Y_0 and Y_3, a much wider range than Y_1 to Y_2. In Figure III it is clear that there is a problem of the proper choice of the instrument, and that the problem should be resolved by setting the money stock at M^* while letting the interest rate end up where it will rather than by setting the interest rate at r^* and letting the money stock end up at whatever level is necessary to obtain r^*.

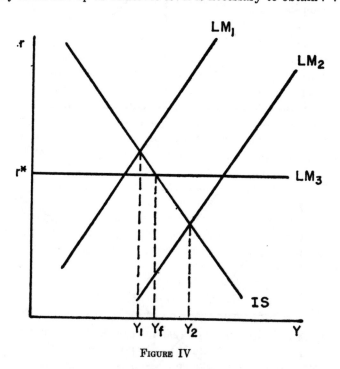

FIGURE IV

In Figure IV the situation is analyzed in which the IS function is stable but the money demand function is randomly shocked. Setting the money stock at M^* will lead to an LM function between LM_1 and LM_2, and income between Y_1 and Y_2, while setting the interest rate at r^* will lead to LM_3 and Y_f. The interest rate is the proper instrument in this case.

In general there will be stochastic disturbances in both the real and the monetary sectors of the economy. In examining the situations represented by Figures III and IV, it appears that in the general case the solution of the instrument problem depends on the relative importance of the random disturbances and on the slopes of the *IS* and *LM* functions, i.e., on the structural parameters of the system. With these general ideas in mind, it is now possible to proceed to a formal model.

III. A Static Stochastic Model

Let us begin by presenting a nonstochastic linear version of the Hicksian *IS-LM* model depicted in Figure I. The model has the two equations

(1a) $\quad Y = a_0 + a_1 r,$ $\qquad a_1 < 0$

(1b) $\quad M = b_0 + b_1 Y + b_2 r,$ $\qquad b_1 > 0, b_2 < 0$

and the variables are all in real terms.[3] Equation (1a), the *IS*-function, is obtained by combining linear consumption and investment equations with the equilibrium condition $Y = C + I$. In equation (1b), the *LM*-function, the left-hand side is the stock of money and the right-hand side is the demand for money. The parameters are not necessarily constant for all time; they may change as a result of fiscal policy measures and other factors. What is assumed is that the parameters are known period by period.

The model has two equations and three variables, Y, M, and r. Monetary policy selects either M or r as the policy instrument so that there are two endogenous variables and one exogenous variable, the policy instrument. Equations (2) and (3) are the reduced forms for the interest rate and money stock instruments, respectively.

(2a) $\quad Y = a_0 + a_1 r$

(2b) $\quad M = b_0 + a_0 b_1 + (a_1 b_1 + b_2) r.$

(3a) $\quad Y = (a_1 b_1 + b_2)^{-1} [a_0 b_2 + a_1 (M - b_0)]$

(3b) $\quad r = (a_1 b_1 + b_2)^{-1} [M - b_0 - a_0 b_1].$

With a desired level of real income of Y_f,[4] from the reduced forms for income we obtain the optimal values for the instrument, r^* or M^*, respectively, as given by equations (4) and (5).

---

3. It can be assumed either that monetary policy can control the real stock of money, at least in the short run, by altering the nominal stock or that the price level is fixed. Alternatively, it could be assumed that the variables in the model are all money magnitudes; in this case, the desired level of income, Y_f, discussed below in real terms, would become instead the desired level of money income such that the economy would be operating at "reasonably" full employment and a "tolerable" rate of price increase. These awkward rationalizations of the economic meaning of the model are, of course, the result of working within a simple model with only the one goal variable, national income.

4. Income above Y_f is undesirable due to resource misallocations at overfull employment or upward pressure on the price level.

(4) $\quad r^*=a_1{}^{-1}(Y_f-a_o)$

(5) $\quad M^*=a_1{}^{-1}[Y_f(a_1b_1+b_2)-a_ob_2+a_1b_o]$.

It is obvious from (2b) that if $r = r^*$, then $M = M^*$ and from (3b) that if $M = M^*$, then $r = r^*$. The policies represented by $M = M^*$ and $r = r^*$ are equivalent in every way; the choice of a policy instrument can be a matter of convenience, preference, or prejudice, but not of substance. In general, the same argument holds for more complicated deterministic models including variables such as free reserves and the level of bank credit.[5]

Now consider the model obtained by adding stochastic terms to the deterministic model above. The model becomes

(6a) $\quad Y=a_o+a_1r+u$

(6b) $\quad M=b_o+b_1Y+b_2r+v$

$\quad\quad$ where $E[u] = E[v] = 0$

$$E[u^2]=\sigma_u{}^2; E[v^2]=\sigma_v{}^2$$

$$E[uv]=\sigma_{uv}=\rho_{uv}\sigma_u\sigma_v.$$

In this model the level of income is a random variable, and in general its probability distribution will depend on whether the money stock or the interest rate is selected as the policy instrument.

It is natural to argue that the selection of the instrument should depend on which instrument minimizes the expected loss from failure of the level of income to equal the desired level. Let us assume a quadratic loss function [6] so that the expected loss, L, is given by

(7) $\quad L=E[(Y-Y_f)^2]$.

It can easily be shown that if the interest rate is the instrument, the minimum expected loss is obtained when $r=r^*$ as given by equation (4); similarly, if the money stock is the instrument, the optimal money stock is $M=M^*$ as given by equation (5).[7] Once the instrument has been selected, the model is one of certainty equivalance under the loss function of equation (7), and the optimal policy in the stochastic model is identical to the optimal policy in the deterministic model.

However, as can be seen from the reduced forms (8) and (9) for interest rate and money stock policies, respectively, in the stochastic

5. In the model presented there is one goal variable and one instrument to be chosen from two possible instruments. In more complicated models, say where there is a choice of two out of three possible instruments and one goal variable, the optimal policy will lie along a line connecting the two instruments chosen. When a point on this line is selected, the value of the variable rejected as an instrument will be determined by the model.

6. See H. Theil, *Optimal Decision Rules for Government and Industry* (Amsterdam: North-Holland, 1964), pp. 2–5, for some comments on the reasons for using a quadratic loss function.

7. *Ibid.*, Ch. 2.

model the two policies are not equivalent as they were in the deterministic model since the stochastic terms of the reduced form equations will depend on which instrument is selected.

(8) $Y = a_0 + a_1 r + u$

$\qquad = Y_f + u \qquad$ when $r = r^*$

(9) $Y = (a_1 b_1 + b_2)^{-1} [a_0 b_2 + a_1 (M - b_0) + b_2 u - a_1 v]$

$\qquad = Y_f + (a_1 b_1 + b_2)^{-1} (b_2 u - a_1 v) \qquad$ when $M = M^*$.

By substituting (8) into the loss function (equation (7)), we obtain the minimum expected loss, L_r, under an interest rate policy, and by substituting (9) into the loss function, we obtain the minimum expected loss, L_M, under a money stock policy, as given by equations (10) and (11).

(10) $L_r = \sigma_u^2$

(11) $L_M = (a_1 b_1 + b_2)^{-2} (a_1^2 \sigma_v^2 - 2 \rho_{uv} a_1 b_2 \sigma_u \sigma_v + b_2^2 \sigma_u^2)$.

Equation (11) has some interesting implications for the importance of the interest sensitivity of the demand for money.[8] From (11) we find that

(12) $\dfrac{\partial L_M}{\partial b_2} = 2 a_1 (a_1 b_1 + b_2)^{-3} \sigma_u \sigma_v \left[b_2 \left(b_1 \dfrac{\sigma_u}{\sigma_v} + \rho_{uv} \right) \right.$

$\qquad \left. - a_1 \left(\dfrac{\sigma_v}{\sigma_u} + b_1 \rho_{uv} \right) \right].$

If $b_1 \dfrac{\sigma_u}{\sigma_v} + \rho_{uv} < 0$, then $\dfrac{\partial L_M}{\partial b_2} > 0$ when $b_2 < 0$.[9]

What this means is that the higher is the interest sensitivity of the demand for money (the lower b_2 is algebraically), the *lower* is the minimum expected loss from a money stock policy. The intuitive explanation for this result (which may on first thought seem peculiar) is as follows: first, note that this result requires $\rho_{uv} < 0$, which means that there is a tendency for disturbances in the two sectors

8. If the model is log linear, then b_2 is the interest elasticity of the demand for money.

9. This result can be seen as follows. First, note that $b_1 \dfrac{\sigma_u}{\sigma_v} + \rho_{uv} < 0$ can only occur if $\rho_{uv} < 0$. Multiplying $b_1 \dfrac{\sigma_u}{\sigma_v} + \rho_{uv}$ by $\dfrac{1}{\rho_{uv}} \dfrac{\sigma_v}{\sigma_u}$ and observing that $\dfrac{b_1}{\rho_{uv}} < b_1 \rho_{uv}$ since $-1 \leq \rho_{uv} < 0$ and $b_1 > 0$, we find that $0 < \dfrac{\sigma_v}{\sigma_u} + \dfrac{b_1}{\rho_{uv}} < \dfrac{\sigma_v}{\sigma_u}$ $+ b_1 \rho_{uv}$. Thus, in (12) the term $(\dfrac{\sigma_v}{\sigma_u} + b_1 \rho_{uv})$ is positive if $(b_1 \dfrac{\sigma_u}{\sigma_v} + \rho_{uv})$ is negative, and in this event $\dfrac{\partial L_M}{\partial b_2}$ is positive since we assume $a_1 < 0$, $b_2 < 0$, $b_1 > 0$.

to be simultaneously expansionary or contractionary. Second, note that σ_v must be relatively large compared to $b_1\sigma_u$. Under these conditions the effect on income of the relatively large disturbances in the monetary sector is smaller, the larger is the interest sensitivity of the demand for money. As will be shown below, in this situation an interest rate policy is superior to a money stock policy.

Another aspect of the interest sensitivity is that in general L_M is at a minimum at a nonzero value of b_2 which may be negative, which means that in some cases a small amount of interest sensitivity is better than none. This fact can be seen by setting (12) equal to zero to find the extremum. The second order conditions assure that this extremum is always a minimum. It is then found that for $b_2 < 0$ at this minimum, it is necessary that $\rho_{uv} + b_1\frac{\sigma_u}{\sigma_v} > 0$ and $b_1\rho_{uv} + \frac{\sigma_v}{\sigma_u} > 0$.

It can also be shown that at this minimum a money stock policy is superior to an interest rate policy. Since the conditions for a minimum L_M to occur at $b_2 < 0$ are likely to be met in practice, these results suggest that some interest sensitivity may well be better than none. Indeed, as shown in the next section this fact may be exploited by deliberately introducing an interest-sensitive supply of money into the model.

The two policies may now be conveniently compared by considering the ratio of their expected losses.

$$(13) \qquad \frac{L_M}{L_r} = (a_1 b_1 + b_2)^{-2}\left(a_1^2\frac{\sigma_v^2}{\sigma_u^2} - 2\rho_{uv}a_1 b_2\frac{\sigma_v}{\sigma_u} + b_2^2\right).$$

It could be argued that much more is known about the monetary sector than about the expenditure sector so that at the current state of economic knowledge σ_v^2 is much smaller than σ_u^2. As can be seen from equation (14), if σ_v/σ_u is small enough $(\sigma_v/\sigma_u < b_1$ is sufficient) the ratio L_M/L_r will be less than one so that a money stock policy would be superior to an interest rate policy.

$$(14) \qquad \frac{L_M}{L_r} = (a_1 b_1 + b_2)^{-2}\left(a_1^2\frac{\sigma_v^2}{\sigma_u^2} - 2\rho_{uv}a_1 b_2\frac{\sigma_v}{\sigma_u} + b_2^2\right)$$

$$= (a_1 b_1 + b_2)^{-2}\left[\left(a_1\frac{\sigma_v}{\sigma_u} + b_2\right)^2 - 2a_1 b_2\frac{\sigma_v}{\sigma_u}(1 + \rho_{uv})\right]$$

$$\leqslant (a_1 b_1 + b_2)^{-2}\left(a_1\frac{\sigma_v}{\sigma_u} + b_2\right)^2.$$

Whether or not this view on the superiority of a money stock policy is correct, the point remains that in a stochastic world one policy may be superior to the other depending on the values of the structural parameters and of the variances of the disturbances. Furthermore,

OPTIMAL CHOICE OF MONETARY POLICY 207

which instrument is optimal may vary over time if the structural and stochastic parameters change.

This analysis, based on the size of σ_v/σ_u, may be compared to the Friedman-Meiselman view that monetary policy is superior to fiscal policy because velocity is more stable than the investment multiplier.[1] In fact, in the model of (6) fiscal policy and an interest rate policy are equivalent in terms of their effects on income since in (6a) fiscal policy affects the term a_o while an interest rate policy affects the term a_1r. But it is important to note that the condition $\sigma_v < \sigma_u$ is not alone sufficient to insure the superiority of the money stock policy.

The stochastic model is one of certainty equivalence in the decision sense but not in the utility sense. Whichever instrument is selected, the optimal decision is the same in the stochastic model as in the certainty model. However, the stochastic model is not equivalent in the utility sense since the level of disutility is zero in the certainty model but nonzero and dependent on the choice of the policy instrument in the stochastic model.

The stochastic terms in the model may be interpreted as arising from a one-period lag in data availability on the level of income. If income data were available instantaneously, then random disturbances would show up immediately in terms of their effects on income, and the policy instrument could be adjusted accordingly, assuming, of course, that policy actions took effect instantaneously. But if information on the goal variable becomes available with a lag, the instantaneous feedback principle is no longer applicable, and it is necessary to think of the goal variable as being a function of the instrument. For monetary policy problems it seems quite reasonable to think of information on money and interest as being continuously available while information on income is available only with a lag.

Thus, the time subscripts on Y, M, and r are all identical in (6a) and (6b), but Y_t is not observable until $t+1$.

Lags in the effects of policy actions may or may not produce a model analytically equivalent to (6a) and (6b); it is necessary to specify the nature of the lags. If production, consumption, and money demand decisions are made one period in advance, the model might be

1. Milton Friedman and David Meiselman, "The Relative Stability of Monetary Velocity and the Investment Multiplier in the United States, 1897–1958," in Commission on Money and Credit, *Stabilization Policies* (Englewood Cliffs, N.J.: Prentice-Hall, 1963), pp. 165–268, esp. pp. 213–16.

$$Y_{t+1} = a_0 + a_1 r_t + u_{t+1}$$
$$M_t = b_0 + b_1 Y_{t+1} + b_2 r_t + v_{t+1}.$$

This model is analytically equivalent to (6a) and (6b). The money demand function may appear a bit strange, but it is possible that the amount of money demanded this period is based on production plans made this period which will determine next period's income.

IV. The Combination Policy

It will be recalled that under the money stock policy there is an optimal value for b_2, the interest sensitivity of the demand for money. Since it would be a most unlikely coincidence for the actual value of b_2 to equal the optimal value, it should be possible to obtain the optimal slope to the LM function by making the supply of money interest sensitive. Whether the supply of money should be positively or negatively related to the interest rate will depend on whether the slope of the LM function with a fixed money stock is too high or too low.

Consider the policy defined in terms of setting values for c'_1 and c'_2 in a money supply equation [2] given by $M = c'_1 + c'_2 r$. However, because the denominators of the optimal c'_1 and c'_2 vanish for certain parameter values, it is convenient to define the money supply function by equation (15) where c_0 is set equal to the common denominator of the optimal c'_1 and c'_2.

$$(15) \qquad c_0 M = c_1 + c_2 r.$$

When (15) is added to the model, there are three equations and three unknowns — Y, r, and M — and the expected loss is minimized by setting the partial derivatives of the loss with respect to c_1 and c_2 equal to zero. The policy instruments may then be said to be the values of c_1 and c_2. We find that the optimal policy is given by

$$(16) \qquad c_0 M = c_1{}^* + c_2{}^* r,$$

where $c_0 = b_1 \sigma_u{}^2 + \sigma_{uv}$

$$c_1{}^* = c_0 (b_0 + b_1 Y_f) + (Y_f - a_0)(\sigma_v{}^2 + b_1 \sigma_{uv})$$
$$c_2{}^* = c_0 b_2 - a_1 (\sigma_v{}^2 + b_1 \sigma_{uv}).$$

Under this combination policy the stochastic term in the reduced form equation for income is affected so that the minimum expected loss, L_0, is found to be

$$(17) \qquad L_0 = \frac{\sigma_u{}^2 \sigma_v{}^2 (1 - \rho_{uv}{}^2)}{\sigma_v + 2 \rho_{uv} b_1 \sigma_u \sigma_v + b_1{}^2 \sigma_u{}^2}.$$

2. It may be objected that this equation represents an impossible policy. The central bank cannot merely observe r and then set M since any change in M will then affect r. Actually, this equation is simply a supply function for money and should be regarded as beset by simultaneity problems neither more nor less than any other supply function.

OPTIMAL CHOICE OF MONETARY POLICY 209

In equation (16) it can be seen that the combination policy becomes a pure interest rate policy when $c_o = 0$, and becomes a pure money stock policy when $c_2^* = 0$.[3] It should be obvious that except in these special cases in which either c_o or c_2^* vanish, the combination policy is superior to both of the pure policies.[4]

The expected losses under the combination policy may be substantially less than the expected losses under either of the pure policies.[5] The explicit specification of a combination policy allows the "fence-sitters" in the debate to stay on the fence and to feel superior in doing so. However, the success of the combination policy depends on knowledge of the parameters of the model, and the combination policy depends on knowledge of more parameters than does a pure money stock or a pure interest rate policy. Furthermore, it is clear from equation (16) that optimal monetary policy may require the central bank to introduce either a direct or an inverse relationship between M and r since the c_o and c_2^* coefficients may be of either the same or opposite signs. Equation (16) is complicated enough that intuition in this matter is to be distrusted; a combination policy based on intuition may be worse than either of the pure policies.

V. A Dynamic Model

The analysis may be extended to more complicated models in which there are lagged responses to the disturbances and policy actions. Considerations involving an investment accelerator or a dependence of consumption on lagged income may produce a model such as

(18a) $\quad Y_t = a_o + a_1 r_t + S_1 Y_{t-1} + S_2 Y_{t-2} + u_t$

3. When there are no disturbances in the monetary section ($\sigma_v^2 = \sigma_{uv} = 0$), the optimal policy is to make the supply function of money the same as the demand function for money at the full employment level of income. At the other extreme, when there are no disturbances in the expenditure sector ($\sigma_u^2 = \sigma_{uv} = 0$), the optimal policy is to set the interest rate at the level required for full employment. These results were anticipated by Martin Bailey, *National Income and the Price Level* (New York: McGraw-Hill, 1962), pp. 154–62. However, in discussing the more general case when disturbances may appear in both sectors, Bailey argues that the source of any particular disturbance, and therefore the proper direction in which to adjust the money stock, may be determined by seeing whether income and interest move together or inversely. This policy prescription is not applicable if, as assumed in this paper, income is observed with a lag.

4. A proof is presented in the Appendix.

5. Assuming that $c_o \neq 0$, the combination policy is quite similar in outlook to the approach urged by Jack M. Guttentag, "The Strategy of Open Market Operations," this *Journal*, LXXX (Feb. 1966), 1–30. The short-run policy reaction to interest rate changes is determined by the value of c_2^*/c_o while the longer-run policy is represented by the value of c_1^*/c_o.

(18b) $\quad M_t = b_0 + b_1 Y_t + b_2 r_t + v_t$

$\quad$ where $\quad E[u_t] = E[v_t] = 0$

$\qquad E[u_t u_s] = \sigma_u^2$ when $t = s$, $= 0$ when $t \neq s$

$\qquad E[v_t v_s] = \sigma_v^2$ when $t = s$, $= 0$ when $t \neq s$

$\qquad E[u_t v_s] = \sigma_{uv}$ when $t = s$, $= 0$ when $t \neq s$.

Since lagged responses are picked up by the lagged income terms, it is assumed that the disturbance terms are serially independent.

At time t, assuming that Y_{t-1} and Y_{t-2} are known, the model may be considered as identical to the model without lags except that the constant term in the *IS* equation becomes

$$a_0 + S_1 Y_{t-1} + S_2 Y_{t-2}.[6]$$

Period by period, then, the optimal level of each of the three policies is given by the same expressions as before except that the constant term a_0 in these expressions is replaced by $a_0 + S_1 Y_{t-1} + S_2 Y_{t-2}$. It is easy to see that if any one of the policies is followed period by period the dependence of income on lagged income will be eliminated.[7]

A policy adjusted period by period might be called an "active" policy. Professor Friedman has argued that a successful active policy is impossible given the current state of knowledge, and that we would be better off with a steady rate of growth of money regardless of current conditions. Such a policy might be called a "passive" policy. The model of this paper involves no economic growth, and so the analog to Friedman's proposal is a money stock fixed permanently. We may also consider a permanent interest rate policy.[8]

Friedman's position is based on his contention that the lags in the effects of monetary policy are long and variable, and so it may

6. At this stage of the argument it would be a trivial matter to add lagged income terms to the money demand equation or lagged interest rate terms to either or both equations. These terms could all be incorporated into the constant terms. While the later analysis would not be affected in any fundamental way by adding lagged income terms to the money demand equations, the presence of both lagged income and lagged interest terms would make the algebra later on difficult and perhaps impossible.

7. In the combination policy, $c_1{}^*$ (though not c_0 and $c_2{}^*$) is itself a random variable depending on Y_{t-1} and Y_{t-2}, and it is therefore necessary to see whether $c_1{}^*$ has a finite mean and variance. If it did not, the policy would presumably not be feasible. However, it is easy to see that $c_1{}^*$ does have a finite mean and variance. The mean and variance of $c_1{}^*$ depend on the means and variances of Y_{t-1} and Y_{t-2} which in turn depend on the means and variances of the disturbances in periods $t-1$ and $t-2$, but in no earlier periods since the dependence of Y on lagged Y is eliminated by the optimal combination policy. Therefore, it is clear that the mean and variance of $c_1{}^*$ exist, and the same argument applies to the interest rate and money stock policies.

8. A third possibility is a permanent combination policy, but I have not worked out the algebra. However, my conjecture is that c_0 and $c_2{}^*$ would have the values as in the static case while $c_1{}^*$ would be the same as in the static case except that a_0 would be replaced by $a_0 + Y_t (S_1 + S_2)$.

well be unfair to analyze the merits of his position within the model given by (18). However, this model does seem to have some relevance to the problem. First, note that Friedman's position does not depend per se on existence of lags in the effects of monetary changes, but rather on the inability to predict the level of income at the time when monetary actions take effect regardless of whether or not this effect occurs with a lag. The longer and more variable the lag, of course, the less accurate are income predictions likely to be. The dynamic model of (18) includes both predictable income changes through the influence of the lagged income terms and unpredictable income changes through the influence of the random terms, and so does represent, at least in part, the nature of the problem that led Friedman to his position.

The second aspect of this model to be noted is that the timing relationship between turning points in money and income is variable due to the random terms u and v even though the partial effect of money on income does not have a variable lag. Thus, the model is consistent with Friedman's findings on the variability of the lag between turning points in money and income.[9] Friedman's argument for a constant rate of growth in the money stock depends on variability in the partial effects of money on income. In passing, it might be mentioned that the only way to obtain evidence on the variability of the partial effects of money on income would be to show either that in a model of the economy the estimated regression coefficients were statistically significantly different from one period to another, or that the variability in the lag in turning points could not occur in a model with constant partial effects of money on income unless a most improbable probability distribution of the disturbance terms existed.

In analyzing passive policies, consider first the interest rate policy of setting $r=r_o$ permanently. It is optimal to set the interest rate according to

(19) $r_o = a_1^{-1}[Y_f(1-S_1-S_2)-a_o],$

and, substituting this expression into (18a), we have

$$Y_t - Y_f = S_1(Y_{t-1} - Y_f) + S_2(Y_{t-2} - Y_f) + u_t, \text{ or}$$

(20) $Z_t - S_1 Z_{t-1} - S_2 Z_{t-2} = u_t, \text{ where } Z_t = Y_t - Y_f.$

From (20) it can be seen that the level of income follows a second-order Markov process around a base level of Y_f.[1]

9. Milton Friedman and Anna J. Schwartz, "Money and Business Cycles," *Review of Economics and Statistics*, Vol. 45, no. 1, pt. 2 (Feb. 1963), 32–64.

1. The model of equation (20) is a stochastic version of Samuelson's multiplier-accelerator model (Paul A. Samuelson, "Interactions Between the Multiplier Analysis and the Principle of Acceleration," *The Review of Economic Statistics*, XXI (May 1939), 75–78).

To solve (20) we need a particular solution, $Z_t = Z'_t$, to (20) and a general solution, $z_t = z'_t$, to its homogenous counterpart

(21) $z_t - S_1 z_{t-1} - S_2 z_{t-2} = 0$, $z_t = Z_t - Z'_1$.

A particular solution to (20) may be found by assuming that

(22) $Z'_t = \sum\limits_{k=0}^{t} Q_k u_{t-k}$,

where the Q_k are yet to be determined. Substituting (22) into (20) we have

$$\sum_{k=0}^{t} Q_k u_{t-k} - S_1 \sum_{k=0}^{t-1} Q_k u_{t-1-k} - S_2 \sum_{k=0}^{t-2} Q_k u_{t-2-k} - u_t = 0, \text{ or}$$

(23) $(Q_0 - 1) u_t + (Q_1 - S_1 Q_0) u_{t-1}$

$$+ \sum_{k=2}^{t} (Q_k - S_1 Q_{k-1} - S_2 Q_{k-2}) u_{t-k} = 0.$$

For (23) to be satisfied for all possible values of u_{t-k}, the coefficient of each u_{t-k} must be zero. In order to find a general expression for Q_k, we must solve the difference equation

(24) $Q_k - S_1 Q_{k-1} - S_2 Q_{k-2} = 0, \quad k = 2, 3, \ldots,$

Equation (24) has the same form as (21) and so its solution provides both the particular solution and the solution to the homogenous counterpart except that the arbitrary constants differ. The general solution to (20) has the form

$$Z_t = Z'_t + z'_t$$

$$= \sum_{k=0}^{t} Q_k u_{t-k} + z'_t,$$

and involves one of the three cases below.

Case 1: $S_1^2 > -4S_2$

     Solution: $Q_k = A_1 \lambda_1{}^k + A_2 \lambda_2{}^k$

            $z'_k = B_1 \lambda_1{}^k + B_2 \lambda_2{}^k$

       where $\lambda_1 = \frac{1}{2}(S_1 + \sqrt{S_1^2 + 4S_2})$

               $\lambda_2 = \frac{1}{2}(S_1 - \sqrt{S_1^2 + 4S_2})$

Case 2: $S_1^2 = -4S^2$

     Solution: $Q_k = (A_1 + kA_2)(\frac{1}{2}S_1)^k$

            $z'_k = (B_1 + kB_2)(\frac{1}{2}S_1)^k$

Case 3: $S_1^2 < -4S_2 \left(\text{i.e. } S_2 < -\left(\dfrac{S_1}{2}\right)^2 \right)$

     Solution: $Q_k = (-S_2)^{\frac{1}{2}k}(A_1 \cos k\,\theta + A_2 \sin k\,\theta)$

            $z'_k = (-S_2)^{\frac{1}{2}k}(B_1 \cos k\,\theta + B_2 \sin k\,\theta)$

       where $\tan \theta = \dfrac{\sqrt{-4S_2 - S_1^2}}{S_1}$.

OPTIMAL CHOICE OF MONETARY POLICY 213

The constants A_1 and A_2, which differ from one case to another, are determined by solving the two equations,

$$Q_o - 1 = 0$$
$$Q_1 - S_1 Q_o = 0.$$

Similarly the constants B_1 and B_2 are obtained by solving the two equations

$$z'_0 = S_1 Z_{-1} + S_2 Z_{-2}$$
$$z'_1 = (S_1{}^2 + S_2) Z_{-1} + S_1 S_2 Z_{-2},$$

where Z_{-1} and Z_{-2} are the initial conditions on income.

The stability conditions on the solution are for Case 1 that $|S_1| < 1 - S_2$, for Case 2 that $|S_1| < 1$, and for Case 3 that $|S_2| < 1$. If the solution is stable the initial income conditions will have a smaller and smaller effect on income as time goes on, and the unconditional mean and variance of Z_t will approach

$$(25) \qquad E[Z_\infty] = E\left[\sum_{k=0}^{\infty} Q_k u_{t-k} \right] = 0$$

$$(26) \qquad \text{Var}[Z_\infty] = E[Z^2{}_\infty] = E\left[\left(\sum_{k=0}^{\infty} Q_k u_{t-k} \right)^2 \right] = \sigma^2{}_u \sum_{k=0}^{\infty} Q^2{}_k.$$

If the stability conditions are not met, the effect of the initial conditions on income will not disappear and the unconditional variance will grow without limit. Since $Z_t = Y_t - Y_f$, the variance of Z_t gives the expected loss with the loss function used before. Even if the loss is defined — i.e., less than infinity — under the passive interest rate policy, the loss will be greater — perhaps far greater — than under the optimal active policy.[2]

Now consider a policy of permanently fixing the money stock at $M_t = M_o$. With the optimal value of M_o we have

$$(27) \qquad Z_t = R_1 Z_{t-1} + R_2 Z_{t-2} + w_t$$
$$\text{where } R_1 = S_1 b_2 (a_1 b_1 + b_2)^{-1}$$
$$R_2 = S_2 b_2 (a_1 b_1 + b_2)^{-1}$$
$$w_t = b_2 (a_1 b_1 + b_2)^{-1} (b_2 u_t - a_1 v_t).$$

Let the particular solution be

$$(28) \qquad Z_t = \sum_{k=0}^{t} P_k w_t,$$

where the P_k are determined by the solution of a difference equation analogous to (24). The general solution also has the same form as before and the stability conditions on R_1 and R_2 are the same as on

2. Under an active interest rate policy the expected loss is $\sigma_u{}^2$ from (10). But from (23) it is clear that $Q_o = 1$ so that the difference of the losses is

$$\sigma_u{}^2 \sum_{k=0}^{\infty} Q_k{}^2 - \sigma_u{}^2 = \sigma_u{}^2 \sum_{k=1}^{\infty} Q_k{}^2 > 0.$$

S_1 and S_2 above. However, since $0 < b_2(a_1b_1+b_2)^{-1} < 1$ under normal assumptions as to the signs of a_1, b_1, and b_2, it is clear that $|R_1| < |S_1|$ and $|R_2| < |S_2|$. This means that although the variance of income might not exist under either policy it is possible that the variance exists when the money stock is set, but not when the interest rate is set. But note that if the variance exists under the interest rate policy, it may be lower than the variance under the money stock policy, since in the latter case we have

$$(29) \qquad E[Z_\infty{}^2] = \sigma_w{}^2 \sum_{k=0}^{\infty} P_k{}^2.$$

When one compares (26) and (29), it is clear that $\Sigma P_k{}^2$ is smaller than $\Sigma Q_k{}^2$, but $\sigma_w{}^2$ may be larger than $\sigma_u{}^2$.

In comparing the active and passive policies, it is clear that the expected loss under the passive policy is greater than under the active policy. While the optimal active and passive policies were in both cases derived under the assumption of known parameters, even if the parameters are not known exactly the analysis suggests that a nonoptimal active policy may still be superior to an optimal passive policy. With incomplete knowledge, a sensible procedure might be to start from a base policy of a fixed money stock (which is most likely superior to a fixed interest rate), and then to move away from this base somewhat cautiously in implementing an active policy.

VI. Concluding Observations

The choice of instruments problem is clearly a consequence of uncertainty, and analysis of the problem requires a stochastic model. The basic model of this paper is the simplest possible model within which the nature of the problem can be carefully defined and a solution determined. It is obvious that while the model provides some insight into the solution of the problem as faced by practical policy-makers, its main value is in clarifying the nature of the problem and suggesting an approach which might be applied to more complete and realistic models.

While the instrument problem has been analyzed as a monetary policy problem, it is worth pointing out that a similar problem arises in fiscal policy. Here the problem is whether the government should set income tax rates allowing tax revenues to be an endogenous variable or set tax receipts (through head taxes or property taxes) allowing the implicit income tax rate to be endogenous. While the income tax is usually viewed as a built-in stablizer, it might be possible to construct a plausible stochastic model in which the property tax stabilized income better than an income tax with the same expected revenue.

Except for a few passing comments no attention has been paid to the very important problem of the effect of uncertainty as to the values of the parameters of the model. In principle what should be done is to treat each parameter as a random variable,[3] but in even the simple model of this paper this approach is analytically intractable due to the large number of variances and co-variances involved, and the existence of products and ratios of random variables in the reduced form equations. A more promising approach might be to employ a sensitivity analysis to see how the results based on known parameters would differ if the parameters differed by plausible amounts from the estimates used in the analysis.

APPENDIX

It is necessary to prove that $L_o \leq L_r$ and $L_c \leq L_M$. Without loss of generality we may assume that $\sigma_u = \sigma_v$ since in equation (6a), the *IS*-function, it is possible to measure Y and u at rates (annual, quarterly, and so on) selected so that $\sigma_u = \sigma_v$; such a change in units will also require adjustments in some of the parameters. In the proof, no separate notation will be introduced for the adjusted parameters, it being understood that the appropriate adjustments have been made.

Under the assumption that $\sigma_u = \sigma_v$, it can be seen from (10) and (17) that

$$(30) \quad \frac{L_o}{L_r} = \frac{(1 - \rho_{uv}^2)}{1 + 2\rho_{uv}b_1 + b_1^2} = \frac{(1 - \rho_{uv})^2}{(1 - \rho_{uv}^2) + (\rho_{uv} + b_1)^2}$$

$$\leq 1 \text{ for } -1 \leq \rho_{uv} \leq 1.$$

If $b_1 = 1$, the denominator in (30) vanishes at $\rho_{uv} = -1$.

However, if $b_1 = 1$ we may write

$$\frac{L_o}{L_r} = \frac{(1 - \rho_{uv}^2)}{2(1 + \rho_{uv})} = \frac{(1 - \rho_{uv})}{2} = 1 \text{ for } \rho_{uv} = -1.$$

Under the assumption that $\sigma_u = \sigma_v$, it can be seen from (11) and (17) that

$$(31) \quad \frac{L_c}{L_M} = \frac{(a_1 b_1 + b_2)^2 (1 - \rho_{uv}^2)}{(a_1^2 - 2\rho_{uv} a_1 b_2 + b_2^2)(1 + 2\rho_{uv}b_1 + b_1^2)}$$

$$= \frac{(a_1 b_1 + b_2)^2 (1 - \rho_{uv})}{(a_1 b_1 + b_2)^2 (1 - \rho_{uv}^2) + [(a_1 - b_1 b_2) + \rho_{uv}(a_1 b_1 - b_2)]^2}$$

$$\leq 1 \text{ for } -1 \leq \rho_{uv} \leq 1.$$

If $b_1 = 1$, the denominator in (31) vanishes at $\rho_{uv} = -1$, and if $a_1 = b_2$, the denominator vanishes at $\rho_{uv} = 1$.

3. See William Brainard, "Uncertainty and the Effectiveness of Policy," *American Economic Review*, Vol. 57 (May 1967), 411–25.

If $b_1 = 1$, we may write

$$\frac{L_c}{L_M} = \frac{(a_1 + b_2)^2 \ (1 - \rho_{uv}^2)}{(a_1 + b_2)^2 \ (1 - \rho_{uv}^2) + [(a_1 - b_2) \ (1 + \rho_{uv})]^2}$$

$$= \frac{(a_1 + b_2)^2 \ (1 - \rho_{uv})}{(a_1 + b_2)^2 \ (1 - \rho_{uv}) + (a_1 - b_2)^2 \ (1 + \rho_{uv})}$$

$$= 1 \text{ at } \rho_{uv} = -1.$$

If $a_1 = b_2$, we may write

$$\frac{L_c}{L_M} = \frac{a_1^2 \ (b_1 + 1)^2 \ (1 - \rho_{uv}^2)}{a_1^2 \ (b_1 + 1)^2 \ (1 - \rho_{uv}^2) + [(a_1 - a_1 b_1) + \rho_{uv}(a_1 b_1 - a_1)]^2}$$

$$= \frac{(b_1 + 1)^2 \ (1 + \rho_{uv})}{(b_1 + 1)^2 \ (1 + \rho_{uv}) + (1 - b_1)^2 \ (1 - \rho_{uv})}$$

$$= 1 \text{ at } \rho_{uv} = 1.$$

BOARD OF GOVERNORS, FEDERAL RESERVE SYSTEM

THE JOURNAL OF
POLITICAL ECONOMY

Volume LXVI   DECEMBER 1958   *Number 6*

AN EXACT CONSUMPTION-LOAN MODEL OF INTEREST WITH OR WITHOUT THE SOCIAL CONTRIVANCE OF MONEY*

PAUL A. SAMUELSON

Massachusetts Institute of Technology

Y FIRST published paper[1] has come of age, and at a time when the subjects it dealt with have come back into fashion. It developed the equilibrium conditions for a rational consumer's lifetime consumption-saving pattern, a problem more recently given by Harrod the useful name of "hump saving" but which Landry, Böhm-Bawerk, Fisher, and others had touched on long before my time.[2] It dealt only with a single individual and did not discuss the mutual determination by all individuals of the

market interest rates which each man had to accept parametrically as given to him.

Now I should like to give a complete general equilibrium solution to the determination of the time-shape of interest rates. This sounds easy, but actually it is very hard, so hard that I shall have to make drastic simplifications in order to arrive at exact results. For while Böhm and Fisher have given us the essential insights into the pure theory of interest, neither they nor other writers seem to have grappled with the following tough problem: in order to define an equilibrium path of interest in a perfect capital market endowed with *perfect certainty*, you have to determine *all* interest rates between now and the end of time; every finite time period points beyond itself!

Some interesting mathematical boundary problems, a little like those in the modern theories of dynamic programming, result from this analysis. And the way is paved for a rigorous attack on a simple model involving money as a store of value and a medium of exchange. My essay concludes with some provocative

* Research aid from the Ford Foundation is gratefully acknowledged.

[1] "A Note on Measurement of Utility," *Review of Economic Studies*, IV (1937), 155–61.

[2] As an undergraduate student of Paul Douglas at Chicago, I was struck by the fact that we might, from the marginal utility schedule of consumptions, deduce saving behavior exactly in the same way that we might deduce gambling behavior. Realizing that, watching the consumer's gambling responses to varying odds, we could deduce his numerical marginal utilities, it occurred to me that, by watching the consumer's saving responses to varying interest rates, we might similarly measure his marginal utilities, and thus the paper was born. (I knew and pointed out, p. 155, n. 2; p. 160, that such a cardinal measurement of utility hinged on a certain refutable "independence" hypothesis.)

remarks about the field of social collusions, a subject of vital importance for political economy and of great analytical interest to the modern theorist.

THE PROBLEM STATED

Let us assume that men enter the labor market at about the age of twenty. They work for forty-five years or so and then live for fifteen years in retirement. (As children they are part of their parents' consumptions, and we take no note of them.) Naturally, they want to consume in their old age, and, in the absence of comprehensive social security—an institution which has important bearing on interest rates and saving—men will want to consume less than they produce during their working years so that they can consume something in the years when they produce nothing.

If there were only Robinson Crusoe, he would hope to put by some durable goods which could be drawn on in his old age. He would, so to speak, want to trade with Mother Nature current consumption goods in return for future consumption goods. And if goods kept perfectly, he could at worst always make the trade through time on a one-to-one basis, and we could say that the interest rate was zero ($i = 0$). If goods kept imperfectly, like ice or radium, Crusoe might have to face a negative real interest rate, $i < 0$. If goods were like rabbits or yeast, reproducing without supervision at compound interest, he would face a positive rate of interest, $i > 0$. This last case is usually considered to be technologically the most realistic one: that is, machines and round-about processes (rather than rabbits) are considered to have a "net productivity," and this is taken to be brute fact. (Böhm himself, after bitterly criticizing naïve productivity theorists and criticizing

Thünen and others for assuming such a fact, ends up with his own celebrated third cause for interest, which also asserts the fact of net productivity. Contrary to much methodological discussion, there is nothing circular about assuming brute facts—that is all we can do; we certainly cannot deduce them, although, admittedly, we can hope by experience to refute falsely alleged facts.)

For the present purpose, I shall make the extreme assumption that nothing will keep at all. Thus no intertemporal trade with Nature is possible (that is, for all such exchanges we would have $i = -1$!). If Crusoe were alone, he would obviously die at the beginning of his retirement years.

But we live in a world where new generations are always coming along. Formerly we used to support our parents in their old age. That is now out of fashion. But cannot men during their productive years give up some of their product to bribe other men to support them in their retirement years? Thus, forty-year-old A gives some of his product to twenty-year-old B, so that when A gets to be seventy-five he can receive some of the product that B is then producing.

Our problem, then, is this: In a stationary population (or, alternatively, one growing in any prescribed fashion) what will be the intertemporal terms of trade or interest rates that will spring up spontaneously in ideally competitive markets?

SIMPLIFYING ASSUMPTIONS

To make progress, let us make convenient assumptions. Break each life up into thirds: men produce one unit of product in period 1 and one unit in period 2; in period 3 they retire and produce nothing. (No one dies in midstream.)

In specifying consumption preferences,

I suppose that each man's tastes can be summarized by an ordinal utility function of the consumptions of the three periods of his life: $U = U(C_1, C_2, C_3)$. This is the same in every generation and has the usual regular indifference-curve concavities, but for much of the argument nothing is said about whether, subjectively, men systematically discount future consumptions or satisfactions. (Thus Böhm's second cause of interest may or may not be operative; it could even be reversed, men being supposed to overvalue the future!)

In addition to ignoring Böhm's second cause of systematic time preference, I am in a sense also denying or reversing his first cause of interest, in that we are *not* supposing that society is getting more prosperous as time passes or that any single man can expect to be more prosperous at a later date in his life, since, on the contrary, during his years of retirement he must look forward to producing even less than during his working years.

Finally, recall our assumption that no goods keep, no trade with Nature being possible, and hence Böhm's third technological cause of interest is being denied.

Under these assumptions, what will be the equilibrium time path of interest rates?

INDIVIDUAL SAVING FUNCTIONS

The simplest case to tackle to answer this question is that of a stationary population, which has always been stationary in numbers and will always be stationary. This ideal case sidesteps the difficult "planning-until-infinity" aspect of the problem. In it births are given by $B_t = B$, the same constant for all positive and negative t.

Now consider any time t. There are B men of age one, B men of age two, and B retired men of age three. Since each

producer produces 1 unit, total product is $B + B$. Now, for convenience of symbols, let $R_t = 1/(1 + i_t)$ be the discount rate between goods (chocolates) of period t traded for chocolates of the next period, $t + 1$. Thus, if $R_t = 0.5$, you must promise me two chocolates tomorrow to get me to part with one chocolate today, the interest rate being 100 per cent per period. If $R_t = 1$, the interest rate is zero, and tomorrow's chocolates cost 1.0 of today's. If $R_t > 1$, say $R_t = 1.5$, the interest rate is negative, and one future chocolate costs 1.5 of today's. (Clearly, R_t is the price of tomorrow's chocolates expressed in terms of today's chocolates as numeraire.)

We seek the equilibrium levels of . . . $R_t, R_{t+1}, \ldots$, that will clear the competitive markets in which present and future goods exchange against each other.

At time t each man who is beginning his life faces[3] the budget equation,

$$C_1 + C_2 R_t + C_3 R_t R_{t+1}$$
$$= 1 + 1R_t + 0R_t R_{t+1} . \tag{1}$$

This merely says that the total discounted value of his life's consumptions must equal the discounted value of his productions. Subject to this constraint, he will, for each given R_t and R_{t+1}, determine an optimal (C_1, C_2, C_3) to maximize $U(C_1, C_2, C_3)$, which we can summarize by the "demand" functions,

$$C_i = C_i(R_t, R_{t+1}) \qquad (i = 1, 2, 3) . \tag{2}$$

[3] I rule out, as I did explicitly in my 1937 paper (p.160), the Ulysses-Strotz-Allais phenomenon whereby time perspective distorts present decisions planned for the future from later actual decisions. Thus, if at the end of period 1 his ordinal preference follows $V(C_1, C_2, C_3)$ rather than $U(C_1, C_2, C_3)$, I am assuming $(\partial V/\partial C_1)/(\partial V/\partial C_2) \equiv (\partial U/\partial C_i)/(\partial U/\partial C_j)$. Hence all later decisions will ratify earlier plans. For a valuable discussion of this problem see R. H. Strotz, "Myopia and Inconsistency in Dynamic Utility Maximization," *Review of Economic Studies*, XXIII (1956), 165–80.

It might be convenient for us to work with "net" or "excess demands" of each man: these are the algebraic differences between what a man consumes and what he produces. Net demands in this sense are the negative of what men usually call "saving," and, in deference to capital theory, I shall work with such "net saving" as defined by

$$S_1 = S_1(R_t, R_{t+1}) = 1 - C_1(R_t, R_{t+1}),$$

$$S_2 = S_2(R_t, R_{t+1}) = 1 - C_2(R_t, R_{t+1}),$$ (3)

$$S_3 = S_3(R_t, R_{t+1}) = 0 - C_3(R_t, R_{t+1}).$$

In old age presumably S_3 is negative, matched by positive youthful saving, so as to satisfy for all (R_t, R_{t+1}) the budget identity,

$$S_1(R_t, R_{t+1}) + R_t S_2(R_t, R_{t+1})$$
$$+ R_t R_{t+1} S_3(R_t, R_{t+1}) = 0.$$ (4)

Of course, these functions are subject to all the restrictions of modern consumption theory of the ordinal utility or revealed preference type. Thus, with consumption in every period being a "superior good," we can infer that $\partial C_3, \partial R_{t+1} > 0$ and $\partial S_3/\partial R_{t+1} < 0$. (This says that lowering the interest rate earned on savings carried over into retirement must increase retirement consumption.) We cannot unambiguously deduce the sign of $\partial S_1/\partial R_t$ and other terms, for the reasons implicit in modern consumption theory.

We can similarly work out the saving functions for men born a period later, which will be of the form $S_i(R_{t+1}, R_{t+2})$, etc., containing, of course, the later interest rates they will face—likewise for earlier interest rates facing men born earlier. Finally, our fundamental condition of clearing the market is this: Total net saving for the community must cancel out to zero in every period. (Remember that no goods keep and that real net investment is impossible, all loans being "consumption" loans.)

At any time t there exist B_t men of the first period, B_{t-1} men of the second period, and B_{t-2} men of the third period. The sum of their savings gives us the fundamental equilibrium condition:

$$0 = B_t S_1(R_t, R_{t+1}) + B_{t-1} S_2(R_{t-1}, R_t)$$
$$+ B_{t-2} S_3(R_{t-2}, R_{t-1}),$$ (5)

for every t. Note that in S_2 we have the interest rates of one earlier period than in S_1, and in S_3 we have still earlier interest rates (in fact, interest rates that are, at time t, already history and no longer to be determined.)

We have such an equation for every t, and if we take any finite stretch of time and write out the equilibrium conditions, we always find them containing discount rates from before the finite period and discount rates from afterward. We never seem to get enough equations: lengthening our time period turns out always to add as many new unknowns as it supplies equations, as will be spelled out later in equations (14).

THE STATIONARY CASE

We can try to cut the Gordian knot by our special assumption of stationariness, namely,

$$\ldots B_{t-1} = B_t = B_{t+1} = \ldots$$

$$= B, \text{ a given constant for all time}$$

$$\ldots R_{t-1} = R_t = R_{t+1} = \ldots$$ (6)

$$= R, \text{ the unknown discount rate.}$$

The first of these is a demographic datum; the second assumption of non-changing interest rates is a conjecture whose consistency we must explore and verify.

AN EXACT CONSUMPTION-LOAN MODEL OF INTEREST 471

Now substituting relations (6) in equation (5), we get one equilibrium equation to determine our one unknown R, namely,

$$0 = BS_1(R, R) + BS_2(R, R) + BS_3(R, R) . \qquad (7)$$

By inspection, we recognize a solution of equation (7) to be $R = 1$, or $i = 0$: that is, zero interest must be one equilibrium rate under our conditions.[4] Why? Because

$$B[S_1(1, 1) + 1S_2(1, 1) + 1S_3(1, 1)] = 0$$

by virtue of the budget identity (4).

Can a common-sense explanation of this somewhat striking result be given? Let me try. In a stationary system everyone goes through the same life-cycle, albeit at different times. Giving over goods now to an older man is figuratively giving over goods to *yourself* when old. At what rate does one give over goods to one's later self? At $R > 1$, or $R < 1$, or $R = 1$? To answer this, note that a chocolate today *is* a chocolate today, and when middle-aged A today gives over a chocolate to old B, there is a one-to-one *physical* transfer of chocolates, none melting in the transfer and none sticking to the hands of a broker. So, heuristically, we see that the hypothetical "transfer *through time*" of the chocolates must be at $R = 1$ with the interest rate i exactly zero.

Note that this result is quite independent of whether or not people have a systematic subjective preference for present consumption over future. Why? Because we have assumed that if *anyone* has such a systematic preference, *everyone* has such a systematic preference. There is no one any different in the system, no outsider—so to speak—to exact

a positive interest rate from the impatient consumers.[5]

A BIOLOGICAL THEORY OF INTEREST AND POPULATION GROWTH

A zero rate of population growth was seen to be consistent with a zero rate of interest for a consumption-loan world. I now turn to the case of a population growing exponentially or geometrically. Now

$$B_t = B(1 + m)^t , \quad \text{with}$$

$$B_{t+1} = (1 + m)B_t = (1 + m)^2 B_{t-1} \dots .$$

For $m > 0$, we have growth; for $m < 0$, decay; for $m = 0$, our previous case of a stationary population. As before, we suppose

$$\dots R_{t-1} = R_t = R_{t+1} = \dots$$

$$= R, \text{ a constant through time.}$$

Now our clearing-of-the-market equation is

$$0 = B(1 + m)^t S_1(R, R)$$

$$+ B(1 + m)^{t-1} S_2(R, R) \quad (8)$$

$$+ B(1 + m)^{t-2} S_3(R, R) ;$$

or, cancelling $B(1 + m)^t$, we have

$$0 = S_1(R, R) + (1 + m)^{-1} S_2(R, R)$$

$$+ (1 + m)^{-2} S_3(R, R) . \quad (9)$$

Recalling our budget identity (4), we realize $R = (1 + m)^{-1}$ or $i = m$ is one root satisfying the equation, giving

$$0 = S_1(R, R) + RS_2(R, R) + R^2 S_3(R, R) .$$

We have therefore established the following paradoxical result:

[4] We shall see that $R = 1$ is not the only root of equation (7) and that there are multiple equilibriums.

[5] If productive opportunities were to exist, Mother Nature would operate as an important outsider, with whom trade could take place, and our conclusion would be modified. But recall our strong postulate that such technological opportunities are non-existent.

THEOREM: Every geometrically growing consumption-loan economy has an equilibrium market rate of interest exactly equal to its biological percentage growth rate.

Thus, if the net reproductive rate gives a population growth of 15 per cent per period, $i = 0.15$ is the corresponding market rate of interest. If, as in Sweden or Ireland, $m < 0$ and population decays, the market rate of interest will be negative, with $i < 0$ and $R > 1$!

OPTIMUM PROPERTY OF THE BIO-LOGICAL INTEREST RATE

The equality of the market rate of interest in a pure consumption-loan world to the rate of population growth was deduced solely from mechanically finding a root of the supply-demand equations that clear the market. Experience often confirms what faith avers: that competitive market relations achieve some kind of an optimum.

Does the saving-consumption pattern given by $S_1(R, R)$, $S_2(R, R)$, $S_3(R, R)$, where $R = 1/(1 + m)$, represent some kind of a social optimum? One would guess that, if it does maximize something, this equilibrium pattern probably maximizes the "lifetime (ordinal) well-being of a representative person, subject to the resources available to him (and to every other representative man) over his lifetime." Or, what seems virtually the same thing, consider a cross-sectional family or clan that has an unchanging age distribution because the group remains in statistical equilibrium, though individuals are born and die. Such a clan will divide its available resources to maximize a welfare function differing only in scale from each man's utility function and will achieve the same result as the biological growth rate.

To test this optimality conjecture, first stick to the stationary population

case. The representative man is thought to maximize $U(C_1, C_2, C_3)$, subject to

$$C_1 + C_2 + C_3 = 1 + 1, \quad (10)$$

$1 + 1$ being the lifetime product available to each man. The solution to this technocratic welfare problem (free in its formulation and solution of all mention of prices or interest rates) requires

$$\frac{\partial U / \partial C_2}{\partial U / \partial C_1} = \frac{\partial U / \partial C_3}{\partial U / \partial C_1}. \quad (11)$$

But this formulation is seen to be identical with that of a single maximizing man facing market discount rates $R_1 = R_2 = 1$. Hence the solution of equations (10) and (11) is exactly that given earlier by equation (3): that is, our present welfare problem has, for its optimality solution,

$$1 - C_1 = S_1(1, 1),$$

$$1 - C_2 = S_2(1, 1),$$

$$0 - C_3 = S_3(1, 1).$$

Now that we have verified our conjecture for the stationary $m = 0$ case, we can prove it for population growing like $B(1 + m)^t$, where $m \gtrless 0$. As before, we maximize $U(C_1, C_2, C_3)$ for the representative man. But what resources are now available to him? Recall that in a growing population the age distribution is permanently skewed in favor of the younger productive ages: society and each clan has an age distribution proportional to $[1, 1/(1 + m), 1/(1 + m)^2]$ and has therefore a per capita output to divide in consumption among the three age classes satisfying

$$C_1 + \frac{1}{1 + m} C_2 + \frac{1}{(1 + m)^2} C_3$$
$$= 1 + \frac{1}{1 + m}. \quad (12)$$

By following a representative man throughout his life and remembering that there are always $(1 + m)^{-1}$ just older than he and $(1 + m)^{-2}$ two periods older, we derive this same "budget" or availibility equation. Subject to equation (12), we maximize $U(C_1, C_2, C_3)$ and necessarily end up with the same conditions as would a competitor facing the biological market interest rate $R_1 = R_2 = 1/(1 + m)$: namely,

$$1 - C_1 = S_1(R, R),$$
$$1 - C_2 = S_2(R, R),$$
$$0 - C_3 = S_3(R, R), \qquad (13)$$

$$R = \frac{1}{1+m}.$$

Hence the identity of the social optimality conditions and the biological market interest theory has been demonstrated.[6]

COMMON-SENSE EXPLANATION OF BIOLOGICAL MARKET INTEREST RATE

Productivity theorists have always related interest to the biological habits of rabbits and cows. And Gustav Cassel long ago developed a striking (but rather nonsensical) biological theory relating

[6] If U has the usual quasi-concavity, this social optimum will be unique—whether U does or does not have the time-symmetry that is sometimes (for concreteness) assumed in later arguments. Not only will the representative man's utility U be maximized, but so will the "total" of social utility enjoyed over a long period of time: specifically, the divergence from attainable bliss

$$[U(C_1, C_2, C_3) - U^*] + [U(C_1, C_2, C_3) - U^*] + \dots$$

over all time will be miminized, where U^* is the utility achieved when $R_1 = 1 = R_2$ and $S_i = S_i(1, 1)$. This theorem may require that we use an ordinal utility indicator that is concave in the C_i, as it is always open to us to do.

Of course, this entire footnote and the related text need obvious modifications if $m \neq 0$.

interest to the life-expectancy of men of means and their alleged propensity to go from maintaining capital to the buying of annuities at an allegedly critical positive i. I seem to be the first, outside a slave economy, to develop a biological theory of interest relating it to the reproductivity of human mothers.

Is there a common-sense market explanation of this (to me at least) astonishing result? I suppose it would go like this: in a growing population men of twenty outnumber men of forty; and retired men are outnumbered by workers more than in the ratio of the work span to the retirement span. With more workers to support them, the aged live better than in the stationary state—the excess being positive interest on their savings.

Such an explanation cannot be deemed entirely convincing. Outside of social security and family altruism, the aged have no claims on the young: cold and selfish competitive markets will not teleologically respect the old; the aged will get only what supply and demand impute to them.

So we might try another more detailed explanation. Recall that men of forty or of period 2 bargain with men of twenty or period 1, trying to bribe the latter to provide them with consumption in their retirement. (Men of over sixty-five or of period 3 can make fresh bargains with no one: after retirement it is too late for them to try to provide for their old age.) In a growing population there are more period 1 men for period 2 men to bargain with; this presumably confers a competitive advantage on period 2 men, the manifestation of it being the positive interest rate.

So might go the explanation. It is at least superficially plausible, and it does qualitatively suggest a positive interest rate when population is growing, although perhaps it falls short of explaining the remarkable quantitative identity between the growth rates of interest and of population.

THE INFINITY PARADOX REVEALED

But will the explanation survive rigorous scrutiny? Is it true, in a growing or in a stationary population, that twenty-year-olds are, in fact, overconsuming so that the middle-aged can provide for their retirement? Specifically, in the stationary case where $R = 1$, is it necessarily true that $S_1(1, 1) < 0$? Study of $U(C_1, C_2, C_3)$ shows how doubtful such a general result would be; thus, if there is no systematic subjective time preference so that U is a function *symmetric* in its arguments, it would be easy to show that $C_1 = C_2 = C_3 = \frac{2}{3}$, with $S_1(1, 1) = S_2(1, 1) = +\frac{1}{3}$ and $S_3(1, 1) = -\frac{2}{3}$. Contrary to our scenario, the middle-aged are *not* turning over to the young what the young will later make good to them in retirement support.

THE TWO-PERIOD CASE

The paradox is delineated more clearly if we suppose but two equal periods of life—work and retirement. Now it becomes *impossible* for *any* worker to find a worker younger than himself to be bribed to support him in old age. Whatever the trend of births, there is but one equilibrium saving pattern possible: during working years, consumption equals product and saving is zero; the same during the brutish years of retirement. What equilibrium interest rate, or R, will prevail? Since no transactions take place, $R = 0/0$, so to speak, and appears rather indeterminate—and rather academic. However, if men desperately want *some* consumption at *all* times, only $R = \infty$ can be regarded as the (virtual) equilibrium rate, with interest equal to -100 per cent per period.[7]

We think we know the right answer just given in the two-period case. Let us test our previous mathematical methods. Now our equations are much as before and can be summarized by:

Maximize $U(C_1, C_2) = U(1 - S_1, 0 - S_2)$

subject to $S_1 + R_t S_2 = 0$.

The resulting saving functions, $S_1(R_t)$ and $S_2(R_t)$, are subject to the budget identity,

$$S_1(R_t) + R_t S_2(R_t) \equiv 0 \text{ for all } R_t. \quad (4')$$

Clearing the market requires

$$0 = B_t S_1(R_t) + B_{t-1} S_2(R_{t-1}) \quad \text{for} \quad (5')$$
$$t = 0, \pm 1, \pm 2, \dots.$$

If $B_t = B(1 + m)^t$ and $R_t = R_{t+1} = \dots = R$, our final equation becomes

$$0 = B\left[S_1(R) + \frac{1}{1+m} S_2(R)\right]. \quad (8')$$

The budget equation $(4')$ assures us that equation $(8')$ has a solution:

$$R = \frac{1}{1+m} \quad \text{or} \quad m = i.$$

with $0 < S_1(R) = -R S_2(R)$.

So the two-period mathematics appears to give us the same answer as before—a biological rate of interest equal to the rate of population growth.

Yet we earlier deduced that *there can be no voluntary saving in a two-period world*. Instead of $S_1 > 0$, we must have $S_1 = 0 = S_2$ with $R = +\infty$. How can we reconcile this with the mathematics?

---

[7] A later numerical example, where $U = \log C_1 + \log C_2 + \log C_3$, shows that cases can arise where no positive R, however large, will clear the market. I adopt the harmless convention of setting $R = \infty$ in every case, even if the limit as $R \to \infty$ does not wipe out the discrepancy between supply and demand.

We substitute $S_1 = 0 = S_2$ in equation (5') or equation (8'), and indeed this does satisfy the clearing-of-the-market equation. Apparently our one equilibrium equation in our one unknown R has more than a single solution! And the relevant one for a free market is *not* that given by our biological or demographic theory of interest, even though our earlier social optimality argument does perfectly fit the two-period case.

THE PARADOX CONTEMPLATED

The transparent two-period case alerts us to the possibility that in the three-period (or n-period) case, the fundamental equation of supply and demand may have multiple solutions. And, indeed, it does.[8] We see that

$$0 = S_1(\infty, \infty) = S_2(\infty, \infty) = S_3(\infty, \infty)$$

is indeed a valid mathematical solution. This raises the following questions:

Is a condition of no saving with dismal retirement consumption and interest rate of -100 per cent per period thinkable as the economically correct equilibrium for a free market?

Surely, the non-myopic middle-aged will do almost anything to make retirement consumption, C_3 non-zero?[9]

One might conjecture that the fact that, in the three-period model, workers can always find younger workers to bargain with is a crucial difference from the two-period case.[10] To investigate the

[8] There is nothing surprising about multiple solutions in economics: not infrequently income effects make possible other intersections, including the possibility of an infinite number where demand and supply curves coincide.

[9] Before answering these questions, it would be well to decide what the word "surely" in the previous sentence means. Surely, no sentence beginning with the word "surely" can validly contain a question mark at its end? However, one paradox is enough for one article, and I shall stick to my economist's last.

problem, we must drop the assumption of a population that is, always has been, and always will be stationary (or exponentially growing or exponentially decaying). For within that ambiguous context $R = 1(R < 1, \ R > 1)$ was indeed an impeccable solution, in the sense that no one can point to a violated equilibrium condition. (Exactly the same can be said of the two-period case, even though we "know" the impeccable solution is economically nonsense.)

We must give mankind a beginning. So, once upon a time, B men were born into the labor force. Then B more. Then B more. Until what? Until . . . ? Or until no more men are born? Must we give mankind an end as well as a beginning? Even the Lord rested after the beginning, so let us tackle one problem at a time and keep births forever constant. Our equilibrium equations, with the constant B's omitted, now become

$$S_1(R_1, R_2) + 0 + 0 = 0,$$

$$S_2(R_1, R_2) + S_1(R_2, R_3) + 0 = 0,$$

$$S_3(R_1, R_2) + S_2(R_2, R_3)$$
$$+ S_1(R_3, R_4) = 0,$$

$$S_3(R_2, R_3) + S_2(R_3, R_4) \qquad (14)$$
$$+ S_1(R_4, R_5) = 0,$$

$$. \ . \ . \ . \ . \ . \ . \ . \ . \ . \ . \ . \ . \ . \ . \ . \ . \ . \ ,$$

$$S_3(R_{t-2}, R_{t-1}) + S_2(R_{t-1}, R_t)$$
$$+ S_1(R_t, R_{t+1}) = 0,$$

$$. \ . \ . \ . \ . \ . \ . \ . \ . \ . \ . \ . \ . \ . \ . \ .$$

We feel that $S_1 \equiv 0 \equiv S_2 \equiv S_3$, while a mathematical solution, is not the economically relevant one. Since $S_1(1, 1)$, $S_2(1, 1)$, and $S_3(1, 1)$ do satisfy the last

[10] By introducing overlap between workers of different ages, the three-period model is essentially equivalent to a general n-period model or to the continuous-time model of real life.

PAUL A. SAMUELSON

of the written equations, we dare hope[11] that the Invisible Hand will ultimately work its way to the socially optimal biological-interest configuration—or that the solution to equation (14) satisfies

$$\lim_{t \to \infty} R_t = 1, \quad S_i(R_t, R_{t+1})$$

$$= S_i(1, 1), \; (i = 1, 2, 3) . \quad (15)$$

THE IMPOSSIBILITY THEOREM

But have we any right to hope that the free market will even ultimately approach the specified social optimum? Does not the two-period case rob us of hope? Will not all the trade that the three-period case makes possible consist of middle-aged period 2 people giving consumption to young period 1 people in return for getting consumption back from them one period later? Do not such voluntary mutual-aid compacts suggest that, if R_t does approach a limit x, it must be such as to make $S_1(x, x) < 0$? Whereas, for many men[12] not too subject to systematic preference for the present over the future (not too affected by Böhm's second cause of interest), we expect $S_1(1, 1) > 0$.

A colleague, whose conjectures are

often better than many people's theorems, has suggested to me that in the three-period or n-period case I am taking too bilateral a view of trade. We might end up with $S_1 > 0$ and encounter no contradictions to voluntary trade by virtue of the fact that young men trade with *anyone* in the market: they do not know or care that all or part of the motive for trade with them comes from the desire of the middle-aged to provide for retirement. The present young are content to be trading with the present old (or, for that matter, with the unborn or dead): all they care about is that their trades take place at the quoted market prices; and, if some kind of triangular or multilateral offsetting among the generations can take place and result in $S_1(R_t, R_{t+1})$ positive and becoming closer and closer to $S_1(1, 1) > 0$, why cannot this happen?

I, too, found the multilateral notion appealing. But the following considerations—of a type I do not recall seeing treated anywhere—suggest to me that the ultimate approach to $R = 1$ and $S_1(1, 1) > 0$ is quite impossible.

List all men from the beginning to time t. All the voluntary trades ever made must be mutually advantageous. If A gives something to B and B does nothing for A directly in return, we know B must be doing something for some C, who does do something good for A. (Of course, C might be more than one man, and there might be many-linked connections within C.)

Now consider a time when $S_1(R_t, R_{t+1})$ has become positive, with $S_2(R_{t-1}, R_t)$ also positive. Young man A is then giving goods to old man B. Young man A expects something in return and will actually two periods later be getting goods from someone. From whom? It certainly cannot be directly from B: B will

---

[11] Our confidence in this would be enhanced if the linear difference equation relating small deviations $r_t = R_t - 1$ had characteristic roots all less than 1 in absolute value. Thus $a_0 r_{t+3} + a_1 r_{t+2} + a_2 r_{t+1} + a_3 r_t = 0$, where the a_i are given in terms of the $S_i(R_t, R_{t+1})$ functions and their partial derivatives, evaluated at $R_t = 1 R_{t+1}$. Logically, this would be neither quite necessary nor sufficient: not sufficient, since the initial R_0, R_1, R_2 might be so far from 1 as to make the linear approximations irrelevant; not necessary, since, with one root less than unity in absolute value, we might ride in toward $R = 1$ on a razor's edge. In any case, as our later numerical example shows, our hope is a vain one.

[12] There is admittedly some econometric evidence that many young adults do dissave, to acquire assets and for other reasons. Some modifications of exposition would have to be made to allow for this.

AN EXACT CONSUMPTION-LOAN MODEL OF INTEREST 477

be dead then. Let it be from someone called C. Can B ever do anything good for such a C, or have in the past done so? No. B only has produce during his first two periods of life, and all the good he can do anyone must be to people who were born before him or just after him. That *never* includes C. So the postulated pattern of $S_1 > 0$ is logically impossible in a free market: and hence $R_t = 1 = R_{t+1}$, as an exact or approximate relation, is impossible. (Note that, for some special pattern of time preference, the competitive solution *might* coincide with the "biological optimum.")

A NUMERICAL EXAMPLE

A concrete case will illustrate all this. The purest Marshallian case of unitary price and income elasticities can be characterized by $U = \log C_1 + \log C_2 + \log C_3$, where all systematic time preference is replaced by *symmetry*.

A maximum of

$$\sum_1^3 \log C_t \text{ subject to} \quad (16)$$

$$C_1 + R_1 C_2 + R_1 R_2 C_3 = 1 + R_1$$

implies

$$R_1 = \frac{\partial U / \partial C_2}{\partial U / \partial C_1} = \frac{1/C_2}{1/C_1},$$

$$R_1 R_2 = \frac{\partial U / \partial C_3}{\partial U / \partial C_1} = \frac{1/C_3}{1/C_1};$$

and, after combining this with the budget equation, we end up with saving functions,

$$S_1(R_1, R_2) = \frac{2}{3} - \frac{R_1}{3},$$

$$S_2(R_1, R_2) = \frac{2}{3} - \frac{1}{3R_1}, \quad (17)$$

$$S_3(R_1, R_2) = 0 - \frac{1}{3R_1 R_2} - \frac{1}{3R_2}.$$

Equations (14) now take the form

$$\frac{2}{3} - \frac{R_1}{3} + 0 + 0 = 0,$$

$$\frac{2}{3} - \frac{1}{3R_1} + \left(\frac{2}{3} - \frac{R_2}{3}\right) + 0 = 0,$$

$$-\frac{1}{3R_1 R_2} - \frac{1}{3R_2} + \left(\frac{2}{3} - \frac{1}{3R_2}\right)$$

$$+ \left(\frac{2}{3} - \frac{R_3}{3}\right) = 0,$$

$$\left(-\frac{1}{3R_2 R_3} - \frac{1}{3R_3}\right) + \left(\frac{2}{3} - \frac{1}{3R_3}\right) \quad (18)$$

$$+ \left(\frac{2}{3} - \frac{R_4}{3}\right) = 0,$$

$$\cdots \cdots \cdots \cdots \cdots$$

$$\left(-\frac{1}{3R_{t-1}R_{t-2}} - \frac{1}{3R_{t-1}}\right)$$

$$+ \left(\frac{2}{3} - \frac{1}{3R_{t-1}}\right) + \left(\frac{2}{3} - \frac{R_t}{3}\right) = 0,$$

$$\cdots \cdots \cdots \cdots \cdots$$

Aside from initial conditions, this can be written in the recursive form,

$$R_t = 4 - \frac{1}{R_{t-1}R_{t-2}} - \frac{2}{R_{t-1}}. \quad (19)$$

Note that $\partial S_1(R_1, R_2) \equiv 0$ made our third-order difference equation degenerate into a second-order difference equation.

If we expand the last equation around $R_{t-2} = 1 = R_{t-1}$, retaining only linear terms and working in terms of deviations from the equilibrium level, $r_t = R_t - 1$, we get the recursive system,

$$r_{t+2} = 3r_{t+1} + r_t. \quad (20)$$

which obviously explodes away from $r = 0$ and $R = 1$ for all small perturbations from such an equilibrium. This confirms our proof that the *social optimum configuration can never here be reached by the competitive market, or even be approached in ever so long a time.*

Where does the solution to (18) eventually go? Its first few R's are numerically calculated to be $[R_1, R_2, R_3, \ldots] = [2, 3\frac{1}{2}, 3\frac{2}{7}, \ldots]$. It is plain that the limiting R_t exceeds 1; hence a negative interest rate i is being asymptotically approached. Substituting $R_{t+2} = R_{t+1} = R_t = x$ in equation (19), we get the following cubic equation to solve for possible equilibrium levels:[13]

$$x = 4 - \frac{1}{x^2} - \frac{2}{x} \quad \text{or}$$

$$x^3 - 4x^2 + 2x + 1 = 0. \tag{21}$$

We know that $x = 1$, the irrelevant optimal level, is one root; so, dividing it out, we end up with

$$(x - 1)(x^2 - 3x - 1) = 0.$$

Solving the quadratic, we have

$$x = \frac{3 \pm \sqrt{9 + 4}}{2}$$

or

$$x = \frac{3}{2} + \frac{\sqrt{13}}{2} = 3.297 \text{ approx}.$$

for the asymptote approached by the free competitive market. The other root, $(3 - \sqrt{13})/2$, corresponds to a negative R, which is economically meaningless, in that it implies that the more we give up of today's consumption, the more we must give up of tomorrow's.

Our meaningful positive root, $R = 3.297$, corresponds to an ultimate negative interest rate,

$$i = \frac{1 - R}{R} = -\frac{2.297}{3.297},$$

[13] Martin J. Bailey has pointed out to me that the budget equation and the clearing-of-the-market equations do, in the stationary state, imply $S_1 = RS_3$ whenever $R \neq 1$, a fact which can be used to give an alternative demonstration of possible equilibrium values.

which implies that consumption loans lose about two-thirds of their principal in one period. This is here the competitive price to avoid retirement starvation.[14]

RECAPITULATION

The task of giving an exact description of a pure consumption-loan interest model is finished. We end up, in the stationary population case, with a negative market interest rate, rather than with the biological zero interest rate corresponding to the social optimum for the representative man. This was proved by the impossibility theorem and verified by an arithmetic example.

A corresponding result will hold for changing population where $m \gtrless 0$. The actual competitive market rate i_m will always be negative and always less than the biological optimality rate m.[15] And

[14] In other examples, this competitive solution would not deviate so much from the $i = m$ biological optimum. But it is important to realize that solutions to equations (14) that come from quasi-concave utility functions—with or without systematic time preference—*cannot* be counted on to approach asymptotically the biological optimum configuration of equation (13).

In this case the linear approximation gives for $r_t = R_t - 3.297$ the recursion relation

$$r_{t+2} = \frac{1}{(3.297)^3} r_{t+1} + \frac{2}{(3.297)^2} r_t.$$

This difference equation has roots easily shown to be less than 1 in absolute value, so the local stability of our competitive equilibrium is assured.

[15] Writing $\lambda = 1/(1 + m)$, our recursion relation (14) becomes

$$0 = S_1(R_t, R_{t+1}) + \lambda S_2(R_{t-1}, R_t)$$
$$+ \lambda^2 S_3(R_{t-2}, R_{t-1}).$$

For the case where $U = \Sigma \log C_i$, our recursion relation (18) becomes

$$R_t = 2(1 + \lambda) - \frac{\lambda^2}{R_{t-1}R_{t-2}} - \frac{\lambda^2}{R_{t-1}} - \frac{\lambda}{R_{t-1}}.$$

Then $x = R_t = R_{t-1} = R_{t-2}$ gives a cubic equation with biological root corresponding to $x = \lambda$ and

increasing the productive years relative to the retirement years of zero product would undoubtedly still leave us with a negative interest rate, albeit one that climbs ever closer to zero.

Is this negative interest rate a hard-to-believe result? Not, I think, when one recalls our extreme and purposely unrealistic assumptions. With Böhm's third technological reason for interest ruled out by assumption, with his second reason involving systematic preference for the present soft-pedaled, and with his first reason reversed (that is, with people expecting to be *poorer* in the future), we should perhaps have been surprised if the market rate had not turned out negative.

Yet, aside from giving the general biological optimum interest rate, our model is an instructive one for a number of reasons.

1. It shows us what interest rates would be implied if the "hump saving" process were acting alone in a world devoid of systematic time preference.[16]

2. It incidentally confirms what modern theorists showed long ago but what is still occasionally denied in the literature, that a zero or negative interest rate is in no sense a *logically* contradictory thing, however bizarre may be the *em-*

$i = m$. The relevant competitive market root is given by

$$x = \frac{2+\lambda}{2} + \sqrt{\frac{(2+\lambda)^2 + 4\lambda}{2}}.$$

Where $m = 0$, $\lambda = 1$, we have $x = 3.297$; for $m \to \infty$, $\lambda \to 0$, $x \to 2$ and $i \to -\frac{1}{2}$; for $m \to -1$, $\lambda \to \infty$, $x \to \infty$ and $i \to -1$. Thus the market rate of interest is always between -1 and $-\frac{1}{2}$, growing as m grows, in agreement with the small husk of truth in our earlier "common-sense explanation."

[16] T. Ophir, of the Massachusetts Institute of Technology and Hebrew University, Jerusalem, has done unpublished work showing how systematic time preference will tend to alter the equilibrium interest rate pattern.

pirical hypotheses that entail a zero or negative rate.

3. It may help us a little to isolate the effects of adding one by one, or together, (*a*) technological investment possibilities, (*b*) innovations that secularly raise productivity and real incomes, (*c*) strong biases toward present goods and against future goods, (*d*) governmental laws and more general collusions than are envisaged in simple laissez faire markets, or (*e*) various aspects of uncertainty. To be sure, other orderings of analysis would also be possible; and these separate processes interact, with the whole not the simple sum of its parts.

4. It points up a fundamental and intrinsic deficiency in a free pricing system, namely, that free pricing gets you on the Pareto-efficiency frontier but by itself has no tendency to get you to positions on the frontier that are ethically optimal in terms of a social welfare function; only by social collusions—of tax, expenditure, fiat, or other type—can an ethical observer hope to end up where he wants to be. (This obvious and ancient point is related to 3*d* above.)

5. The present model enables us to see one "function" of money from a new slant—as a social compact that can provide optimal old age social security. (This is also related to 3*d* above.)

For the rest of this essay, I shall develop aspects of the last two of these themes.

SOCIAL COMPACTS AND THE OPTIMUM

If each man insists on a *quid pro quo*, we apparently continue until the end of time, with each worse off than in the social optimum, biological interest case. Yet how easy it is by a simple change in the rules of the game to get to the optimum. Let mankind enter into a Hobbes-Rousseau social contract in which the young are assured of their retirement subsistence if they will today support the aged, such support to be guaranteed by a draft on the yet-unborn. Then the social optimum can be achieved within one lifetime, and our equations (14) will become

$$S_1(1, 1) + S_2(1, 1) + S_3(1, 1) = 0$$

from $t = 3$ on.

We economists have been told[17] that what we are to economize on is love or altruism, this being a scarce good in our imperfect world. True enough, in the sense that we want what there is to go as far as possible. But it is also the task of political economy to point out where common rules in the form of self-imposed fiats can attain higher positions on the social welfare functions prescribed for us by ethical observers.

The Golden Rule or Kant's Categorical Imperative (enjoining like people to follow the common pattern that makes each best off) are often not self-enforcing: if all but one obey, the one may gain selfish advantage by disobeying—which is where the sheriff comes in: *we* politically invoke force on *ourselves*, attempting to make an unstable equilibrium a stable one.[18]

Once social coercion or contracting is admitted into the picture, the present problem disappears. The reluctance of the young to give to the old what the old can never themselves directly or indirectly repay is overcome. Yet the young never suffer, since their successors come under the same requirement. Everybody ends better off. It is as simple as that.[19]

[17] D. H. Robertson, *What Does the Economist Maximize?* (a keynote address at the Columbia bicentennial celebrations, May, 1954), published by the Trustees of the University in the *Proceedings of the Conference, 1955* (New York: Doubleday & Co.) and reprinted as chap. ix in D. H. Robertson, *Economic Commentaries* (London: Staples, 1956).

The economics of social collusions is a rich field for analysis, involving fascinating predictive and normative properties. Thus, when society *acts as if* it were maximizing certain functions, we can predict the effect upon equilibrium of specified exogenous disturbances. And certain patterns of thought appropriate to a single mind become appropriate,

[18] Now, admittedly, there is usually lacking in the real world the axes of symmetry needed to make all this an easy process. In a formulation elsewhere, I have shown some of the requirements for an optimal theory of public expenditure of the Sax-Wicksell-Lindahl-Musgrave-Bowen type, and the failure of the usual voting and signaling mechanisms to converge to an optimum solution (see "The Pure Theory of Public Expenditure," *Review of Economics and Statistics*, XXXVI [November, 1954], 387–89, and "Diagrammatic Exposition of Public Expenditure," *ibid.*, XXXVII [November, 1955], 350–56). Such a model is poles apart from the pure case in which Walrasian laissez faire happens to be optimal. I should be prepared to argue that a good deal of what is important and interesting in the real world lies between these extreme poles, perhaps in between in the sense of displaying properties that are a blending of the polar properties. But such discussion must await another time.

[19] How can the competitive configuration with negative interest rates be altered to everyone's advantage? Does not this deny the Pareto optimality of perfect competition, which is the least (and most) we can expect from it? Here we encounter one more paradox, which no doubt arises from the "infinity" aspect of our model. If we assume a large finite span to the human race—say 1 million generations—then the final few generations face the equations

$$S_1(R_{T-1}, \infty) + S_2(R_{T-2}, R_{T-1})$$
$$+ S_3(R_{T-3}, R_{T-2}) = 0,$$

$$S_2(R_{T-1}, \infty) + S_3(R_{T-2}, R_{T-1}) + 0 = 0,$$

$$S_3(R_{T-1}, \infty) + 0 + 0 = 0,$$

$$\text{where} \quad T = 1,000,000.$$

If we depart from the negative interest rate pattern, the final young will be cheated by the demise of the human race. Should such a cheating of one generation 30 million years from now perpetually condemn society to a suboptimal configuration? Perfect competition shrugs its shoulders at such a question and (not improperly) sticks to its Pareto optimality.

AN EXACT CONSUMPTION-LOAN MODEL OF INTEREST 481

even though we reject the notion of a group mind. (Example: developed social security could give rise to the same bias toward increasing population that exists among farmers and close family groups, where children are wanted as a means of old age support.)

The economics of collusion provides an important field of study for the theorist. Such collusions can be important elements of strength in the struggle for existence. Reverence for life, in the Schweitzer sense of respecting ants and flowers, might be a handicap in the Darwinian struggle for existence. (And, since the reverencer tends to disappear, the ants may not be helped much in the long run.) But culture in which altruism abounds—because men do not think to behave like atomistic competitors or because men have by custom and law entered into binding social contracts— may have great survival and expansion powers.

An essay could be written on the welfare state as a complicated device for self- or reinsurance. (From this view, the graduated income tax becomes in part a device for reducing *ex ante* variance.) That the Protestant Ethic should have been instrumental in creating individualistic capitalism one may accept; but that it should stop there is not necessarily plausible.[20] What made Jeremy Bentham a Benthamite in 1800, one suspects, might in 1900 have made him a Fabian (and do we not see a lot in common in the personalities of James Mill and Friedrich Engels?).

Much as you and I may dislike government "interferences" in economic life, we must face the positive fact that the moti-

vations for higher living standards that a free market channels into Walrasian equilibrium when the special conditions for that pattern happen to be favorable —these same motivations often lead to social collusions and myriad uses of the apparatus of the state. For good or evil, these may not be aberrations from laissez faire, but theorems entailed by its intrinsic axioms.

CONCLUSION: MONEY AS A SOCIAL CONTRIVANCE

Let me conclude by applying all these considerations to an analysis of the role of money in our consumption-loan world. In it nothing kept. All ice melted, and so did all chocolates. (If non-depletable land existed, it must have been superabundant.) Workers could not carry goods over into their retirement years.

There is no arguing with Nature. But what is to stop man—or rather men— from printing oblongs of paper or stamping circles of shell. These units of money can keep.[21] (Even if ink fades, this could be true.) With ideal clearing arrangements, money as a medium of exchange might have little function. But remember that a money medium of exchange is itself a rather efficient clearing arrangement.

So suppose men officially through the state, or unofficially through custom, make a grand consensus on the use of these greenbacks as a money of exchange. Now the young and middle-aged do have something to hold and to carry over into their retirement years. And note this: as long as the new current generations of

[20] Recall the Myrdal thesis that the austere planned economies of Europe are Protestant, the Catholic countries being individualistic.

[21] I have been asked whether introducing durable money does not violate my fiat against durable goods and trades with Nature. All that I must insist on is that the new durable moneys (or records) be themselves quite worthless for consumption. The essence of them as money is that they are valued only for what they will fetch in exchange.

workers do not repudiate the old money, this gives workers of one epoch a claim on workers of a later epoch, even though no real *quid pro quo* (other than money) is possible.

We then find this remarkable fact: without legislating social security or entering into elaborate social compacts, society by using money will go from the non-optimal negative-interest-rate configuration to the optimal biological-interest-rate configuration. How does this happen? I shall try to give only a sketchy account that does not pretend to be rigorous.

Take the stationary population case with $m = 0$. With total money M constant and the flow of goods constant, the price level can be expected very soon to level off and be constant. The productive invest their hump savings in currency; in their old age they disinvest this currency, turning it over to the productive workers in return for sustenance.

With population growing like $(1 + m)^t$, output will come to grow at that rate. Fixed M will come to mean prices falling like $1/(1 + m)^t$. Each dollar saved today will thus yield a *real* rate of interest of exactly m per period—just what the biological social-optimality configuration calls for. Similarly, when $m < 0$ and population falls, rising prices will create the desired negative real rate of interest equal to m.

In short, the use of money can itself be regarded as a social compact.[22] When economists say that one of the functions of money is to act as a store of wealth and that one of money's desirable properties is constancy of value (as measured by constancy of average prices), we are entitled to ask: How do you know this? Why *should* prices be stable? On what tablets is that injunction written? Perhaps the function of money, if it is to serve as an optimal store of wealth, is so to change in its value as to create that optimal pattern of lifetime saving which could otherwise be established only by alternative social contrivances.[23]

I do not pretend to pass judgment on the policies related to all this. But I do suggest for economists' further research the difficult analysis of capital models which grapple with the fact that each and every today is followed by a tomorrow.

[22] In terms of immediate self-interest the existing productive workers should perhaps unilaterally repudiate the money upon which the aged hope to live in retirement. (Compare the Russian and Belgium calling-in of currencies.) So a continuing social compact is required. (Compare, too, current inflationary trends which do give the old less purchasing power than many of them had counted on.)

[23] Conversely, with satisfactory social security programs, the necessity for having secular stable prices so that the retired are taken care of can be lightened. Even after extreme inflations, social security programs can re-create themselves anew astride the community's indestructible real tax base.

[31]

TECHNICAL PROGRESS, CAPITAL FORMATION, AND ECONOMIC GROWTH*

By ROBERT M. SOLOW

Massachusetts Institute of Technology

Introduction

The goal of this paper is an answer to the question: How much fixed investment is necessary to support alternative rates of growth of potential output in the United States in the near future? Notice that I said "necessary to support" and not "sufficient to generate." I believe that a high rate of capital formation is required if the growth of aggregate productivity and output is to accelerate, but I do not believe that it is all that is required. Notice also that I said "potential output" and not "realized output." The relation between investment and output is two sided, as I think I once heard my friend Evsey Domar say, and I am concerned here with the supply side only. Whether any particular required rate of investment will be accompanied by a high enough level of final demand to use the resulting capacity is another question. And how a particular required rate of investment can in fact be induced is yet another. Neither will be answered in this paper.

I shall try to deduce an answer to my question by estimating an aggregate production function, because I do not know any other way to go about it. One aggregate production function is pretty much like another, I admit, and this one has only a few distinctive markings. They are: (1) the data differ a little from those normally used in this kind of enterprise; (2) it is assumed that *all* technological progress needs to be "embodied" in newly produced capital goods before there can be any effect on output; (3) a sharp distinction is drawn between actual output and potential output, and the method includes a built-in estimate of the gap between them.

The next section of the paper sets out the assumptions of this approach. Then I shall briefly describe the data, present some alternative estimates of the production function, and draw the implications for capital requirements.

Assumptions and Theory

I assume that new technology can be introduced into the production process *only* through gross investment in new plant and equipment.

* All the work in this paper was done by Thomas Rothenberg and Richard Attiyeh of M.I.T., Yale, and the staff of the Council of Economic Advisers.

This is certainly not literally true. No one knows whether it is more or less true than the exactly opposite assumption that technical progress makes new and old capital goods more productive in the same way and in the same proportion. I have worked both sides of the street in different papers, and I will produce estimates on both assumptions in this paper. That seems to me to be the moral equivalent of Edward Denison's suspiciously round assumption that half of new technology is the "embodied" kind and half the "disembodied" kind. The most casual kind of reflection suggests to me that embodied technological progress is by a substantial margin the more important kind.

Suppose that capital goods produced in any year are 100λ per cent more productive than those produced the year before. Suppose also that if a gross investment of $I(v)$ is made in year v, the amount surviving in a later year t will be $B(t - v)$. Under the further assumption that labor and machines of various vintages are arranged in such a way as to yield maximum output (or equivalently that all workers receive the same wage regardless of the age of their equipment) it can be shown that the stock of surviving capital goods of different vintage and productivity can be summarized for production-function purposes in an "equivalent stock of capital." The equivalent stock of capital adds up the survivors of each vintage after weighting them by the appropriate productivity improvement factor. To be precise, the equivalent stock of capital in year t is

$$(1) \qquad J(t) = \sum_{v=-\infty}^{t} (1 + \lambda)^v B(t - v) I(v)$$

Potential output is a function of the available equivalent stock of capital and the available input of labor $N(t)$, say

$$(2) \qquad P(t) = F(J(t), N(t))$$

No explicit mention of technical progress is needed; it is already wrapped up in J. What we observe, however, is not $P(t)$ but actual output $A(t)$. It is tempting to try to make some estimate of potential output and then to use it in estimating the production function. But since what one expects from the production function is a statement about potential output, it seems a little circular to impose an independently calculated measure of potential output to begin with. I have tried to get around this difficulty by a device which owes a lot to some of Arthur Okun's ideas.

Actual output falls below potential output because employment is less than the available supply of labor and because some capital stands idle. There is a logical pitfall here. If it is assumed—as I have tacitly done in (2)—that labor and already existing capital are substitutable for each other, then in principle capital should never be idle unless its marginal value product has fallen to zero (if depreciation occurs with use rather than with time, I should say marginal net product). Otherwise it would pay to use more capital with the current input of labor; the extra product would provide at least some quasi-rent. Yet we believe there to be such a thing as idle capacity in periods of economic slack. The paradox is easily resolved in a model which permits virtual substitution of labor and capital *before* capital goods take concrete form, but not after. I have analyzed such a model [3] but I do not at the moment see any direct way of using it in empirical work. So I shall simply assume, as an approximation, that the ratio of actual to potential output is a function of the unemployment rate. (The unemployment rate I shall be using is the difference between the "full employment" supply of man-hours and the number of man-hours actually worked, expressed as a ratio of the full employment supply. It differs from the ordinary labor-force concept in a number of ways—for example it can become negative, and did so in 1942-44, because the number of man-hours worked exceeded the normal supply.) If I let $u(t)$ stand for the unemployment rate:

$$(3) \qquad A(t) = f(u(t))P(t) = f(u)F(J, N)$$

With a convenient choice of functional forms for $f(u)$ and $F(J, N)$, I can hope simultaneously to estimate the production function for potential output, and the curve which relates the degree of slack to the unemployment rate. The raw materials are time series of actual output, the full employment supply of labor, and the equivalent stock of capital, to be described in a moment.

To simplify computations, I have used the Cobb-Douglas function with constant returns to scale for $F(J, N)$. For $f(u)$ I have used what amounts to the half of a normal curve lying to the right of the peak. This choice has the double advantage of being workable and of having the right general shape. One would want, I think, to have a kind of diminishing returns to the reduction of unemployment after a point, and this occurs as the normal curve flattens out near its peak. Also, any linear approximation near usual unemployment levels tends to show actual output dropping to zero when the unemployment rate reaches 30 per cent or so, and the normal curve avoids this.

With those specializations, my production function now reads:

$$(4) \qquad A = a10^{b+cu+du^2}J^\alpha N^{1-\alpha}$$

though I shall fit it in the form:

$$(4') \qquad A/N = a10^{b+cu+du^2}(J/N)^\alpha.$$

or

$$(4'') \qquad \log(A/N) = \log a + b + cu + du^2 + \alpha \log(J/N).$$

In (4″) there are two constant terms, one belonging to F and one to f. They can be separated as soon as I make a statistical definition of "full employment." It happens that the measure of unemployment used in this paper coincides numerically with the usual labor force measure when they are both equal to about 4 per cent. That figure has become, at least temporarily, the conventional description of full employment, and I adopt it here. Now I must have actual output equal to potential output at full employment. This implies

$$f(.04) = 1 \quad \text{or} \quad b + .04c + (.04)^2d = 0$$

From estimates of c and d I can calculate b, and then from (4″) I can find a.

With all constants estimated it is possible to ask and answer such questions as: given the expected increase in the supply of man-hours, and given the already determinate mortality of existing capital, how much gross investment is necessary to increase *potential* output by 3 or 4 or 5 per cent in the next year?

Data

Several time series measuring the "equivalent stock of capital" were constructed along the lines of equation (1), with alternative trial values of λ. The case $\lambda = 0$ is, of course, the plain stock of capital. All are expressed in 1954 prices. Stock and equivalent stock figures were computed separately for plant and equipment—sometimes using different values of λ for each component, on the chance that equipment improves in productivity more rapidly than plant—with mortality calculated according to the schedules devised by George Terborgh. Because the plant and equipment series are quite highly correlated, I did not try to use them as separate inputs in the production function. Instead, every stock of capital or equivalent stock of capital figure in my regressions is actually the sum of a stock of plant and a stock of equipment, each generated from gross investment data with its own mortality curve and its own value of λ. The investment series used is consistent with "producers' durable goods" plus "other construction" in the national accounts, with the exception that religious, educational, hospital and institutional construction are excluded. (Dwellings are excluded from the stock of capital, which is intended to be a measure of privately-owned business plant and equipment.)

The output concept comparable to this measure of capital stock is gross national product minus the product originating in general government, government enterprises, households and institutions, rest of the world, and services of houses: This defines a reasonably close approximation to the output produced by the privately-owned stock of plant and equipment. It is expressed in 1954 prices.

The series for "full employment man-hours" is essentially due to Knowles [2]. This is based on the age and sex distribution of the population together with smoothed trends in participation rates and annual hours worked. Some minor adjustments were made, particularly to eliminate government employees since the output and capital series are restricted to the private business economy. Analogous adjustments were made to the BLS series on man-hours worked in the private economy, to restrict the coverage approximately to that involved in the other data used in the analysis.

Estimated Production Functions

Equation (1) defines the equivalent stock of capital for any constant rate of increase in the productivity of capital goods. As noted earlier, I have experimented with different improvement factors for plant and equipment separately and then added the two series. The regression results I shall report here use the following six combinations:

	J_0	J_1	J_2	J_3	J_4	J_5
λ plant	0	.02	.02	.02	.03	.03
λ equipment	0	.02	.03	.04	.03	.04

The multiple regressions themselves are given in the following table: The parameters are designated as in (4), with standard errors following in parentheses, except that $f(u)$ was actually estimated as $10^{b+cu+d(u+.130)^2}$.

Inspection of Table 1 yields some obvious generalizations.

(a) From the similarity of the estimated values of α for the equations with J_2 and J_4 and for those with J_3 and J_5, it seems clear that more depends on the improvement factor for equipment than on that for plant. This is associated with the fact that between 1929 and 1961 the ordinary stock of plant increased by about 50 per cent while the stock of equipment grew by almost 170 per cent.

(b) The estimated elasticity of output with respect to the equivalent stock of capital declines as the improvement factor (particularly that for equipment) increases, for obvious reasons.

(c) Very low values for the improvement factor lead to implausible values for α. One gets nonsense results unless considerable weight is given to technological progress.

(d) The estimated curve relating realized to potential output is not very sensitive to alternative assumptions about the improvement factor.

THE LAGGING U.S. GROWTH RATE   81

TABLE 1

	$\log a$	b	c	d	α	R^2	Standard Error of Estimate
J_0	$-.4179$	$.0460$	$-.1244\,(.2016)$	$-1.344\,(.413)$	$1.2377\,(.0993)$	$.9622$	$.0322$
J_1	$-.3934$	$.0395$	$-.2814\,(.1524)$	$-\ .979\,(.315)$	$.6323\,(.0364)$	$.9789$	$.0241$
J_2	$-.3328$	$.0382$	$-.3187\,(.1465)$	$-\ .879\,(.304)$	$.4990\,(.0274)$	$.9806$	$.0230$
J_3	$-.2956$	$.0370$	$-.3386\,(.1398)$	$-\ .813\,(.291)$	$.4026\,(.0221)$	$.9825$	$.0220$
J_4	$-.3888$	$.0387$	$-.3097\,(.1427)$	$-\ .909\,(.295)$	$.5054\,(.0270)$	$.9816$	$.0225$
J_5	$-.0375$	$.0375$	$-.3319\,(.1381)$	$-\ .838\,(.287)$	$.4160\,(.0214)$	$.9828$	$.0217$

(*e*) The multiple correlation is a little higher and the standard error of estimate a little smaller for the larger values of λ. But because the estimates of α change in an offsetting way, goodness of fit is a poor way of distinguishing among neighboring values of λ.

It will be interesting to compare the conclusions flowing from estimates of (4) with those derived on the assumption that all technological progress is "disembodied," falling alike on new and old capital goods and therefore not requiring investment to generate an increase in productivity. For this purpose I have also estimated the production functions

(5) $$A = a(1 + \mu)^t J_0^\alpha N^{1-\alpha} 10^{b+cu+d(u+.130)^2}$$

with the result

(5′) $$A = 1.10(1.025)^t J_0^{.11} N^{.89} 10^{.0365-.251u-.888(u+.130)^2}.$$

The squared correlation is .9945. The elasticity of output with respect to J_0 is about equal to its standard error. Essentially, output per man-hour just rises at $2\frac{1}{2}$ per cent a year.

Actual and Potential Output

A useful by-product of this procedure is a built-in estimate of the ratio of actual to potential output as a function of the unemployment rate. It must be remembered that the measure of unemployment I am using is not the conventional one. I define the unemployment rate in any year as the difference between the estimated full employment supply of man-hours and the number of man-hours actually worked, expressed as a fraction of the full employment supply of man-hours. This should be in principle a better measure of the excess supply of labor, for two reasons. In the first place, when the demand for labor is slack some people leave the measured labor force although they would willingly take work if they thought work were available. This kind of "unemployment" represents excess capacity. Second, involuntary part-time work, though it does not show up as unemployment in the official statistics, does affect the alternative concept. On the other hand, the usual labor force statistics undoubtedly contain less error than the ones used here.

A plot of the two measures of the unemployment rate against each other shows that most points fall along a smooth nonlinear curve. It happens by chance that the two measures coincide approximately at an unemployment rate of 4 per cent, which is the conventional definition of "full employment" I am using. Columns 1 and 2 of Table 2 give a few selected corresponding values of u (the unemployment rate used in this paper) and u^* (the usual labor force unemployment rate).

It is also the case, mentioned earlier, that the regression equations using different equivalent stocks give very similar curves relating the ratio of actual to potential output to the unemployment rate. The ratios corresponding to J_4 and J_5, and those corresponding to equation (5) are given in columns 3, 4, and 5 of Table 2.

TABLE 2

u	u^*	A/P J_4	A/P J_5	A/P (5)	A/P Okun's Law
−.13	.01	1.200	1.203	1.172	1.096
−.03	.02	1.094	1.094	1.084	1.064
.00	.03	1.054	1.054	1.051	1.032
.02	.035	1.028	1.025	1.027	1.016
.04	.04	1.000	1.000	1.000	1.000
.06	.05	.971	.971	.976	.968
.08	.06	.941	.942	.949	.936
.10	.07	.911	.912	.921	.904
.27	.21	.645	.652	.671	.456

The only other systematic attempt to relate the gap between actual and potential output to the unemployment rate is Okun's Law [1] which states that the percentage excess of potential over actual output is 3.2 times the excess of the (conventional) unemployment rate over 4 per cent. In my notation, Okun's Law states that

$$\frac{P-A}{P} = 3.2\,(u^* - .04).$$

Okun himself, it should be noted, has used this relation only for the period since 1955. The ratio of actual to potential output read from this equation is shown in the last column of Table 2.

It is altogether remarkable that Okun's Law and the approach used in this paper give very similar results for conventional unemployment rates between 3 and 7 per cent, despite the fact that they are based on entirely different data (and the fact that u relates to private employment and u^* to total). It is only natural that they should differ for extremely high unemployment rates and extremely low ones. I introduced the possibility of considerable curvature into this approach because I wanted to allow for diminishing returns as the unemployment rate becomes very low. But as Table 2 shows, at very low levels of unemployment, the approach in this paper indicates a greater excess of actual over normal full employment potential than does Okun's Law. The required curvature is actually in the equations; the apparent paradox arises because the man-hours figures allow for the supernormal increase in labor force and hours worked during the war years of very low unemployment.

Investment Requirements for Economic Growth

With the unemployment rate fixed at $u = .04$, any one of the estimated production functions states that potential output is constrained by the currently available input of labor and by the whole history of capital formation. If the American economy can and must move along such a function in the next few years, the growth of productive potential is tied in a specific way to the growth of the labor supply and the rate of investment. Movements in the supply of hours of work are usually taken as given. That leaves the volume of investment as the most important determinant of growth which is actually open to influence by policy. (There is also the equally important possibility of influencing the rate of technological progress, λ; but that leads to an entirely different set of questions.)

The movement of full employment man-hours for the entire economy in the next few years can be estimated with reasonable accuracy from demographic trends. It is less easy to estimate the supply of man-hours to the private economy, because that is less purely a matter of demography. Public employment has been gaining relative to private employment in recent years, and since there is no reason to expect a reversal of this trend, it is safe to conclude that the supply of labor to the private economy will rise more slowly than the total. With the labor force expected to grow at about 1.7 per cent per year and average annual hours worked declining at an annual rate of some 0.3-0.4 per cent, the supply of potential man-hours is likely to increase at about 1.3-1.4 per cent a year in the near future. This is a more rapid rate of increase than in the decade just past. But the supply of labor to the private economy will rise more slowly than that. Between 1950 and 1960, our series for the supply of potential man-hours to the private economy rose at an average annual rate between 0.4 and 0.5 per cent. For looking ahead, I have made alternative calculations with an annual increase in labor supply of 0.65 per cent and 1.0 per cent.

With this growth in labor input, a substantial amount of investment is needed just to keep capital per man-hour constant. Suppose that some $2\frac{1}{2}$ per cent of the capital stock is retired each year. (I am speaking now of the ordinary capital stock, with $\lambda = 0$.) Then with a capital-output ratio of about $1\frac{3}{4}$, $4\frac{1}{2}$ per cent of private GNP must be invested just to replace worn-out capital, and between $5\frac{1}{2}$ and 6 per cent of GNP must be invested (depending on the assumed rate of growth of the labor force) to keep capital per man-hour constant. A slightly higher rate of investment would be needed to keep capital per worker from falling.

When we deal with an equivalent stock of capital the calculations are a little more complicated but the results not very different. The annual mortality of "equivalent capital" can be calculated. For J_3 and J_5 it runs just over 3 per cent of the equivalent stock; for J_4 it is about $2\frac{1}{2}$ per cent. The capital-output ratio is much higher because the improvement factor makes the equivalent stock considerably higher than the capital stock itself. Working against this is the fact that a dollar's worth of investment is more potent, creating more than "a dollar's worth" of equivalent capital.

Generally speaking, the result is that the maintenance of capital intensity—and the accompanying achievement of low rates of growth of output—can be obtained with a somewhat slighter investment burden than consideration of the ordinary stock of capital would suggest.

To attain a high rate of growth of output, the equivalent stock of capital must grow faster than the input of labor. Additional investment now performs a function beyond the widening process as the labor force increases and the conventional deepening process as the capital-intensity of production increases. The third function is, of course, what one might call quickening: the carrying into production of new technology as represented by the improvement factor. Table 3 shows—for 1960-61 values of the variables—the percentage of business GNP which must be invested gross to permit different rates of growth of output. The calculations are shown for J_3, J_4, and J_5 with the two alternative rates of growth of the labor force mentioned earlier.

In interpreting these figures it should be remembered that the output concept used here covers about 80 per cent of the total gross national product. Also the omission of various kinds of institutional construction reduces the gross investment total to about 93 per cent of "producers' durable equipment" plus "other construction" in the national accounts. Thus an investment quota corresponding to the ratio of business fixed investment to GNP would be about 86 per cent of the number given in Table 3. With this adjustment, the estimates in the table seem to be of the right order of magnitude. They suggest that a necessary condition for increasing the rate of growth of output from

TABLE 3

INVESTMENT QUOTAS FOR ALTERNATIVE GROWTH RATES

Growth Rate	3%	3½%	4%	4½%	5%
J_3					
Slow growth in man-hours.............	9.9	11.2	12.4	13.8	15.0
Fast growth in man-hours.............	9.2	10.4	11.7	13.1	14.3
J_4					
Slow growth in man-hours.............	9.0	10.2	11.4	12.5	13.7
Fast growth in man-hours.............	8.5	9.8	10.9	12.0	13.2
J_5					
Slow growth in man-hours.............	10.1	11.3	12.6	13.9	15.3
Fast growth in man-hours.............	9.4	10.8	12.0	13.3	14.7

about 3½ per cent annually to 4½ per cent annually may be a 20-25 per cent increase in the investment quota from the range 10-11 per cent of business GNP to the range 12-14 per cent of business GNP. J_4 gives both a lower required investment quota and a smaller relative increase to get from 3½ to 4½ per cent growth than do J_3 and J_5. Alternative improvement factors have only a minor effect on the implied investment requirements because the estimated elasticity changes to make a partial compensation.

Rough calculations show that to maintain an accelerated rate of growth throughout a decade requires a slowly rising savings-investment quota. But the rise is slow and the average investment quota only slightly above the initial figure shown in Table 3.

By comparison, the production function (5), which makes technological change a pure "residual," gives altogether different results. The high time trend—a residual increase in output of 2½ per cent annually with labor and capital constant—and the low elasticity of output with respect to capital imply that a fairly rapid rate of growth of output per man-hour is achievable with very little investment but that a visibly higher rate of growth can be supported only by an unrealistically high investment rate. For example, with the slower rate of growth of the labor force, (5) says that a 3 per cent increase in potential output is achievable with a slight decrease in the capital stock. The gross investment implied is about 3½ per cent of potential output; the net investment is actually negative. But to lift the rate of growth to 4 per cent a year would require an investment quota of almost 20 per cent of potential output. These implications seem wholly unrealistic to me, and they suggest that the "embodied" model is a better one. But I must admit that there is nothing in the analysis I have given which "proves" that (4) is a better model of production than (5).

Entirely apart from all statistical difficulties, one must admit the possibility that our economy is not free to move back and forth along a production function like (4) or even (5). An attempt to accelerate movement out along the function may have the effect of shifting the function itself. For one thing, a sharply higher rate of investment may bring about premature scrapping of old equipment. Second, there may be limits even in a mature economy to the speed with which the system can adjust to large inflows of new capital. Third, a change in the investment quota is itself a change in the composition of output; changes in the composition of output may also have the effect of shifting the function bodily, though it would be difficult to make an a priori judgment about the nature of the shift. This reflection suggests the wisdom of trying to make such analyses of the productivity of investment sector by sector. This would place a greater strain on the availability of data, but might in compensation yield important conclusions about the best sectoral composition of investment.

Conclusion

Capital formation is not the only source of growth in productivity. Investment is at best a necessary condition for growth, surely not a sufficient condition. Recent study has indicated the importance of such activities as research, education, and public health. But while economists are now convinced of the significance of these factors in the process of economic growth, we are still a long way from having any quantitative estimate of the pay-off to society of resources devoted to research, education, and improvements in allocative efficiency. Since such estimates must form the foundation for a national allocation of resources in the interests of economic growth, their provision by hook or by crook presents a research problem of great theoretical and practical interest. The object of this paper is to make a start in that job for the much easier and prosaic case of tangible capital formation.

REFERENCES

1. "The American Economy in 1961: Problems and Policies," in "January 1961 Economic Report of the President and the Economic Situation and Outlook," hearings before the Joint Economic Committee (87th Cong., 1st sess., 1961), pp. 324, 375.
2. James W. Knowles, "Potential Economic Growth in the United States," Study Paper No. 20, prepared for the Joint Economic Committee in connection with the Study of Employment, Growth and Price Levels (86th Cong., 2d sess., 1960).
3. Robert M. Solow, "Substitution and Fixed Proportions in the Theory of Capital," to appear in *Rev. of Econ. Studies,* 1962.

[32]

Aggregate Dynamics and Staggered Contracts

John B. Taylor

Columbia University

Staggered wage contracts as short as 1 year are shown to be capable of generating the type of unemployment persistence which has been observed during postwar business cycles in the United States. A contract multiplier causes business cycles to persist beyond the length of the longest contract, and a diffusion of shocks across contracts causes the persistence to increase for several periods before diminishing. A persistence of inflation is also generated by the contracts. This persistence is represented as a reduced-form distributed-lag wage equation in which the lag coefficients have a pure-expectations component and an inertia component due to the overhang of outstanding contracts. Using rational expectations to separate these components suggests that aggregate demand may have a greater impact on inflation than the simple reduced-form estimates would indicate.

A distinctive feature of recent theoretical models of macroeconomic fluctuations is the emphasis on partial rigidities, either in the form of information lags or temporary inflexibility of prices and wages. These rigidities have been remarkably successful in explaining observed correlations between such aggregates as inflation and unemployment, despite the constraints of rational expectations and a fixed natural rate of unemployment. Indeed, statistical Phillips curves are an essential property of these models.[1]

I am grateful to Guillermo Calvo and Edmund Phelps for extensive discussions and to Larry Christiano for valuable research assistance. This research is supported by a grant from the National Science Foundation.

[1] Models which have stressed informational rigidities include Lucas (1973, 1975), Sargent and Wallace (1975), and Barro (1976, 1978). Models which have stressed wage or price rigidities include Fischer (1977) and Phelps and Taylor (1977). A recent paper by Hall (1977) incorporates such rigidities but leaves open whether they are informa-

[*Journal of Political Economy*, 1980, vol. 88, no. 1]

As is well known, however, these models have been unable to explain the observed serial correlation in unemployment without the imposition of additional sources of persistence—either exogenous serial correlation of shocks or capital formation lags. Neither informational rigidities nor temporary wage and price contracts, therefore, have seemed capable of independently generating the kind of serial persistence observed in most modern economies.

This paper considers a rational expectations model in which wage contracts are the only source of rigidity, yet which is capable of endogenously generating serial correlation in unemployment which significantly outlasts the duration of the longest contract. Hence, contracts which last only about 1 year can generate the degree of cyclical persistence which has been observed in the United States during the postwar period. Two key assumptions underlie the model:[2] (1) wage contracts are staggered, that is, not all wage decisions in the economy are made at the same time; and (2) when making wage decisions, firms (and unions) look at the wage rates which are set at other firms and which will be in effect during their own contract period. Because of the staggering, some firms will have established their wage rates prior to the current negotiations, but others will establish their wage rates in future periods. Hence, when considering relative wages, firms and unions must look both forward and backward in time to see what other workers will be paid during their own contract period. In effect, each contract is written relative to other contracts, and this causes shocks to be passed on from one contract to another—a sort of "contract multiplier." In statistical terms the overlapping contracts cause unemployment to follow a mixed autoregressive–moving-average process, rather than the relatively low-order moving-average process found in previous contract models. The mixed process implies that the impact of shocks on unemployment will first rise for several periods before decreasing toward zero—a lag shape which is characteristic of the unemployment rate in the United States.

The concern of this paper, however, is not solely with endogenous persistence of unemployment. As will be shown below, contract for-

---

tion or contract based. The lack of persistence in models with contract-based rigidities has not been emphasized as much as in models based on information lags. An examination of the latter three papers will indicate, however, that persistence of unemployment is very short without exogenous serial correlation. Sargent (1977) and Fischer (1979) are two recent papers which examine this persistence problem.

[2] The 2-period version of this contract model was suggested as a device to explain the existence of lagged inflation rates in a rational expectations Phillips curve by Taylor (1979). The implications of a multiperiod version of the contract equation for the design of guideposts to reduce inflation while maintaining full employment are discussed in Phelps (1978). Further references to similar types of models are given in Phelps (1978).

mation in this model generates an inertia of wages which parallels the persistence of unemployment. The econometric specification of this inertia is a wage equation which includes a distributed lag of past wage rates—much like an expectations-augmented Phillips curve. In contrast to other Phillips curves, however, the distributed lag of past wages incorporates not only the expectations of future wage decisions but also the overhang of previous wage decisions. Given the assumptions of the model, this lag shape has a predictable form: it declines steadily over the length of the lag and at a decreasing rate. Moreover, the lag shape depends on economic policy. A more accommodative monetary policy, for example, tends to increase the sum of the lag weights and thereby increase the serial persistence of wages.

This dependence of parameters on policy, a property which has been emphasized by Lucas (1976) in a related context, has both econometric and policy implications. It suggests that it will be difficult to estimate the structural parameters of the model without a knowledge of the aggregate-demand policy rule. It also suggests that the Phillips-curve policy trade-off will depend on expectations of policy in future periods, a point which has been discussed by Fellner (1976). In particular, because wage determination is both forward and backward looking, aggregate demand may have a greater effect on inflation than current models of the Phillips curve would suggest. One advantage of the model specified here is that it permits one to calculate the size of this expectations effect.

Section I introduces the structural model, and Section II derives the rational expectations reduced-form contract equations. Because of certain symmetries in the contract equations and the policy rule, we are able to make use of factorization theorems which frequently arise in time-series analysis to derive explicit relationships among the reduced-form parameters, the structural parameters, and the policy rule. The spectral density function of the contract wages is derived and shown to be a convenient way to describe their stochastic properties when contracts are fairly long. Section III describes the persistence effects generated by the model with 2-, 3-, or 4-quarter contracts and compares these with the actual persistence of unemployment in the United States. In Section IV the effect of aggregate demand on wages, as implied by a particular policy rule, is compared with the conventional short-run Phillips-curve approach for a certain set of parameter values. This comparison provides a way of separating the impact of wage expectations from pure wage inertia.

I. The Contract Determination Equation

As mentioned above, overlapping contracts are a key assumption behind the persistence effects generated by this model. And while price contracts are potentially as important as wage contracts, we will focus on wage contracts in this paper. We consider an economy in which all wage contracts are N periods long and a constant fraction $1/N$ of all firms determine their wage contracts in any given time period.[3] A contract is assumed to specify (implicitly or explicitly) a fixed nominal wage rate which will apply for the duration of the contract; employment is then determined by fluctuations in the demand for labor, given this nominal wage during the contract period. Let x_t be the logarithm of the wage rate specified in contracts beginning in period t. Then x_t, which applies to $1/N$ of the firms, will remain in effect until period $t + N - 1$, when it will be changed to x_{t+N}. (While for some purposes it might be useful to attach another index to x_t in order to represent a particular group of firms, such a notation would be cumbersome and does not directly relate to the results presented here. It should be noted, however, that while x_t and x_{t+N} refer to the same group of firms, x_t and x_{t+s} for $s < N$ refer to different groups of firms.)

If contracts are set in this way, they will clearly overlap each other. At the time that a given wage contract is in the process of being set, there will be an overhang of contracts set in the last $N - 1$ periods which will still be in effect during part of the current contract period. Moreover, during the next $N - 1$ periods, contracts will be written which will also be in effect during part of the current contract period. Wage rates set in the current period should reflect the wage rates set in these previous and future contracts. They serve as a base for determining the relative wage of the current contract. A simple and plausible wage-setting procedure which weights other wage rates proportionally to the number of periods they overlap with the current contract period, and which is sensitive to excess demand in the labor market, is then given by the log-linear form

$$x_t = \sum_{s=1}^{N-1} b_s x_{t-s} + \sum_{s=1}^{N-1} b_s \hat{x}_{t+s} + \frac{h}{N} \sum_{s=0}^{N-1} \hat{e}_{t+s} + \epsilon_t, \tag{1}$$

where e_t is a measure of excess demand in the labor market ($e_t = 0$ represents full employment), h is a positive parameter, and ϵ_t is a random shock, which will be assumed to be serially uncorrelated. (The "hat" over a variable represents the mathematical conditional expectation operator, given information through time $t - 1$.) The weights on the future and lagged contract wages are given by $b_s = (N$

---

[3] This uniform distribution assumption is made for simplicity. A nonuniform distribution (as long as it is not degenerate with all contracts set in 1 period) would introduce seasonal effects which, while important from a practical point of view, would not alter the general qualitative features of the model. In this regard it is interesting to note that the *Economist* has recently suggested that the distribution of contract negotiation in the United Kingdom be made less uniform, presumably to reduce overlapping.

$-1)^{-1} (1 - s/N), s = 1, 2, \ldots, N - 1$. They decline linearly into the past and future, and they sum to one. Contracts close to the current contract are given most weight, while contracts in the more distant past or future are given less weight. The symmetric linear decline is a result of our assumption that these past and future wages are weighted proportionally to the number of periods they overlap with x_t. For example, if contracts are N periods long, then $\hat{x}_{t+s}$ and x_{t-s}, for $s < N$, will overlap with x_t for $N - s$ periods each. The total number of overlapping periods for all contracts is, therefore, $2 \Sigma_{s=1}^{N-1} (N - s) = (N - 1)N$. The contracts $\hat{x}_{t+s}$ and x_{t-s} should therefore each be weighted by $N - s$ divided by $(N - 1)N$, which defines the b-weights. The proportional weighting scheme does not allow for either discounting effects which would lead to a sharper decline on future weights or forgetting effects which would lead to a sharper decline on past weights.

In addition to past and future wages, equation (1) indicates that the current contract wage will be sensitive to expected labor market conditions during the contract period; that is, x_t will respond to $\hat{e}_t$, $\hat{e}_{t+1}$, $\ldots, \hat{e}_{t+N-1}$. Equation (1) implies that all of these periods are weighted equally and with a weight $1/N$. (Of course, $1/N$ could be incorporated in the parameter h, but we leave it explicit so that excess-demand effects can be held constant when we consider changes in the contract length N.) It should be noted that only expected and not actual excess demand in period t enters equation (1); it would be a relatively easy matter to include current e_t in equation (1) and thereby permit the wage contract to react simultaneously to actual market conditions in the current period.

Our assumption that the contract wage rate x_t is fixed for the entire length of the contract implies heavy front-end loading. That is, the entire wage adjustment occurs in the first period. Available information on explicit long-term union contracts indicates that front-end loading is not generally this extreme. However, casual observation suggests that most implicit contracts, which appear to be about 1 year in duration, are front-end loaded in this way.

In order to obtain a solution for x_t from equation (1), it is necessary to model the determinants of the excess demand for labor e_t and the relationship between contract wages and prices. A very simple model which achieves this end is given by

$$y_t + p_t = m_t + v_t, \tag{2}$$

$$p_t = \frac{1}{N} \sum_{i=0}^{N-1} x_{t-i}, \tag{3}$$

$$e_t = g_2 y_t, \tag{4}$$

$$m_t = g_3 p_t, \tag{5}$$

JOURNAL OF POLITICAL ECONOMY

6

where p_t = log of aggregate price level, y_t = log of real output less log of full-employment output, m_t = log of nominal money balances less the log of full-employment money balances, and v_t = random velocity shock. Equation (2) is a simple quantity-theory representation of aggregate demand. It is written in deviation form; hence, $y_t = 0$ represents full-employment output. The assumption that the elasticity of real balances with respect to output is one introduces no loss of generality, as will become clear below. The log of velocity v_t is assumed to be a serially uncorrelated shock; this will highlight other persistence effects of the model.

Equation (3) states that the aggregate price level is determined by a simple proportional markup over the average wage; hence, we abstract from the important problem of real wage and productivity changes. The term $N^{-1} \sum_{i=0}^{N-1} x_{t-i}$ is the logarithm of the geometric average of the contract wages in effect at time t. Equation (4) is a simple production relationship which states that excess demand for labor is a simple proportion of the deviation of output from trend or full-employment output.

Equation (5) is the policy rule; $g_3 = 0$ corresponds to a fixed money supply while $g_3 > 0$ allows for some accommodating increase in the money supply in response to price increases. By substituting (4) into (1) and (5) into (2), we arrive at a simple two-equation representation of the model:

$$x_t = \sum_{s=1}^{N-1} b_s x_{t-s} + \sum_{s=1}^{N-1} b_s \hat{x}_{t+s} + \frac{\gamma}{N} \sum_{s=0}^{N-1} \hat{y}_{t+s} + \epsilon_t, \tag{6}$$

$$y_t = -\beta p_t + v_t, \tag{7}$$

where $\gamma = hg_2$ and $\beta = (1 - g_3)$. The parameter γ is the major structural parameter of the model. It represents the sensitivity of wages to aggregate-demand policy. The policy parameter β measures how accommodative aggregate-demand policy is to changes in the price level from its long-run equilibrium level. We now turn to the derivation of the rational expectations solution of the model.

II. The Reduced-Form Contract Equation

Derivation

In order to eliminate the expectation variables in equation (6), we make use of the aggregate-demand policy rule (eq. [7]) and the definition of the aggregate price level in equation (3). That is, we substitute the conditional expectation of output

$$\hat{y}_{t+s} = -\beta \hat{p}_{t+s} = -\frac{\beta}{N} \sum_{i=0}^{n} \hat{x}_{t+s-i} \tag{8}$$

STAGGERED CONTRACTS   7

into equation (6) to obtain

$$x_t = \sum_{s=1}^{n} b_s x_{t-s} + \sum_{s=1}^{n} b_s \hat{x}_{t+s} - \frac{\beta\gamma}{N^2} \sum_{s=0}^{n} \sum_{i=0}^{n} \hat{x}_{t+s-i} + \epsilon_t, \tag{9}$$

where $n = N - 1$. Equation (9) involves only the log of the contract wage x_t and its expectations. It states that the current contract will be influenced by relative wage effects (represented by the first two sums in eq. [9]) and also by the impact of the wage settlements on aggregate demand, as implied by the policy rule (this influence is represented by the double sum in eq. [9]).

Taking expectations on both sides of equation (9), conditional on information available in period $t - 1$, and noting the identity,[4]

$$\frac{1}{N^2} \sum_{s=0}^{n} \sum_{i=0}^{n} \hat{x}_{t+s-i} = \frac{n}{N} \sum_{s=1}^{n} b_s \hat{x}_{t-s} + \frac{\hat{x}_t}{N} + \frac{n}{N} \sum_{s=1}^{n} b_s \hat{x}_{t+s}, \tag{10}$$

where the b-weights are as in Section I, we have

$$\left(1 + \frac{\beta\gamma}{N}\right)\hat{x}_t = \left(1 - \frac{n\beta\gamma}{N}\right) \sum_{s=1}^{n} b_s \hat{x}_{t-s} + \left(1 - \frac{n\beta\gamma}{N}\right) \sum_{s=1}^{n} b_s \hat{x}_{t+s}. \tag{11}$$

Dividing through by $[1 - (n\beta\gamma/N)]$ and rearranging terms reduces equation (11) to

$$\sum_{s=1}^{n} b_s \hat{x}_{t-s} - c\hat{x}_t + \sum_{s=1}^{n} b_s \hat{x}_{t+s} = 0, \tag{12}$$

where $c = (N + \beta\gamma)/(N - n\beta\gamma)$. Note that c is the only parameter of equation (12) which depends on either the policy or the structural parameters of the model. We assume that $0 \leq \beta\gamma$ so that $|c| \geq 1$. Using the lag-operator notation ($L^s x_t = x_{t-s}$), and defining the polynomial

$$B(L) = \sum_{s=-n}^{n} b_s L^s, \tag{13}$$

where $b_0 = -c$ and $b_{-s} = b_s, s = 1, 2, \ldots, n$, equation (12) can be rewritten

$$B(L)\hat{x}_t = 0. \tag{14}$$

Obtaining a unique rational expectations solution to equation (14) involves some technical considerations. The polynomial $B(L)$ has negative as well as positive powers of L; however, because of its symmetry ($b_s = b_{-s}$), it can be factored into a product of a polynomial in L and the same polynomial in L^{-1}; that is,

$$B(L) = \lambda A(L)A(L^{-1}), \tag{15}$$

---

[4] This identity is easily established using induction. Note that N times eq. (10) is an average of a sum, that is, a Cesaro sum in the contract wage.

where λ is a normalization constant and

$$A(L) = \sum_{s=0}^{n} \alpha_s L^s, \tag{16}$$

with $\alpha_0 = 1$. The canonical representation in equation (15) follows directly from factorization theorems for symmetric polynomials (see Anderson 1971, p. 224, e.g.), which frequently arise in the theory of stochastic processes. (It may be helpful to note that the problem of obtaining the factorization in eq. [15] is identical with the problem of obtaining the moving-average representation of a stochastic process given its autocovariance function or correlogram. The polynomial [13] would be the autocovariance-generating function and the coefficient of $A[L]$ would be the coefficients of the moving-average representation.)

From the factorization (15) we can obtain a unique rational expectations solution to (14) by imposing the usual stability condition and thereby choosing the polynomial $A(L)$ which corresponds to the roots of $B(L)$ that lie outside the unit circle.[5] (Again, the analogy from stochastic processes is helpful here: our assumption of stability corresponds to the assumption of invertibility of a moving-average process, which is enough to give a unique representation.) Having chosen $A(L)$ in this fashion, we can then divide equation (14) by $\lambda A(L^{-1})$ to obtain

$$A(L)\hat{x}_t = 0. \tag{17}$$

A comparison of (17) with (9) indicates that the rational expectations reduced-form stochastic difference equation for the contract wage is

$$A(L)x_t = \epsilon_t, \tag{18}$$

or, writing the lagged contracts on the right-hand side of the equation,

$$x_t = a_1 x_{t-1} + a_2 x_{t-2} + \ldots + a_n x_{t-n} + \epsilon_t, \tag{19}$$

where $a_i = -\alpha_i$, $i = 1, \ldots, n$.

Note that there is an explicit set of constraints which the structural parameters γ and β, working through the parameter $b_0 = -c$, put on this reduced-form equation. These constraints can be derived by equating the coefficients of the polynomials on the left- and right-hand side of (15) to obtain:

---

[5] Let $\lambda_i, i = 1, \ldots, n$ be the roots of $B(L)$ which lie outside or on the unit circle; then λ_i^{-1} are the roots of $B(L)$ which lie within or on the unit circle. The coefficients of $A(L)$ are therefore equal to the coefficients of the corresponding powers of L in $\Pi_{i=1}^{n} (L - \lambda_i)$.

$$-c = \lambda(1 + \alpha_1^2 + \alpha_2^2 + \ldots + \alpha_n^2)$$

$$b_1 = \lambda(\alpha_1 + \alpha_1\alpha_2 + \alpha_2\alpha_3 + \ldots + \alpha_{n-1}\alpha_n)$$

$$b_2 = \lambda(\alpha_2 + \alpha_1\alpha_3 + \alpha_2\alpha_4 + \ldots + \alpha_{n-2}\alpha_n)$$

.

.

.   (20)

$$b_{n-1} = \lambda(\alpha_{n-1} + \alpha_1\alpha_n)$$

$$b_n = \lambda\alpha_n,$$

or, more compactly,

$$b_s = \lambda \sum_{u=0}^{n-s} \alpha_u\alpha_{u+s}, \qquad s = 0, 1, 2, \ldots, n.$$

There is only one structural parameter (c) in these equations; hence, regardless of the number of lag coefficients α_i, there is only 1 degree of freedom; only the product of γ and β matters. If c is known, then the entire lag distribution is known.

The relationship between the reduced-form weights and the structural lag and lead weights is shown in figure 1 for the case of $c = 1$, the full-employment rule. Note that in this case both the b-weights and the a-weights sum to one. Since the reduced form can only be backward looking, it must capture both the backward-looking and forward-looking features of the structural form. Hence, the sum of the lag weights for the reduced form is twice as large as the sum of the lag weights for the structural form. The area between the reduced-form lag weights and the structural lag weights in figure 1 represents the component of the reduced form which is due to expectational effects, while the remaining component represents pure wage-inertia effects. As will be shown below, policy can affect the reduced-form lag weights by altering the expectations component. For example, a less accommodative policy can reduce the expectations component and even make it negative; that is, policy can push the reduced-form lag weights below the structural lag weights.

It is interesting to note that the expectations component is much larger for short lags than for longer lags. This is a property of the optimality of the rational forecasts. Hence, the reduced-form lag declines much more quickly than the structural form.

A striking characteristic of the reduced-form contract-wage equation (19) is that it does not include a measure of excess demand. The impact of excess demand on wage behavior is captured in the lag coefficients. If we had assumed *actual* excess demand influences wage behavior along with *expected* excess demand in the basic structural

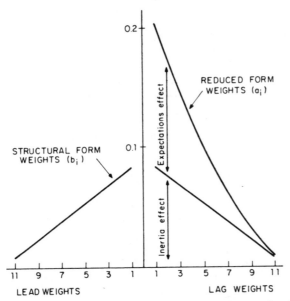

FIG. 1.—Relationship between structural contract wage equation and reduced form

equation (1), then excess-demand effects would be visible in equation (20). But even then, only unexpected excess demand would matter. Although the aggregate-demand side of this model is very simple, this feature of the wage equation is suggestive of the difficulties which are inherent in econometric attempts to estimate the impact of aggregate demand on wage behavior. If the unemployment rate were inserted on the right-hand side of a regression equation similar to (19), the estimated coefficient of the unemployment rate would have a probability limit of zero.

Shape of the Lag Distribution

The constraints in equation (20) indicate that the wage equation is sensitive to policy and the length of contracts. In order to illustrate how the lag shape depends on policy and on contract length, we have tabulated the theoretical lag distribution for 3-, 4-, and 12-period contracts and for alternative values of $\gamma\beta$. These are shown in table 1 and figure 2. Note that the lag coefficients are all positive and decline at a decreasing rate for all contract lengths and all values of $\beta\gamma$. This convexity is a result of the linearity of the structural weights. With this type of autoregressive lag shape, one would not expect to find overshooting effects; but, since the stochastic difference equation has

TABLE 1

THEORETICAL LAG DISTRIBUTIONS FOR ALTERNATIVE CONTRACT LENGTHS

$\beta\gamma =$	.0	.1	.2	.3
		3-Period Contracts		
a_1	.732	.464	.375	.313
a_2	.268	.188	.158	.135
		4-Period Contracts		
a_1	.572	.361	.290	.240
a_2	.308	.210	.173	.146
a_3	.120	.089	.076	.065
		12-Period Contracts		
a_1	.206	.128	.101	.082
a_2	.176	.113	.090	.073
a_3	.149	.098	.079	.064
a_4	.123	.083	.068	.056
a_5	.101	.070	.057	.047
a_6	.080	.057	.047	.039
a_7	.062	.045	.038	.032
a_8	.045	.034	.029	.025
a_9	.032	.024	.021	.018
a_{10}	.019	.015	.013	.011
a_{11}	.009	.007	.006	.005

complex roots, we should also examine the spectral density function for signs of cyclical behavior. This is done in the following section.

As policy gets less accommodative (β increases), or as the sensitivity of wages to excess demand increases (γ increases), the lag distribution is pushed toward zero. While the sum of the lag weights is one when $\beta\gamma = 0$, it is less than one when $\beta\gamma > 0$. Hence, a larger $\beta\gamma$ tends to reduce the serial correlation of wages.

Spectral Density of the Contract Wage

A convenient way to analyze the behavior of the contract wage is through its spectral density, which has a simple analytic representation. According to equation (18), x_t follows an nth-order autoregression. Hence, if σ^2 is the variance of ϵ_t, then the spectral density of x_t is given by

$$f(\omega) = \frac{\sigma^2}{2\pi} \left| \sum_{s=0}^{n} \alpha_s e^{i\omega(n-s)} \right|^{-2} \qquad (-\pi < \omega < \pi). \qquad (21)$$

The advantage of looking at the spectral density of x_t is that the squared modulus of the complex sum in (21) involves the same non-

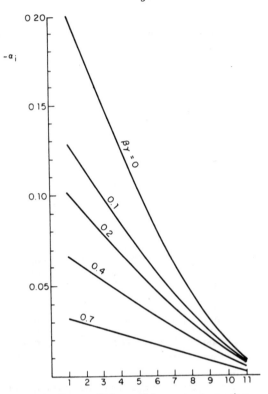

FIG. 2.—Lag coefficients of the contract equation

linear functions of the α coefficients that were found on the right-hand side of (20). Hence, we can utilize the formulas in (20) to obtain:

$$
\begin{aligned}
f(\omega) &= \frac{\sigma^2}{2\pi} \left[\frac{b_0}{\lambda} + \frac{2}{\lambda n} \sum_{s=1}^{n} \left(1 - \frac{s}{N} \right) \cos s\omega \right]^{-1} \\
&= \frac{\sigma^2}{2\pi} \left[\frac{b_0}{\lambda} - \frac{1}{\lambda n} + \frac{2}{\lambda n} \left(\frac{\sin^2 \frac{1}{2}\omega N}{2N \sin^2 (\frac{1}{2}\omega)} \right) \right]^{-1}.
\end{aligned}
\tag{22}
$$

The second equality in (20) follows from a trigonometric identity which arises in the analysis of Fourier series (see Lanczos 1966, p. 56). The expression $(\sin^2 \frac{1}{2}\omega N)(2\pi N \sin^2 \frac{1}{2}\omega)^{-1}$ is known as Fejer's kernel and frequently occurs in studies of the serial correlation properties of averages.[6]

We know from the first equation of (20) that $\lambda < 0$; hence, $f(\omega)$ will have maxima and minima at the same values of ω as Fejer's kernel.

---

[6] See Anderson (1971, pp. 508–9) for a description of the qualitative features of Fejer's kernel. We make use of these features in analyzing eq. (22).

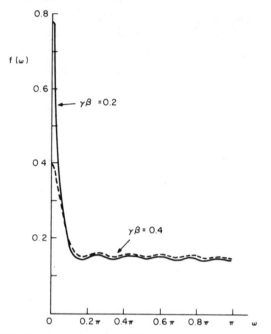

Fig. 3.—Spectral density of 12-period contract equation

Considering only the positive ω, the spectral density function has a maximum at $\omega = 0$, relative minima at $k\pi/N$, for $k = 2, 4, 6, \ldots$, and relative maxima approximately at $\omega = k\pi/N$, for $k = 1, 3, 5, \ldots$. If N is odd, then π is a relative maximum. The locations of these relative maxima and minima remain the same for all values of the parameter c, that is, for all policy rules. A sketch of the spectral density function for two values of $\beta\gamma$ is shown in figure 3. Note that as policy becomes less accommodative, the area under the curve is reduced, indicating the variance of the contract wage is reduced. However, the reduction in variance occurs only at low frequencies, and there is a slight increase in the variance at the higher frequencies.

The relative maxima of the spectral density in the higher frequencies are small compared with the maximum at $\omega = 0$. Hence, the contract wage has the typical spectral shape of an economic time series: no sharp peaks occur anywhere except at the zero frequency. In this sense, the persistence effects of the overlapping contracts—given the policy rule and our assumption of linearly declining weights in the structural equation—would not be expected to generate overshooting endogenously. As is shown below, however, the aggregate wage and price level follows an autoregressive–moving-average process which can have the appearance of overshooting: the impact of a shock on the wage level can increase from its initial value for a number of periods before diminishing toward zero.

III. Aggregate Dynamics and the Persistence of Unemployment

Equations describing the macroeconomic dynamics of the model can be derived by aggregating the contract wages to determine the aggregate wage and price level. Let

$$D(L) = \frac{1}{N} \sum_{s=0}^{n} L^s \qquad (23)$$

be the unweighted moving-average operator. Then, from the definition of the aggregate price level in equation (3) of Section I,

$$p_t = D(L)x_t. \qquad (24)$$

Substitution of (24) into the contract wage equation (19) yields the aggregate price equation

$$A(L)p_t = D(L)\epsilon_t. \qquad (25)$$

Hence, the price level follows an autoregressive–moving-average process, ARMA (n,n). The autoregressive part of the process is the same as that of the contract equation (19). In a deterministic perfect foresight version of this model, the aggregate equation would therefore be described by the same difference equation as the contract wages. Given equation (25), the behavior of aggregate output can easily be determined from the aggregate-demand equation (7), that is,

$$y_t = -\beta p_t + v_t. \qquad (26)$$

Aggregate output, therefore, has the same basic stochastic structure as the price level. Of course, the realizations of output will look much different than those of the price level. The larger β is, the larger the output fluctuations relative to price fluctuations will be. And, except for the influence of velocity shocks, output and prices will tend to move in opposite directions. This result follows directly from our simple quantity theory of aggregate demand combined with a fixed rule for money-supply behavior. In the extreme case of the fixed and known money supply ($\beta = 1$), real output must fall by the same proportion that the price level rises.

Persistence Effects

The potential for this model to exhibit high serial correlation in unemployment is evident in equations (25) and (26). Recall that the unemployment rate is assumed to be proportional to y_t. The autoregressive terms in equation (25) prevent the serial correlation between y_t and y_{t+s} from hitting zero as soon as s is greater than the contract length. Instead, the correlation between y_t and y_{t+s} diminishes gradually and approaches zero only asymptotically as $s \to \infty$. If the sum of the autoregressive coefficients in (25) is large, then the serial correlation will remain high for very long lags.

These general features can be illustrated in the case of two-period contracts ($N = 2$). In this case, equation (25) becomes

$$p_t = a_1 p_{t-1} + \frac{\epsilon_t}{2} + \frac{\epsilon_{t-1}}{2}, \qquad 0 \leqslant a_1 \leqslant 1. \tag{27}$$

From (20), $a_1 \equiv - \alpha_1 = c - \sqrt{c^2 - 1}$. The ARMA (1,1) model in (27) can be inverted in order to represent p_t as a function of the ϵ_t only. That is,

$$p_t = \frac{1}{2}[\epsilon_t + \psi_1 \epsilon_{t-1} + \psi_2 \epsilon_{t-2} + \ldots], \tag{28}$$

where

$$\psi_i = a_1^{i-1}(1 + a_1), i = 1, 2, \ldots. \tag{29}$$

From equation (26), output then has the moving-average representation

$$y_t = v_t - \frac{\beta}{2}[\epsilon_t + \psi_1 \epsilon_{t-1} + \psi_2 \epsilon_{t-2} + \ldots]. \tag{30}$$

According to equation (29), the ψ weights increase for one lag before decreasing geometrically to zero. If a_1 were close to 1, as it would be if $\gamma\beta$ were small, then the ψ weights would decline to zero very slowly and y_t would show high correlation. On the other hand, if $\gamma\beta$ were large, the serial correlation would be weaker but would nevertheless converge to zero only asymptotically.

It is instructive to compare the type of serial persistence generated by this model with the observed serial persistence of unemployment in the United States. The ψ weights in the moving-average representation (30) are useful for this purpose. Table 2 compares the ψ weights implied by the model with the actual ψ weights for the unemployment rate for the case where velocity shocks are negligible ($v_t = 0$). The estimated ψ weights were obtained by first estimating an ARMA (2,1) process for the quarterly unemployment rate for males 20 and over (to avoid labor force composition shifts), and then by writing this process in pure moving-average form.[7] The resulting ψ weights for the sample period 1954:1 through 1976:4 are given in

---

[7] The ARMA model was $u_t = 1.39 u_{t-1} - .49 u_{t-2} + r_t + .27 r_{t-1}$, where u_t is the quarterly unemployment rate and r_t is the serially uncorrelated error term. Nelson (1972) found this same model adequate for the 1947:1–1966:4 period.

TABLE 2

THEORETICAL AND OBSERVED SERIAL
PERSISTENCE OF UNEMPLOYMENT
(Quarterly Moving-Average Representation)

| | THEORETICAL ψ_i | | | OBSERVED ψ_i |
LAG	$N = 2$	$N = 3$	$N = 4$	(1954:1–1976:4)
0	1.00	1.00	1.00	1.00
1	1.64	1.46	1.36	1.66
2	1.05	1.86	1.73	1.82
3	.67	1.13	1.99	1.71
4	.43	.87	1.20	1.48
5	.27	.61	1.00	1.21
6	.17	.45	.79	.96
7	.11	.32	.60	.73
8	.07	.23	.47	.55
9	.05	.17	.37	.40
10	.03	.12	.28	.28

NOTE.—The observed ψ_i are obtained by estimating an ARMA (2,1) model for the unemployment rate for males 20 and over and inverting it to obtain the pure moving-average form; the theoretical weights are described in the text. $\beta = .5$, $\gamma = .2$; contract length: $N = 2$, 3, or 4 quarters.

the fourth column of table 2. The estimated ψ weights show a tendency to rise for the first few quarters and then decline fairly steadily.

The theoretical weights are reported in the first three columns of table 2 for contract lengths of 2, 3, and 4 quarters, respectively. These have been calculated using the parametric assumption that $\beta = .5$ and $\gamma = .2$ (or, more generally, that $\gamma\beta = .1$). The results for the 3- and 4-quarter contracts appear quite similar to the observed serial correlation in unemployment. The lag weights rise for the first few quarters before beginning to diminish rather rapidly. However, the case of 2-quarter contracts appears to give substantially less serial correlation. To some extent, these results are dependent on our parameter choice; for example, a larger value for $\beta\gamma$ would reduce persistence but would not change the general humped shape of the lag distribution. In any case, the results show the capability of this type of contract model to explain the observed persistence in unemployment—even when there is no other source of persistence and contract lengths are reasonably short.

A Statistical Phillips Curve[8]

An essential requirement of a theoretical macromodel is that it exhibits a statistical Phillips curve. Although the model of this paper in-

[8] This section owes much to discussions I have had with Edmund Phelps on this subject.

cludes a monetary policy rule which forces a positive correlation
between the price level and the unemployment rate, there does exist a
negative correlation between the change in the price level and the
unemployment rate. To see this, consider the covariance between y_t
and $p_{t+1} - p_t$ for the case of $N = 2$. If this covariance is positive, then
there is a statistical Phillips curve. From equation (28),

$$p_{t+1} - p_t = \frac{1}{2}\left[\epsilon_{t+1} + \sum_{i=0}^{\infty}(\psi_i - \psi_{i-1})\epsilon_{t-i}\right], \tag{31}$$

and the covariance between y_t and $p_{t+1} - p_t$ is

$$\begin{aligned}
E[y_t(p_{t+1} - p_t)] &= -\beta\left[(\psi_1 - 1) + \sum_{i=2}^{\infty}(\psi_i - \psi_{i-1})\psi_{i-1}\right]\frac{\sigma^2}{4} \\
&= -\beta\left[a_1 + \sum_{i=0}^{\infty}a_1^{2i}(a_1 - 1)(1 + a_1)^2\right]\frac{\sigma^2}{4} \\
&= -\beta[a_1 - (1 + a_1)]\frac{\sigma^2}{4} \\
&= \beta\frac{\sigma^2}{4},
\end{aligned} \tag{32}$$

which is positive. Hence, during boom periods, when output is above
the full-employment level, inflation will be higher on the average.
Note that the size of this covariance depends directly on aggregate-
demand policy. (Recall the assumption that price shocks and velocity
shocks are uncorrelated. If there is a positive correlation between v_t
and ϵ_t, then the above covariance would be larger.) The theoretical
regression coefficient of $p_{t+1} - p_t$ on y_t is given by $\beta/2$. Hence, the more
accommodative is aggregate-demand policy, the flatter is the statistical
Phillips curve.

Stabilization Policy

The policy problem in this model is one of stabilizing the fluctuations
of output about its full-employment level and fluctuations of the price
level about its steady state level. The dimensions of the problem are
evident in equations (25) and (26). According to (26), when the
aggregate-demand reaction parameter is zero, the variance of output
is at its minimum value, which is equal to the variance of v_t. However,
when $\beta = 0$ the variance of the price level is infinite, for then the sum
of the autoregressive weights in equation (25) is one. As the value of β
is increased, the variance of the price level will fall and the variance of
output will rise. The resulting trade-off between the variability of
output and prices is illustrated in table 3 for the case of $N = 2$; the σ_y
and σ_p columns refer to the standard deviation of output and the

TABLE 3

ALTERNATIVE POLICIES WITH 2-PERIOD CONTRACTS

				σ_y	
$\beta\gamma$	c	a_1	σ_p	$\gamma = .2$	$\gamma = .4$
.01	1.010	.868	3.89	1.02	1.004
.04	1.041	.752	2.84	1.15	1.04
.12	1.128	.606	2.25	1.68	1.21
.20	1.222	.520	2.04	2.27	1.43
.40	1.500	.382	1.78	3.70	2.04
.60	1.857	.292	1.68	5.14	2.71

price level, respectively. The standard deviation of output is given for two values of γ. Note that the larger γ is, the more favorable is the trade-off: for the same level of price variability, the variance of output can be smaller if the sensitivity of price and wages to excess demand is high. This improvement in the trade-off is uniform over its entire range and is some measure of the gain from more responsive prices.[9]

IV. Wage Expectations versus Wage Inertia

As was discussed in Section II, lagged wages appear on the right-hand side of the reduced-form wage equation in this model for two reasons: they represent the expectations of future wages and the overhang of past wages. Using the rational expectations assumption, these two components can be sorted out, as was illustrated in figure 1. One of the results of this decomposition is that the expectations component depends, in an explicit way, on the aggregate-demand policy rule. For this reason, the policy implications of this model are much different from models where either there is no expectations component—wage determination is purely backward looking—or where the expectations component is based on adaptive or extrapolative expectations schemes. The purpose of this section is to explore this difference.[10]

We begin by maintaining the assumption that the underlying rate

[9] The stabilization problem considered by Taylor (1979) involves smoothing fluctuations in the inflation rate about a constant target, rather than the log of the price level about a constant trend as in this paper.

[10] Similar expectational effects have been discussed by Fellner (1976, p. 117), though with more emphasis on making the aggregate-demand policy rule credible. If credibility cannot be established by direct announcement, then there will be a transition period during which the behavior of the economy might be a weighted average of the two sets of columns in table 4. Public learning during the transition would be similar to that discussed in Taylor (1975).

of inflation is zero, so that the steady-state average price level is constant. One of the objectives of demand policy is to stabilize fluctuations of prices (or wages) about this constant level. (The case of a rising-price path can be considered using similar techniques.) It will be convenient to consider the problem within the context of a single realization of a price shock which raises, say, the aggregate price level above its equilibrium value. The objective of policy, therefore, is to bring the price level back to equilibrium. The appropriate rate of return to equilibrium will depend on the relative weights of prices and output in the social welfare function: a quick return if prices have a high weight, or a slow return if output has a high weight.

Assume that $N = 2$ and that an aggregate-demand policy rule of the form discussed in this paper is in force when this price shock occurs. This rule might have been the result of decisions made within the political process and which planned for such shocks, so that when the shock occurs there is no pressure to change the rule. For illustration purposes, assume that the rule is $\beta = .5$, that $\gamma = .2$, and that $\epsilon_1 = 10$ percent ($\epsilon_s = 0, s > 1$). If $p_0 = 0$ and $\epsilon_0 = 0$ (i.e., the price level was in equilibrium before the shock), then $p_1 = 5$ and p_t follows the path

$$p_t = a_1 p_{t-1} + \frac{\epsilon_t}{2} + \frac{\epsilon_{t-1}}{2}, \qquad t = 2, 3, \ldots, \tag{33}$$

where $a_1 = .63$. The path for output is then given by $y_1 = -2.5$, and

$$y_t = -.5 p_t, \qquad t = 2, 3, \ldots. \tag{34}$$

For these numerical values, the two paths are given in table 4. The convergence of the price level to equilibrium is relatively quick despite the accommodating strategy. If β were greater than .5, the return would be faster, but the loss of output would be larger; conversely if β were less than .5.

To compare these results with a model which does not incorporate forward-looking wage determination or which is based on extrapolative expectations, consider equation (1) in the case of $N = 2$,

$$x_t = \frac{1}{2}(x_{t-1} + \hat{x}_{t+1}) + \frac{\gamma}{2}(\hat{y}_t + \hat{y}_{t+1}) + \epsilon_t. \tag{35}$$

A modification of equation (35) to eliminate forward looking is

$$x_t = \frac{1}{2}(x_{t-1} + x_{t-1}) + \frac{\gamma}{2}(y_{t-1} + y_{t-1}) + \epsilon_t, \tag{36}$$

or simply

$$x_t = x_{t-1} + \gamma y_{t-1} + \epsilon_t. \tag{37}$$

TABLE 4

Comparison of Aggregate-Demand Effects on
Price Behavior with Rational and
Extrapolative Expectations
(Percent Deviations from Trend)

t	Rational Expectations (Eq. [34])		Extrapolative Expectations (Eq. [38])	
	p_t	y_t	p_t	y_t
0	.00	.00	.00	.00
1	5.00	−2.50	5.00	−2.50
2	8.15	−4.08	9.75	−4.08
3	5.13	−2.57	9.09	−2.57
4	3.23	−1.62	8.43	−1.62
5	2.03	−1.02	8.01	−1.02
6	1.28	−.64	7.75	−.64
7	.81	−.41	7.58	−.41
8	.51	−.26	7.48	−.26
9	.32	−.16	7.41	−.16
10	.20	−.10	7.37	−.10

Hence, either current wage negotiations ignore future developments or they simply extrapolate current developments by forecasting x_{t+1} with x_{t-1} and y_{t+1} with y_{t-1}. The aggregate price level is then given by

$$p_t = p_{t-1} + \frac{\gamma}{2}(y_{t-1} + y_{t-2}) + \frac{\epsilon_t}{2}\frac{\epsilon_{t-1}}{2}. \tag{38}$$

The policy implications of equation (38) are clearly much different from equation (34). The path of the price level using (38) is given in table 4 for the same path of output considered above (starting with p_0 = 0, y_0 = 0, and ϵ_0 = 0). It is evident that the reduction in the price level is much smaller than in the case of rational forward-looking expectations; according to equation (38), a much larger loss of output would be required to bring the price level back to the target path at the same rate implied by equation (34). Price stability appears to be very costly when expectations are not rational or contracts do not look forward. The difference between the two models provides a simple measure of the "expectation bonus" which comes from rational anticipatory wage determination. The difference indicates that rational expectations matter greatly—despite the existence of contracts—for macroeconomic stabilization. It also indicates the need to determine empirically whether wage-contract decisions rationally anticipate in this way.

V. Concluding Remarks

The analysis of this paper has centered on a stationary economy with staggered overlapping wage contracts and rational expectations. The aggregate dynamics of this economy—when subject to continual demand and price shocks—were examined under alternative monetary policy rules. In order to emphasize endogenous persistence effects, these shocks were assumed to be serially uncorrelated.

The results of the analysis can be summarized as follows. Persistence of unemployment similar to that observed in the United States can be generated by the model when contracts are 3 or 4 quarters long and there are no other sources of persistence. The time shape of the dynamic impact of shocks on unemployment—rising for several quarters before tapering off—is characteristic both of the estimated process for unemployment and the theoretical process implied by the model. Moreover, the model generates a persistence of wages and prices which gives rise to a statistical Phillips curve and which presents a policy trade-off between price stability and output stability. The persistence of wages has both an expectational component and an inertia component, and these can be decomposed using the rational expectations approach. Policy affects the behavior of wages and employment by altering the expectations component of persistence. Hence, the econometric wage equations depend on the policy rule, and the estimated impact of aggregate demand on wages will be biased, unless expectations of policy in future periods are accounted for.

By viewing the logarithms of the price level, the contract wage, and the money supply as deviations from a linear trend, all the results presented here carry over to an inflationary economy. The policy problem then would be to stabilize prices as well as output about an exponentially growing target path. Given an aggregate-demand policy rule, price shocks above this path are followed by lower rates of inflation and higher unemployment, until the price level returns to the target path; conversely with negative price shocks. The statistical Phillips curve derived in Section III would be evident in the data left by these paths if the econometrician were careful to take deviations of the inflation rate from the underlying inflation rate before computing the regressions. This Phillips curve would convey little information about the sensitivity of wages or prices to excess demand, however. This sensitivity would be implicit in the reduced-form wage equations (again in deviation from trend form) derived in Section II, but it could not be extracted without knowledge of the policy rule. Finally, aggregate-demand policy makes a substantial difference for the behavior of output, wages, and prices. The choice of a target rule for aggregate-demand policy is therefore no less important than the choice of a target unemployment rate or a target inflation rate. It should therefore be considered as carefully in the political process as the other two targets typically are.

Appendix

The Reduced-Form Contract Equation When Shocks Are Correlated

In order to emphasize the persistence generated by the staggered contracts, we have assumed that both velocity shocks and wage shocks are serially uncorrelated. In some applications, however, one might want to allow for the possibility that these shocks are correlated. The purpose of this Appendix is to show how the solution technique introduced in Section II can be used to handle the case of serially correlated shocks.

Let the wage shock ϵ_t and the velocity shock v_t in equations (6) and (7) of the text be represented as

$$\epsilon_t = \sum_{i=0}^{\infty} \delta_i u_{t-i} \tag{A1}$$

and

$$v_t = \sum_{i=0}^{\infty} \theta_i \eta_{t-i}, \tag{A2}$$

where (u_t, η_t) is a serially uncorrelated random vector with zero mean and where $\delta_0 = \theta_0 = 1$. Using this serial correlation structure to forecast output as in equation (8) and substituting into equation (6) gives

$$x_t = \sum_{s=1}^{n} b_s x_{t-s} + \sum_{s=1}^{n} b_s \hat{x}_{t+s} - \frac{\beta\gamma}{N^2} \sum_{s=0}^{n} \sum_{i=0}^{n} \hat{x}_{t+s-i} + \frac{\gamma}{N} \sum_{i=1}^{\infty} \rho_i \hat{\eta}_{t-i} + \sum_{i=0}^{\infty} \delta_i u_{t-i}, \tag{A3}$$

where $\rho_i = \sum_{s=i}^{n+i} \theta_s$. Taking expectations on both sides of (A3) and using the identity (10) yields

$$\sum_{s=1}^{n} b_s \hat{x}_{t-s} - c\hat{x}_t + \sum_{s=1}^{n} b_s \hat{x}_{t+s} = -\left(1 - \frac{n\beta\gamma}{N}\right)^{-1} \left(\frac{\gamma}{N} \sum_{i=1}^{\infty} \rho_i \hat{\eta}_{t-i} + \sum_{i=1}^{\infty} \delta_i \hat{u}_{t-1}\right). \tag{A4}$$

Using the lag polynomial notation as in Section II, this can be written

$$B(L)\hat{x}_t = -\left(1 - \frac{n\beta\gamma}{N}\right)^{-1}\left[\frac{\gamma}{N} R(L)\hat{\eta}_t + \Delta(L)\hat{u}_t\right], \tag{A5}$$

where $R(L) = \sum_{i=1}^{\infty} \rho_i L^i$ and $\Delta(L) = \sum_{i=1}^{\infty} \delta_i L^i$. The polynomial $B(L)$ is the same as that in equation (14). Hence, it can be factored as $B(L) = \lambda A(L)A(L^{-1})$; and by dividing both sides of (A5) by $\lambda A(L^{-1})$, we have

$$A(L)\hat{x}_t = -\lambda^{-1}\left(1 - \frac{n\beta\gamma}{N}\right)^{-1}\left[\frac{\gamma}{N} H(L)\hat{\eta}_t + G(L)\hat{u}_t\right], \tag{A6}$$

where $H(L)$ is a polynomial obtained by omitting all terms involving nonpositive powers of L in the polynomial $[A(L^{-1})]^{-1}R(L)$, and $G(L)$ is a polynomial obtained by omitting all terms involving nonpositive powers of L in the polynomial $[A(L^{-1})]^{-1}\Delta(L)$. The nonpositive powers of L cancel because $L^{-s}\hat{\eta}_t = \hat{\eta}_{t+s} = 0$ for $s \geq 0$ and $L^{-s}\hat{u}_t = \hat{u}_{t+s} = 0$ for $s \geq 0$, since the expectations are conditional on information through period $t - 1$ and η_t and u_t are each serially uncorrelated. Comparing (A6) with (A3) indicates that the reduced-form contract equation is given by

$$A(L)x_t = -\lambda^{-1}\left(1 - \frac{n\beta\gamma}{N}\right)^{-1}\left[\frac{\gamma}{N}H(L)\eta_t + G(L)u_t\right] + u_t. \qquad (A7)$$

Equation (A7) determines the current contract in terms of past contracts, past shocks, and the current contract shock. From this relationship the behavior of the aggregate price level and aggregate output can be derived following the techniques described in Section II.

References

Anderson, Theodore W. *The Statistical Analysis of Times Series*. New York: Wiley, 1971.

Barro, Robert J. "Rational Expectations and the Role of Monetary Policy." *J. Monetary Econ.* 2 (January 1976): 1–32.

———. "A Capital Market in an Equilibrium Business Cycle Model." Mimeographed. Univ. Rochester, Dept. Econ., 1978.

Fellner, William J. *Towards a Reconstruction of Macroeconomics: Problems of Theory and Policy*. Washington: American Enterprise Inst., 1976.

Fischer, Stanley. "Long-Term Contracts, Rational Expectations, and the Optimal Money Supply Rule." *J.P.E.* 85, no. 1 (February 1977): 191–206.

———. "Anticipations and the Nonneutrality of Money." *J.P.E.* 87, no. 2 (April 1979): 225–52.

Hall, R. E. "Expectations Errors, Unemployment, and Wage Inflation." Mimeographed. Center Advanced Study Behavioral Sci., Stanford Univ., 1977.

Lanczos, Cornelius. *Discourse on Fourier Series*. New York: Hafner, 1966.

Lucas, Robert E., Jr. "Some International Evidence on Output-Inflation Tradeoffs." *A.E.R.* 63, no. 3 (June 1973): 326–34.

———. "An Equilibrium Model of the Business Cycle." *J.P.E.* 83, no. 6 (December 1975): 1113–44.

———. "Econometric Policy Evaluation: A Critique." In *The Phillips Curve and Labor Markets*, edited by Karl Brunner and Allan H. Meltzer. Amsterdam: North-Holland, 1976.

Nelson, Charles R. "The Prediction Performance of the FRB-MIT-PENN Model of the U.S. Economy." *A.E.R.* 62, no. 5 (December 1972): 902–17.

Phelps, Edmund S. "Disinflation without Recession: Adaptive Guideposts and Monetary Policy." *Weltwirtschaftliches Archiv* 114 (December 1978): 783–809.

Phelps, Edmund S., and Taylor, John B. "Stabilizing Powers of Monetary Policy under Rational Expectations." *J.P.E.* 85, no. 1 (February 1977): 163–90.

Sargent, Thomas J. "The Persistence of Aggregate Employment and the Neutrality of Money." Mimeographed. Univ. Minnesota, Dept. Econ., 1977.

Sargent, Thomas J., and Wallace, Neil. " 'Rational' Expectations, the Optimal Monetary Instrument, and the Optimal Money Supply Rule." *J.P.E.* 83, no. 2 (April 1975): 241–54.

Taylor, John B. "Monetary Policy during a Transition to Rational Expectations." *J.P.E.* 83, no. 5 (October 1975): 1009–21.

———. "Estimation and Control of a Macroeconomic Model with Rational Expectations." *Econometrica* 47 (September 1979): 1267–86.

Name Index